# BAREFOOT GEN

## VOLUME FOUR:
## OUT OF THE ASHES

### KEIJI NAKAZAWA

### Translated by Project Gen

**LAST GASP OF SAN FRANCISCO**

Barefoot Gen: A Cartoon Story of Hiroshima
Volume Four: Out of the Ashes

By Keiji Nakazawa

Published by Last Gasp of San Francisco
777 Florida Street, San Francisco, California, 94110
www.lastgasp.com

First serialized under the title *Hadashi no Gen* in Japan, 1972-3.
Published by Last Gasp with a new translation, 2005.
First hardcover Last Gasp edition, 2016.
ISBN 978-0-86719-834-8

Translation by Project Gen
Volume 4 Translators: Kiyoko Nishita, Kyoko Honda, Alan Gleason,
Joanne Higashi, Tomoko Shimotomai.

Project Gen Volunteers: Namie Asazuma, Kazuko Futakuchi, Michael
Gordon, Yukari Kimura, Nobutoshi Kohara, Nante Kotta, George Stenson,
Michiko Tanaka, Kazuko Yamada.

Edited by Alan Gleason and Colin Turner
Production: Colin Turner
Cover design: Evan Hayden

Printed in China by Prolong Press Ltd.

For more information visit www.barefootgen.net

# The Birth of Barefoot Gen

## Keiji Nakazawa

The atomic bomb exploded 600 meters above my hometown of Hiroshima on August 6, 1945 at 8:15 a.m. I was a little over a kilometer away from the epicenter, standing at the back gate of Kanzaki Primary School, when I was hit by a terrible blast of wind and searing heat. I was six years old. I owe my life to the school's concrete wall. If I hadn't been standing in its shadow, I would have been burned to death instantly by the 5,000-degree heat flash. Instead, I found myself in a living hell, the details of which remain etched in my brain as if it happened yesterday.

My mother, Kimiyo, was eight months pregnant. She was on the second floor balcony of our house, had just finished hanging up the wash to dry, and was turning to go back inside when the bomb exploded. The blast blew the entire balcony, with my mother on it, into the alley behind our house. Miraculously, my mother survived without a scratch.

The blast blew our house flat. The second floor collapsed onto the first, trapping my father, my sister Eiko, and my brother Susumu under it. My brother had been sitting in the front doorway, playing with a toy ship. His head was caught under the rafter over the doorway. He frantically kicked his legs and cried out for my mother. My father, trapped inside the house, begged my mother to do something. My sister had been crushed by a rafter and killed instantly.

My mother frantically tried to lift the rafters off them, but she wasn't strong enough to do it by herself. She begged passersby to stop and help, but nobody would. In that atomic hell, people could only think of their own survival; they had no time for anyone else. My mother tried everything she could, but to no avail. Finally, in despair, she sat down in the doorway, clutching my crying brother and helplessly pushing at the rafter that was crushing him.

The fires that followed the blast soon reached our house. It was quickly enveloped in flame. My brother yelled that he was burning; my father kept begging my mother to get some help. My mother, half-mad with grief and desperation, sobbed that she would stay and die with them. But our next-door neighbor found my mother just in time and dragged her away.

For the rest of her days, my mother never forgot the sound of the voices of her husband and son, crying out for her to save them. The shock sent my mother into labor, and she gave birth to a daughter by the side of the road that day. She named the baby Tomoko. But Tomoko died only four months later -- perhaps from malnutrition, perhaps from radiation sickness, we didn't know.

After escaping the flames near the school, I found my mother there by the roadside with her newborn baby. Together we sat and watched the scenes of hell unfolding around us.

My father had been a painter of lacquer work and traditional-style Japanese painting. He was also a member of an anti-war theater group that performed plays like Gorky's "The Lower Depths." Eventually the thought police arrested the entire troupe and put them in the Hiroshima Prefectural Prison. My father was held there for a year and a half. Even when I was a young child, my father constantly told me that Japan had been stupid and reckless to start the war.

Thanks, no doubt, to my father's influence, I enjoyed drawing from an early age. After the war I began reading Osamu Tezuka's comic magazine *Shin-Takarajima* (*New Treasure Island*); that had a huge impact on me. I began slavishly copying Tezuka's drawings and turned into a manga maniac. Hiroshima was an empty, burnt-out wasteland and we went hungry every day, but when I drew comics, I was happy and forgot everything else. I vowed early on to become a professional cartoonist when I grew up.

In 1961 I pursued my dream by moving to Tokyo. A year later I published my first cartoon serial in the manga monthly *Shonen Gaho* (*Boys' Pictorial*). From then on I was a full-time cartoonist.

In 1966, after seven years of illness, my mother died in the A-Bomb Victims Hospital in Hiroshima. When I went to the crematorium to collect her ashes, I was shocked. There were no bones left in my mother's ashes, as there normally are after a cremation. Radioactive cesium from the bomb had eaten away at her bones to the point that they disintegrated. The bomb had even deprived me of my mother's bones. I was overcome with rage. I vowed that I would never forgive the Japanese militarists who started the war, nor the Americans who had so casually dropped the bomb on us.

I began drawing comics about the A-bomb as a way to avenge my mother. I vented my anger through a "Black" series of six manga published in an adult manga magazine, starting with *Kuroi Ame ni Utarete* (*Struck by Black Rain*). Then I moved to *Shukan Shonen Jump* (*Weekly Boys' Jump*), where I began a series of works about the war and the A-bomb starting with *Aru Hi Totsuzen ni* (*One Day, Suddenly*). When the monthly edition of *Jump* launched a series of autobiographical works by its cartoonists, I was asked to lead off with my own story. My 45-page manga auto-biography was titled *Ore wa Mita* (*I Saw It*). My editor at *Jump*, Tadasu Nagano, commenting that I must have more to say that wouldn't fit in 45 pages, urged me to draw a longer series based on my personal experiences. I gratefully began the series right away. That was in 1972.

I named my new story *Hadashi no Gen* (*Barefoot Gen*). The young protagonist's name, Gen, has several meanings in Japanese. It can mean the "root" or "origin" of something, but also "elemental" in the sense of an atomic element, as well as a "source" of vitality and happiness. I envisioned Gen as barefoot, standing firmly atop the burnt-out rubble of Hiroshima, raising his voice against war and nuclear weapons. Gen is my alter ego, and his family is just like my own. The episodes in *Barefoot Gen* are all based on what really happened to me or to other people in Hiroshima.

Human beings are foolish. Thanks to bigotry, religious fanaticism, and the greed of those who traffic in war, the Earth is never at peace, and the specter of nuclear war is never far away. I hope that Gen's story conveys to its readers the preciousness of peace and the courage we need to live strongly, yet peacefully. In *Barefoot Gen*, wheat appears as a symbol of that strength and courage. Wheat pushes its shoots up through the winter frost, only to be trampled again and again. But the trampled wheat sends strong roots into the earth and grows straight and tall. And one day, that wheat bears fruit.

# BAREFOOT GEN

## OUT OF THE ASHES

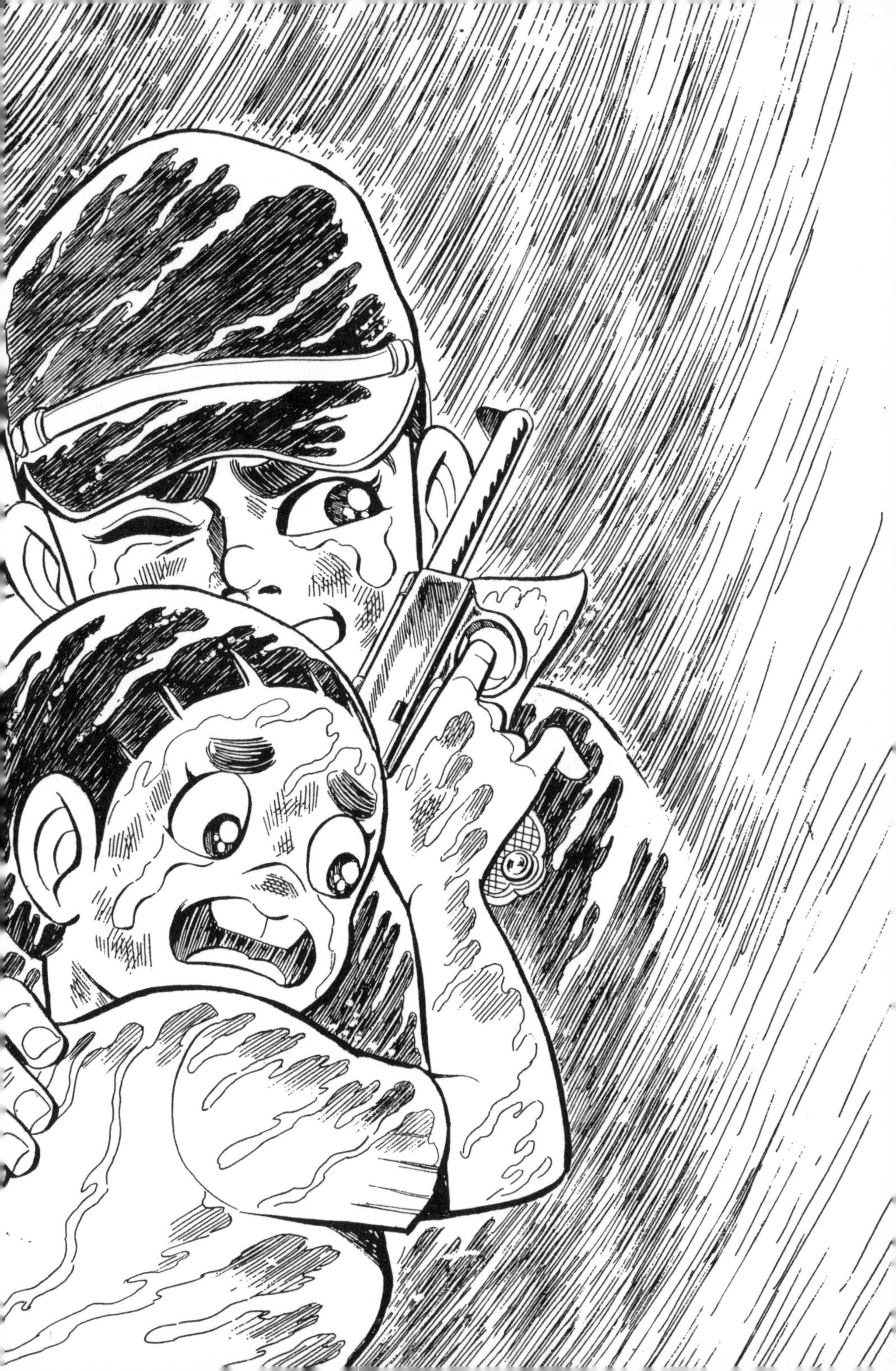

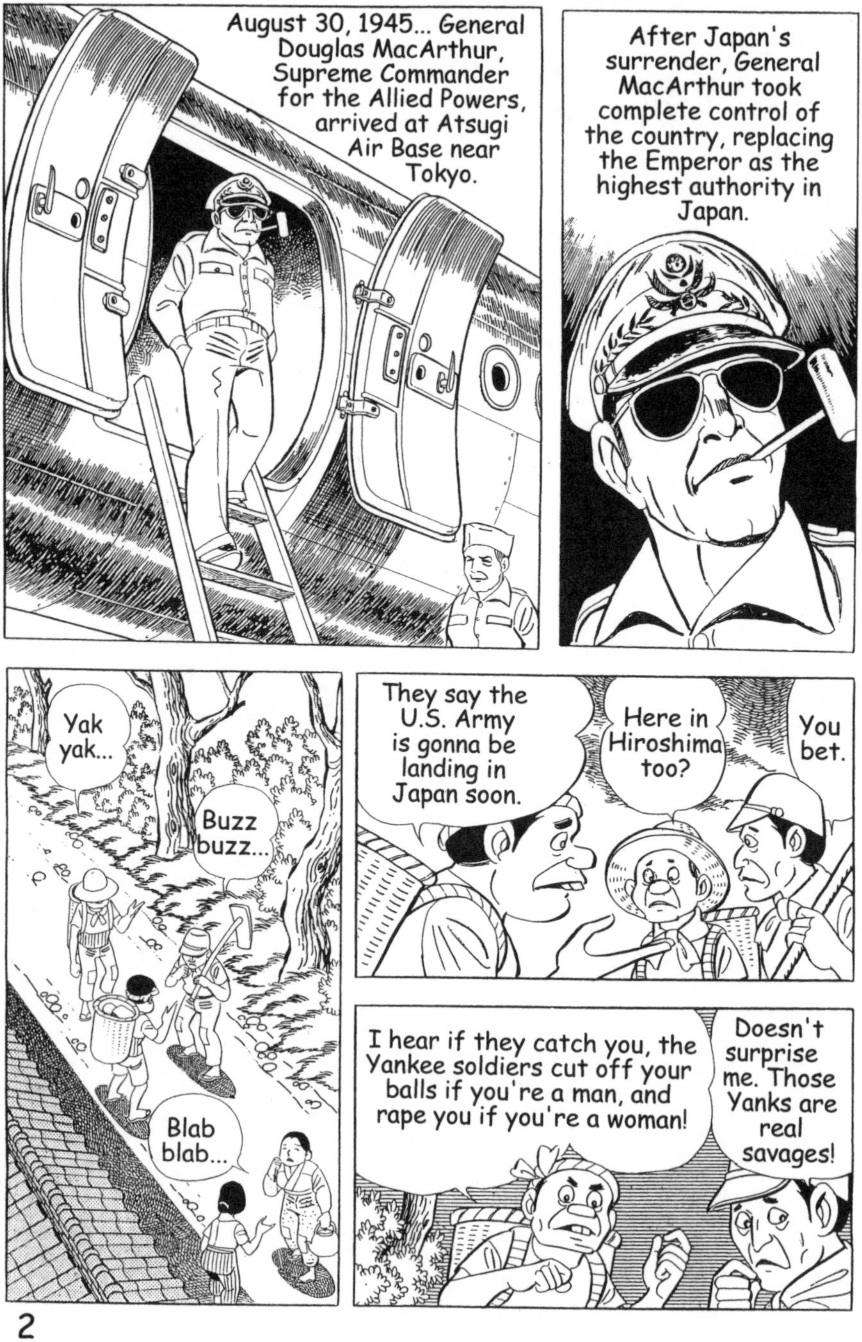
August 30, 1945... General Douglas MacArthur, Supreme Commander for the Allied Powers, arrived at Atsugi Air Base near Tokyo.
After Japan's surrender, General MacArthur took complete control of the country, replacing the Emperor as the highest authority in Japan.
Yak yak...
Buzz buzz...
Blab blab...
They say the U.S. Army is gonna be landing in Japan soon.
Here in Hiroshima too?
You bet.
I hear if they catch you, the Yankee soldiers cut off your balls if you're a man, and rape you if you're a woman!
Doesn't surprise me. Those Yanks are real savages!

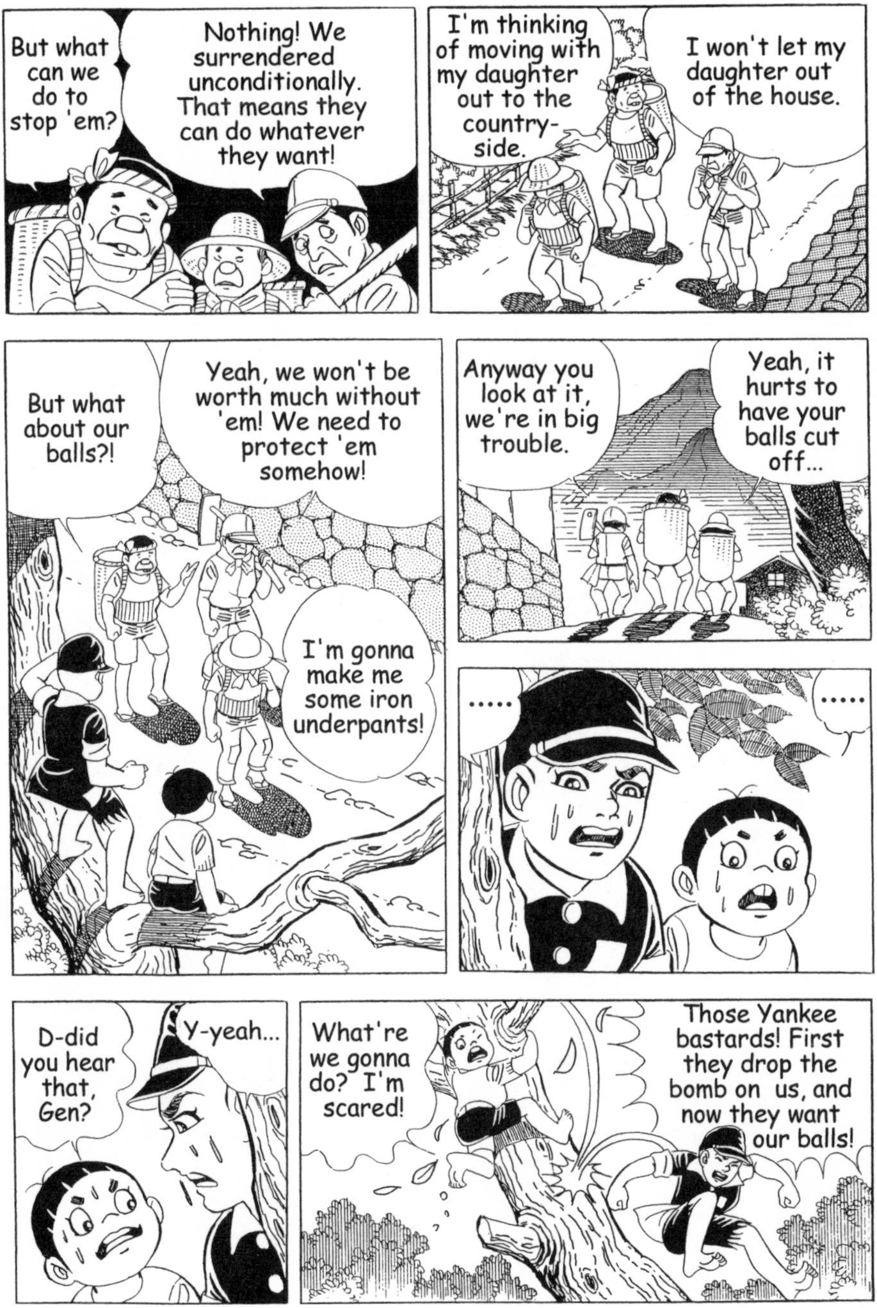
But what can we do to stop 'em?
Nothing! We surrendered unconditionally. That means they can do whatever they want!
I'm thinking of moving with my daughter out to the country-side.
I won't let my daughter out of the house.
But what about our balls?!
Yeah, we won't be worth much without 'em! We need to protect 'em somehow!
I'm gonna make me some iron underpants!
Anyway you look at it, we're in big trouble.
Yeah, it hurts to have your balls cut off...
.....
.....
D-did you hear that, Gen?
Y-yeah...
What're we gonna do? I'm scared!
Those Yankee bastards! First they drop the bomb on us, and now they want our balls!

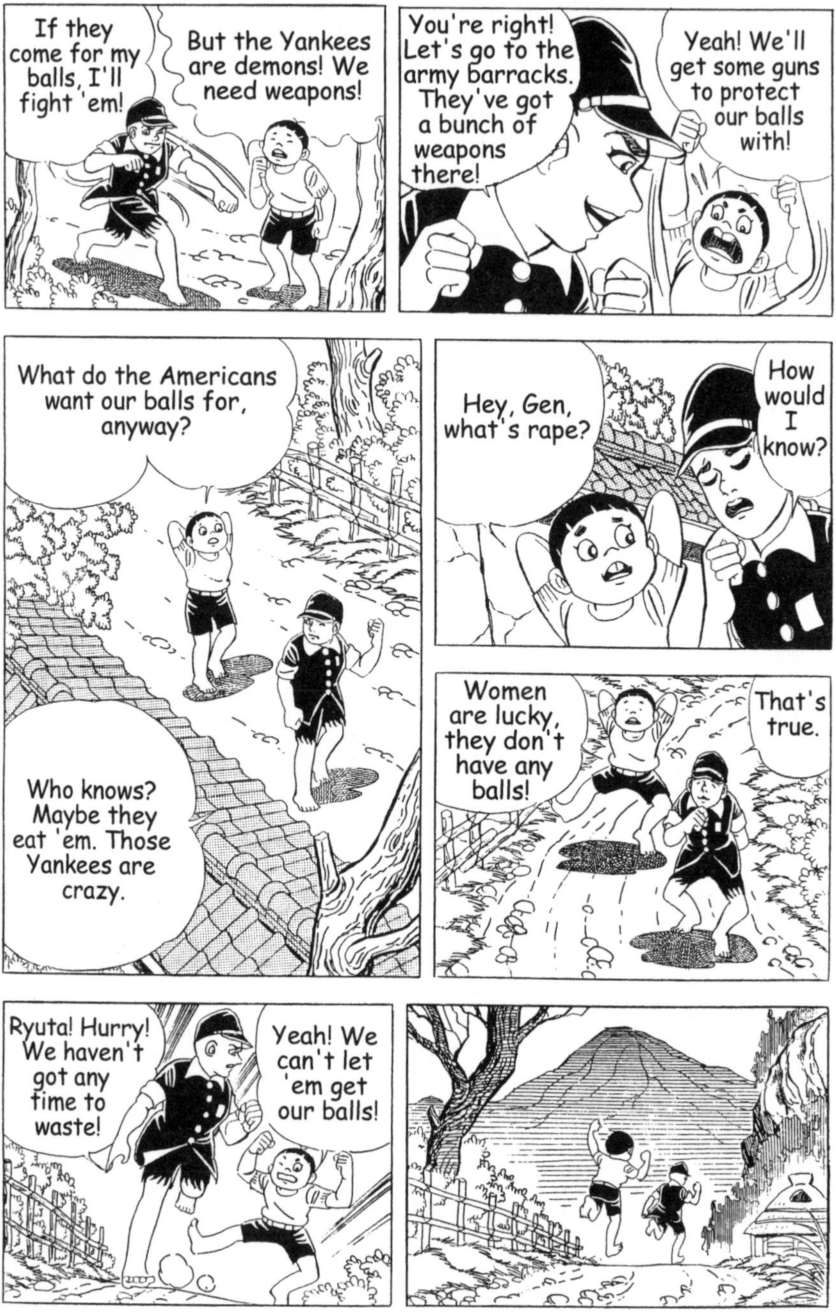

If they come for my balls, I'll fight 'em!
But the Yankees are demons! We need weapons!
You're right! Let's go to the army barracks. They've got a bunch of weapons there!
Yeah! We'll get some guns to protect our balls with!
What do the Americans want our balls for, anyway?
Who knows? Maybe they eat 'em. Those Yankees are crazy.
Hey, Gen, what's rape?
How would I know?
Women are lucky, they don't have any balls!
That's true.
Ryuta! Hurry! We haven't got any time to waste!
Yeah! We can't let 'em get our balls!

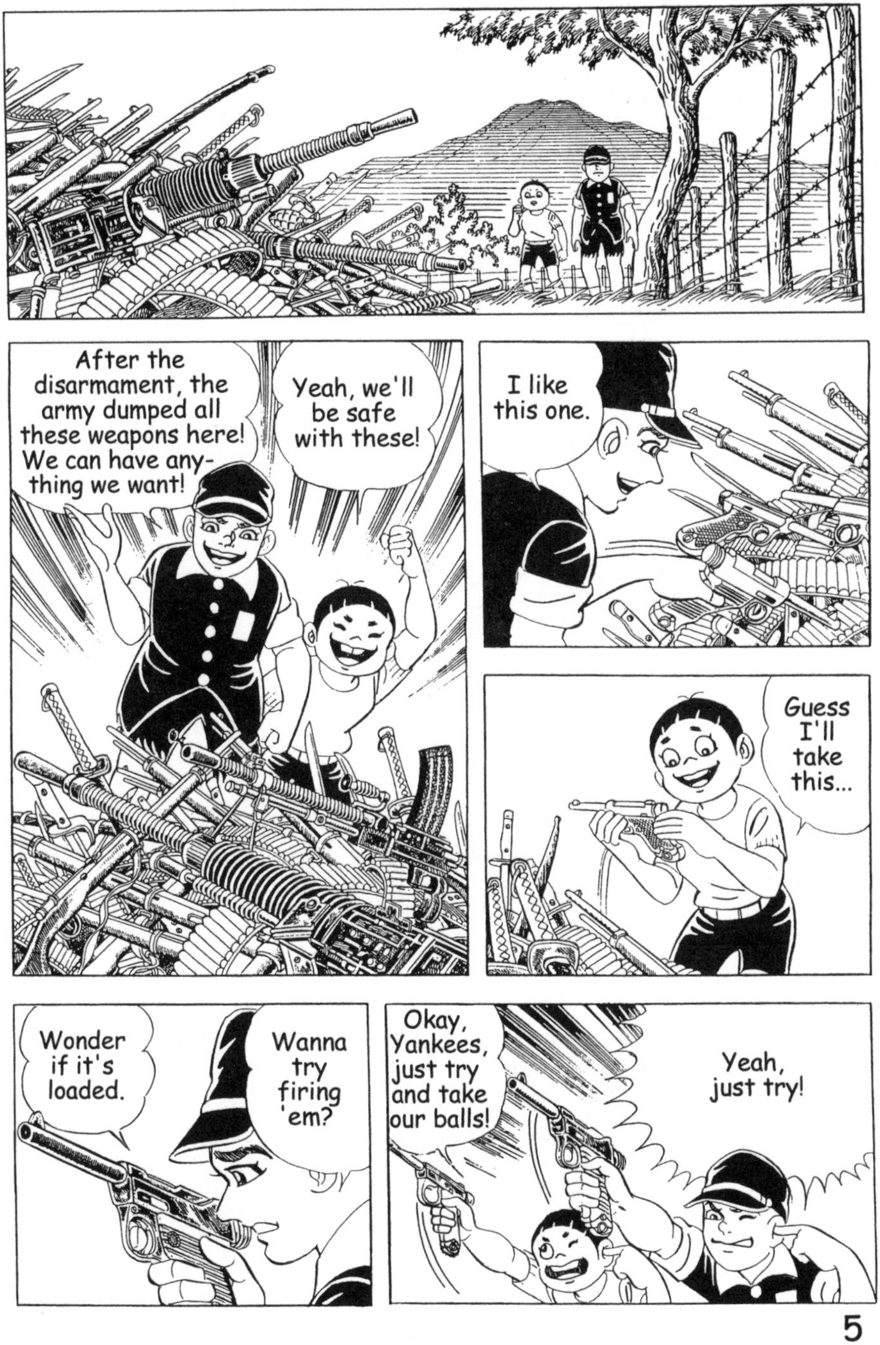

After the disarmament, the army dumped all these weapons here! We can have any-thing we want!
Yeah, we'll be safe with these!
I like this one.
Guess I'll take this...
Wonder if it's loaded.
Wanna try firing 'em?
Okay, Yankees, just try and take our balls!
Yeah, just try!

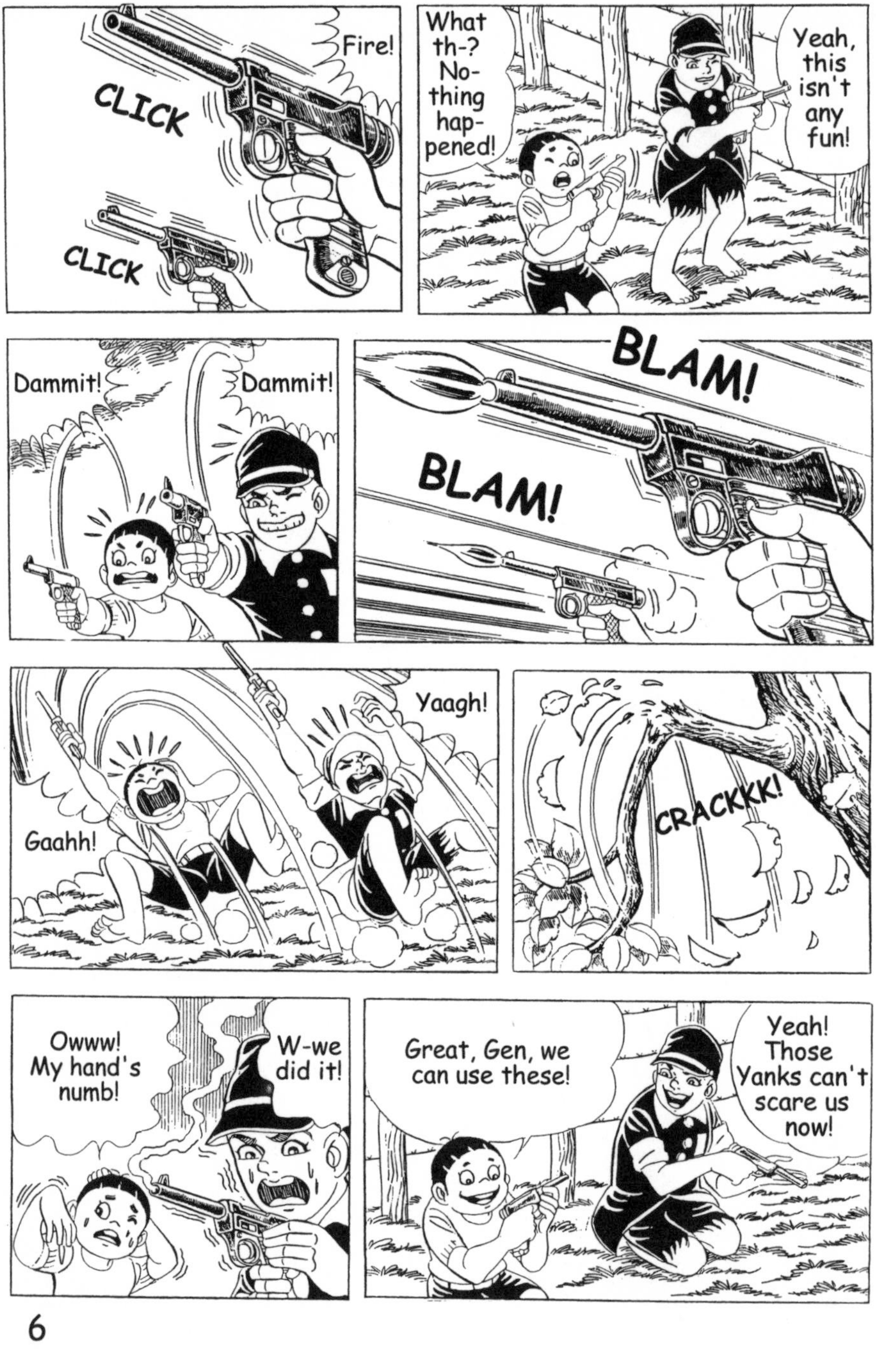
Fire!
CLICK
CLICK
What th-? No-thing hap-pened!
Yeah, this isn't any fun!
Dammit!
Dammit!
BLAM!
BLAM!
Gaahh!
Yaagh!
CRACKKK!
Owww! My hand's numb!
W-we did it!
Great, Gen, we can use these!
Yeah! Those Yanks can't scare us now!

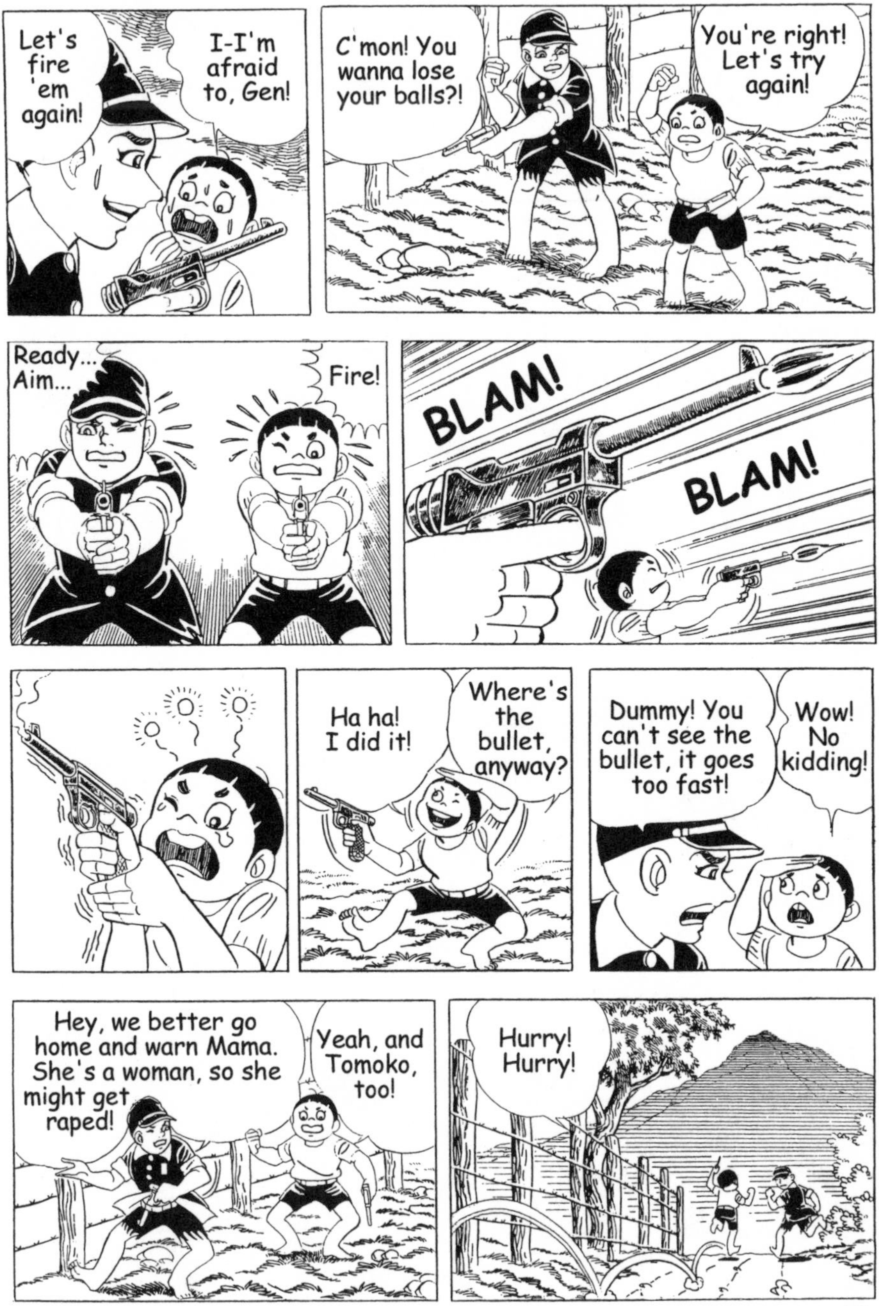
Let's fire 'em again!
I-I'm afraid to, Gen!
C'mon! You wanna lose your balls?!
You're right! Let's try again!
Ready... Aim...
Fire!
BLAM!
BLAM!
Ha ha! I did it!
Where's the bullet, anyway?
Dummy! You can't see the bullet, it goes too fast!
Wow! No kidding!
Hey, we better go home and warn Mama. She's a woman, so she might get raped!
Yeah, and Tomoko, too!
Hurry! Hurry!

Look out! Look out! The Yanks are coming to take our balls!

Mama! Bad news!

Urk!

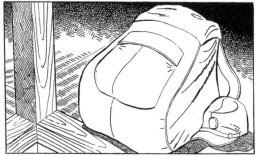

K-Koji! It's you, isn't it!

Yahoo! My big brother's back from the prep pilot school!

Hurrah! Hurrah!

.....

Koji! W-what's the matter?

8

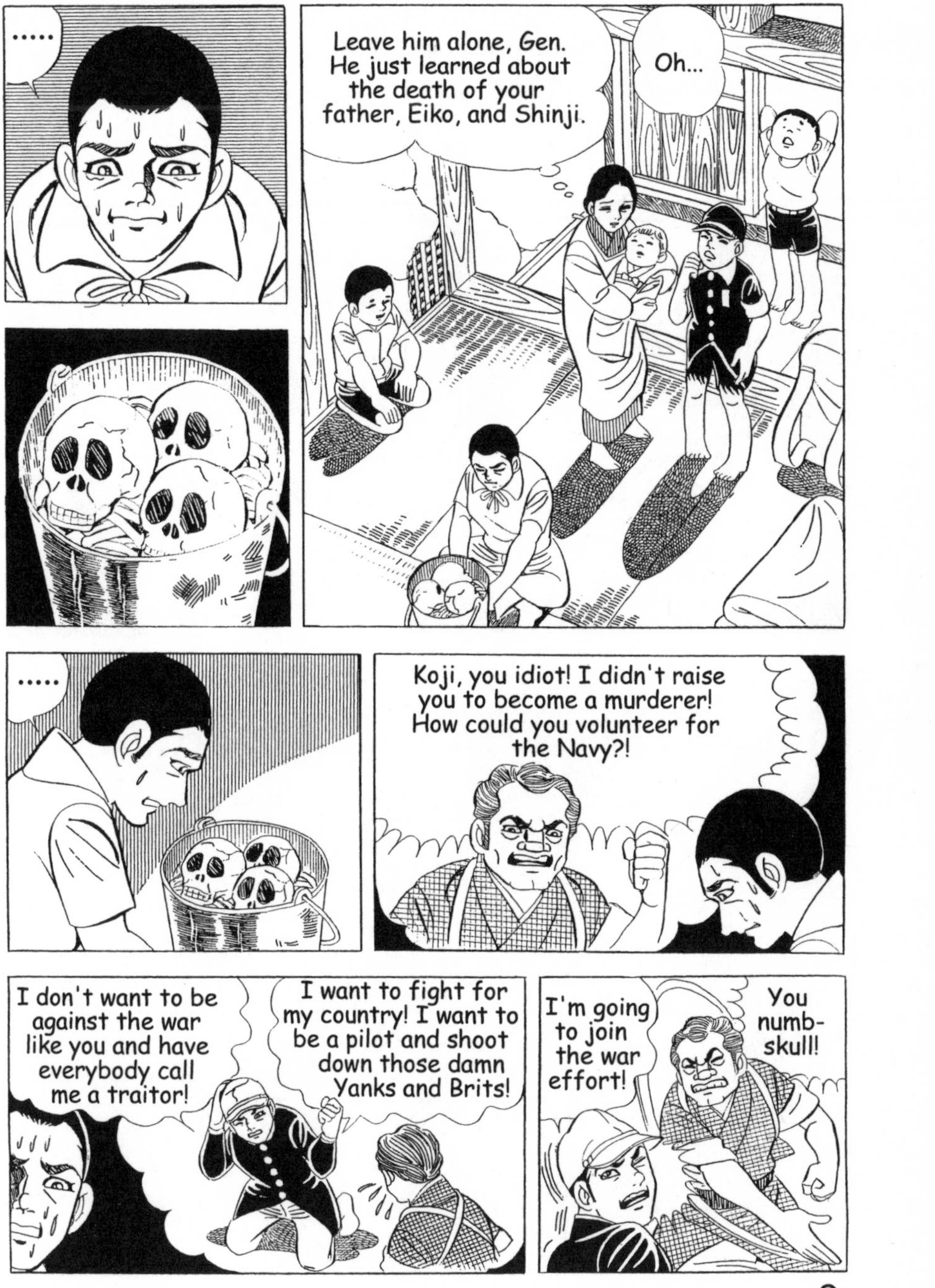

......
Leave him alone, Gen. He just learned about the death of your father, Eiko, and Shinji.
Oh...
......
Koji, you idiot! I didn't raise you to become a murderer! How could you volunteer for the Navy?!
I don't want to be against the war like you and have everybody call me a traitor!
I want to fight for my country! I want to be a pilot and shoot down those damn Yanks and Brits!
I'm going to join the war effort!
You numb-skull!

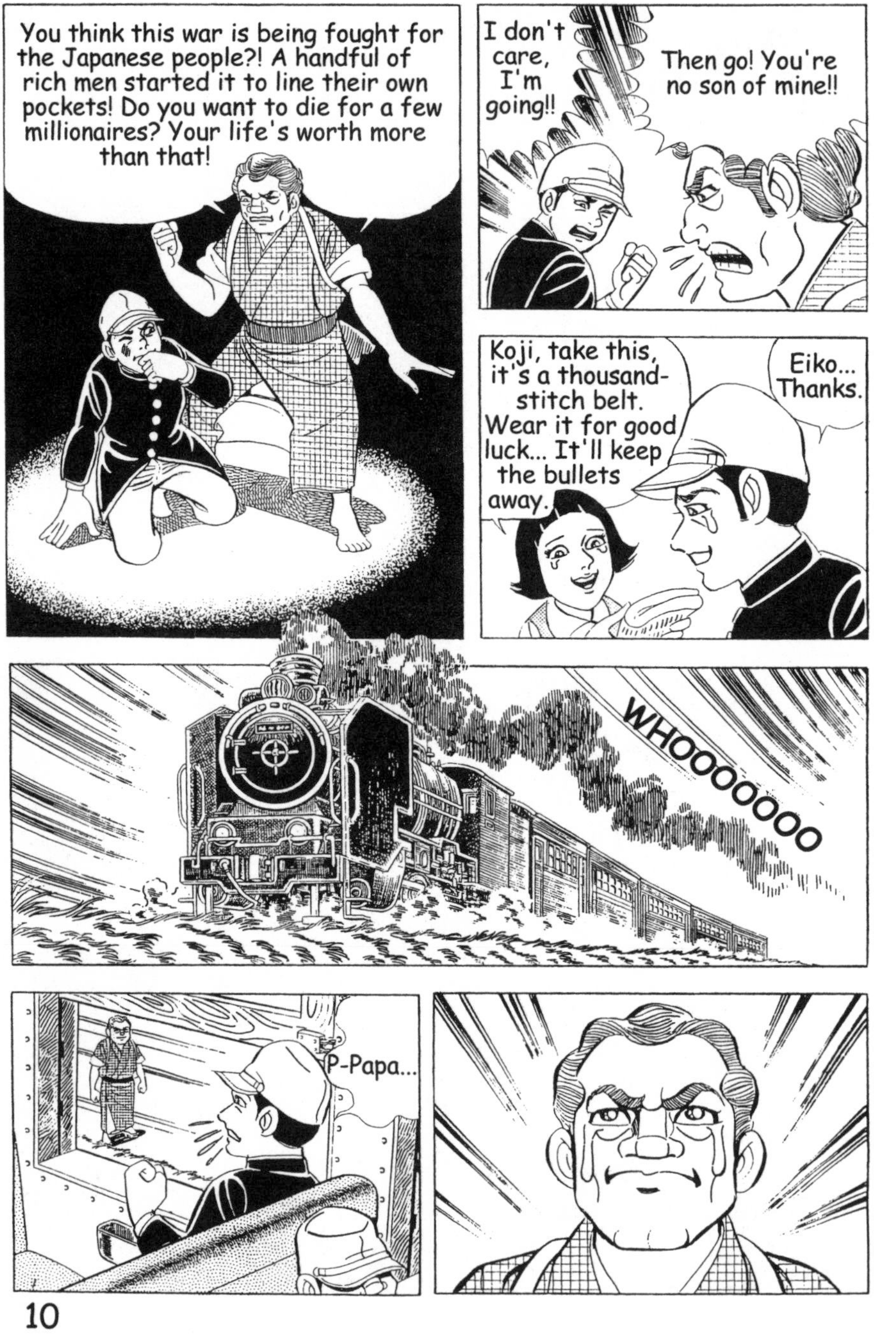
You think this war is being fought for the Japanese people?! A handful of rich men started it to line their own pockets! Do you want to die for a few millionaires? Your life's worth more than that!
I don't care, I'm going!!
Then go! You're no son of mine!!
Koji, take this, it's a thousand-stitch belt. Wear it for good luck... It'll keep the bullets away.
Eiko... Thanks.
WHOOOOOOOO
P-Papa...

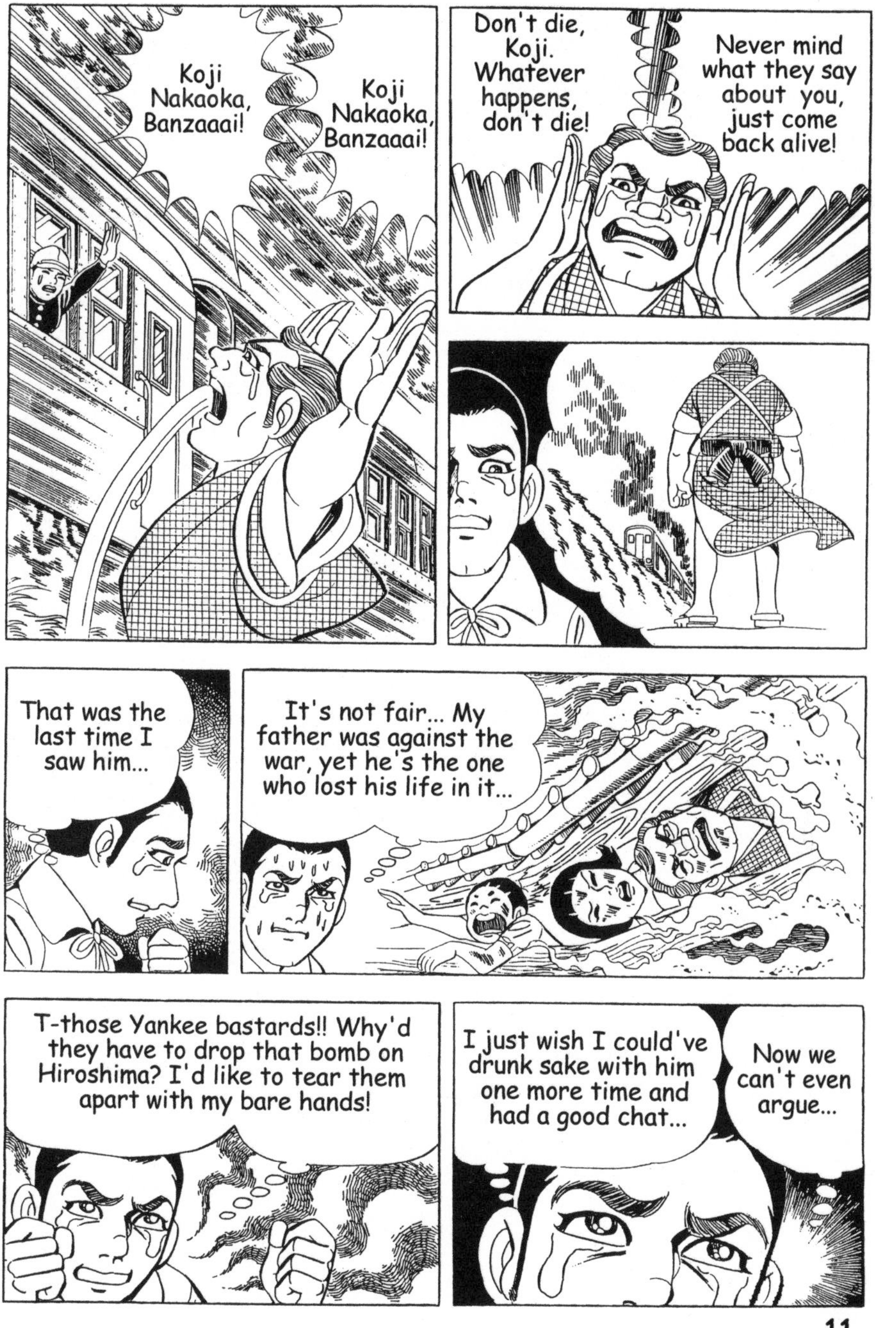
Koji Nakaoka, Banzaaai!
Koji Nakaoka, Banzaaai!
Don't die, Koji. Whatever happens, don't die!
Never mind what they say about you, just come back alive!
That was the last time I saw him...
It's not fair... My father was against the war, yet he's the one who lost his life in it...
T-those Yankee bastards!! Why'd they have to drop that bomb on Hiroshima? I'd like to tear them apart with my bare hands!
I just wish I could've drunk sake with him one more time and had a good chat...
Now we can't even argue...

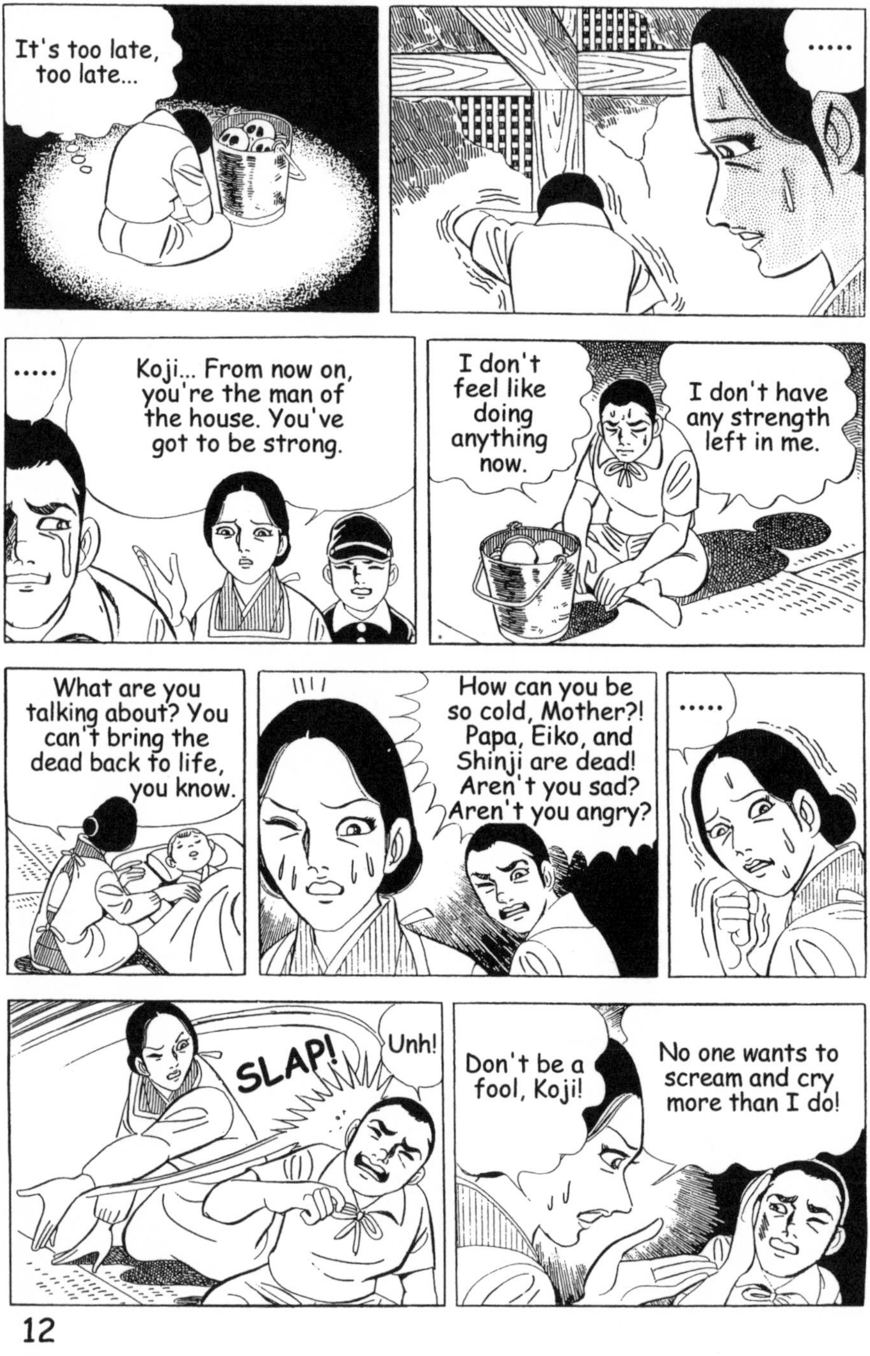
It's too late, too late...
.....
.....
Koji... From now on, you're the man of the house. You've got to be strong.
I don't feel like doing anything now.
I don't have any strength left in me.
What are you talking about? You can't bring the dead back to life, you know.
How can you be so cold, Mother?! Papa, Eiko, and Shinji are dead! Aren't you sad? Aren't you angry?
.....
SLAP!
Unh!
Don't be a fool, Koji!
No one wants to scream and cry more than I do!

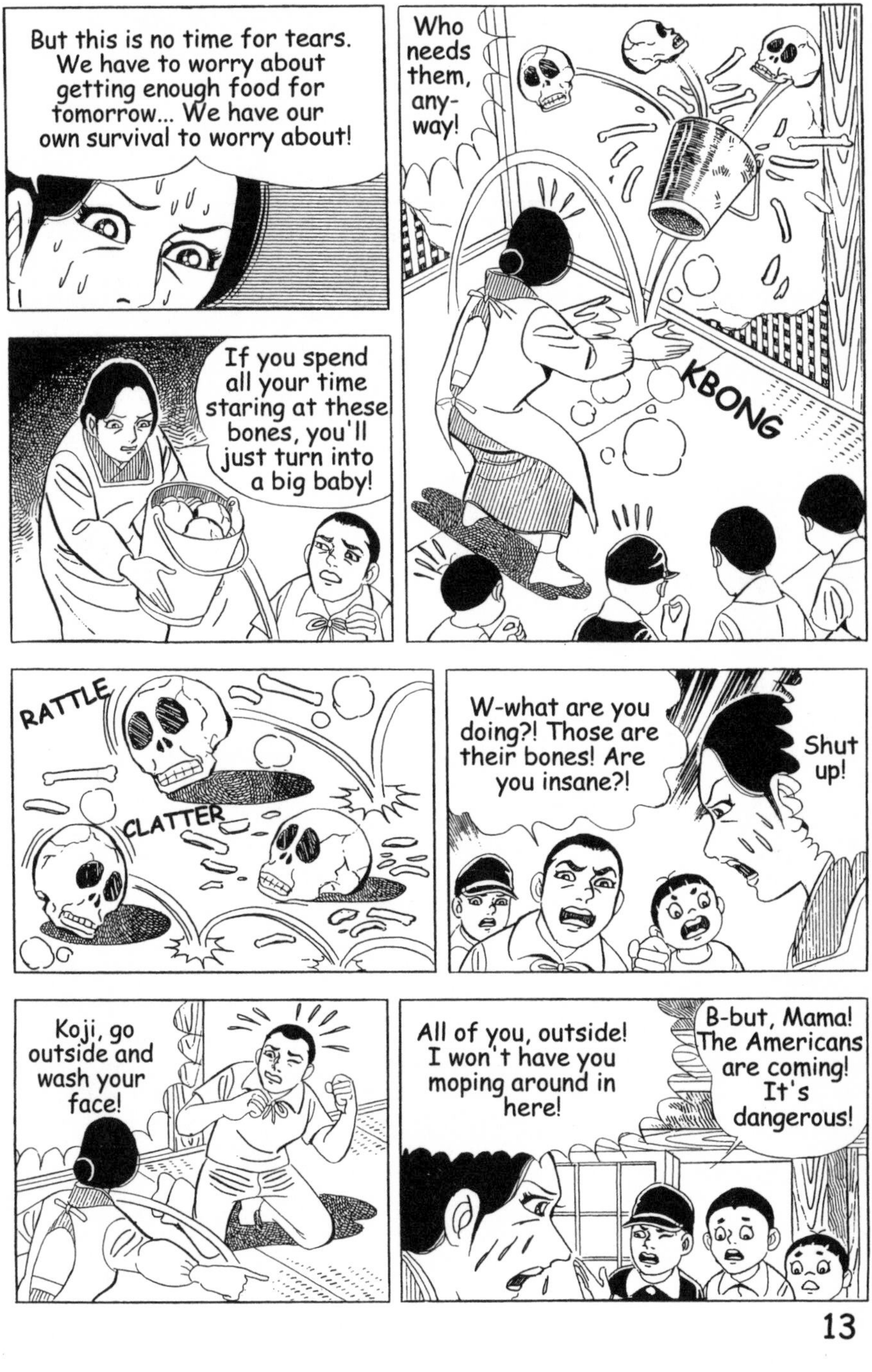
But this is no time for tears. We have to worry about getting enough food for tomorrow... We have our own survival to worry about!
Who needs them, any-way!
KBONG
If you spend all your time staring at these bones, you'll just turn into a big baby!
RATTLE
CLATTER
W-what are you doing?! Those are their bones! Are you insane?!
Shut up!
Koji, go outside and wash your face!
All of you, outside! I won't have you moping around in here!
B-but, Mama! The Americans are coming! It's dangerous!

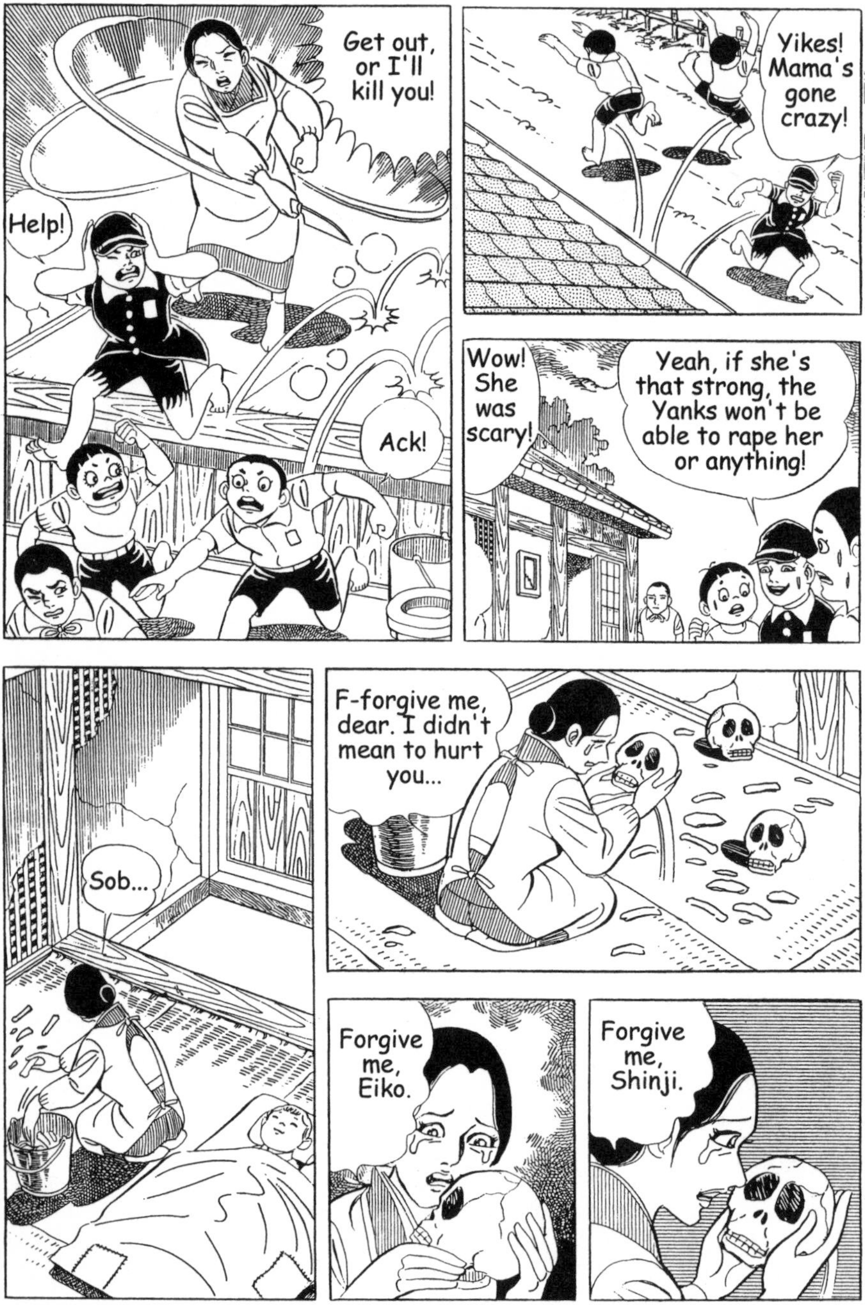
Get out, or I'll kill you!
Help!
Ack!
Yikes! Mama's gone crazy!
Wow! She was scary!
Yeah, if she's that strong, the Yanks won't be able to rape her or anything!
Sob...
F-forgive me, dear. I didn't mean to hurt you...
Forgive me, Eiko.
Forgive me, Shinji.

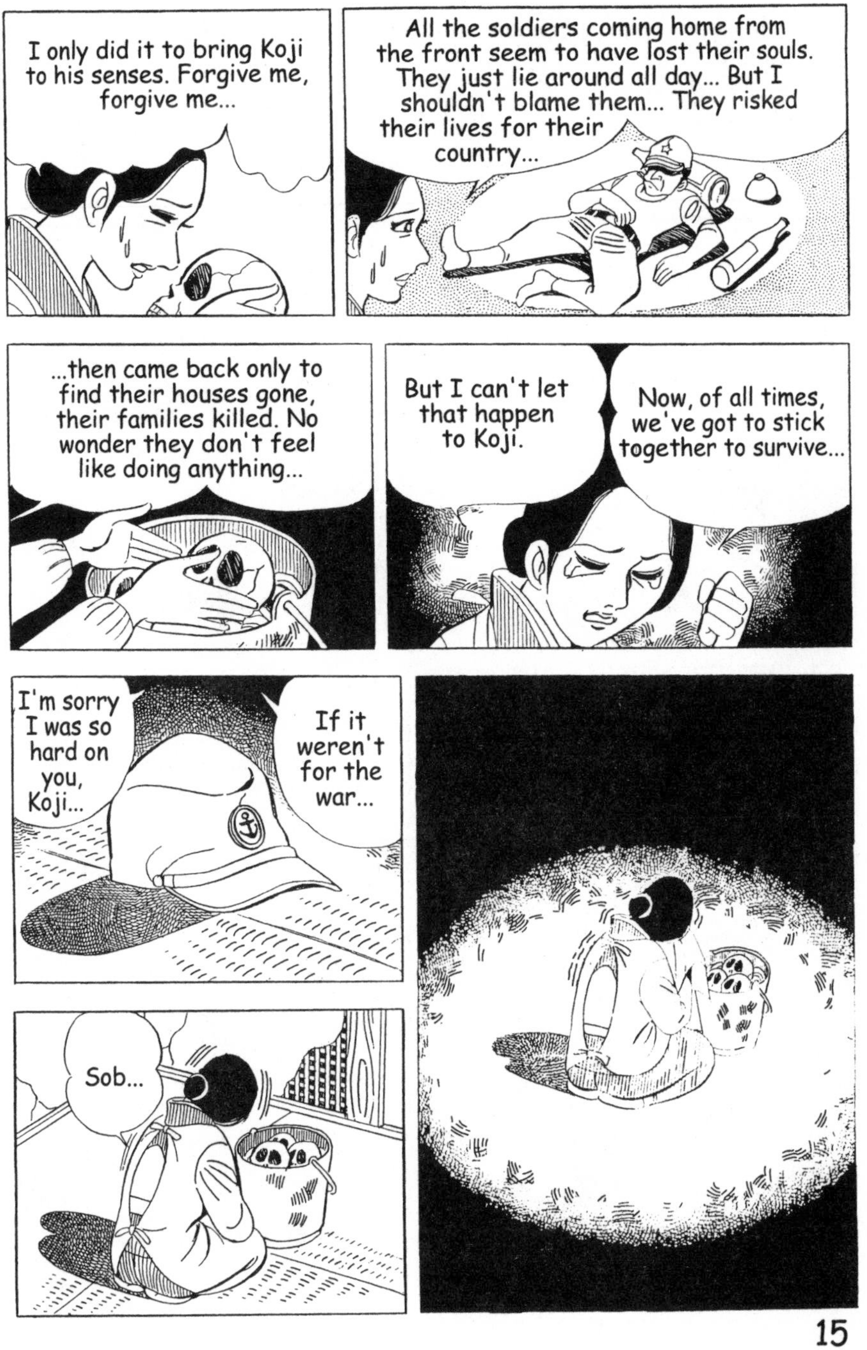
I only did it to bring Koji to his senses. Forgive me, forgive me...
All the soldiers coming home from the front seem to have lost their souls. They just lie around all day... But I shouldn't blame them... They risked their lives for their country...
...then came back only to find their houses gone, their families killed. No wonder they don't feel like doing anything...
But I can't let that happen to Koji.
Now, of all times, we've got to stick together to survive...
I'm sorry I was so hard on you, Koji...
If it weren't for the war...
Sob...

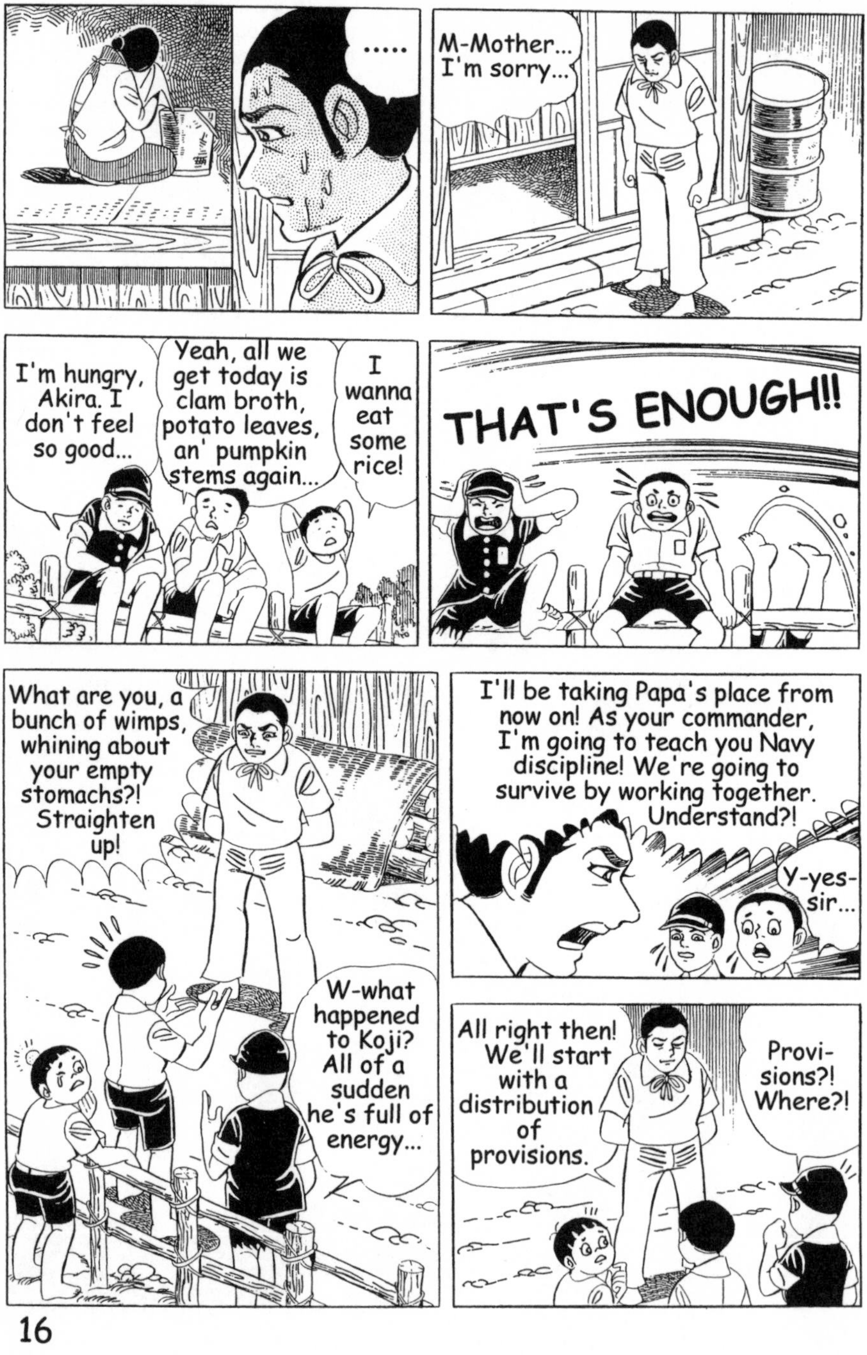
.....
M-Mother... I'm sorry...
I'm hungry, Akira. I don't feel so good...
Yeah, all we get today is clam broth, potato leaves, an' pumpkin stems again...
I wanna eat some rice!
THAT'S ENOUGH!!
What are you, a bunch of wimps, whining about your empty stomachs?! Straighten up!
W-what happened to Koji? All of a sudden he's full of energy...
I'll be taking Papa's place from now on! As your commander, I'm going to teach you Navy discipline! We're going to survive by working together. Understand?!
Y-yes-sir...
All right then! We'll start with a distribution of provisions.
Provi-sions?! Where?!

Go look in my knapsack.

Aye aye, Cap'n Koji, sir! Right away!!

Hee hee hee!

Boy oh boy!

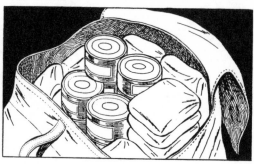

Yahoo!! Canned food!!

Biscuits!

And rice!!

Yow! I'm so happy I'm gonna wet my pants!!

Akira, Gen, Shinji... I mean Ryuta!... Go ahead and help yourselves. Today marks a fresh start for the Nakaoka family!

You've made your crew very happy, Cap'n Koji!

Aye aye, sir!

17

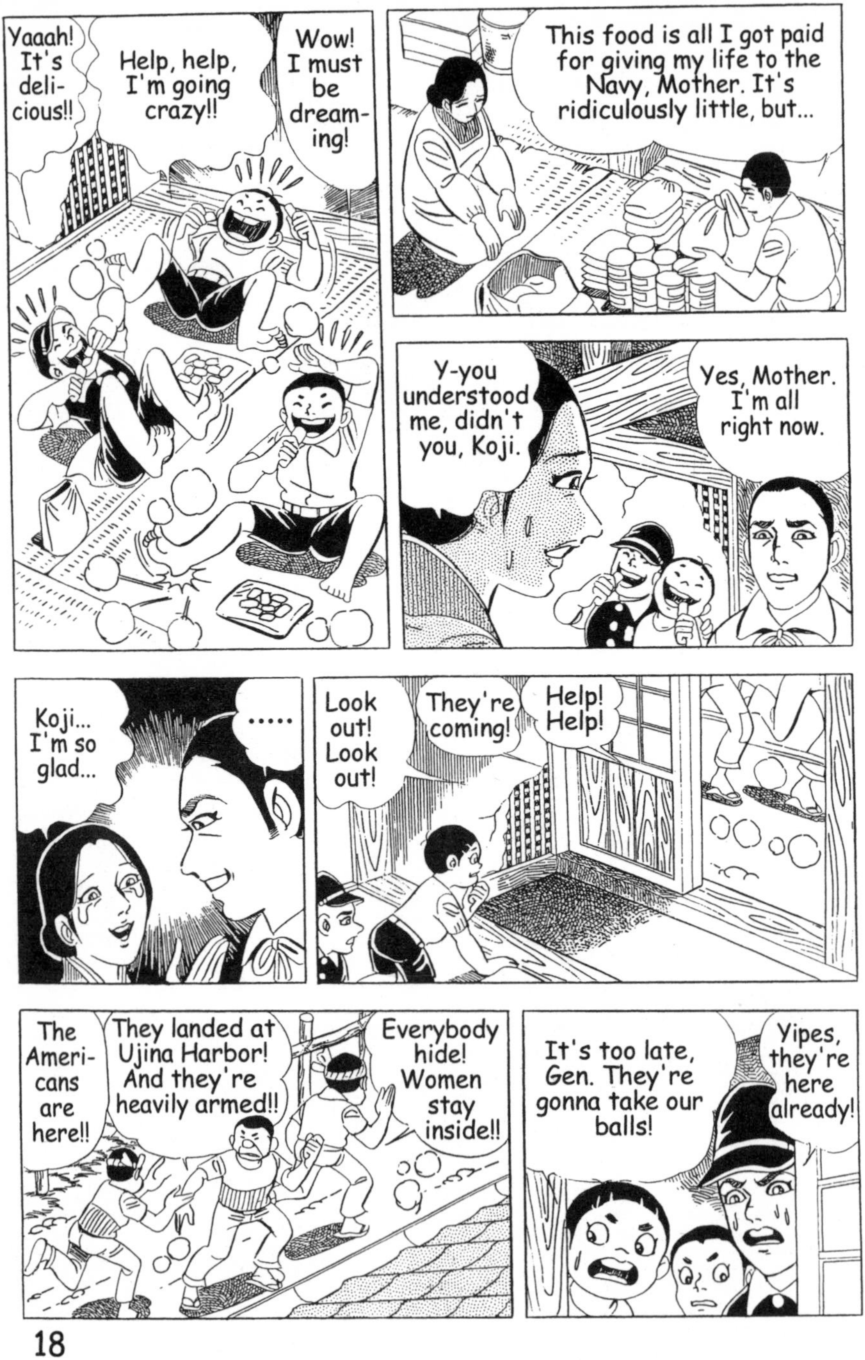
Yaaah! It's deli-cious!!
Help, help, I'm going crazy!!
Wow! I must be dream-ing!
This food is all I got paid for giving my life to the Navy, Mother. It's ridiculously little, but...
Y-you understood me, didn't you, Koji.
Yes, Mother. I'm all right now.
Koji... I'm so glad...
.....
Look out! Look out!
They're coming!
Help! Help!
The Ameri-cans are here!!
They landed at Ujina Harbor! And they're heavily armed!!
Everybody hide! Women stay inside!!
It's too late, Gen. They're gonna take our balls!
Yipes, they're here already!

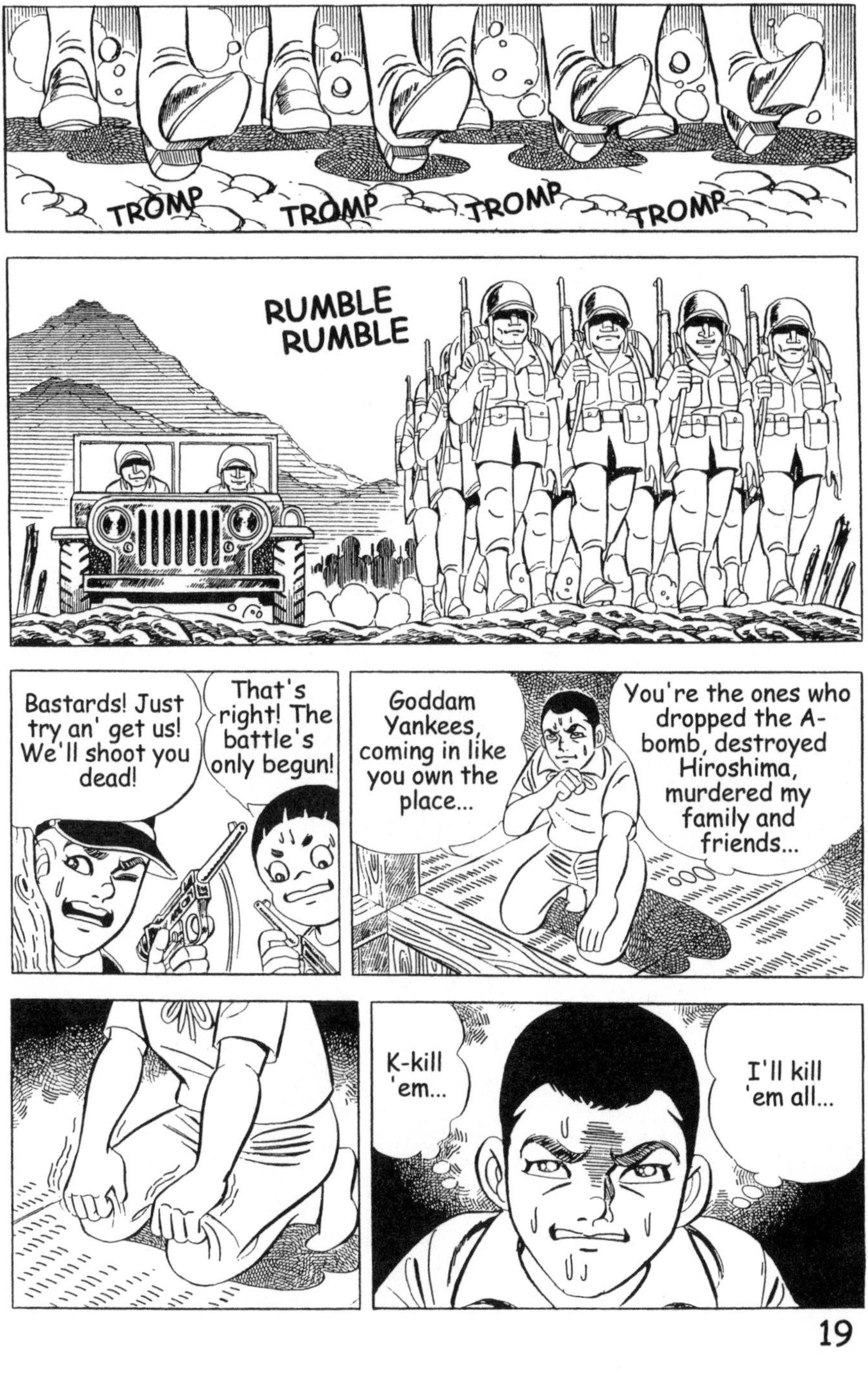
TROMP
TROMP
TROMP
TROMP
RUMBLE RUMBLE
Bastards! Just try an' get us! We'll shoot you dead!
That's right! The battle's only begun!
Goddam Yankees, coming in like you own the place...
You're the ones who dropped the A-bomb, destroyed Hiroshima, murdered my family and friends...
K-kill 'em...
I'll kill 'em all...

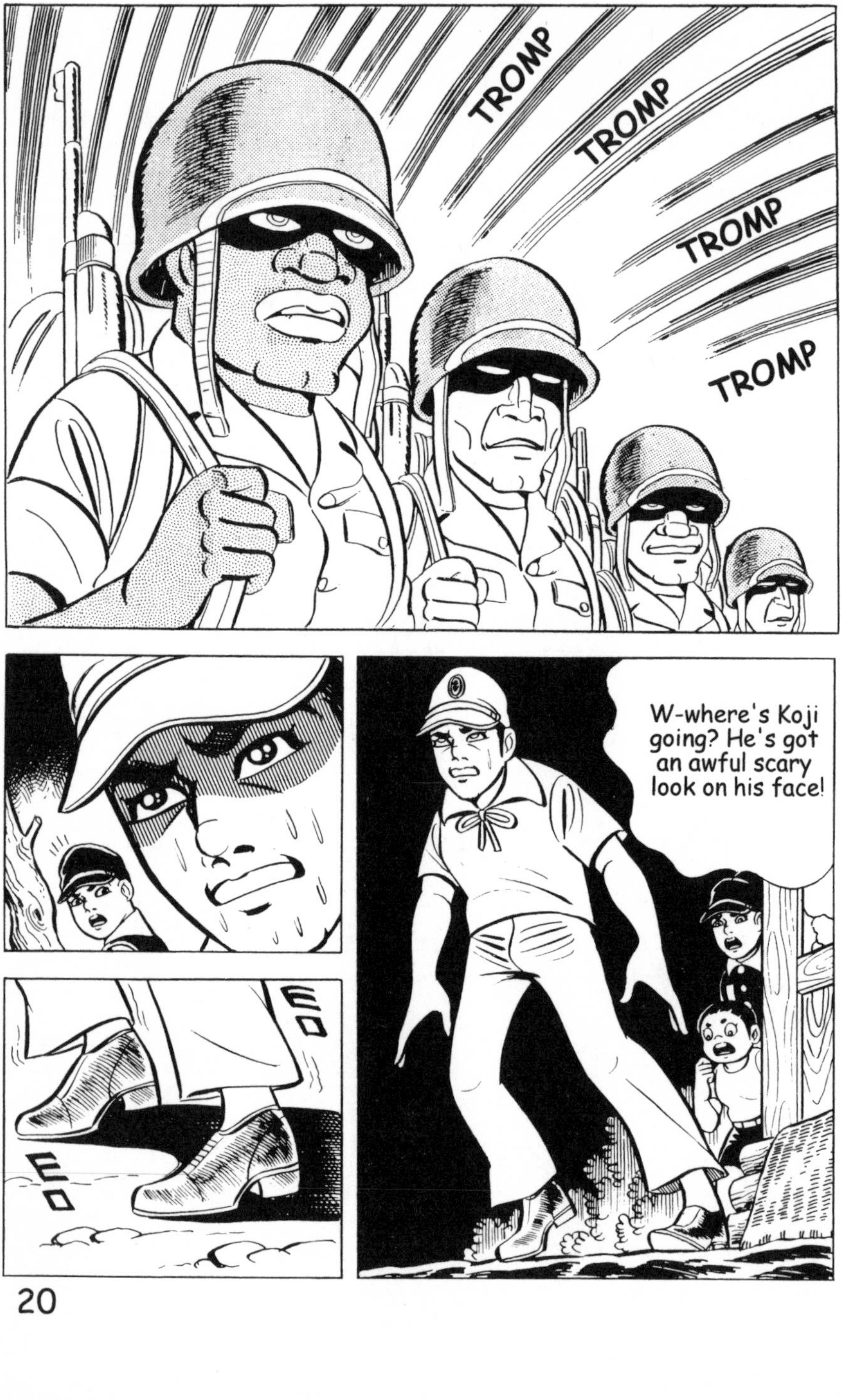
TROMP
TROMP
TROMP
TROMP
W-where's Koji going? He's got an awful scary look on his face!

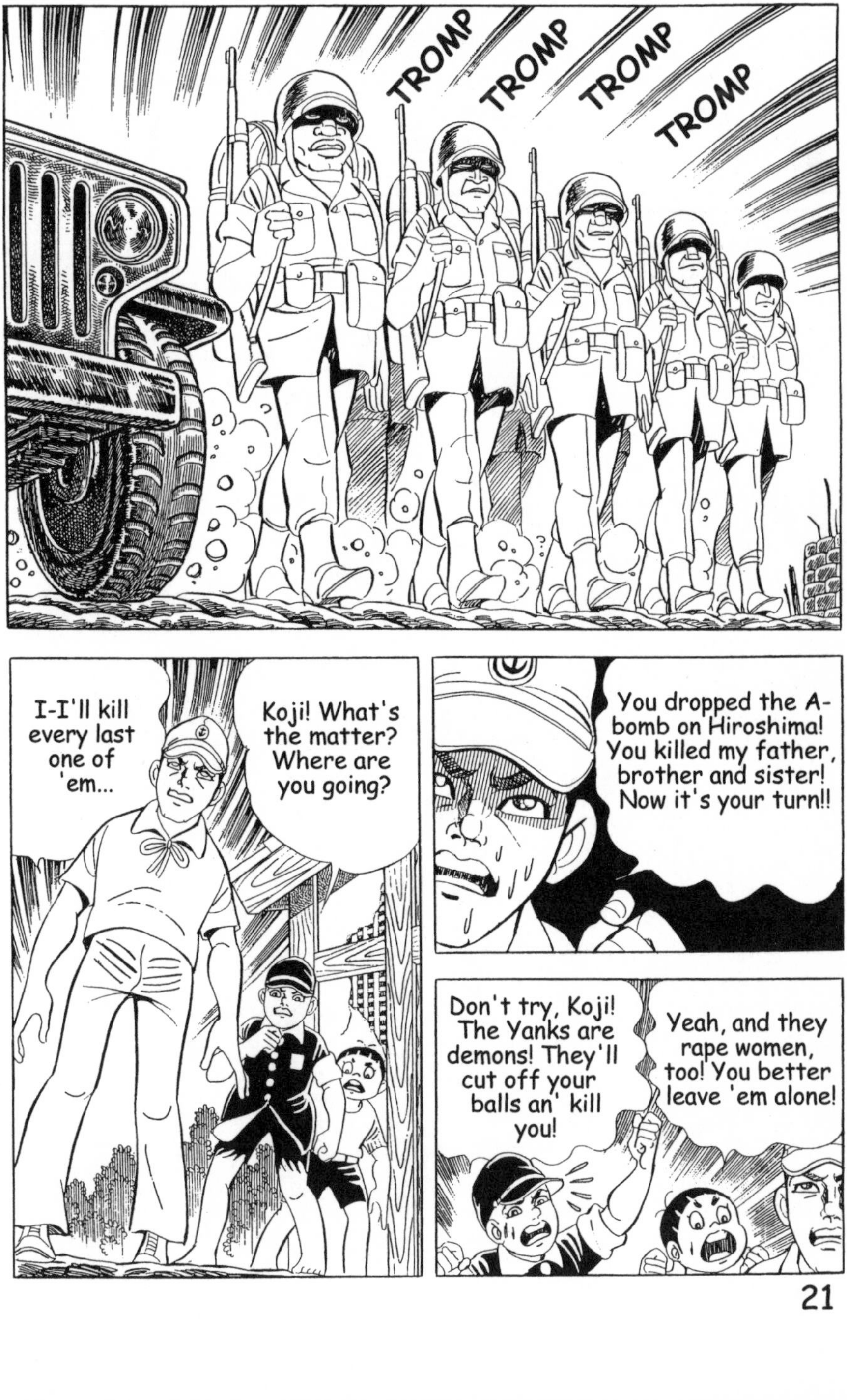
TROMP
TROMP
TROMP
TROMP
I-I'll kill every last one of 'em...
Koji! What's the matter? Where are you going?
You dropped the A-bomb on Hiroshima! You killed my father, brother and sister! Now it's your turn!!
Don't try, Koji! The Yanks are demons! They'll cut off your balls an' kill you!
Yeah, and they rape women, too! You better leave 'em alone!

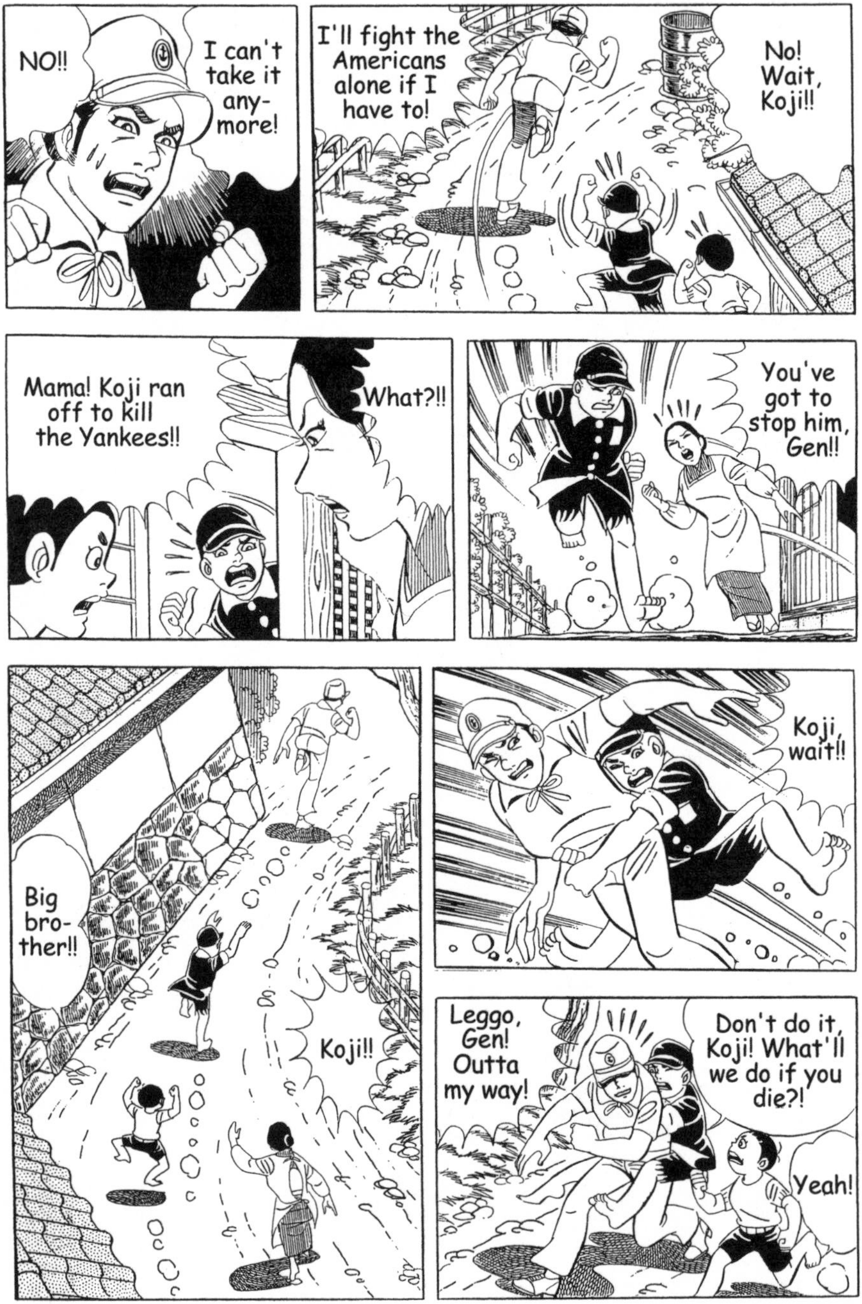
NO!!
I can't take it any-more!
I'll fight the Americans alone if I have to!
No! Wait, Koji!!
Mama! Koji ran off to kill the Yankees!!
What?!!
You've got to stop him, Gen!!
Big bro-ther!!
Koji!!
Koji, wait!!
Leggo, Gen! Outta my way!
Don't do it, Koji! What'll we do if you die?!
Yeah!

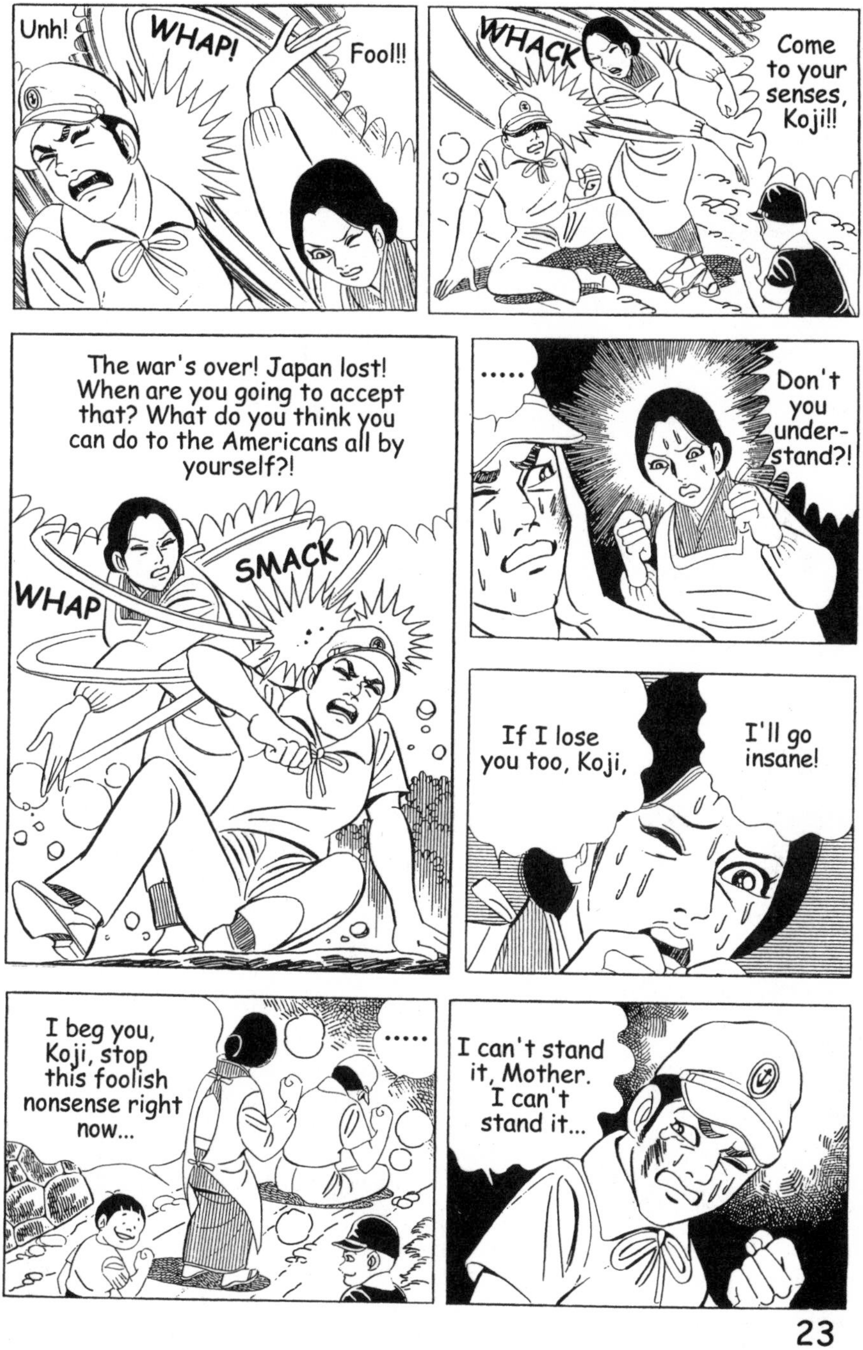
Unh!
WHAP!
Fool!!
WHACK
Come to your senses, Koji!!
The war's over! Japan lost! When are you going to accept that? What do you think you can do to the Americans all by yourself?!
WHAP
SMACK
.....
Don't you under-stand?!
If I lose you too, Koji,
I'll go insane!
I beg you, Koji, stop this foolish nonsense right now...
.....
I can't stand it, Mother. I can't stand it...

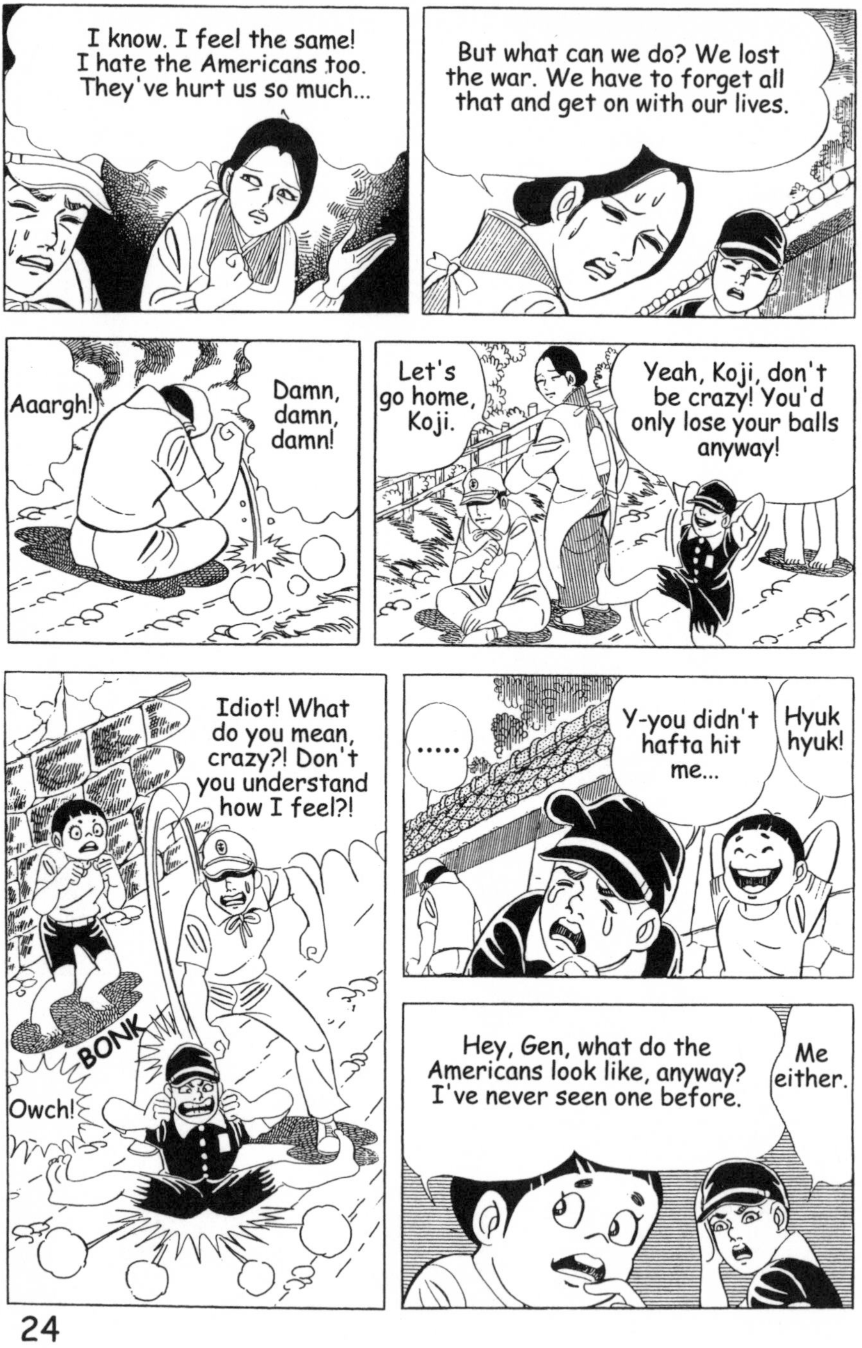
I know. I feel the same! I hate the Americans too. They've hurt us so much...
But what can we do? We lost the war. We have to forget all that and get on with our lives.
Aaargh!
Damn, damn, damn!
Let's go home, Koji.
Yeah, Koji, don't be crazy! You'd only lose your balls anyway!
Idiot! What do you mean, crazy?! Don't you understand how I feel?!
BONK
Owch!
.....
Y-you didn't hafta hit me...
Hyuk hyuk!
Hey, Gen, what do the Americans look like, anyway? I've never seen one before.
Me either.

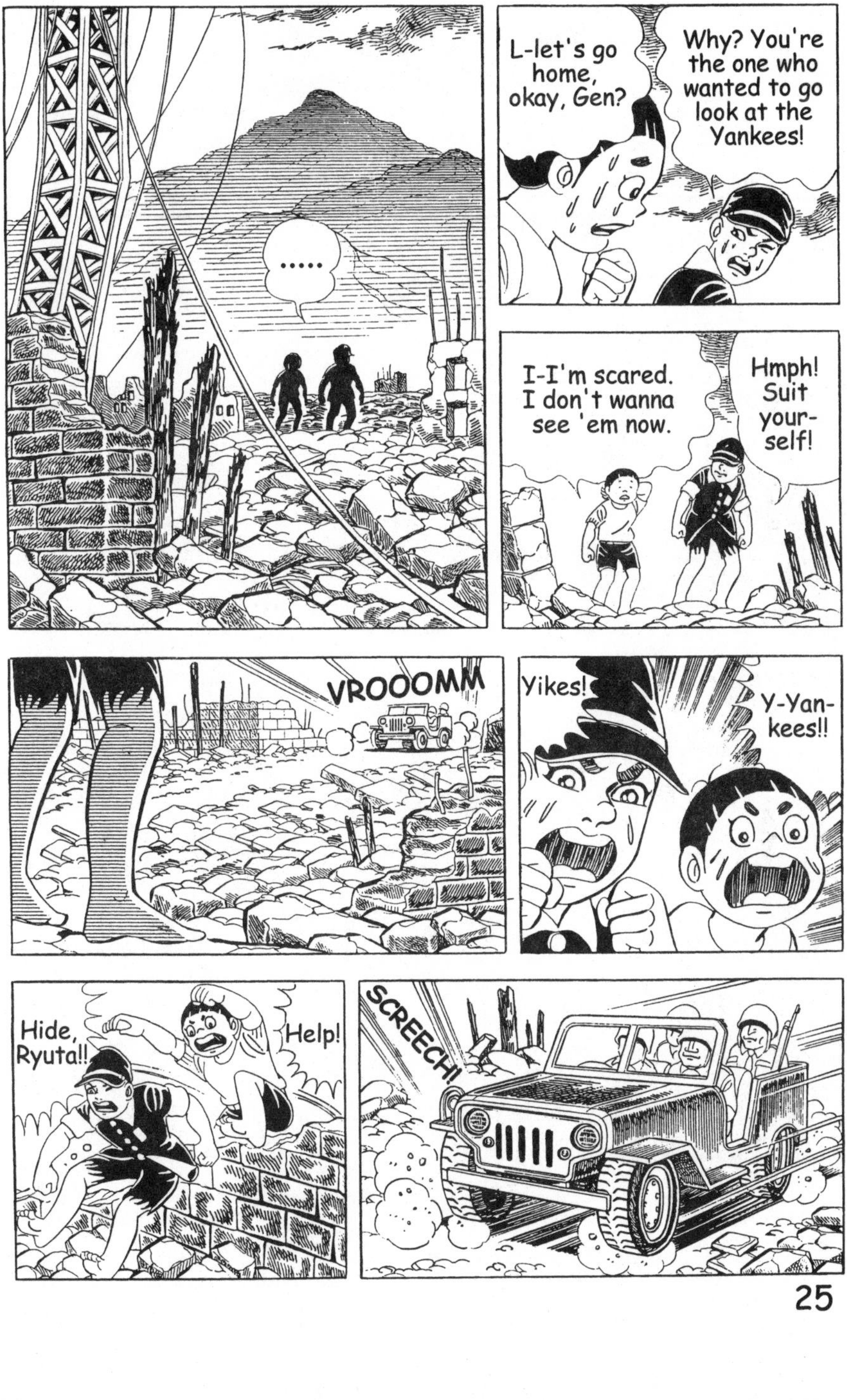
......
L-let's go home, okay, Gen?
Why? You're the one who wanted to go look at the Yankees!
I-I'm scared. I don't wanna see 'em now.
Hmph! Suit your-self!
VROOOMM
Yikes!
Y-Yan-kees!!
Hide, Ryuta!!
Help!
SCREECH!!

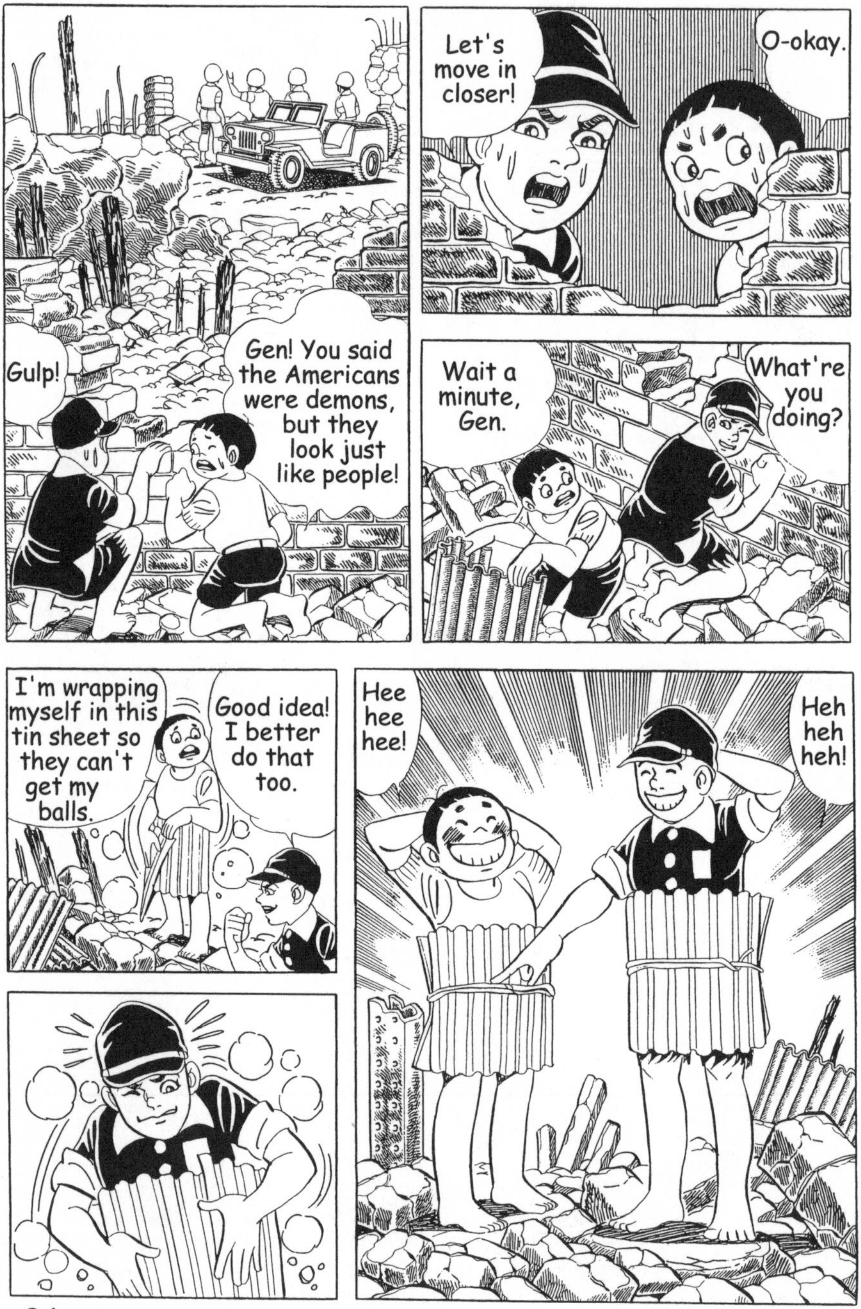
Let's move in closer!
O-okay.
Gulp!
Gen! You said the Americans were demons, but they look just like people!
Wait a minute, Gen.
What're you doing?
I'm wrapping myself in this tin sheet so they can't get my balls.
Good idea! I better do that too.
Hee hee hee!
Heh heh heh!

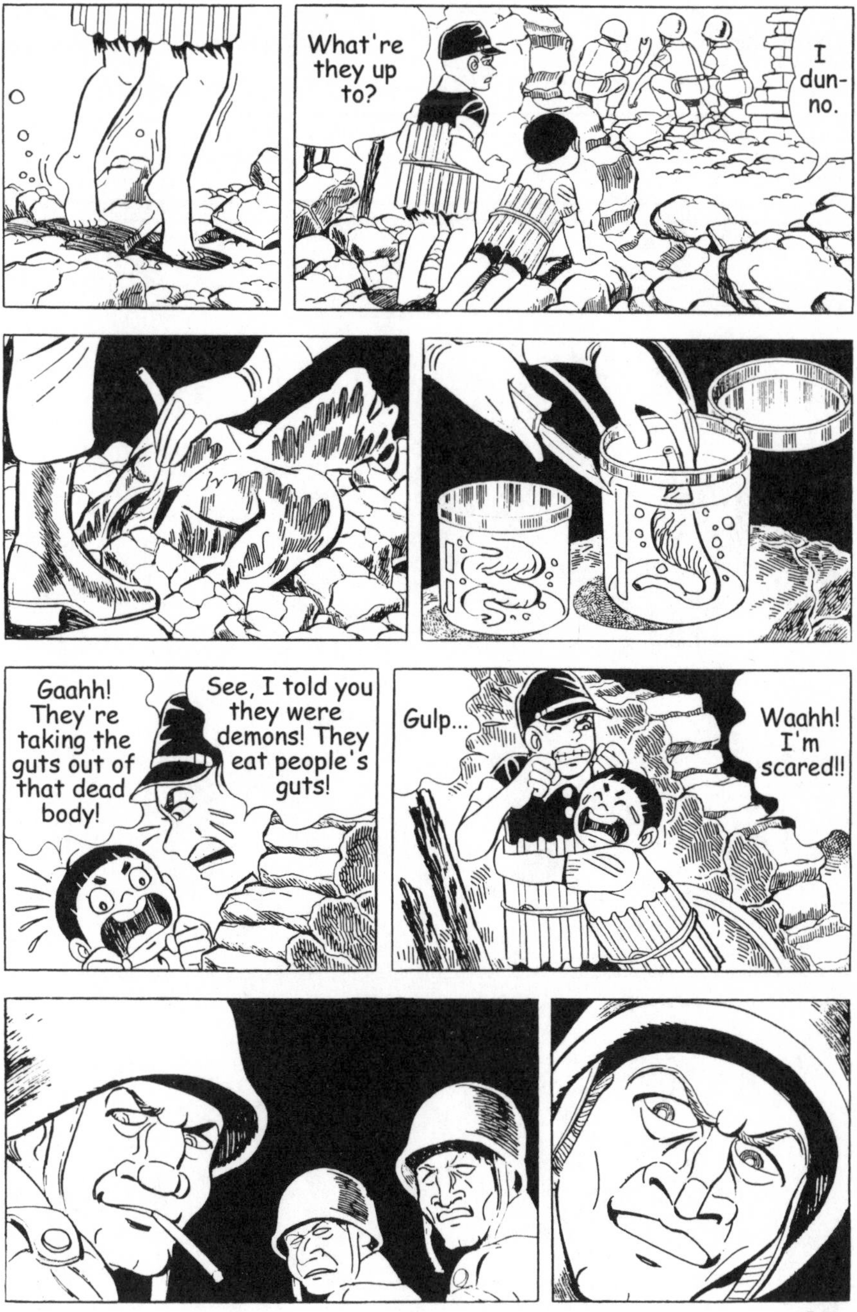
What're they up to?
I dun-no.
Gaahh! They're taking the guts out of that dead body!
See, I told you they were demons! They eat people's guts!
Gulp...
Waahh! I'm scared!!

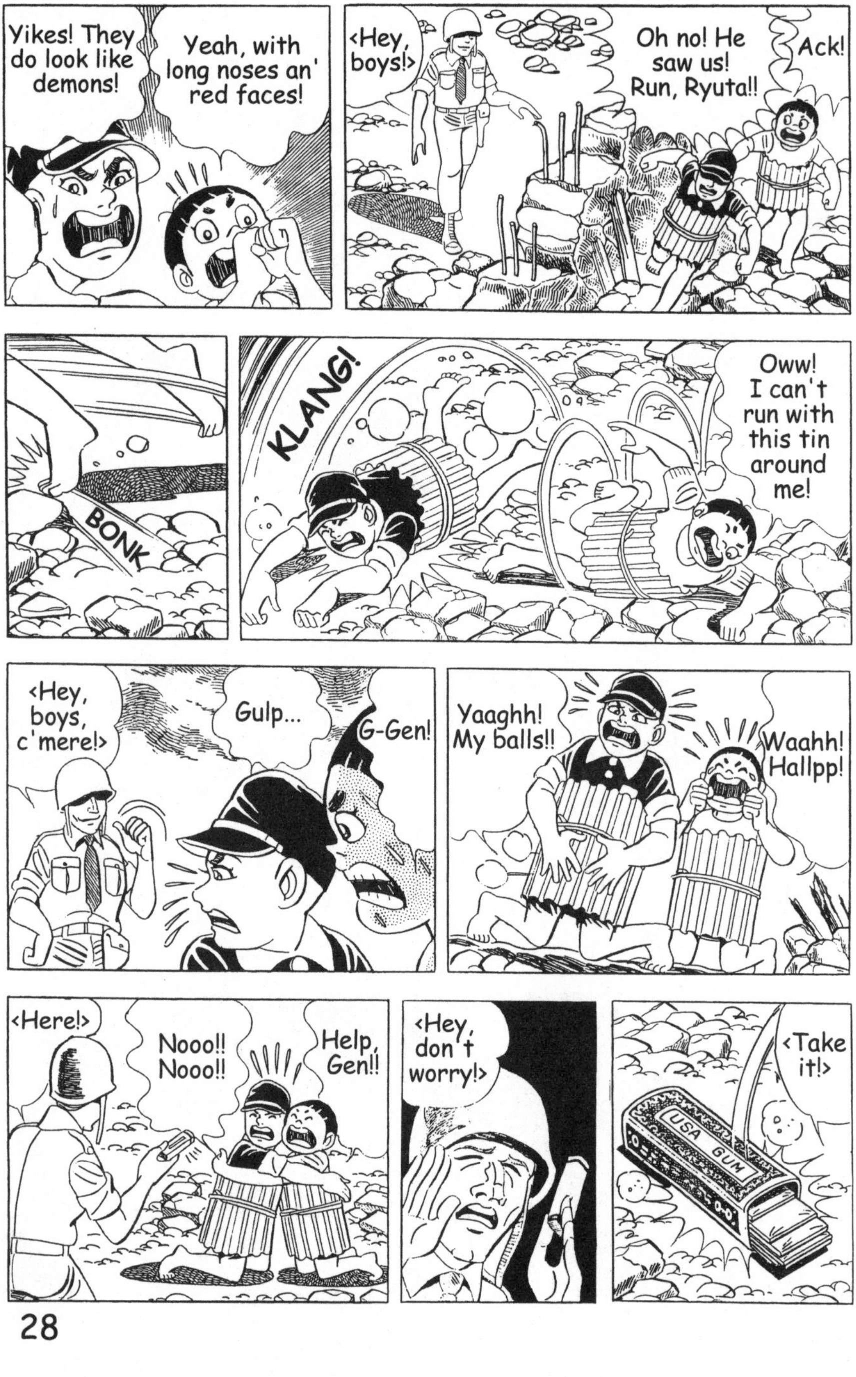

Yikes! They do look like demons!
Yeah, with long noses an' red faces!
<Hey, boys!>
Oh no! He saw us! Run, Ryuta!!
Ack!
BONK
KLANG!
Oww! I can't run with this tin around me!
<Hey, boys, c'mere!>
Gulp...
G-Gen!
Yaaghh! My balls!!
Waahh! Hallpp!
<Here!>
Nooo!! Nooo!!
Help, Gen!!
<Hey, don't worry!>
<Take it!>
USA GUM

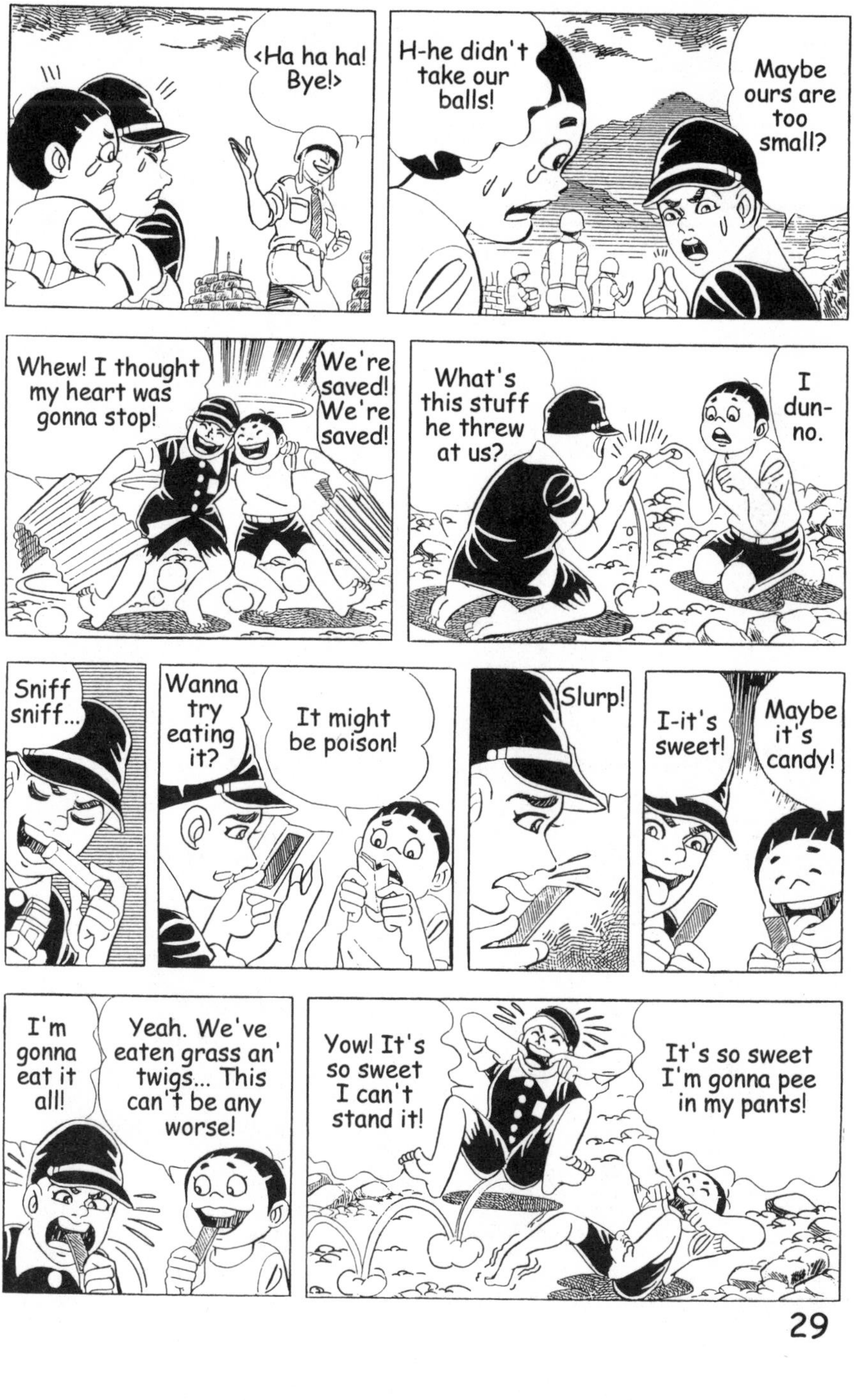
‹Ha ha ha! Bye!›
H-he didn't take our balls!
Maybe ours are too small?
Whew! I thought my heart was gonna stop!
We're saved! We're saved!
What's this stuff he threw at us?
I dun-no.
Sniff sniff...
Wanna try eating it?
It might be poison!
Slurp!
I-it's sweet!
Maybe it's candy!
I'm gonna eat it all!
Yeah. We've eaten grass an' twigs... This can't be any worse!
Yow! It's so sweet I can't stand it!
It's so sweet I'm gonna pee in my pants!

But why do they want people's guts when they have good stuff like this to eat?

Search me...

As soon as the Americans landed in Hiroshima, they began collecting materials for their A-bomb research--everything from pebbles to the innards of corpses.

And they made sure that news about the effects of the A-bomb did not reach the rest of the world. In this way the Americans covered up the terrible crime they had committed in Hiroshima.

Worst of all was the plight of the people who survived the bomb. Abandoned by everyone else, they were left alone to endure the pain of their burned and irradiated bodies.

Yak yak...

CHEW CHEW

CHEW CHEW CHEW

Blah blah...

Y'mean they didn't take your balls?!

You guys are real hot shots, takin' candy from the Yankees!

Har-rumph!

Ahem!

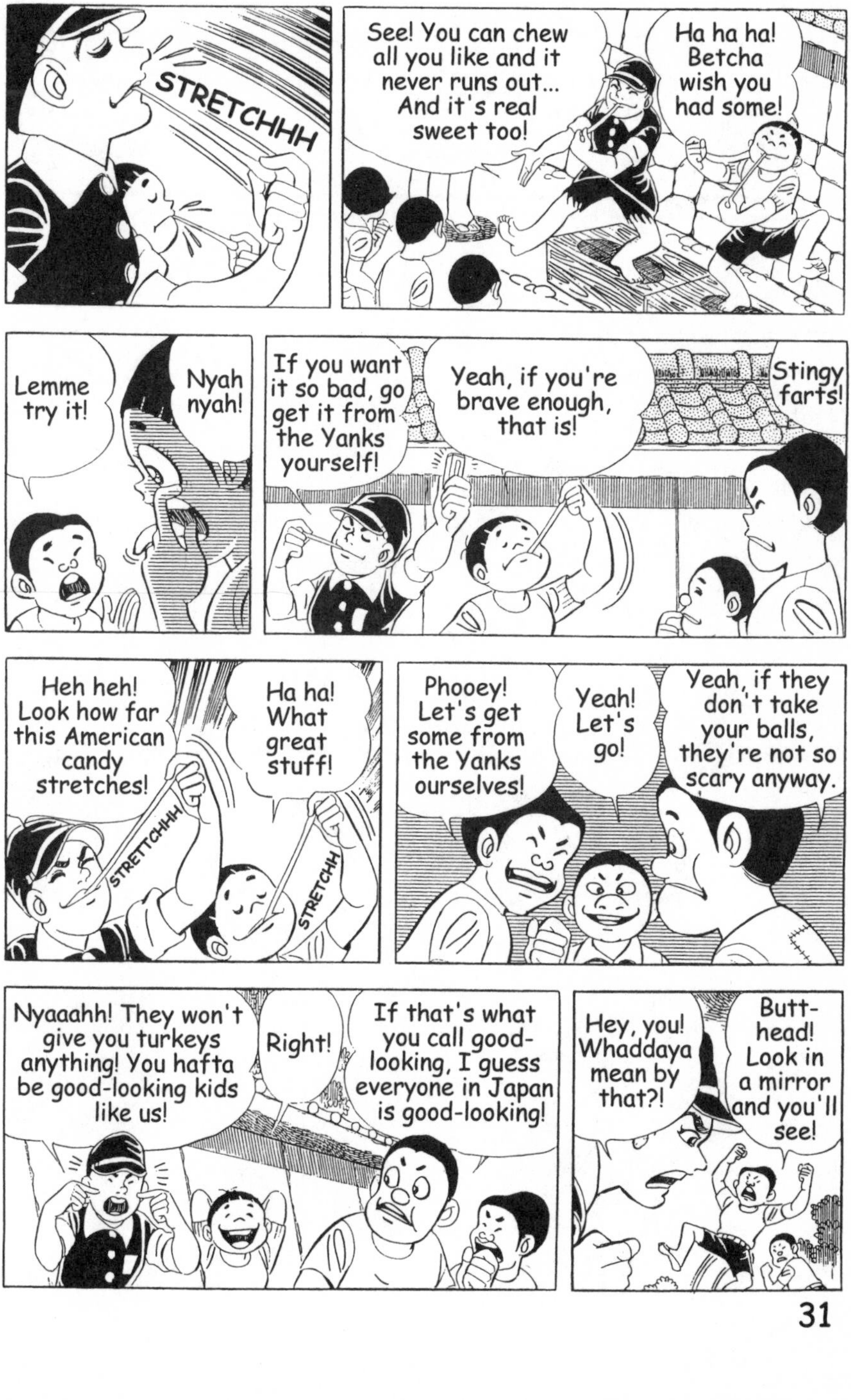
STRETCHHH
See! You can chew all you like and it never runs out... And it's real sweet too!
Ha ha ha! Betcha wish you had some!
Lemme try it!
Nyah nyah!
If you want it so bad, go get it from the Yanks yourself!
Yeah, if you're brave enough, that is!
Stingy farts!
Heh heh! Look how far this American candy stretches!
Ha ha! What great stuff!
STRETTCHHH
STRETCHH
Phooey! Let's get some from the Yanks ourselves!
Yeah! Let's go!
Yeah, if they don't take your balls, they're not so scary anyway.
Nyaaahh! They won't give you turkeys anything! You hafta be good-looking kids like us!
Right!
If that's what you call good-looking, I guess everyone in Japan is good-looking!
Hey, you! Whaddaya mean by that?!
Butt-head! Look in a mirror and you'll see!

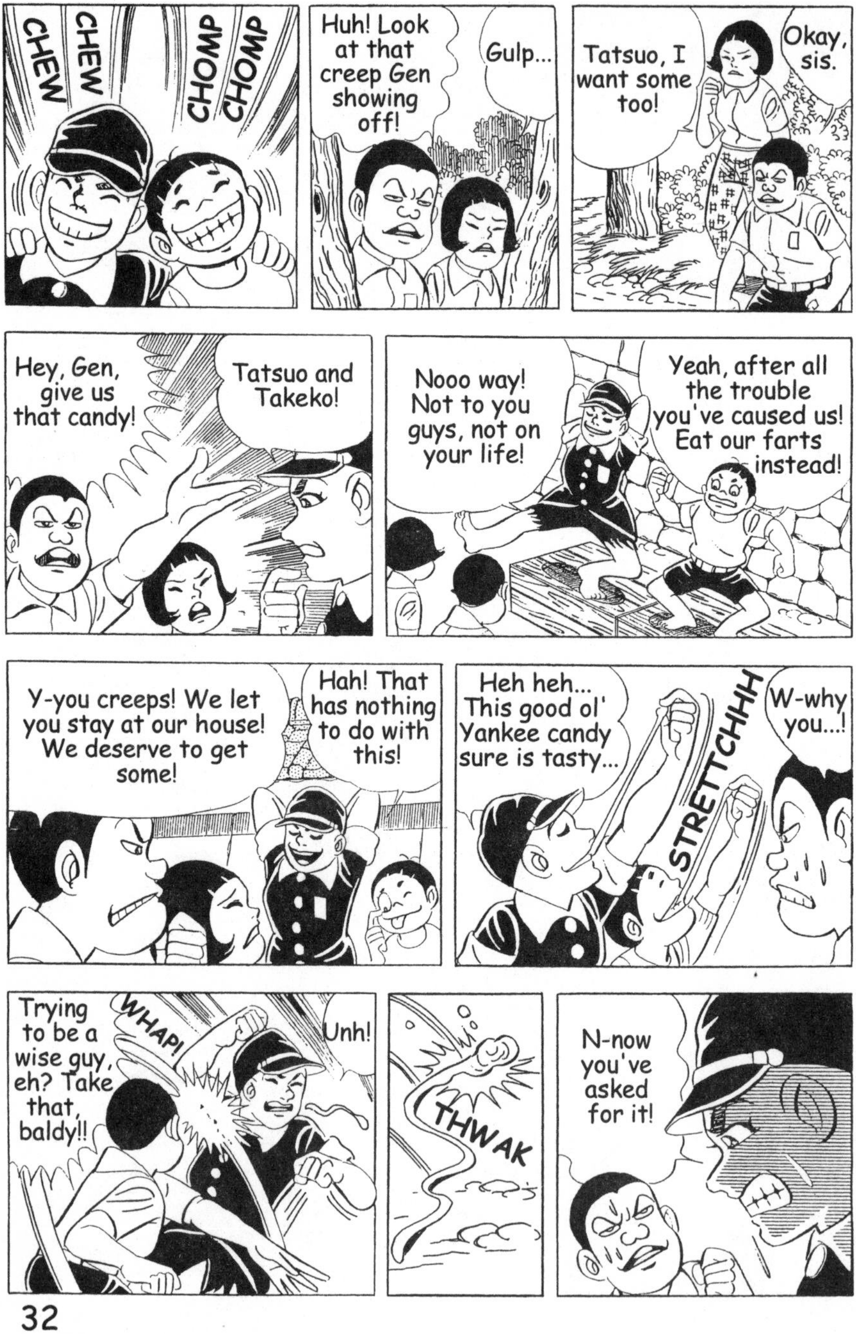
CHEW CHEW
CHOMP CHOMP
Huh! Look at that creep Gen showing off!
Gulp...
Tatsuo, I want some too!
Okay, sis.
Hey, Gen, give us that candy!
Tatsuo and Takeko!
Nooo way! Not to you guys, not on your life!
Yeah, after all the trouble you've caused us! Eat our farts instead!
Y-you creeps! We let you stay at our house! We deserve to get some!
Hah! That has nothing to do with this!
Heh heh... This good ol' Yankee candy sure is tasty...
STRETTCHHH
W-why you...!
Trying to be a wise guy, eh? Take that, baldy!!
WHAP!
Unh!
THWAK
N-now you've asked for it!

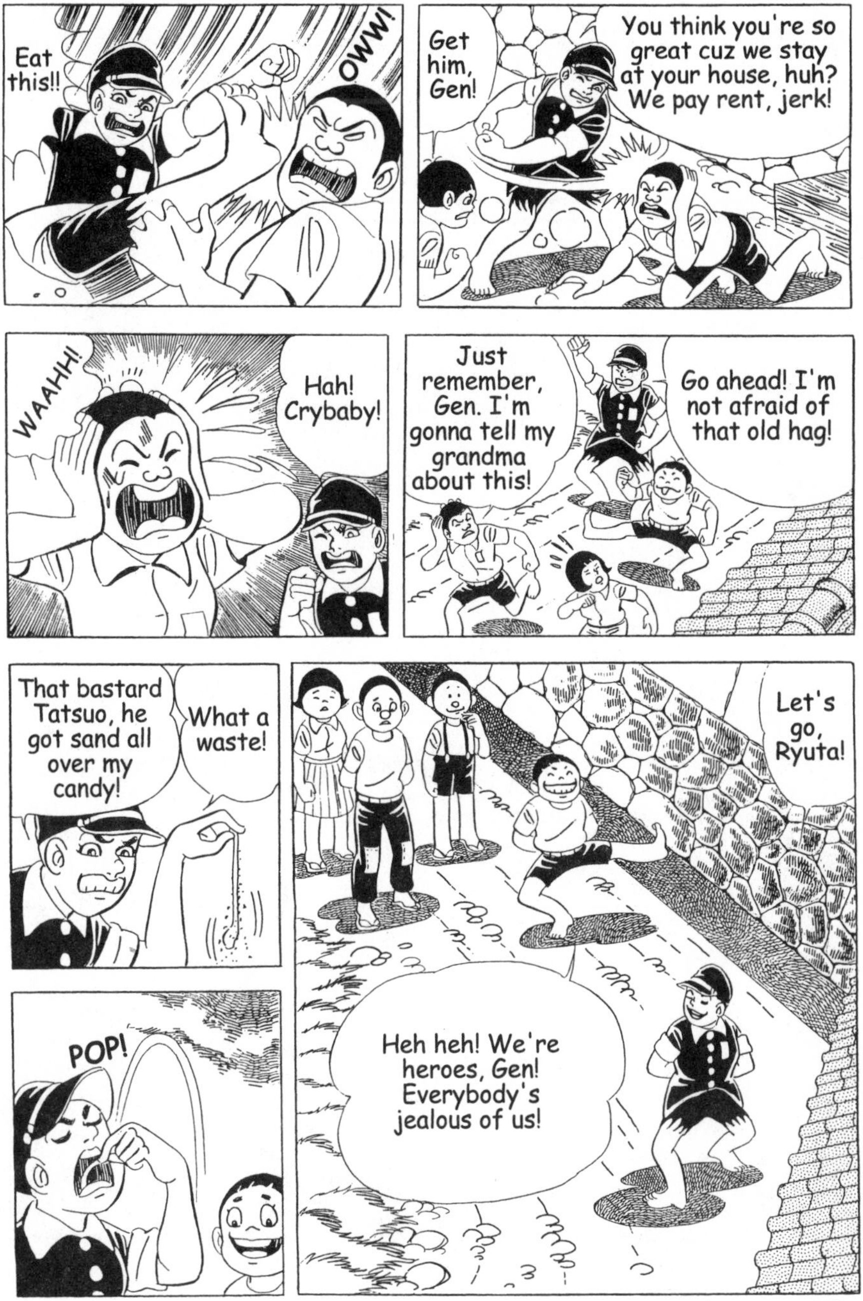
Eat this!!
OWW!
Get him, Gen!
You think you're so great cuz we stay at your house, huh? We pay rent, jerk!
WAAHH!
Hah! Crybaby!
Just remember, Gen. I'm gonna tell my grandma about this!
Go ahead! I'm not afraid of that old hag!
That bastard Tatsuo, he got sand all over my candy!
What a waste!
POP!
Let's go, Ryuta!
Heh heh! We're heroes, Gen! Everybody's jealous of us!

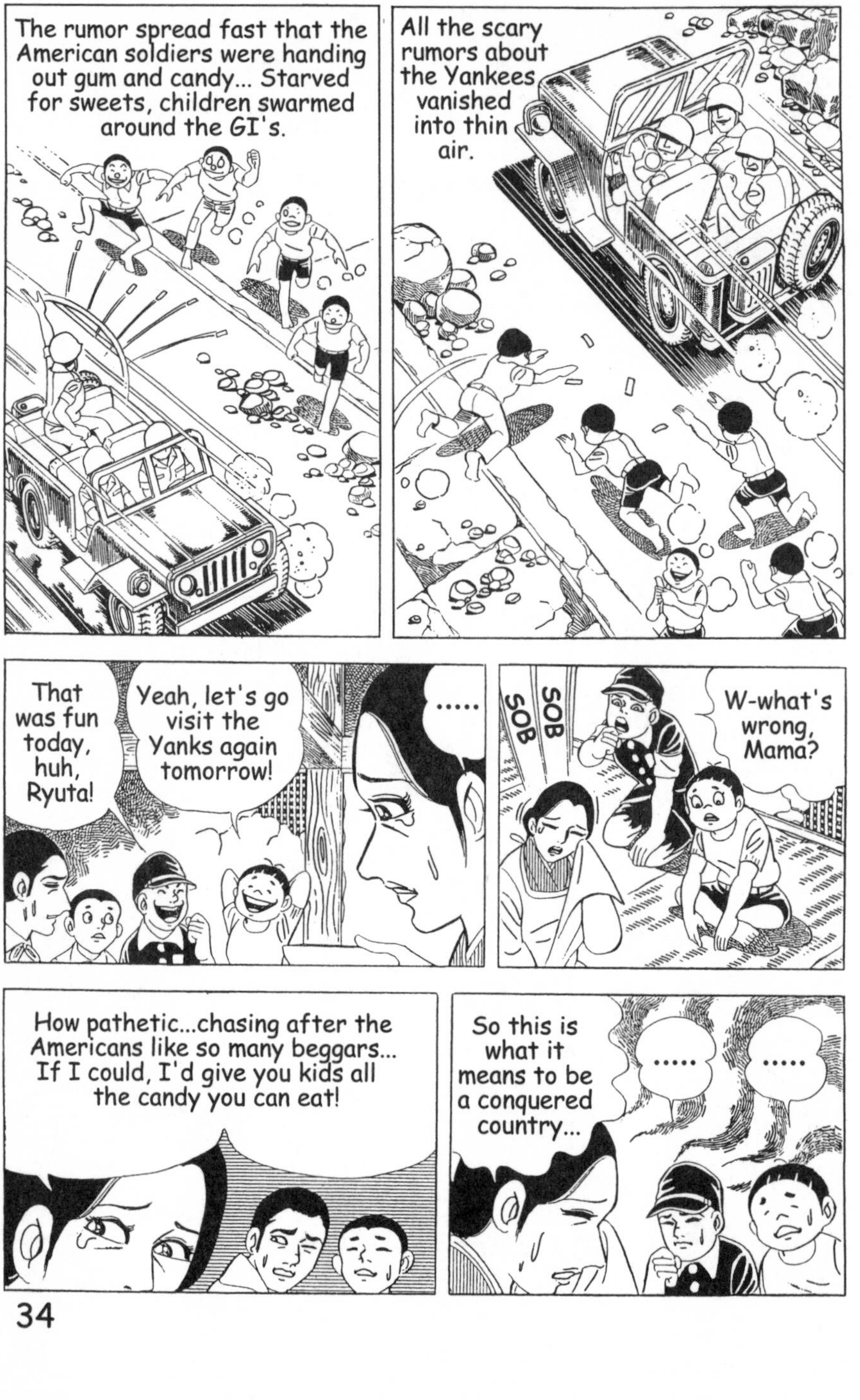
The rumor spread fast that the American soldiers were handing out gum and candy... Starved for sweets, children swarmed around the GI's.
All the scary rumors about the Yankees vanished into thin air.
That was fun today, huh, Ryuta!
Yeah, let's go visit the Yanks again tomorrow!
.....
SOB
SOB
W-what's wrong, Mama?
How pathetic...chasing after the Americans like so many beggars... If I could, I'd give you kids all the candy you can eat!
So this is what it means to be a conquered country...
.....
.....

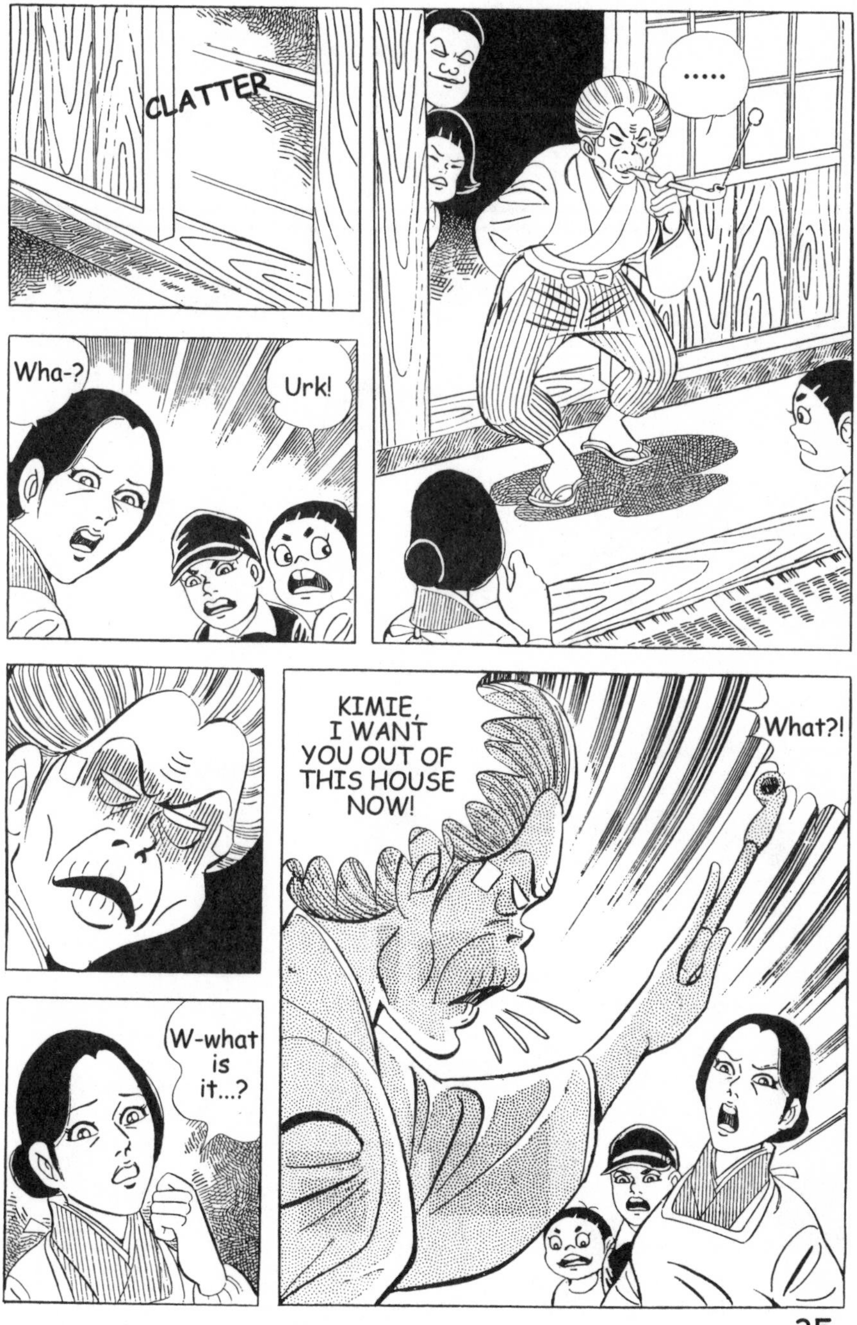
CLATTER
......
Wha-?
Urk!
KIMIE, I WANT YOU OUT OF THIS HOUSE NOW!
What?!
W-what is it...?

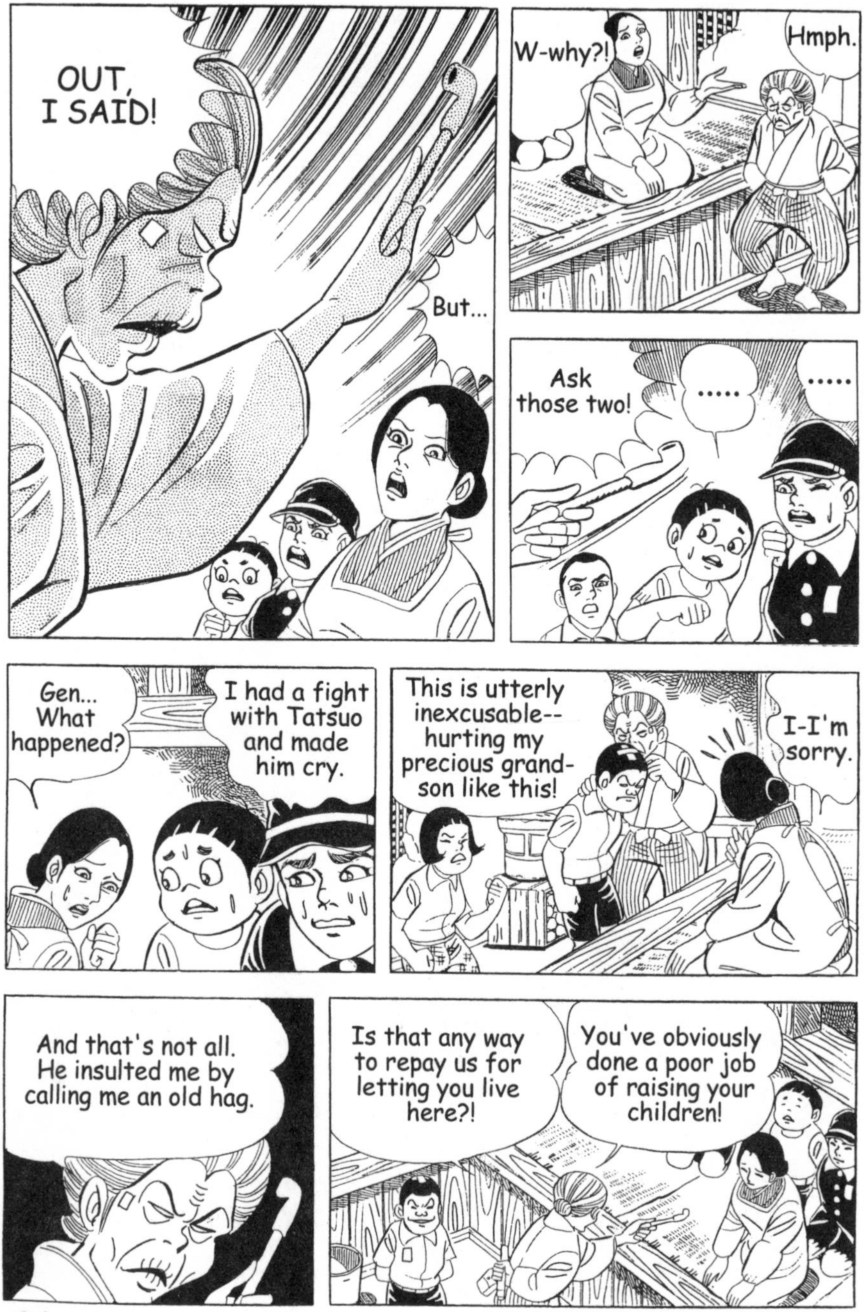
OUT, I SAID!
But...
W-why?!
Hmph.
Ask those two!
.....
.....
Gen... What happened?
I had a fight with Tatsuo and made him cry.
This is utterly inexcusable-- hurting my precious grand-son like this!
I-I'm sorry.
And that's not all. He insulted me by calling me an old hag.
Is that any way to repay us for letting you live here?!
You've obviously done a poor job of raising your children!

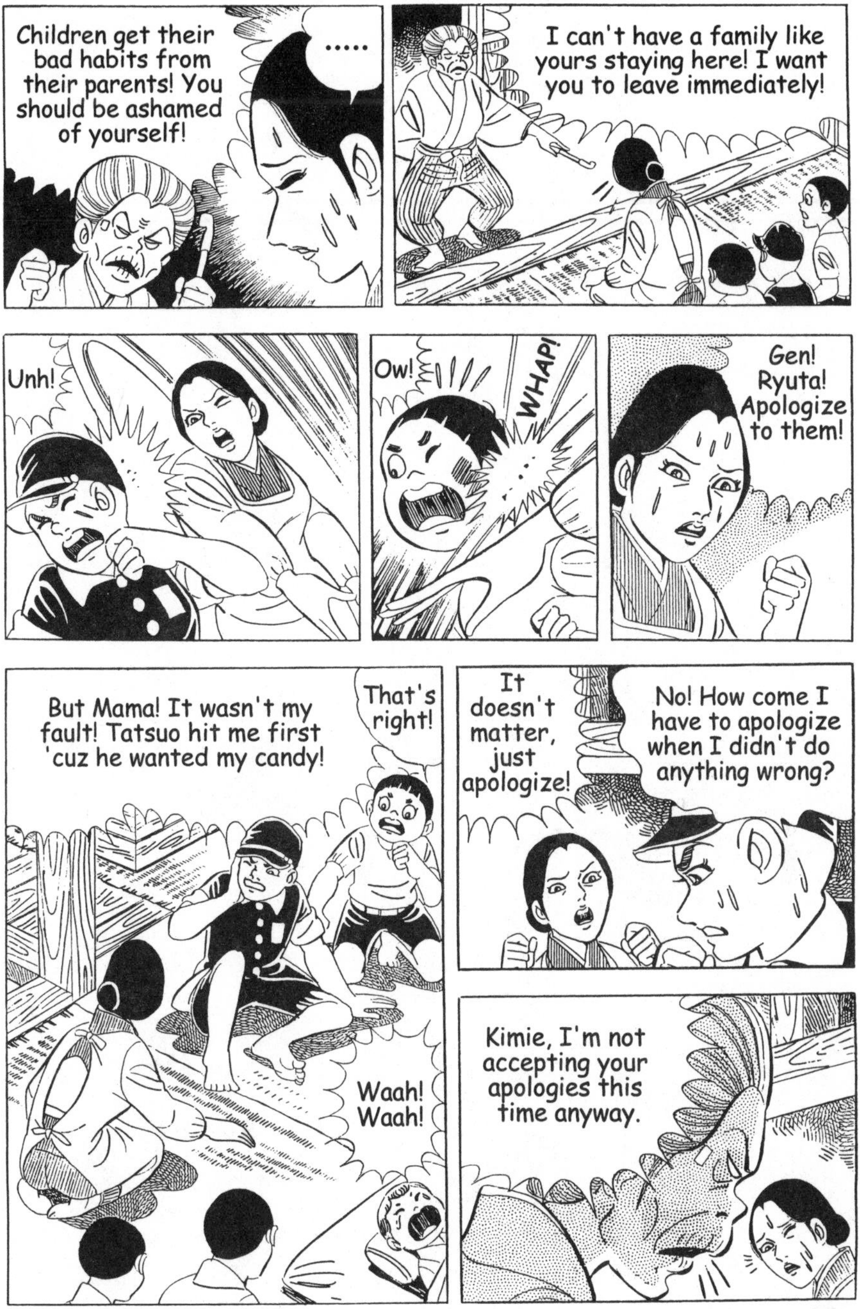
Children get their bad habits from their parents! You should be ashamed of yourself!
.....
I can't have a family like yours staying here! I want you to leave immediately!
Unh!
Ow!
WHAP!
Gen! Ryuta! Apologize to them!
But Mama! It wasn't my fault! Tatsuo hit me first 'cuz he wanted my candy!
That's right!
Waah! Waah!
It doesn't matter, just apologize!
No! How come I have to apologize when I didn't do anything wrong?
Kimie, I'm not accepting your apologies this time anyway.

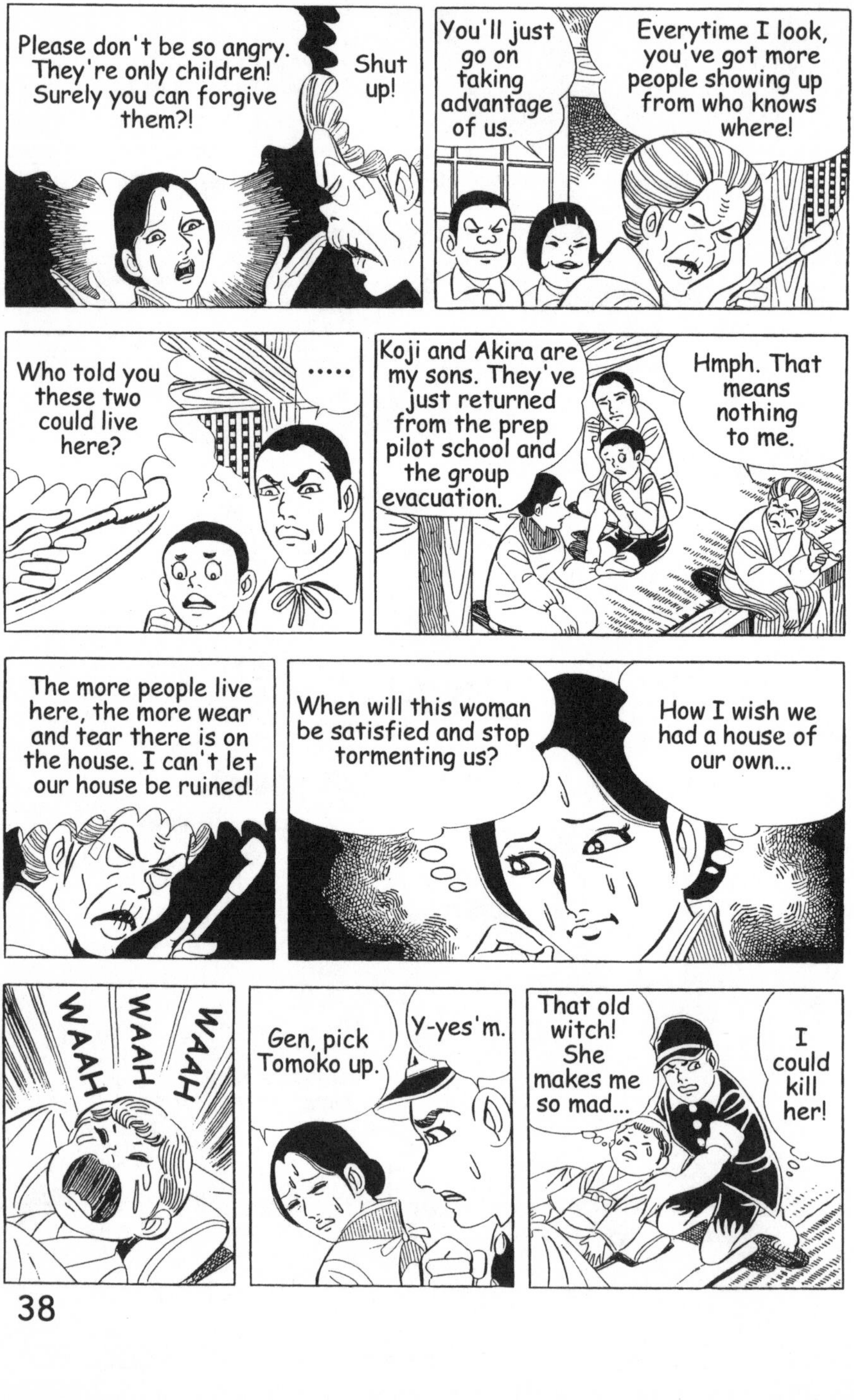
Please don't be so angry. They're only children! Surely you can forgive them?!
Shut up!
You'll just go on taking advantage of us.
Everytime I look, you've got more people showing up from who knows where!
Who told you these two could live here?
.....
Koji and Akira are my sons. They've just returned from the prep pilot school and the group evacuation.
Hmph. That means nothing to me.
The more people live here, the more wear and tear there is on the house. I can't let our house be ruined!
When will this woman be satisfied and stop tormenting us?
How I wish we had a house of our own...
WAAH
WAAH
WAAH
Gen, pick Tomoko up.
Y-yes'm.
That old witch! She makes me so mad...
I could kill her!

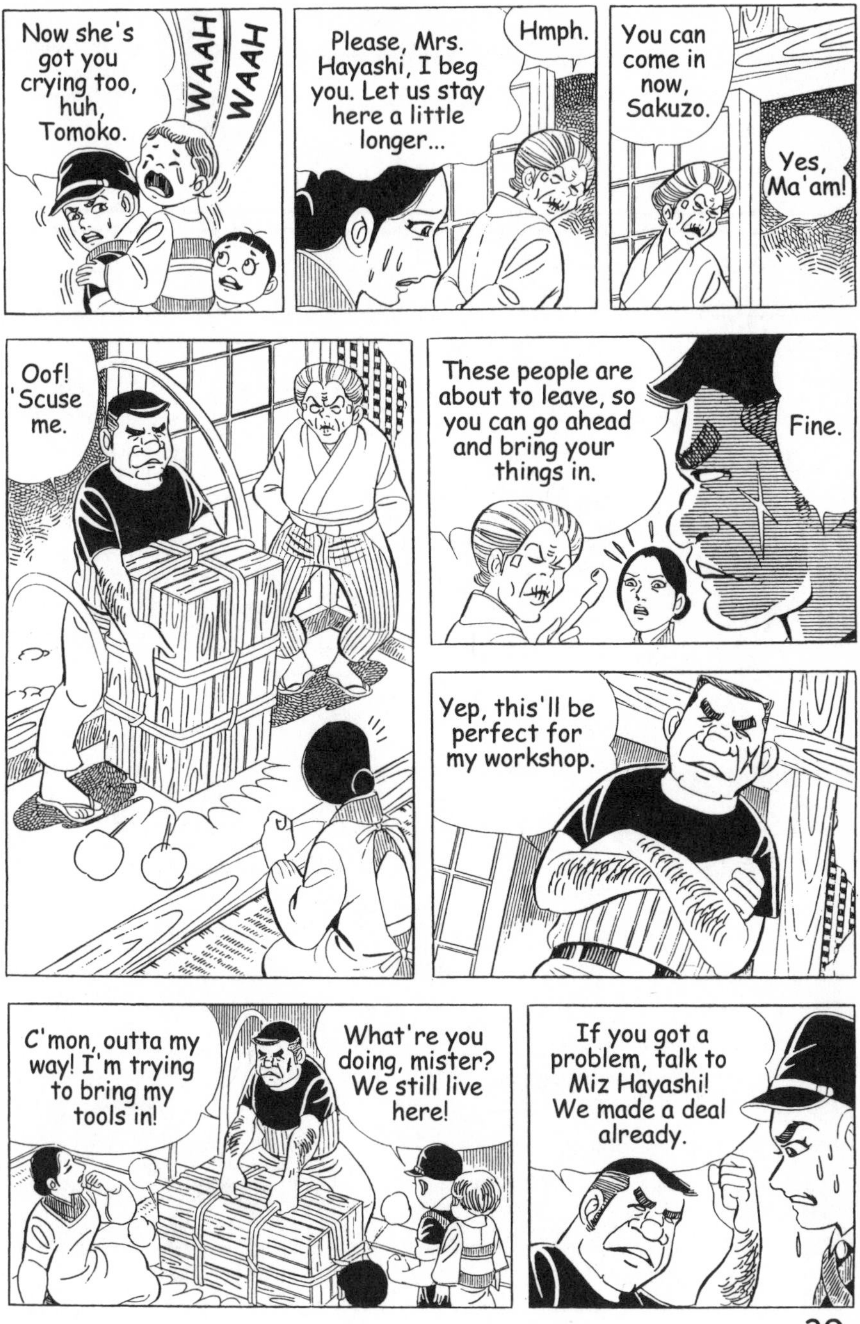
Now she's got you crying too, huh, Tomoko.
WAAH WAAH
Please, Mrs. Hayashi, I beg you. Let us stay here a little longer...
Hmph.
You can come in now, Sakuzo.
Yes, Ma'am!
Oof! 'Scuse me.
These people are about to leave, so you can go ahead and bring your things in.
Fine.
Yep, this'll be perfect for my workshop.
C'mon, outta my way! I'm trying to bring my tools in!
What're you doing, mister? We still live here!
If you got a problem, talk to Miz Hayashi! We made a deal already.

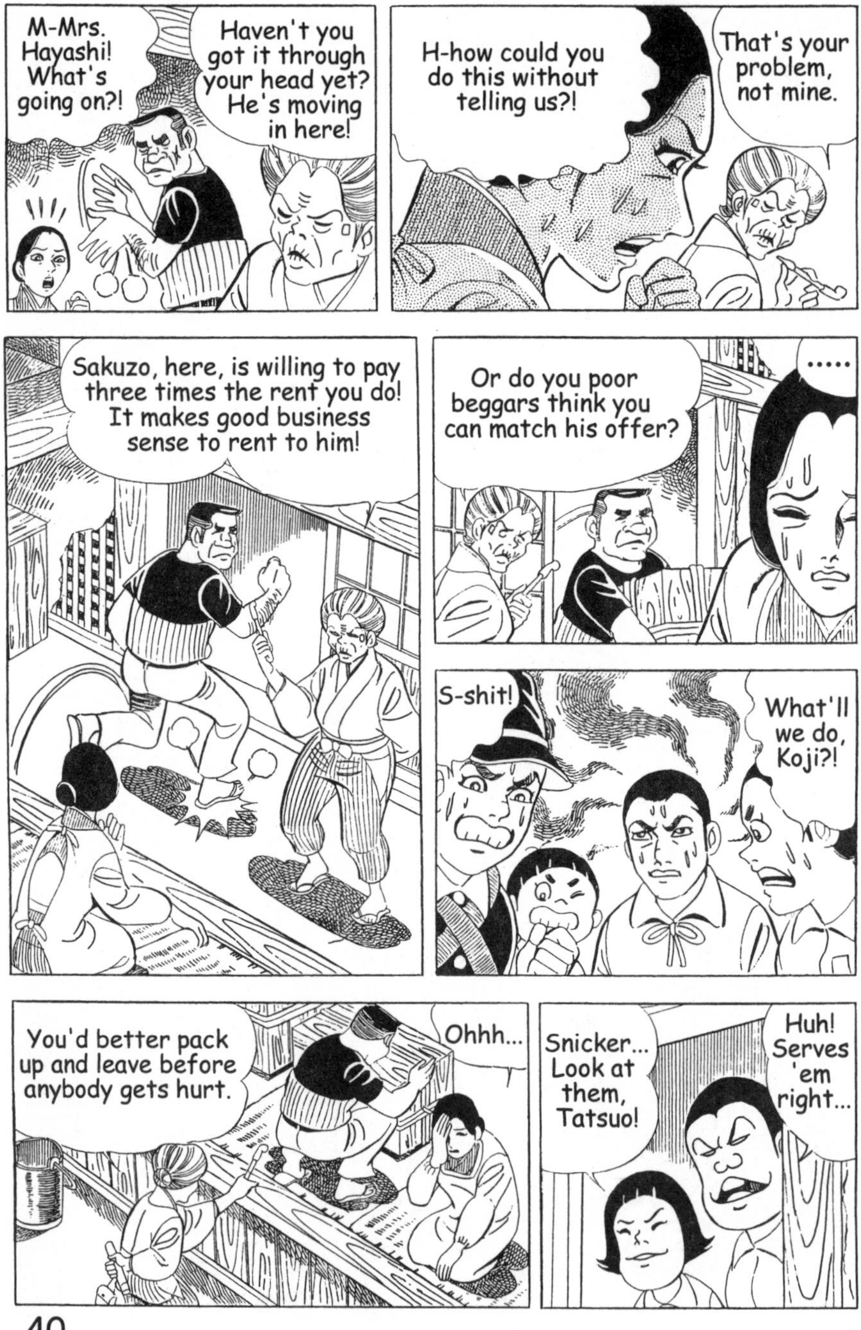
M-Mrs. Hayashi! What's going on?!
Haven't you got it through your head yet? He's moving in here!
H-how could you do this without telling us?!
That's your problem, not mine.
Sakuzo, here, is willing to pay three times the rent you do! It makes good business sense to rent to him!
Or do you poor beggars think you can match his offer?
.....
S-shit!
What'll we do, Koji?!
You'd better pack up and leave before anybody gets hurt.
Ohhh...
Snicker... Look at them, Tatsuo!
Huh! Serves 'em right...

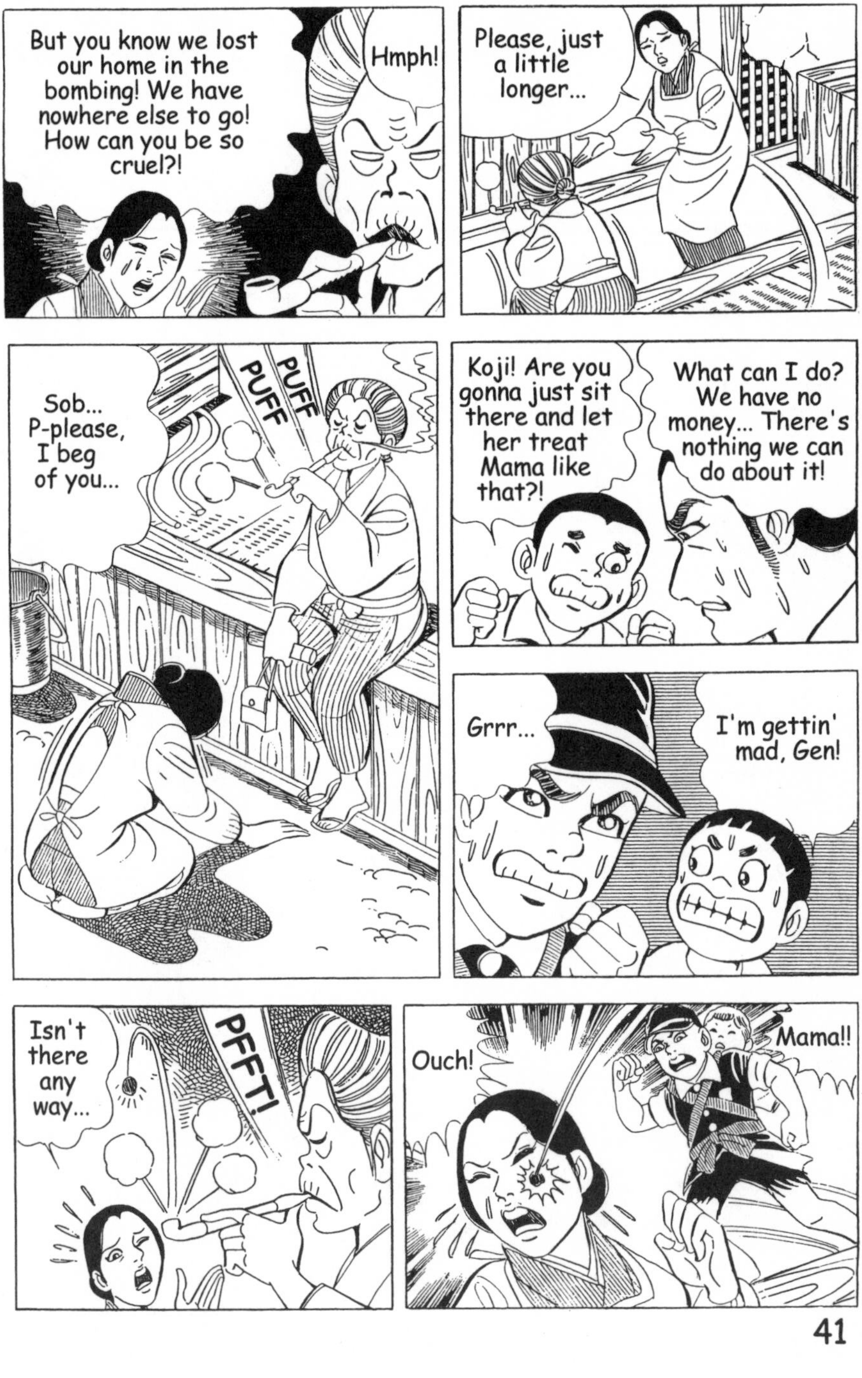
But you know we lost our home in the bombing! We have nowhere else to go! How can you be so cruel?!
Hmph!
Please, just a little longer...
Sob... P-please, I beg of you...
PUFF
PUFF
Koji! Are you gonna just sit there and let her treat Mama like that?!
What can I do? We have no money... There's nothing we can do about it!
Grrr...
I'm gettin' mad, Gen!
Isn't there any way...
PFFT!
Ouch!
Mama!!

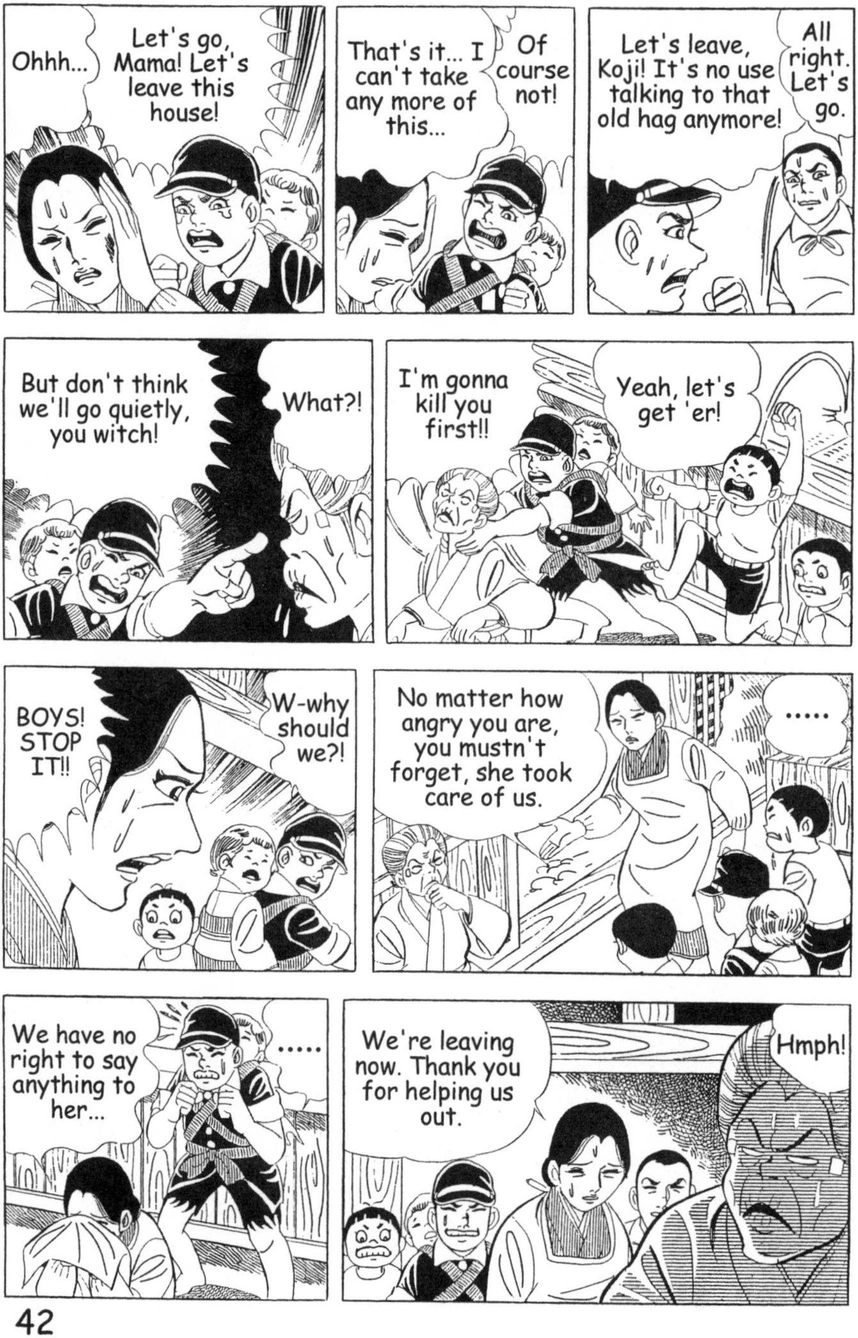

Ohhh...
Let's go, Mama! Let's leave this house!
That's it... I can't take any more of this...
Of course not!
Let's leave, Koji! It's no use talking to that old hag anymore!
All right. Let's go.
But don't think we'll go quietly, you witch!
What?!
I'm gonna kill you first!!
Yeah, let's get 'er!
BOYS! STOP IT!!
W-why should we?!
No matter how angry you are, you mustn't forget, she took care of us.
.....
We have no right to say anything to her...
.....
We're leaving now. Thank you for helping us out.
Hmph!

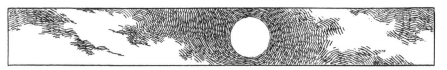

What are we gonna do now, Mama?

What a sorry lot we are... First of all, we have to find a place to live...

Ah!

Akira! Where are Gen and Ryuta?

Huh?! They were here a minute ago!

Those little trouble-makers! Where could they have gone?

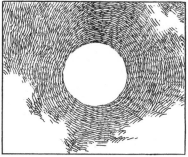

43

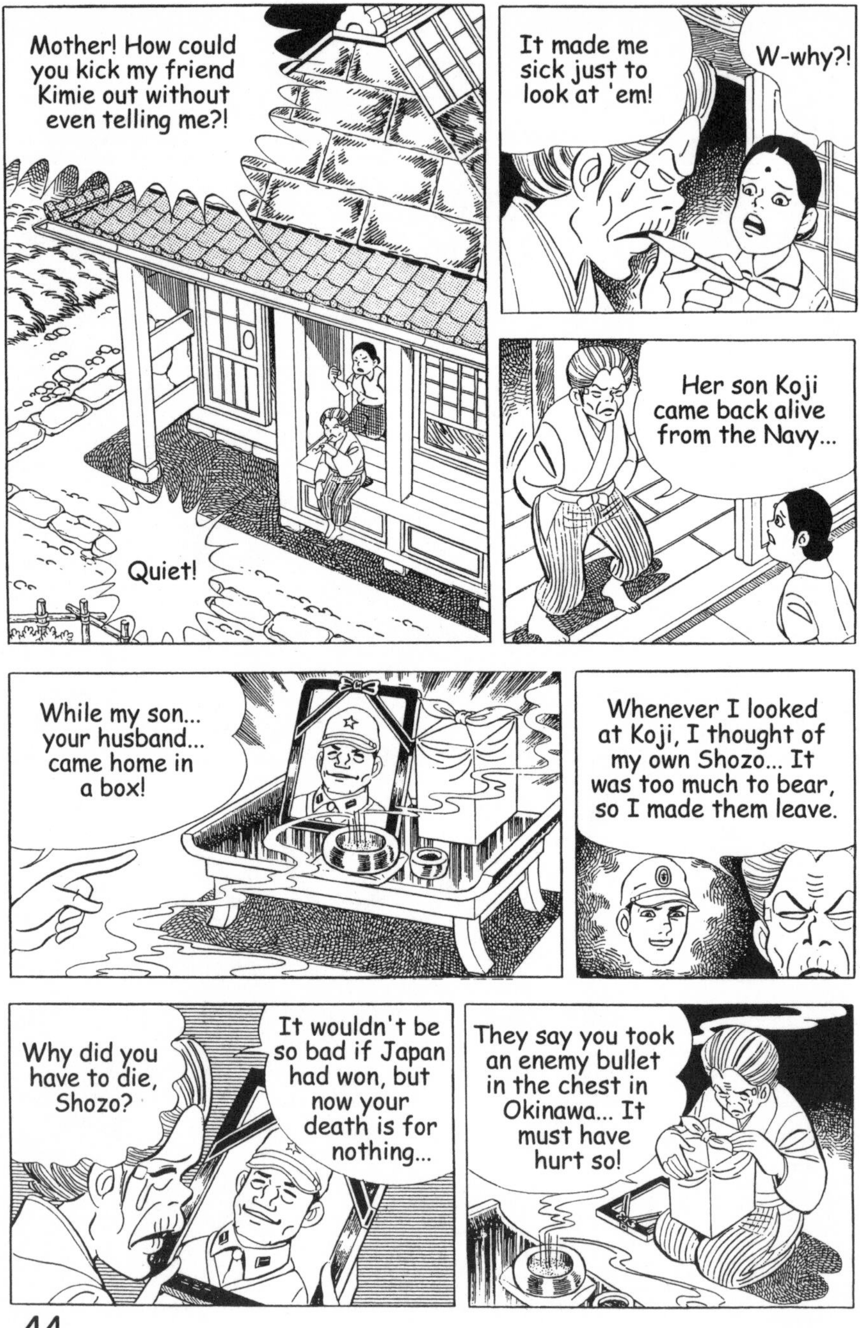
Mother! How could you kick my friend Kimie out without even telling me?!
Quiet!
It made me sick just to look at 'em!
W-why?!
Her son Koji came back alive from the Navy...
While my son... your husband... came home in a box!
Whenever I looked at Koji, I thought of my own Shozo... It was too much to bear, so I made them leave.
Why did you have to die, Shozo?
It wouldn't be so bad if Japan had won, but now your death is for nothing...
They say you took an enemy bullet in the chest in Okinawa... It must have hurt so!

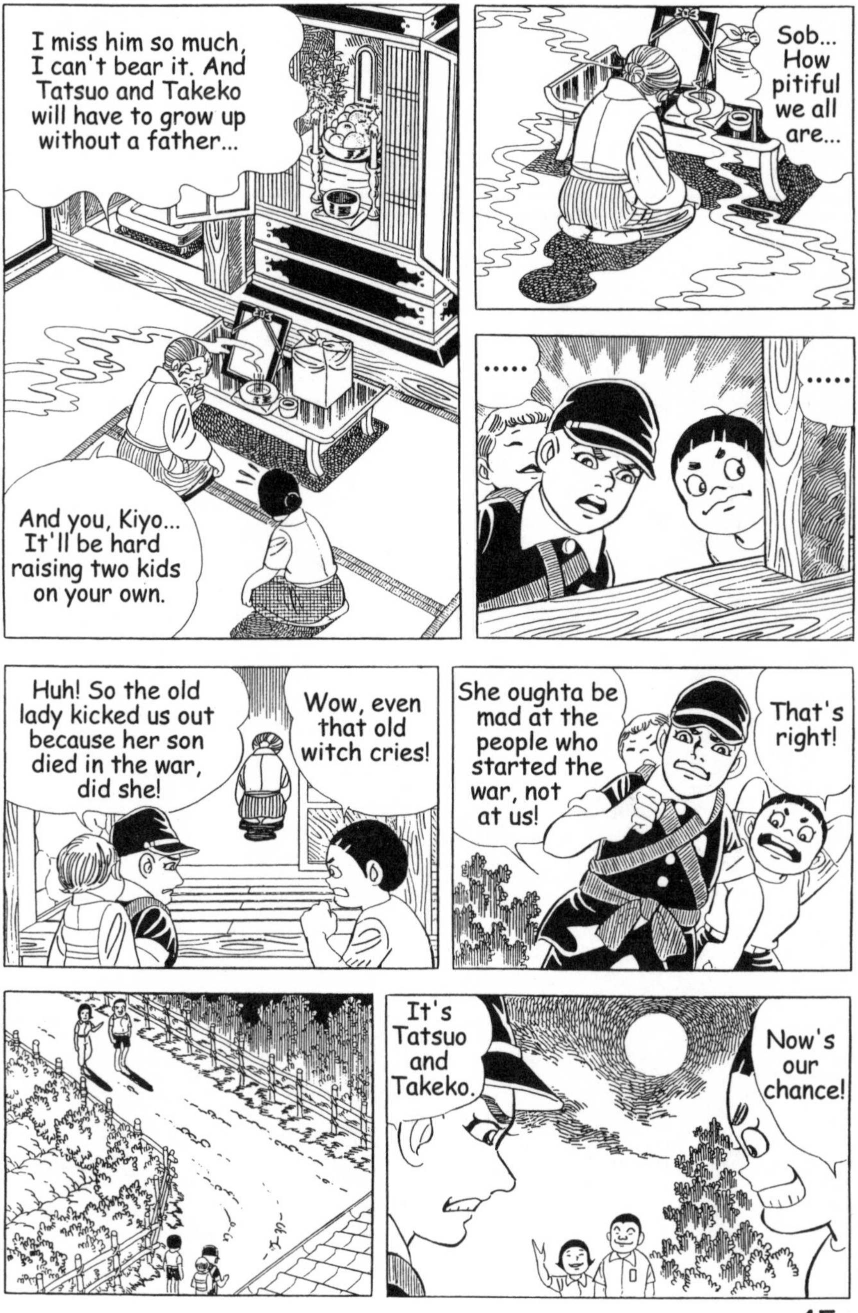
I miss him so much, I can't bear it. And Tatsuo and Takeko will have to grow up without a father...
And you, Kiyo... It'll be hard raising two kids on your own.
Sob... How pitiful we all are...
.....
.....
Huh! So the old lady kicked us out because her son died in the war, did she!
Wow, even that old witch cries!
She oughta be mad at the people who started the war, not at us!
That's right!
It's Tatsuo and Takeko.
Now's our chance!

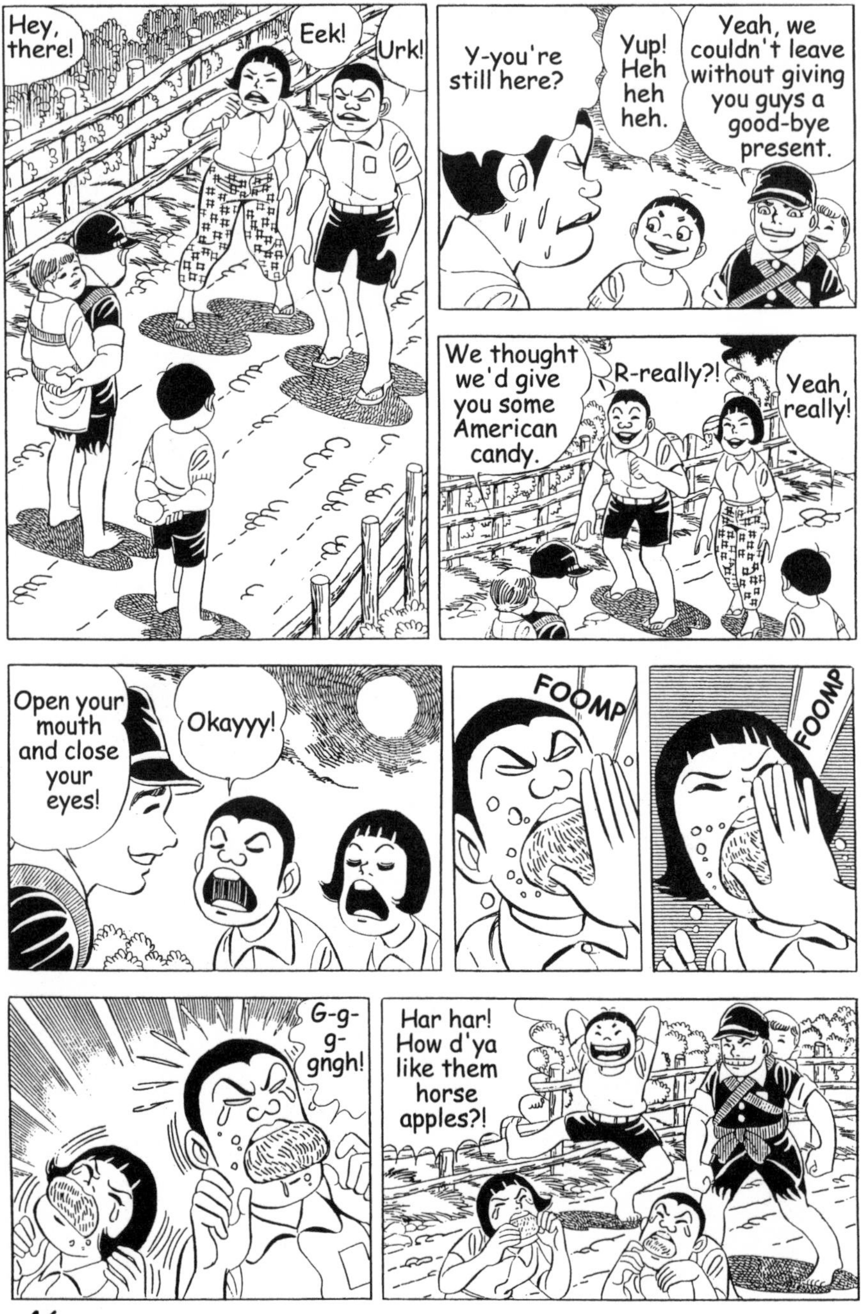
Hey, there!
Eek!
Urk!
Y-you're still here?
Yup! Heh heh heh.
Yeah, we couldn't leave without giving you guys a good-bye present.
We thought we'd give you some American candy.
R-really?!
Yeah, really!
Open your mouth and close your eyes!
Okayyy!
FOOMP
FOOMP
G-g-g-gngh!
Har har! How d'ya like them horse apples?!

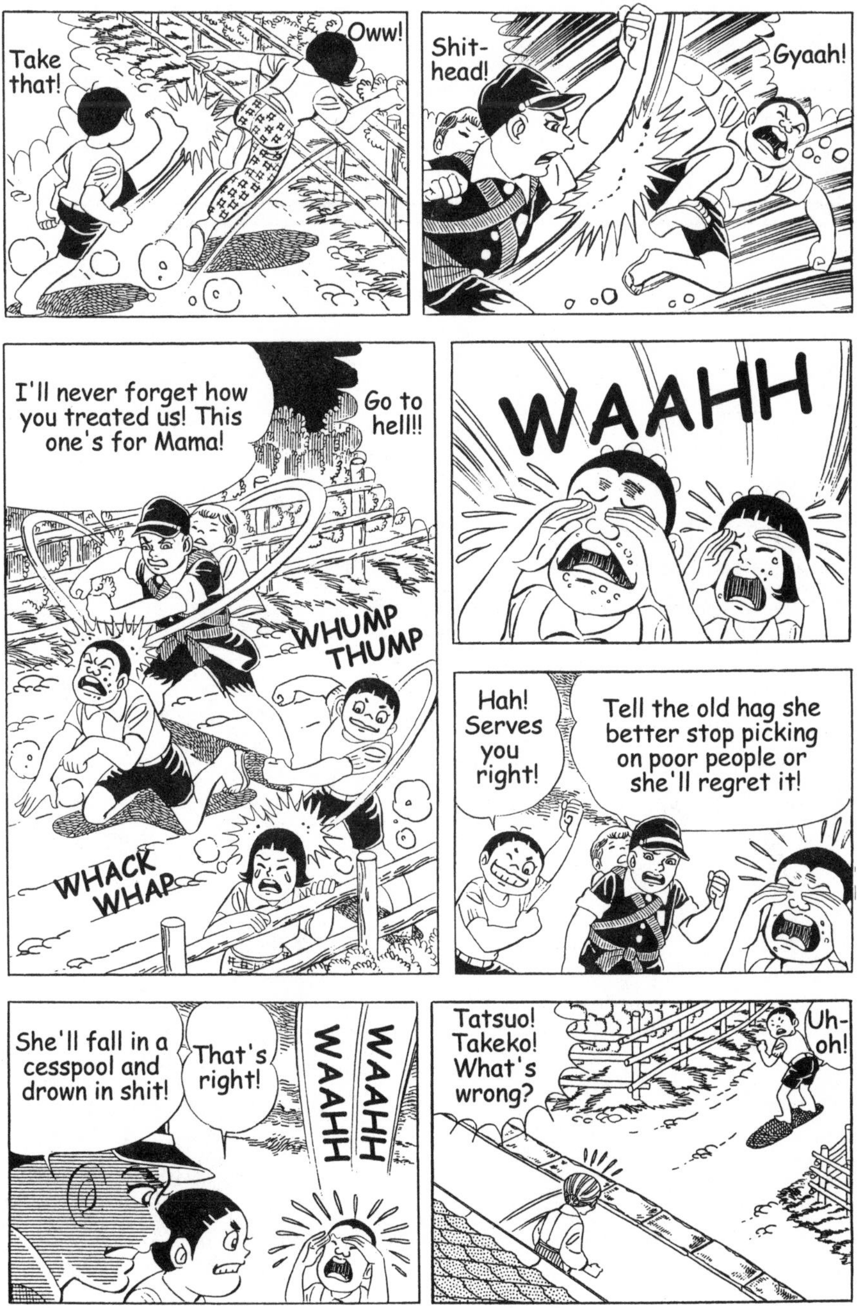

Take that!
Oww!
Shit-head!
Gyaah!
I'll never forget how you treated us! This one's for Mama!
Go to hell!!
WHUMP THUMP
WHACK WHAP
WAAHH
Hah! Serves you right!
Tell the old hag she better stop picking on poor people or she'll regret it!
She'll fall in a cesspool and drown in shit!
That's right!
WAAHH WAAHH
Tatsuo! Takeko! What's wrong?
Uh-oh!

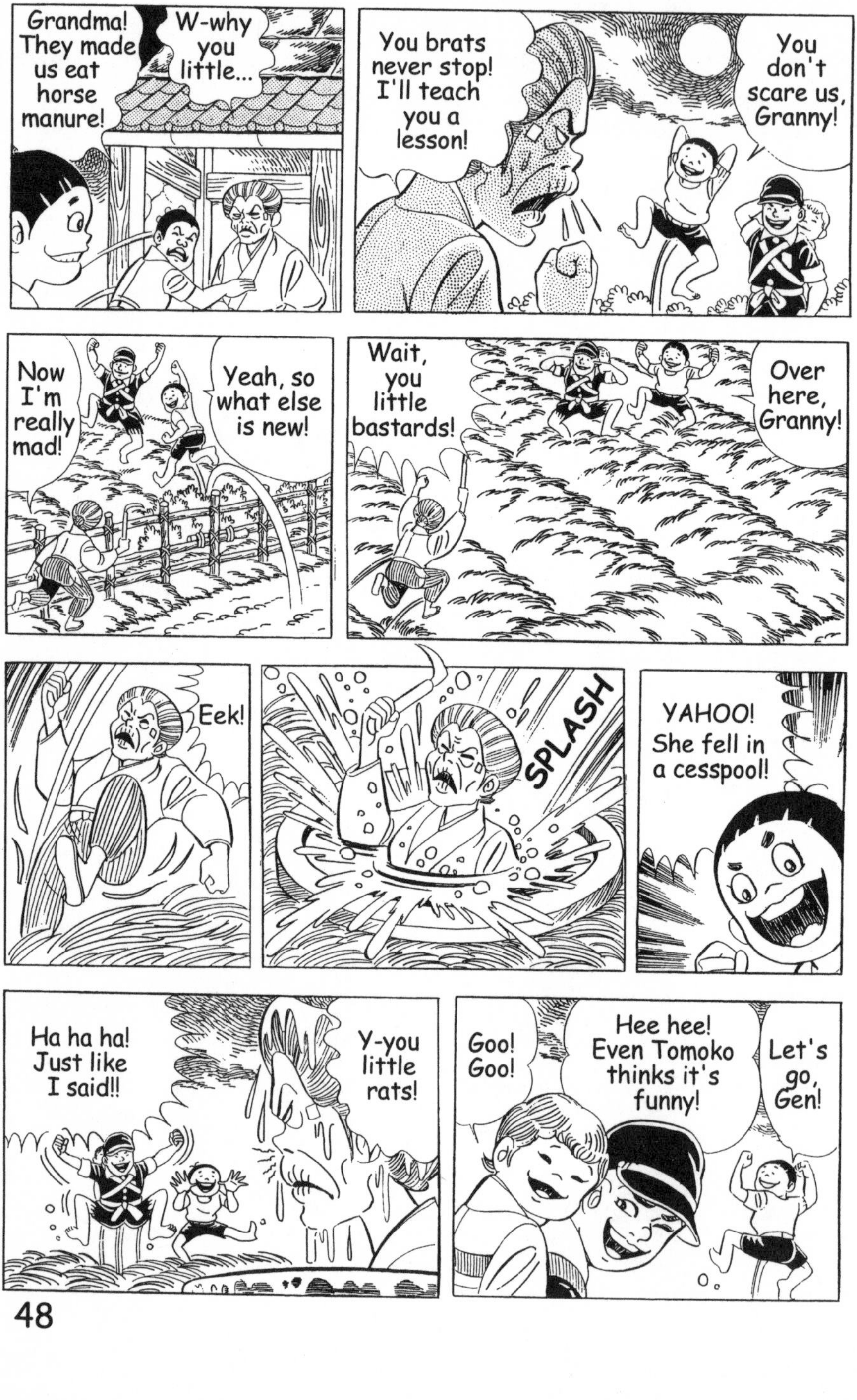
Grandma! They made us eat horse manure!
W-why you little...
You brats never stop! I'll teach you a lesson!
You don't scare us, Granny!
Now I'm really mad!
Yeah, so what else is new!
Wait, you little bastards!
Over here, Granny!
Eek!
SPLASH
YAHOO! She fell in a cesspool!
Ha ha ha! Just like I said!!
Y-you little rats!
Goo! Goo!
Hee hee! Even Tomoko thinks it's funny!
Let's go, Gen!

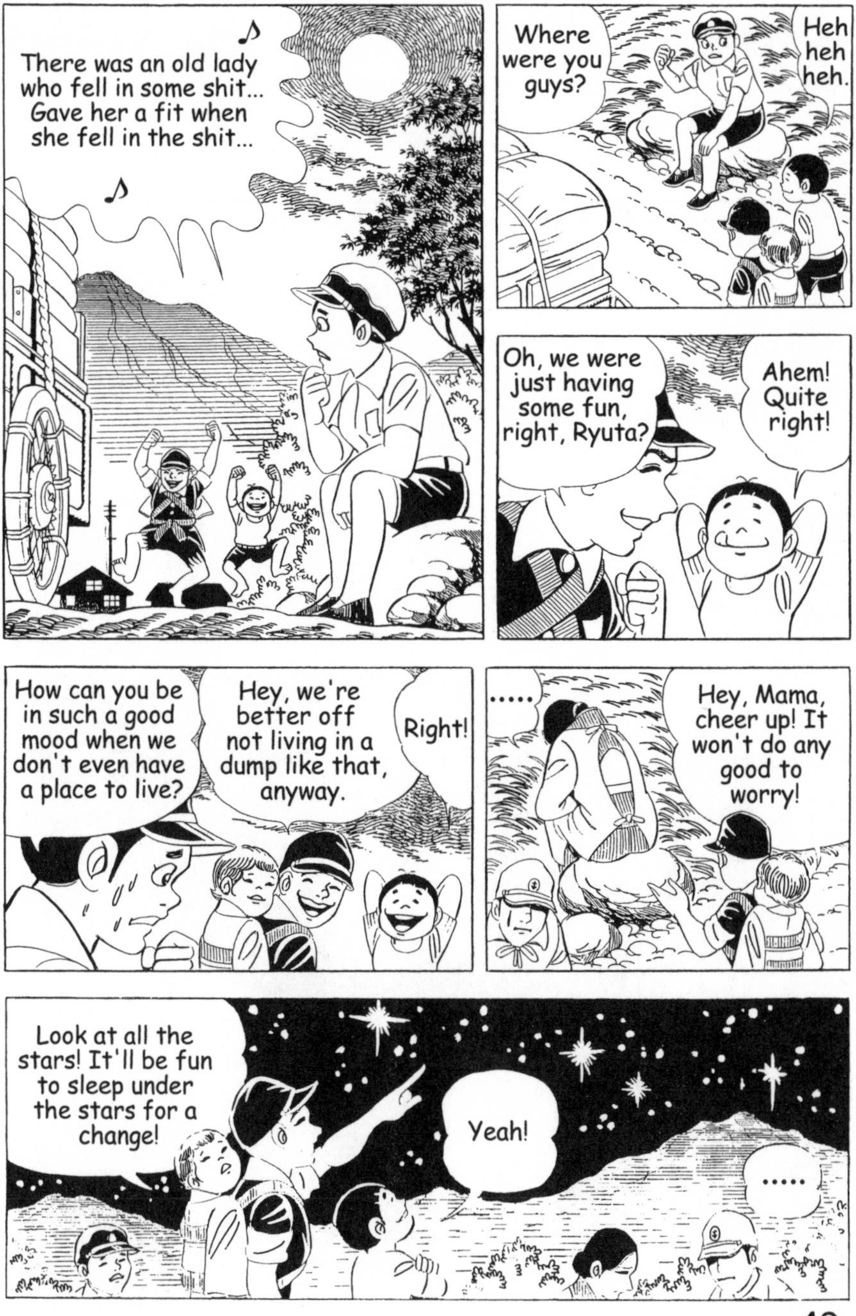
There was an old lady who fell in some shit... Gave her a fit when she fell in the shit...
Where were you guys?
Heh heh heh.
Oh, we were just having some fun, right, Ryuta?
Ahem! Quite right!
How can you be in such a good mood when we don't even have a place to live?
Hey, we're better off not living in a dump like that, anyway.
Right!
.....
Hey, Mama, cheer up! It won't do any good to worry!
Look at all the stars! It'll be fun to sleep under the stars for a change!
Yeah!
.....

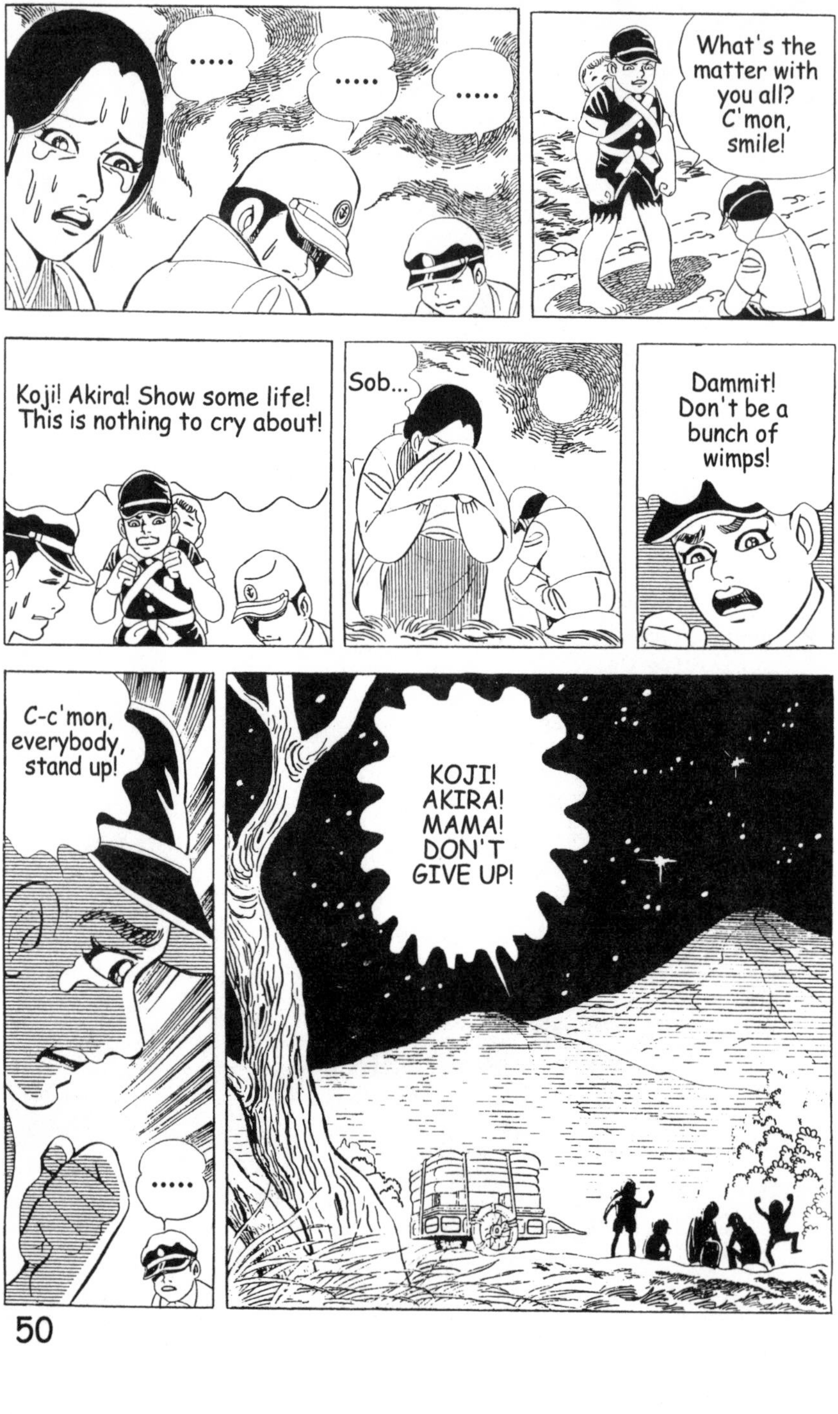
.....
.....
.....
What's the matter with you all? C'mon, smile!
Koji! Akira! Show some life! This is nothing to cry about!
Sob...
Dammit! Don't be a bunch of wimps!
C-c'mon, everybody, stand up!
.....
KOJI! AKIRA! MAMA! DON'T GIVE UP!

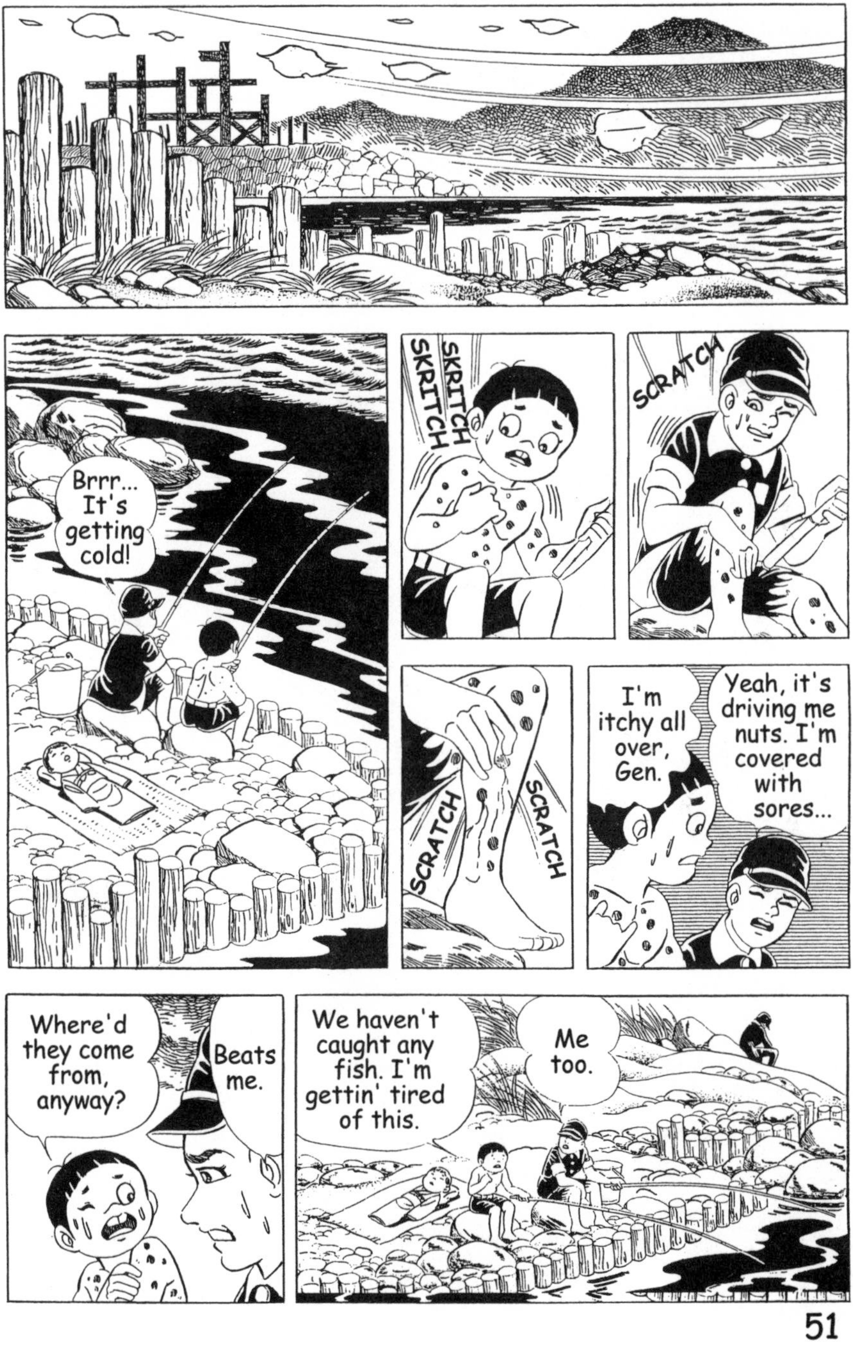
Brrr... It's getting cold!
SKRITCH
SKRITCH
SCRATCH
SCRATCH
SCRATCH
I'm itchy all over, Gen.
Yeah, it's driving me nuts. I'm covered with sores...
Where'd they come from, anyway?
Beats me.
We haven't caught any fish. I'm gettin' tired of this.
Me too.

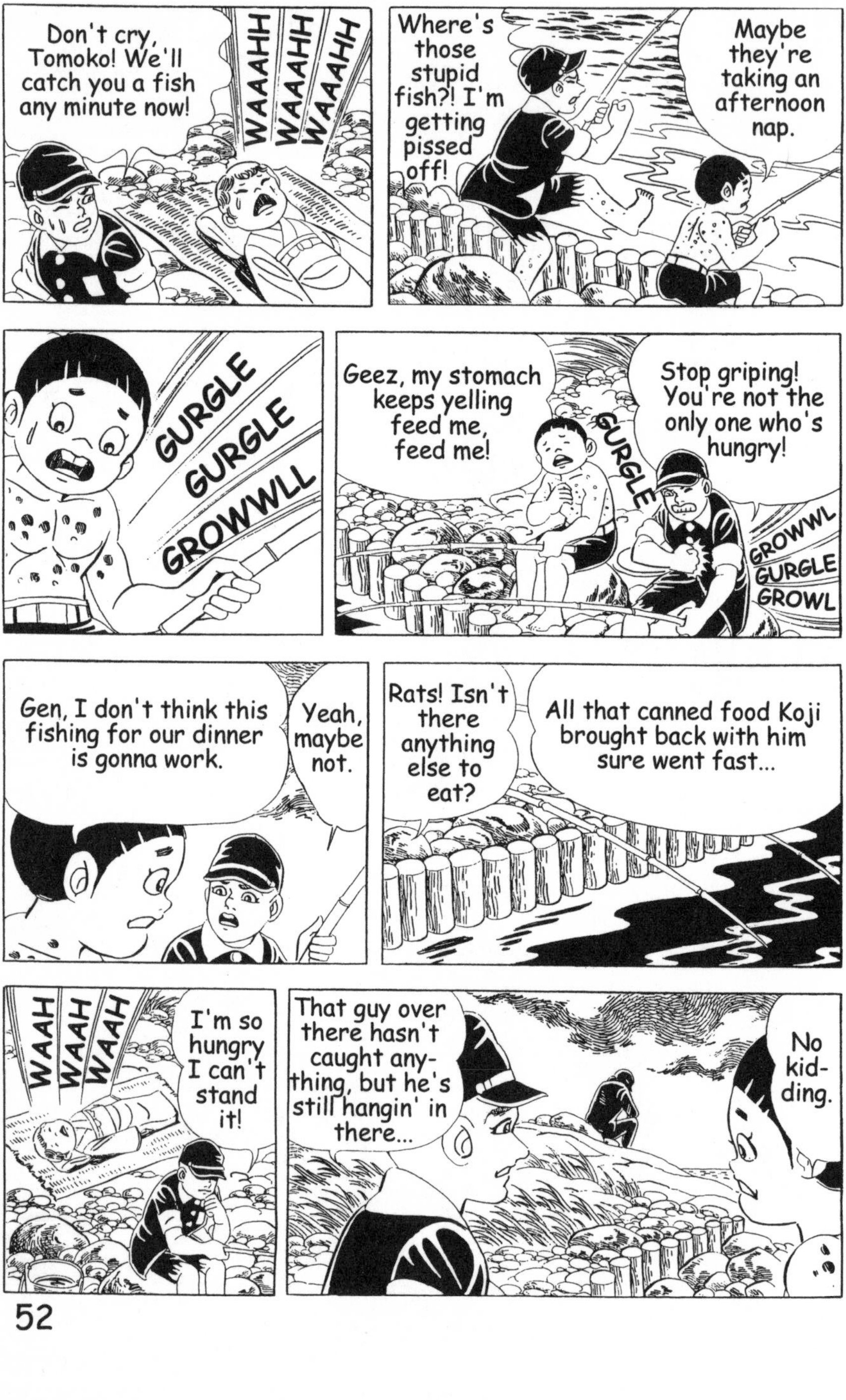
Don't cry, Tomoko! We'll catch you a fish any minute now!
WAAAHH WAAAHH WAAAHH
Where's those stupid fish?! I'm getting pissed off!
Maybe they're taking an afternoon nap.
GURGLE GURGLE GROWWLL
Geez, my stomach keeps yelling feed me, feed me!
GURGLE
Stop griping! You're not the only one who's hungry!
GROWWL GURGLE GROWL
Gen, I don't think this fishing for our dinner is gonna work.
Yeah, maybe not.
Rats! Isn't there anything else to eat?
All that canned food Koji brought back with him sure went fast...
WAAH WAAH WAAH
I'm so hungry I can't stand it!
That guy over there hasn't caught any-thing, but he's still hangin' in there...
No kid-ding.

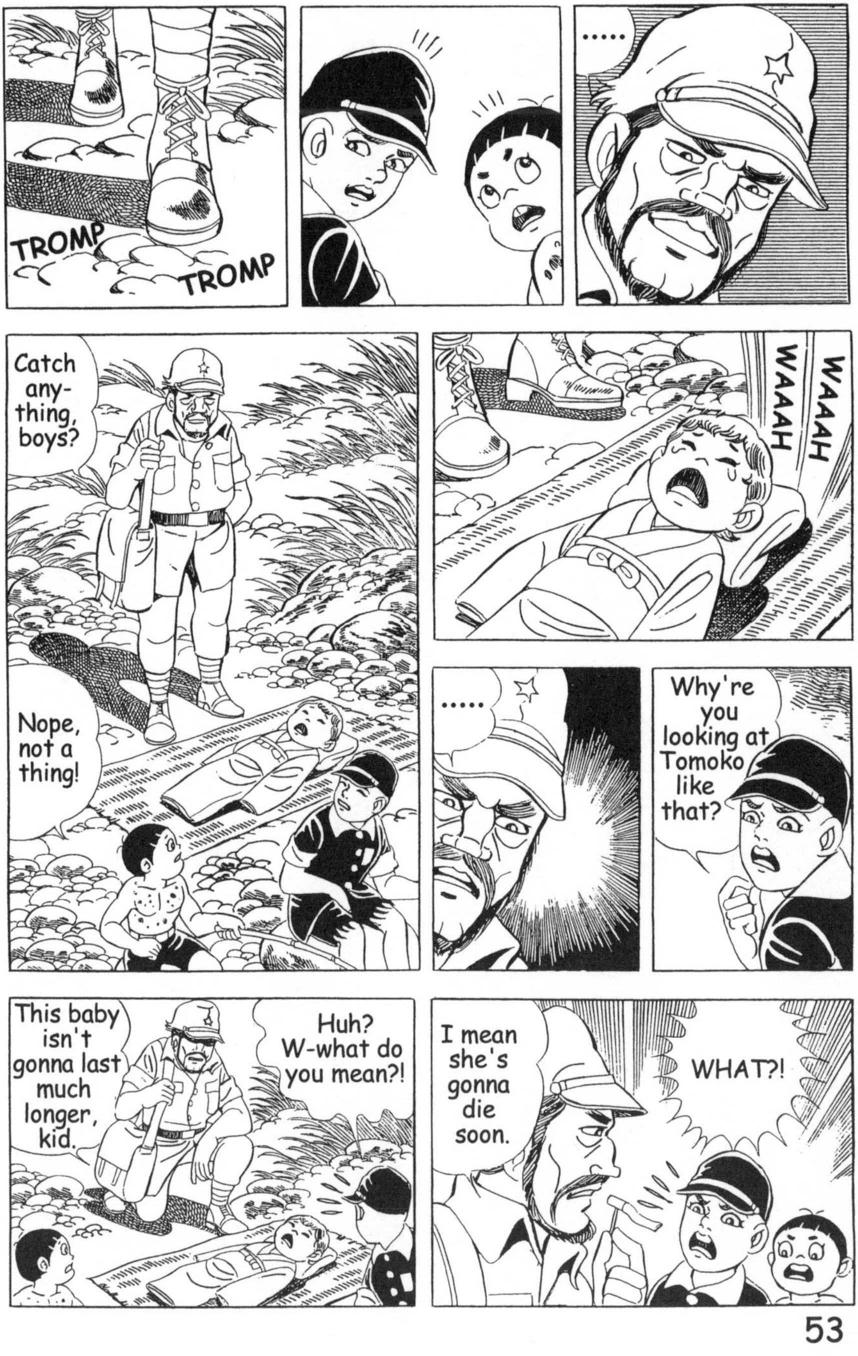

TROMP
TROMP
.....
Catch anything, boys?
Nope, not a thing!
WAAAH
WAAAH
.....
Why're you looking at Tomoko like that?
This baby isn't gonna last much longer, kid.
Huh? W-what do you mean?!
I mean she's gonna die soon.
WHAT?!

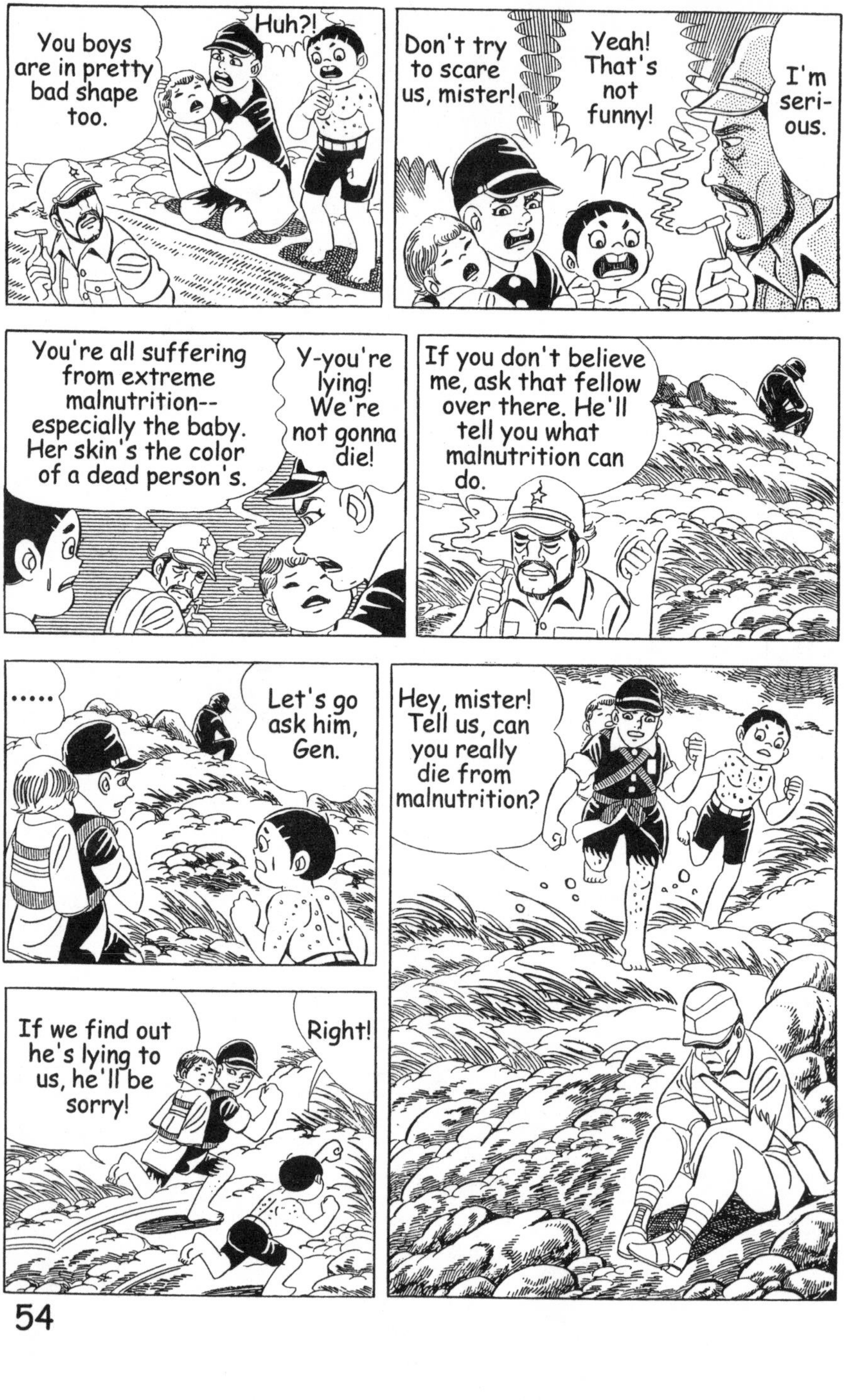
You boys are in pretty bad shape too.
Huh?!
Don't try to scare us, mister!
Yeah! That's not funny!
I'm seri-ous.
You're all suffering from extreme malnutrition-- especially the baby. Her skin's the color of a dead person's.
Y-you're lying! We're not gonna die!
If you don't believe me, ask that fellow over there. He'll tell you what malnutrition can do.
.....
Let's go ask him, Gen.
If we find out he's lying to us, he'll be sorry!
Right!
Hey, mister! Tell us, can you really die from malnutrition?

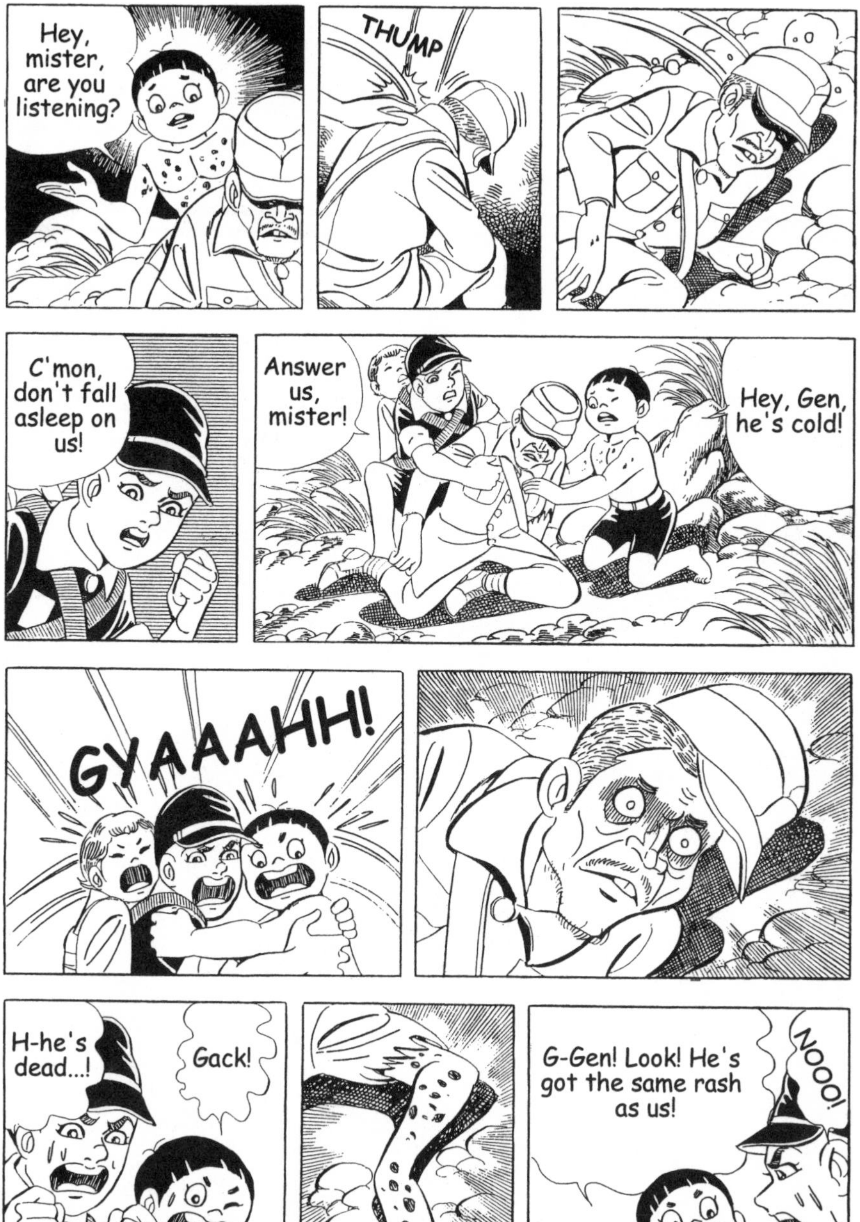
Hey, mister, are you listening?
THUMP
C'mon, don't fall asleep on us!
Answer us, mister!
Hey, Gen, he's cold!
GYAAAHH!
H-he's dead...!
Gack!
G-Gen! Look! He's got the same rash as us!
NOOO!

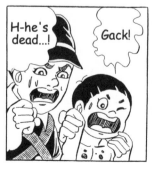

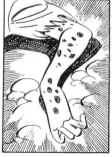

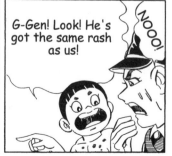

Yaagh! Hallpp!

So now you know what malnutrition can do, eh!

..... .....

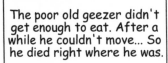

The poor old geezer didn't get enough to eat. After a while he couldn't move... So he died right where he was.

When I was in the war, I saw plenty of soldiers die of malnutrition. So I know what it looks like.

And you're gonna end up like him if you don't watch out!

H-how do you get rid of m-mal-nutri-tion...?

By getting lots of nutrition, of course.

Hm?

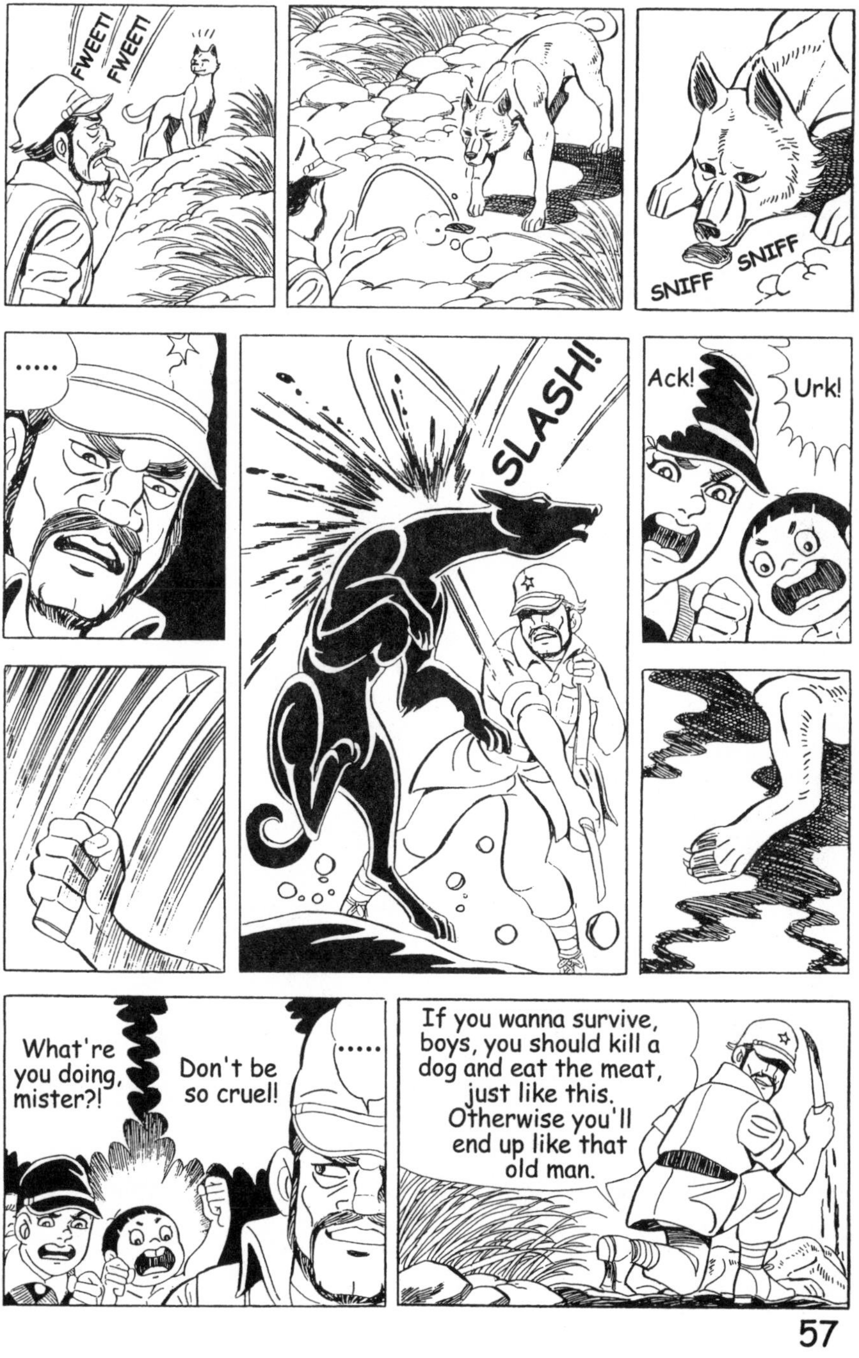
FWEET!
FWEET!
SNIFF
SNIFF
.....
SLASH!
Ack!
Urk!
What're you doing, mister?!
Don't be so cruel!
.....
If you wanna survive, boys, you should kill a dog and eat the meat, just like this. Otherwise you'll end up like that old man.

We humans can't live without meat or fish. We need the protein.

So if you don't wanna die, catch yourselves a dog and eat it.

Heh heh... Dog meat doesn't taste half bad, you know.

.....

Urghh!

MUNCH CHOMP

Want some?

N-no thanks!

Hmph... This is no time to put on airs... not these days!

You boys better find some meat to eat real quick. That'll get rid of your rash. And if you don't feed that baby something nourishing right away, she's gonna die.

Heh heh heh... Good luck!

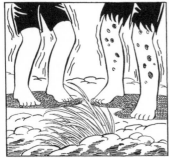

Waahh! Gen, I don't wanna die!!

WAAH WAAH WAAH

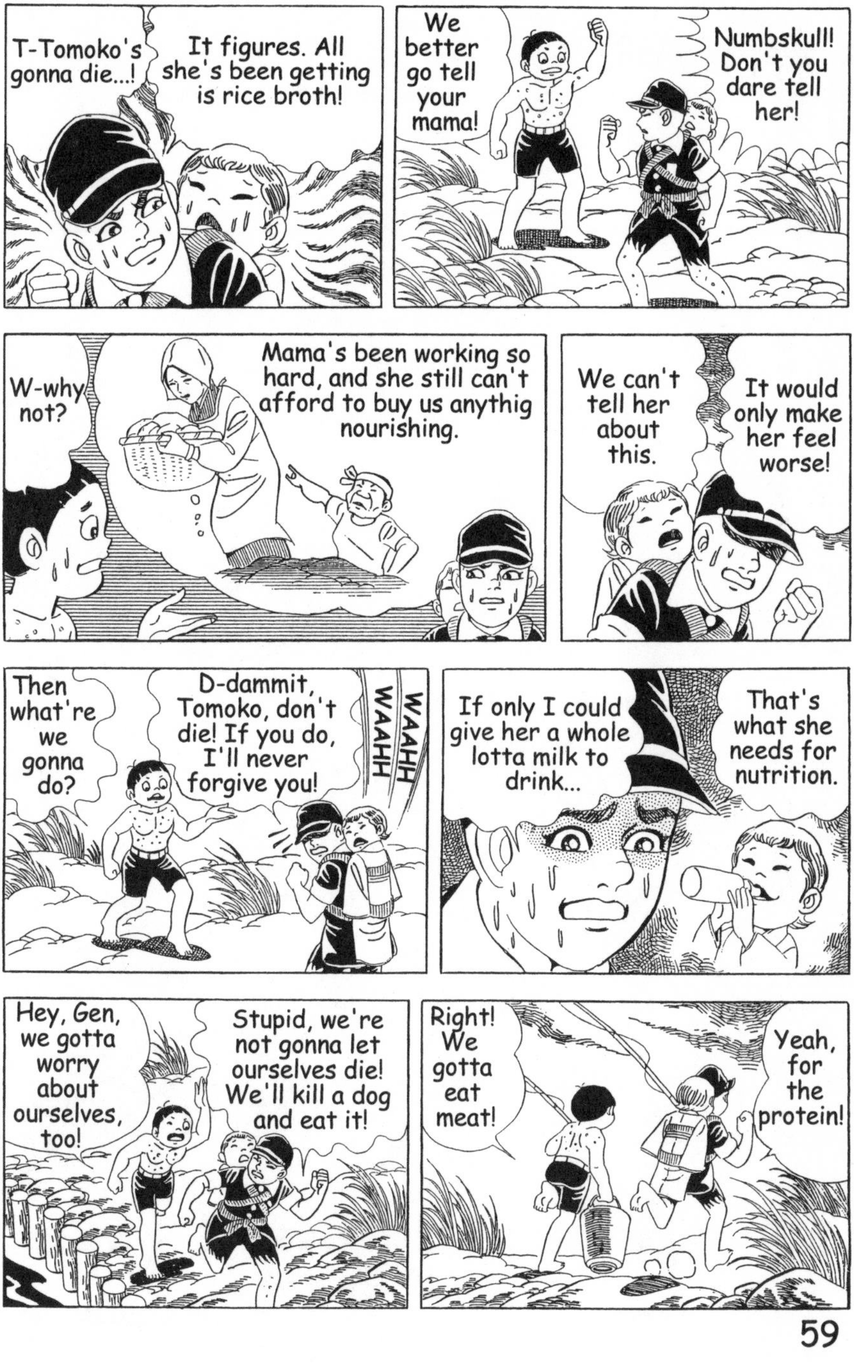
T-Tomoko's gonna die...!
It figures. All she's been getting is rice broth!
We better go tell your mama!
Numbskull! Don't you dare tell her!
W-why not?
Mama's been working so hard, and she still can't afford to buy us anythig nourishing.
We can't tell her about this.
It would only make her feel worse!
Then what're we gonna do?
D-dammit, Tomoko, don't die! If you do, I'll never forgive you!
WAAHH WAAHH
If only I could give her a whole lotta milk to drink...
That's what she needs for nutrition.
Hey, Gen, we gotta worry about ourselves, too!
Stupid, we're not gonna let ourselves die! We'll kill a dog and eat it!
Right! We gotta eat meat!
Yeah, for the protein!

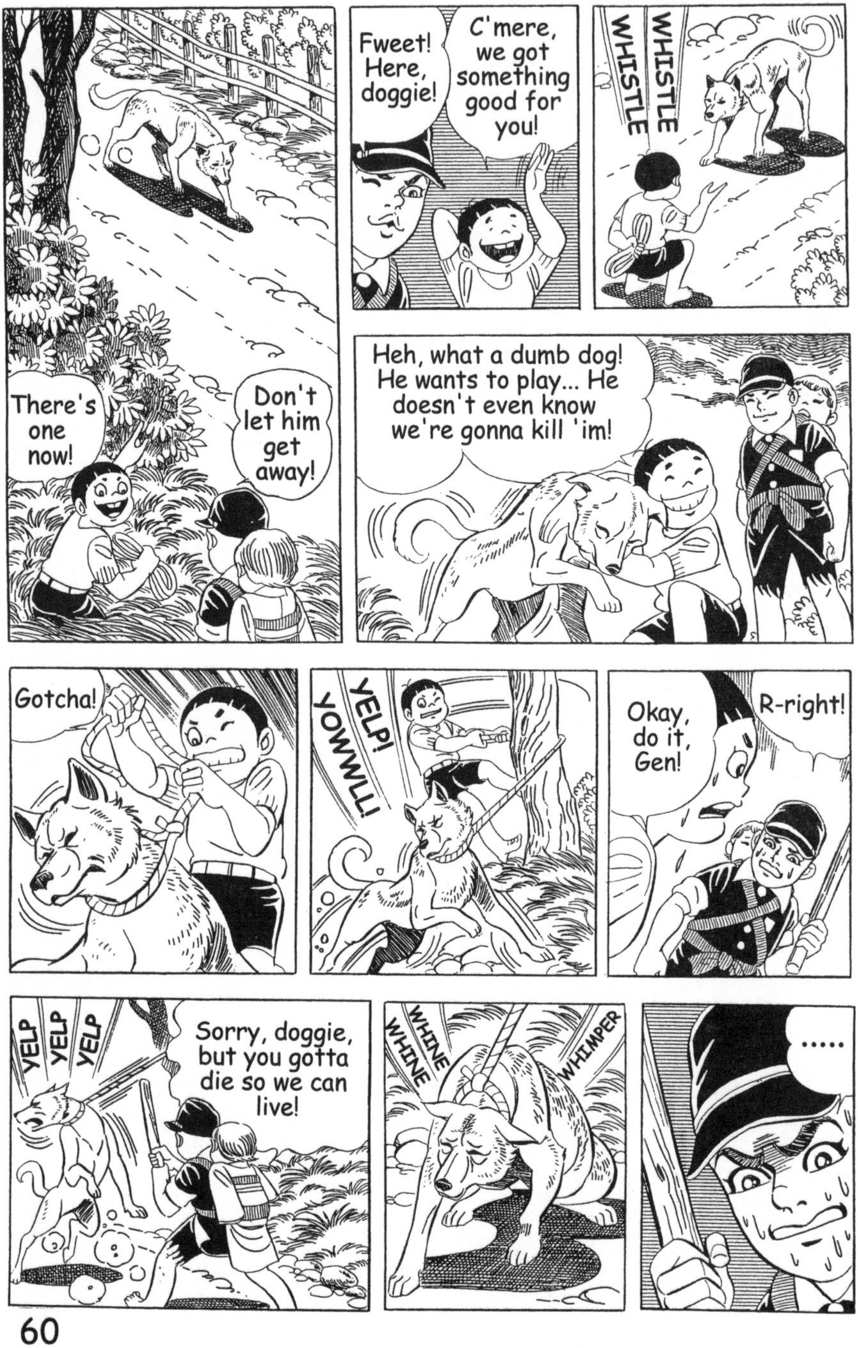
There's one now!
Don't let him get away!
Fweet! Here, doggie!
C'mere, we got something good for you!
WHISTLE
WHISTLE
Heh, what a dumb dog! He wants to play... He doesn't even know we're gonna kill 'im!
Gotcha!
YELP!
YOWWLL!
Okay, do it, Gen!
R-right!
YELP
YELP
YELP
Sorry, doggie, but you gotta die so we can live!
WHINE
WHINE
WHIMPER
.....

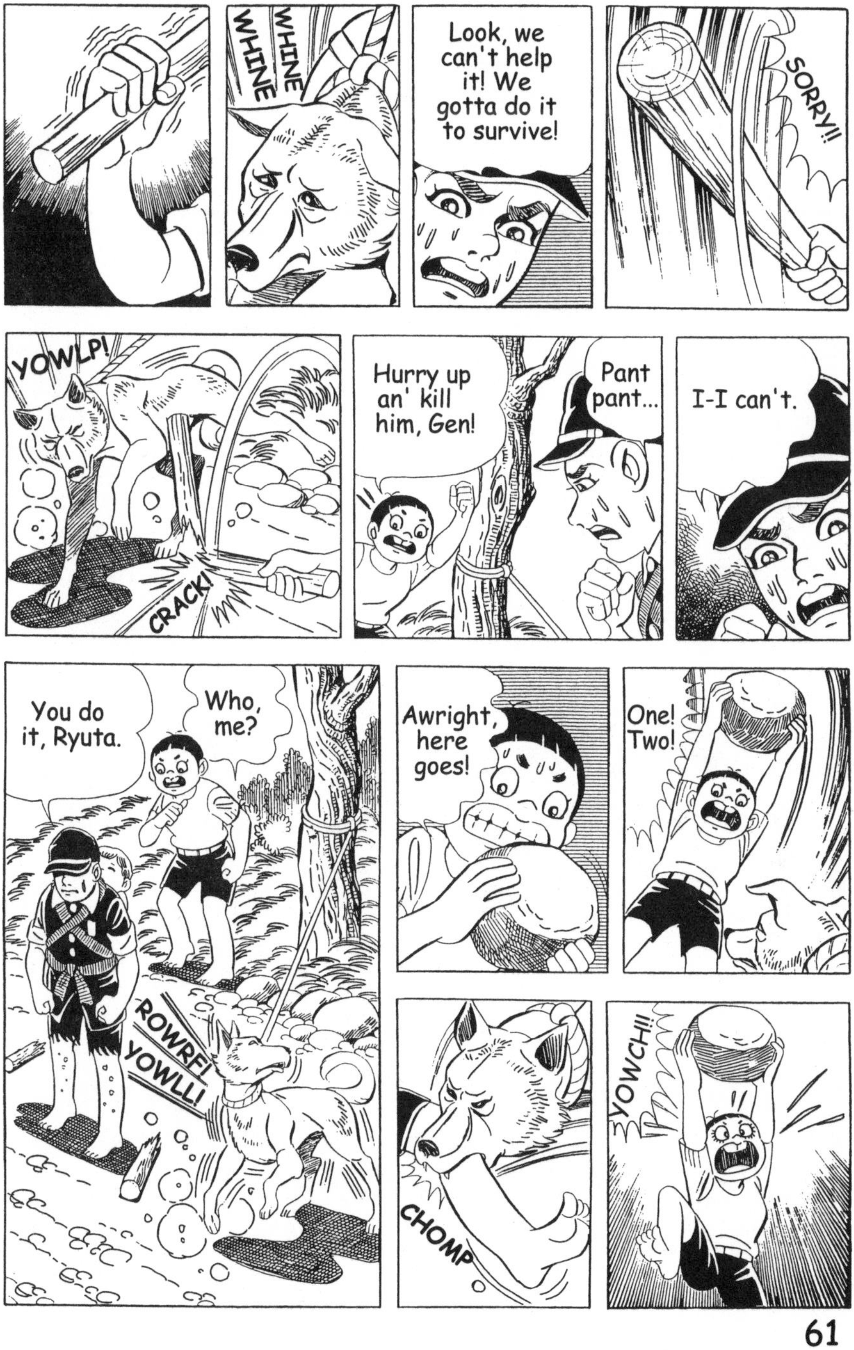
WHINE
WHINE
Look, we can't help it! We gotta do it to survive!
SORRY!!
YOWLP!
CRACK!
Hurry up an' kill him, Gen!
Pant pant...
I-I can't.
You do it, Ryuta.
Who, me?
ROWRF!
YOWLL!
Awright, here goes!
One! Two!
CHOMP
YOWCH!!

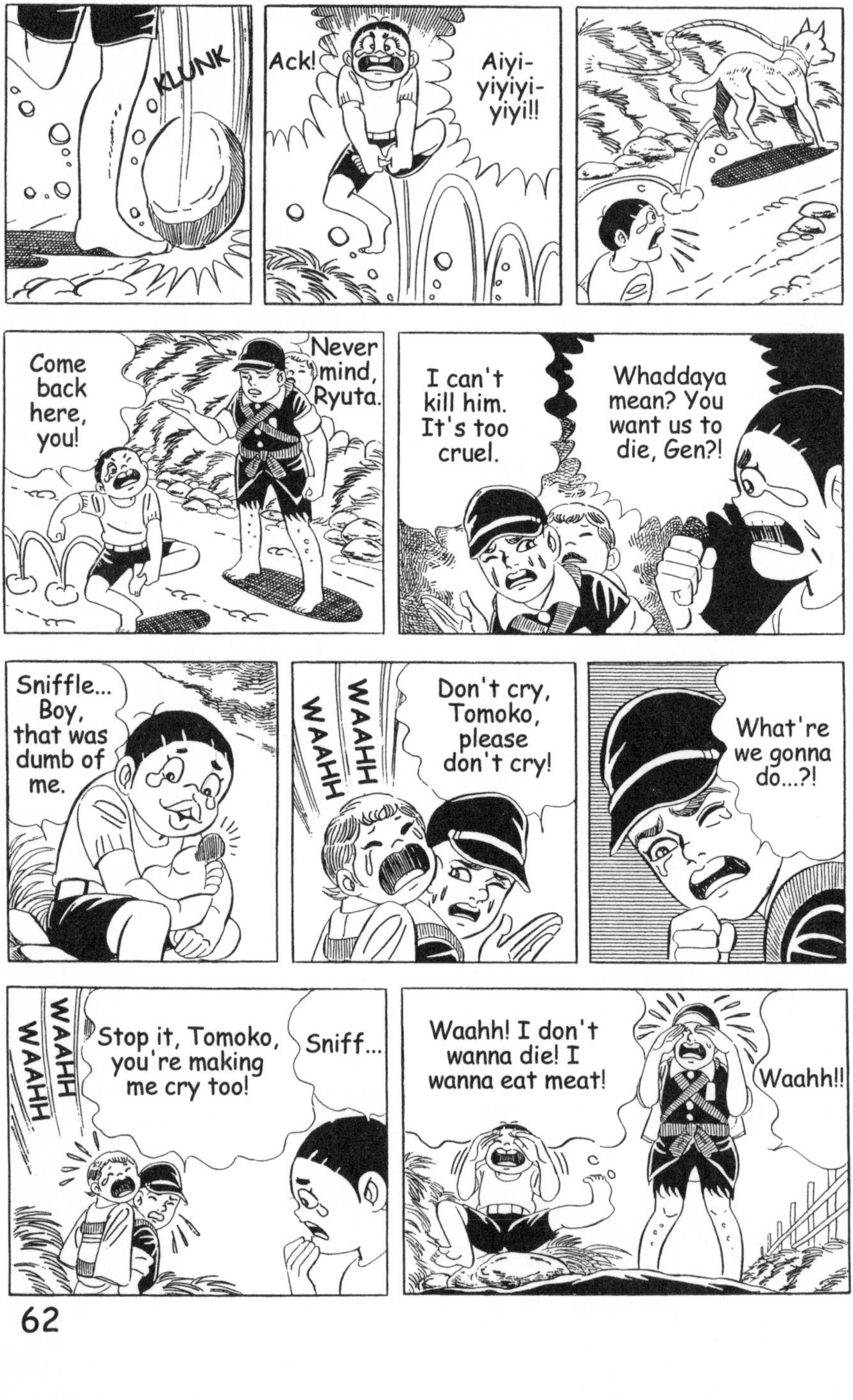
KLUNK
Ack!
Aiyi-yiyiyi-yiyi!!
Come back here, you!
Never mind, Ryuta.
I can't kill him. It's too cruel.
Whaddaya mean? You want us to die, Gen?!
Sniffle... Boy, that was dumb of me.
WAAHH WAAHH
Don't cry, Tomoko, please don't cry!
What're we gonna do...?!
WAAHH WAAHH
Stop it, Tomoko, you're making me cry too!
Sniff...
Waahh! I don't wanna die! I wanna eat meat!
Waahh!!

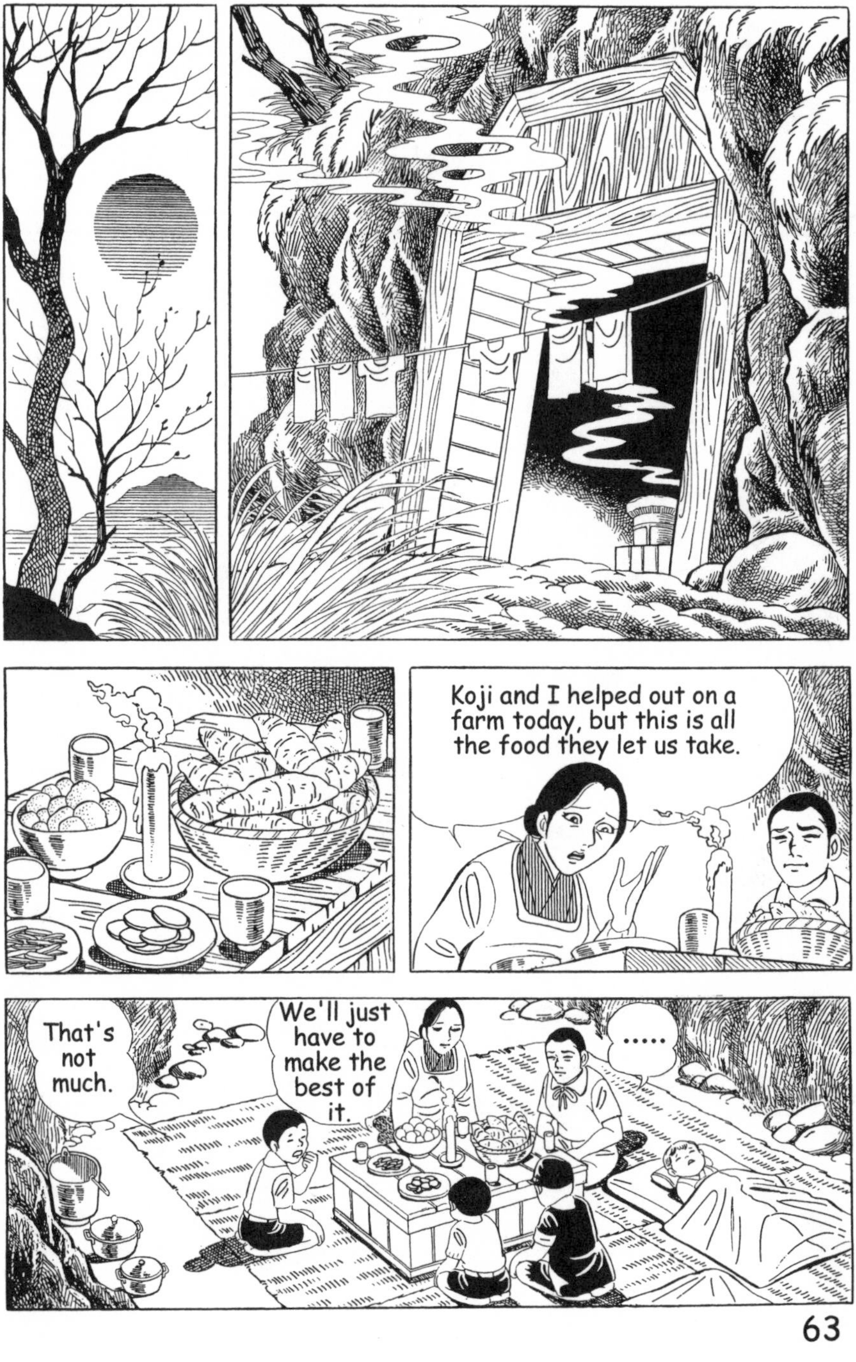
Koji and I helped out on a farm today, but this is all the food they let us take.
That's not much.
We'll just have to make the best of it.
.....

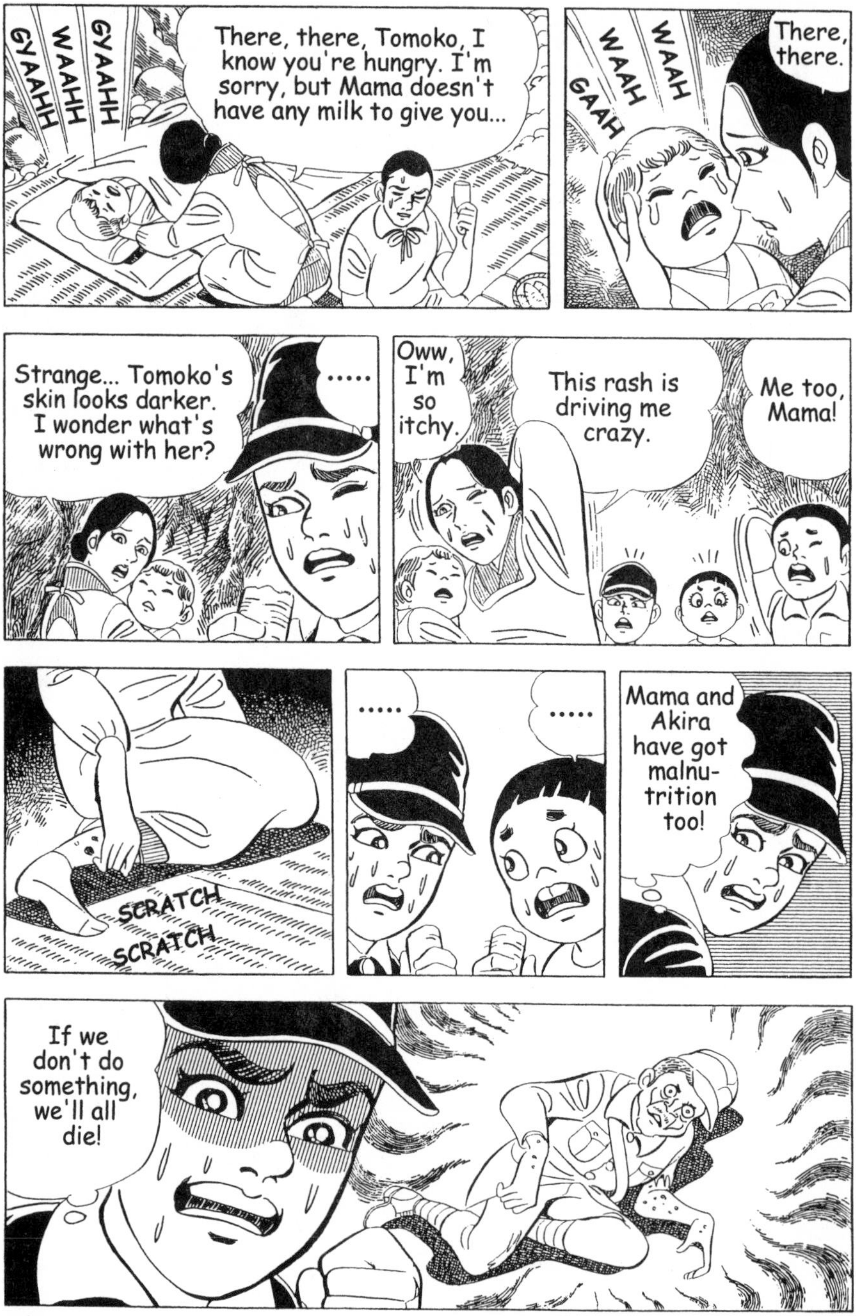
GYAAHH
WAAHH
GYAAHH
There, there, Tomoko, I know you're hungry. I'm sorry, but Mama doesn't have any milk to give you...
WAAH
WAAH
GAAH
There, there.
Strange... Tomoko's skin looks darker. I wonder what's wrong with her?
.....
Oww, I'm so itchy.
This rash is driving me crazy.
Me too, Mama!
SCRATCH
SCRATCH
.....
.....
Mama and Akira have got malnu-trition too!
If we don't do something, we'll all die!

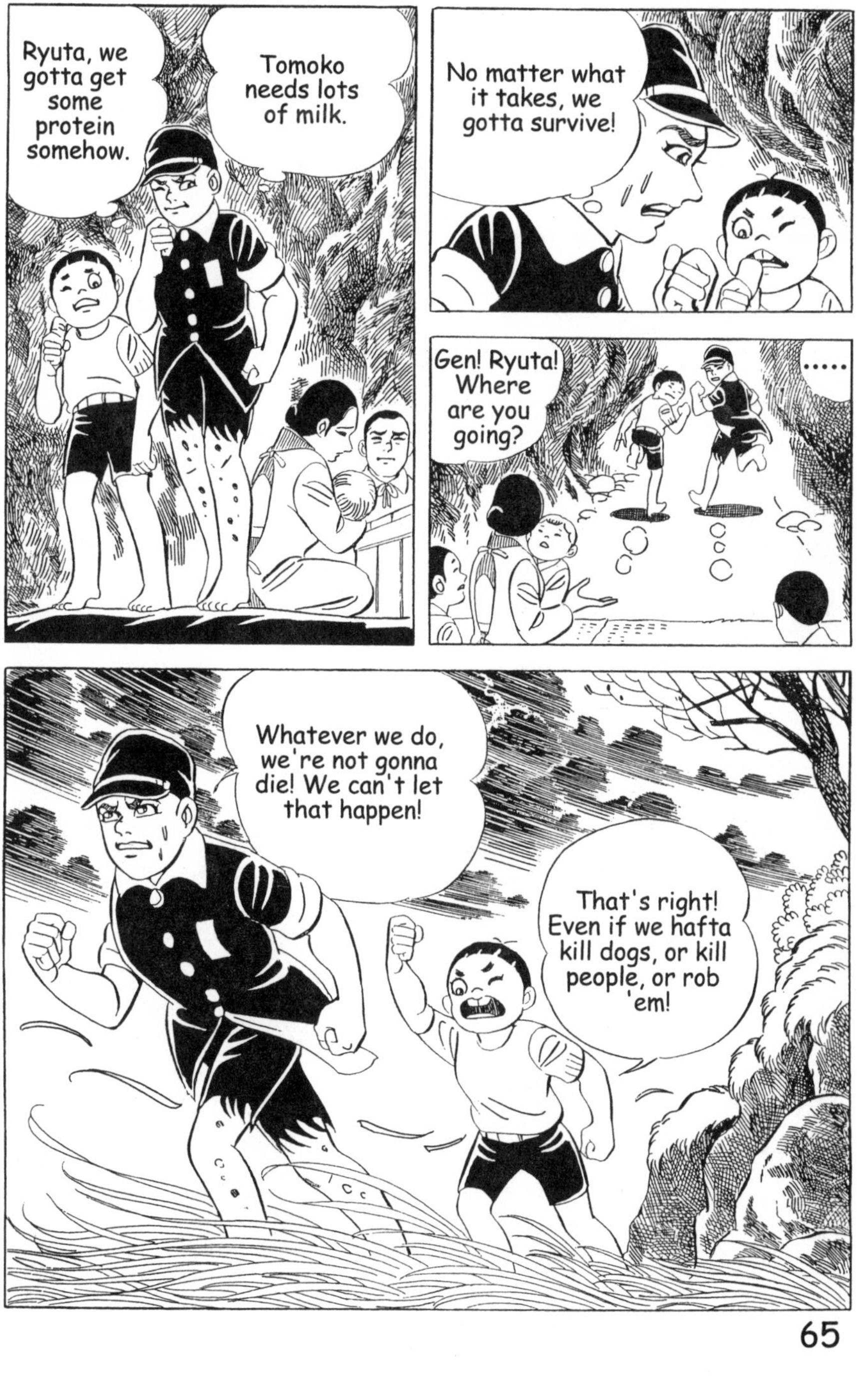
Ryuta, we gotta get some protein somehow.
Tomoko needs lots of milk.
No matter what it takes, we gotta survive!
Gen! Ryuta! Where are you going?
.....
Whatever we do, we're not gonna die! We can't let that happen!
That's right! Even if we hafta kill dogs, or kill people, or rob 'em!

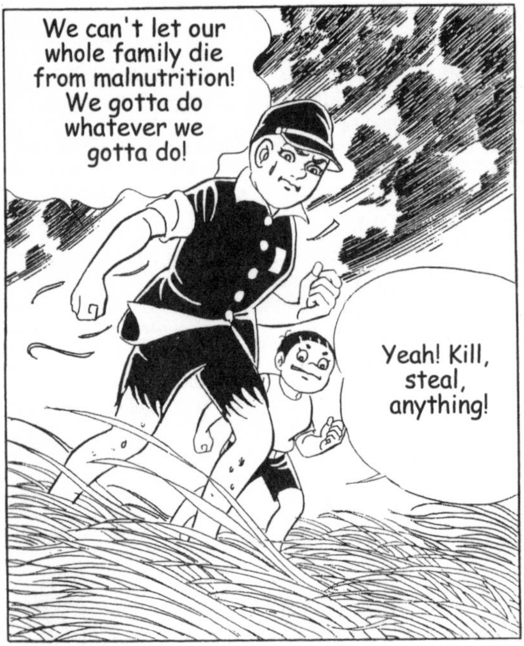
We can't let our whole family die from malnutrition! We gotta do whatever we gotta do!
Yeah! Kill, steal, anything!
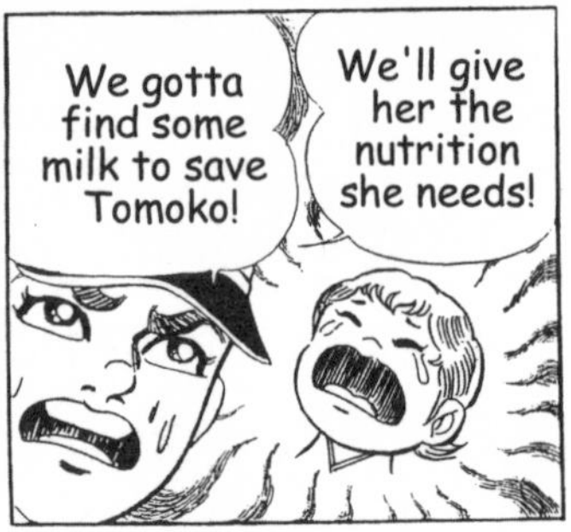
We gotta find some milk to save Tomoko!
We'll give her the nutrition she needs!
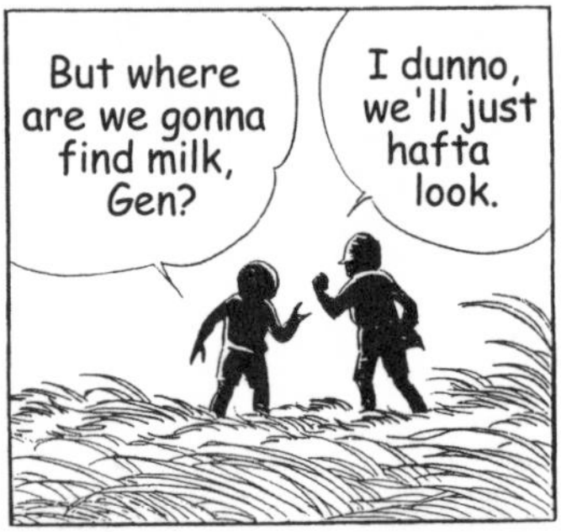
But where are we gonna find milk, Gen?
I dunno, we'll just hafta look.
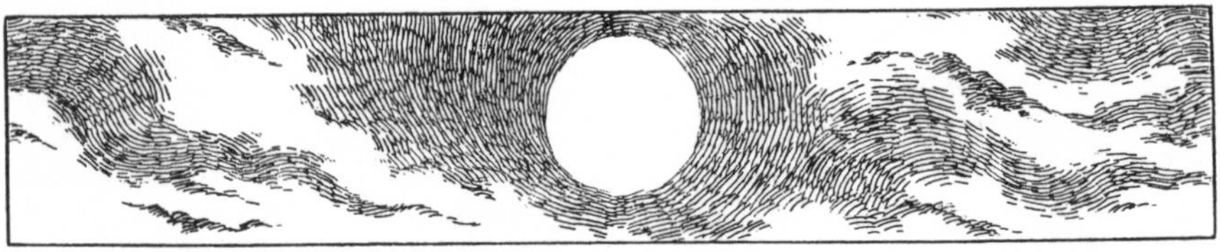
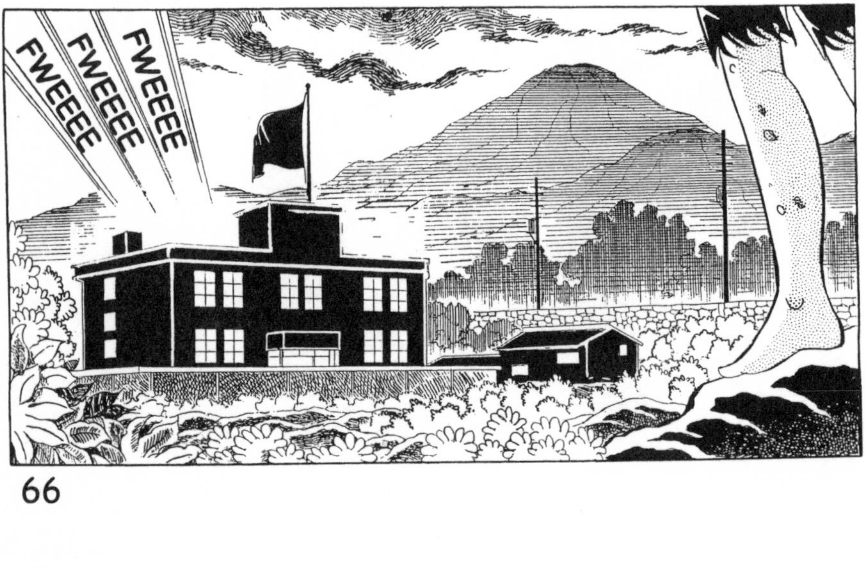
FWEEEEE
FWEEEEE
FWEEEEE

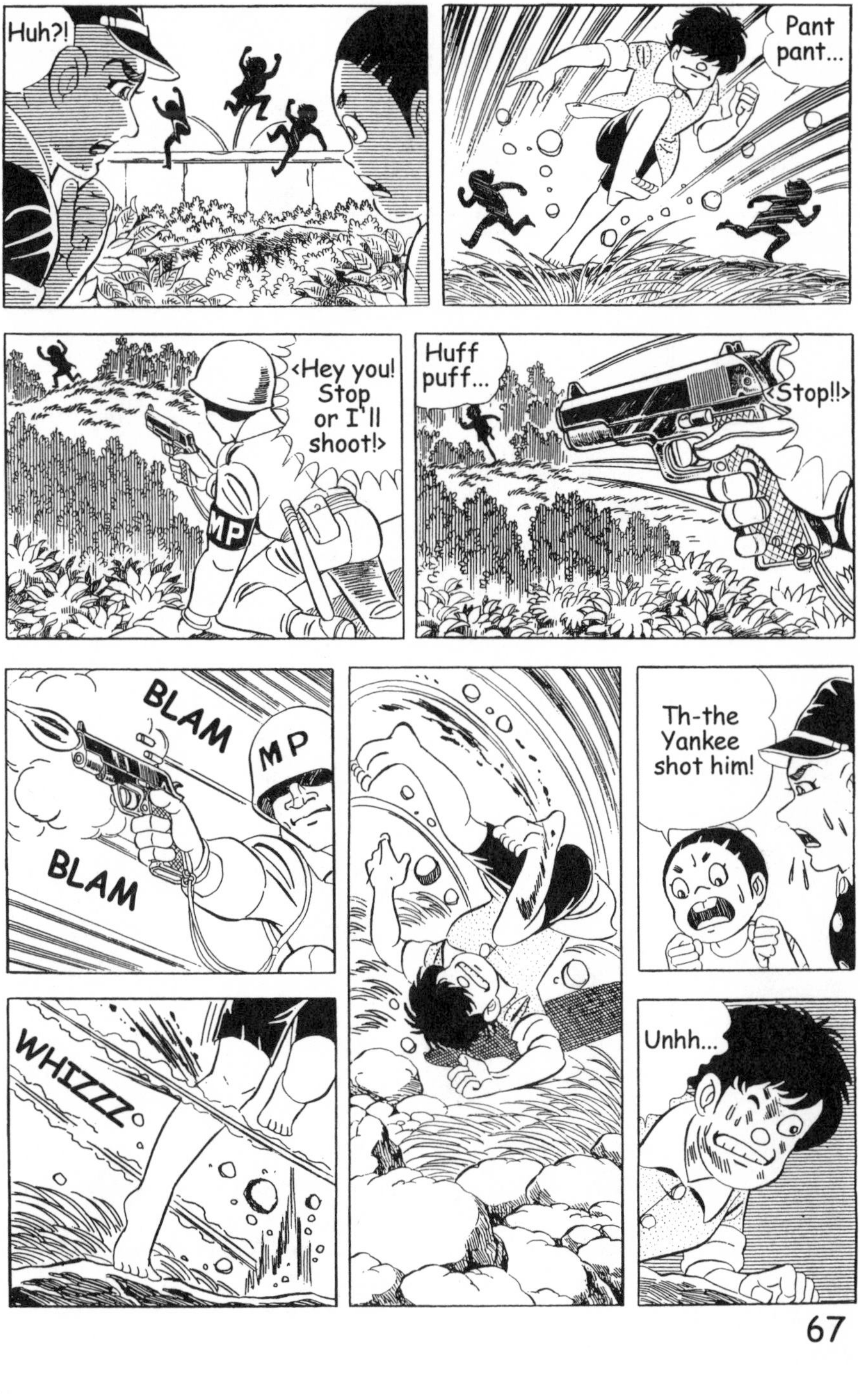

Huh?!
Pant pant...
<Hey you! Stop or I'll shoot!>
Huff puff...
<Stop!!>
BLAM
BLAM
WHIZZZZ
Th-the Yankee shot him!
Unhh...

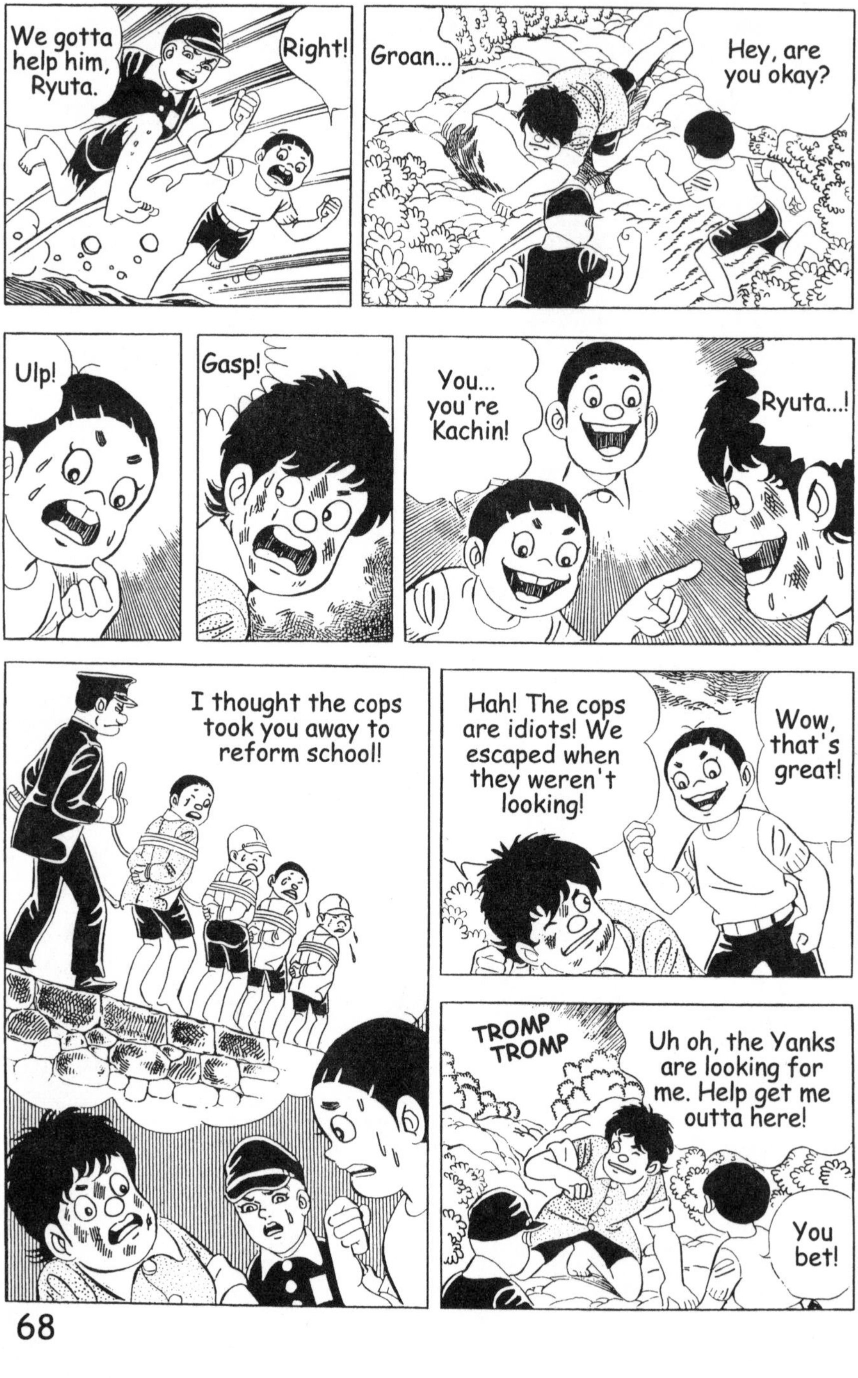

We gotta help him, Ryuta.
Right!
Groan...
Hey, are you okay?
Ulp!
Gasp!
You... you're Kachin!
Ryuta...!
I thought the cops took you away to reform school!
Hah! The cops are idiots! We escaped when they weren't looking!
Wow, that's great!
TROMP TROMP
Uh oh, the Yanks are looking for me. Help get me outta here!
You bet!

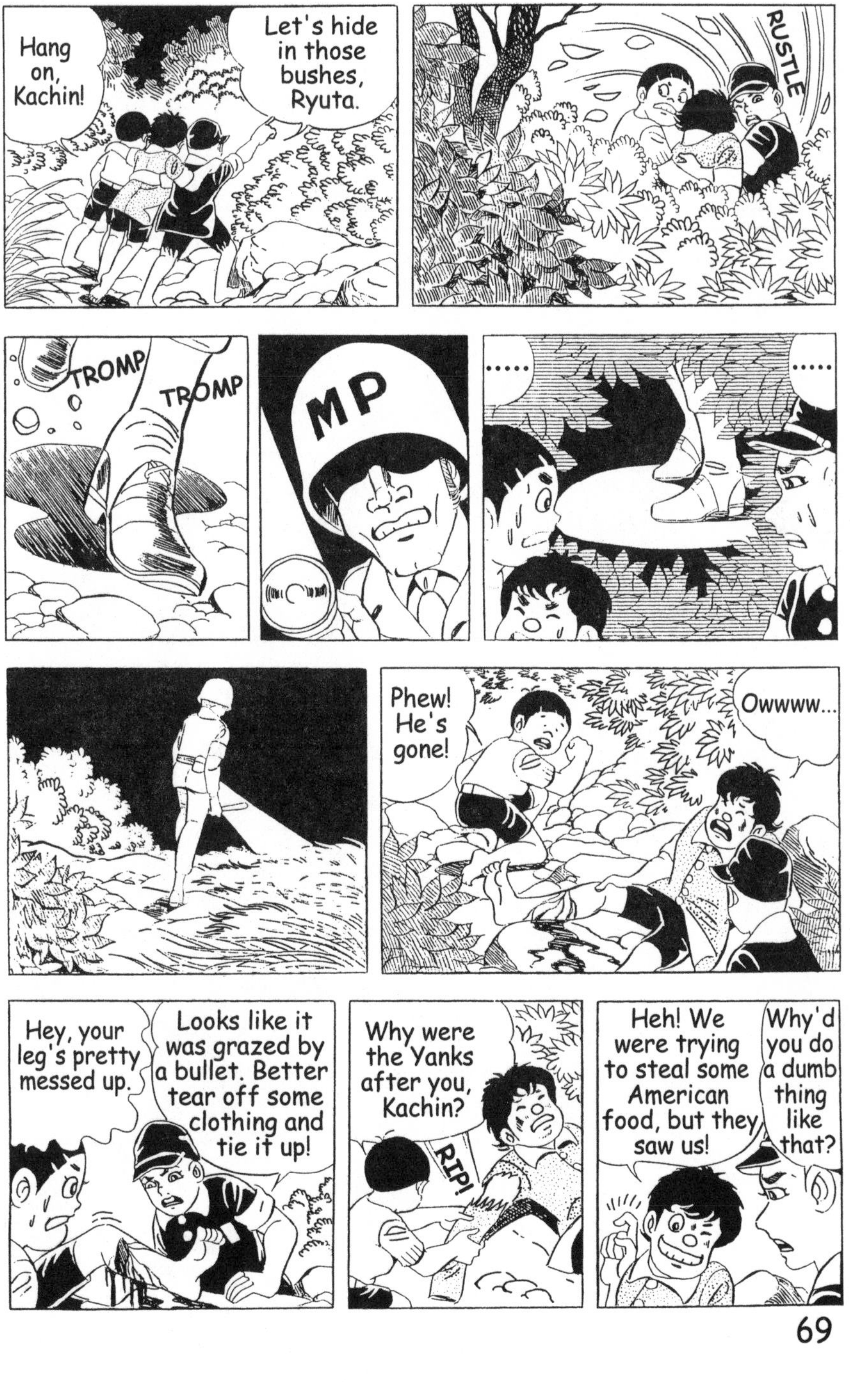
Hang on, Kachin!
Let's hide in those bushes, Ryuta.
RUSTLE
TROMP
TROMP
MP
.....
.....
Phew! He's gone!
Owwww...
Hey, your leg's pretty messed up.
Looks like it was grazed by a bullet. Better tear off some clothing and tie it up!
Why were the Yanks after you, Kachin?
RIP!
Heh! We were trying to steal some American food, but they saw us!
Why'd you do a dumb thing like that?

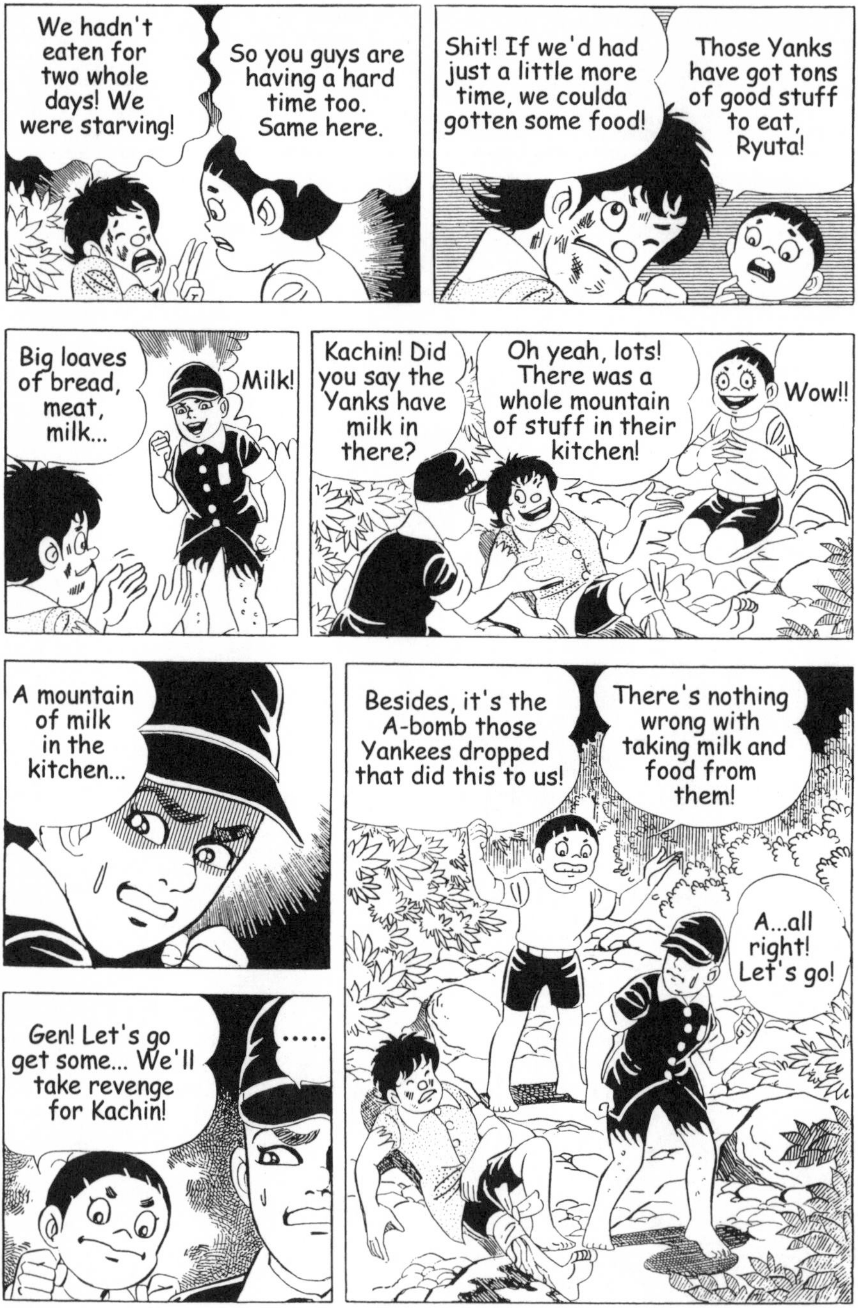
We hadn't eaten for two whole days! We were starving!
So you guys are having a hard time too. Same here.
Shit! If we'd had just a little more time, we coulda gotten some food!
Those Yanks have got tons of good stuff to eat, Ryuta!
Big loaves of bread, meat, milk...
Milk!
Kachin! Did you say the Yanks have milk in there?
Oh yeah, lots! There was a whole mountain of stuff in their kitchen!
Wow!!
A mountain of milk in the kitchen...
Gen! Let's go get some... We'll take revenge for Kachin!
.....
Besides, it's the A-bomb those Yankees dropped that did this to us!
There's nothing wrong with taking milk and food from them!
A...all right! Let's go!

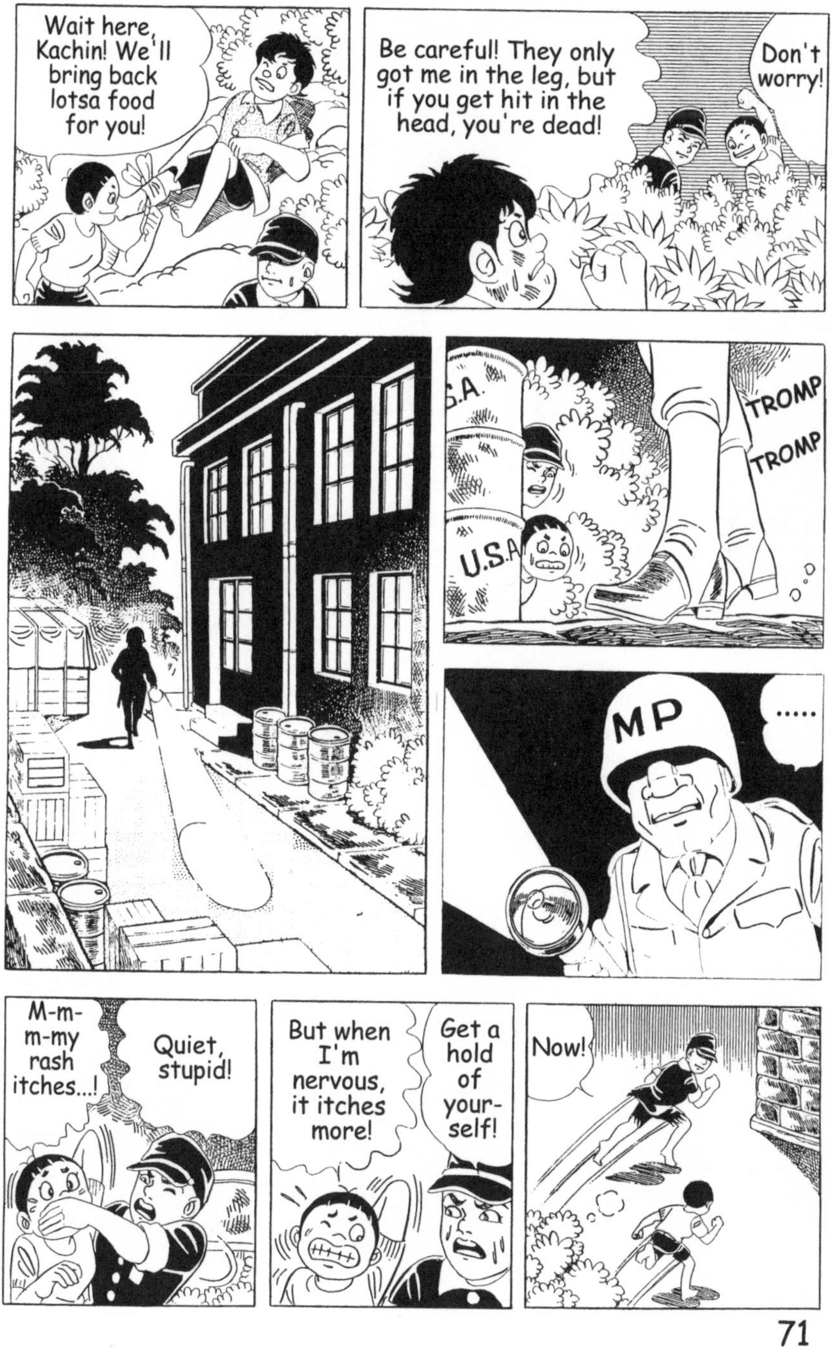
Wait here, Kachin! We'll bring back lotsa food for you!
Be careful! They only got me in the leg, but if you get hit in the head, you're dead!
Don't worry!
S.A.
U.S.A
TROMP
TROMP
MP
.....
M-m-m-my rash itches...!
Quiet, stupid!
But when I'm nervous, it itches more!
Get a hold of your-self!
Now!

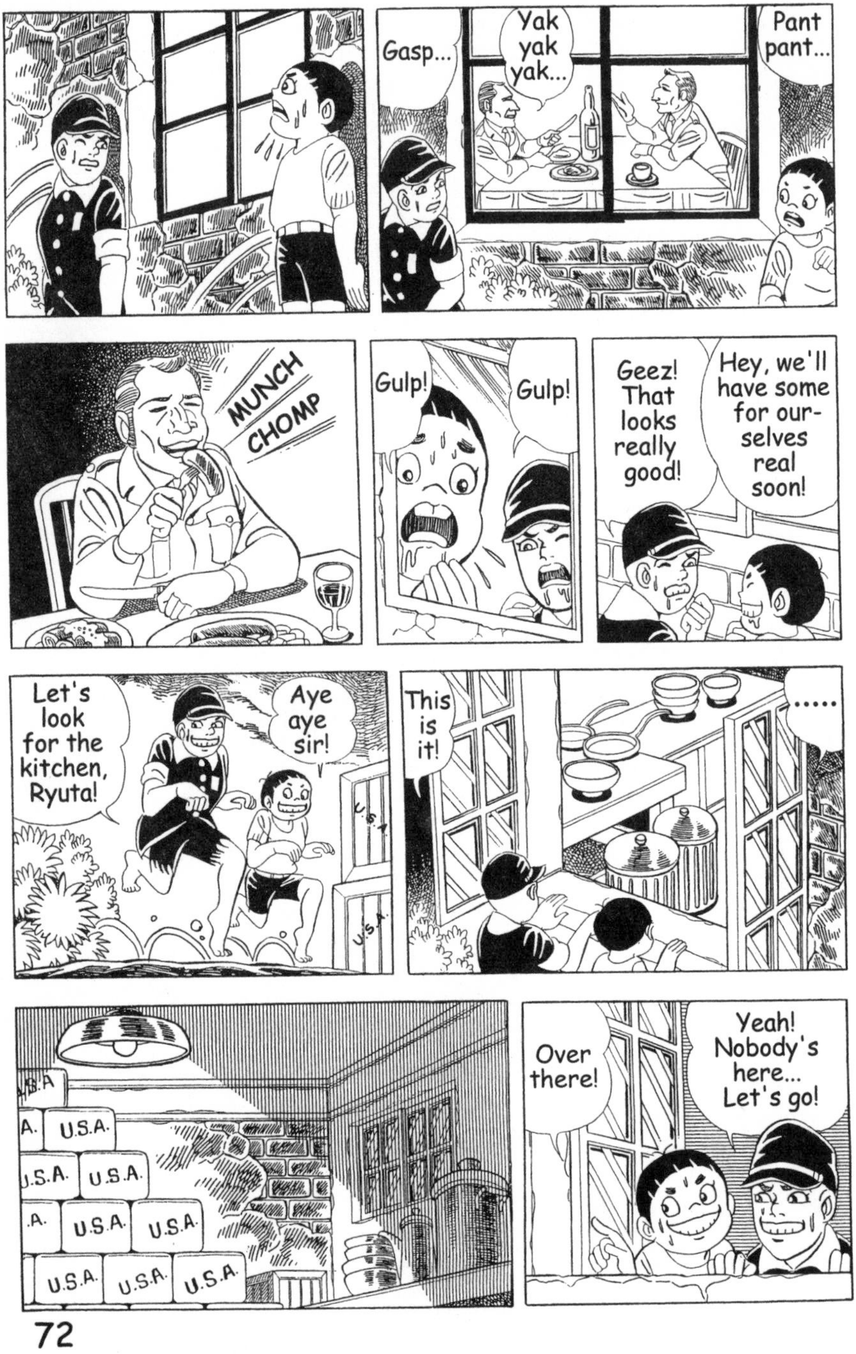
Gasp...
Yak yak yak...
Pant pant...
MUNCH
CHOMP
Gulp!
Gulp!
Geez! That looks really good!
Hey, we'll have some for our-selves real soon!
Let's look for the kitchen, Ryuta!
Aye aye sir!
U.S.A.
U.S.A.
This is it!
.....
U.S.A.
U.S.A.
U.S.A.
U.S.A.
U.S.A.
U.S.A.
U.S.A.
U.S.A.
Over there!
Yeah! Nobody's here... Let's go!

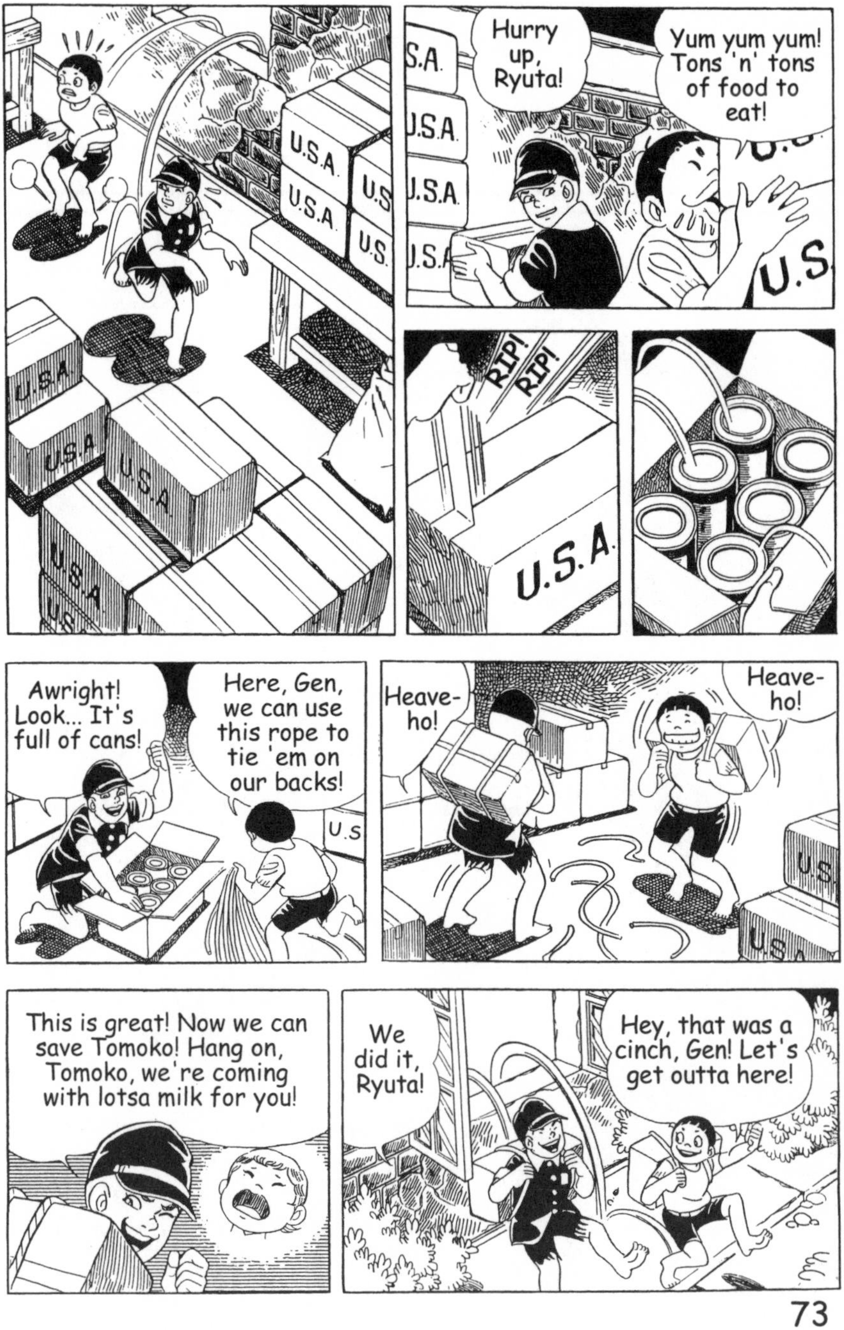
U.S.A
Hurry up, Ryuta!
Yum yum yum! Tons 'n' tons of food to eat!
RIP! RIP!
U.S.A.
Awright! Look... It's full of cans!
Here, Gen, we can use this rope to tie 'em on our backs!
Heave-ho!
Heave-ho!
This is great! Now we can save Tomoko! Hang on, Tomoko, we're coming with lotsa milk for you!
We did it, Ryuta!
Hey, that was a cinch, Gen! Let's get outta here!

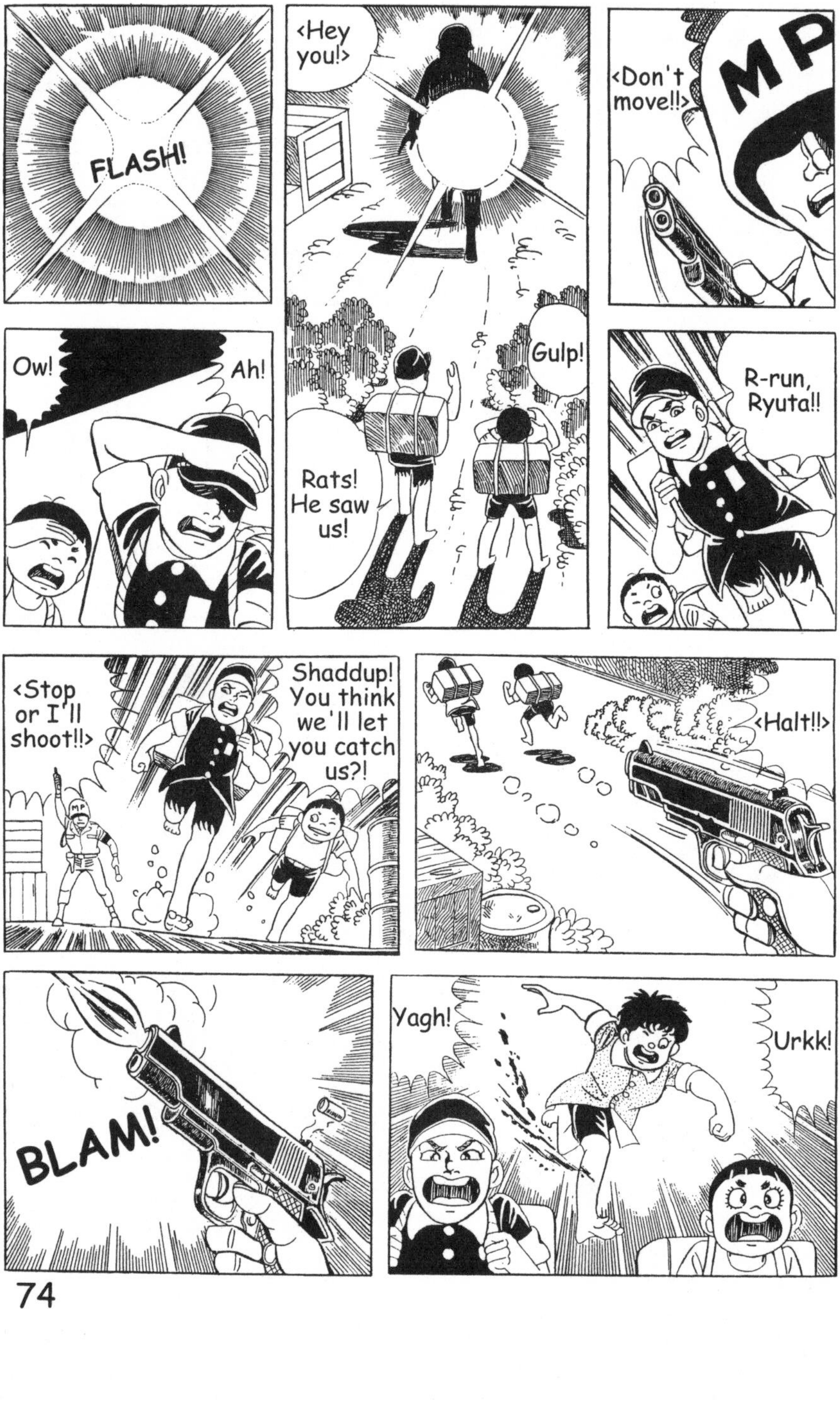
FLASH!
Ow!
Ah!
<Hey you!>
Gulp!
Rats! He saw us!
<Don't move!!>
MP
R-run, Ryuta!!
<Stop or I'll shoot!!>
Shaddup! You think we'll let you catch us?!
<Halt!!>
BLAM!
Yagh!
Urkk!

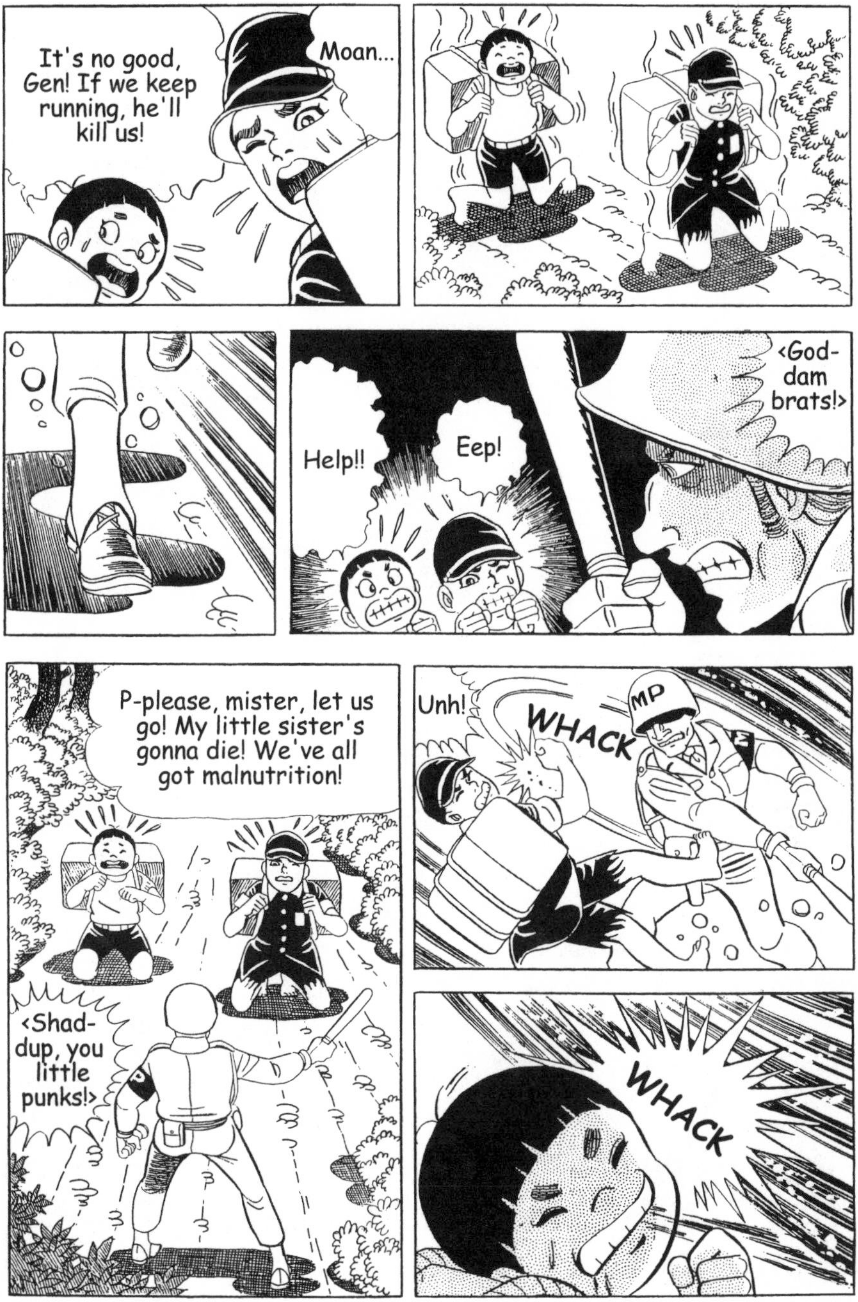
It's no good, Gen! If we keep running, he'll kill us!
Moan...
Help!!
Eep!
<God-dam brats!>
P-please, mister, let us go! My little sister's gonna die! We've all got malnutrition!
<Shad-dup, you little punks!>
Unh!
WHACK
MP
WHACK

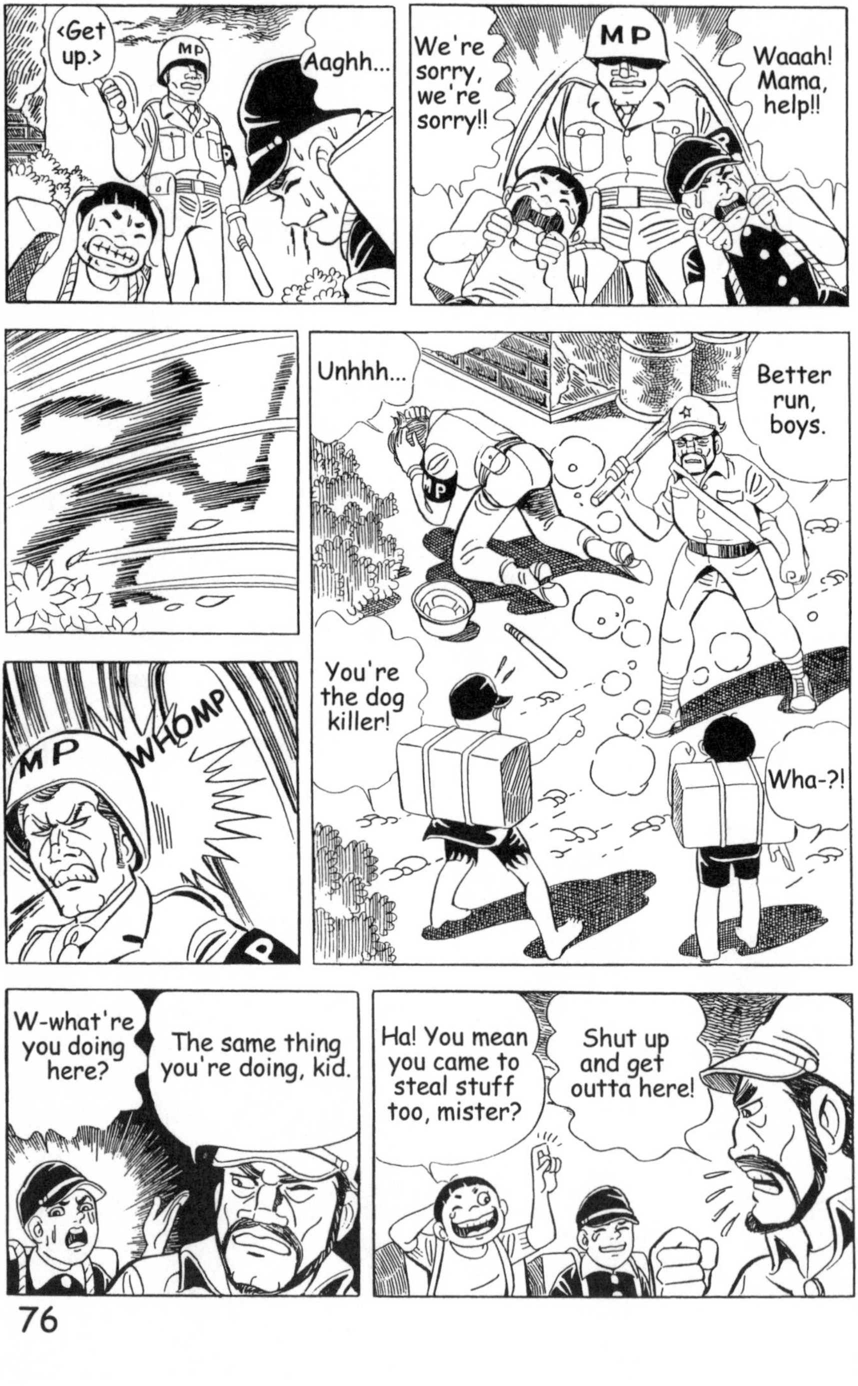
<Get up.>
Aaghh...
We're sorry, we're sorry!!
Waaah! Mama, help!!
WHOMP
Unhhh...
Better run, boys.
You're the dog killer!
Wha-?!
W-what're you doing here?
The same thing you're doing, kid.
Ha! You mean you came to steal stuff too, mister?
Shut up and get outta here!

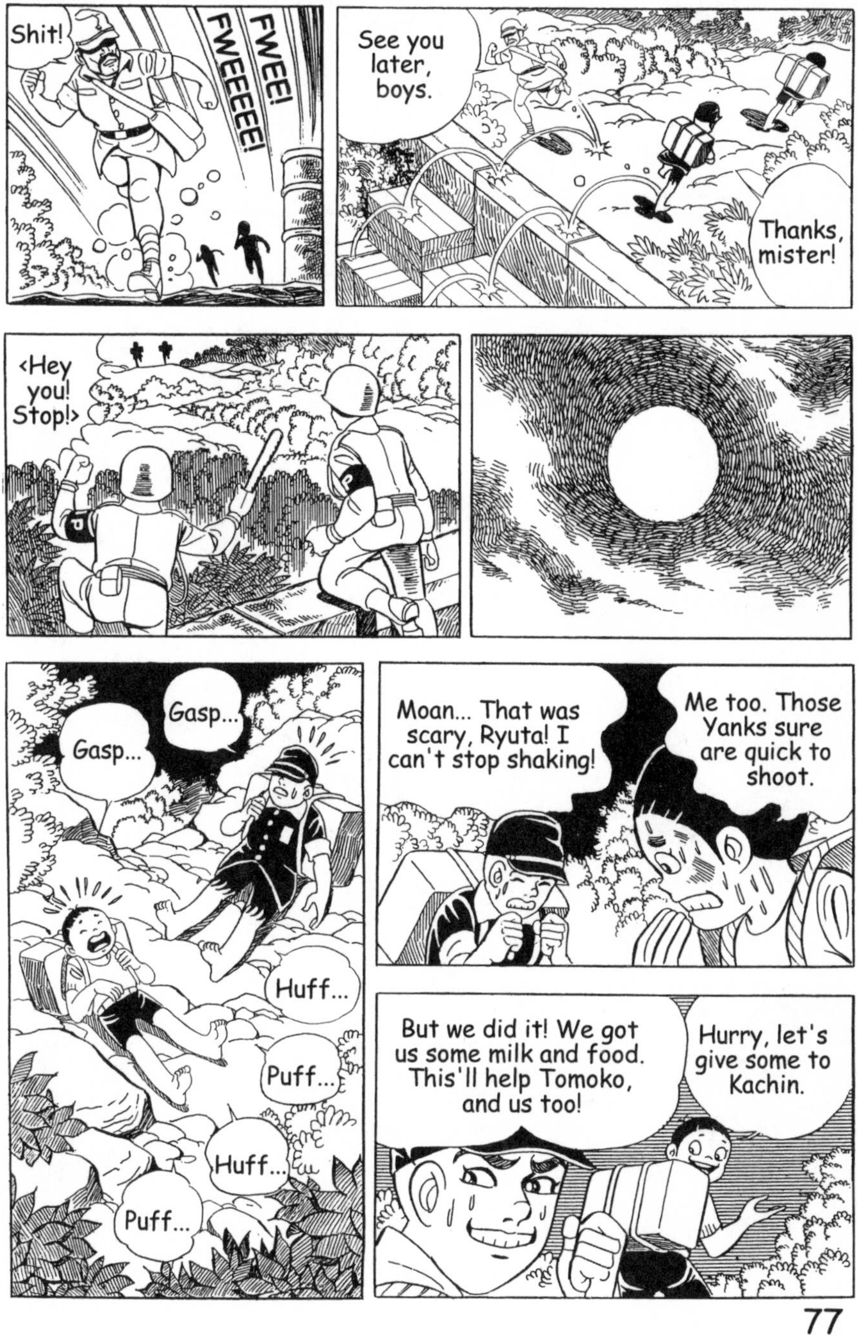
Shit!
FWEE! FWEEEEEE!
See you later, boys.
Thanks, mister!
‹Hey you! Stop!›
Gasp...
Gasp...
Huff...
Puff...
Huff...
Puff...
Moan... That was scary, Ryuta! I can't stop shaking!
Me too. Those Yanks sure are quick to shoot.
But we did it! We got us some milk and food. This'll help Tomoko, and us too!
Hurry, let's give some to Kachin.

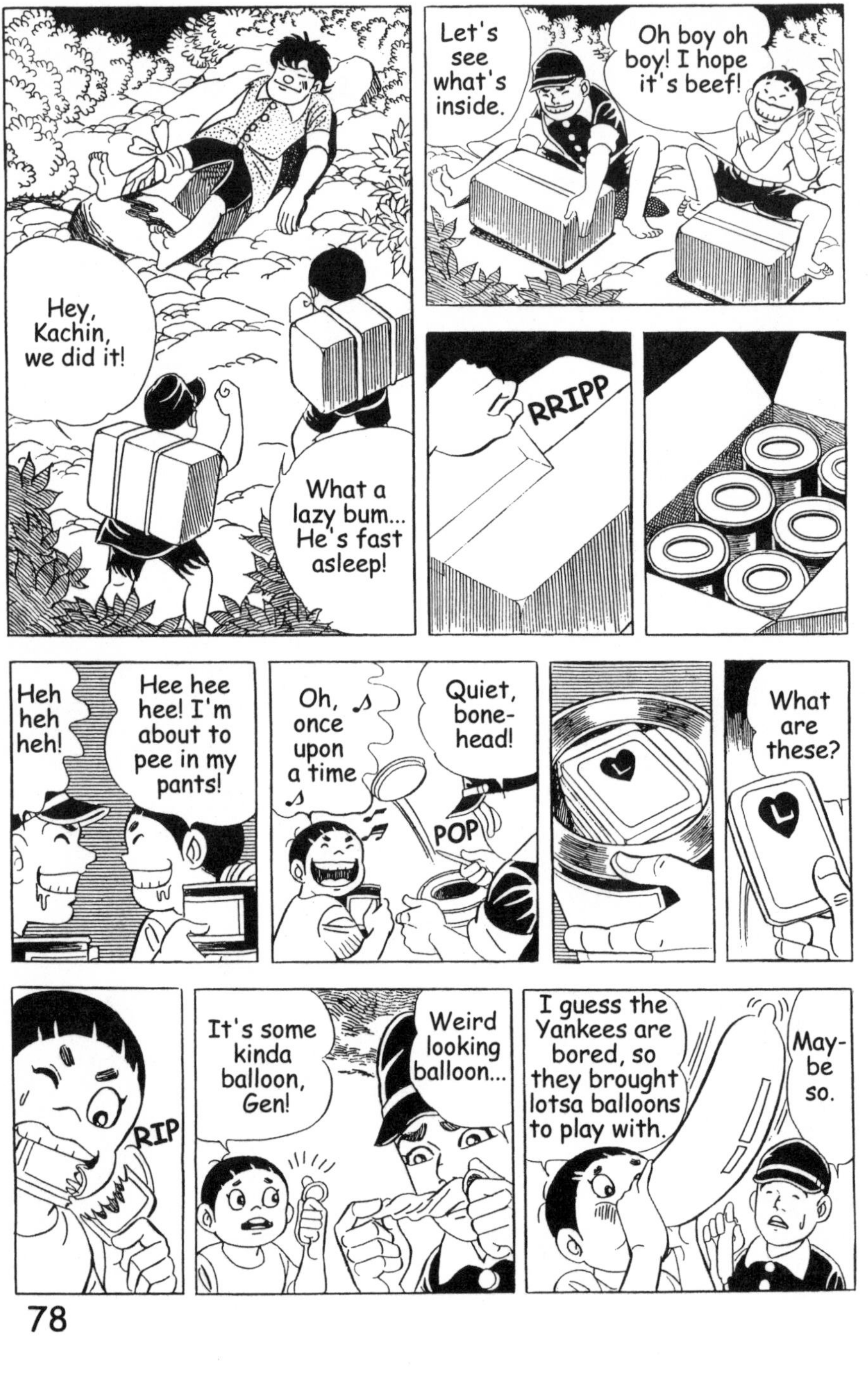
Hey, Kachin, we did it!
What a lazy bum... He's fast asleep!
Let's see what's inside.
Oh boy oh boy! I hope it's beef!
RRIPP
Heh heh heh!
Hee hee hee! I'm about to pee in my pants!
Oh, once upon a time
Quiet, bone-head!
POP
What are these?
RIP
It's some kinda balloon, Gen!
Weird looking balloon...
I guess the Yankees are bored, so they brought lotsa balloons to play with.
May-be so.

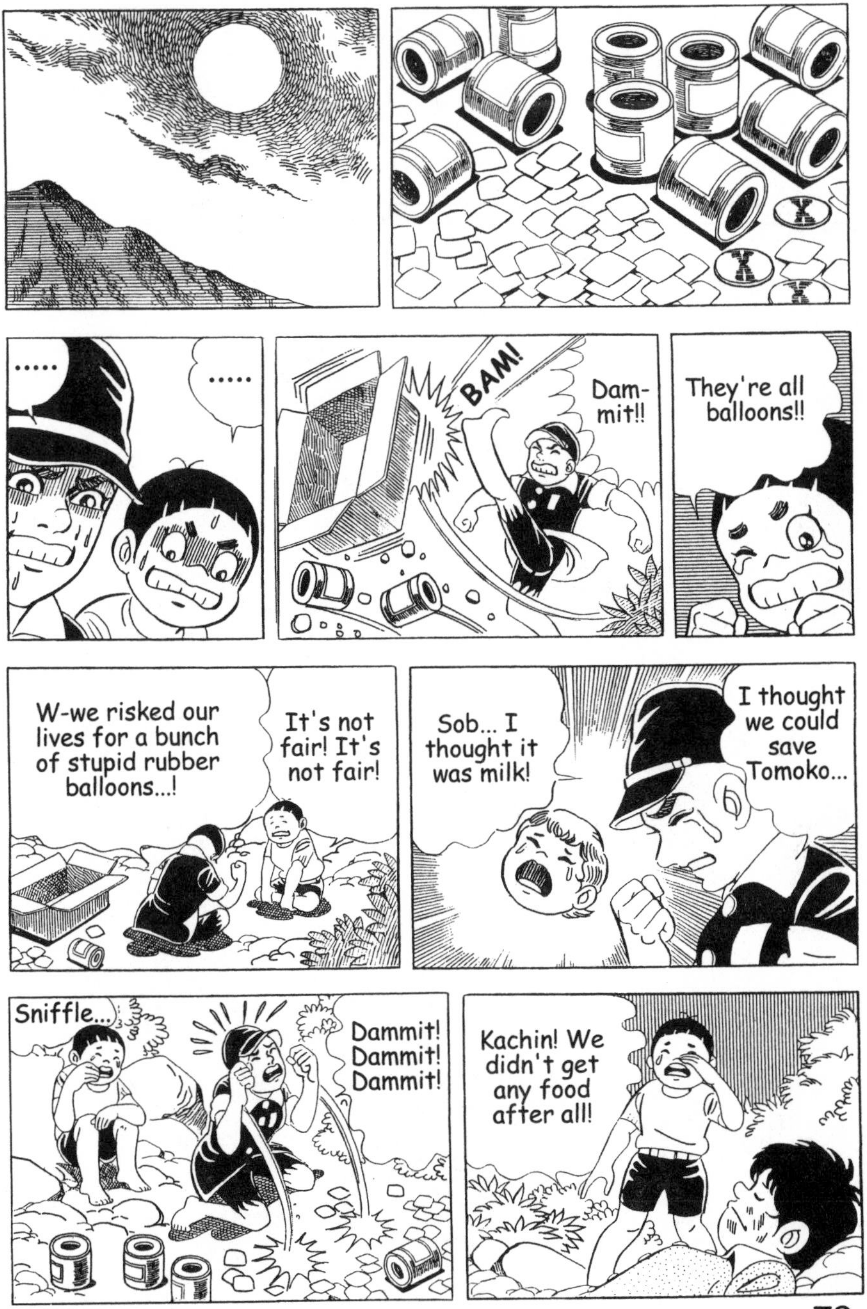
......
......
BAM!
Dam-mit!!
They're all balloons!!
W-we risked our lives for a bunch of stupid rubber balloons...!
It's not fair! It's not fair!
Sob... I thought it was milk!
I thought we could save Tomoko...
Sniffle...
Dammit! Dammit! Dammit!
Kachin! We didn't get any food after all!

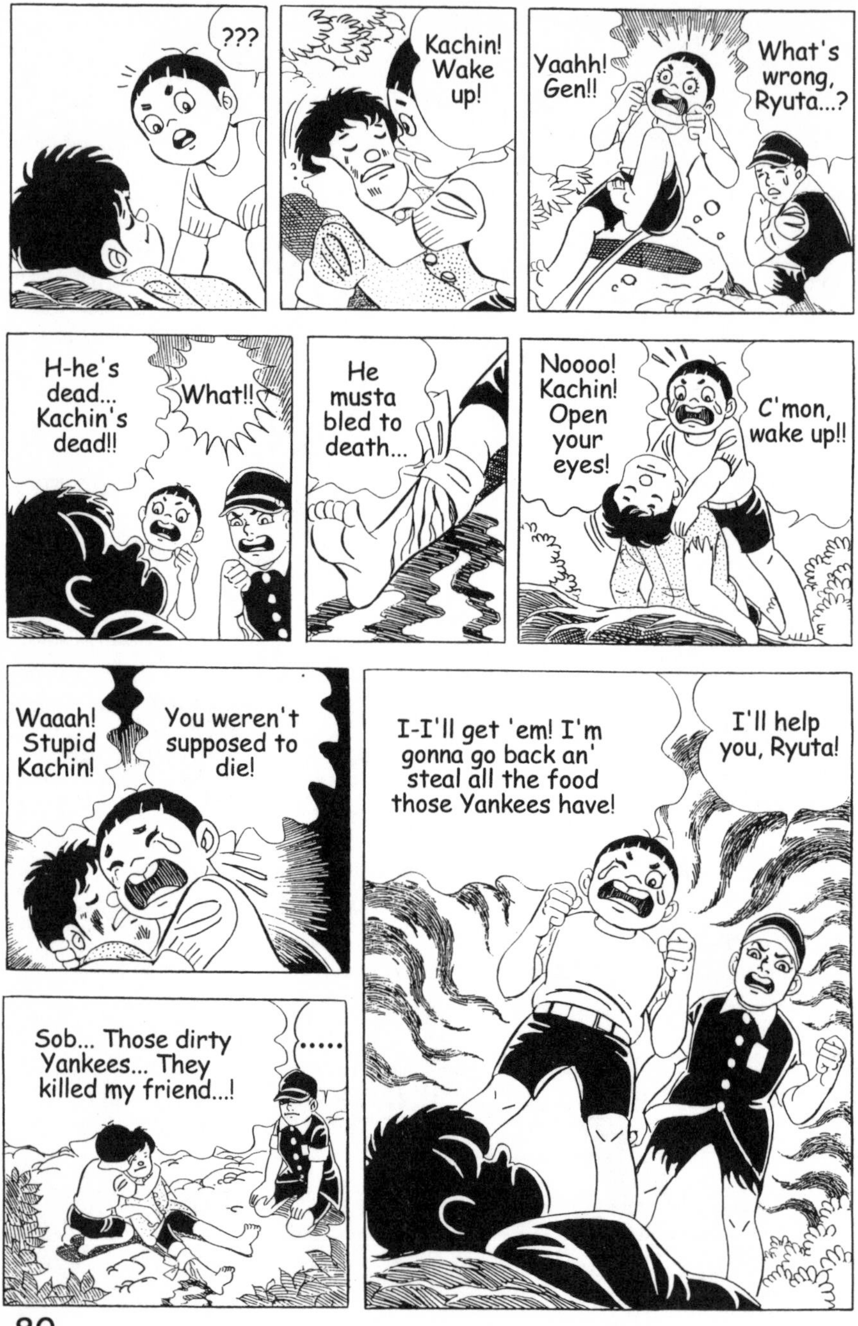
???
Kachin! Wake up!
Yaahh! Gen!!
What's wrong, Ryuta...?
H-he's dead... Kachin's dead!!
What!!
He musta bled to death...
Noooo! Kachin! Open your eyes!
C'mon, wake up!!
Waaah! Stupid Kachin!
You weren't supposed to die!
Sob... Those dirty Yankees... They killed my friend...!
.....
I-I'll get 'em! I'm gonna go back an' steal all the food those Yankees have!
I'll help you, Ryuta!

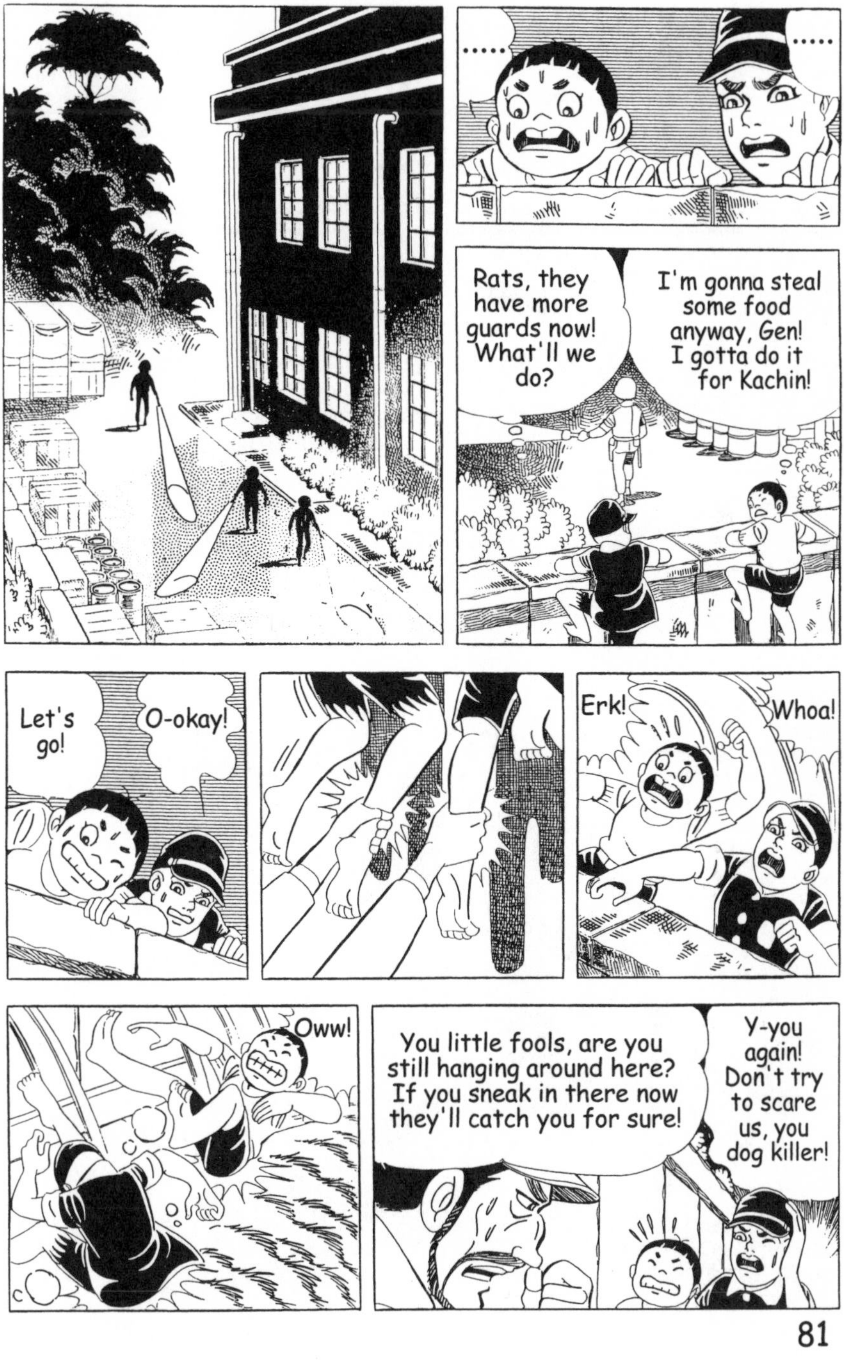

......
......
Rats, they have more guards now! What'll we do?
I'm gonna steal some food anyway, Gen! I gotta do it for Kachin!
Let's go!
O-okay!
Erk!
Whoa!
Oww!
You little fools, are you still hanging around here? If you sneak in there now they'll catch you for sure!
Y-you again! Don't try to scare us, you dog killer!

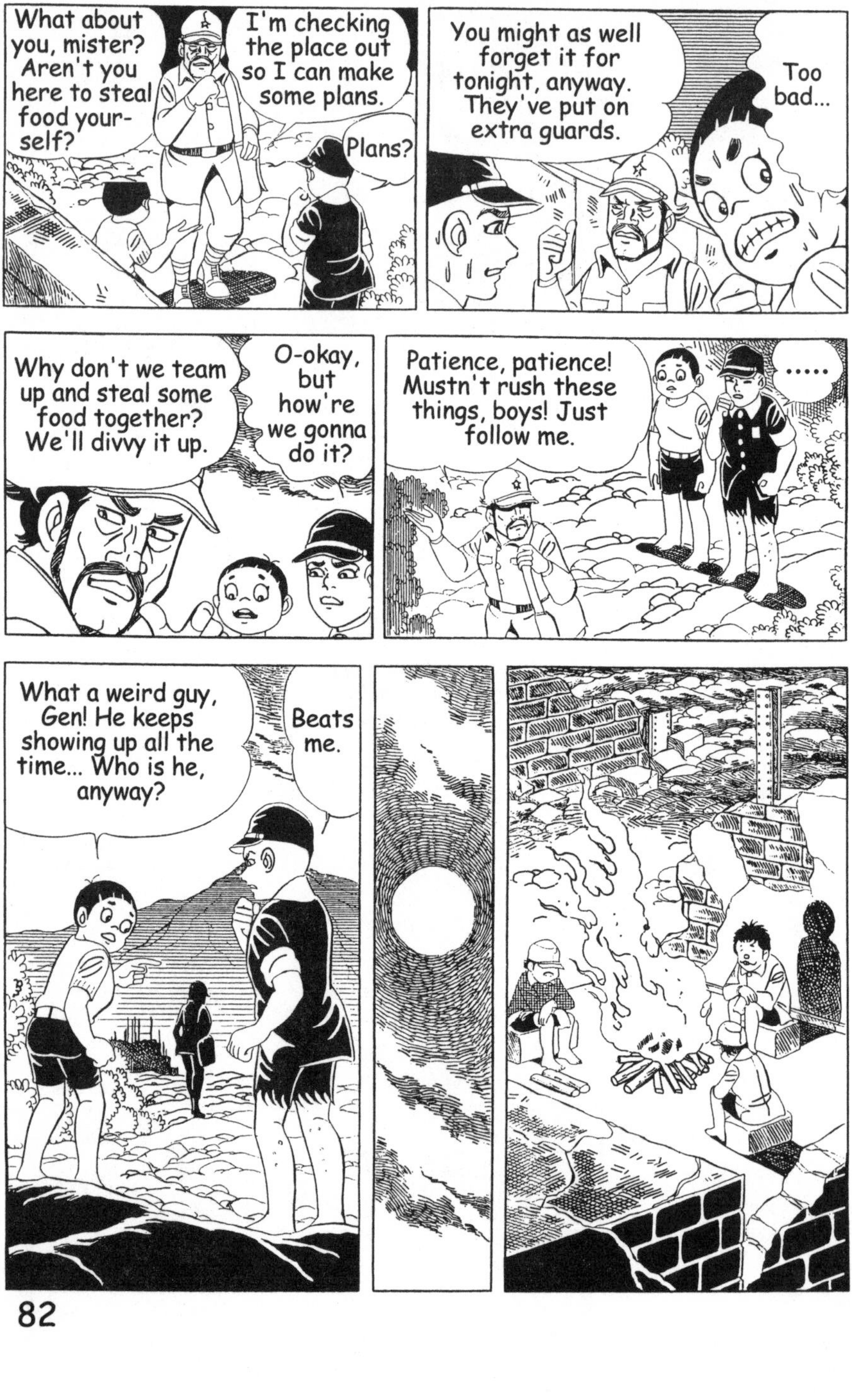
What about you, mister? Aren't you here to steal food your-self?
I'm checking the place out so I can make some plans.
Plans?
You might as well forget it for tonight, anyway. They've put on extra guards.
Too bad...
Why don't we team up and steal some food together? We'll divvy it up.
O-okay, but how're we gonna do it?
Patience, patience! Mustn't rush these things, boys! Just follow me.
.....
What a weird guy, Gen! He keeps showing up all the time... Who is he, anyway?
Beats me.

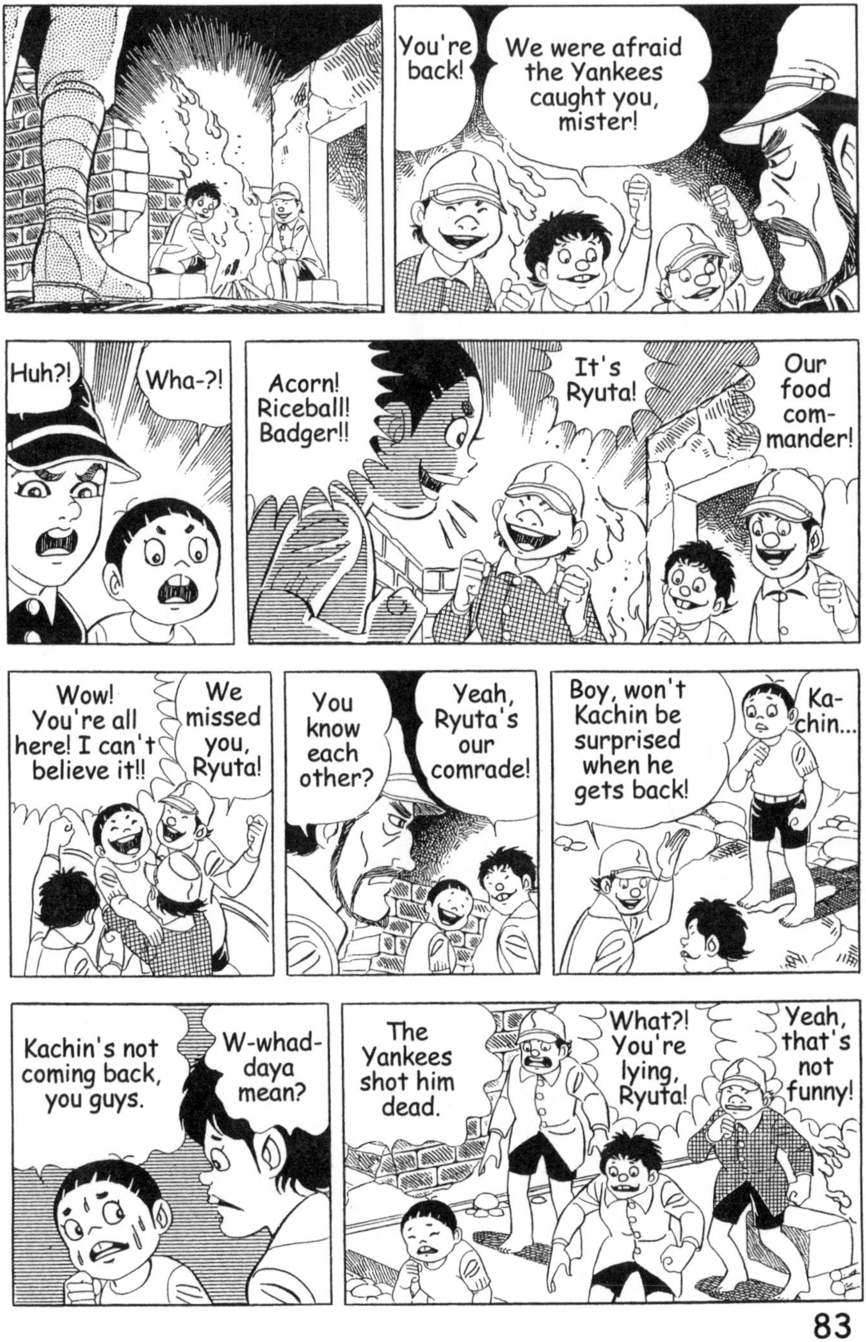
You're back!
We were afraid the Yankees caught you, mister!
Huh?!
Wha-?!
Acorn! Riceball! Badger!!
It's Ryuta!
Our food com-mander!
Wow! You're all here! I can't believe it!!
We missed you, Ryuta!
You know each other?
Yeah, Ryuta's our comrade!
Boy, won't Kachin be surprised when he gets back!
Ka-chin...
Kachin's not coming back, you guys.
W-whad-daya mean?
The Yankees shot him dead.
What?! You're lying, Ryuta!
Yeah, that's not funny!

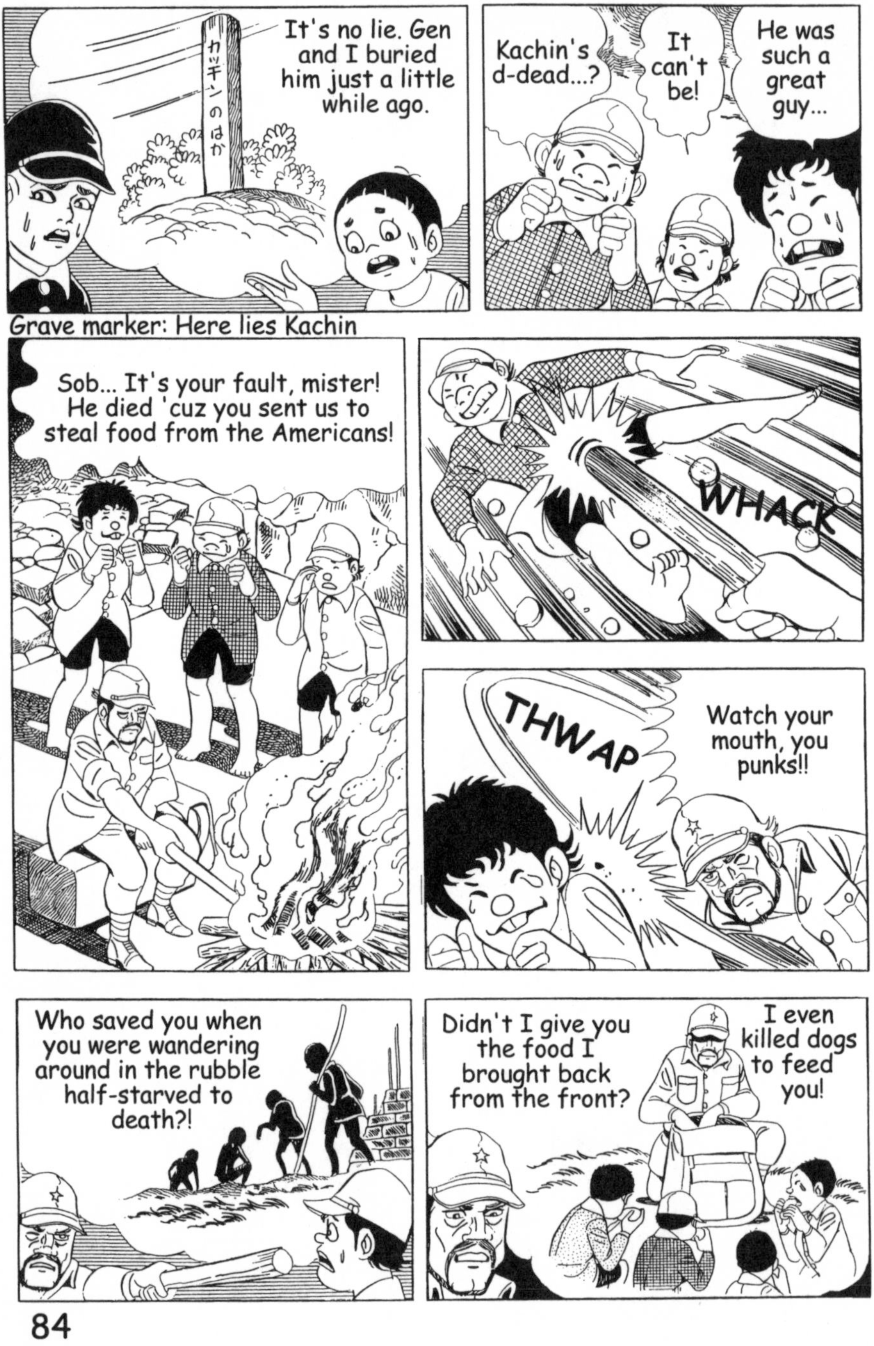
カッチンのはか
It's no lie. Gen and I buried him just a little while ago.
Grave marker: Here lies Kachin
Kachin's d-dead...?
It can't be!
He was such a great guy...
Sob... It's your fault, mister! He died 'cuz you sent us to steal food from the Americans!
WHACK
THWAP
Watch your mouth, you punks!!
Who saved you when you were wandering around in the rubble half-starved to death?!
Didn't I give you the food I brought back from the front?
I even killed dogs to feed you!

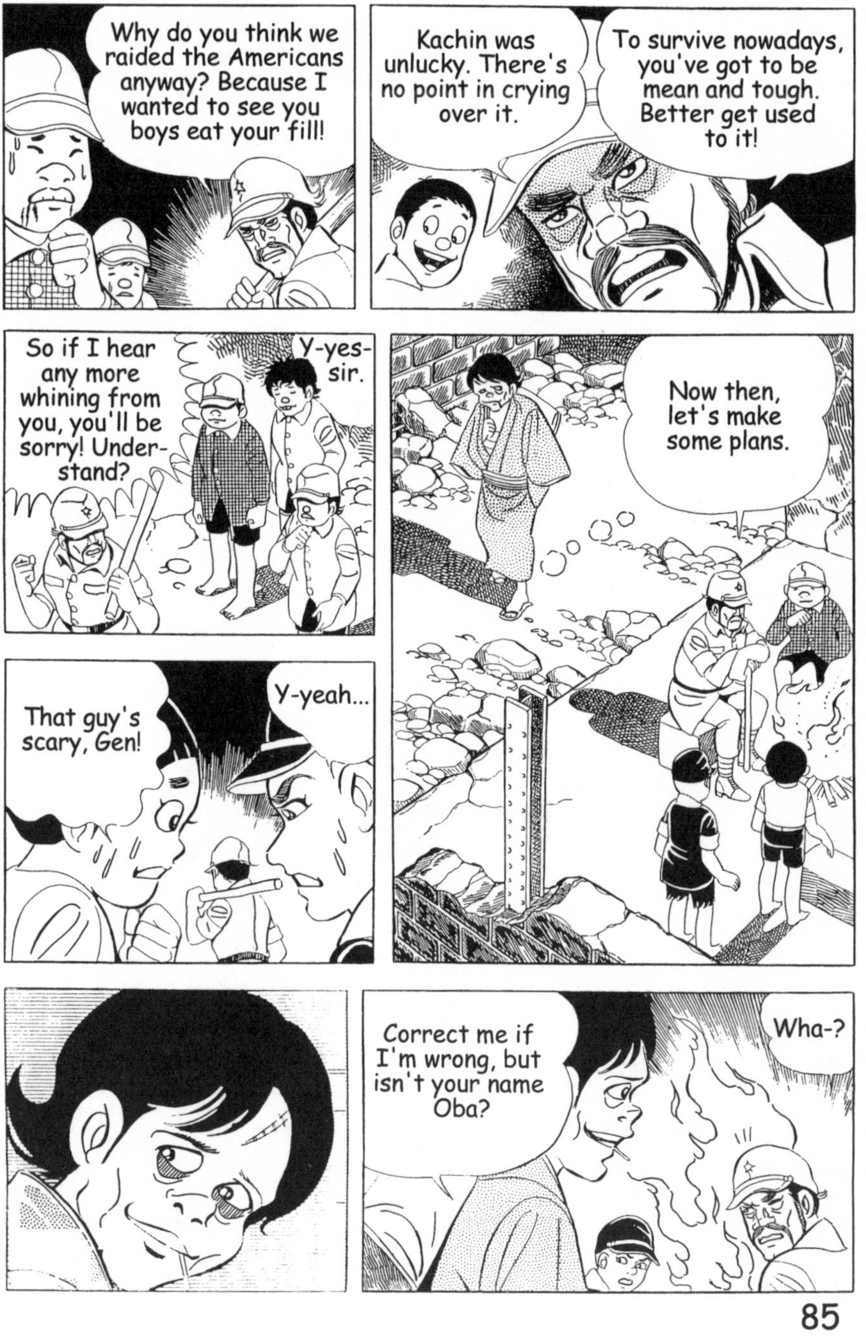
Why do you think we raided the Americans anyway? Because I wanted to see you boys eat your fill!
Kachin was unlucky. There's no point in crying over it.
To survive nowadays, you've got to be mean and tough. Better get used to it!
So if I hear any more whining from you, you'll be sorry! Under-stand?
Y-yes-sir.
That guy's scary, Gen!
Y-yeah...
Now then, let's make some plans.
Correct me if I'm wrong, but isn't your name Oba?
Wha-?

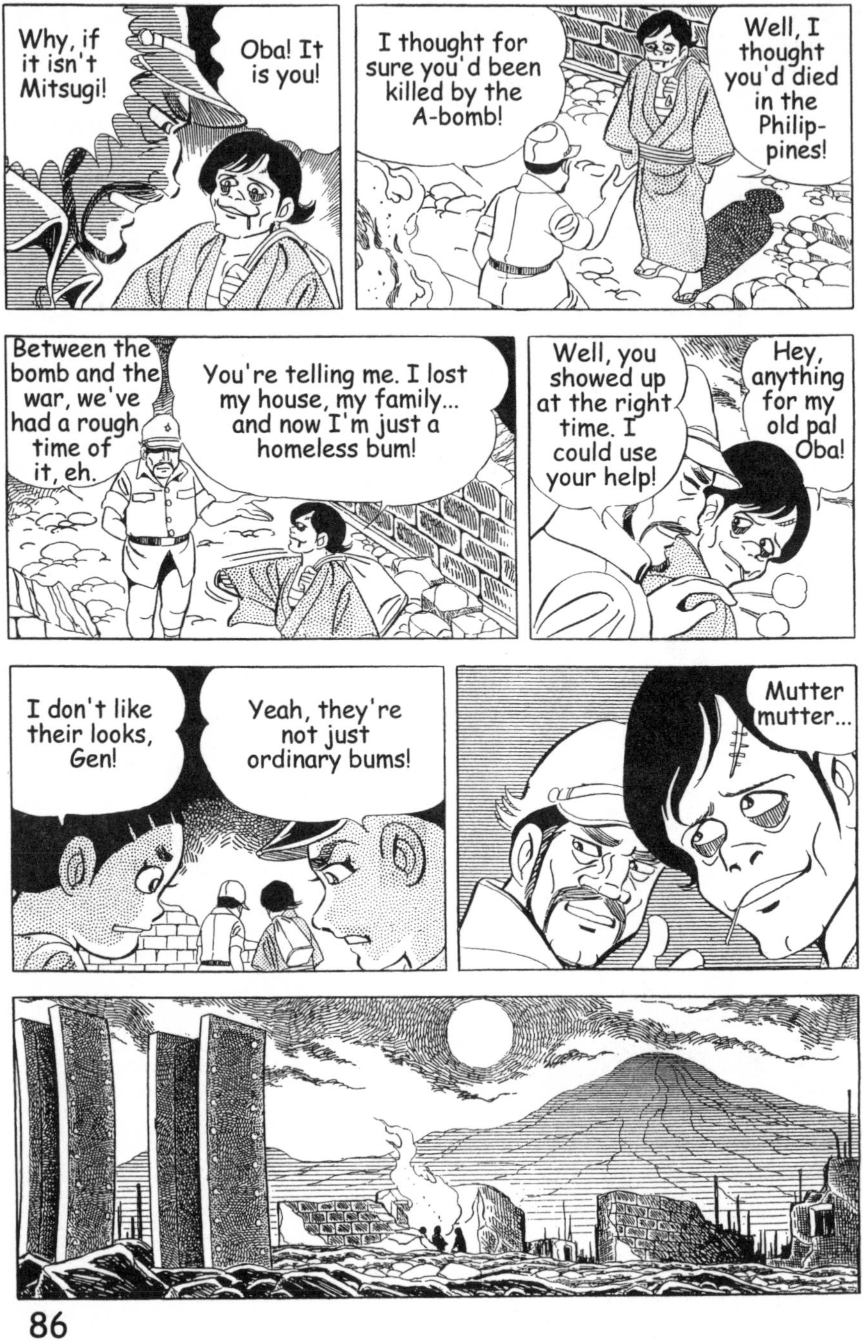
Why, if it isn't Mitsugi!
Oba! It is you!
I thought for sure you'd been killed by the A-bomb!
Well, I thought you'd died in the Philip-pines!
Between the bomb and the war, we've had a rough time of it, eh.
You're telling me. I lost my house, my family... and now I'm just a homeless bum!
Well, you showed up at the right time. I could use your help!
Hey, anything for my old pal Oba!
I don't like their looks, Gen!
Yeah, they're not just ordinary bums!
Mutter mutter...

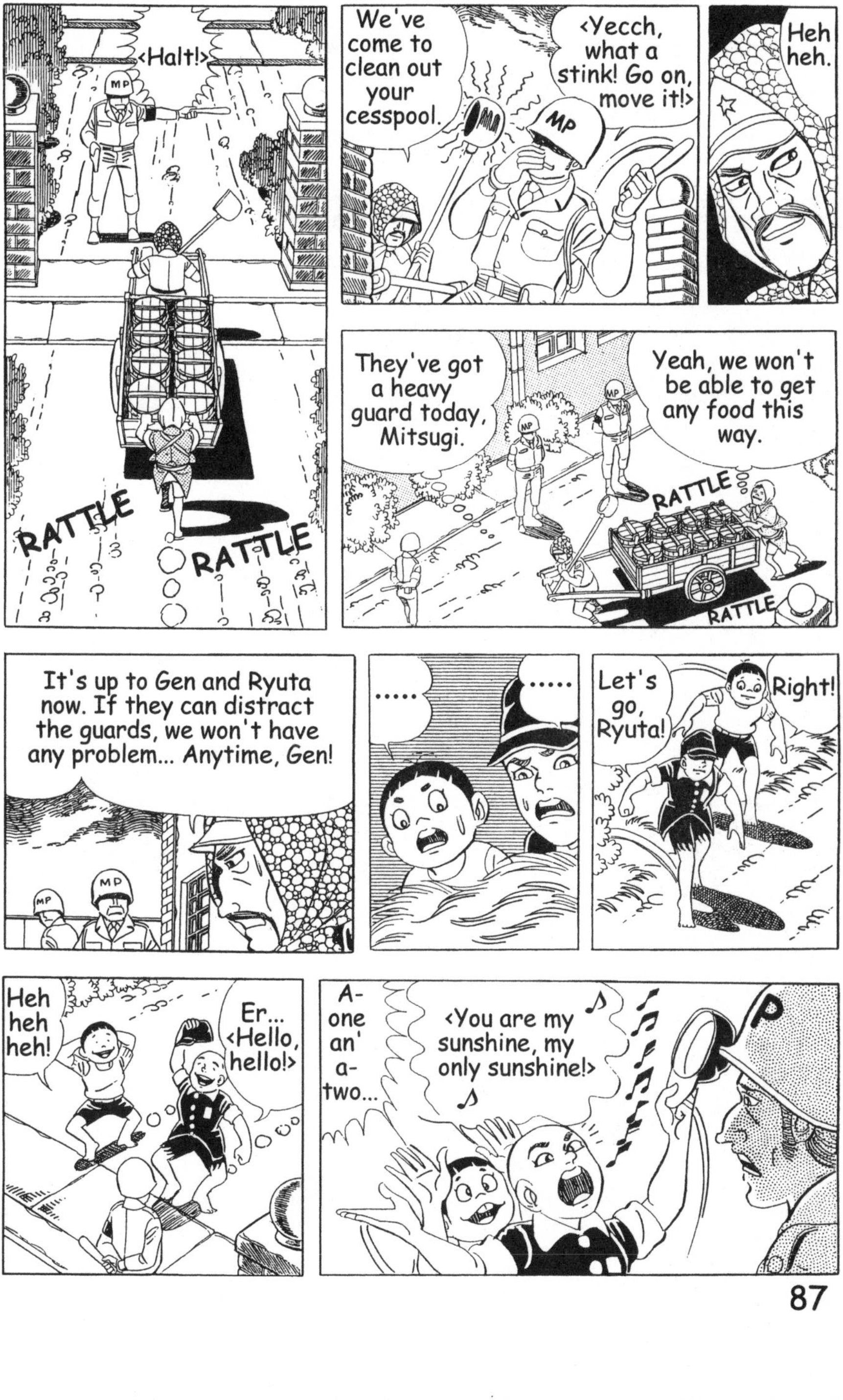
<Halt!>
RATTLE
RATTLE
We've come to clean out your cesspool.
<Yecch, what a stink! Go on, move it!>
Heh heh.
They've got a heavy guard today, Mitsugi.
Yeah, we won't be able to get any food this way.
RATTLE
RATTLE
It's up to Gen and Ryuta now. If they can distract the guards, we won't have any problem... Anytime, Gen!
.....
.....
Let's go, Ryuta!
Right!
Heh heh heh!
Er... <Hello, hello!>
A-one an' a-two...
<You are my sunshine, my only sunshine!>

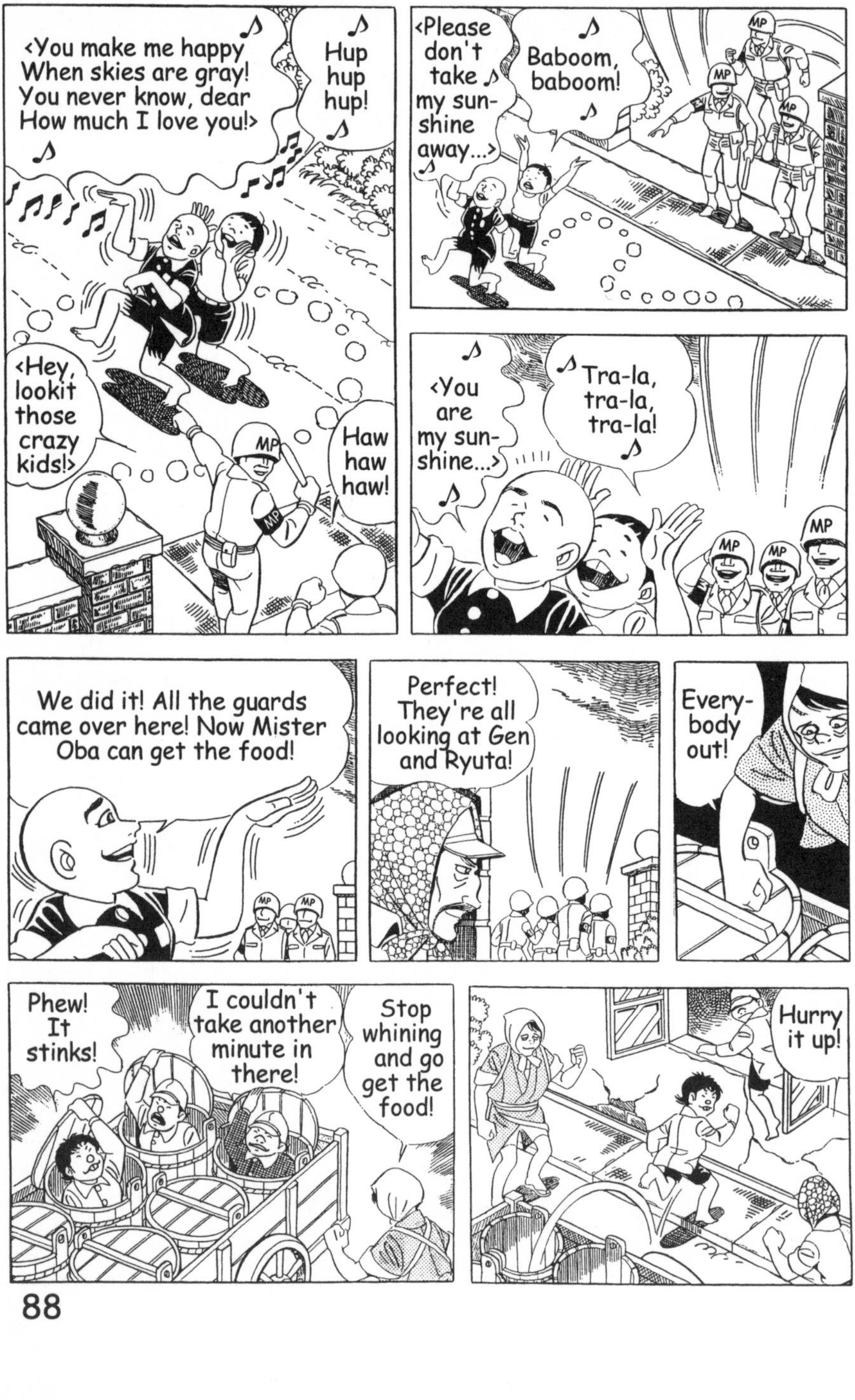

<You make me happy When skies are gray! You never know, dear How much I love you!>
Hup hup hup!
<Hey, lookit those crazy kids!>
Haw haw haw!
<Please don't take my sunshine away...>
Baboom, baboom!
<You are my sunshine...>
Tra-la, tra-la, tra-la!
We did it! All the guards came over here! Now Mister Oba can get the food!
Perfect! They're all looking at Gen and Ryuta!
Everybody out!
Phew! It stinks!
I couldn't take another minute in there!
Stop whining and go get the food!
Hurry it up!

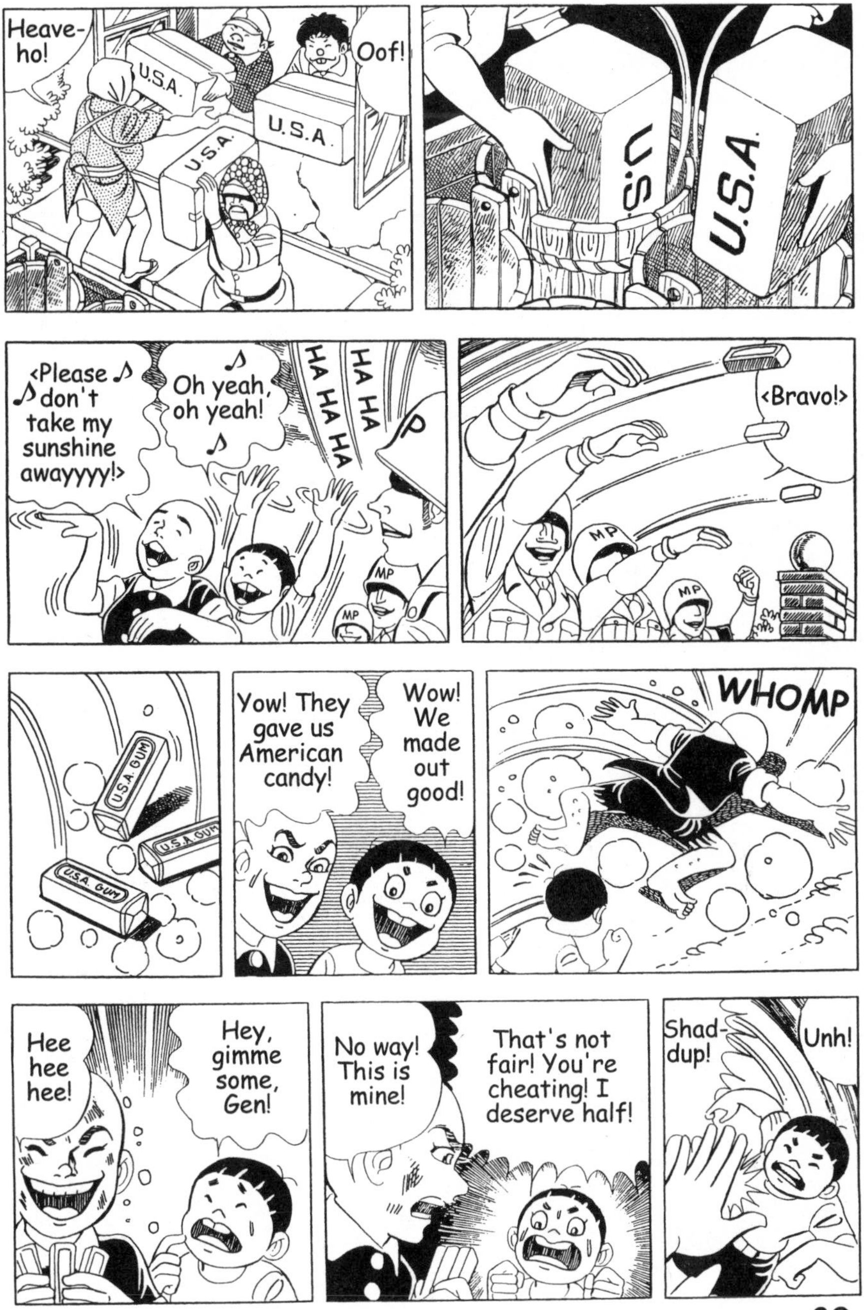
Heave-ho!
Oof!
U.S.A.
U.S.A.
U.S.A.
U.S.A.
U.S.A.
<Please ♪ ♪ don't take my sunshine awayyyy!>
♪ Oh yeah, oh yeah! ♪
HA HA HA HA HA
MP
MP
<Bravo!>
MP
MP
U.S.A. GUM
U.S.A. GUM
U.S.A. GUM
Yow! They gave us American candy!
Wow! We made out good!
WHOMP
Hee hee hee!
Hey, gimme some, Gen!
No way! This is mine!
That's not fair! You're cheating! I deserve half!
Shad-dup!
Unh!

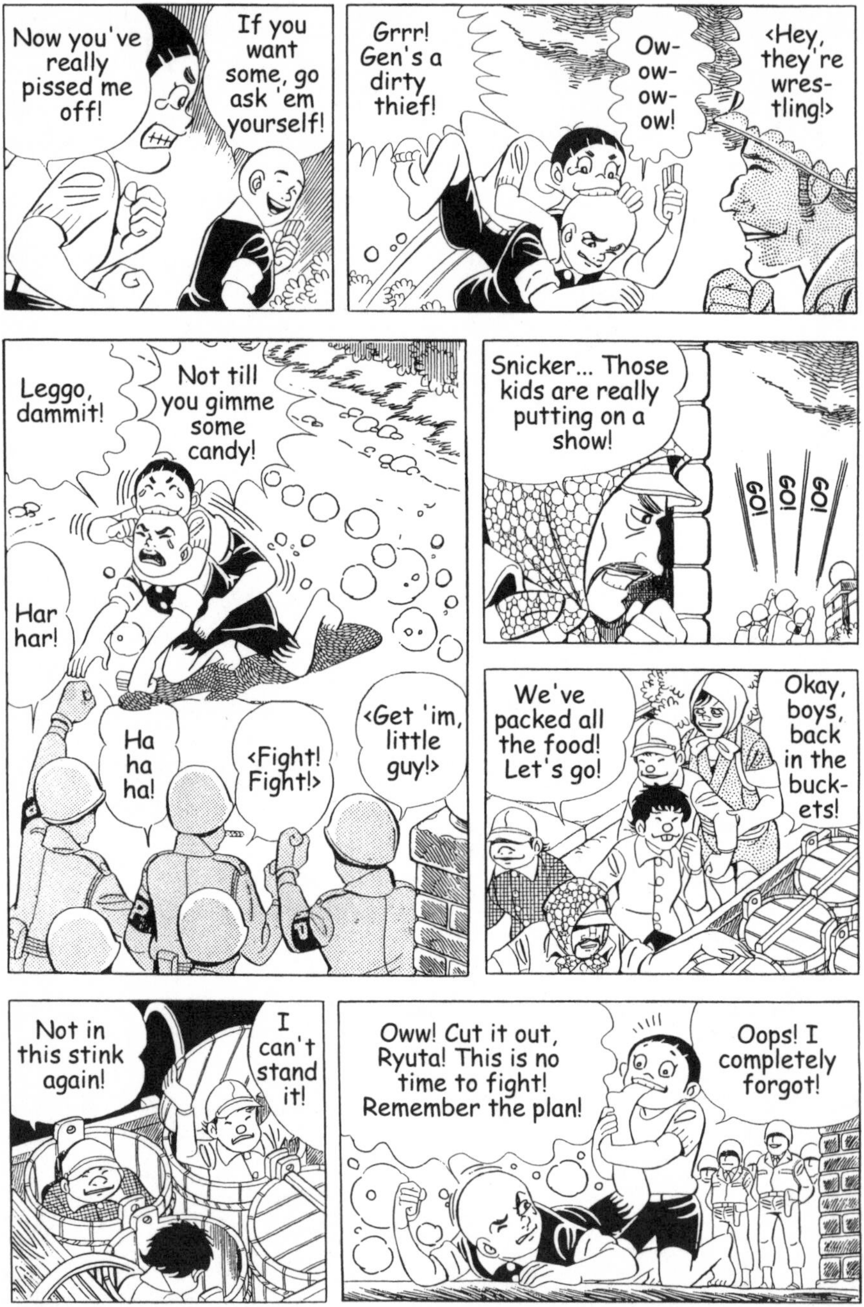
Now you've really pissed me off!
If you want some, go ask 'em yourself!
Grrr! Gen's a dirty thief!
Ow-ow-ow-ow!
<Hey, they're wres-tling!>
Leggo, dammit!
Not till you gimme some candy!
Har har!
Ha ha ha!
<Fight! Fight!>
<Get 'im, little guy!>
Snicker... Those kids are really putting on a show!
GO! GO! GO!
We've packed all the food! Let's go!
Okay, boys, back in the buck-ets!
Not in this stink again!
I can't stand it!
Oww! Cut it out, Ryuta! This is no time to fight! Remember the plan!
Oops! I completely forgot!

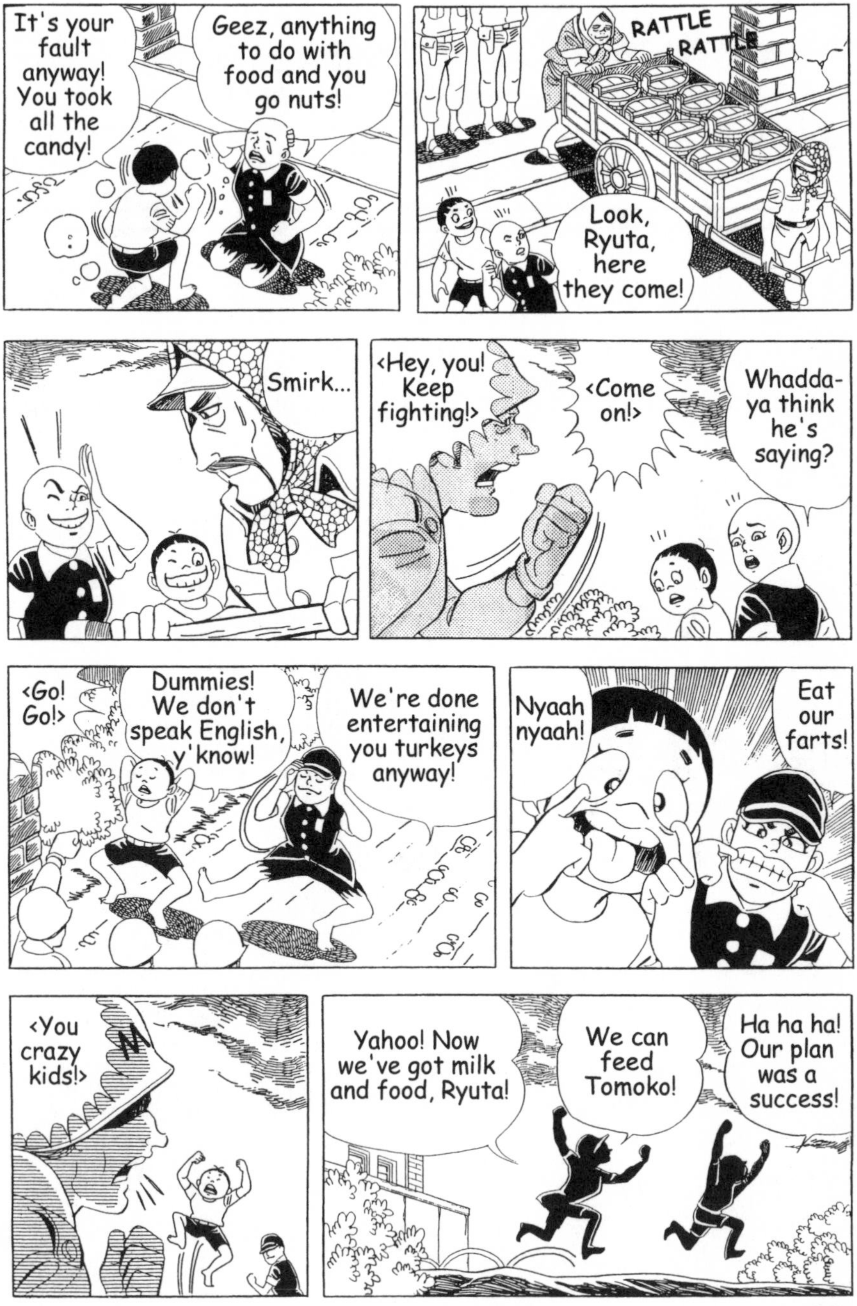
It's your fault anyway! You took all the candy!
Geez, anything to do with food and you go nuts!
RATTLE RATTLE
Look, Ryuta, here they come!
Smirk...
<Hey, you! Keep fighting!>
<Come on!>
Whadda-ya think he's saying?
<Go! Go!>
Dummies! We don't speak English, y'know!
We're done entertaining you turkeys anyway!
Nyaah nyaah!
Eat our farts!
<You crazy kids!>
Yahoo! Now we've got milk and food, Ryuta!
We can feed Tomoko!
Ha ha ha! Our plan was a success!

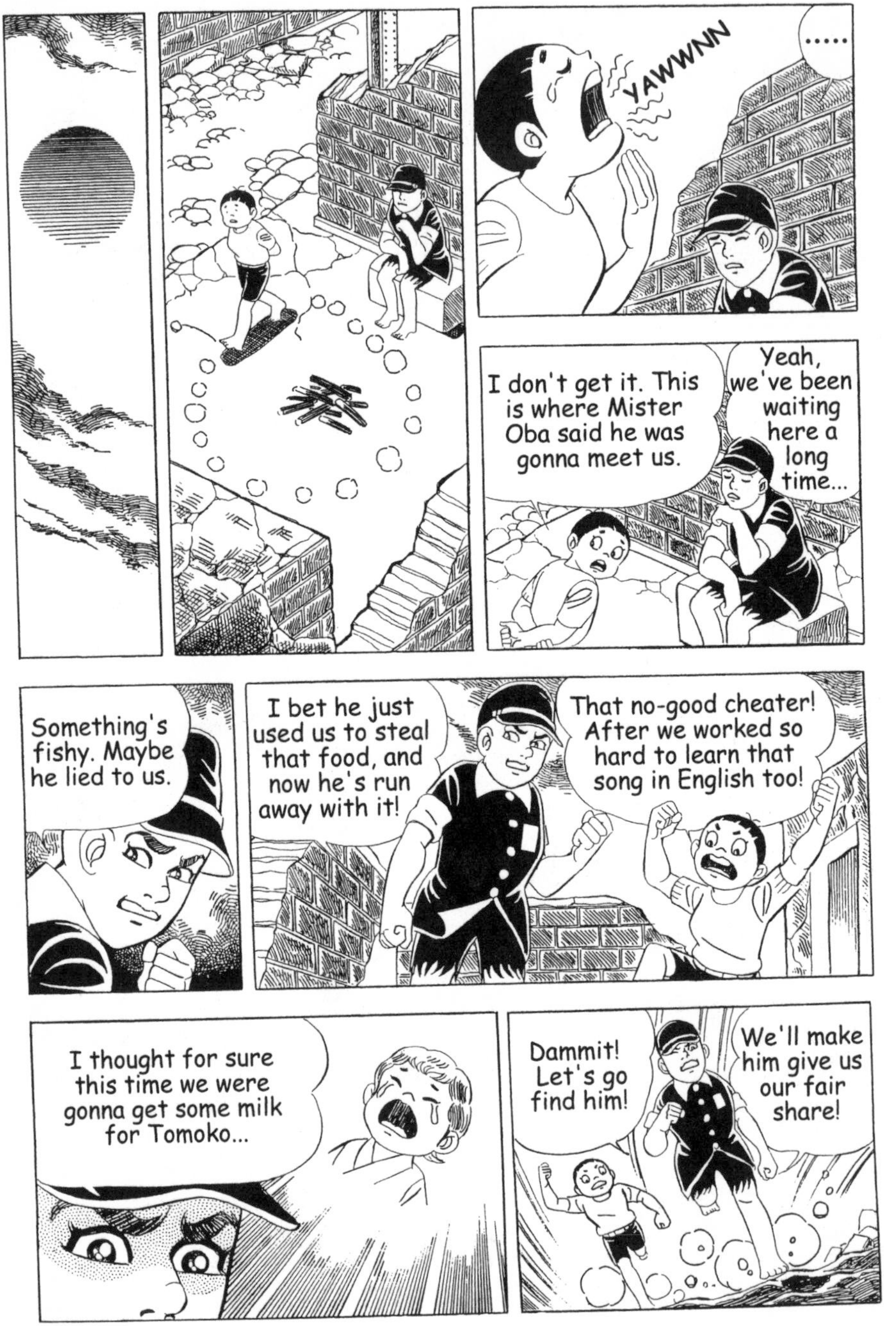
YAWWNN
.....
I don't get it. This is where Mister Oba said he was gonna meet us.
Yeah, we've been waiting here a long time...
Something's fishy. Maybe he lied to us.
I bet he just used us to steal that food, and now he's run away with it!
That no-good cheater! After we worked so hard to learn that song in English too!
I thought for sure this time we were gonna get some milk for Tomoko...
Dammit! Let's go find him!
We'll make him give us our fair share!

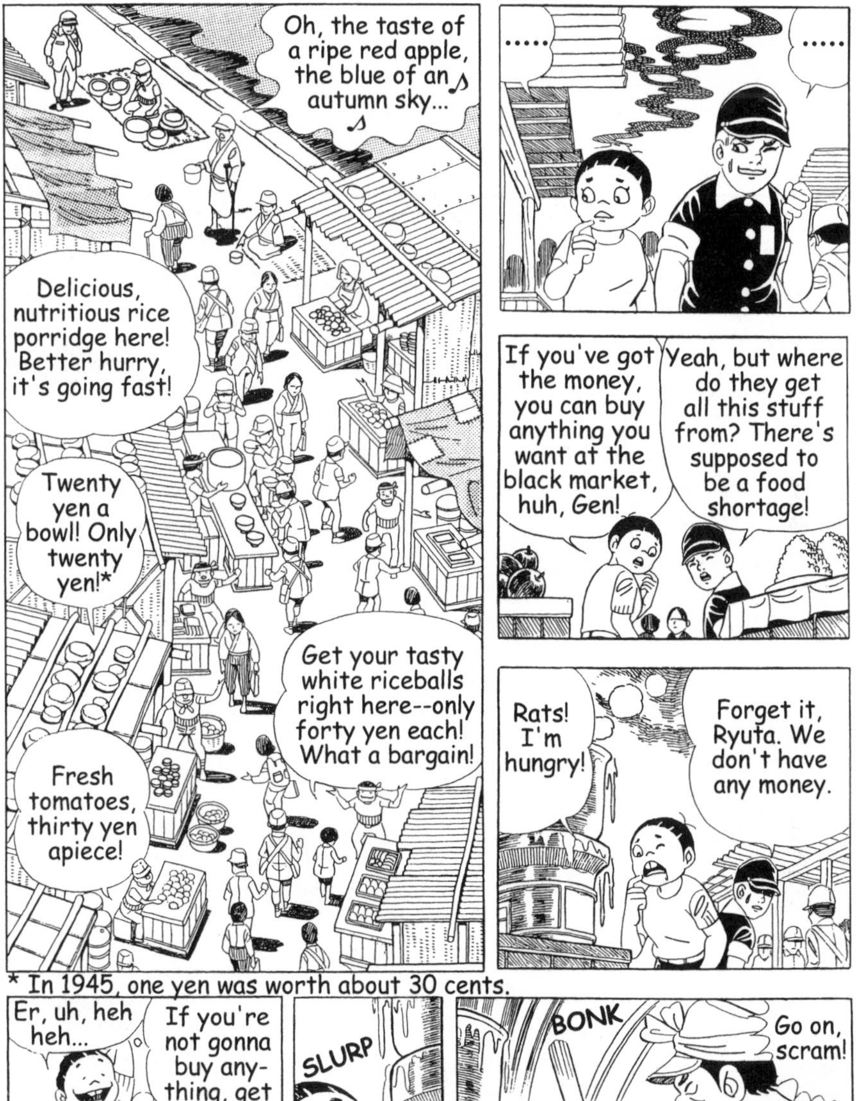
Oh, the taste of a ripe red apple, the blue of an autumn sky...
Delicious, nutritious rice porridge here! Better hurry, it's going fast!
Twenty yen a bowl! Only twenty yen!*
Get your tasty white riceballs right here--only forty yen each! What a bargain!
Fresh tomatoes, thirty yen apiece!
.....
.....
If you've got the money, you can buy anything you want at the black market, huh, Gen!
Yeah, but where do they get all this stuff from? There's supposed to be a food shortage!
Rats! I'm hungry!
Forget it, Ryuta. We don't have any money.

* In 1945, one yen was worth about 30 cents.

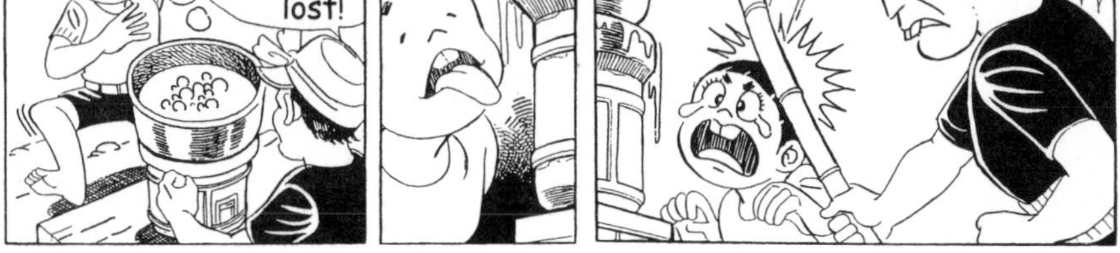
Er, uh, heh heh...
If you're not gonna buy any-thing, get lost!
SLURP
BONK
Go on, scram!

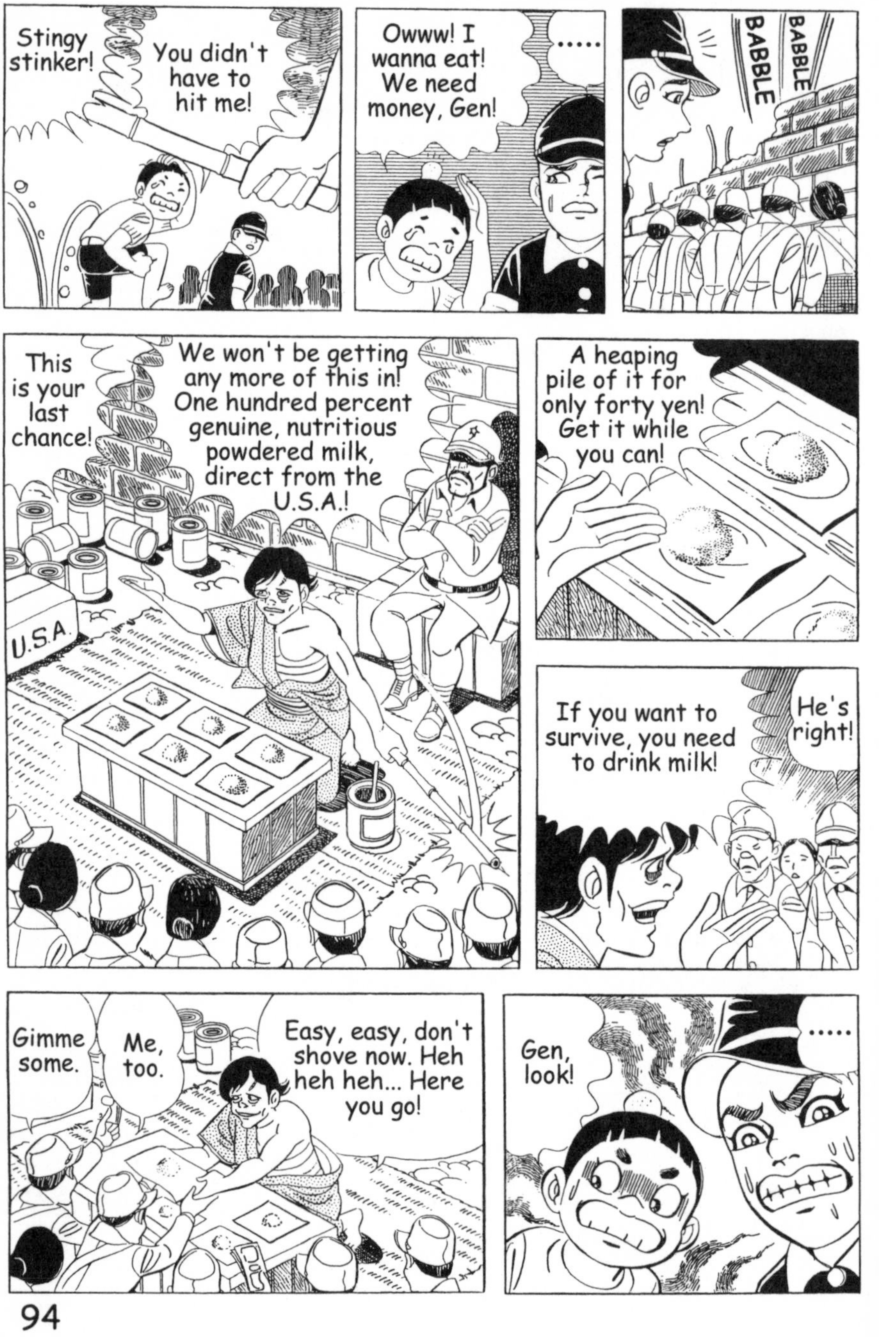
Stingy stinker!
You didn't have to hit me!
Owww! I wanna eat! We need money, Gen!
.....
BABBLE
BABBLE
This is your last chance!
We won't be getting any more of this in! One hundred percent genuine, nutritious powdered milk, direct from the U.S.A.!
U.S.A.
A heaping pile of it for only forty yen! Get it while you can!
If you want to survive, you need to drink milk!
He's right!
Gimme some.
Me, too.
Easy, easy, don't shove now. Heh heh heh... Here you go!
Gen, look!
.....

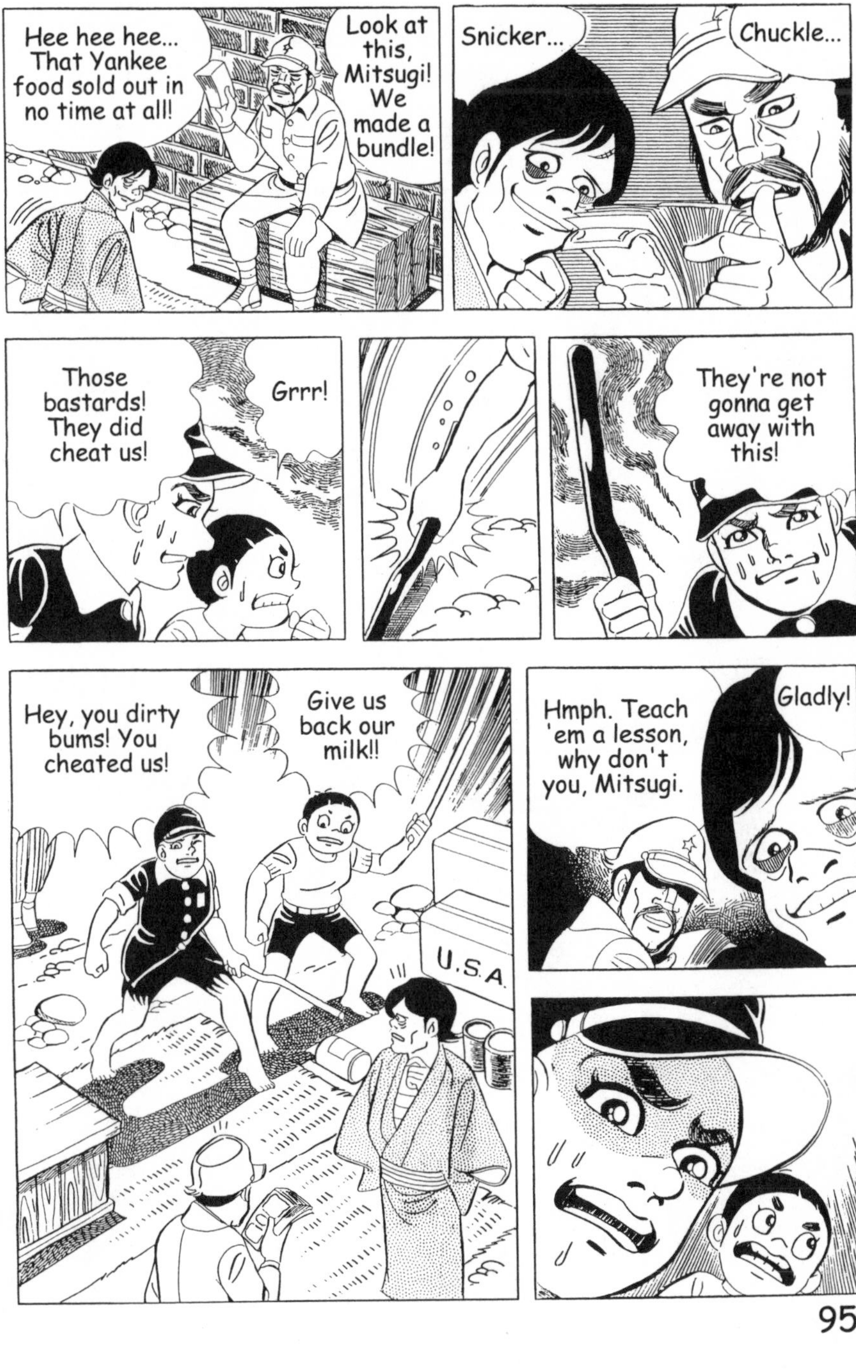

Hee hee hee... That Yankee food sold out in no time at all!
Look at this, Mitsugi! We made a bundle!
Snicker...
Chuckle...
Those bastards! They did cheat us!
Grrr!
They're not gonna get away with this!
Hey, you dirty bums! You cheated us!
Give us back our milk!!
U.S.A.
Hmph. Teach 'em a lesson, why don't you, Mitsugi.
Gladly!

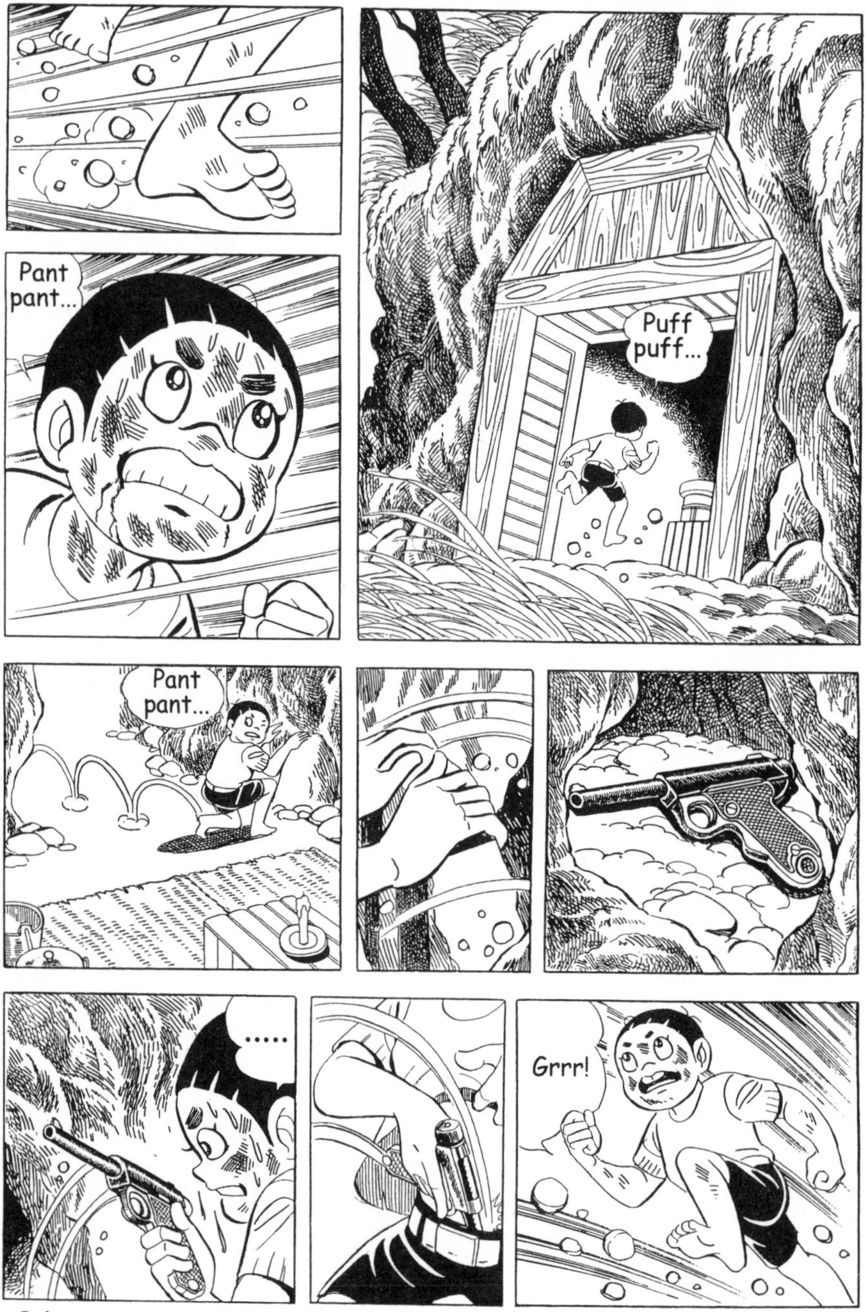
Pant pant...
Puff puff...
Pant pant...
.....
Grrr!

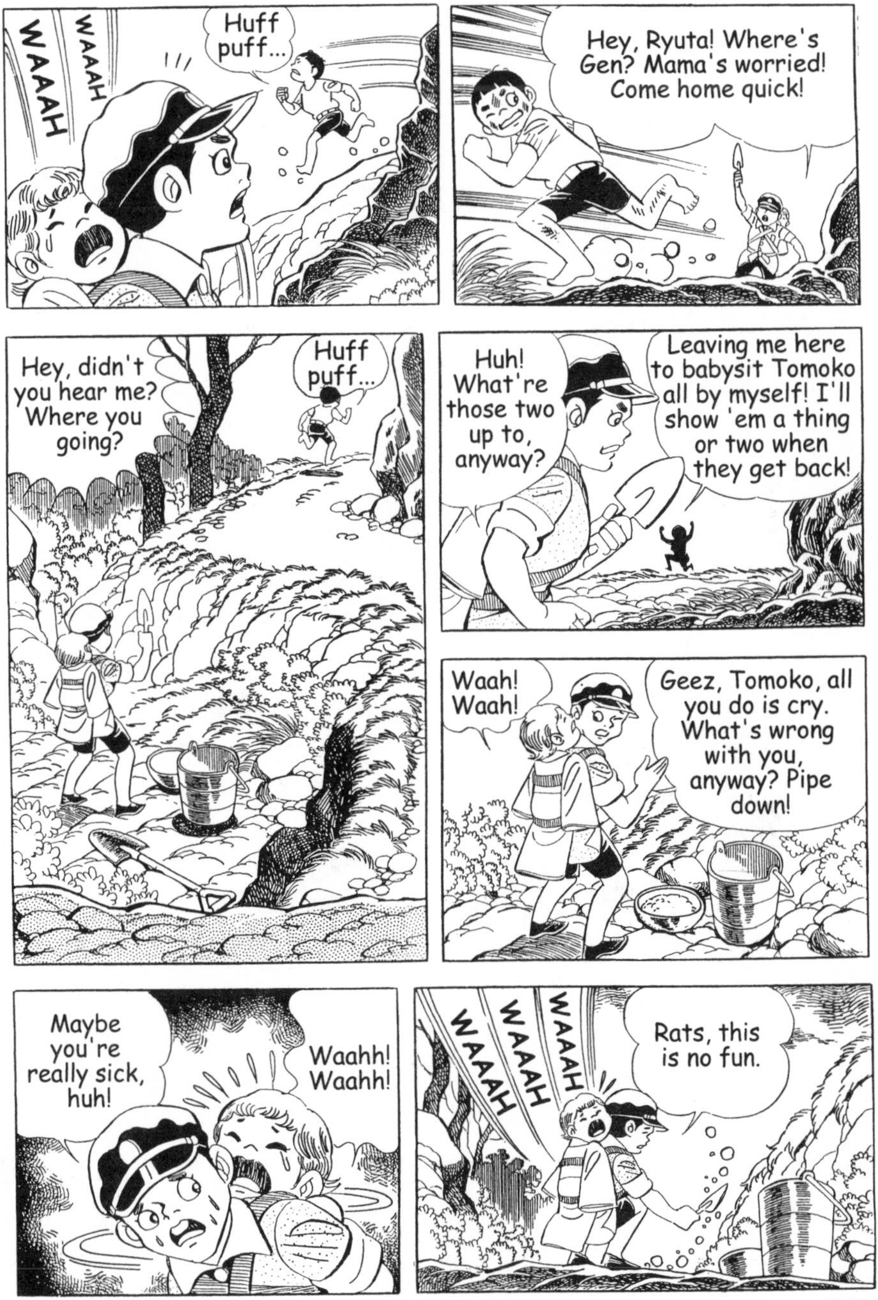
WAAAH
WAAAH
Huff puff...
Hey, Ryuta! Where's Gen? Mama's worried! Come home quick!
Hey, didn't you hear me? Where you going?
Huff puff...
Huh! What're those two up to, anyway?
Leaving me here to babysit Tomoko all by myself! I'll show 'em a thing or two when they get back!
Waah! Waah!
Geez, Tomoko, all you do is cry. What's wrong with you, anyway? Pipe down!
Maybe you're really sick, huh!
Waahh! Waahh!
WAAAH
WAAAH
WAAAH
Rats, this is no fun.

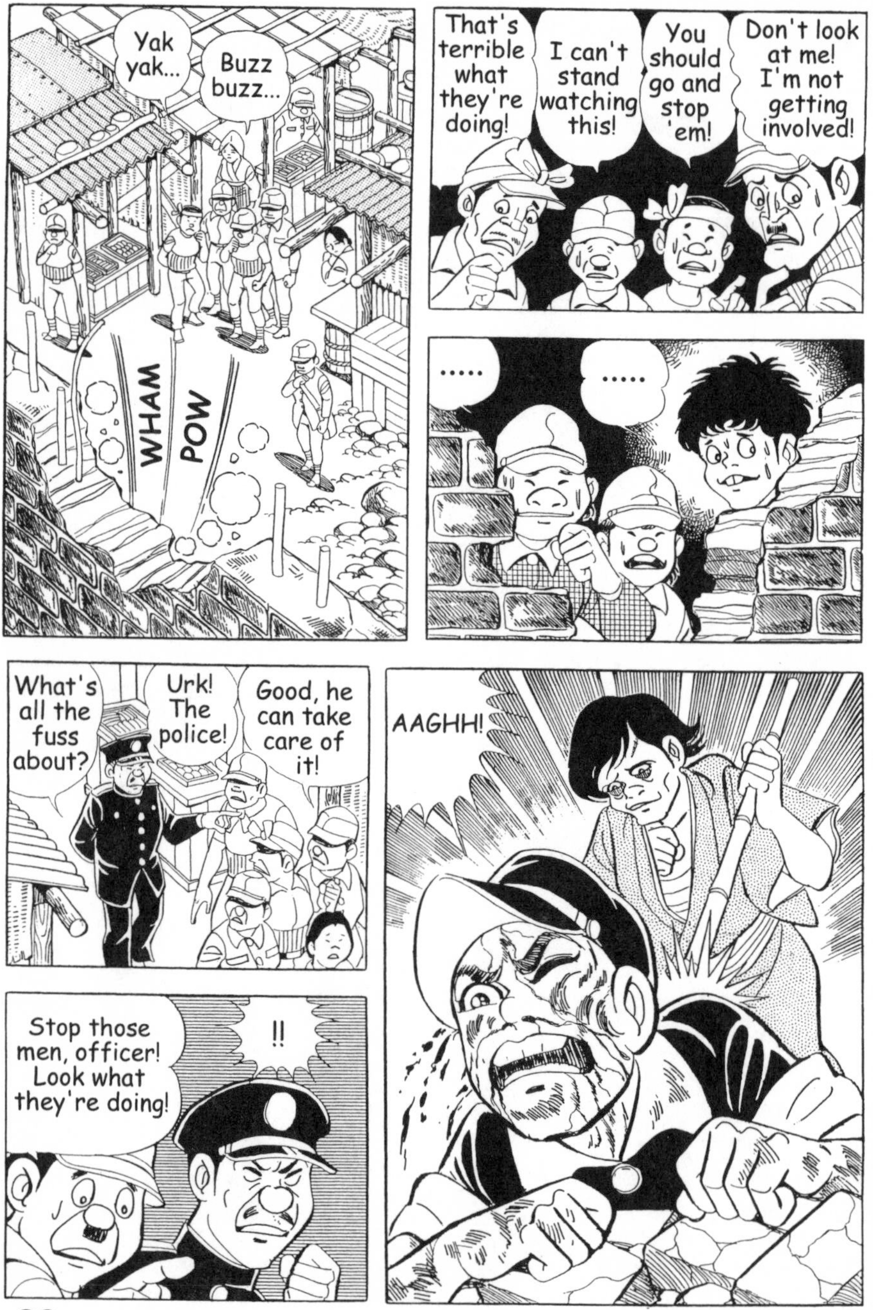
Yak yak...
Buzz buzz...
WHAM
POW
That's terrible what they're doing!
I can't stand watching this!
You should go and stop 'em!
Don't look at me! I'm not getting involved!
.....
.....
What's all the fuss about?
Urk! The police!
Good, he can take care of it!
Stop those men, officer! Look what they're doing!
!!
AAGHH!

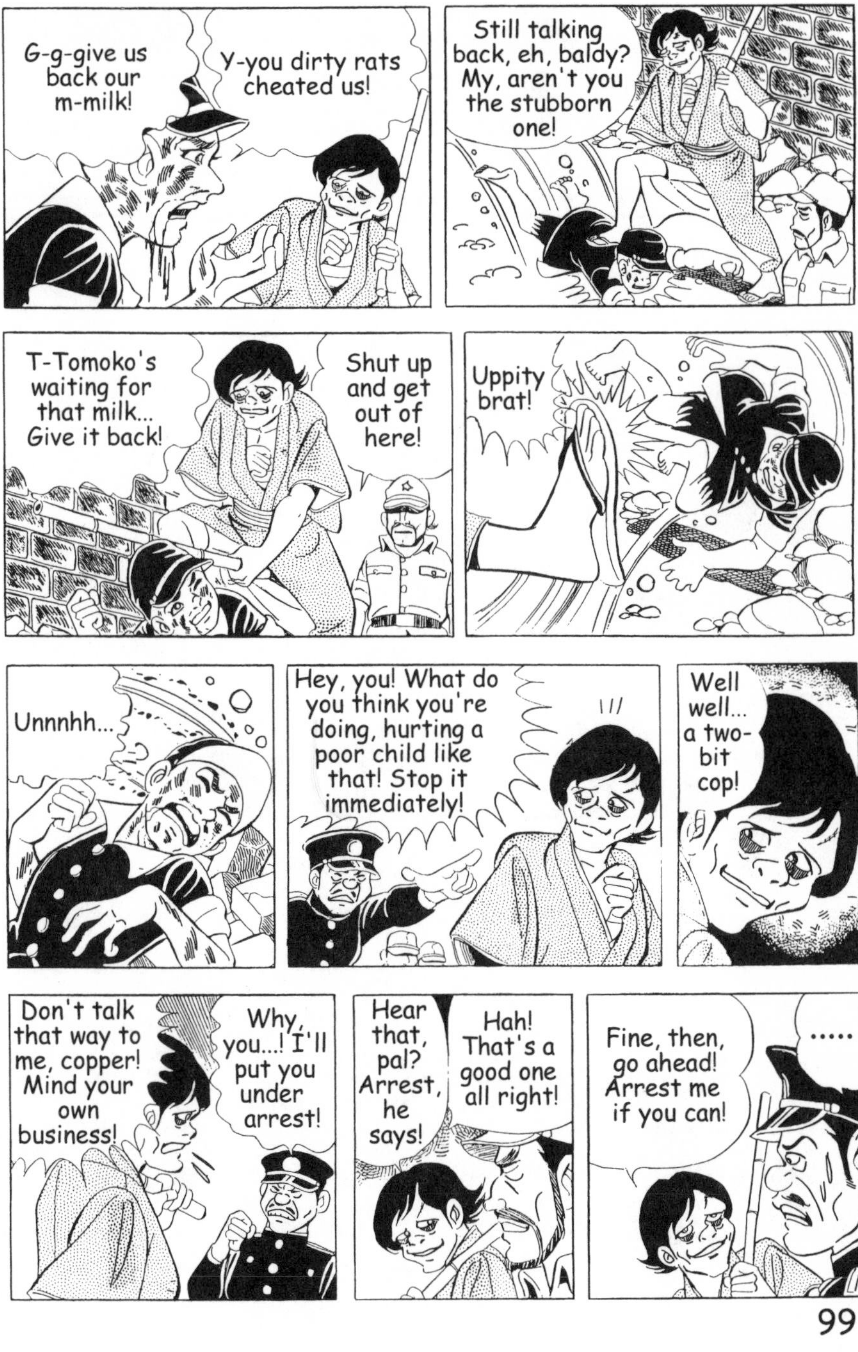
G-g-give us back our m-milk!
Y-you dirty rats cheated us!
Still talking back, eh, baldy? My, aren't you the stubborn one!
T-Tomoko's waiting for that milk... Give it back!
Shut up and get out of here!
Uppity brat!
Unnnhh...
Hey, you! What do you think you're doing, hurting a poor child like that! Stop it immediately!
Well well... a two-bit cop!
Don't talk that way to me, copper! Mind your own business!
Why, you...! I'll put you under arrest!
Hear that, pal? Arrest, he says!
Hah! That's a good one all right!
Fine, then, go ahead! Arrest me if you can!
.....

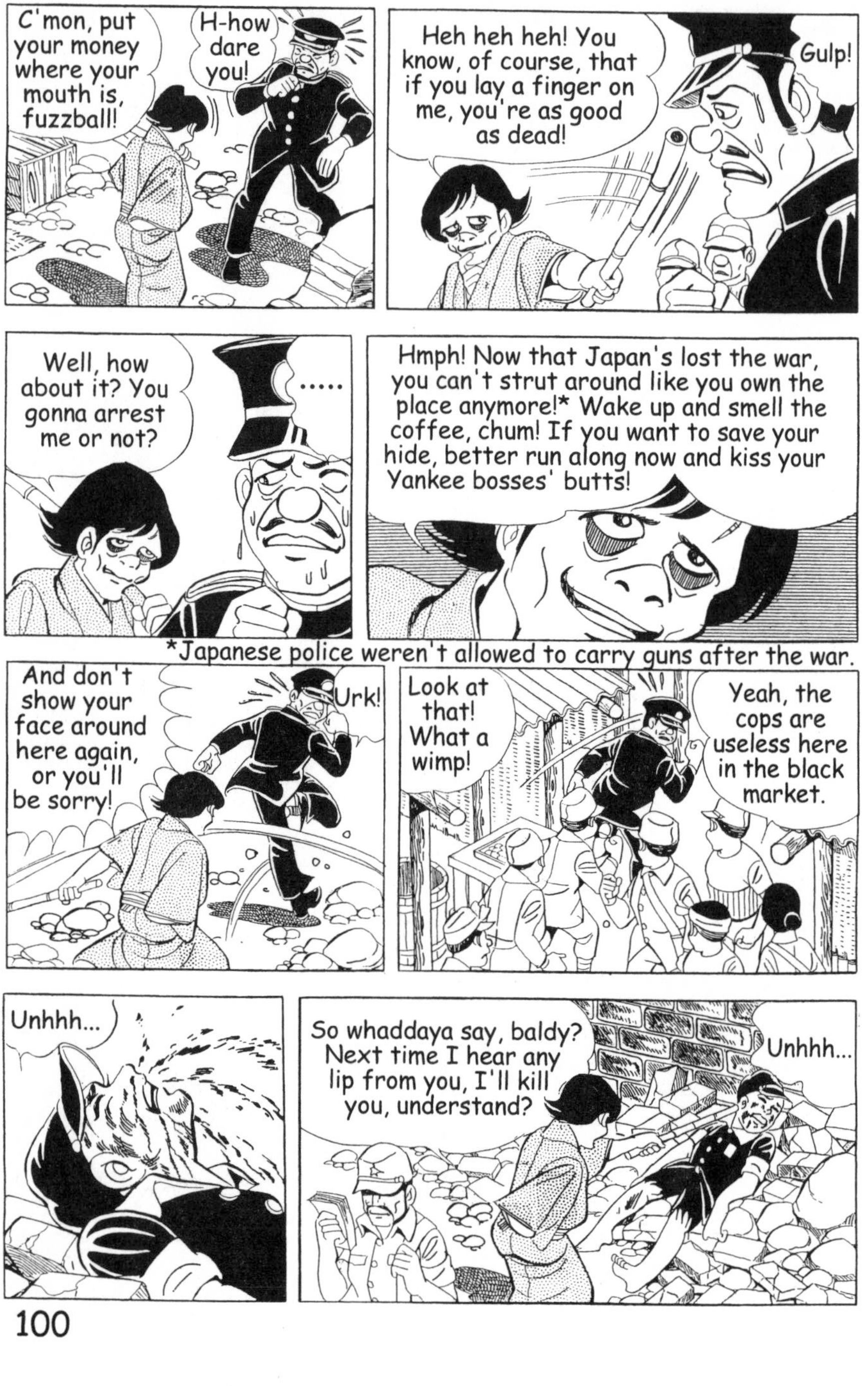
C'mon, put your money where your mouth is, fuzzball!
H-how dare you!
Heh heh heh! You know, of course, that if you lay a finger on me, you're as good as dead!
Gulp!
Well, how about it? You gonna arrest me or not?
.....
Hmph! Now that Japan's lost the war, you can't strut around like you own the place anymore!* Wake up and smell the coffee, chum! If you want to save your hide, better run along now and kiss your Yankee bosses' butts!
*Japanese police weren't allowed to carry guns after the war.
And don't show your face around here again, or you'll be sorry!
Urk!
Look at that! What a wimp!
Yeah, the cops are useless here in the black market.
Unhhh...
So whaddaya say, baldy? Next time I hear any lip from you, I'll kill you, understand?
Unhhh...

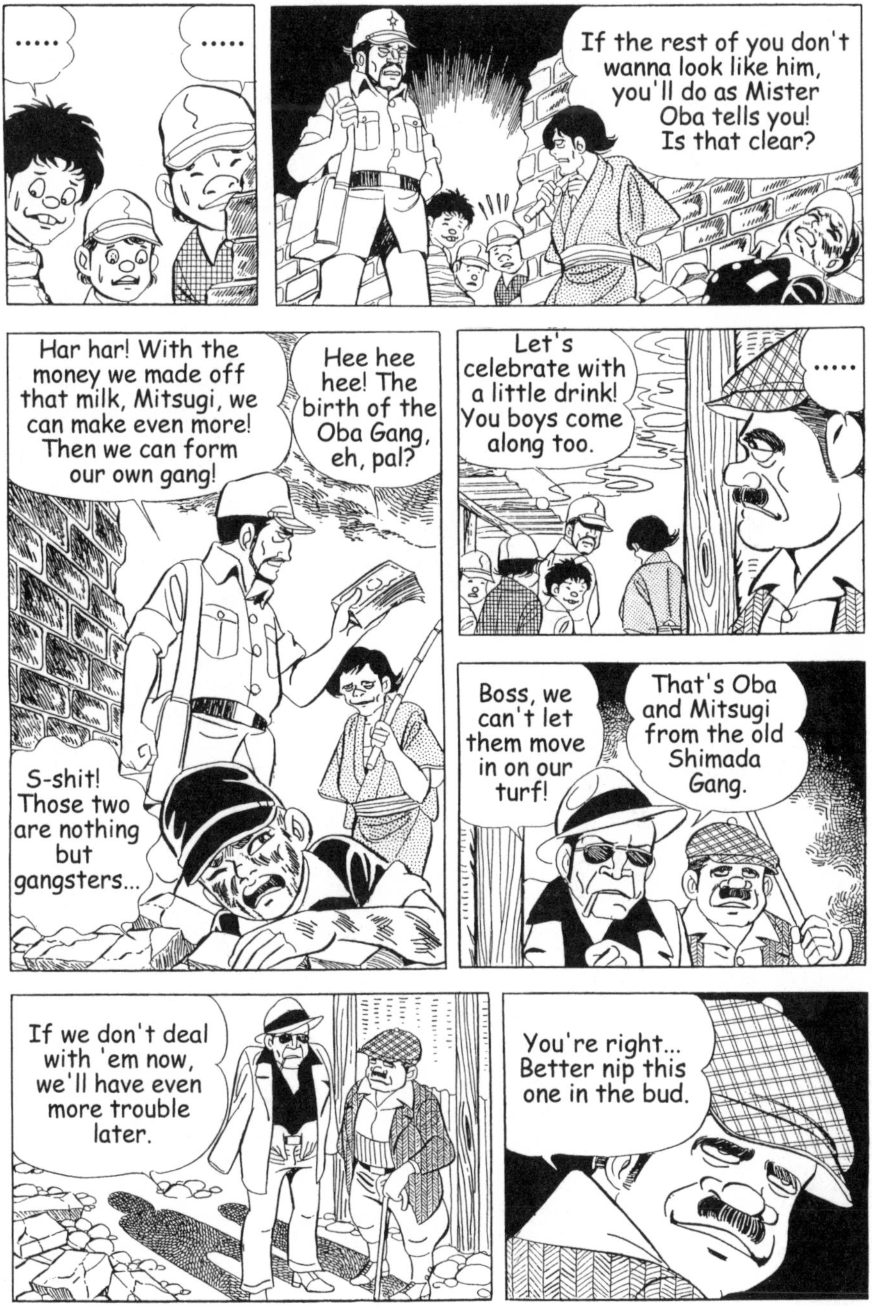

.....
.....
If the rest of you don't wanna look like him, you'll do as Mister Oba tells you! Is that clear?
Har har! With the money we made off that milk, Mitsugi, we can make even more! Then we can form our own gang!
Hee hee hee! The birth of the Oba Gang, eh, pal?
S-shit! Those two are nothing but gangsters...
Let's celebrate with a little drink! You boys come along too.
.....
Boss, we can't let them move in on our turf!
That's Oba and Mitsugi from the old Shimada Gang.
If we don't deal with 'em now, we'll have even more trouble later.
You're right... Better nip this one in the bud.

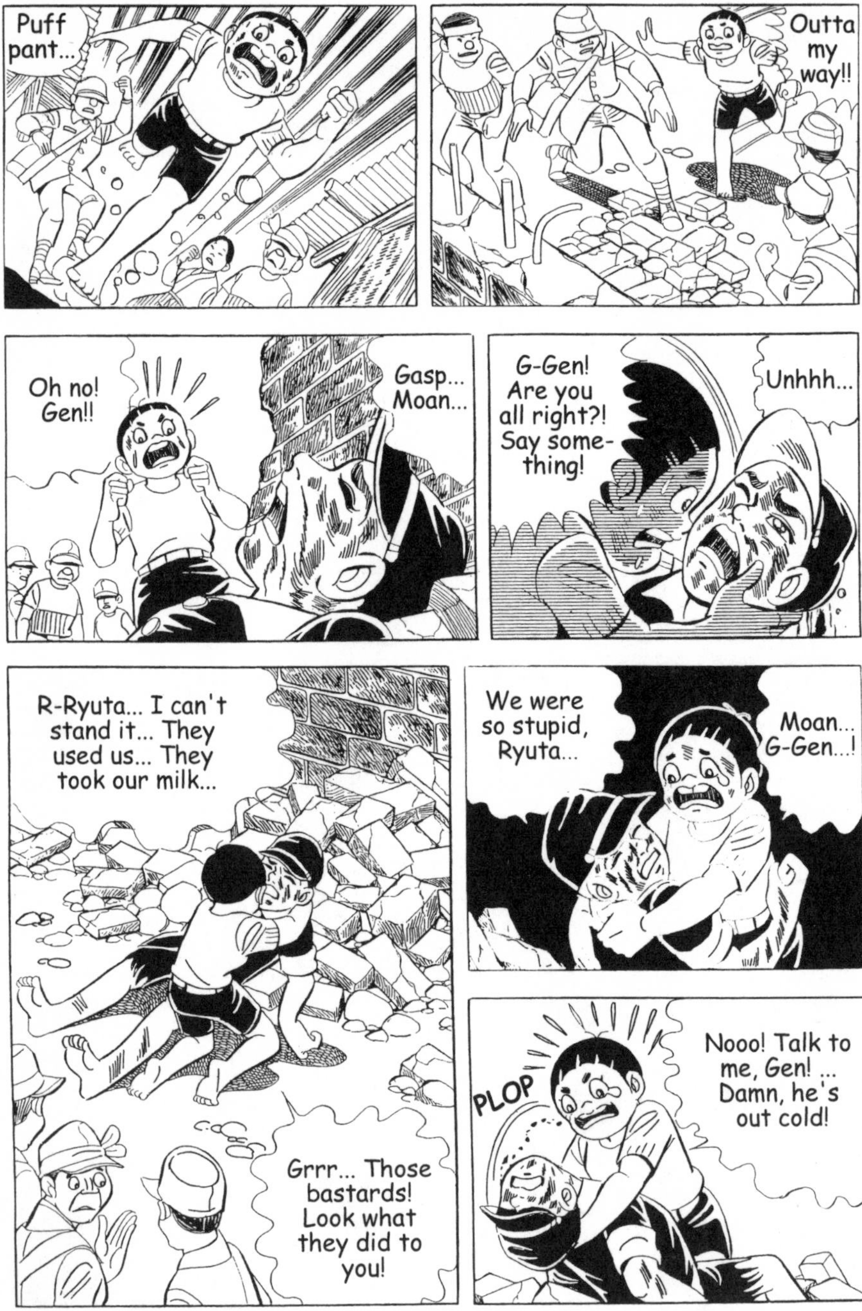

Puff pant...
Outta my way!!
Oh no! Gen!!
Gasp... Moan...
G-Gen! Are you all right?! Say some-thing!
Unhhh...
R-Ryuta... I can't stand it... They used us... They took our milk...
Grrr... Those bastards! Look what they did to you!
We were so stupid, Ryuta...
Moan... G-Gen...!
PLOP
Nooo! Talk to me, Gen! ... Damn, he's out cold!

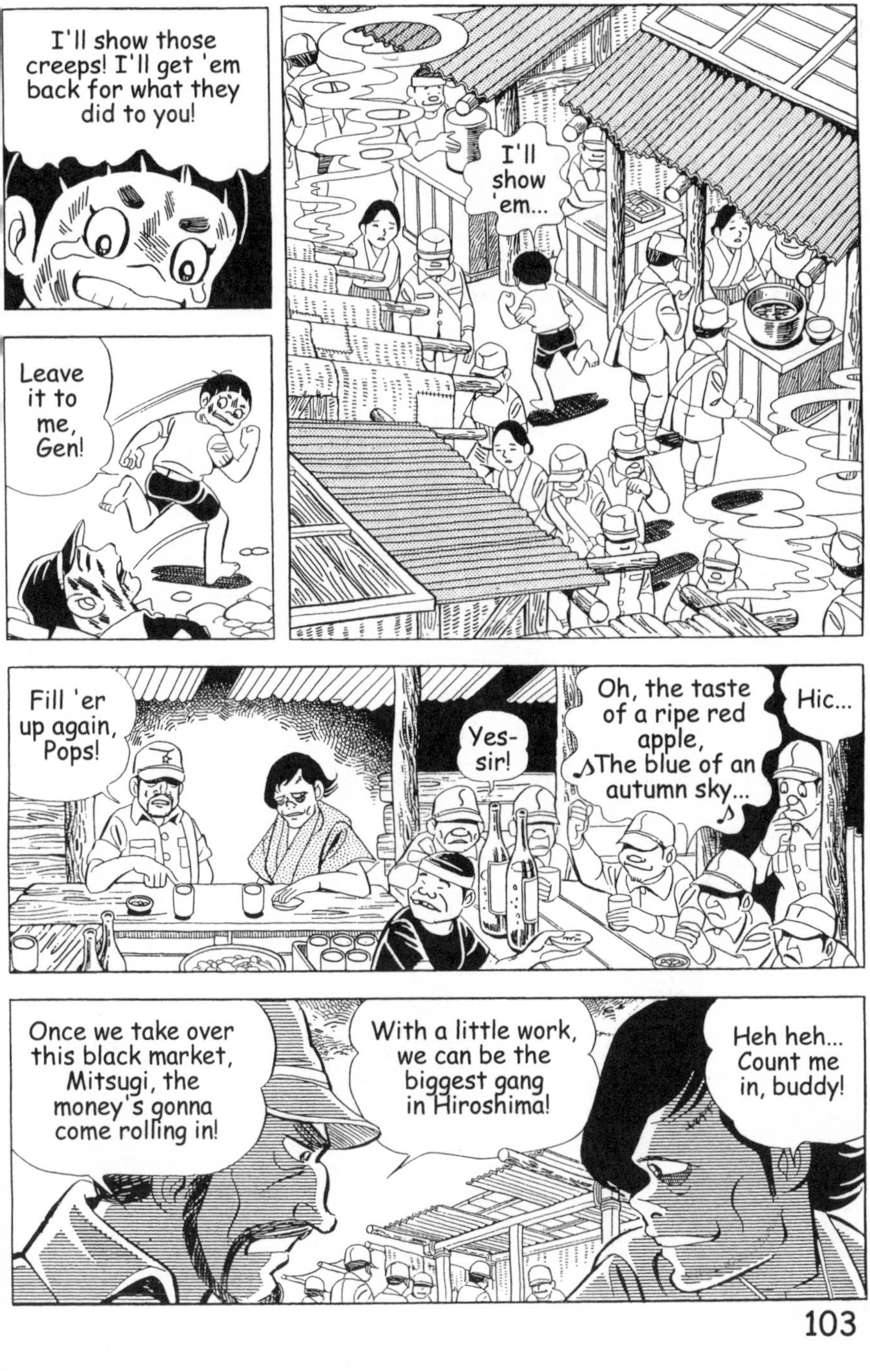
I'll show those creeps! I'll get 'em back for what they did to you!
I'll show 'em...
Leave it to me, Gen!
Fill 'er up again, Pops!
Yes-sir!
Oh, the taste of a ripe red apple, ♪The blue of an autumn sky...♪
Hic...
Once we take over this black market, Mitsugi, the money's gonna come rolling in!
With a little work, we can be the biggest gang in Hiroshima!
Heh heh... Count me in, buddy!

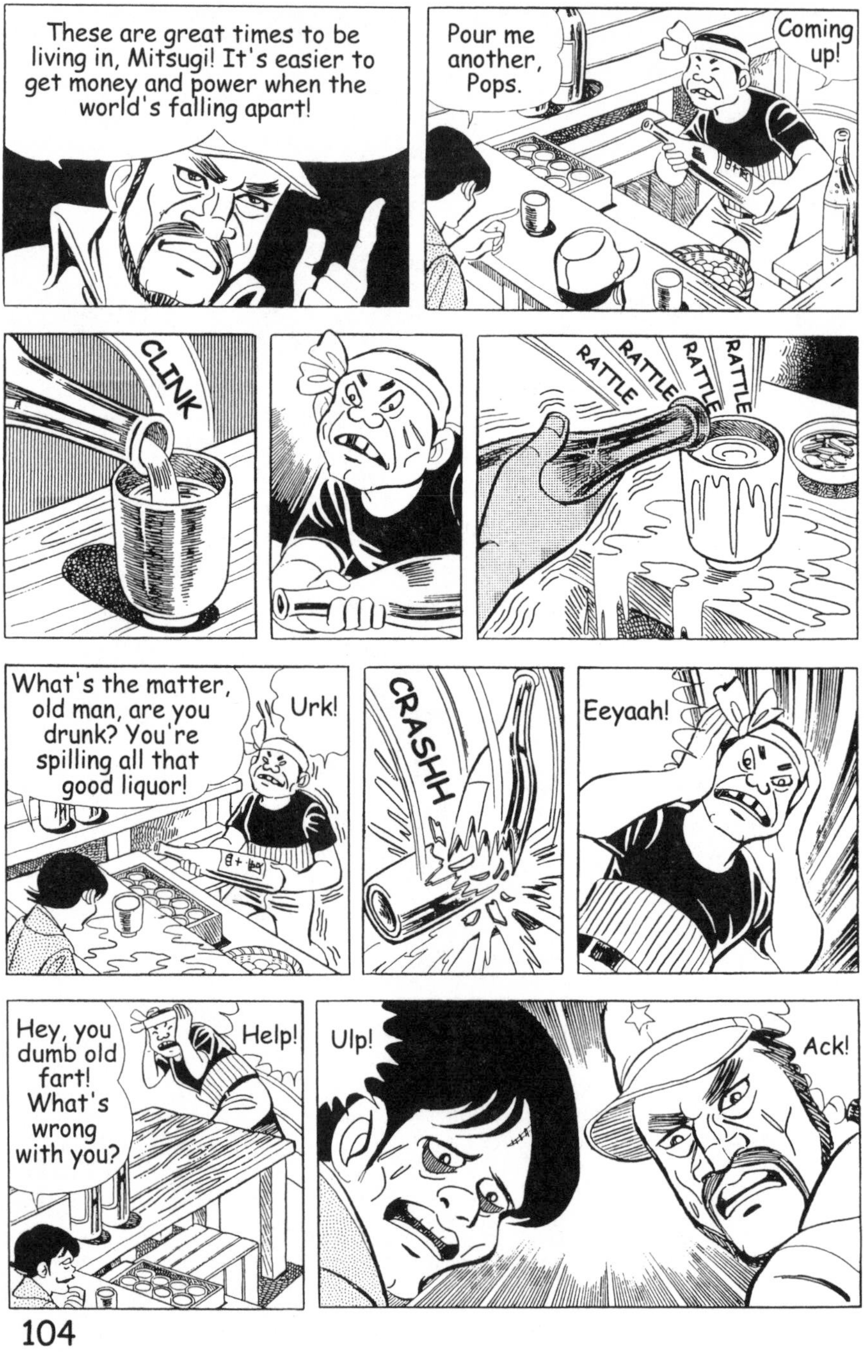
These are great times to be living in, Mitsugi! It's easier to get money and power when the world's falling apart!
Pour me another, Pops.
Coming up!
CLINK
RATTLE
RATTLE
RATTLE
RATTLE
What's the matter, old man, are you drunk? You're spilling all that good liquor!
Urk!
CRASHH
Eeyaah!
Hey, you dumb old fart! What's wrong with you?
Help!
Ulp!
Ack!

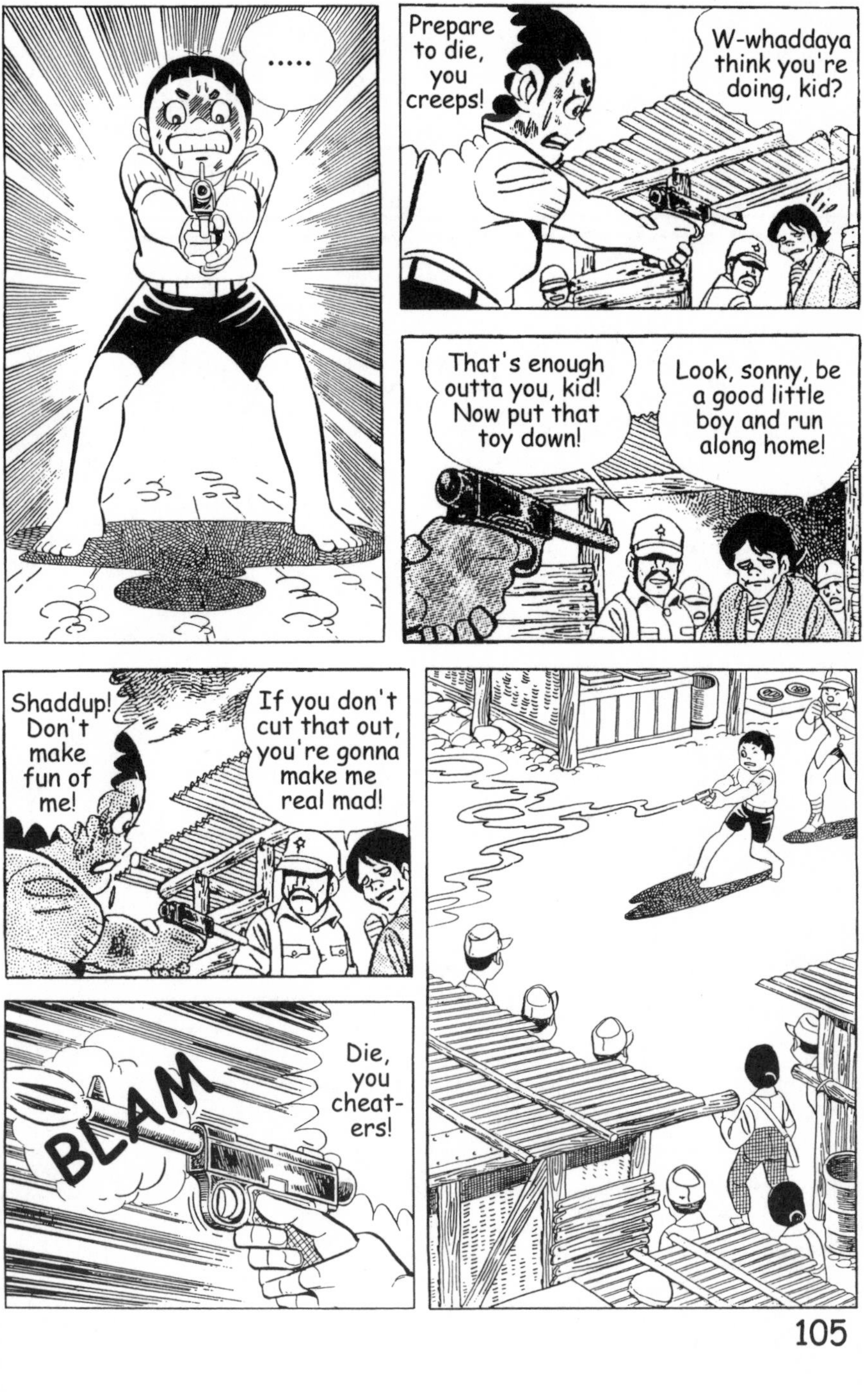
.....
Prepare to die, you creeps!
W-whaddaya think you're doing, kid?
That's enough outta you, kid! Now put that toy down!
Look, sonny, be a good little boy and run along home!
Shaddup! Don't make fun of me!
If you don't cut that out, you're gonna make me real mad!
BLAM
Die, you cheat-ers!

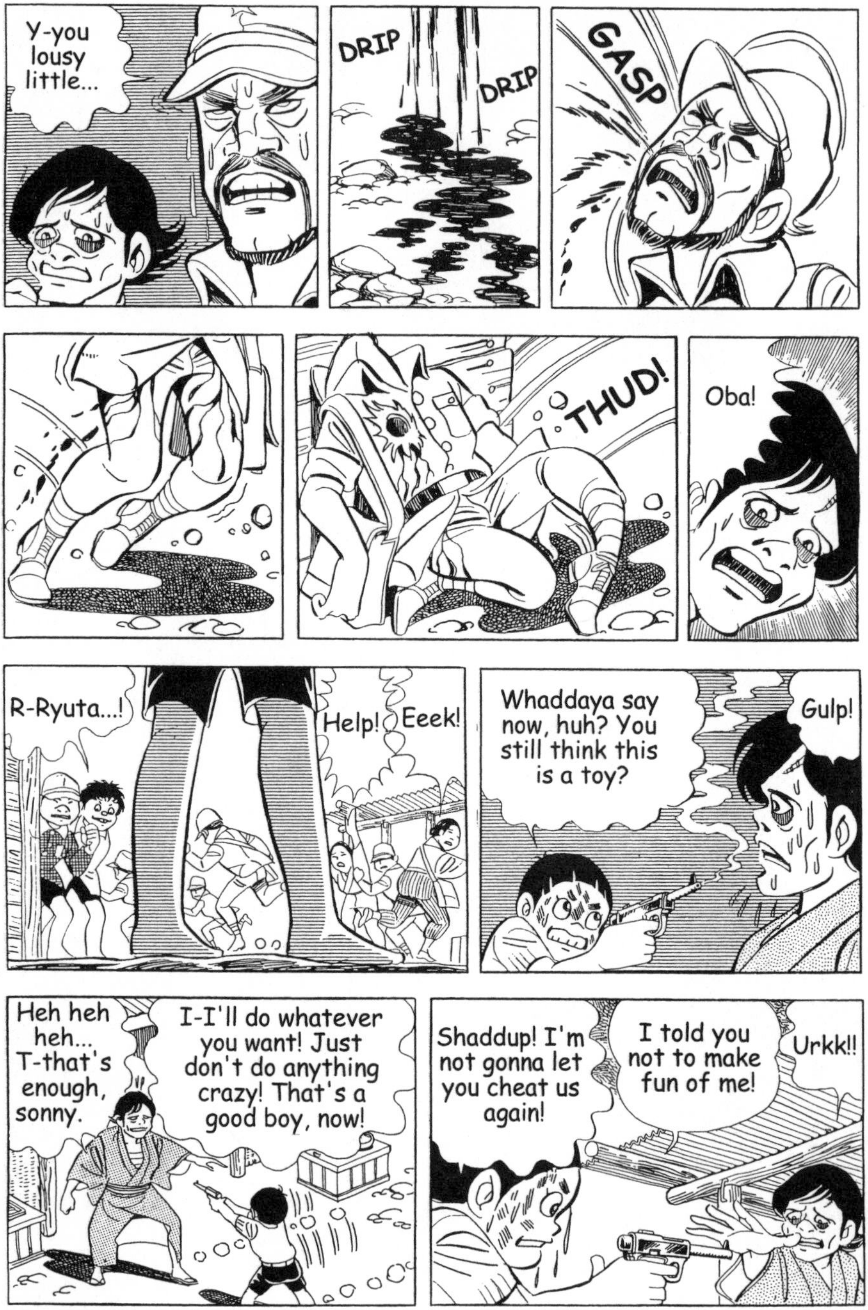
Y-you lousy little...
DRIP
DRIP
GASP
THUD!
Oba!
R-Ryuta...!
Help!
Eeek!
Whaddaya say now, huh? You still think this is a toy?
Gulp!
Heh heh heh... T-that's enough, sonny.
I-I'll do whatever you want! Just don't do anything crazy! That's a good boy, now!
Shaddup! I'm not gonna let you cheat us again!
I told you not to make fun of me!
Urkk!!

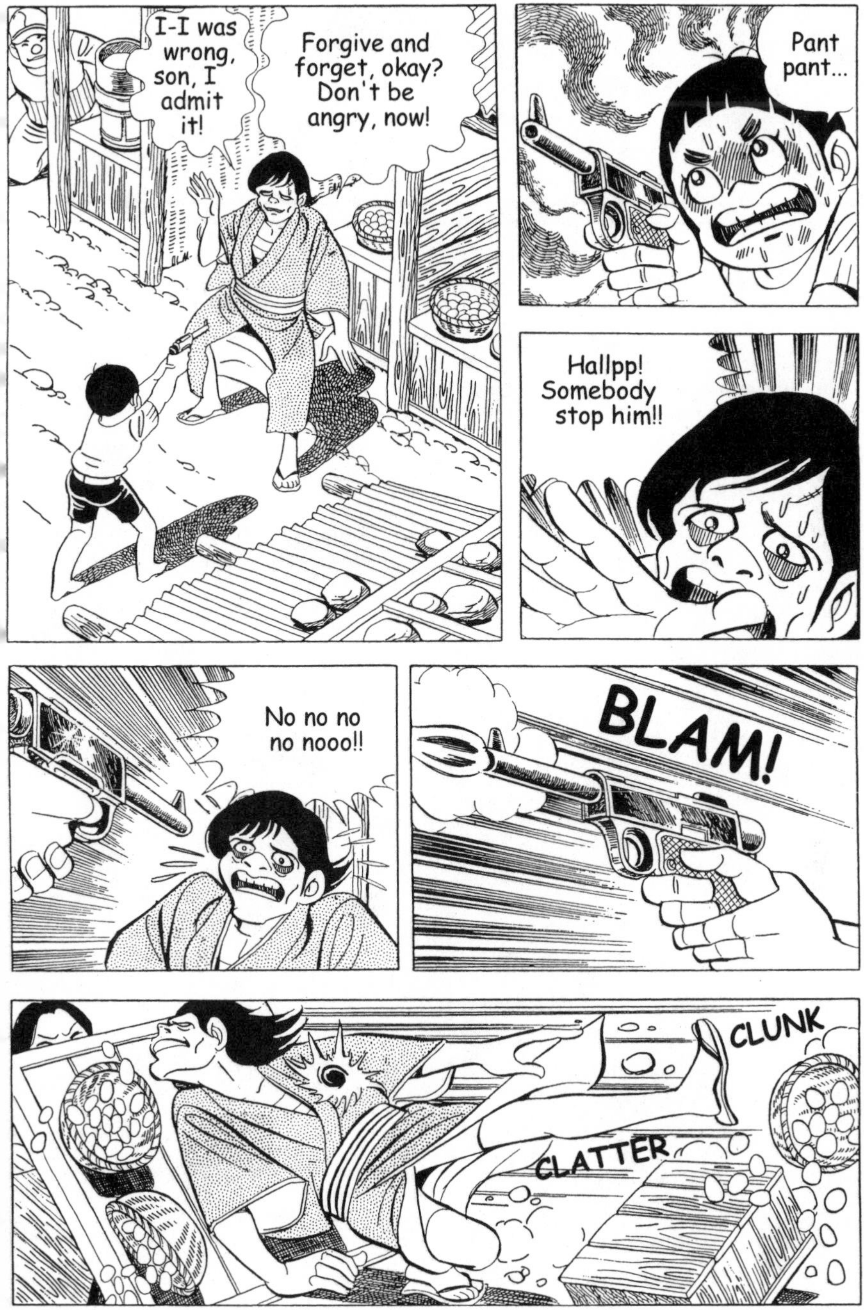
I-I was wrong, son, I admit it!
Forgive and forget, okay? Don't be angry, now!
Pant pant...
Hallpp! Somebody stop him!!
No no no no nooo!!
BLAM!
CLUNK
CLATTER

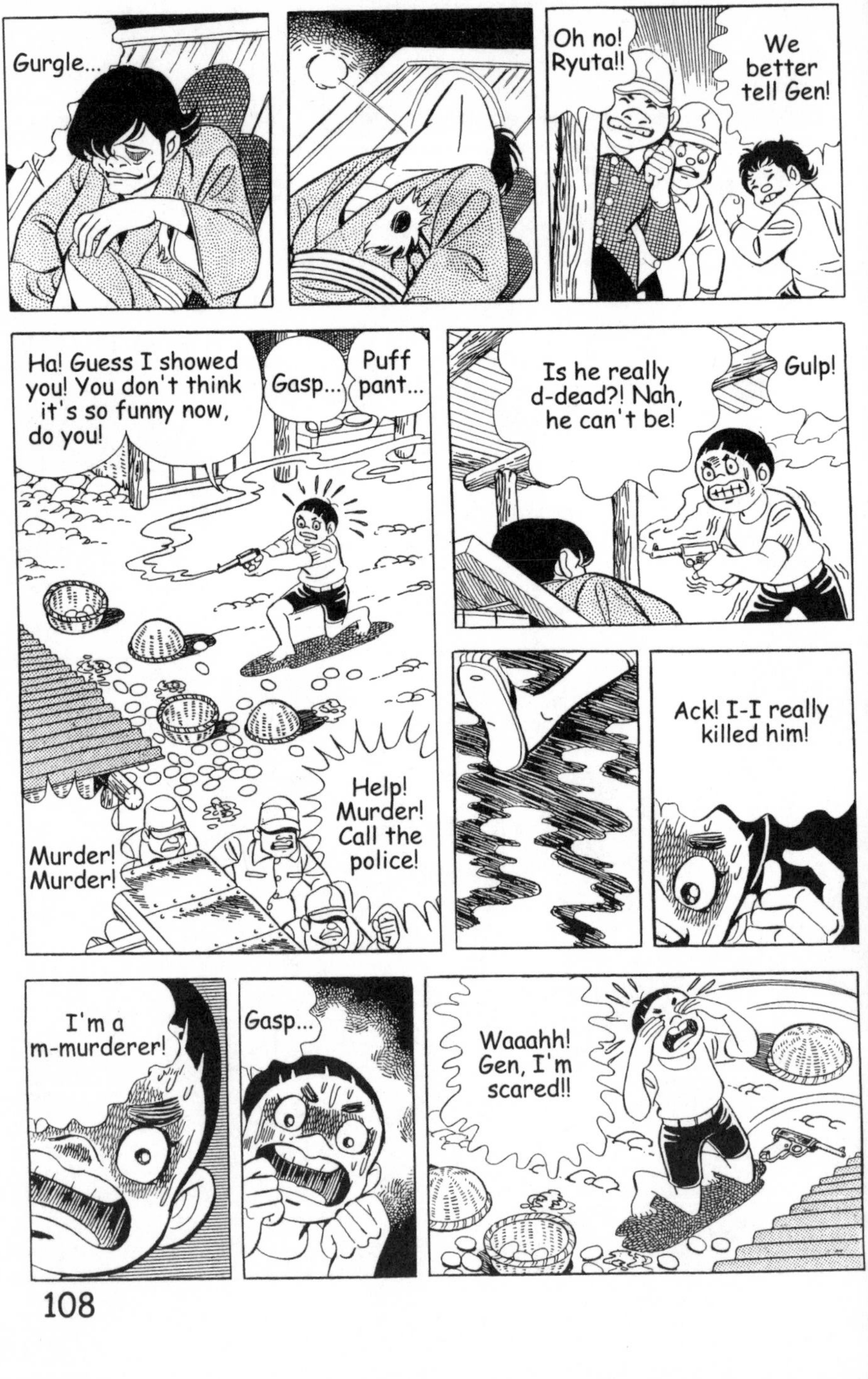
Gurgle...
Oh no! Ryuta!!
We better tell Gen!
Ha! Guess I showed you! You don't think it's so funny now, do you!
Gasp...
Puff pant...
Help! Murder! Call the police!
Murder! Murder!
Is he really d-dead?! Nah, he can't be!
Gulp!
Ack! I-I really killed him!
I'm a m-murderer!
Gasp...
Waaahh! Gen, I'm scared!!

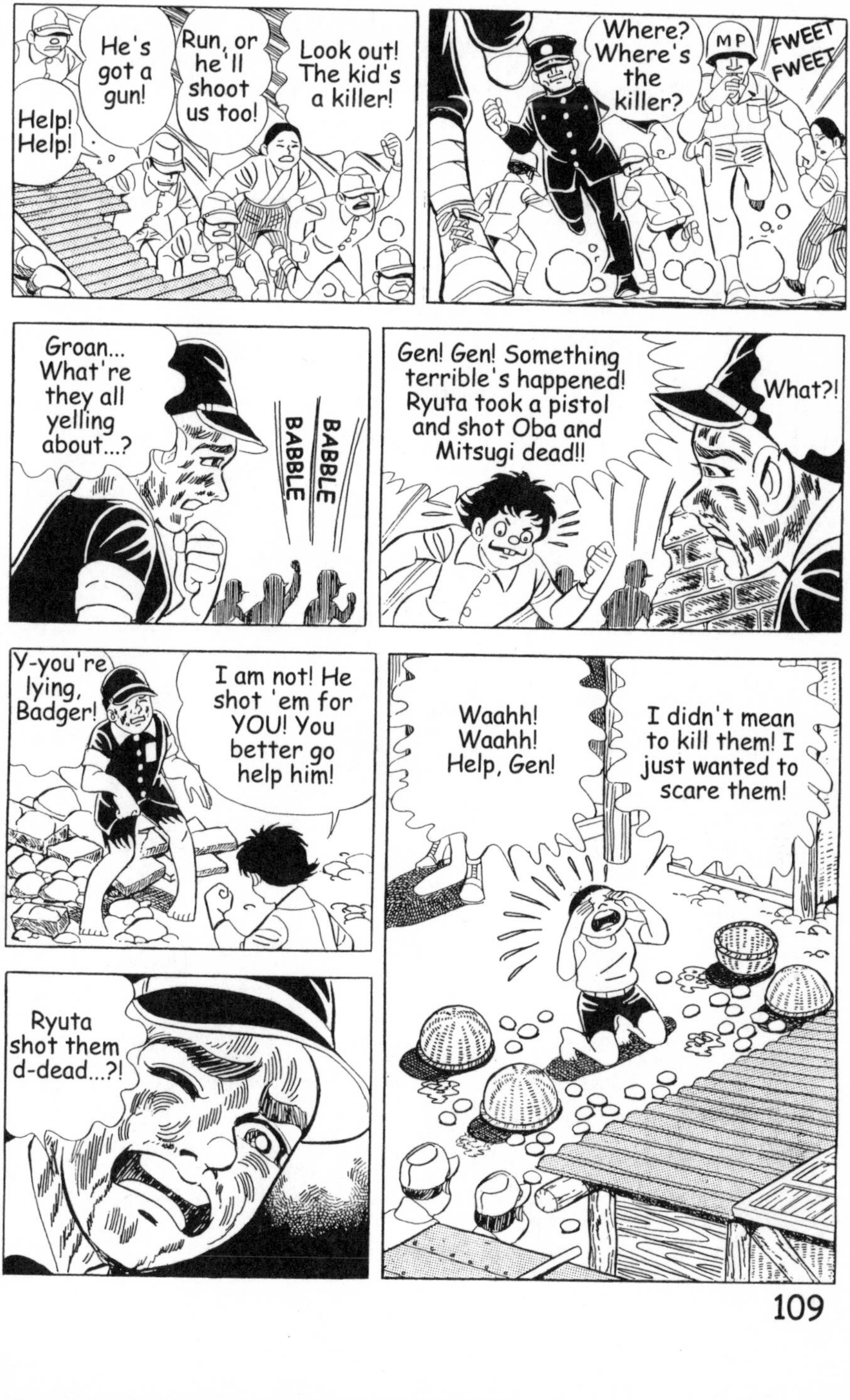
Help! Help!
He's got a gun!
Run, or he'll shoot us too!
Look out! The kid's a killer!
Where? Where's the killer?
MP
FWEET FWEET
Groan... What're they all yelling about...?
BABBLE BABBLE
Gen! Gen! Something terrible's happened! Ryuta took a pistol and shot Oba and Mitsugi dead!!
What?!
Y-you're lying, Badger!
I am not! He shot 'em for YOU! You better go help him!
Waahh! Waahh! Help, Gen!
I didn't mean to kill them! I just wanted to scare them!
Ryuta shot them d-dead...?!

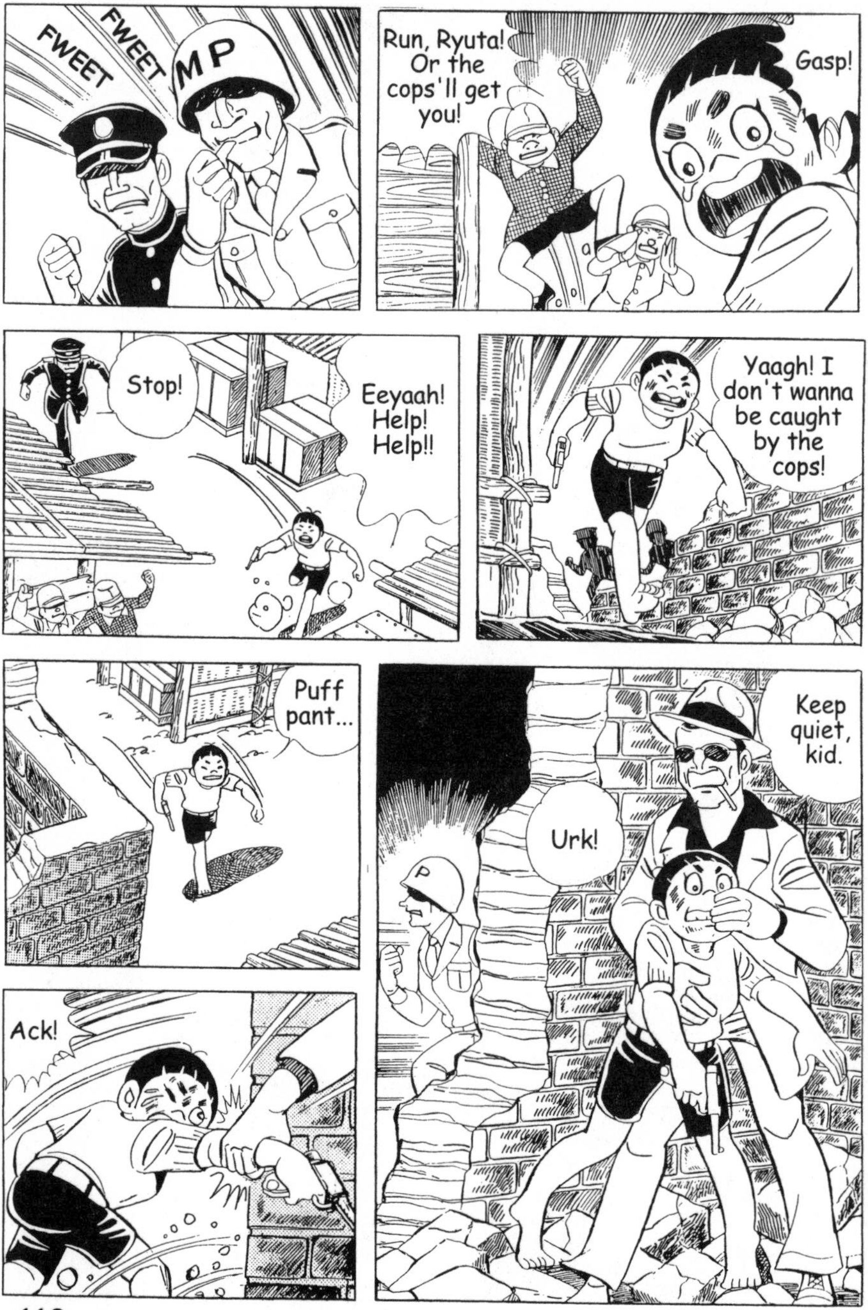
FWEET
FWEET
MP
Run, Ryuta! Or the cops'll get you!
Gasp!
Stop!
Eeyaah! Help! Help!!
Yaagh! I don't wanna be caught by the cops!
Puff pant...
Ack!
Keep quiet, kid.
Urk!
P

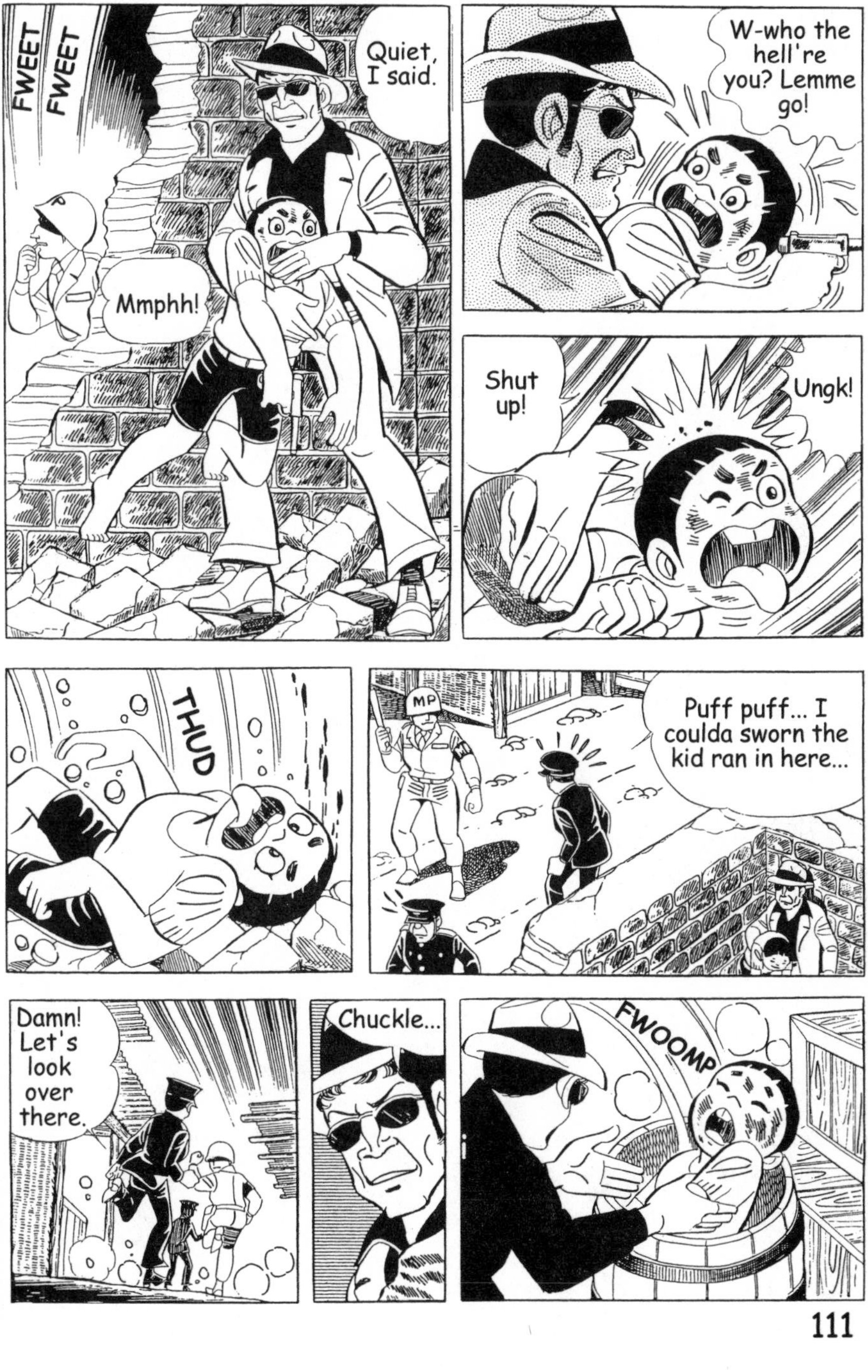
FWEET
FWEET
Quiet, I said.
Mmphh!
W-who the hell're you? Lemme go!
Shut up!
Ungk!
THUD
Puff puff... I coulda sworn the kid ran in here...
MP
Damn! Let's look over there.
Chuckle...
FWOOMP

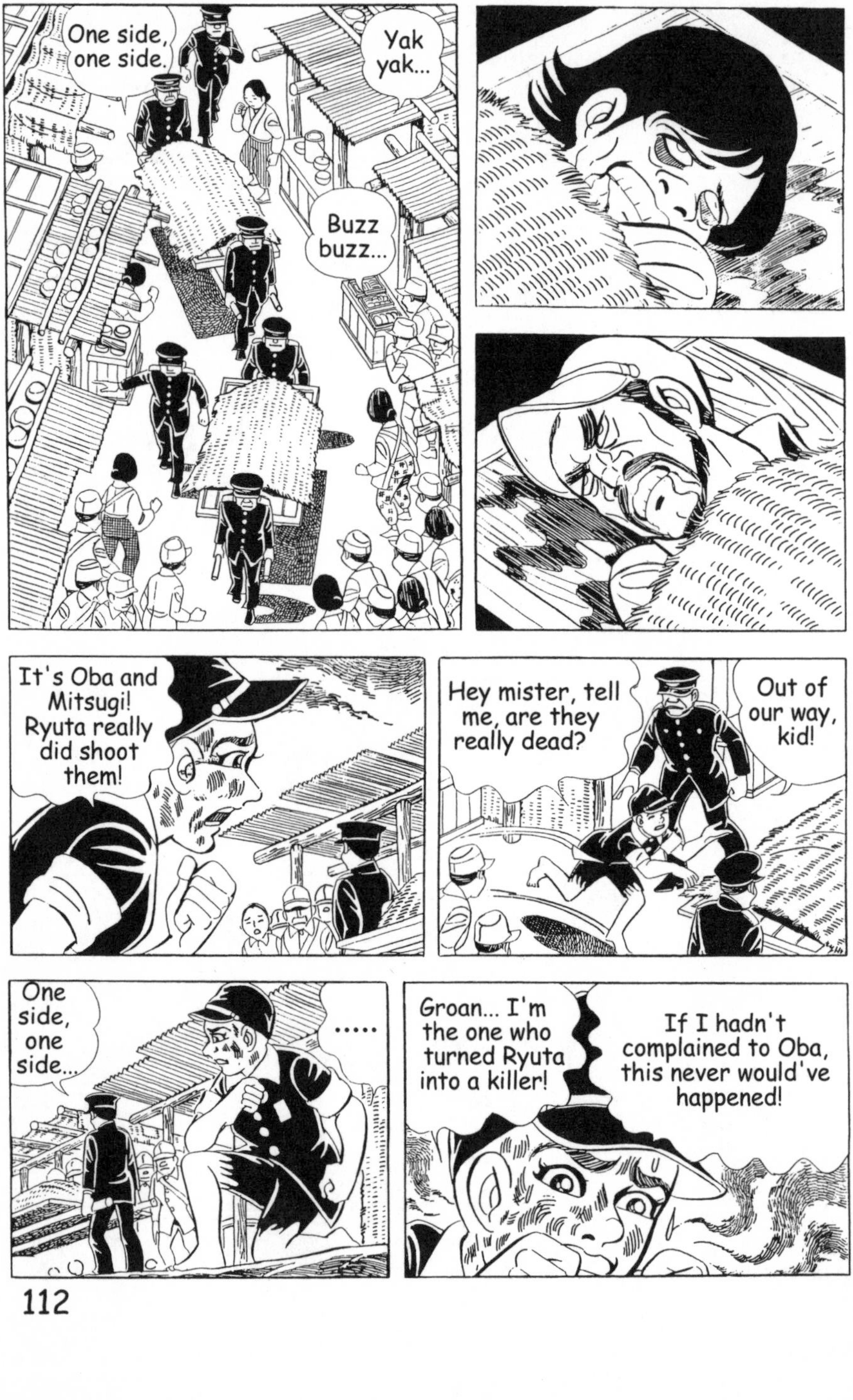
One side, one side.
Yak yak...
Buzz buzz...
It's Oba and Mitsugi! Ryuta really did shoot them!
Hey mister, tell me, are they really dead?
Out of our way, kid!
One side, one side...
.....
Groan... I'm the one who turned Ryuta into a killer!
If I hadn't complained to Oba, this never would've happened!

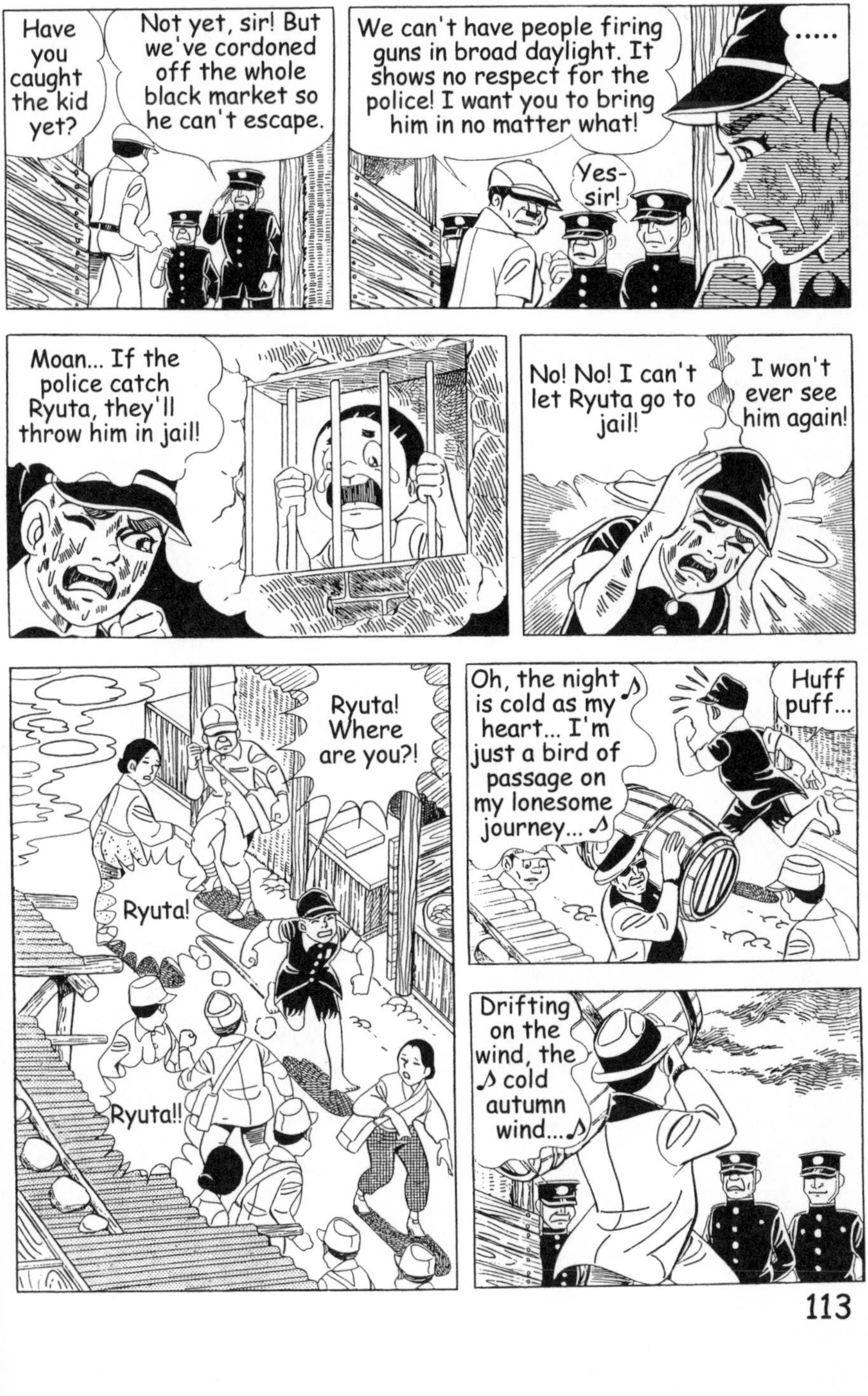
Have you caught the kid yet?
Not yet, sir! But we've cordoned off the whole black market so he can't escape.
We can't have people firing guns in broad daylight. It shows no respect for the police! I want you to bring him in no matter what!
Yes-sir!
.....
Moan... If the police catch Ryuta, they'll throw him in jail!
No! No! I can't let Ryuta go to jail!
I won't ever see him again!
Ryuta! Where are you?!
Ryuta!
Ryuta!!
Oh, the night ♪ is cold as my heart... I'm just a bird of passage on my lonesome journey... ♪
Huff puff...
Drifting on the wind, the ♪ cold autumn wind... ♪

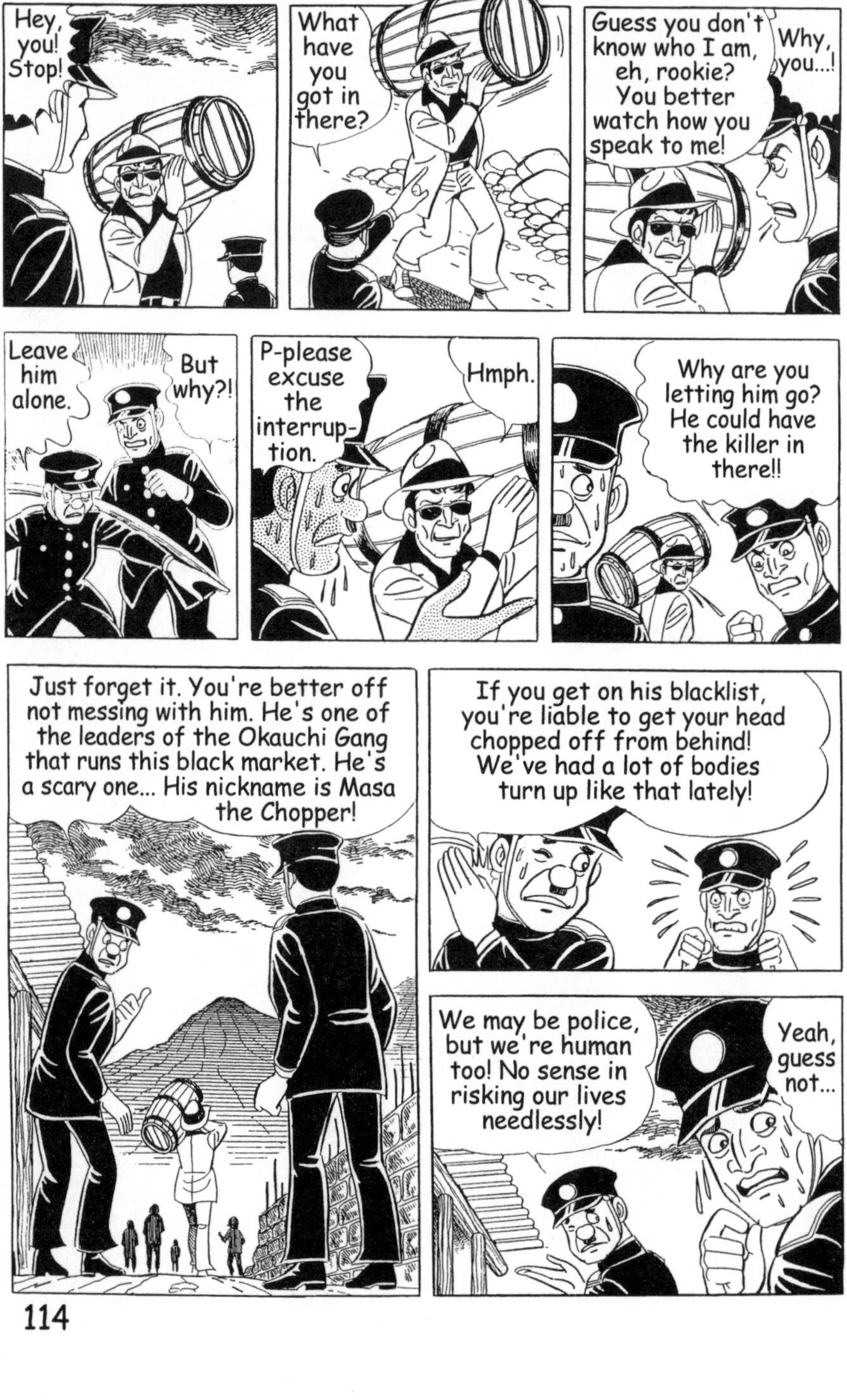

Hey, you! Stop!
What have you got in there?
Guess you don't know who I am, eh, rookie? You better watch how you speak to me!
Why, you...!
Leave him alone.
But why?!
P-please excuse the interruption.
Hmph.
Why are you letting him go? He could have the killer in there!!
Just forget it. You're better off not messing with him. He's one of the leaders of the Okauchi Gang that runs this black market. He's a scary one... His nickname is Masa the Chopper!
If you get on his blacklist, you're liable to get your head chopped off from behind! We've had a lot of bodies turn up like that lately!
We may be police, but we're human too! No sense in risking our lives needlessly!
Yeah, guess not...

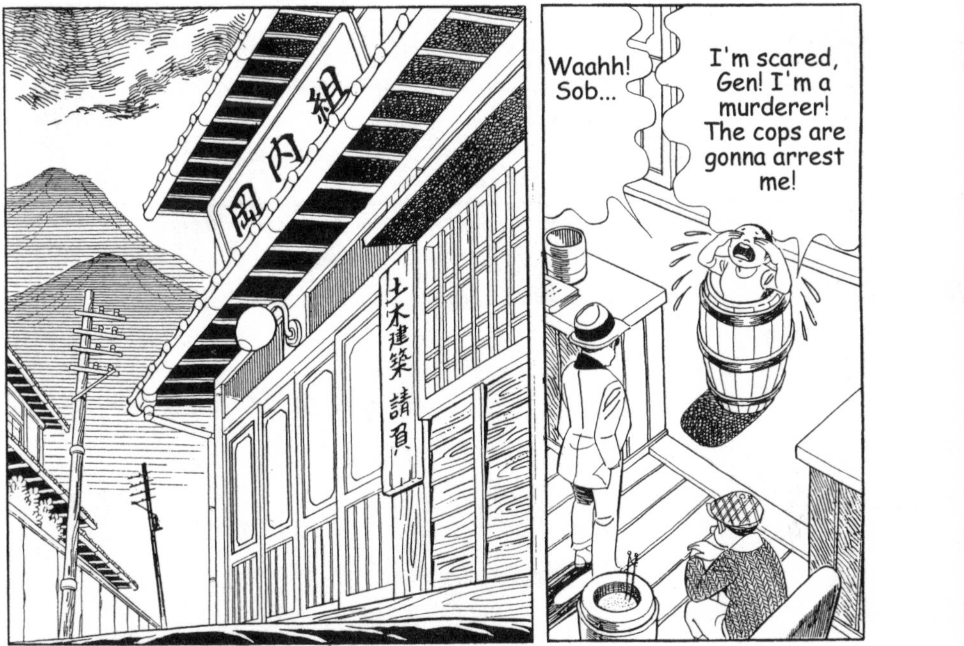
岡内組
土木建築 請負
Waahh! Sob...
I'm scared, Gen! I'm a murderer! The cops are gonna arrest me!

Signs: Okauchi & Co., General Contractors

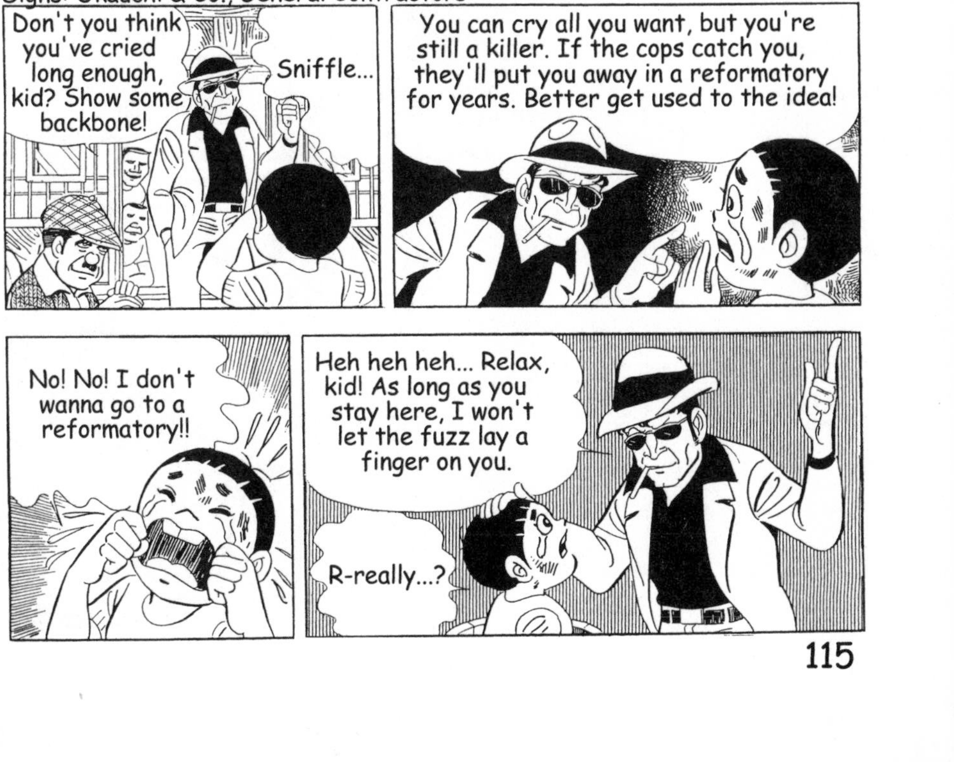
Don't you think you've cried long enough, kid? Show some backbone!
Sniffle...
You can cry all you want, but you're still a killer. If the cops catch you, they'll put you away in a reformatory for years. Better get used to the idea!
No! No! I don't wanna go to a reformatory!!
Heh heh heh... Relax, kid! As long as you stay here, I won't let the fuzz lay a finger on you.
R-really...?

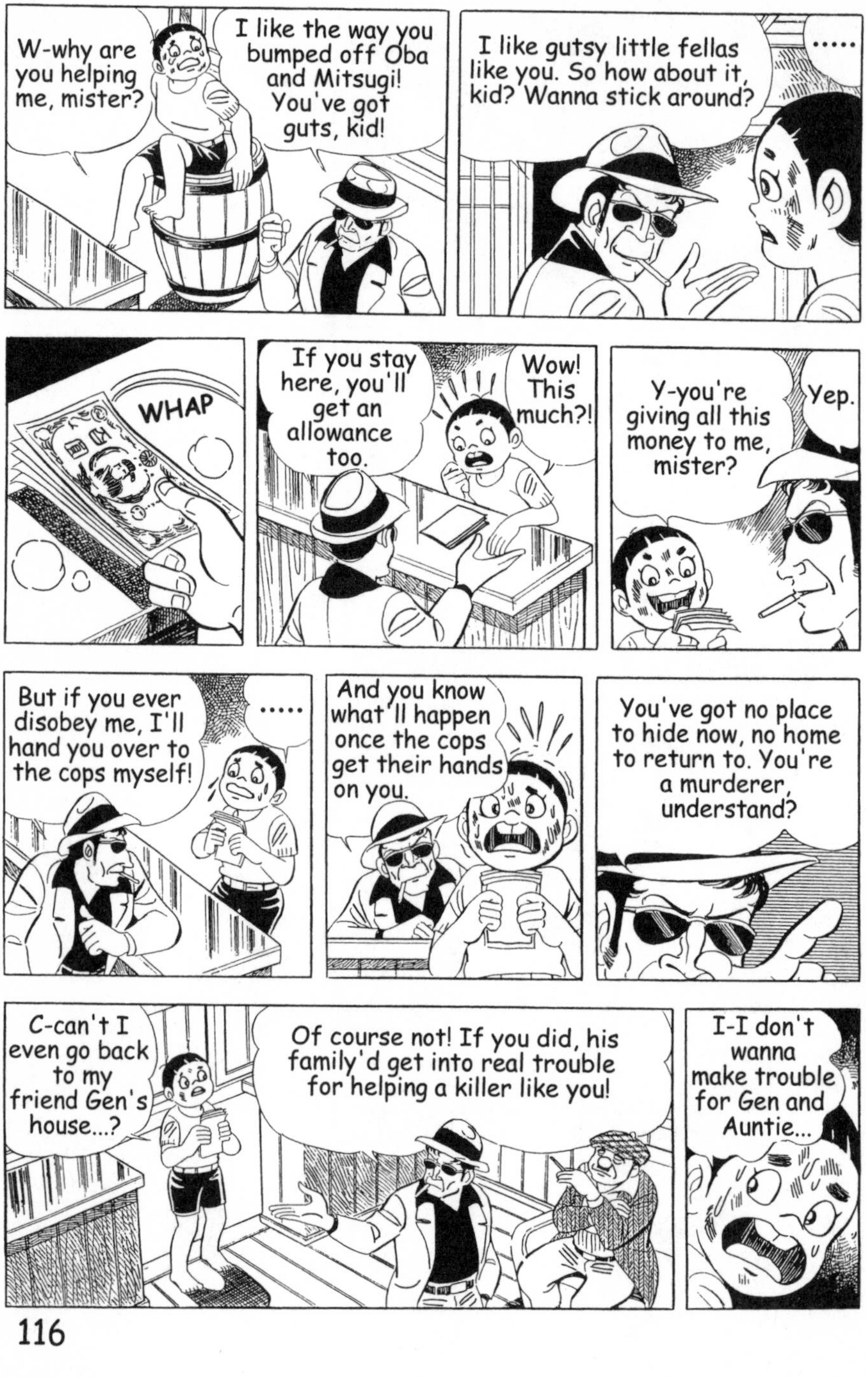
W-why are you helping me, mister?
I like the way you bumped off Oba and Mitsugi! You've got guts, kid!
I like gutsy little fellas like you. So how about it, kid? Wanna stick around?
.....
WHAP
If you stay here, you'll get an allowance too.
Wow! This much?!
Y-you're giving all this money to me, mister?
Yep.
But if you ever disobey me, I'll hand you over to the cops myself!
.....
And you know what'll happen once the cops get their hands on you.
You've got no place to hide now, no home to return to. You're a murderer, understand?
C-can't I even go back to my friend Gen's house...?
Of course not! If you did, his family'd get into real trouble for helping a killer like you!
I-I don't wanna make trouble for Gen and Auntie...

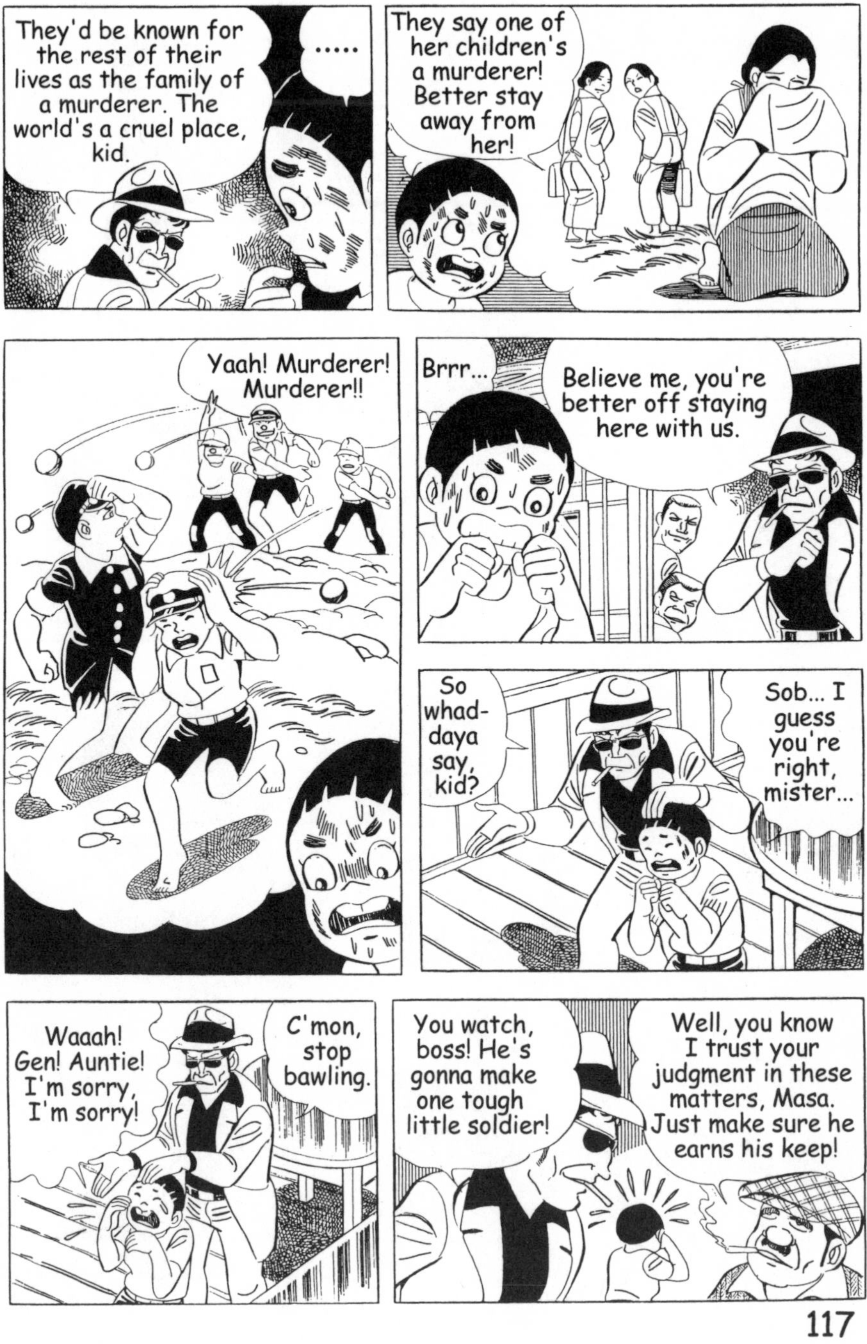

They'd be known for the rest of their lives as the family of a murderer. The world's a cruel place, kid.
.....
They say one of her children's a murderer! Better stay away from her!
Yaah! Murderer! Murderer!!
Brrr...
Believe me, you're better off staying here with us.
So whaddaya say, kid?
Sob... I guess you're right, mister...
Waaah! Gen! Auntie! I'm sorry, I'm sorry!
C'mon, stop bawling.
You watch, boss! He's gonna make one tough little soldier!
Well, you know I trust your judgment in these matters, Masa. Just make sure he earns his keep!

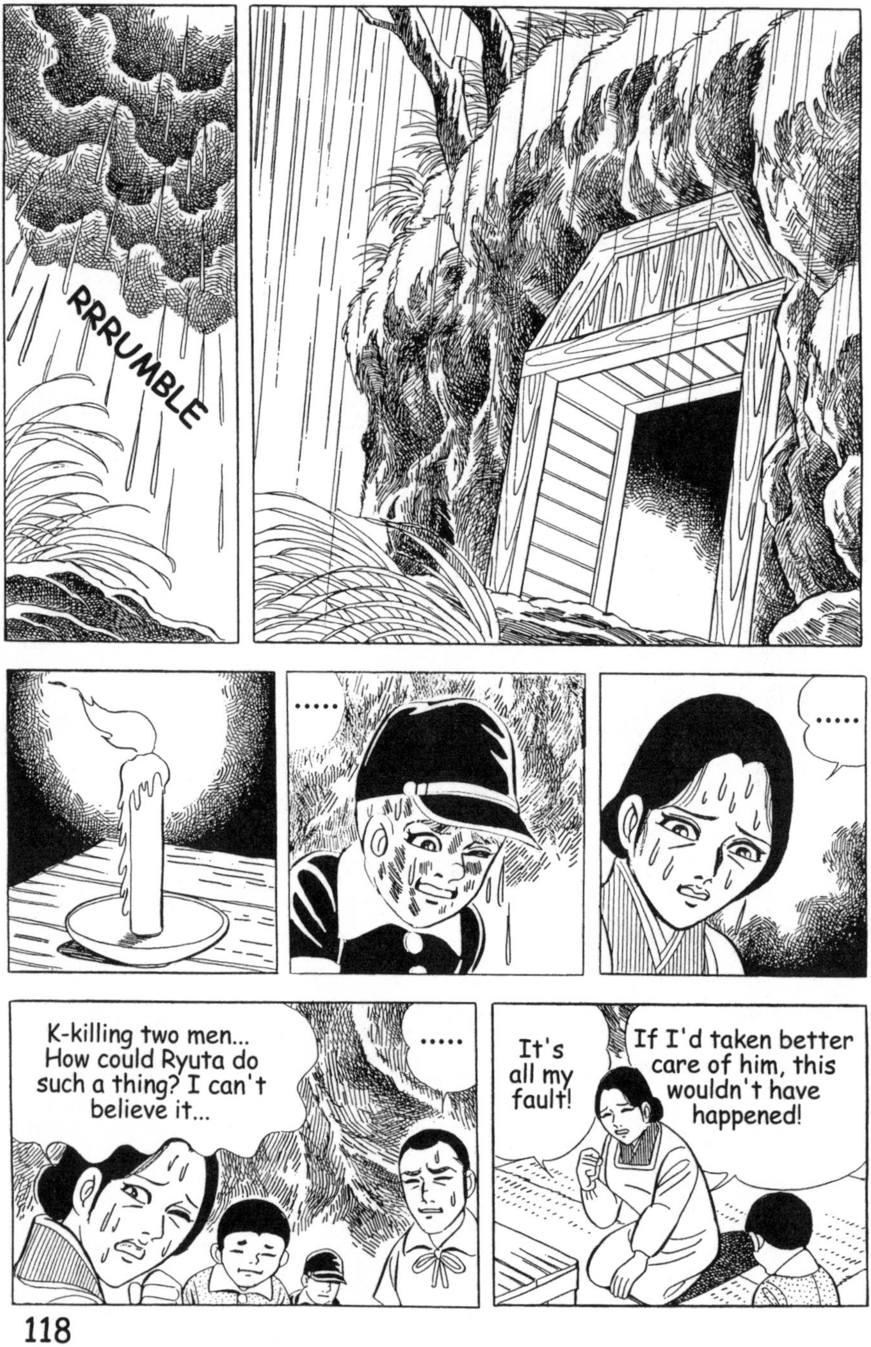
RRRUMBLE
.....
.....
K-killing two men... How could Ryuta do such a thing? I can't believe it...
.....
It's all my fault!
If I'd taken better care of him, this wouldn't have happened!

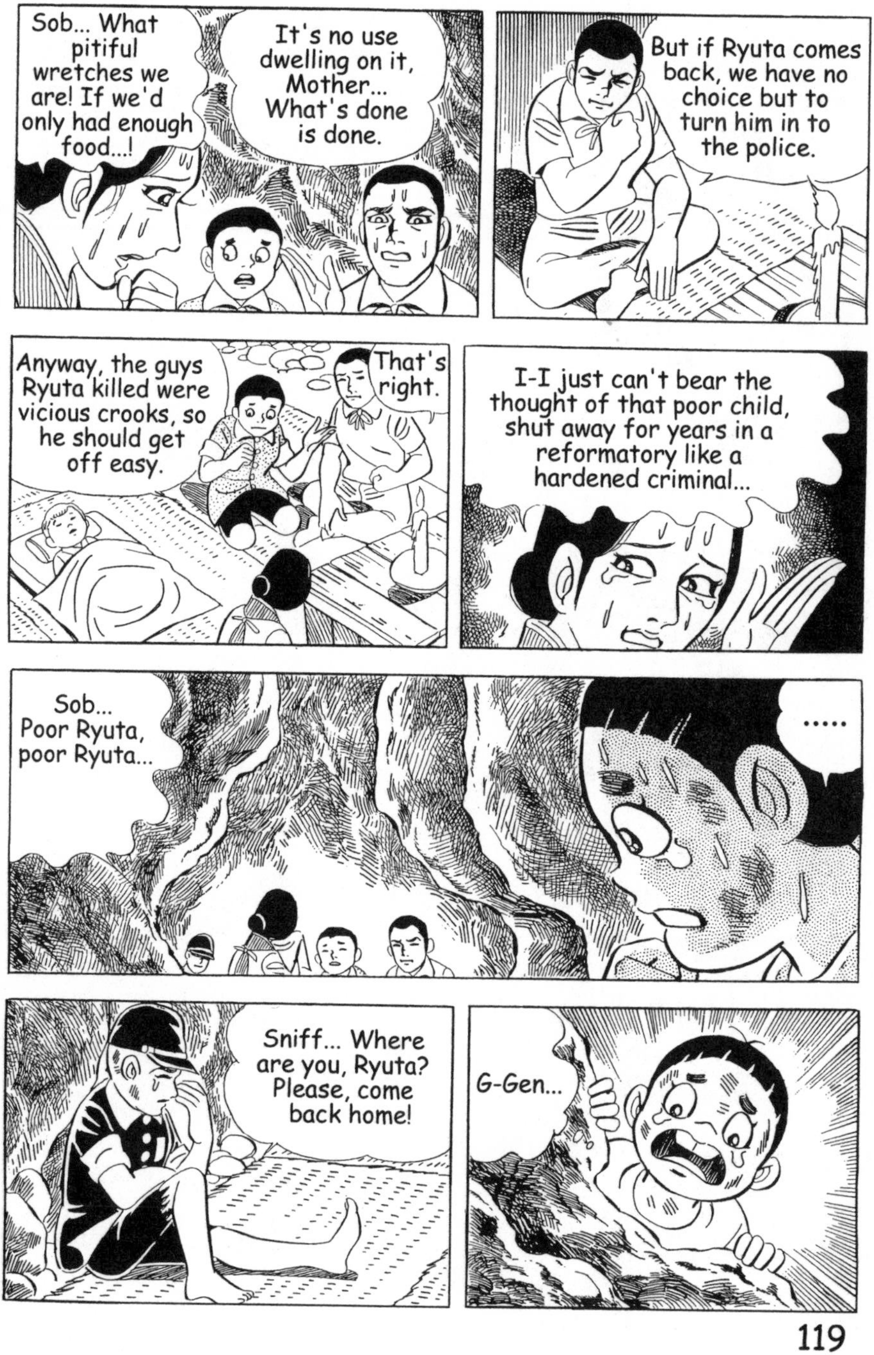
Sob... What pitiful wretches we are! If we'd only had enough food...!
It's no use dwelling on it, Mother... What's done is done.
But if Ryuta comes back, we have no choice but to turn him in to the police.
Anyway, the guys Ryuta killed were vicious crooks, so he should get off easy.
That's right.
I-I just can't bear the thought of that poor child, shut away for years in a reformatory like a hardened criminal...
Sob... Poor Ryuta, poor Ryuta...
.....
Sniff... Where are you, Ryuta? Please, come back home!
G-Gen...

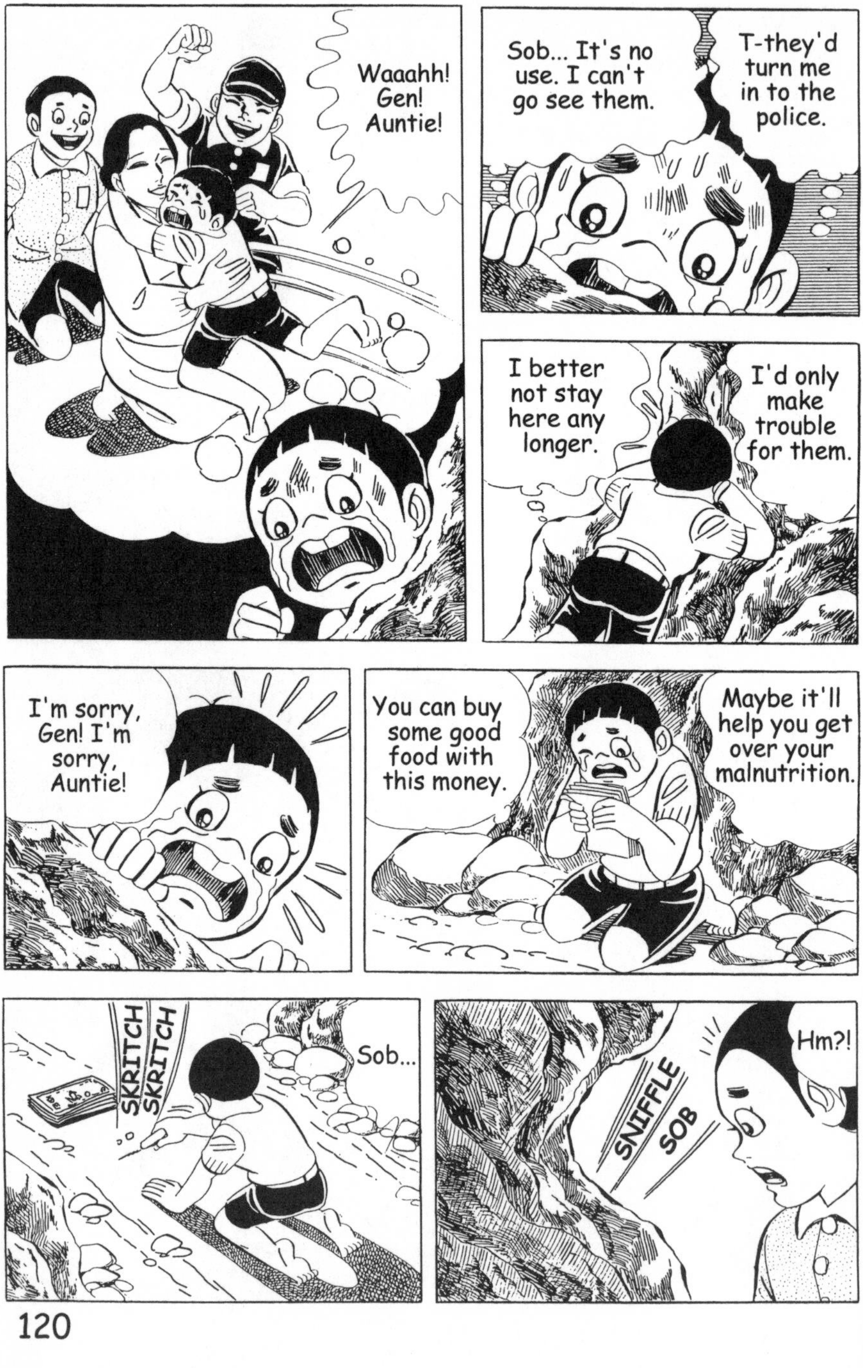
Waaahh! Gen! Auntie!
Sob... It's no use. I can't go see them.
T-they'd turn me in to the police.
I better not stay here any longer.
I'd only make trouble for them.
I'm sorry, Gen! I'm sorry, Auntie!
You can buy some good food with this money.
Maybe it'll help you get over your malnutrition.
SKRITCH SKRITCH
Sob...
SNIFFLE SOB
Hm?!

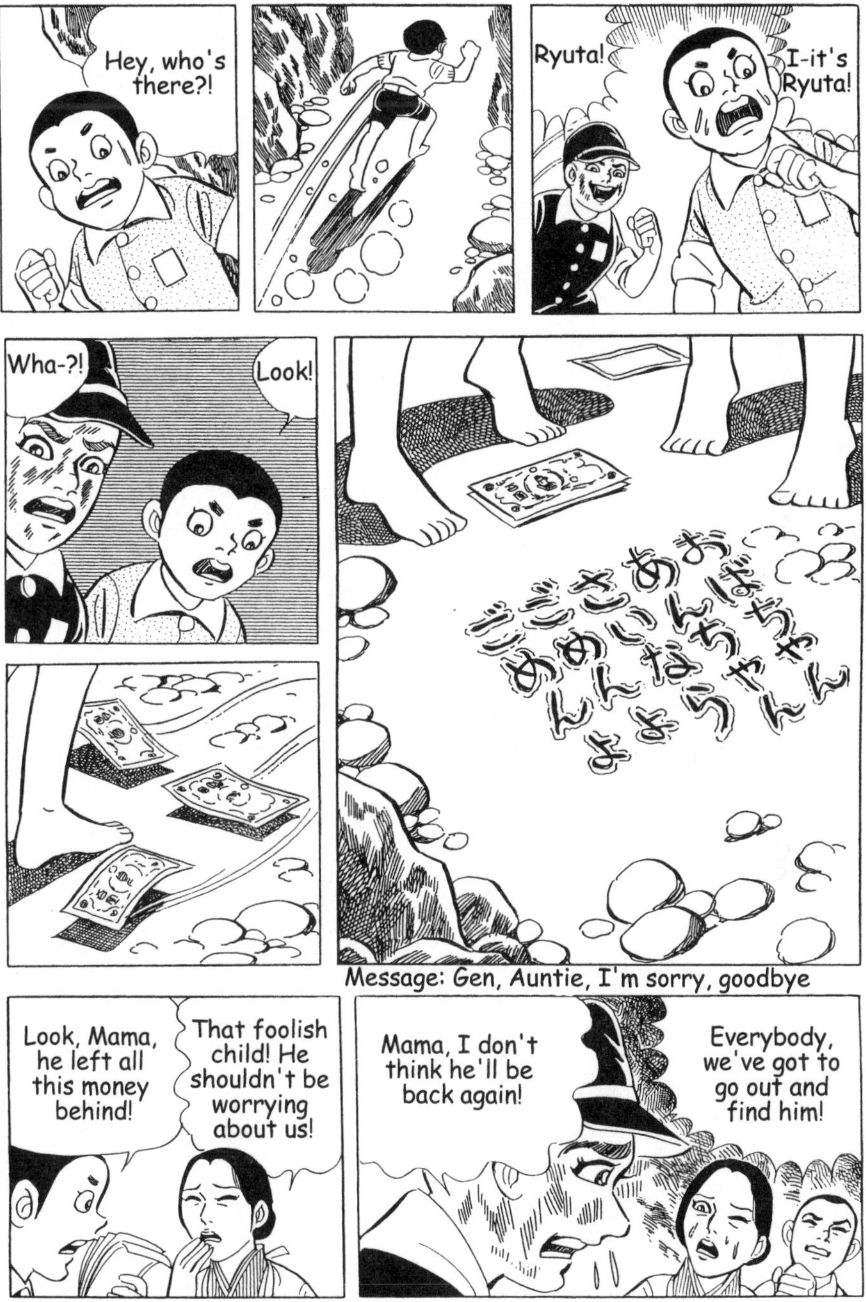
Hey, who's there?!
Ryuta!
I-it's Ryuta!
Wha-?!
Look!
おばちゃん
あんちゃん
さいなら
ごめんよ
ごめんよ
Message: Gen, Auntie, I'm sorry, goodbye
Look, Mama, he left all this money behind!
That foolish child! He shouldn't be worrying about us!
Mama, I don't think he'll be back again!
Everybody, we've got to go out and find him!

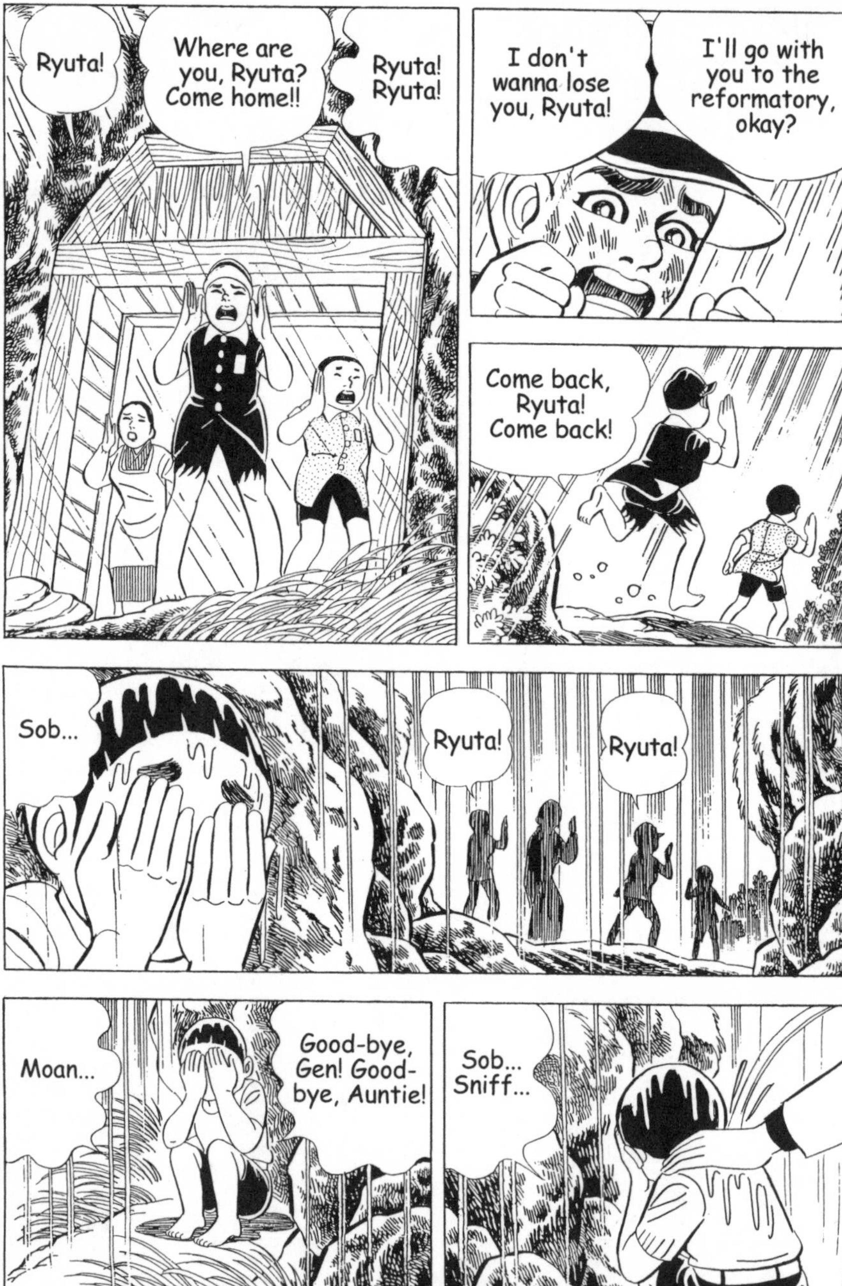
Ryuta!
Where are you, Ryuta? Come home!!
Ryuta! Ryuta!
I don't wanna lose you, Ryuta!
I'll go with you to the reformatory, okay?
Come back, Ryuta! Come back!
Sob...
Ryuta!
Ryuta!
Moan...
Good-bye, Gen! Good-bye, Auntie!
Sob... Sniff...

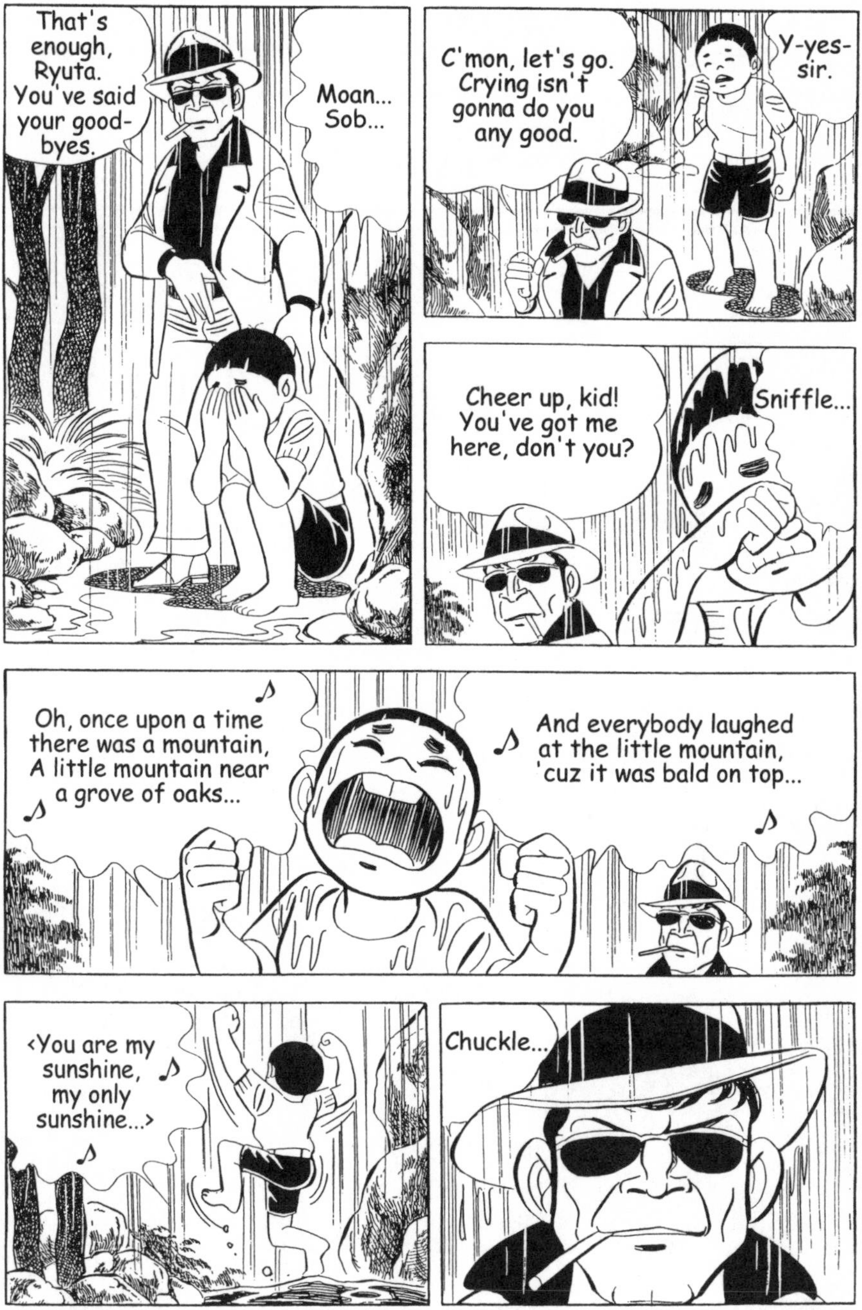

That's enough, Ryuta. You've said your good-byes.
Moan... Sob...
C'mon, let's go. Crying isn't gonna do you any good.
Y-yes-sir.
Cheer up, kid! You've got me here, don't you?
Sniffle...
Oh, once upon a time there was a mountain, A little mountain near a grove of oaks...
And everybody laughed at the little mountain, 'cuz it was bald on top...
<You are my sunshine, my only sunshine...>
Chuckle...

Yep, this kid is gonna help make us some money!

These bomb orphans are real handy when there's dirty work to be done... They're used to anything!

♪<You make me happy w-when skies are gray...>

WAAAHHHH!!

WAAHH! WAAHH!

That's enough whining!

Waahh! Ryuta, come back!!

RYUTA! RYUTA!

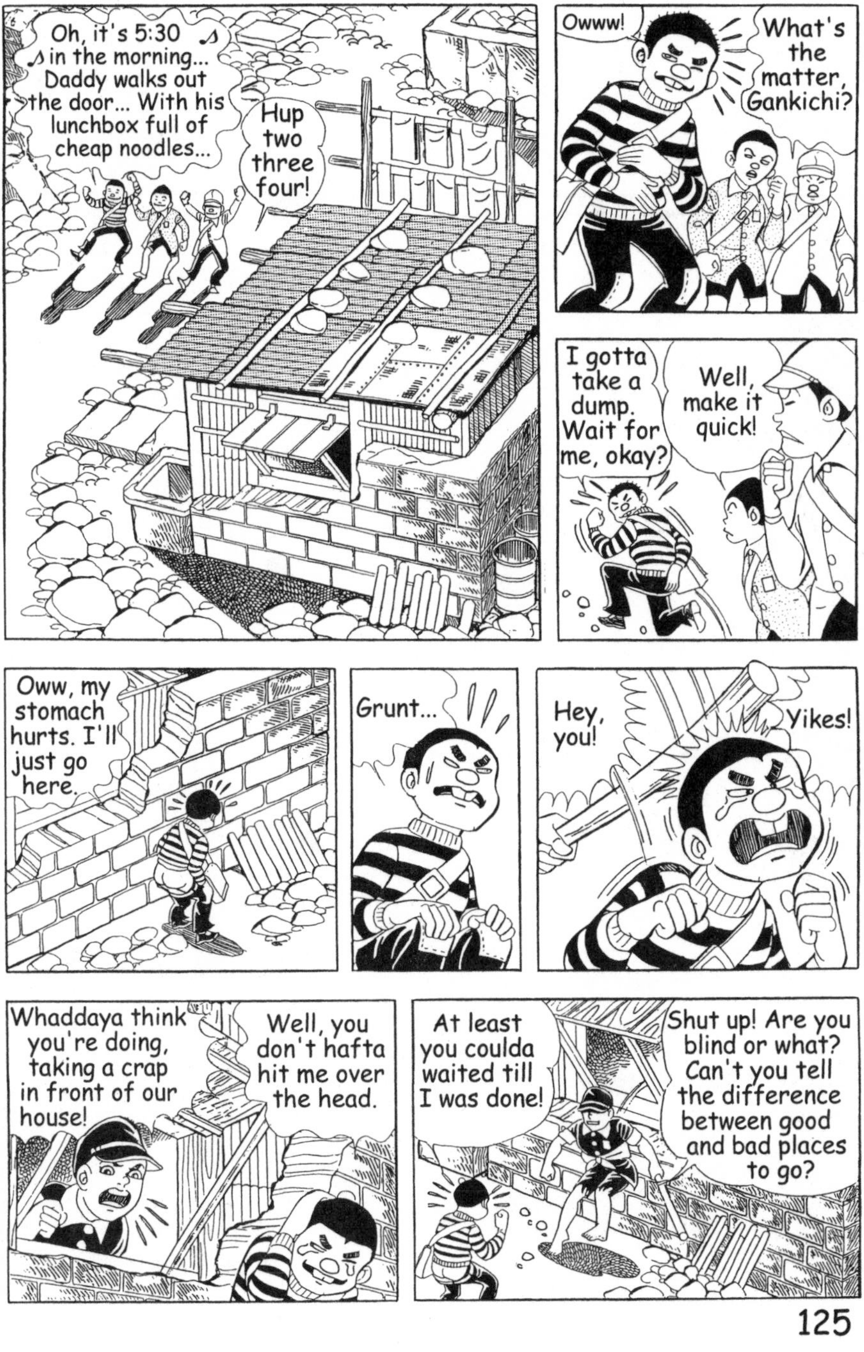
Oh, it's 5:30 in the morning... Daddy walks out the door... With his lunchbox full of cheap noodles...
Hup two three four!
Owww!
What's the matter, Gankichi?
I gotta take a dump. Wait for me, okay?
Well, make it quick!
Oww, my stomach hurts. I'll just go here.
Grunt...
Hey, you!
Yikes!
Whaddaya think you're doing, taking a crap in front of our house!
Well, you don't hafta hit me over the head.
At least you coulda waited till I was done!
Shut up! Are you blind or what? Can't you tell the difference between good and bad places to go?

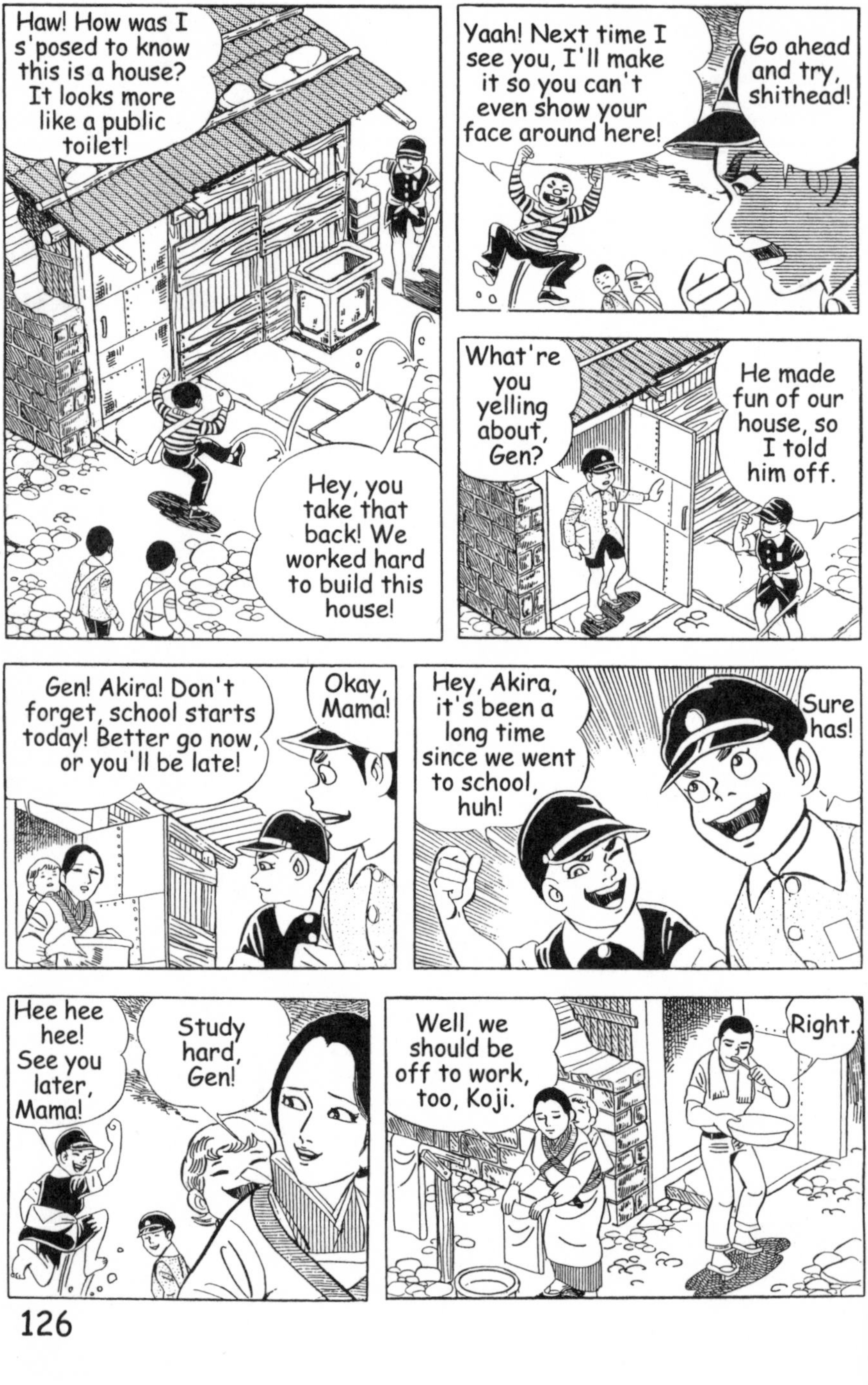
Haw! How was I s'posed to know this is a house? It looks more like a public toilet!
Hey, you take that back! We worked hard to build this house!
Yaah! Next time I see you, I'll make it so you can't even show your face around here!
Go ahead and try, shithead!
What're you yelling about, Gen?
He made fun of our house, so I told him off.
Gen! Akira! Don't forget, school starts today! Better go now, or you'll be late!
Okay, Mama!
Hey, Akira, it's been a long time since we went to school, huh!
Sure has!
Hee hee hee! See you later, Mama!
Study hard, Gen!
Well, we should be off to work, too, Koji.
Right.

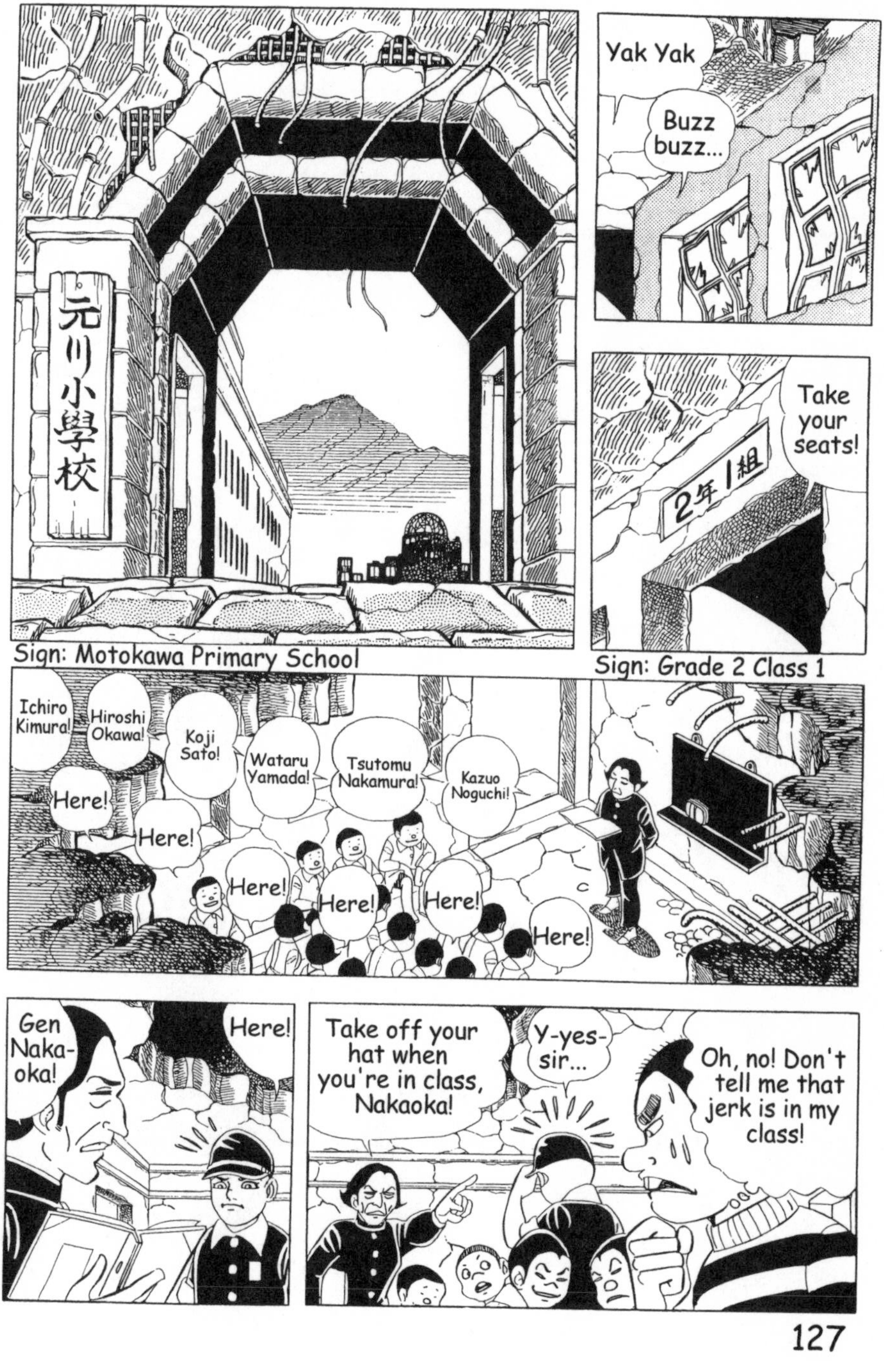

元川小學校
Sign: Motokawa Primary School
Yak Yak
Buzz buzz...
Take your seats!
2年1組
Sign: Grade 2 Class 1
Ichiro Kimura!
Here!
Hiroshi Okawa!
Here!
Koji Sato!
Here!
Wataru Yamada!
Here!
Tsutomu Nakamura!
Here!
Kazuo Noguchi!
Here!
Gen Naka-oka!
Here!
Take off your hat when you're in class, Nakaoka!
Y-yes-sir...
Oh, no! Don't tell me that jerk is in my class!

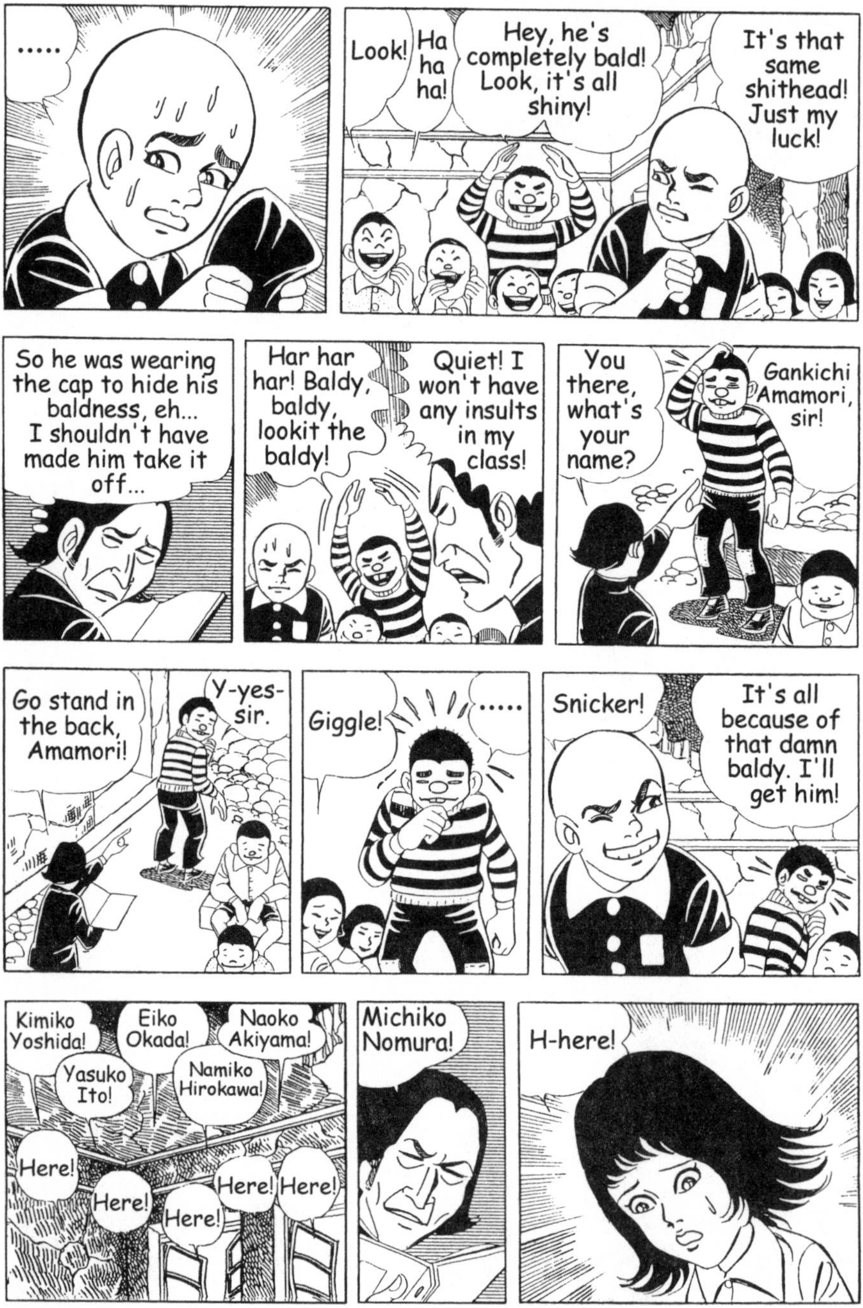
.....
Look!
Ha ha ha!
Hey, he's completely bald! Look, it's all shiny!
It's that same shithead! Just my luck!
So he was wearing the cap to hide his baldness, eh... I shouldn't have made him take it off...
Har har har! Baldy, baldy, lookit the baldy!
Quiet! I won't have any insults in my class!
You there, what's your name?
Gankichi Amamori, sir!
Go stand in the back, Amamori!
Y-yes-sir.
Giggle!
.....
Snicker!
It's all because of that damn baldy. I'll get him!
Kimiko Yoshida!
Eiko Okada!
Naoko Akiyama!
Yasuko Ito!
Namiko Hirokawa!
Here!
Here!
Here!
Here!
Here!
Michiko Nomura!
H-here!

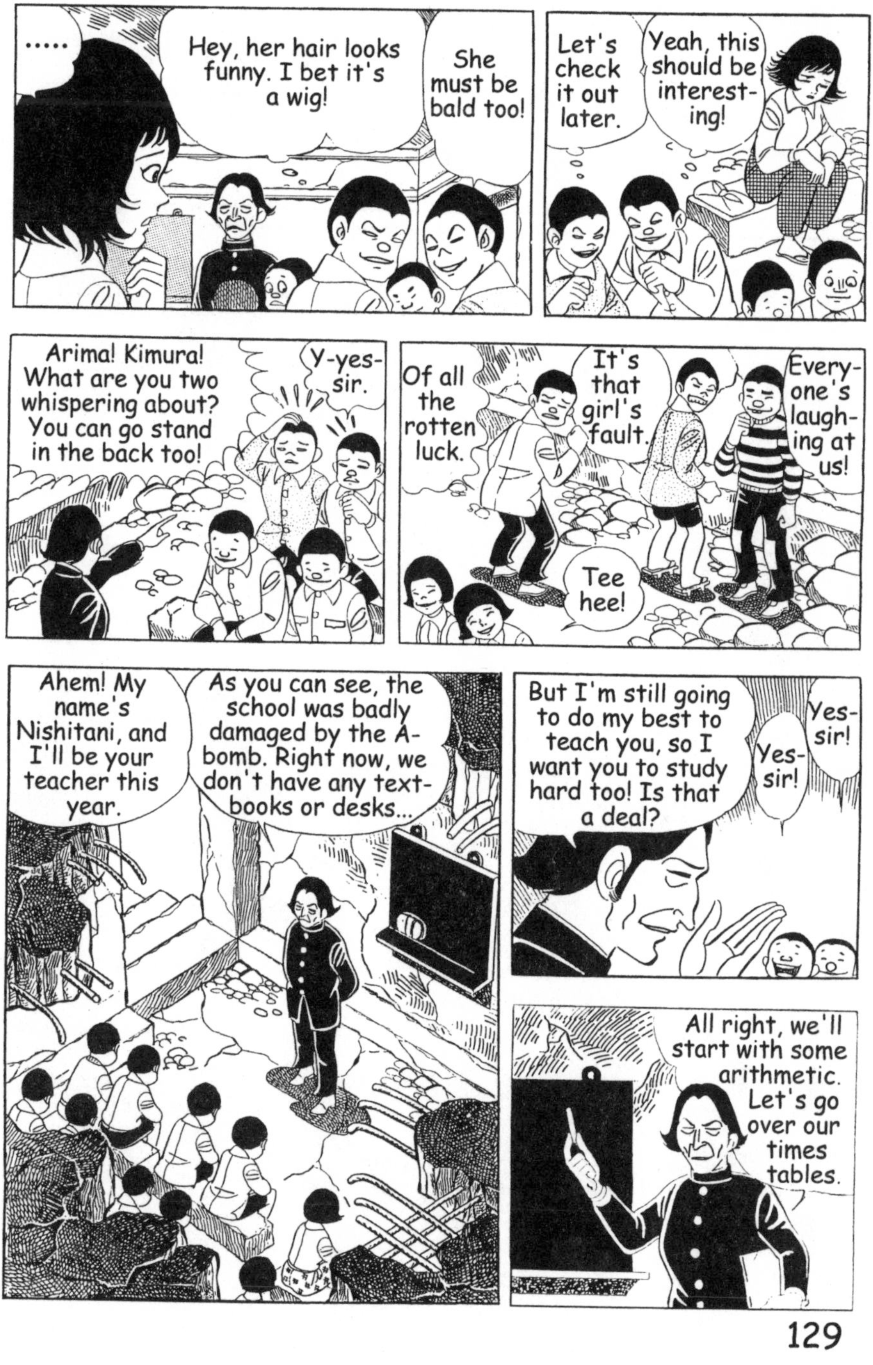
.....
Hey, her hair looks funny. I bet it's a wig!
She must be bald too!
Let's check it out later.
Yeah, this should be interest-ing!
Arima! Kimura! What are you two whispering about? You can go stand in the back too!
Y-yes-sir.
Of all the rotten luck.
It's that girl's fault.
Every-one's laugh-ing at us!
Tee hee!
Ahem! My name's Nishitani, and I'll be your teacher this year.
As you can see, the school was badly damaged by the A-bomb. Right now, we don't have any text-books or desks...
But I'm still going to do my best to teach you, so I want you to study hard too! Is that a deal?
Yes-sir!
Yes-sir!
All right, we'll start with some arithmetic. Let's go over our times tables.

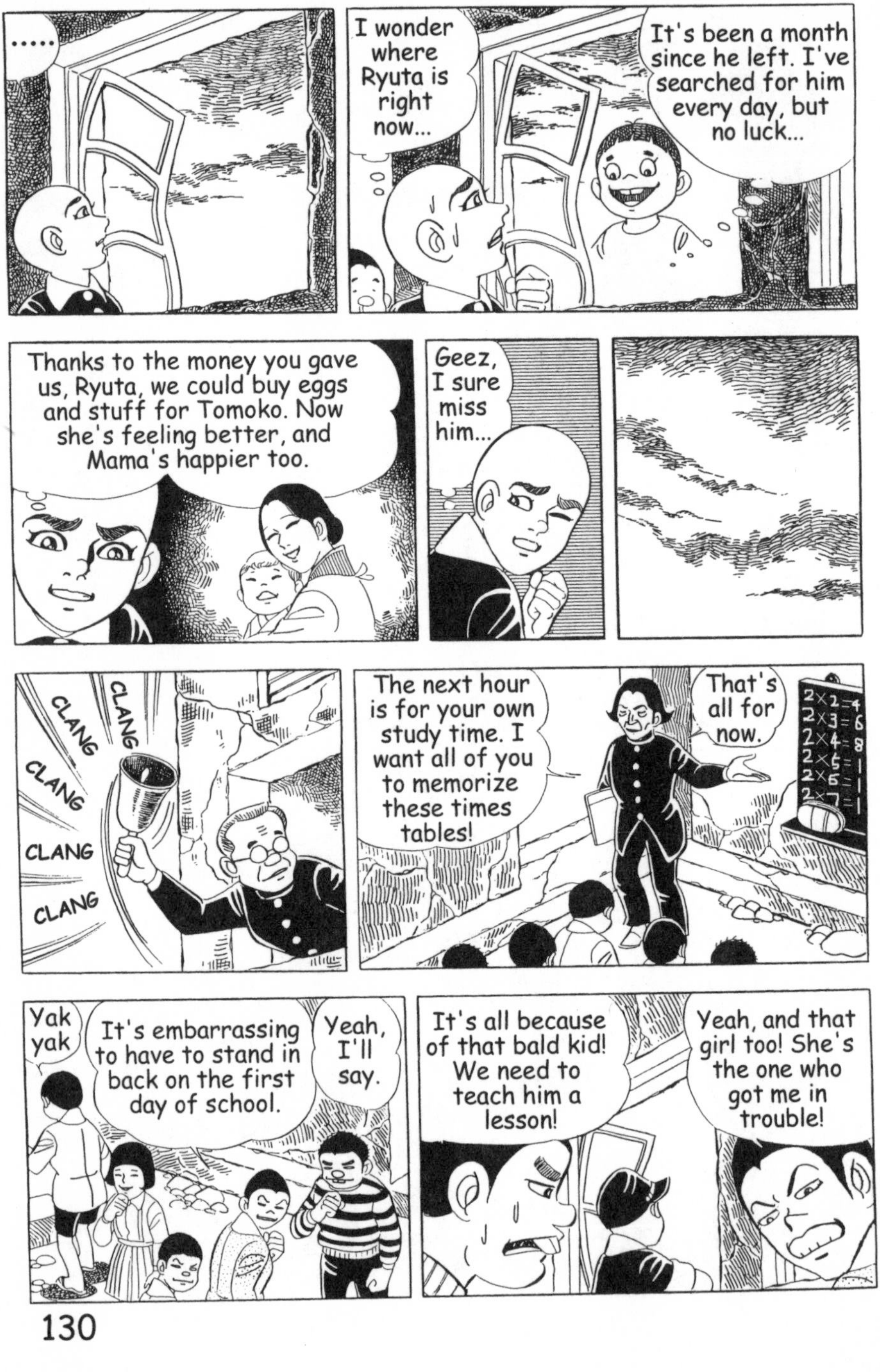

......
I wonder where Ryuta is right now...
It's been a month since he left. I've searched for him every day, but no luck...
Thanks to the money you gave us, Ryuta, we could buy eggs and stuff for Tomoko. Now she's feeling better, and Mama's happier too.
Geez, I sure miss him...
CLANG
CLANG
CLANG
CLANG
CLANG
The next hour is for your own study time. I want all of you to memorize these times tables!
That's all for now.
2×2=4
2×3=6
2×4=8
2×5=1
2×6=1
2×7=1
Yak yak
It's embarrassing to have to stand in back on the first day of school.
Yeah, I'll say.
It's all because of that bald kid! We need to teach him a lesson!
Yeah, and that girl too! She's the one who got me in trouble!

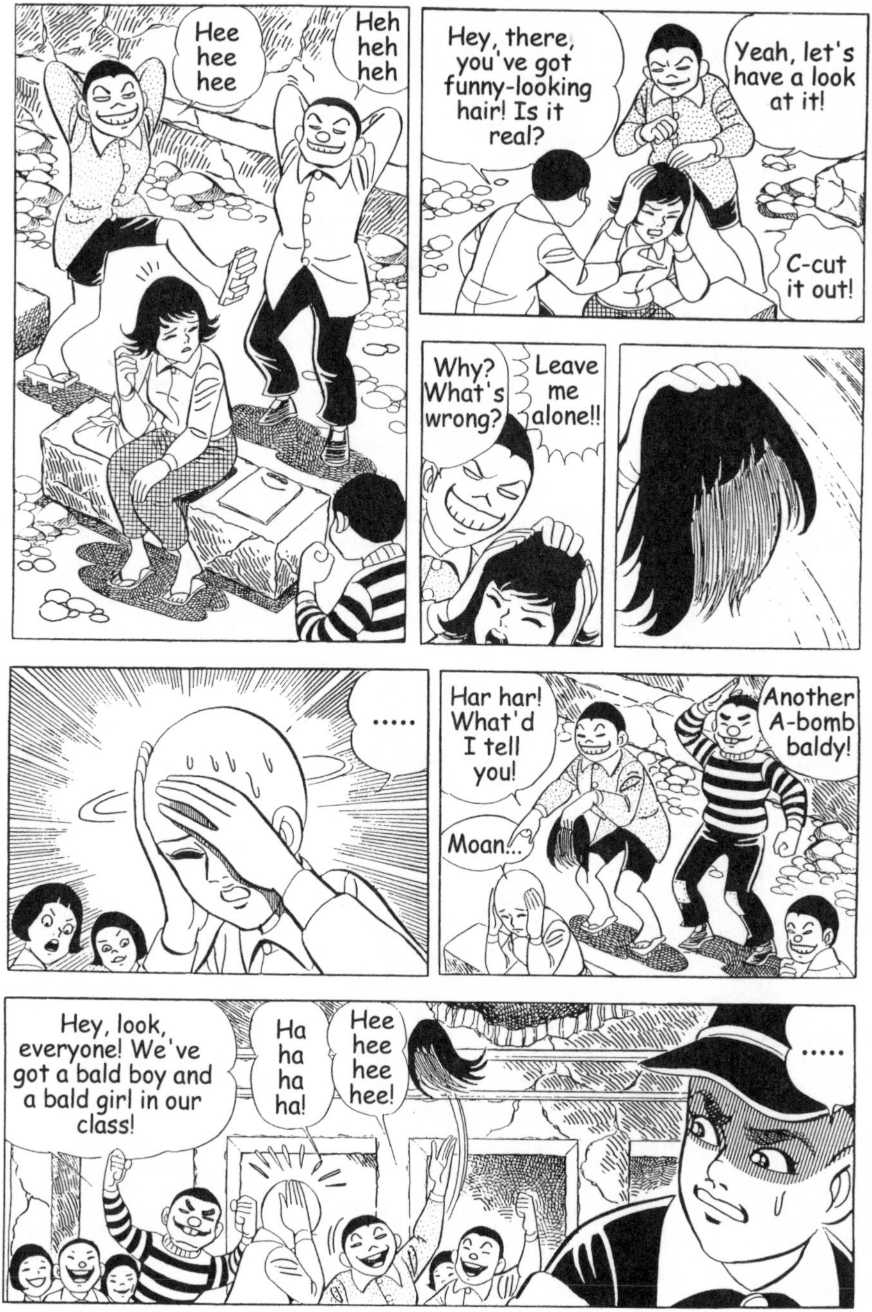
Hee hee hee
Heh heh heh
Hey, there, you've got funny-looking hair! Is it real?
Yeah, let's have a look at it!
C-cut it out!
Why? What's wrong?
Leave me alone!!
.....
Har har! What'd I tell you!
Another A-bomb baldy!
Moan...
Hey, look, everyone! We've got a bald boy and a bald girl in our class!
Ha ha ha ha!
Hee hee hee hee!
.....

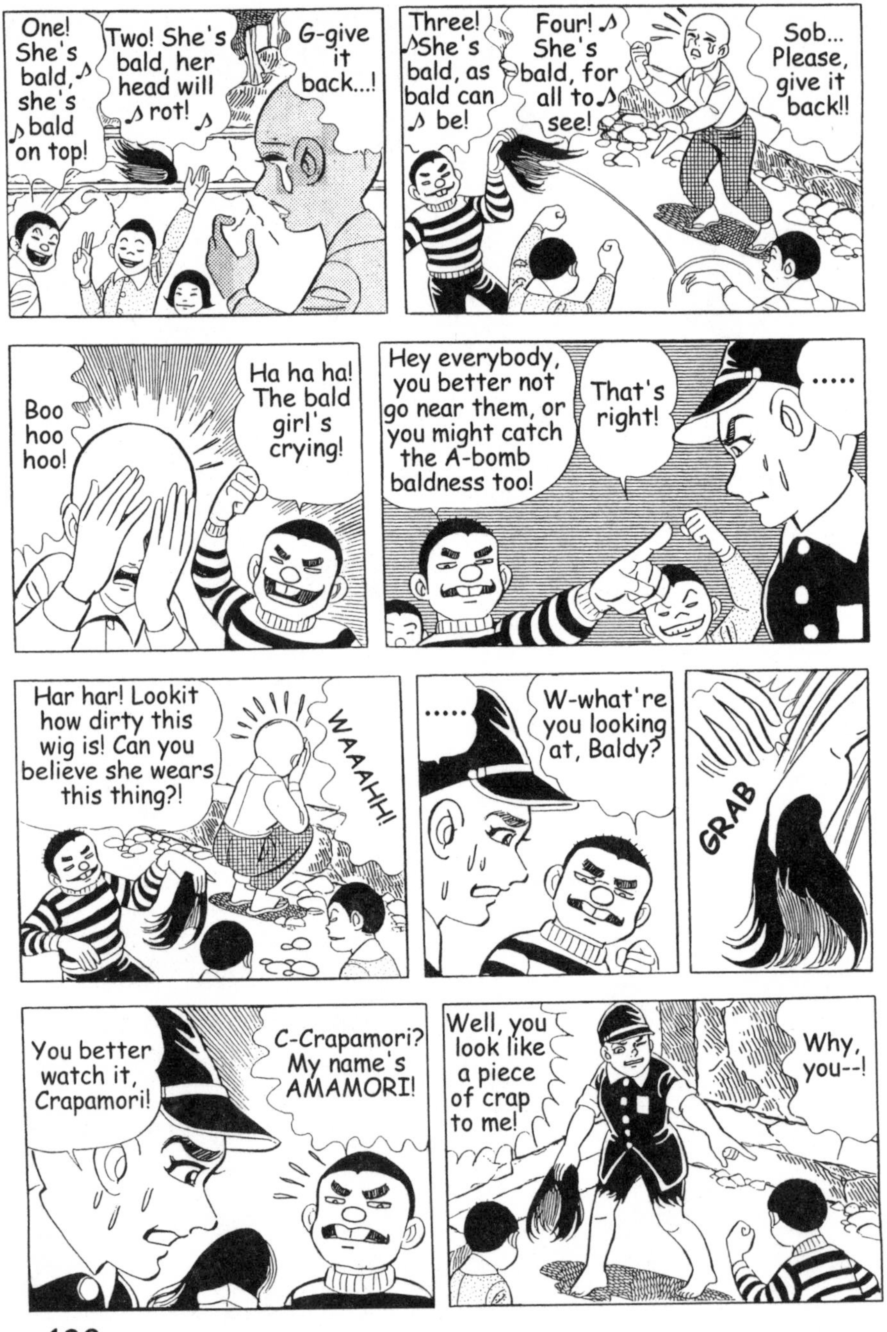
One! She's bald, ♪ she's ♪ bald on top!
Two! She's bald, her head will ♪ rot! ♪
G-give it back...!
Three! ♪ She's bald, as bald can ♪ be!
Four! ♪ She's bald, for all to ♪ see!
Sob... Please, give it back!!
Boo hoo hoo!
Ha ha ha! The bald girl's crying!
Hey everybody, you better not go near them, or you might catch the A-bomb baldness too!
That's right!
.....
Har har! Lookit how dirty this wig is! Can you believe she wears this thing?!
WAAAHH!
.....
W-what're you looking at, Baldy?
GRAB
You better watch it, Crapamori!
C-Crapamori? My name's AMAMORI!
Well, you look like a piece of crap to me!
Why, you--!

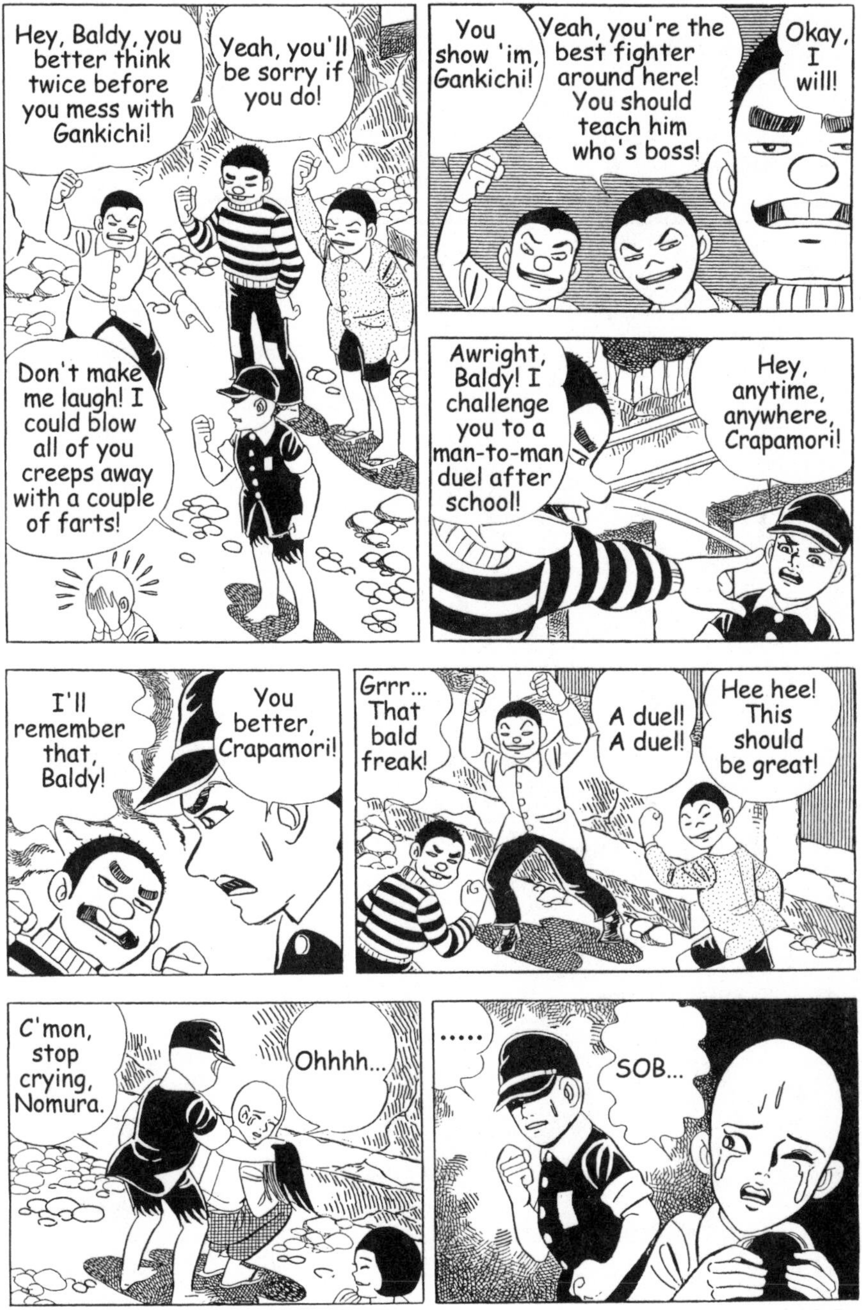
Hey, Baldy, you better think twice before you mess with Gankichi!
Yeah, you'll be sorry if you do!
Don't make me laugh! I could blow all of you creeps away with a couple of farts!
You show 'im, Gankichi!
Yeah, you're the best fighter around here! You should teach him who's boss!
Okay, I will!
Awright, Baldy! I challenge you to a man-to-man duel after school!
Hey, anytime, anywhere, Crapamori!
I'll remember that, Baldy!
You better, Crapamori!
Grrr... That bald freak!
A duel! A duel!
Hee hee! This should be great!
C'mon, stop crying, Nomura.
Ohhhh...
.....
SOB...

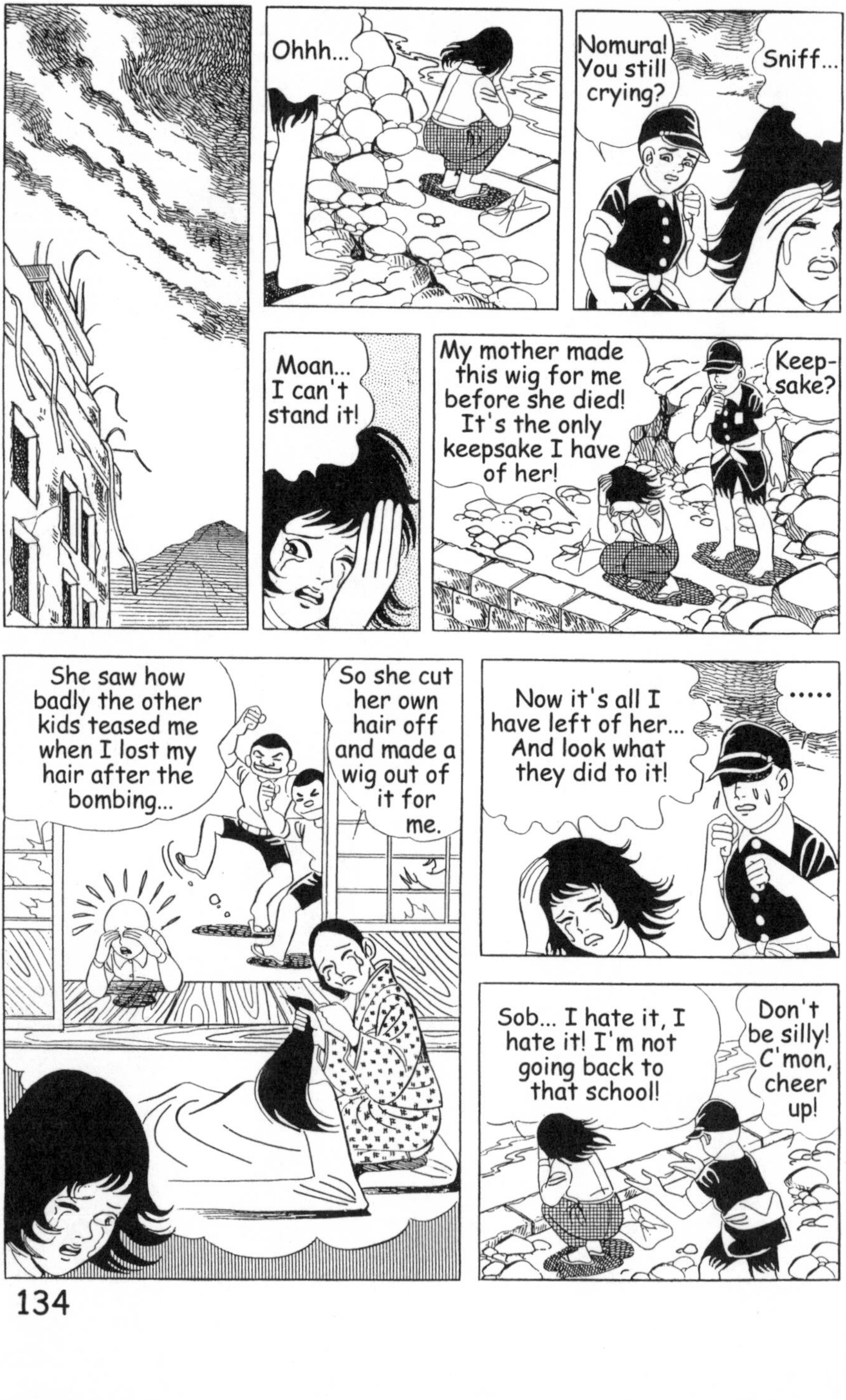
Ohhh...
Nomura! You still crying?
Sniff...
Moan... I can't stand it!
My mother made this wig for me before she died! It's the only keepsake I have of her!
Keep-sake?
She saw how badly the other kids teased me when I lost my hair after the bombing...
So she cut her own hair off and made a wig out of it for me.
Now it's all I have left of her... And look what they did to it!
.....
Sob... I hate it, I hate it! I'm not going back to that school!
Don't be silly! C'mon, cheer up!

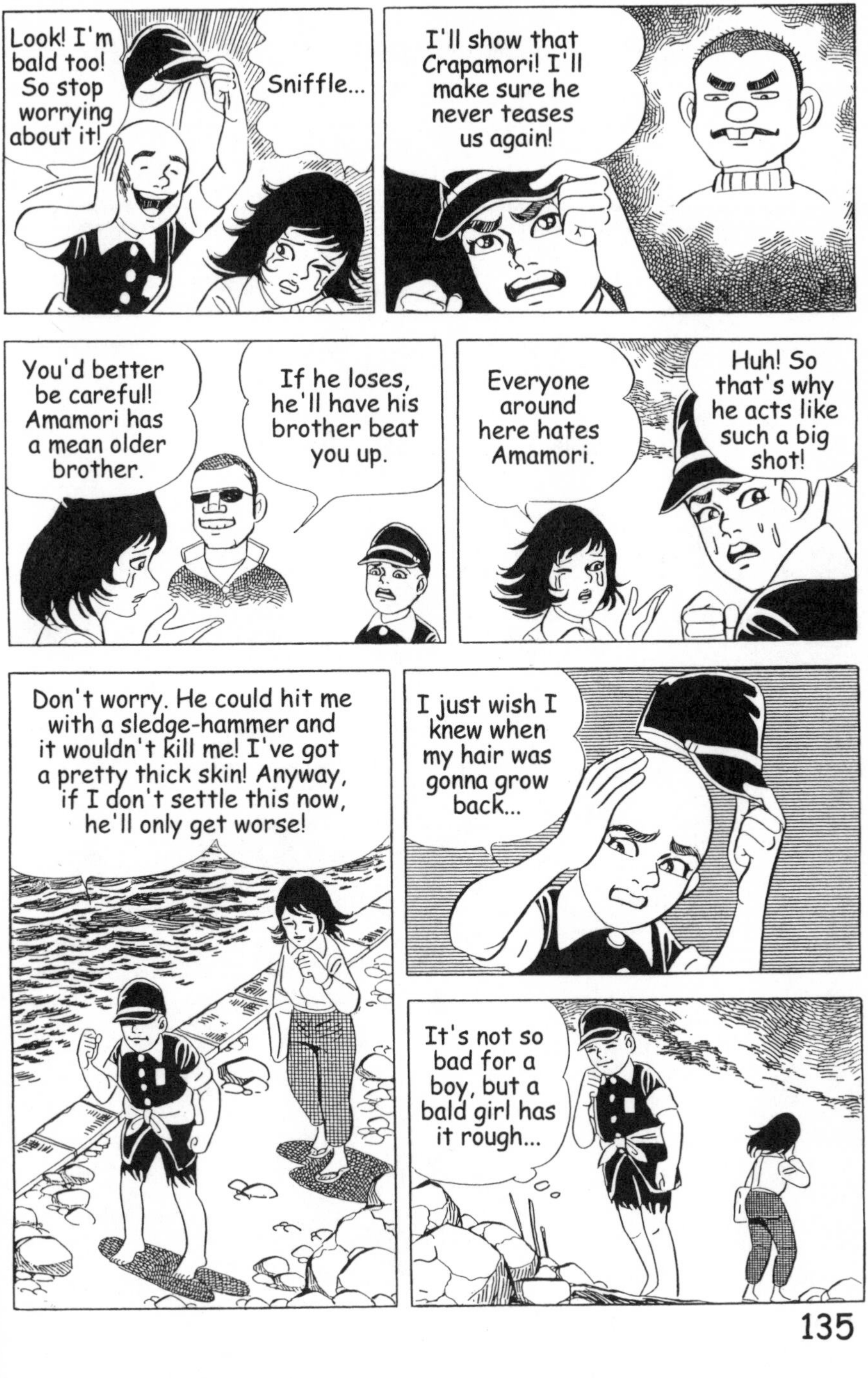
Look! I'm bald too! So stop worrying about it!
Sniffle...
I'll show that Crapamori! I'll make sure he never teases us again!
You'd better be careful! Amamori has a mean older brother.
If he loses, he'll have his brother beat you up.
Everyone around here hates Amamori.
Huh! So that's why he acts like such a big shot!
Don't worry. He could hit me with a sledge-hammer and it wouldn't kill me! I've got a pretty thick skin! Anyway, if I don't settle this now, he'll only get worse!
I just wish I knew when my hair was gonna grow back...
It's not so bad for a boy, but a bald girl has it rough...

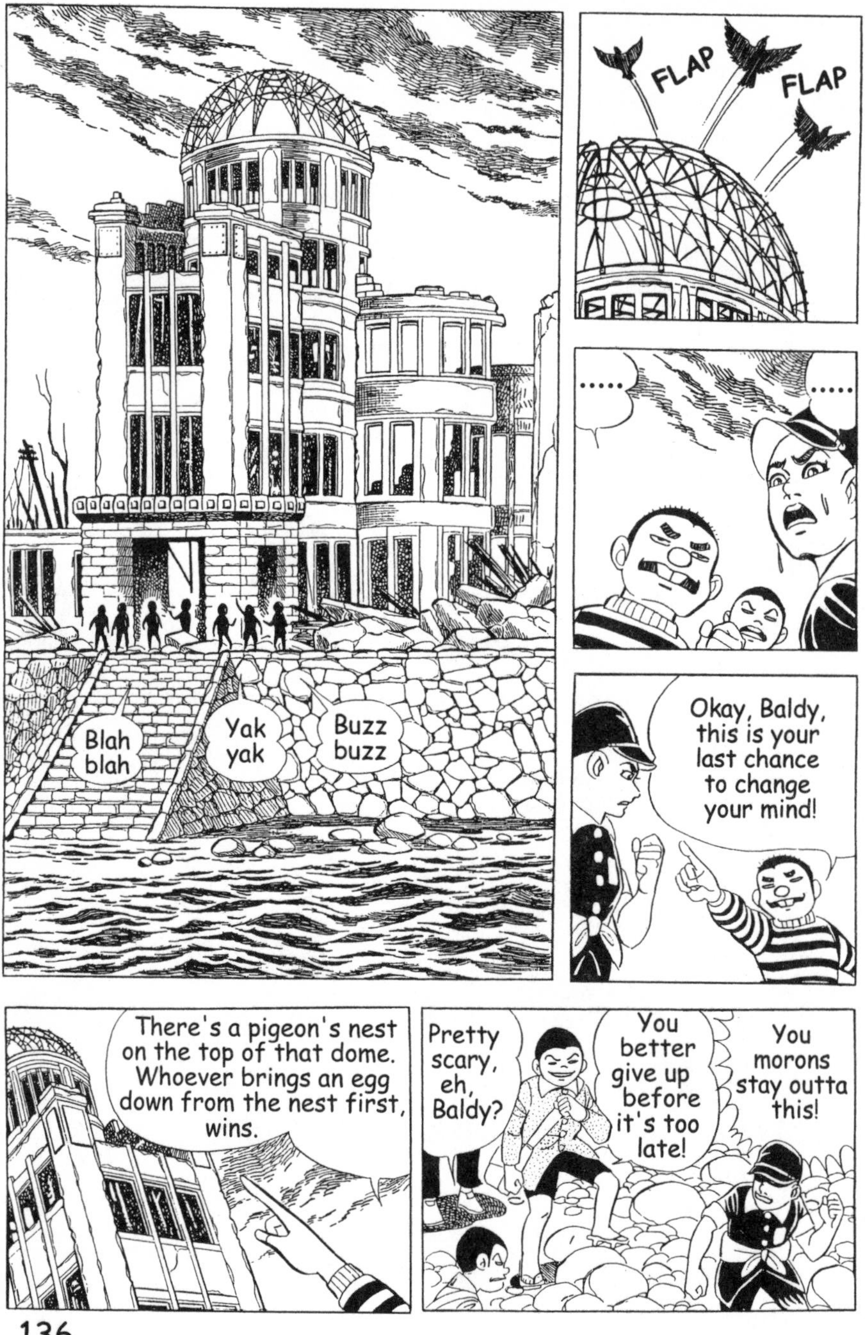
Blah blah
Yak yak
Buzz buzz
FLAP
FLAP
.....
.....
Okay, Baldy, this is your last chance to change your mind!
There's a pigeon's nest on the top of that dome. Whoever brings an egg down from the nest first, wins.
Pretty scary, eh, Baldy?
You better give up before it's too late!
You morons stay outta this!

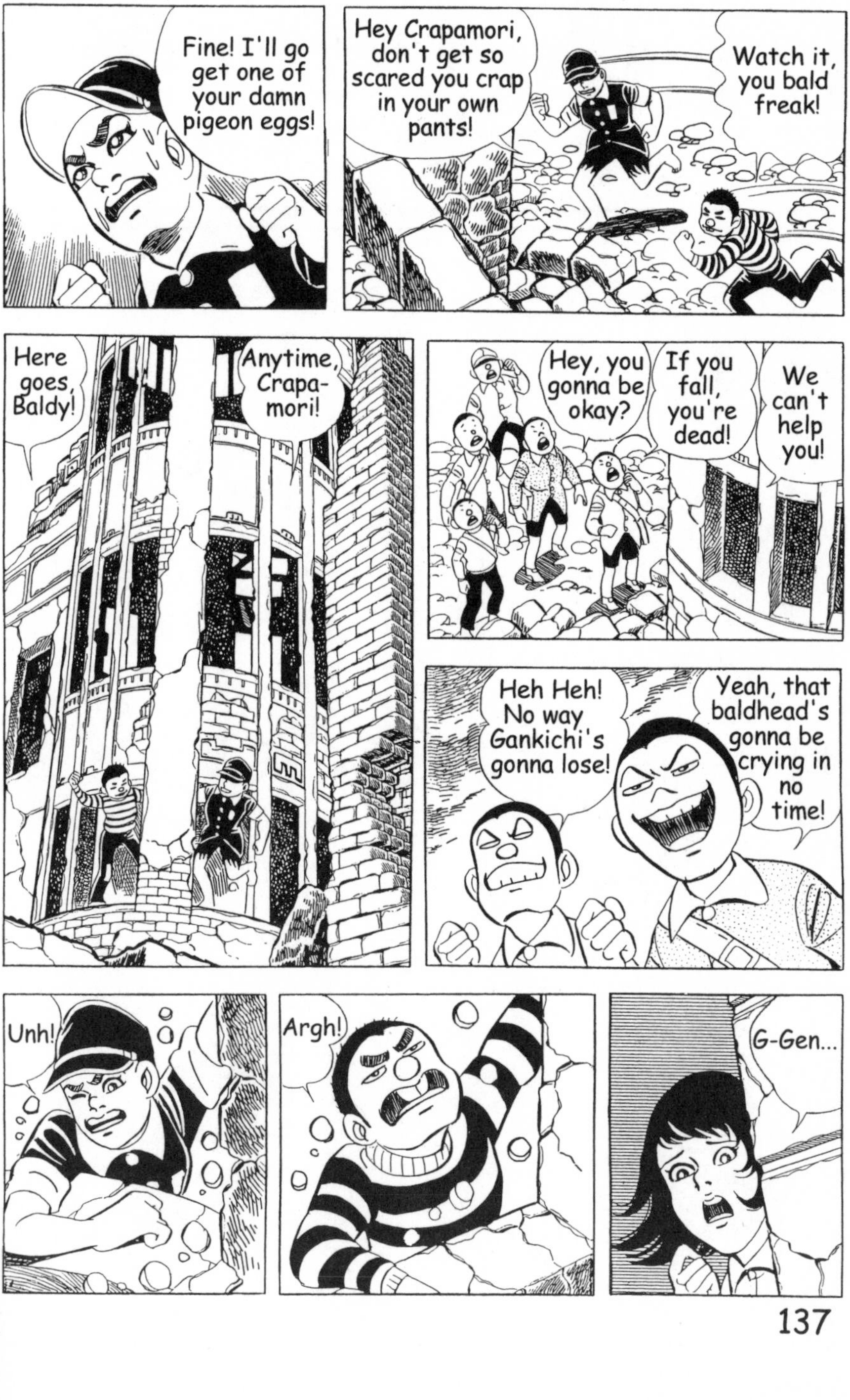

Fine! I'll go get one of your damn pigeon eggs!
Hey Crapamori, don't get so scared you crap in your own pants!
Watch it, you bald freak!
Here goes, Baldy!
Anytime, Crapamori!
Hey, you gonna be okay?
If you fall, you're dead!
We can't help you!
Heh Heh! No way Gankichi's gonna lose!
Yeah, that baldhead's gonna be crying in no time!
Unh!
Argh!
G-Gen...

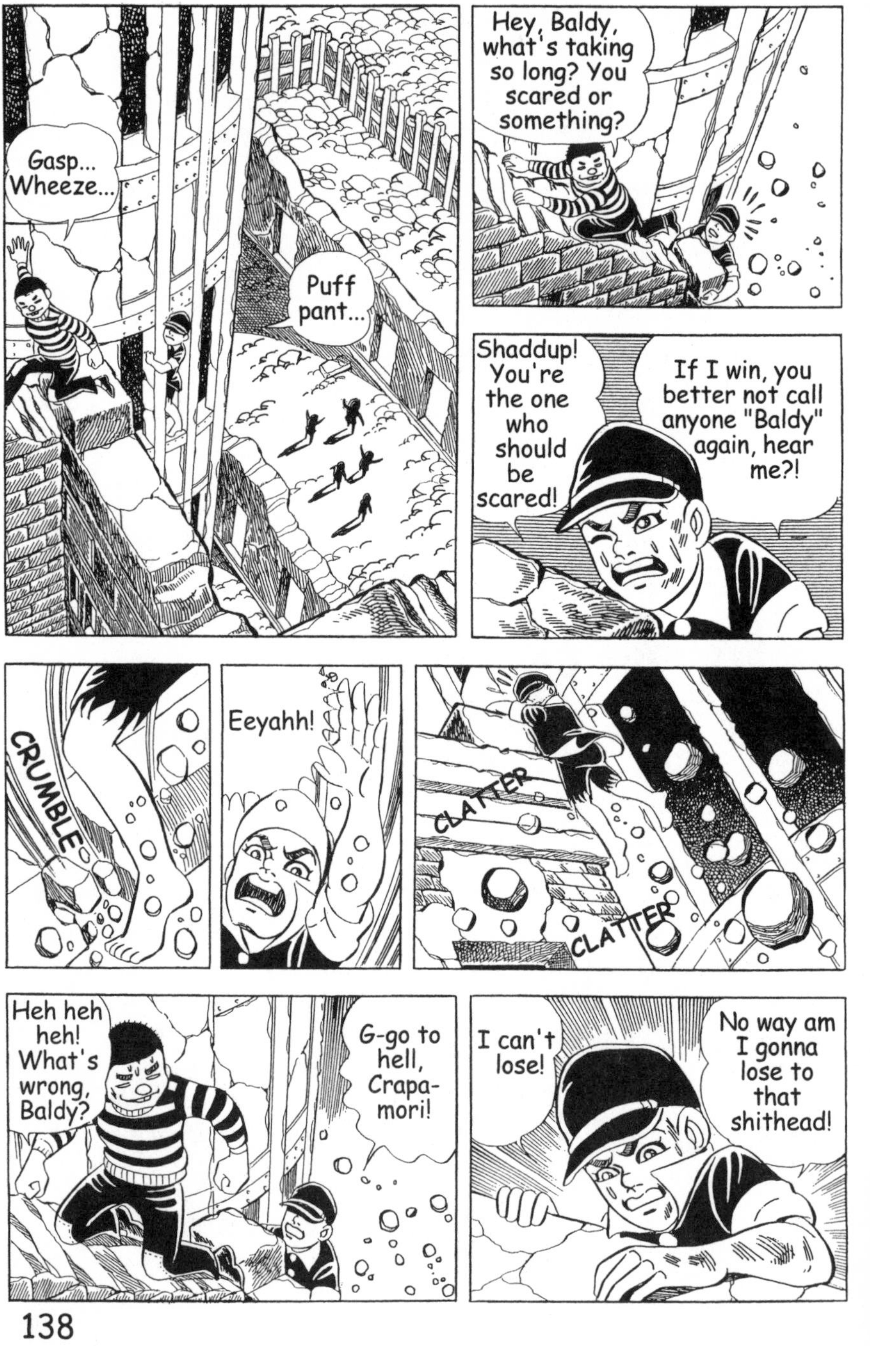
Gasp... Wheeze...
Puff pant...
Hey, Baldy, what's taking so long? You scared or something?
Shaddup! You're the one who should be scared!
If I win, you better not call anyone "Baldy" again, hear me?!
CRUMBLE
Eeyahh!
CLATTER
CLATTER
Heh heh heh! What's wrong, Baldy?
G-go to hell, Crapamori!
I can't lose!
No way am I gonna lose to that shithead!

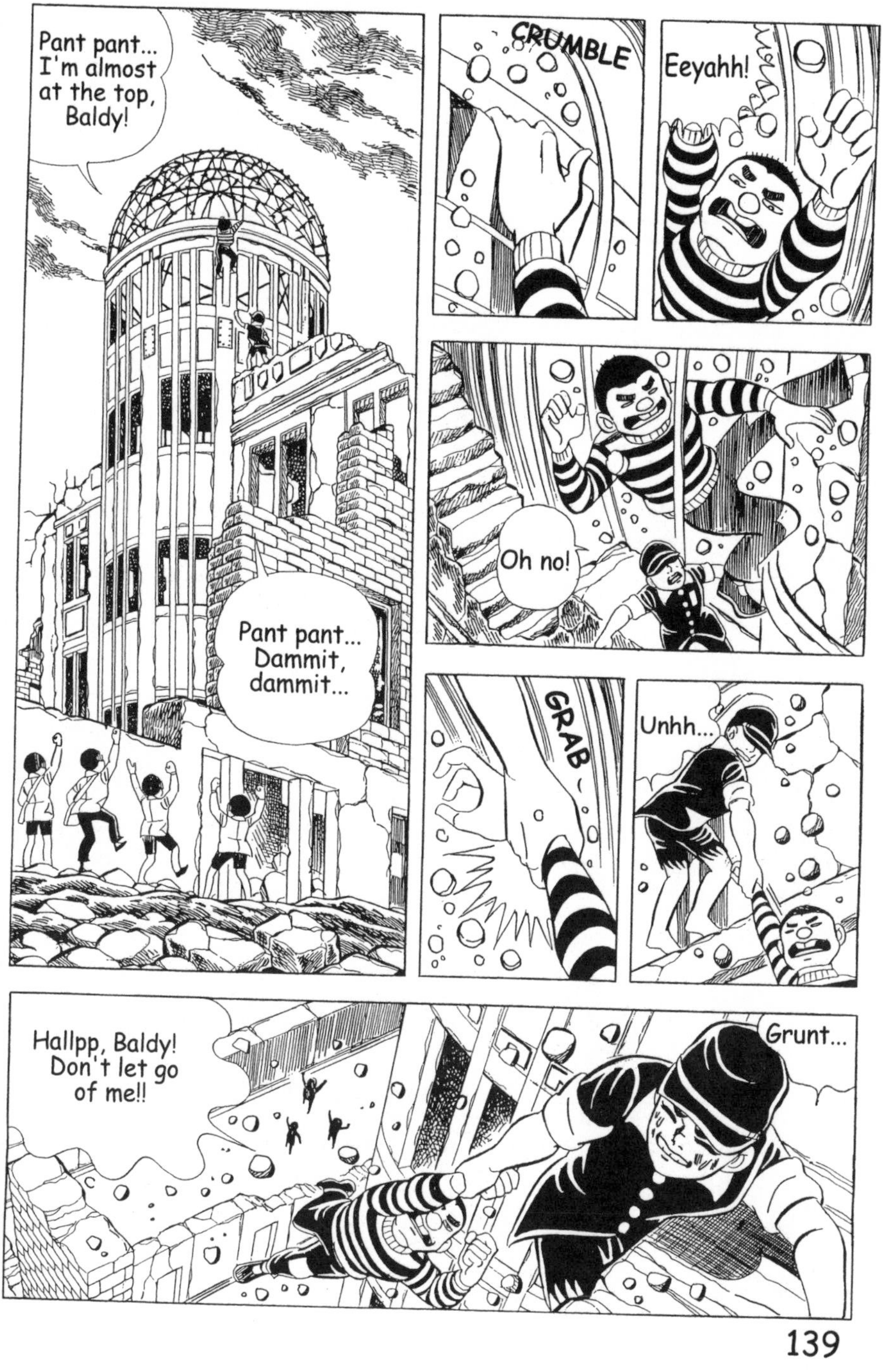
Pant pant... I'm almost at the top, Baldy!
Pant pant... Dammit, dammit...
CRUMBLE
Eeyahh!
Oh no!
GRAB
Unhh...
Hallpp, Baldy! Don't let go of me!!
Grunt...

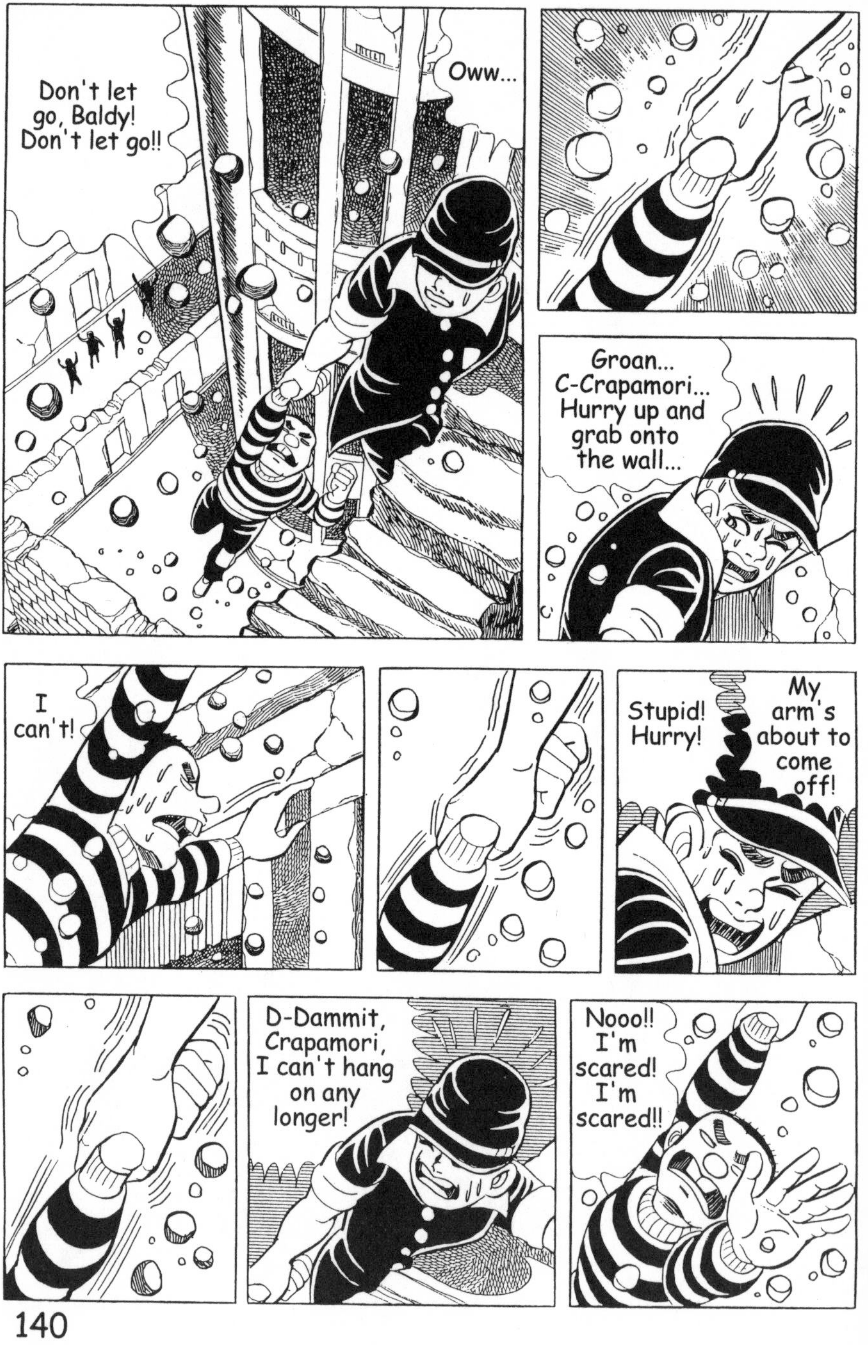
Don't let go, Baldy! Don't let go!!
Oww...
Groan... C-Crapamori... Hurry up and grab onto the wall...
I can't!
Stupid! Hurry!
My arm's about to come off!
D-Dammit, Crapamori, I can't hang on any longer!
Nooo!! I'm scared! I'm scared!!

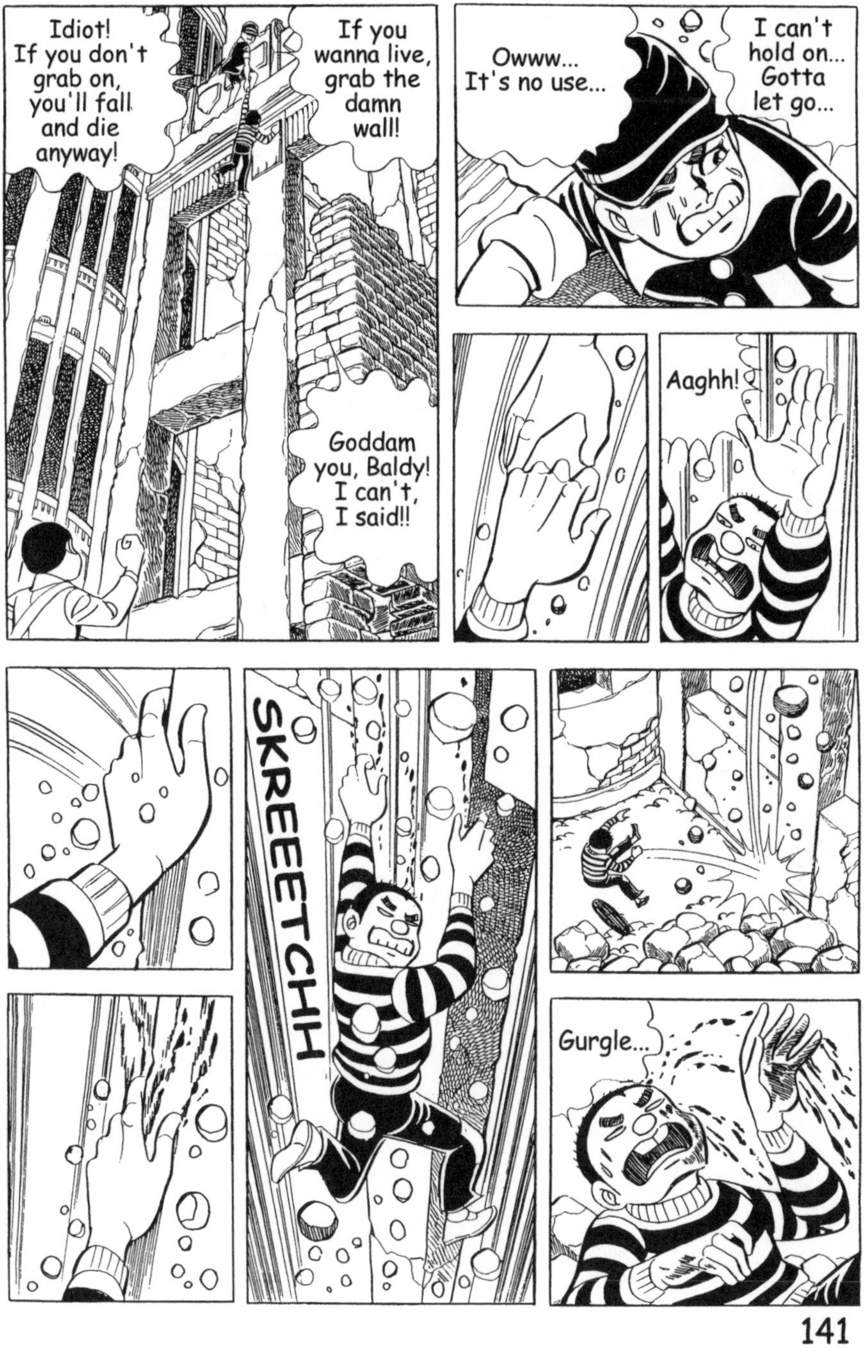
Idiot! If you don't grab on, you'll fall and die anyway!
If you wanna live, grab the damn wall!
Goddam you, Baldy! I can't, I said!!
Owww... It's no use...
I can't hold on... Gotta let go...
Aaghh!
SKREEETCHH
Gurgle...

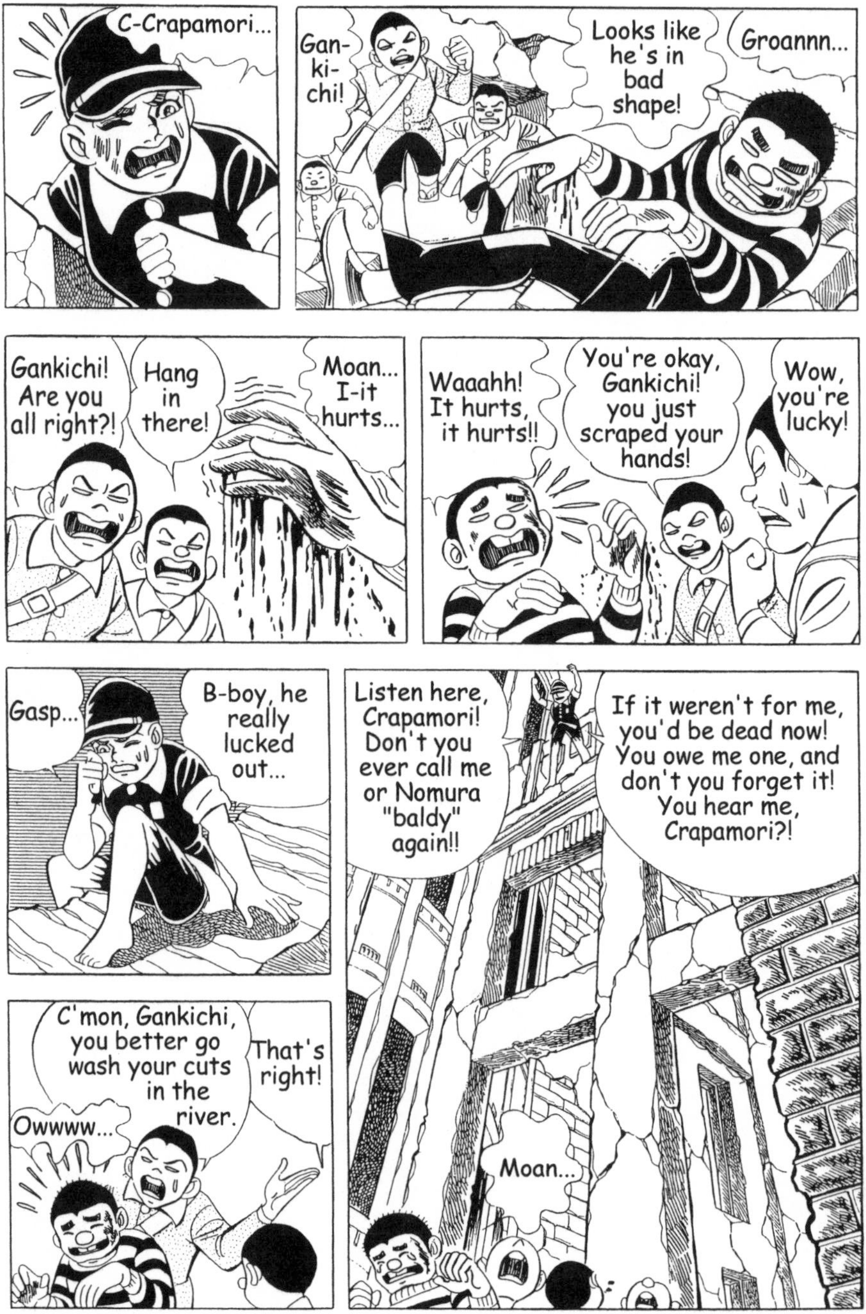
C-Crapamori...
Gan-
ki-
chi!
Looks like he's in bad shape!
Groannn...
Gankichi! Are you all right?!
Hang in there!
Moan... I-it hurts...
Waaahh! It hurts, it hurts!!
You're okay, Gankichi! you just scraped your hands!
Wow, you're lucky!
Gasp...
B-boy, he really lucked out...
Listen here, Crapamori! Don't you ever call me or Nomura "baldy" again!!
If it weren't for me, you'd be dead now! You owe me one, and don't you forget it! You hear me, Crapamori?!
Moan...
C'mon, Gankichi, you better go wash your cuts in the river.
That's right!
Owwww...

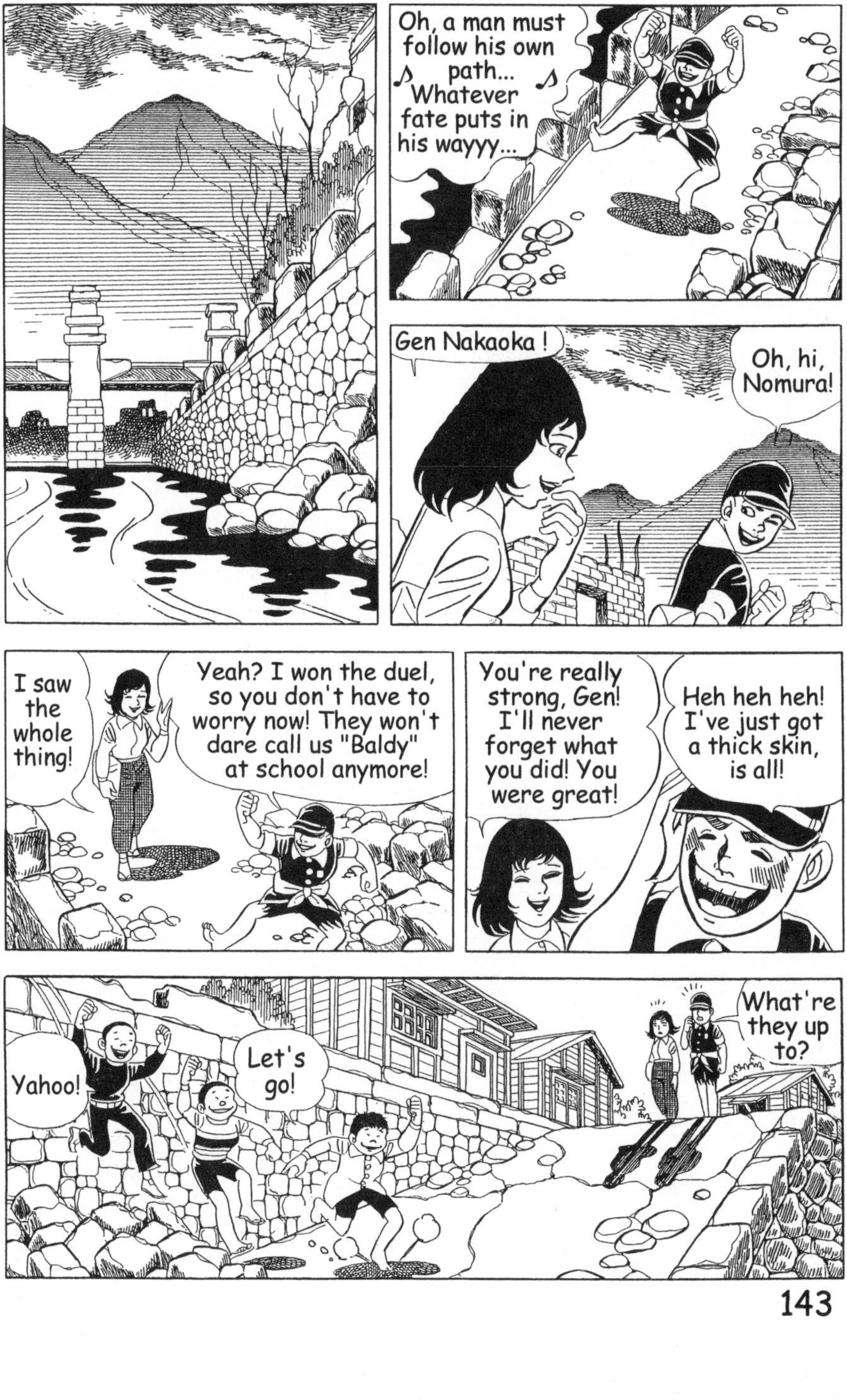

♪ Oh, a man must follow his own path... ♪ Whatever fate puts in his wayyy...
Gen Nakaoka !
Oh, hi, Nomura!
I saw the whole thing!
Yeah? I won the duel, so you don't have to worry now! They won't dare call us "Baldy" at school anymore!
You're really strong, Gen! I'll never forget what you did! You were great!
Heh heh heh! I've just got a thick skin, is all!
Yahoo!
Let's go!
What're they up to?

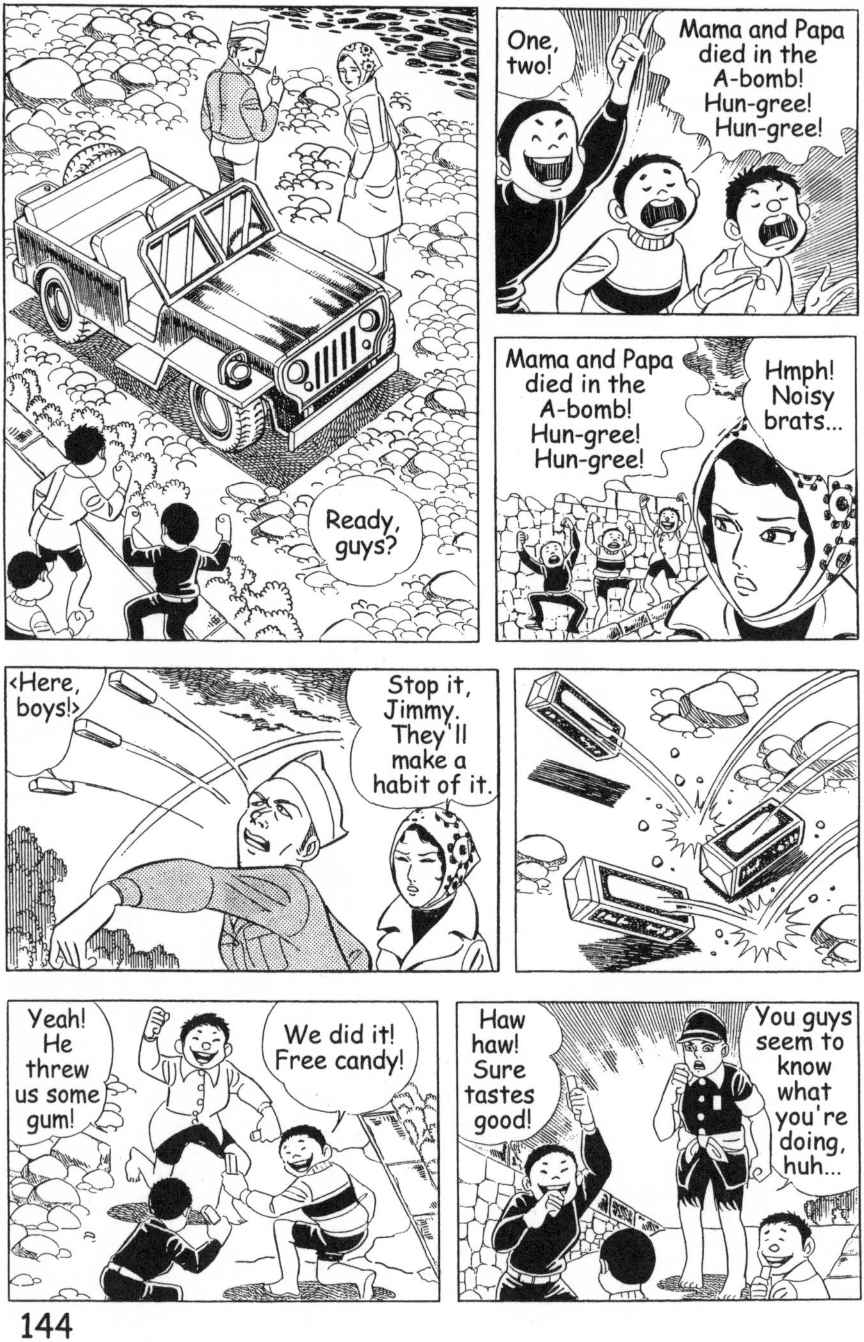
Ready, guys?
One, two!
Mama and Papa died in the A-bomb! Hun-gree! Hun-gree!
Mama and Papa died in the A-bomb! Hun-gree! Hun-gree!
Hmph! Noisy brats...
‹Here, boys!›
Stop it, Jimmy. They'll make a habit of it.
Yeah! He threw us some gum!
We did it! Free candy!
Haw haw! Sure tastes good!
You guys seem to know what you're doing, huh...

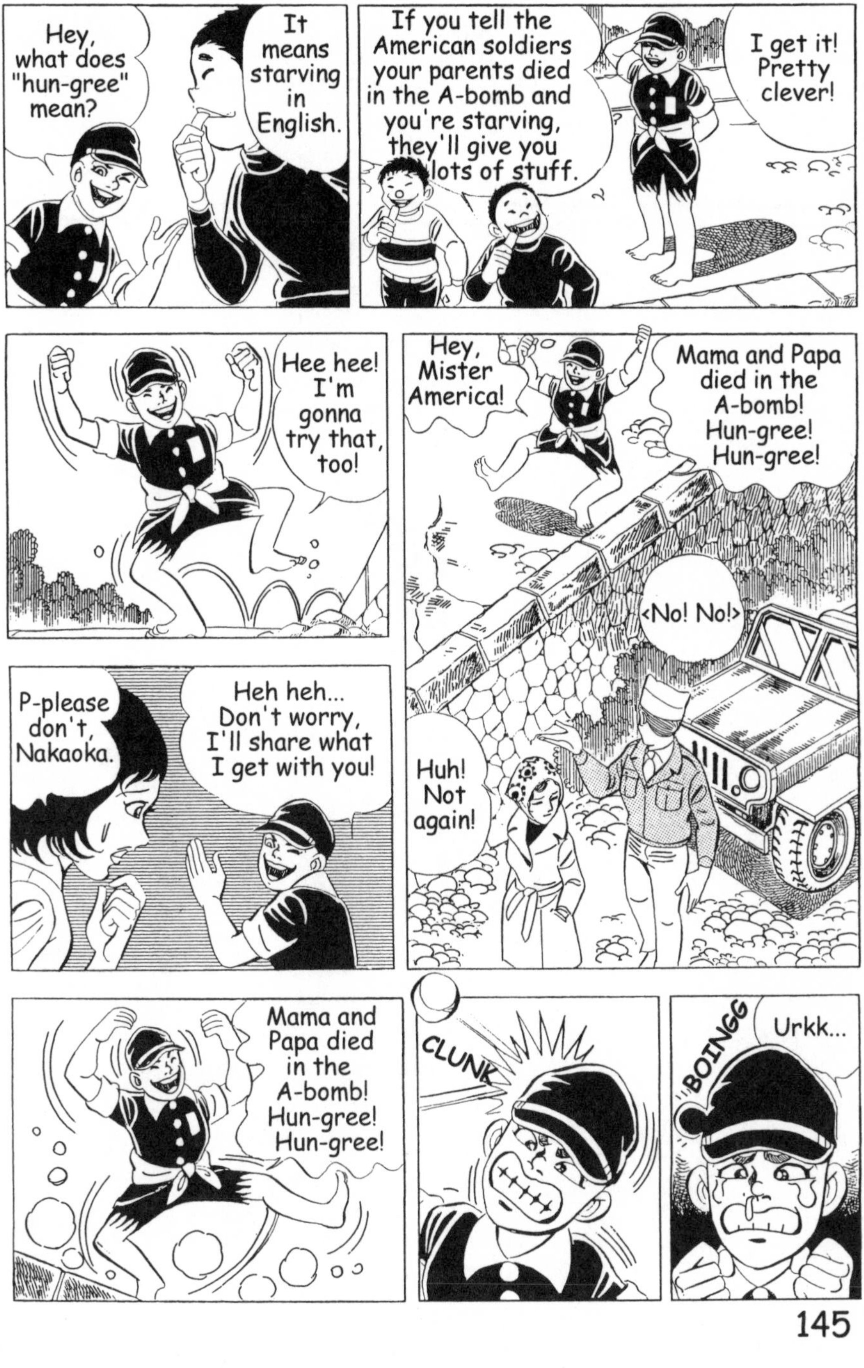
Hey, what does "hun-gree" mean?
It means starving in English.
If you tell the American soldiers your parents died in the A-bomb and you're starving, they'll give you lots of stuff.
I get it! Pretty clever!
Hee hee! I'm gonna try that, too!
Hey, Mister America!
Mama and Papa died in the A-bomb! Hun-gree! Hun-gree!
<No! No!>
Huh! Not again!
P-please don't, Nakaoka.
Heh heh... Don't worry, I'll share what I get with you!
Mama and Papa died in the A-bomb! Hun-gree! Hun-gree!
CLUNK
BOINGG
Urkk...

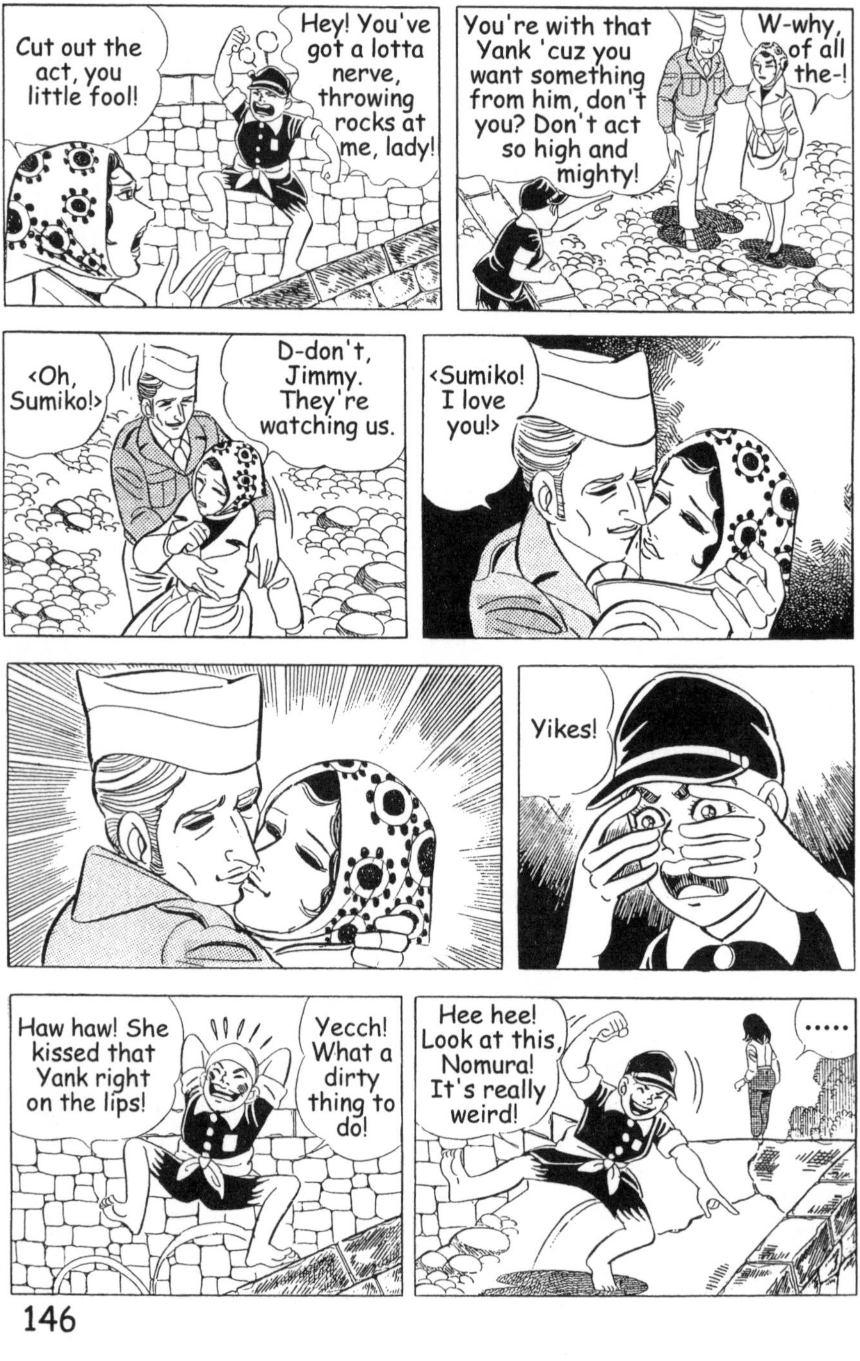
Cut out the act, you little fool!
Hey! You've got a lotta nerve, throwing rocks at me, lady!
You're with that Yank 'cuz you want something from him, don't you? Don't act so high and mighty!
W-why, of all the-!
<Oh, Sumiko!>
D-don't, Jimmy. They're watching us.
<Sumiko! I love you!>
Yikes!
Haw haw! She kissed that Yank right on the lips!
Yecch! What a dirty thing to do!
Hee hee! Look at this, Nomura! It's really weird!
.....

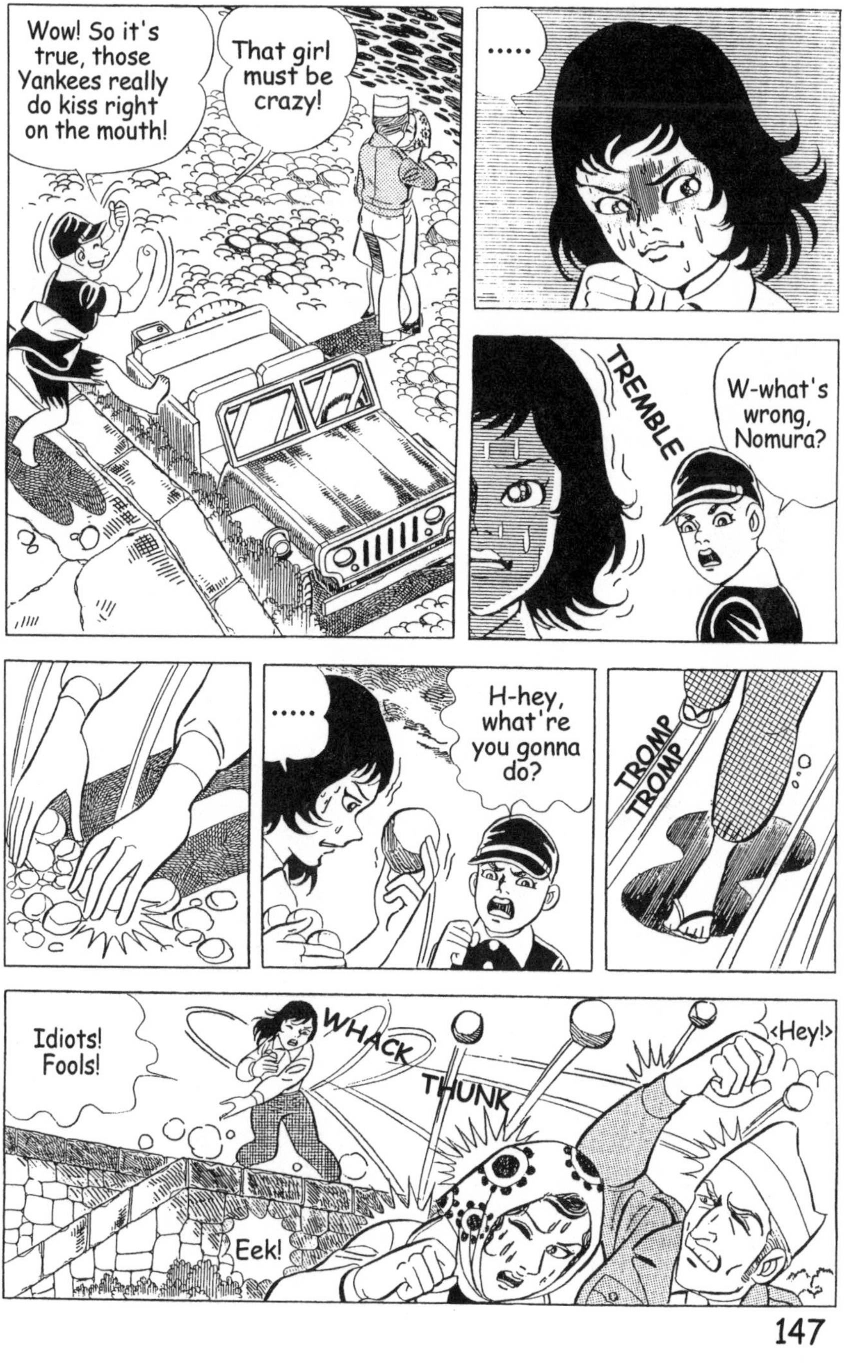
Wow! So it's true, those Yankees really do kiss right on the mouth!
That girl must be crazy!
.....
TREMBLE
W-what's wrong, Nomura?
.....
H-hey, what're you gonna do?
TROMP TROMP
Idiots! Fools!
WHACK
THUNK
<Hey!>
Eek!

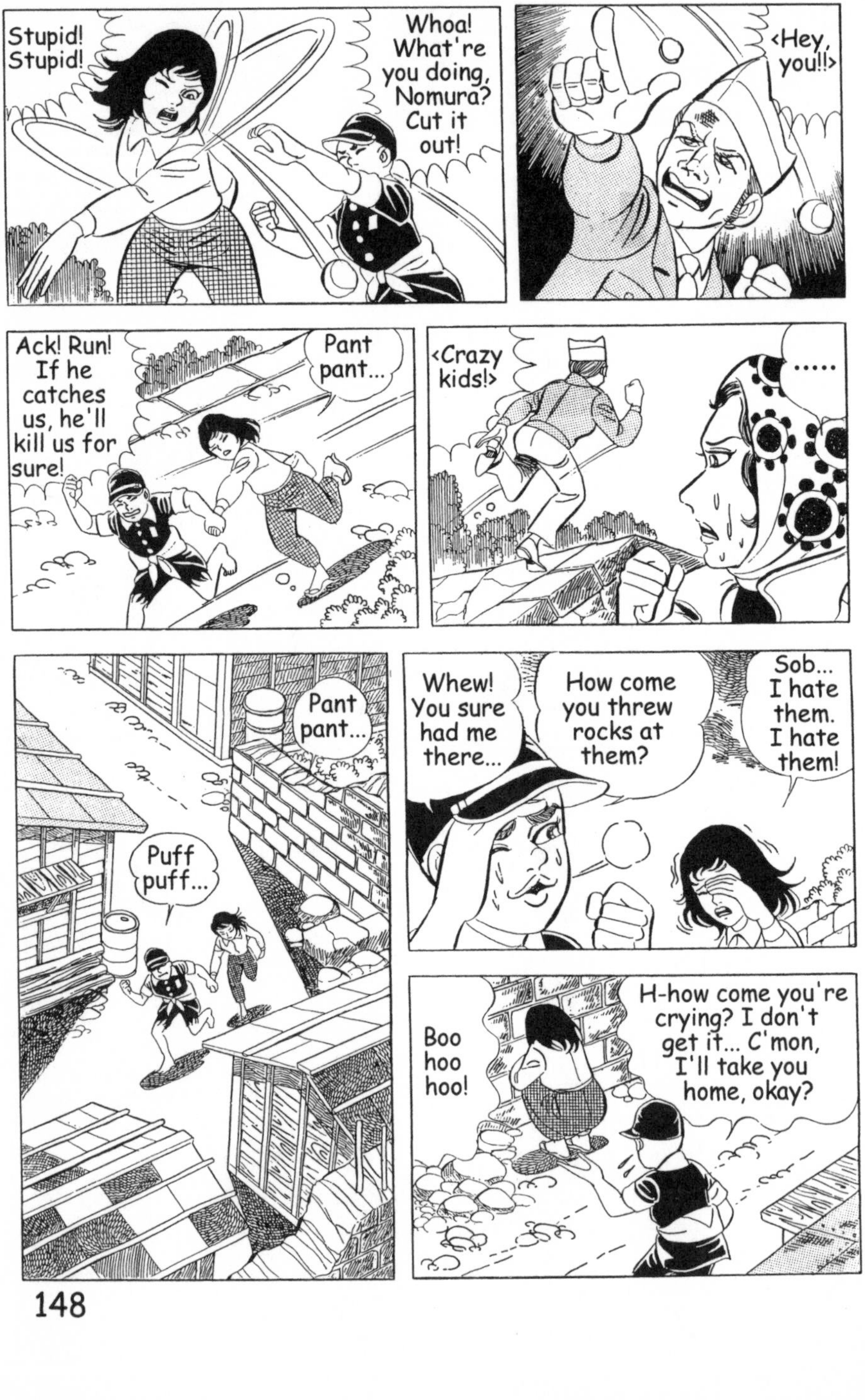

Stupid! Stupid!
Whoa! What're you doing, Nomura? Cut it out!
‹Hey, you!!›
Ack! Run! If he catches us, he'll kill us for sure!
Pant pant...
‹Crazy kids!›
.....
Pant pant...
Puff puff...
Whew! You sure had me there...
How come you threw rocks at them?
Sob... I hate them. I hate them!
Boo hoo hoo!
H-how come you're crying? I don't get it... C'mon, I'll take you home, okay?

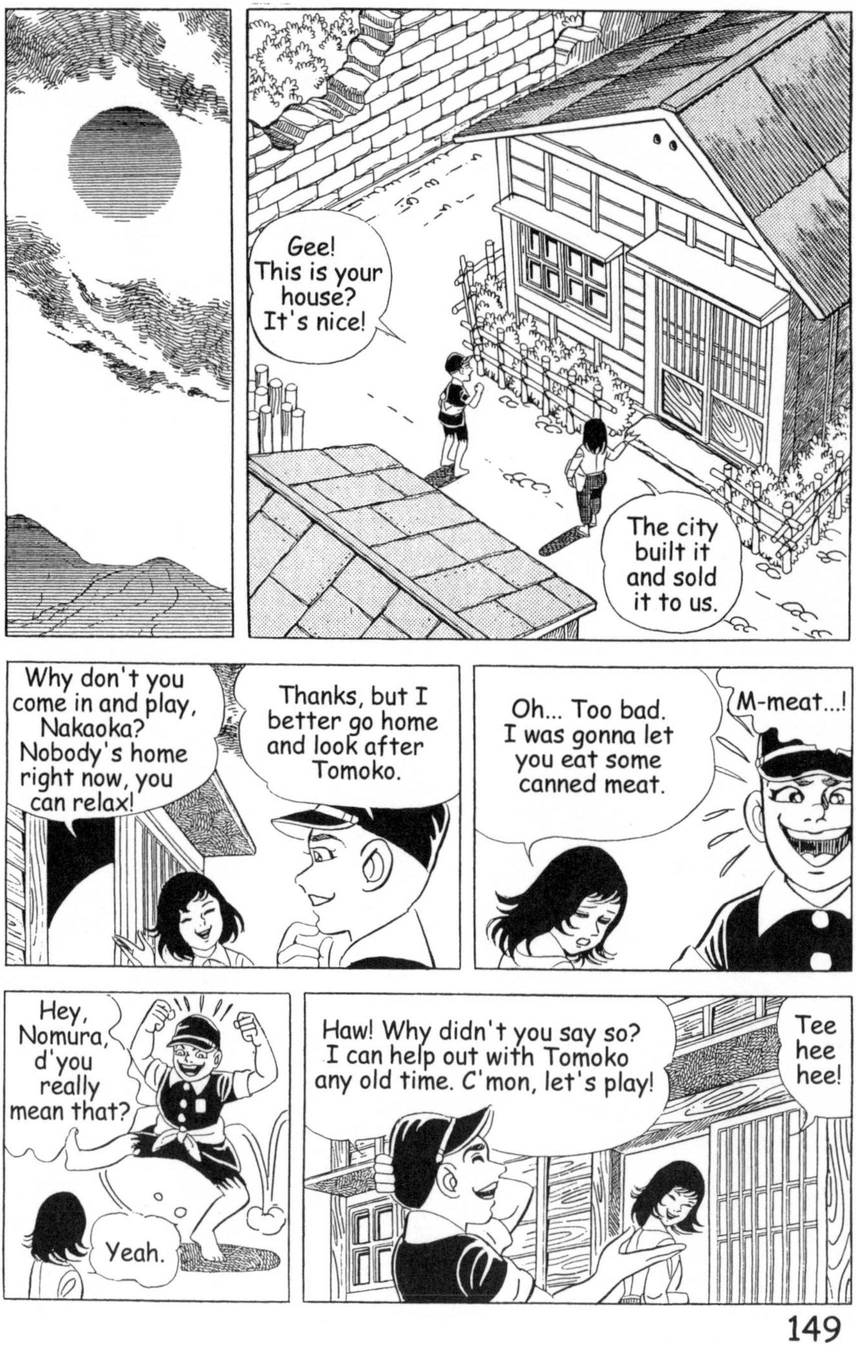
Gee! This is your house? It's nice!
The city built it and sold it to us.
Why don't you come in and play, Nakaoka? Nobody's home right now, you can relax!
Thanks, but I better go home and look after Tomoko.
Oh... Too bad. I was gonna let you eat some canned meat.
M-meat...!
Hey, Nomura, d'you really mean that?
Yeah.
Haw! Why didn't you say so? I can help out with Tomoko any old time. C'mon, let's play!
Tee hee hee!

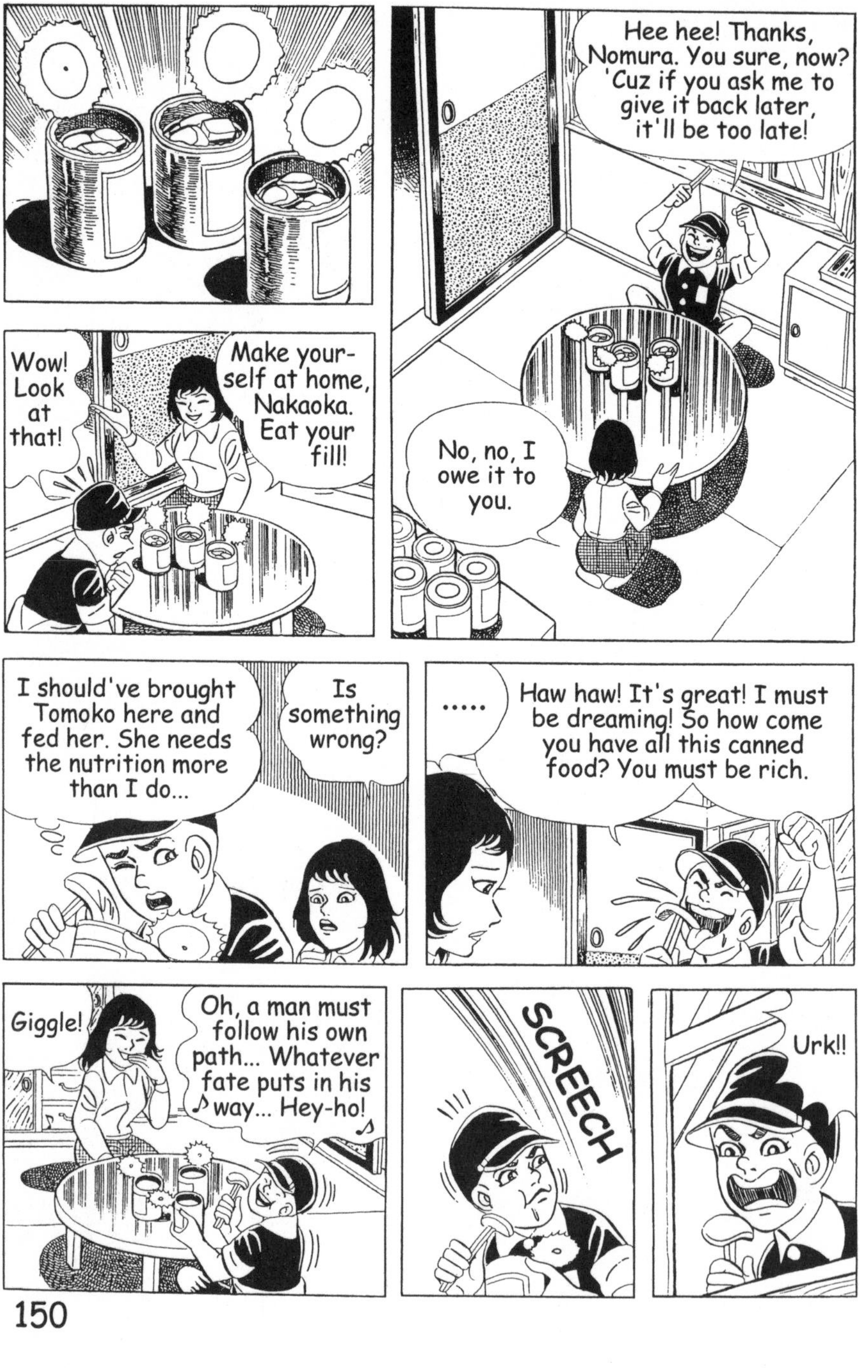
Wow! Look at that!
Make your-self at home, Nakaoka. Eat your fill!
Hee hee! Thanks, Nomura. You sure, now? 'Cuz if you ask me to give it back later, it'll be too late!
No, no, I owe it to you.
I should've brought Tomoko here and fed her. She needs the nutrition more than I do...
Is something wrong?
.....
Haw haw! It's great! I must be dreaming! So how come you have all this canned food? You must be rich.
Giggle!
Oh, a man must follow his own path... Whatever fate puts in his ♪way... Hey-ho! ♪
SCREECH
Urk!!

Oh no! T-the Yank and that girl have come after us!

Hurry, Nomura, we better run for it!

CLATTER

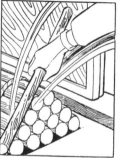

Ack!

.....

H-hey! W-what're you-?!

151

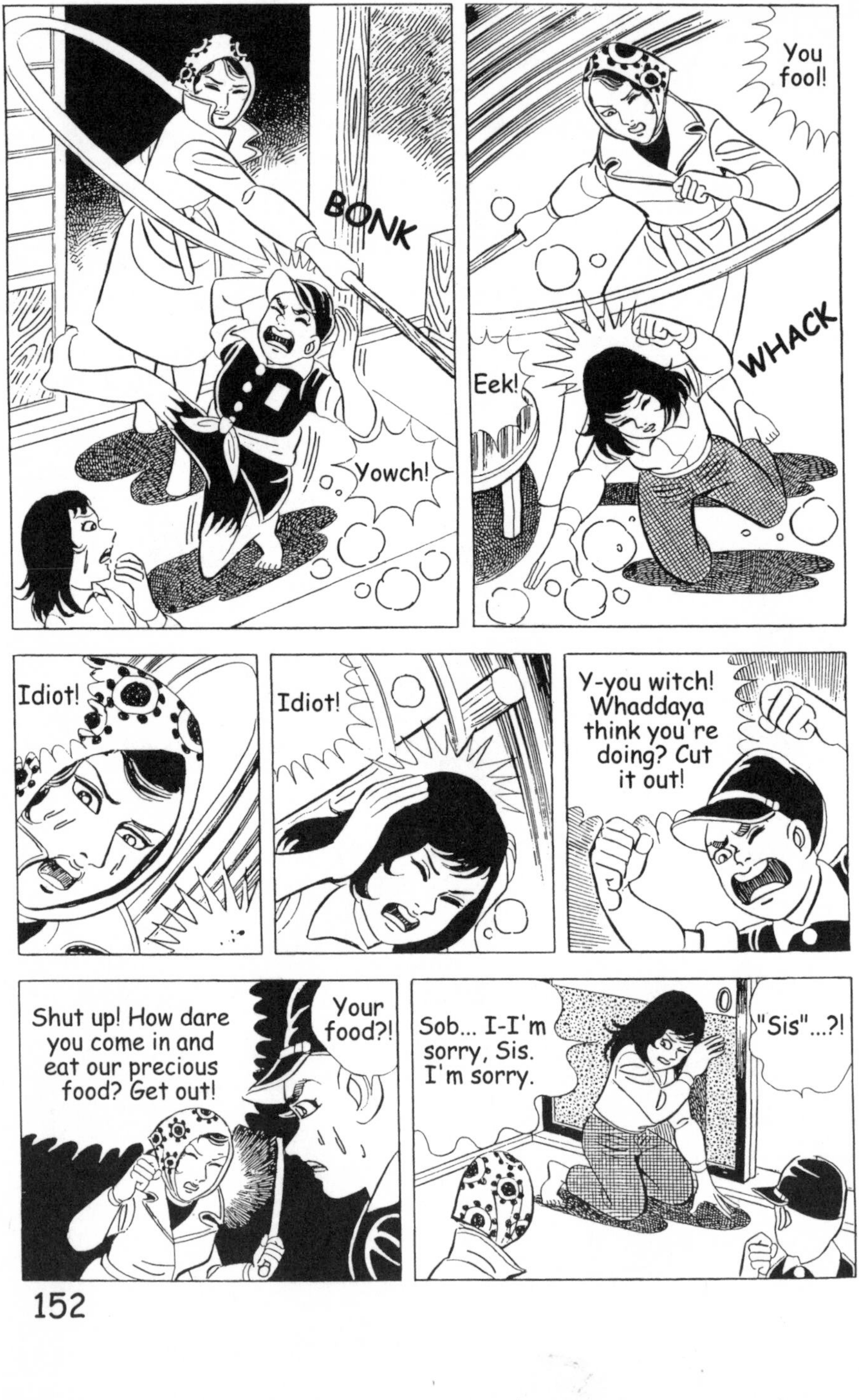
BONK
Yowch!
You fool!
WHACK
Eek!
Idiot!
Idiot!
Y-you witch! Whaddaya think you're doing? Cut it out!
Shut up! How dare you come in and eat our precious food? Get out!
Your food?!
Sob... I-I'm sorry, Sis. I'm sorry.
"Sis"...?!

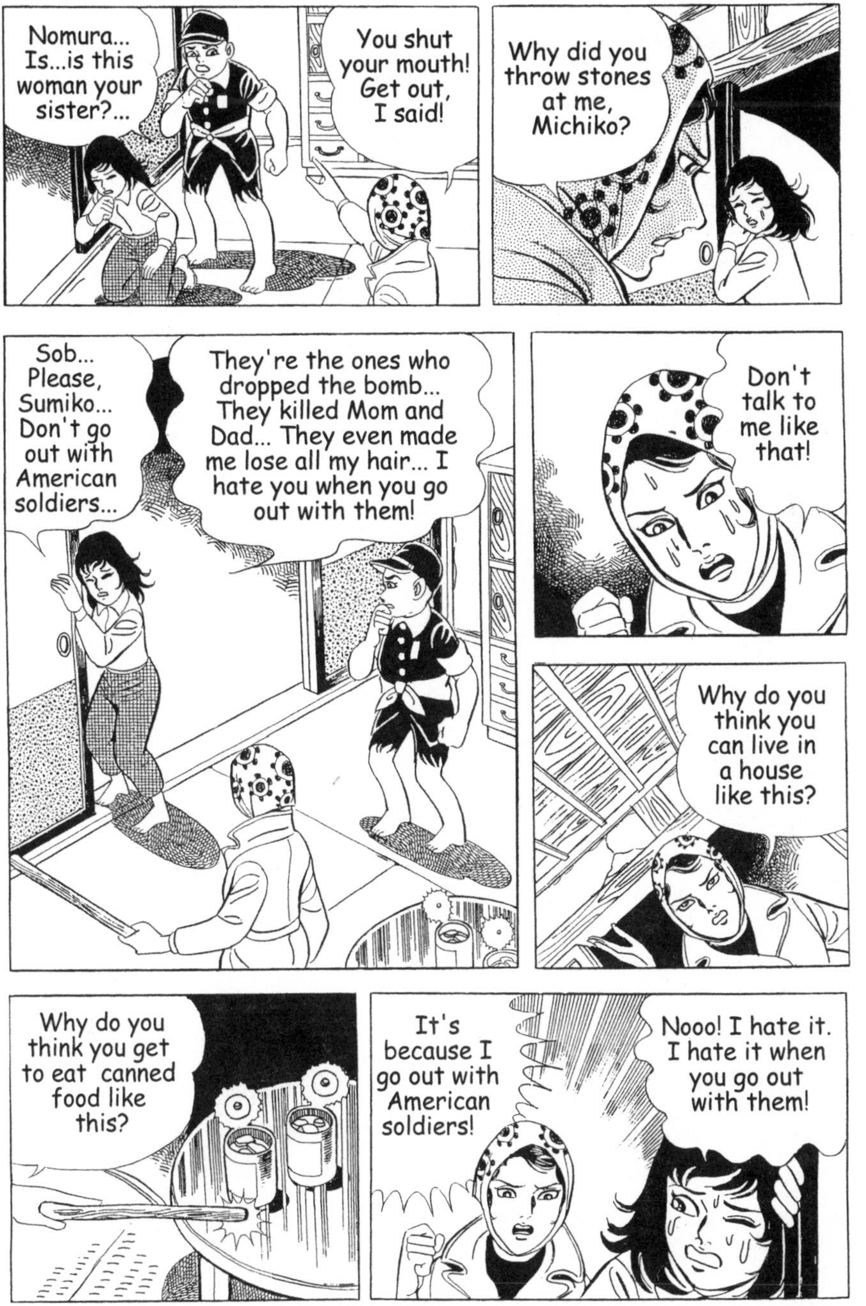

Nomura... Is...is this woman your sister?...
You shut your mouth! Get out, I said!
Why did you throw stones at me, Michiko?
Sob... Please, Sumiko... Don't go out with American soldiers...
They're the ones who dropped the bomb... They killed Mom and Dad... They even made me lose all my hair... I hate you when you go out with them!
Don't talk to me like that!
Why do you think you can live in a house like this?
Why do you think you get to eat canned food like this?
It's because I go out with American soldiers!
Nooo! I hate it. I hate it when you go out with them!

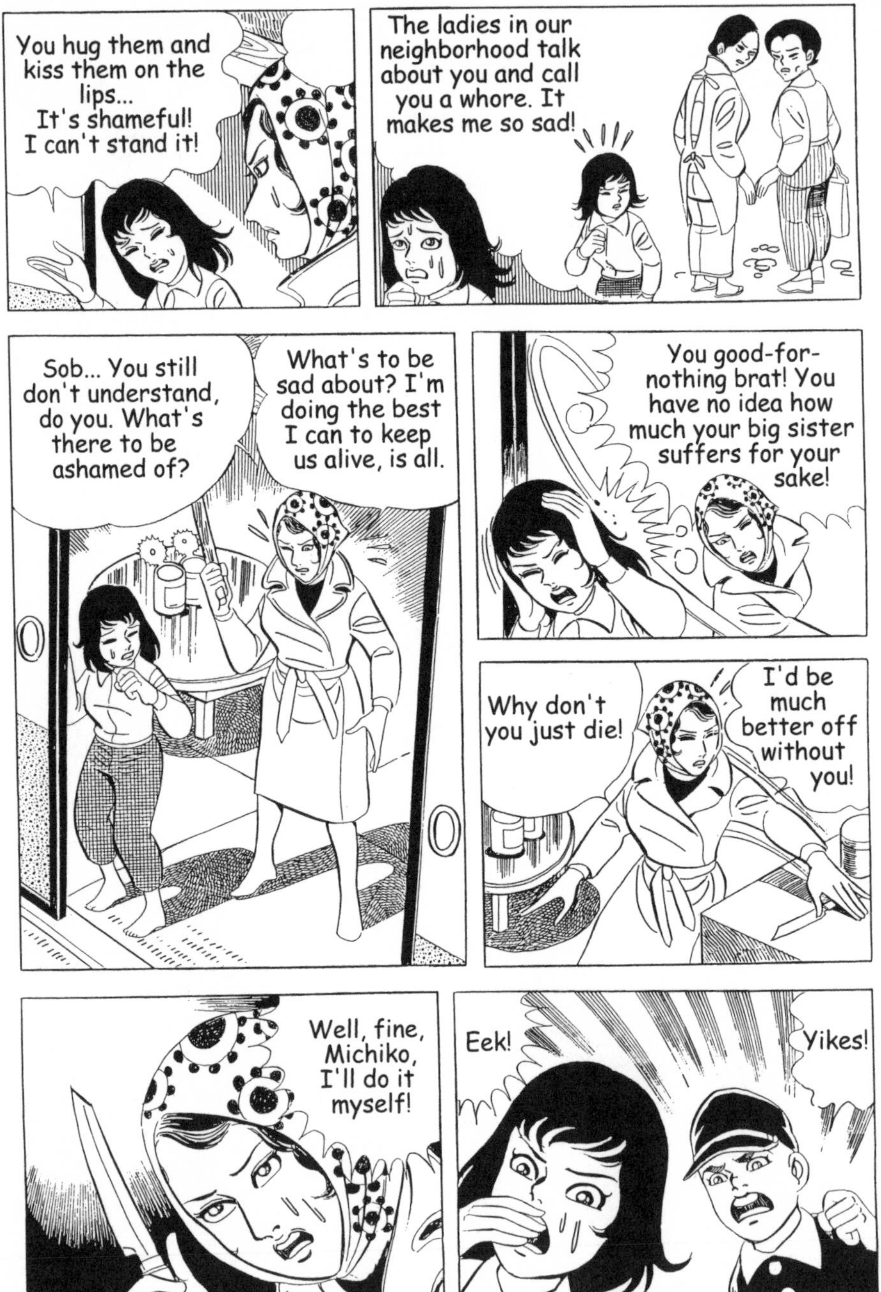
You hug them and kiss them on the lips... It's shameful! I can't stand it!
The ladies in our neighborhood talk about you and call you a whore. It makes me so sad!
Sob... You still don't understand, do you. What's there to be ashamed of?
What's to be sad about? I'm doing the best I can to keep us alive, is all.
You good-for-nothing brat! You have no idea how much your big sister suffers for your sake!
Why don't you just die!
I'd be much better off without you!
Well, fine, Michiko, I'll do it myself!
Eek!
Yikes!

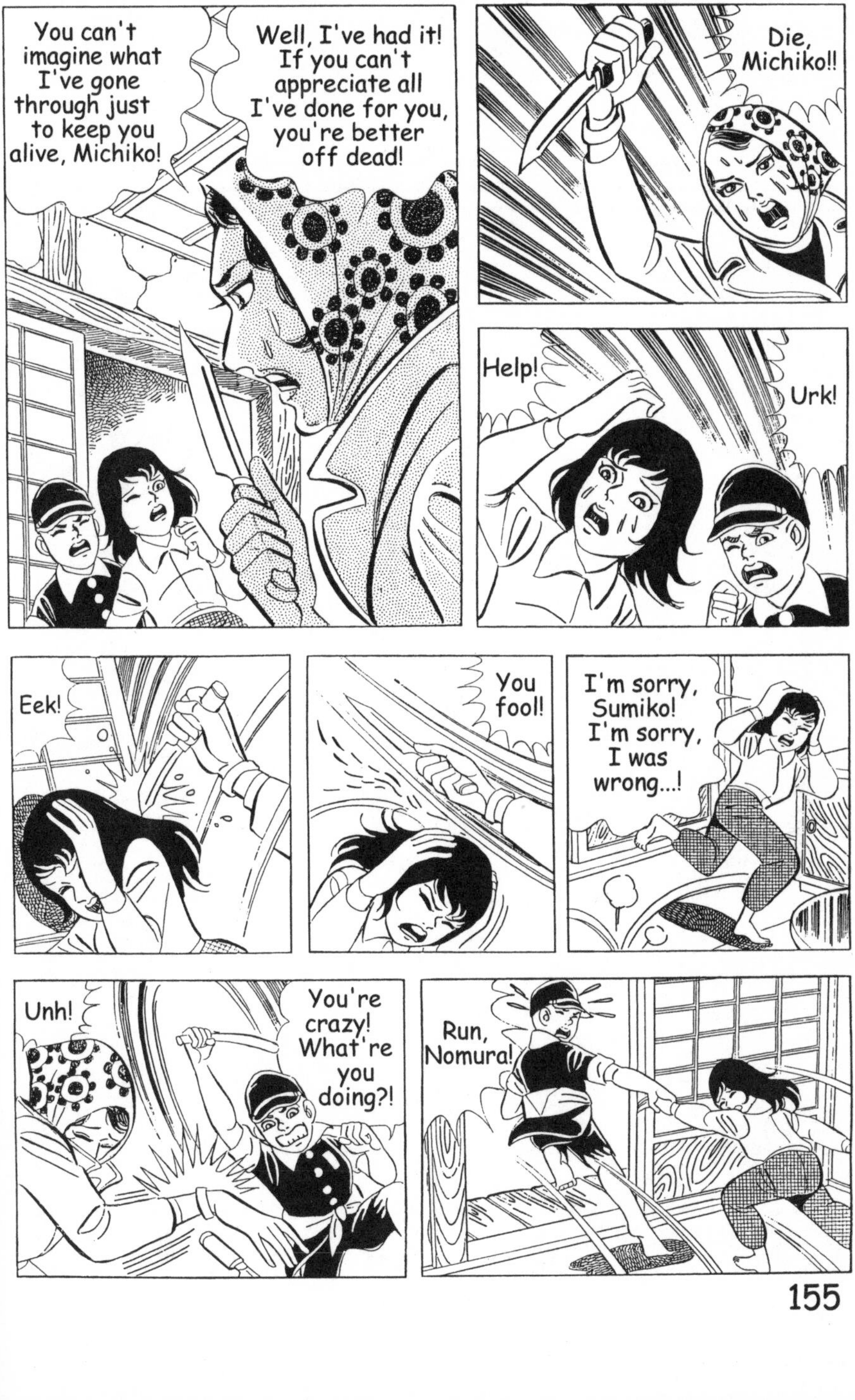
You can't imagine what I've gone through just to keep you alive, Michiko!
Well, I've had it! If you can't appreciate all I've done for you, you're better off dead!
Die, Michiko!!
Help!
Urk!
Eek!
You fool!
I'm sorry, Sumiko! I'm sorry, I was wrong...!
Unh!
You're crazy! What're you doing?!
Run, Nomura!

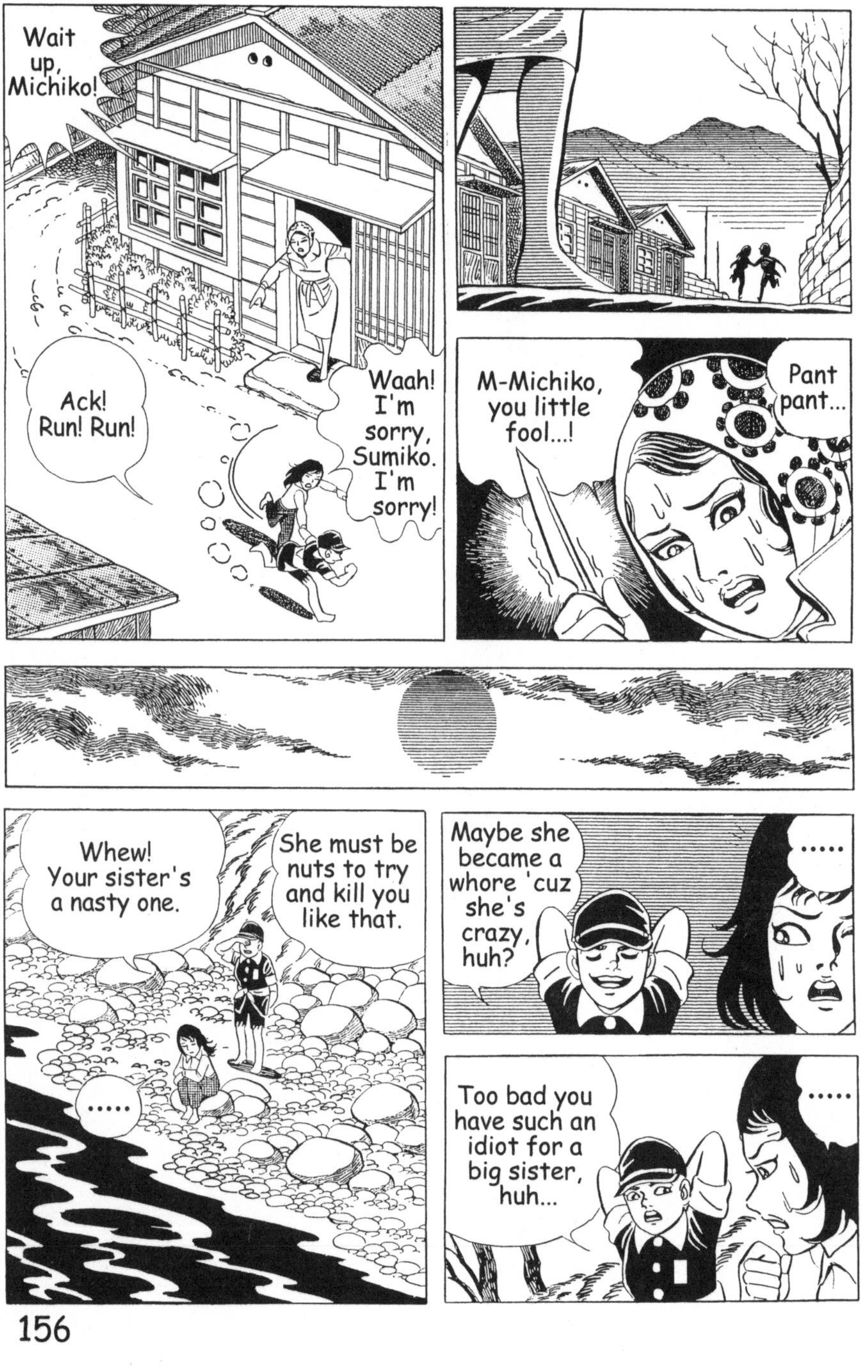
Wait up, Michiko!
Ack! Run! Run!
Waah! I'm sorry, Sumiko. I'm sorry!
M-Michiko, you little fool...!
Pant pant...
Whew! Your sister's a nasty one.
She must be nuts to try and kill you like that.
.....
Maybe she became a whore 'cuz she's crazy, huh?
.....
Too bad you have such an idiot for a big sister, huh...
.....

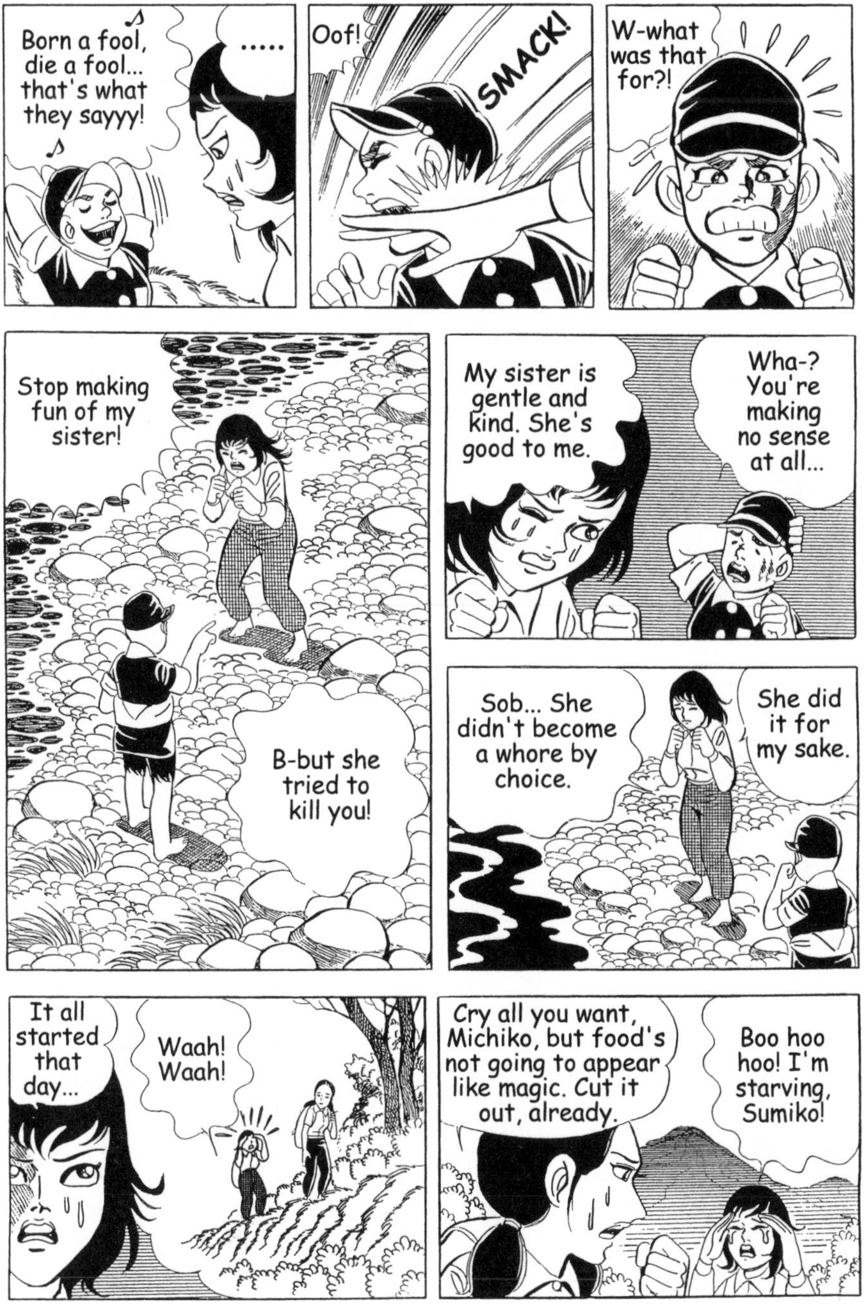

Born a fool, die a fool... that's what they sayyy!
.....
Oof!
SMACK!
W-what was that for?!
Stop making fun of my sister!
B-but she tried to kill you!
My sister is gentle and kind. She's good to me.
Wha-? You're making no sense at all...
Sob... She didn't become a whore by choice.
She did it for my sake.
It all started that day...
Waah! Waah!
Cry all you want, Michiko, but food's not going to appear like magic. Cut it out, already.
Boo hoo hoo! I'm starving, Sumiko!

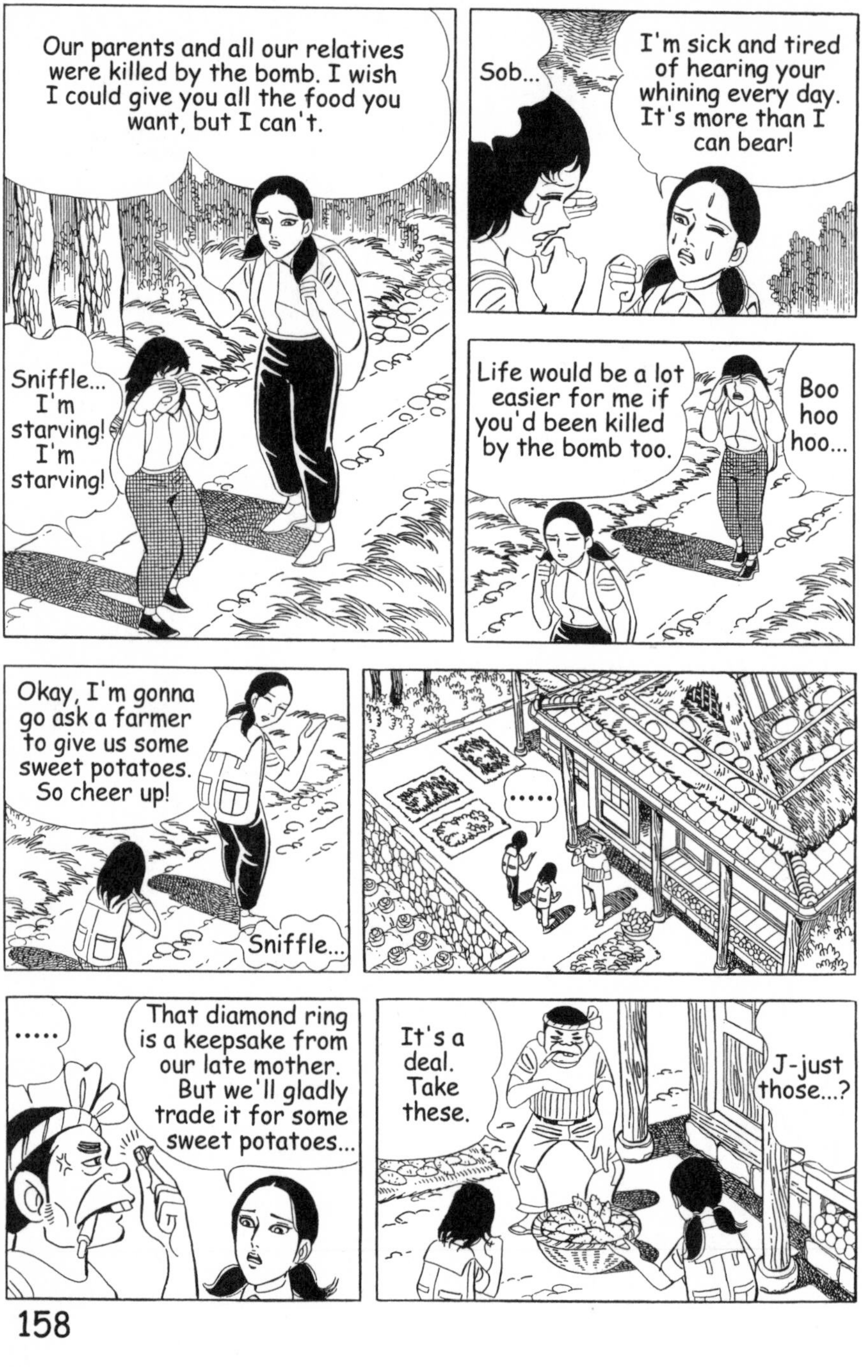
Our parents and all our relatives were killed by the bomb. I wish I could give you all the food you want, but I can't.
Sniffle... I'm starving! I'm starving!
Sob...
I'm sick and tired of hearing your whining every day. It's more than I can bear!
Life would be a lot easier for me if you'd been killed by the bomb too.
Boo hoo hoo...
Okay, I'm gonna go ask a farmer to give us some sweet potatoes. So cheer up!
Sniffle...
.....
.....
That diamond ring is a keepsake from our late mother. But we'll gladly trade it for some sweet potatoes...
It's a deal. Take these.
J-just those...?

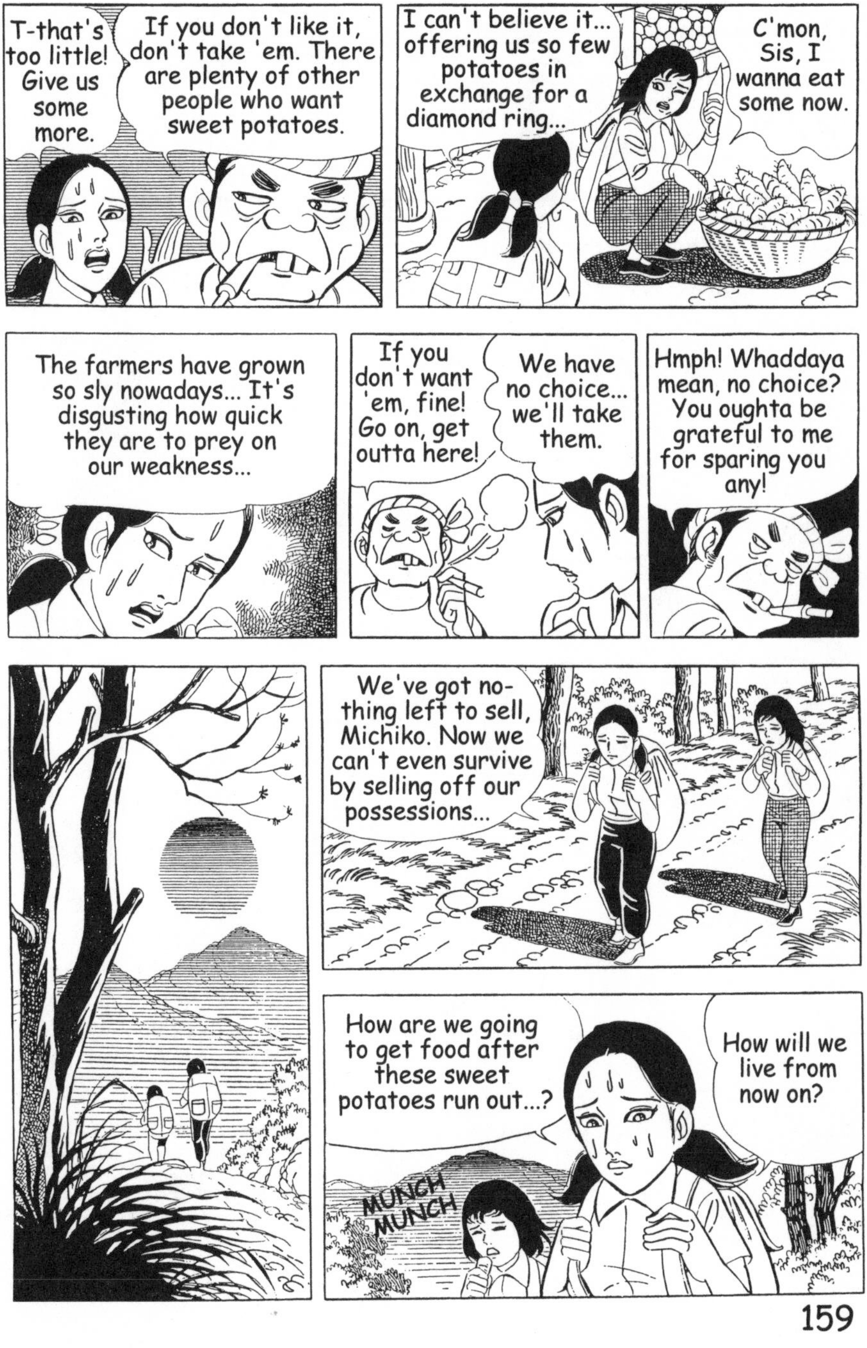
T-that's too little! Give us some more.
If you don't like it, don't take 'em. There are plenty of other people who want sweet potatoes.
I can't believe it... offering us so few potatoes in exchange for a diamond ring...
C'mon, Sis, I wanna eat some now.
The farmers have grown so sly nowadays... It's disgusting how quick they are to prey on our weakness...
If you don't want 'em, fine! Go on, get outta here!
We have no choice... we'll take them.
Hmph! Whaddaya mean, no choice? You oughta be grateful to me for sparing you any!
We've got nothing left to sell, Michiko. Now we can't even survive by selling off our possessions...
How are we going to get food after these sweet potatoes run out...?
How will we live from now on?
MUNCH MUNCH

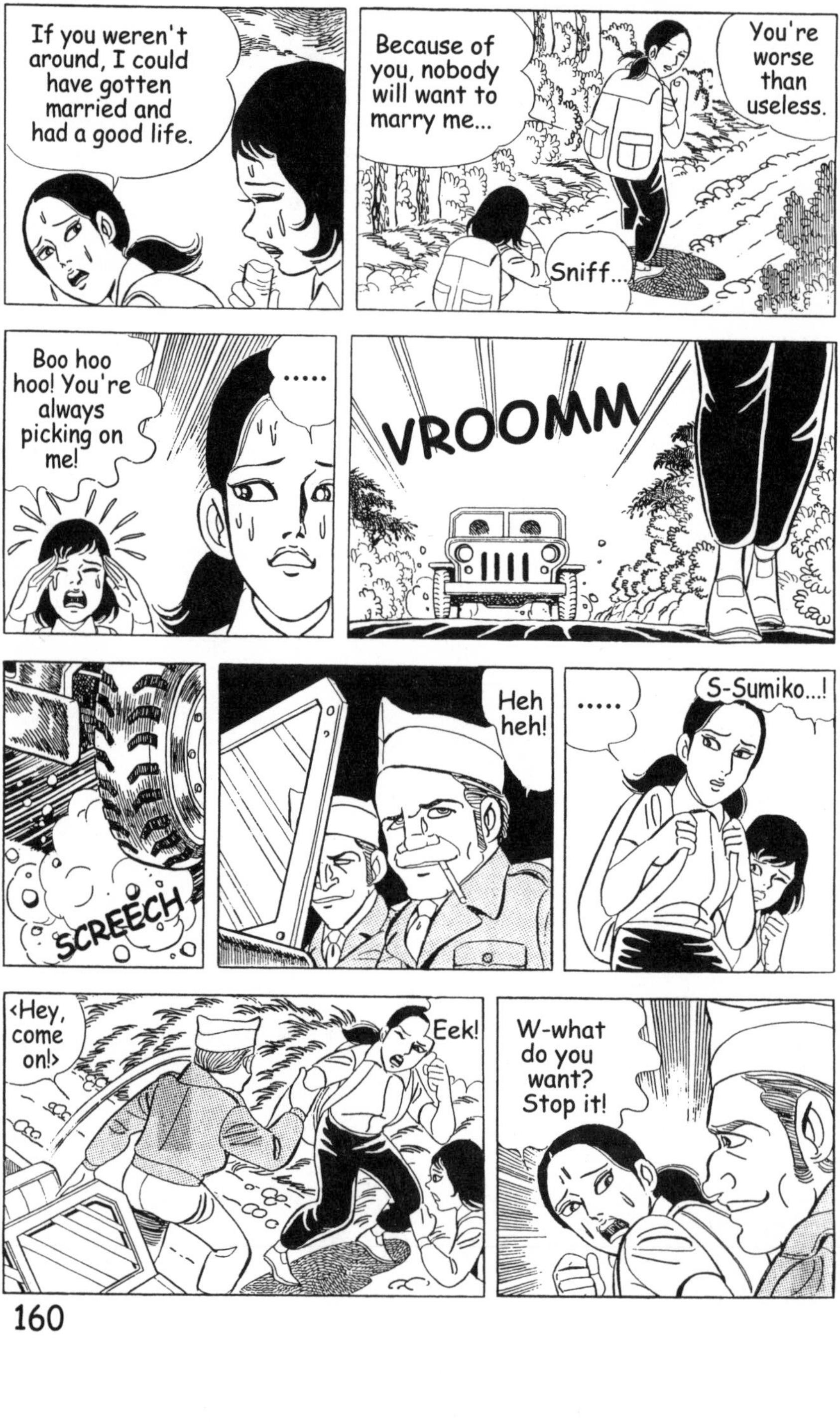
If you weren't around, I could have gotten married and had a good life.
Because of you, nobody will want to marry me...
You're worse than useless.
Sniff...
Boo hoo hoo! You're always picking on me!
.....
VROOMM
SCREECH
Heh heh!
.....
S-Sumiko...!
‹Hey, come on!›
Eek!
W-what do you want? Stop it!

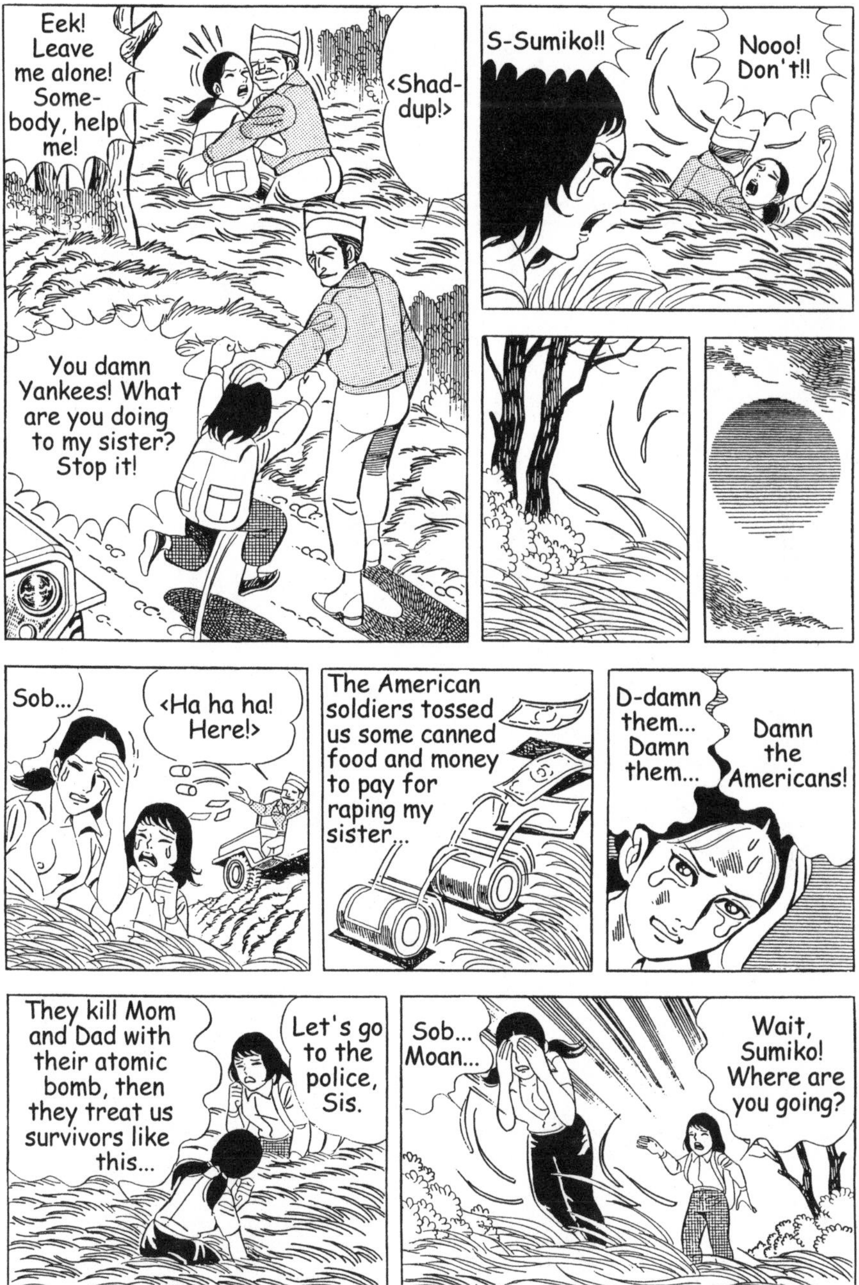
Eek! Leave me alone! Some-body, help me!
<Shad-dup!>
You damn Yankees! What are you doing to my sister? Stop it!
S-Sumiko!!
Nooo! Don't!!
Sob...
<Ha ha ha! Here!>
The American soldiers tossed us some canned food and money to pay for raping my sister...
D-damn them... Damn them...
Damn the Americans!
They kill Mom and Dad with their atomic bomb, then they treat us survivors like this...
Let's go to the police, Sis.
Sob... Moan...
Wait, Sumiko! Where are you going?

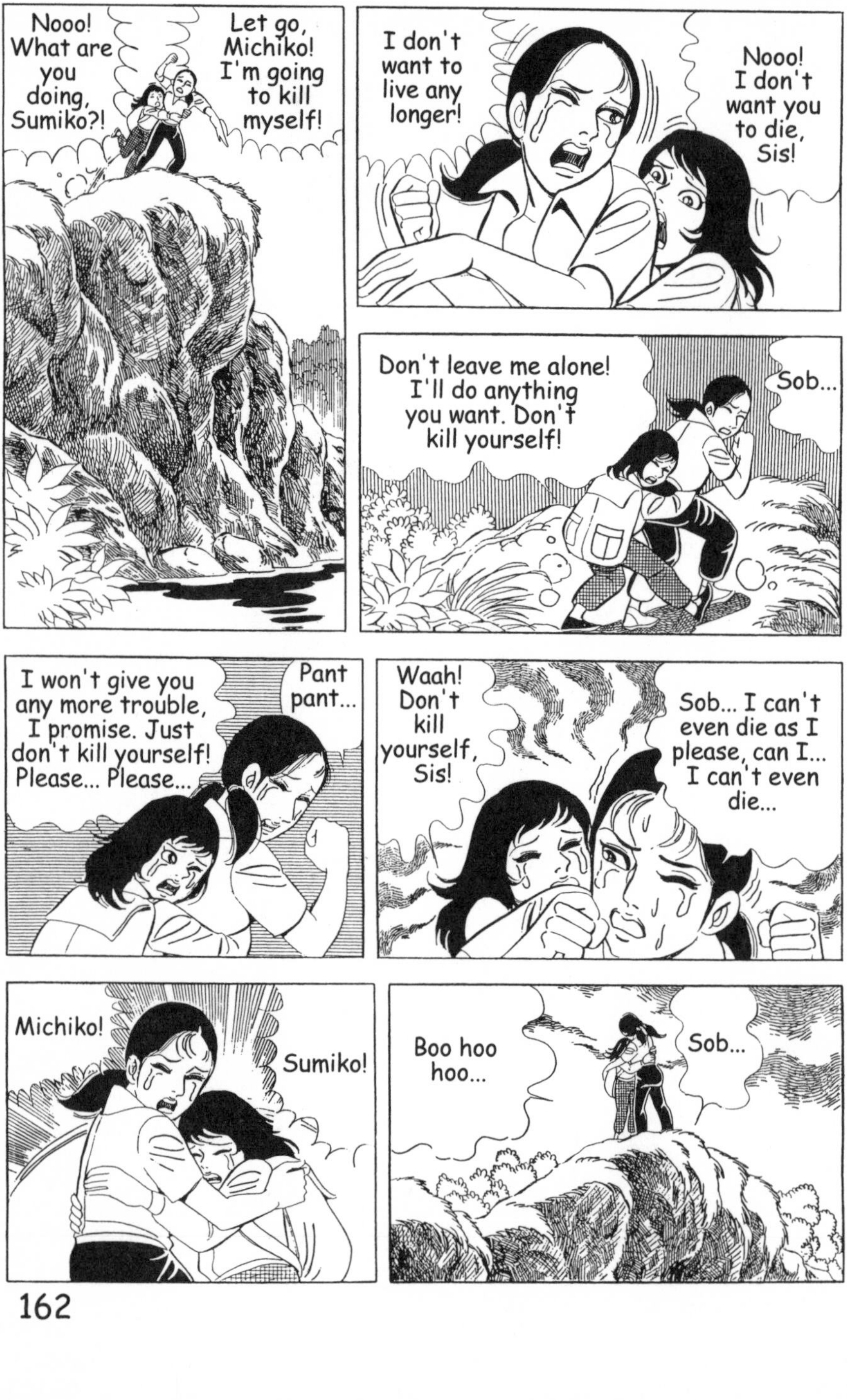
Nooo! What are you doing, Sumiko?!
Let go, Michiko! I'm going to kill myself!
I don't want to live any longer!
Nooo! I don't want you to die, Sis!
Don't leave me alone! I'll do anything you want. Don't kill yourself!
Sob...
I won't give you any more trouble, I promise. Just don't kill yourself! Please... Please...
Pant pant...
Waah! Don't kill yourself, Sis!
Sob... I can't even die as I please, can I... I can't even die...
Michiko!
Sumiko!
Boo hoo hoo...
Sob...

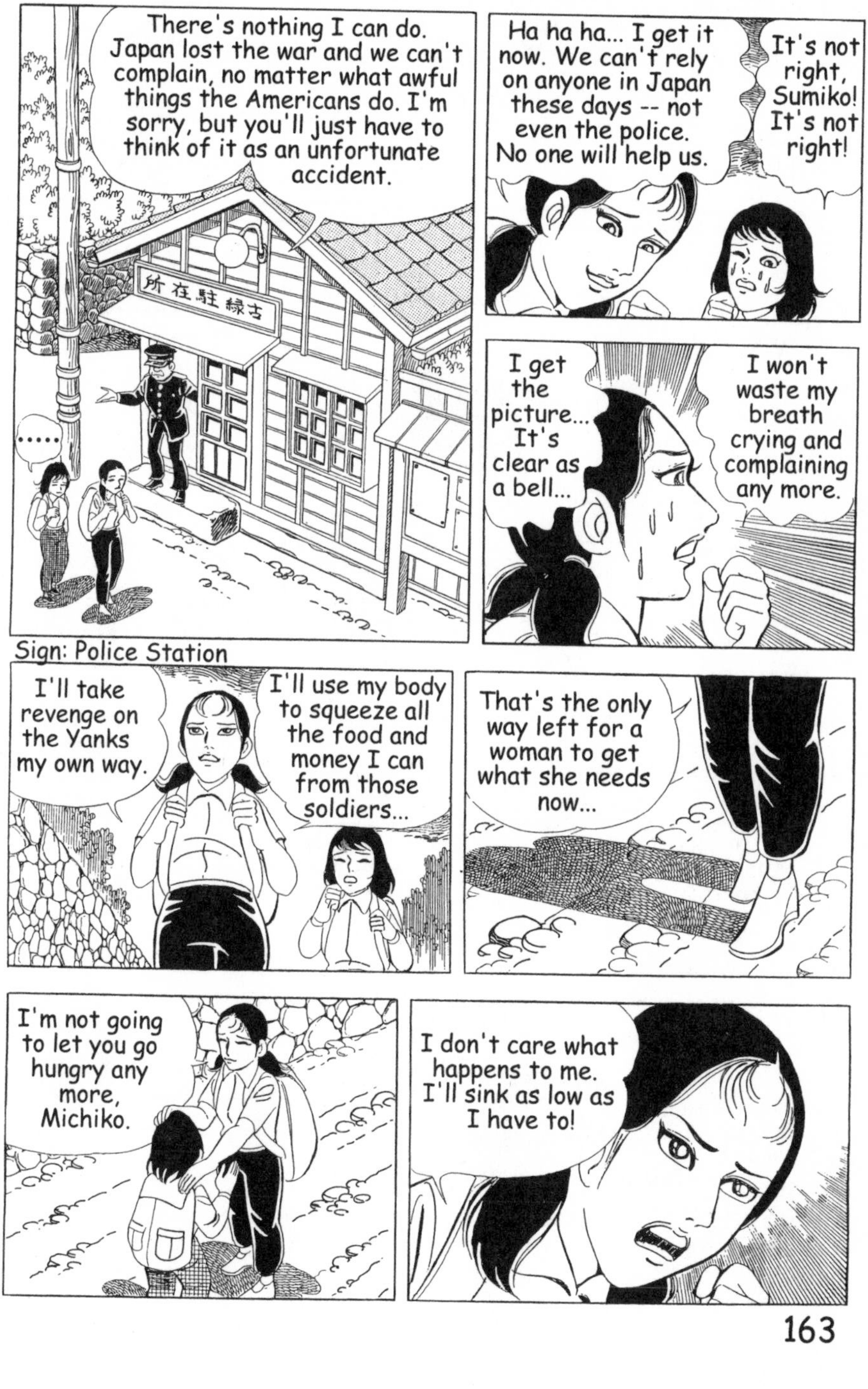
There's nothing I can do. Japan lost the war and we can't complain, no matter what awful things the Americans do. I'm sorry, but you'll just have to think of it as an unfortunate accident.
古緑駐在所
......
Sign: Police Station
Ha ha ha... I get it now. We can't rely on anyone in Japan these days -- not even the police. No one will help us.
It's not right, Sumiko! It's not right!
I get the picture... It's clear as a bell...
I won't waste my breath crying and complaining any more.
I'll take revenge on the Yanks my own way.
I'll use my body to squeeze all the food and money I can from those soldiers...
That's the only way left for a woman to get what she needs now...
I'm not going to let you go hungry any more, Michiko.
I don't care what happens to me. I'll sink as low as I have to!

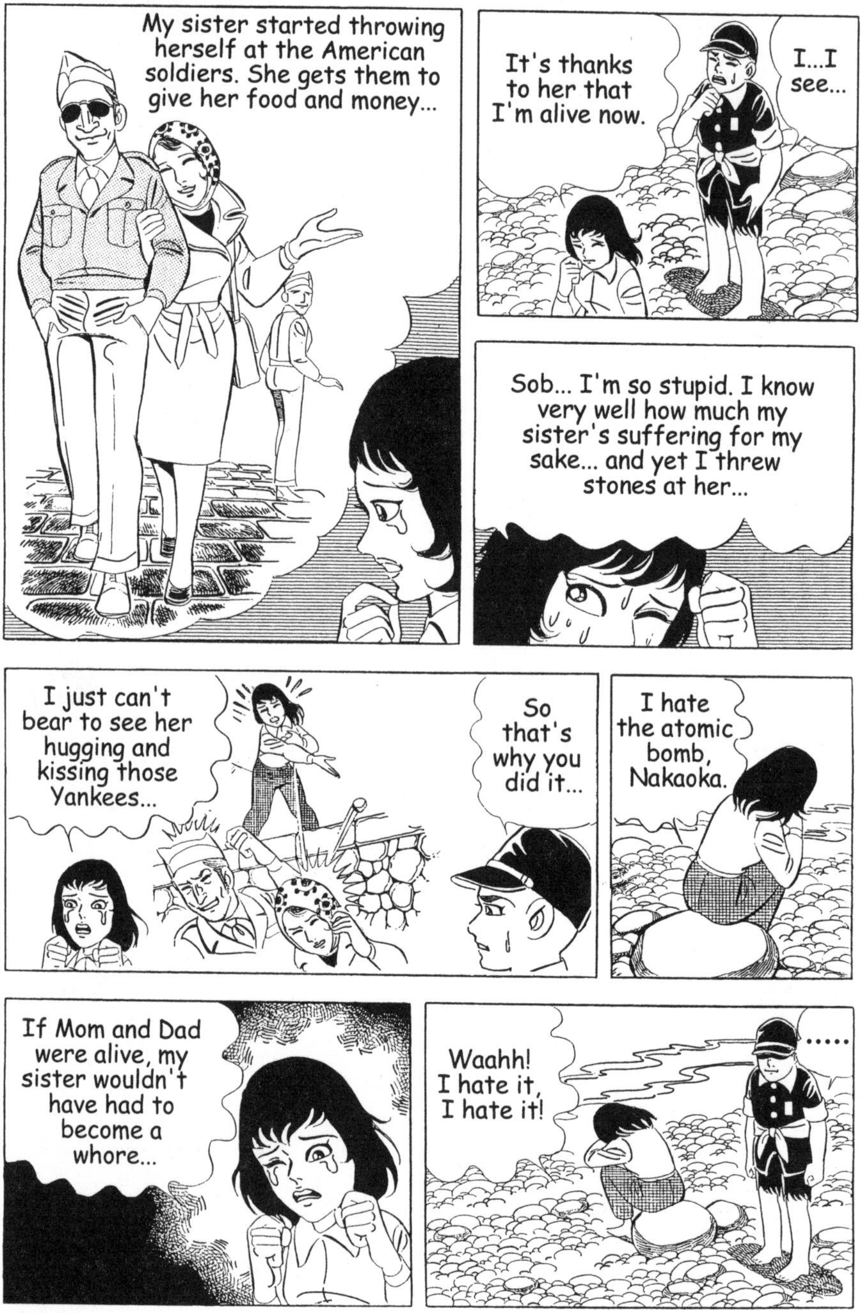
My sister started throwing herself at the American soldiers. She gets them to give her food and money...
It's thanks to her that I'm alive now.
I...I see...
Sob... I'm so stupid. I know very well how much my sister's suffering for my sake... and yet I threw stones at her...
I just can't bear to see her hugging and kissing those Yankees...
So that's why you did it...
I hate the atomic bomb, Nakaoka.
If Mom and Dad were alive, my sister wouldn't have had to become a whore...
Waahh! I hate it, I hate it!
.....

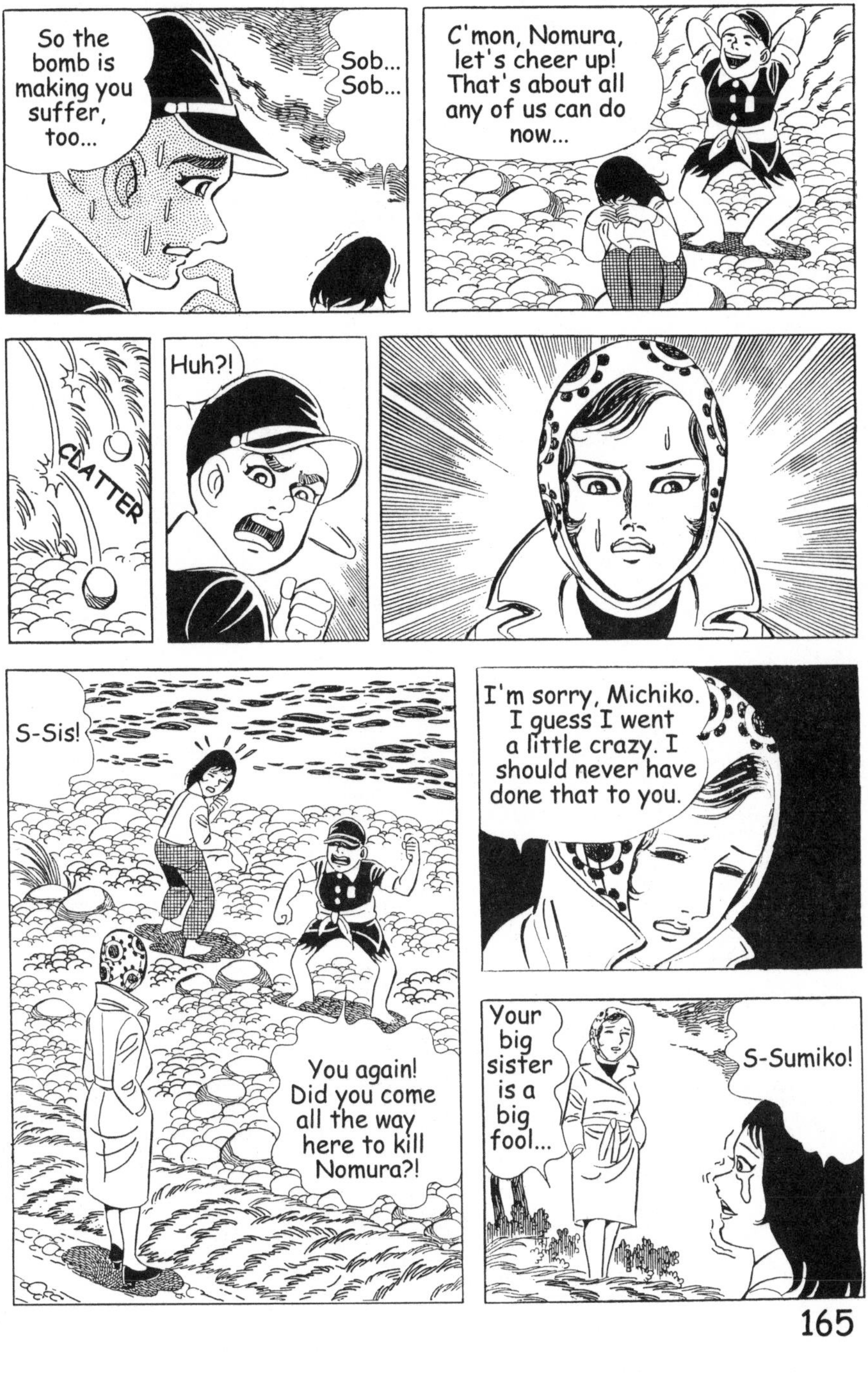
So the bomb is making you suffer, too...
Sob... Sob...
C'mon, Nomura, let's cheer up! That's about all any of us can do now...
CLATTER
Huh?!
S-Sis!
You again! Did you come all the way here to kill Nomura?!
I'm sorry, Michiko. I guess I went a little crazy. I should never have done that to you.
Your big sister is a big fool...
S-Sumiko!

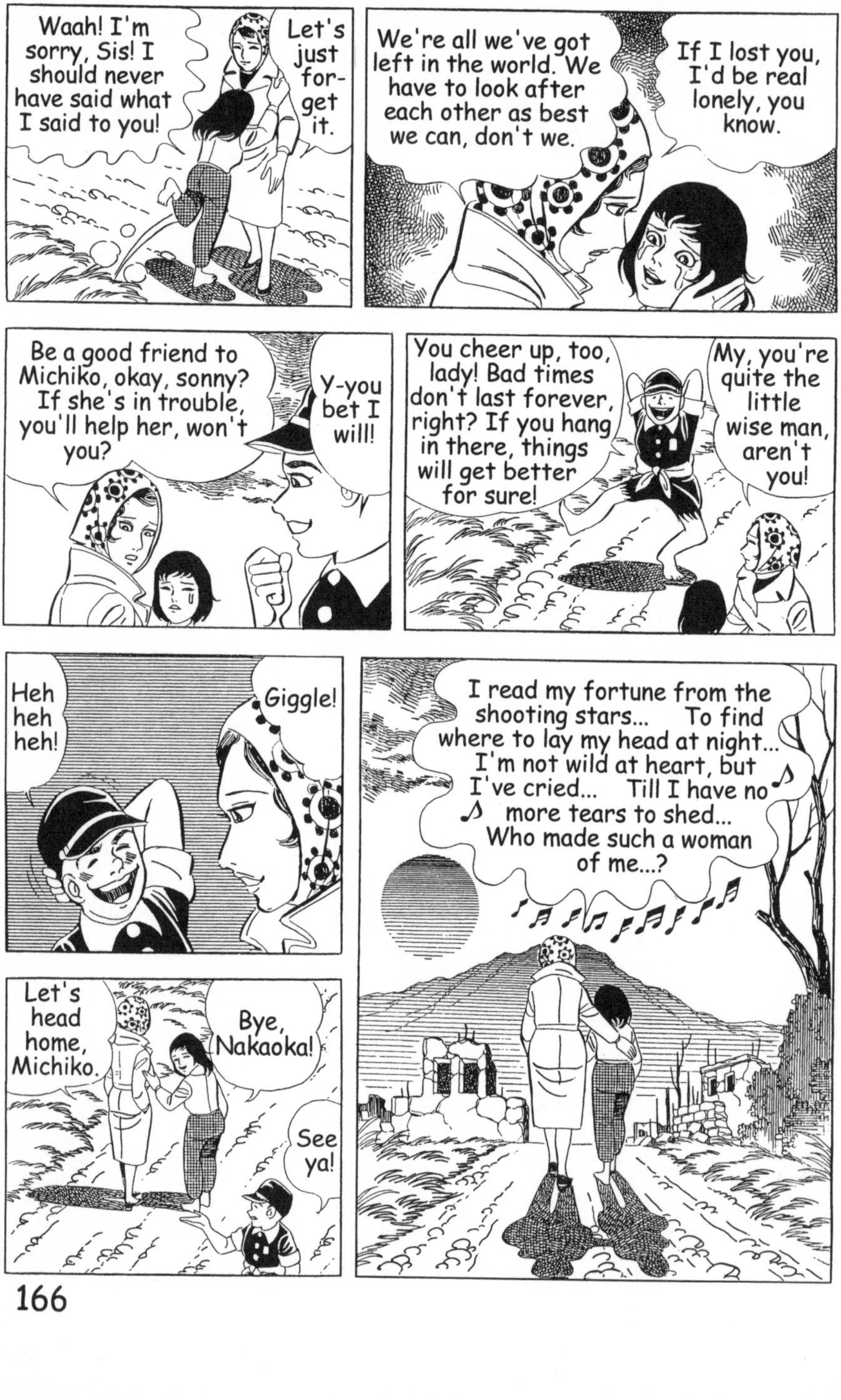

Waah! I'm sorry, Sis! I should never have said what I said to you!
Let's just for-get it.
We're all we've got left in the world. We have to look after each other as best we can, don't we.
If I lost you, I'd be real lonely, you know.
Be a good friend to Michiko, okay, sonny? If she's in trouble, you'll help her, won't you?
Y-you bet I will!
You cheer up, too, lady! Bad times don't last forever, right? If you hang in there, things will get better for sure!
My, you're quite the little wise man, aren't you!
Heh heh heh!
Giggle!
I read my fortune from the shooting stars... To find where to lay my head at night... I'm not wild at heart, but I've cried... Till I have no more tears to shed... Who made such a woman of me...?
Let's head home, Michiko.
Bye, Nakaoka!
See ya!

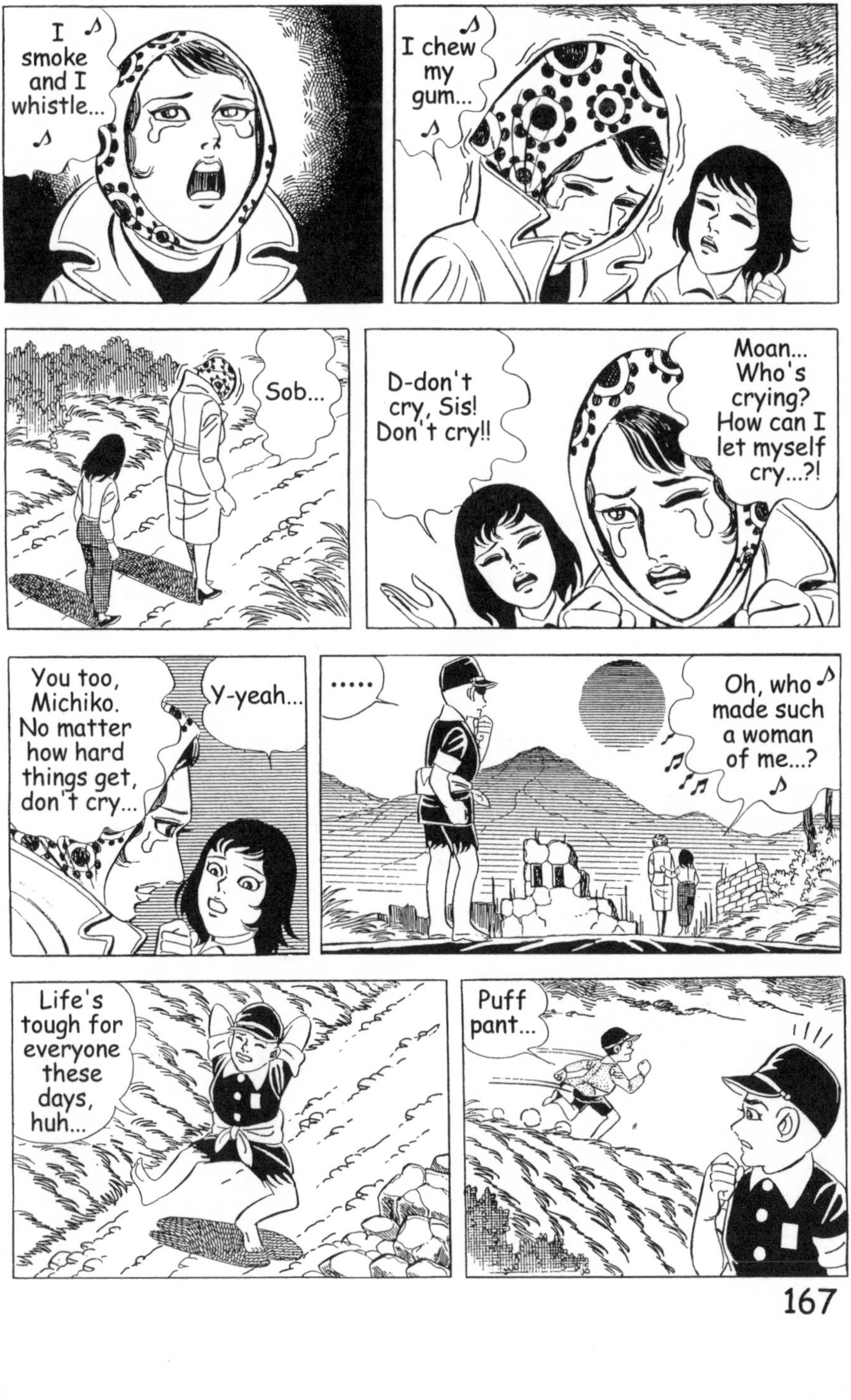
I smoke and I whistle...
I chew my gum...
Sob...
D-don't cry, Sis! Don't cry!!
Moan... Who's crying? How can I let myself cry...?!
You too, Michiko. No matter how hard things get, don't cry...
Y-yeah...
.....
Oh, who made such a woman of me...?
Life's tough for everyone these days, huh...
Puff pant...

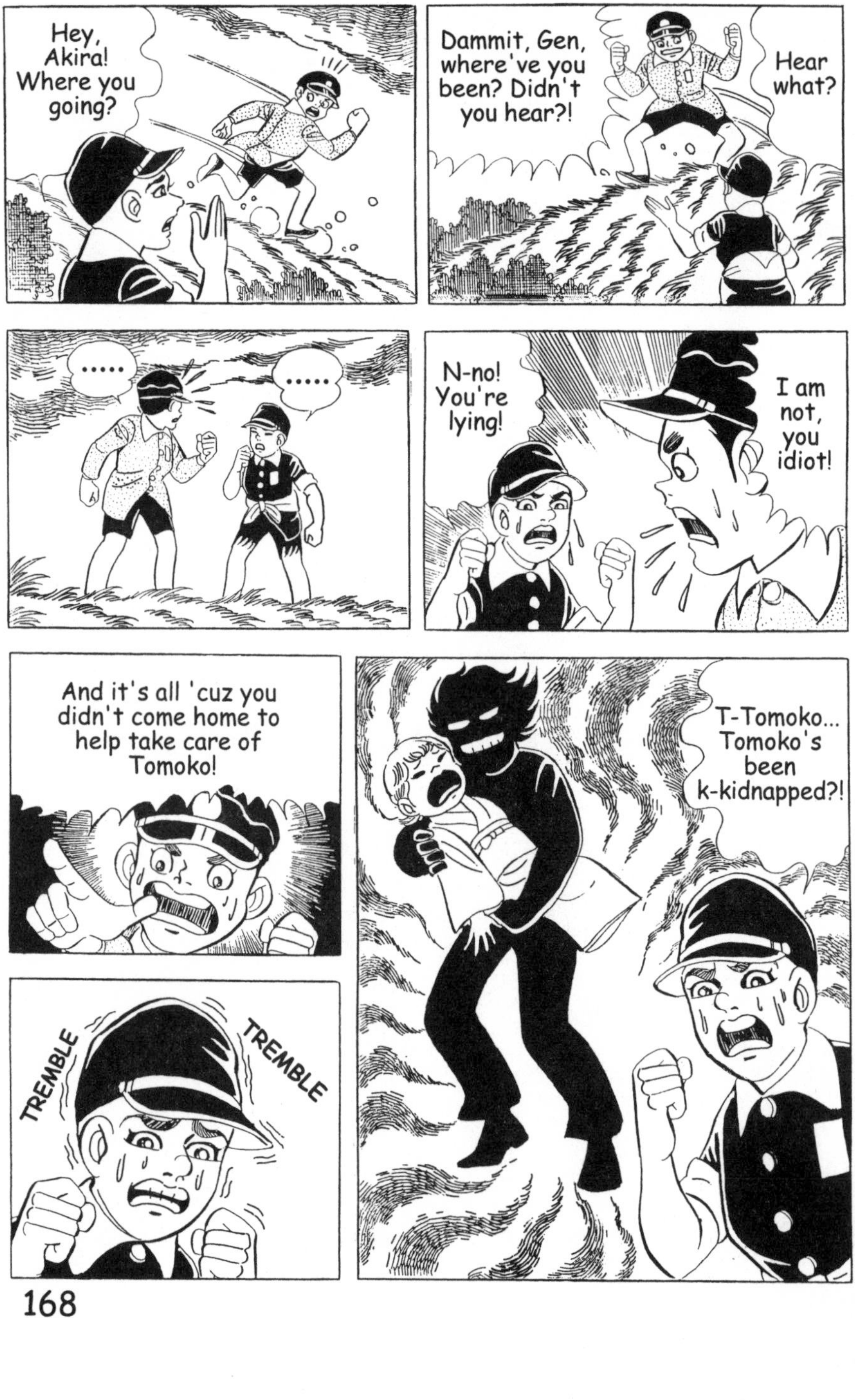
Hey, Akira! Where you going?
Dammit, Gen, where've you been? Didn't you hear?!
Hear what?
.....
.....
N-no! You're lying!
I am not, you idiot!
And it's all 'cuz you didn't come home to help take care of Tomoko!
TREMBLE
TREMBLE
T-Tomoko... Tomoko's been k-kidnapped?!

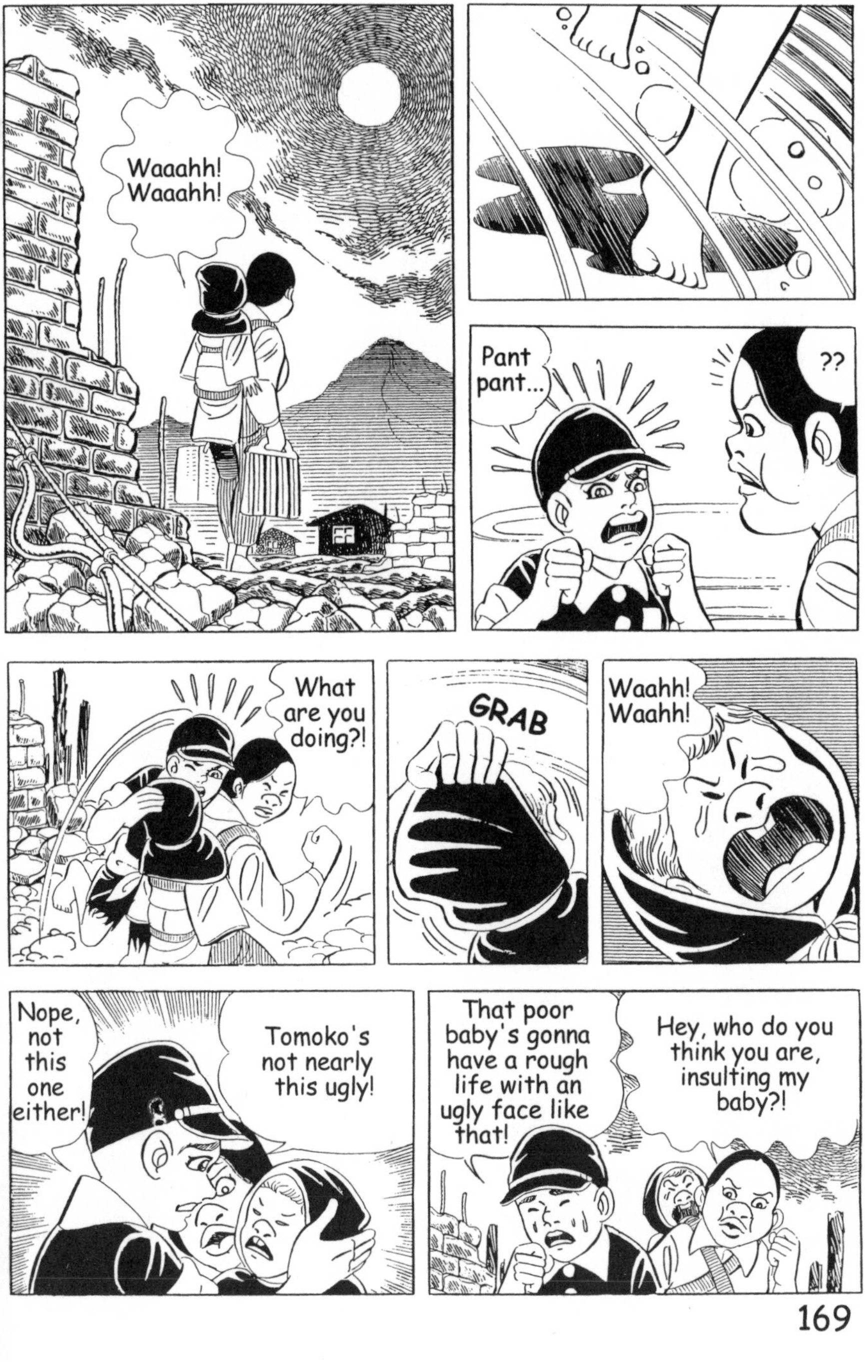
Waaahh! Waaahh!
Pant pant...
??
What are you doing?!
GRAB
Waahh! Waahh!
Nope, not this one either!
Tomoko's not nearly this ugly!
That poor baby's gonna have a rough life with an ugly face like that!
Hey, who do you think you are, insulting my baby?!

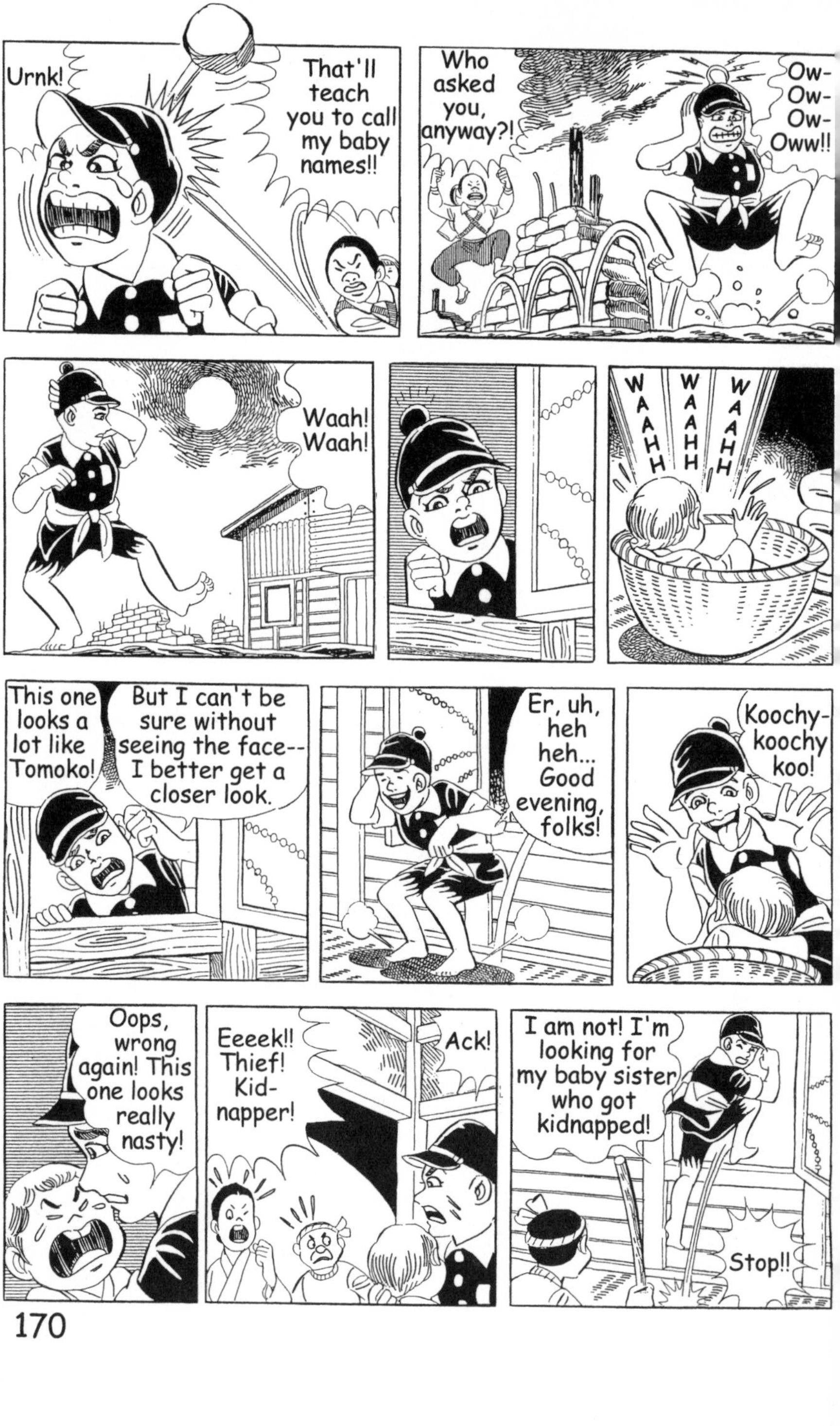
Urnk!
That'll teach you to call my baby names!!
Who asked you, anyway?!
Ow-Ow-Ow-Oww!!
Waah! Waah!
WAAHH
WAAHH
WAAHH
This one looks a lot like Tomoko!
But I can't be sure without seeing the face--I better get a closer look.
Er, uh, heh heh... Good evening, folks!
Koochy-koochy koo!
Oops, wrong again! This one looks really nasty!
Eeeek!! Thief! Kid-napper!
Ack!
I am not! I'm looking for my baby sister who got kidnapped!
Stop!!

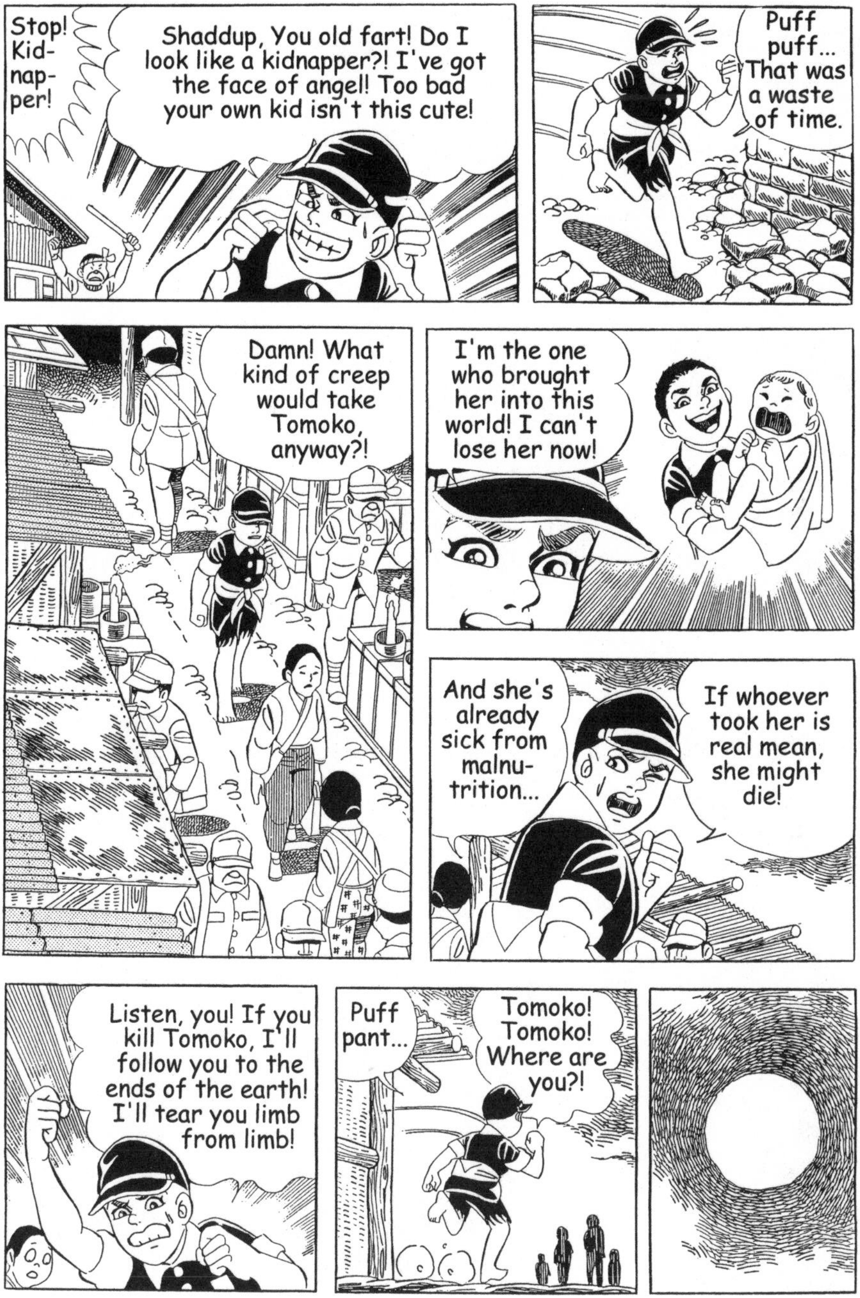
Stop! Kid-nap-per!
Shaddup, You old fart! Do I look like a kidnapper?! I've got the face of angel! Too bad your own kid isn't this cute!
Puff puff... That was a waste of time.
Damn! What kind of creep would take Tomoko, anyway?!
I'm the one who brought her into this world! I can't lose her now!
And she's already sick from malnu-trition...
If whoever took her is real mean, she might die!
Listen, you! If you kill Tomoko, I'll follow you to the ends of the earth! I'll tear you limb from limb!
Puff pant...
Tomoko! Tomoko! Where are you?!

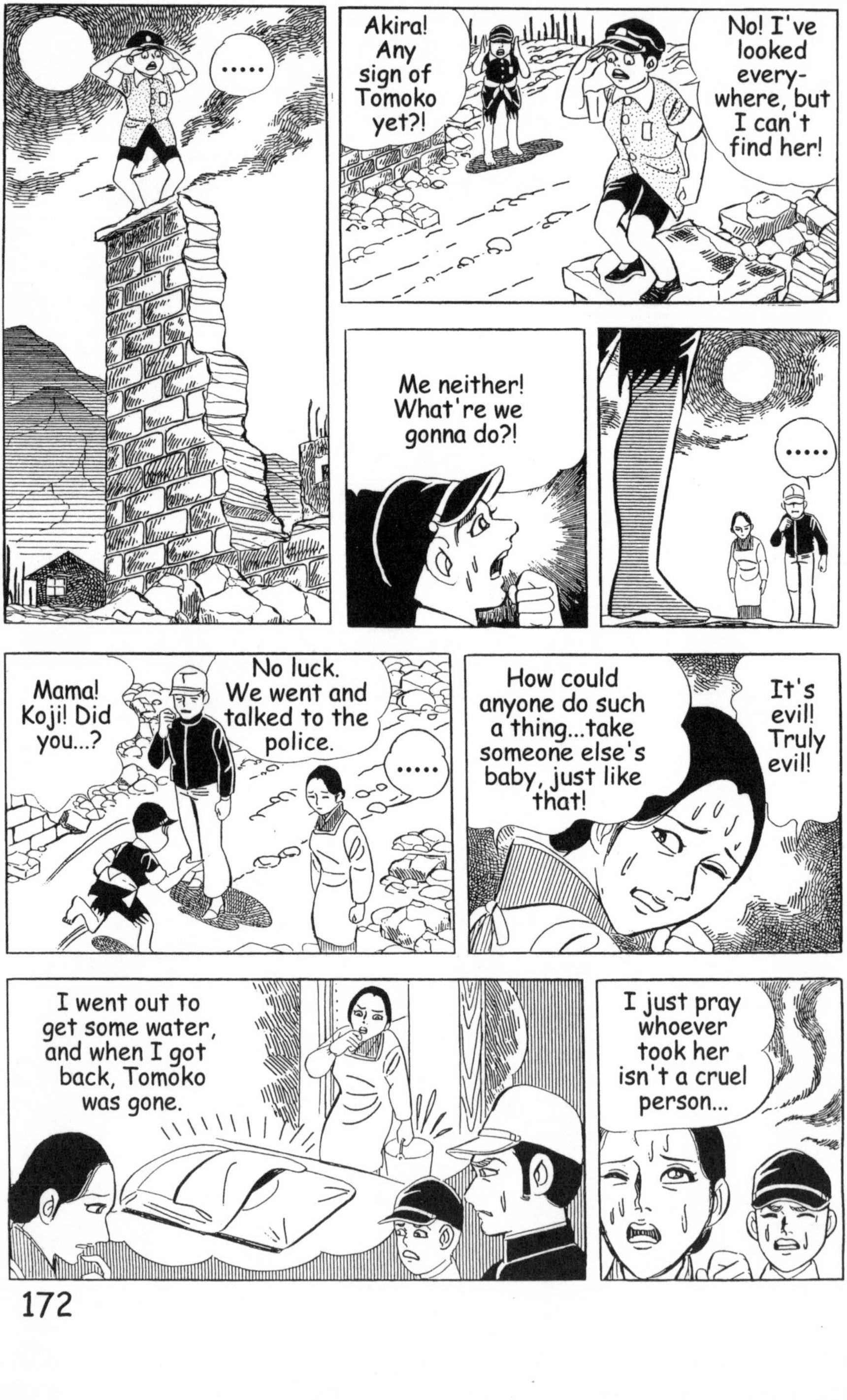
.....
Akira! Any sign of Tomoko yet?!
No! I've looked every-where, but I can't find her!
Me neither! What're we gonna do?!
.....
Mama! Koji! Did you...?
No luck. We went and talked to the police.
.....
How could anyone do such a thing...take someone else's baby, just like that!
It's evil! Truly evil!
I went out to get some water, and when I got back, Tomoko was gone.
I just pray whoever took her isn't a cruel person...

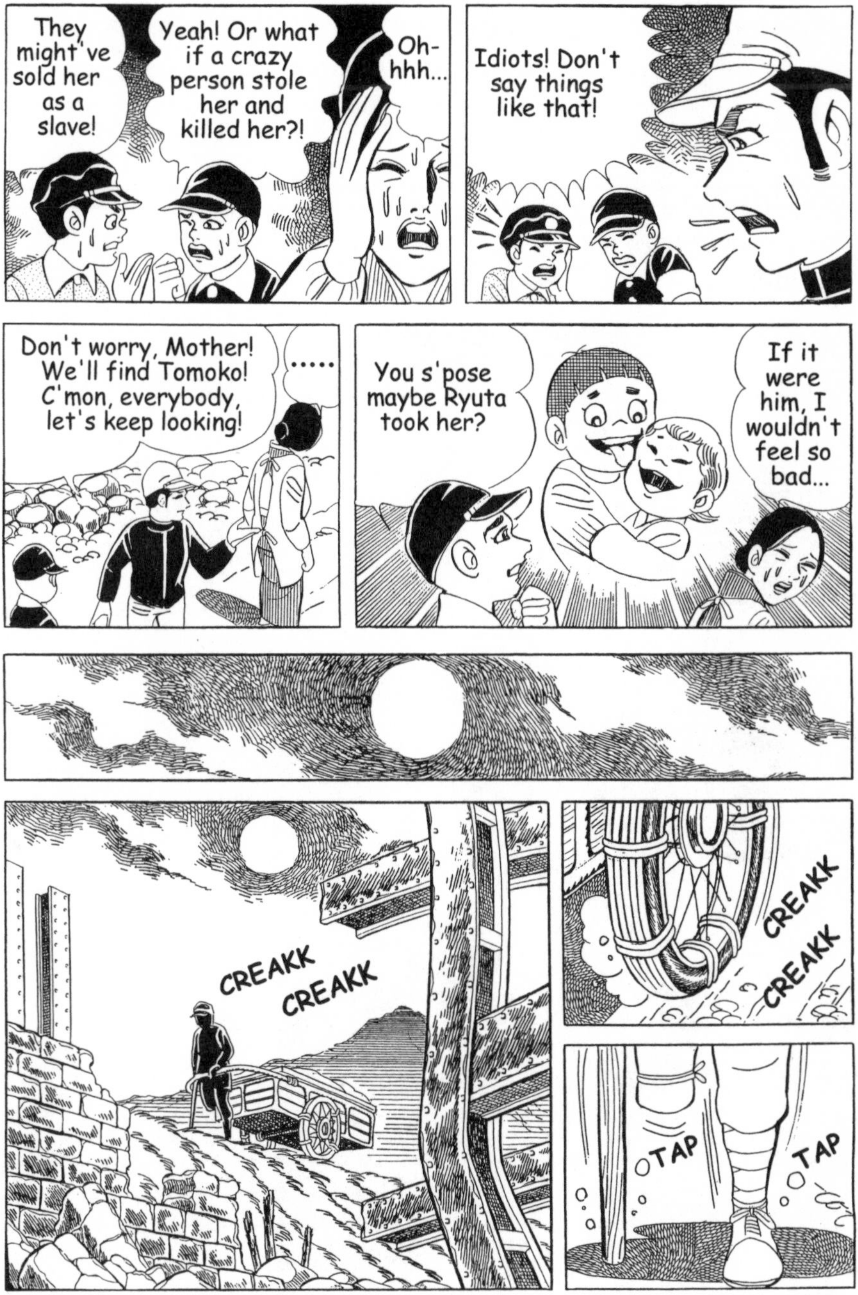
They might've sold her as a slave!
Yeah! Or what if a crazy person stole her and killed her?!
Oh-hhh...
Idiots! Don't say things like that!
Don't worry, Mother! We'll find Tomoko! C'mon, everybody, let's keep looking!
.....
You s'pose maybe Ryuta took her?
If it were him, I wouldn't feel so bad...
CREAKK
CREAKK
CREAKK
CREAKK
TAP
TAP

CREAKK

CREAKK

WAAHH WAAHH WAAHH WAAHH

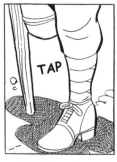

TAP

Waahh!
Waahh!

C'mon,
hush up
now.

.....

WAAAH

WAAAH

WAAAH

WAAAHH WAAAHH

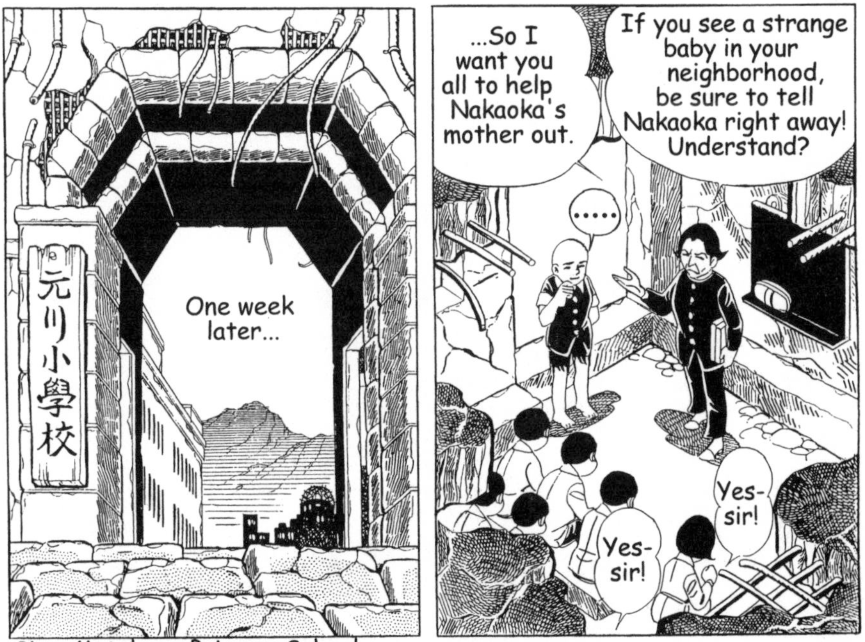
元川小學校
One week later...
...So I want you all to help Nakaoka's mother out.
If you see a strange baby in your neighborhood, be sure to tell Nakaoka right away! Understand?
.....
Yes-sir!
Yes-sir!
Sign: Motokawa Primary School

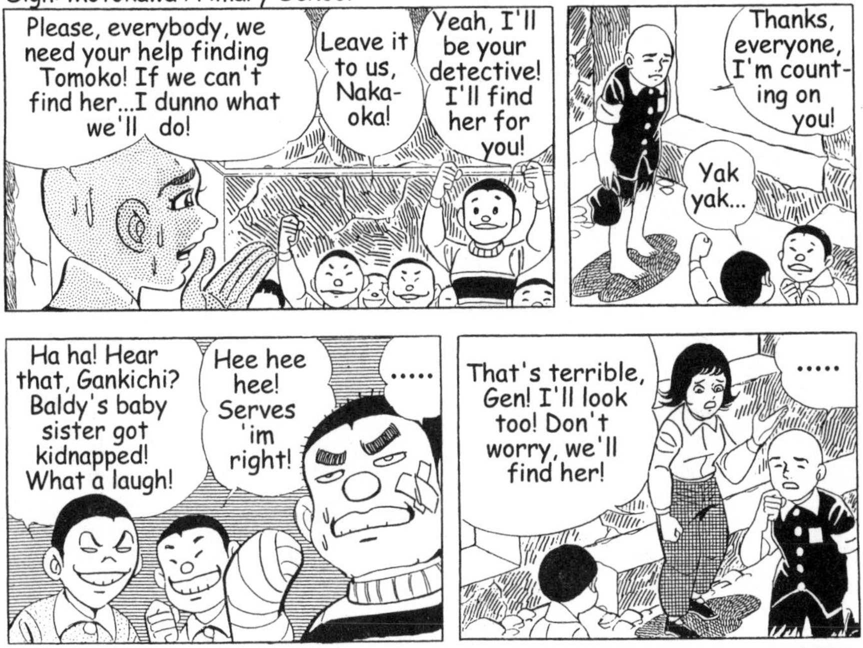
Please, everybody, we need your help finding Tomoko! If we can't find her...I dunno what we'll do!
Leave it to us, Naka-oka!
Yeah, I'll be your detective! I'll find her for you!
Thanks, everyone, I'm count-ing on you!
Yak yak...
Ha ha! Hear that, Gankichi? Baldy's baby sister got kidnapped! What a laugh!
Hee hee hee! Serves 'im right!
.....
That's terrible, Gen! I'll look too! Don't worry, we'll find her!
.....

Whoever took her must be a real monster!

.....

Hey, Nakaoka, you oughta go pray at the Daikakuji Temple!

Why's that, Nakamura?

When my aunt's baby disappeared, my mom prayed to the Buddha and they found the baby right away. It'll work for your baby, too!

That's just a superstition!

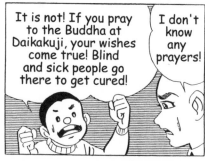

It is not! If you pray to the Buddha at Daikakuji, your wishes come true! Blind and sick people go there to get cured!

I don't know any prayers!

Just try it. You don't have to believe in it!

Pray-ing, huh...?

Hey, Baldy!

What do you want, Crapa-mori?

What does your baby sister look like?

Y-you mean you'll help look for her? Wow, thanks!

.....

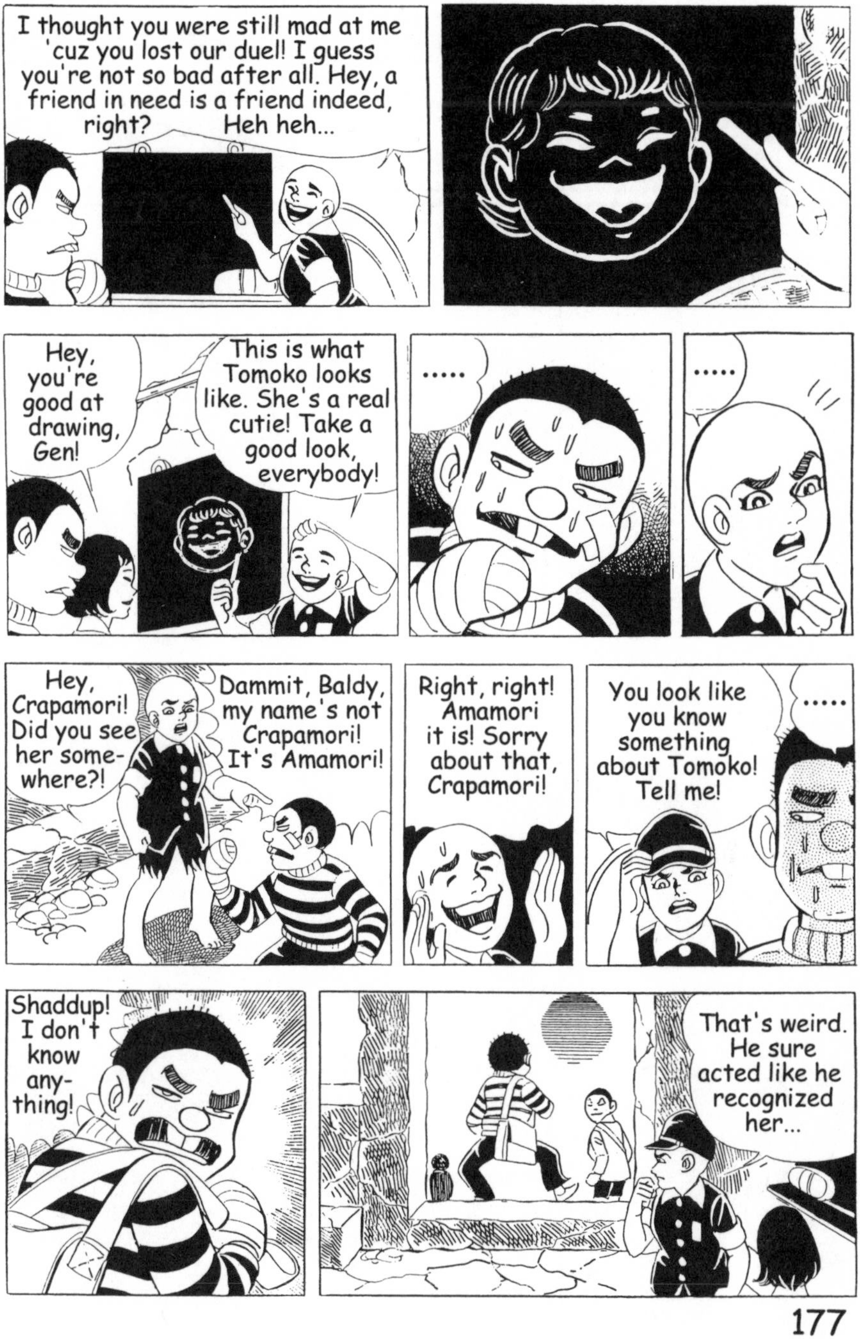
I thought you were still mad at me 'cuz you lost our duel! I guess you're not so bad after all. Hey, a friend in need is a friend indeed, right? Heh heh...
Hey, you're good at drawing, Gen!
This is what Tomoko looks like. She's a real cutie! Take a good look, everybody!
.....
.....
Hey, Crapamori! Did you see her some-where?!
Dammit, Baldy, my name's not Crapamori! It's Amamori!
Right, right! Amamori it is! Sorry about that, Crapamori!
You look like you know something about Tomoko! Tell me!
.....
Shaddup! I don't know any-thing!
That's weird. He sure acted like he recognized her...

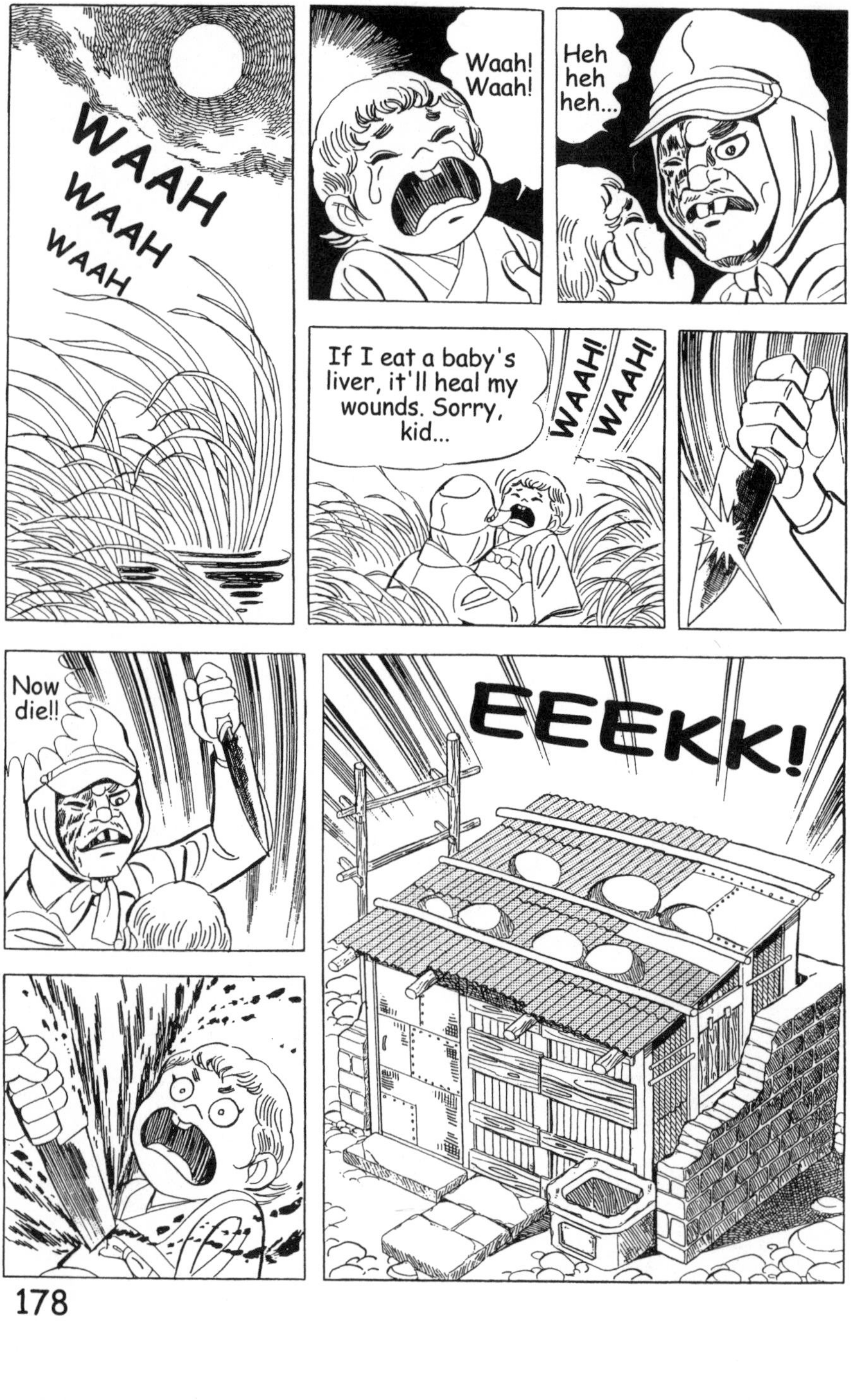
WAAH
WAAH
WAAH
Waah! Waah!
Heh heh heh...
If I eat a baby's liver, it'll heal my wounds. Sorry, kid...
WAAH!
WAAH!
Now die!!
EEEKK!

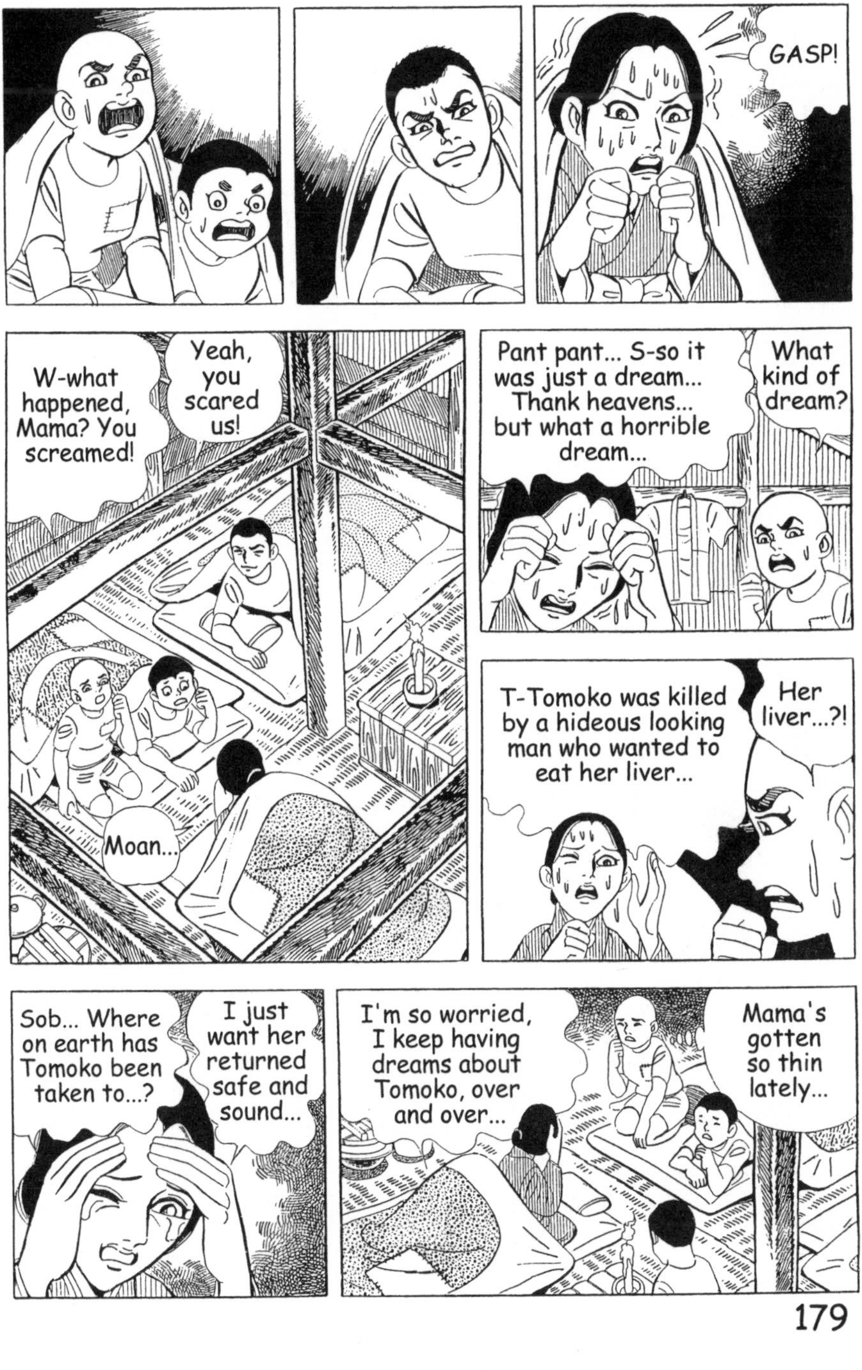
GASP!
W-what happened, Mama? You screamed!
Yeah, you scared us!
Moan...
Pant pant... S-so it was just a dream... Thank heavens... but what a horrible dream...
What kind of dream?
T-Tomoko was killed by a hideous looking man who wanted to eat her liver...
Her liver...?!
Sob... Where on earth has Tomoko been taken to...?
I just want her returned safe and sound...
I'm so worried, I keep having dreams about Tomoko, over and over...
Mama's gotten so thin lately...

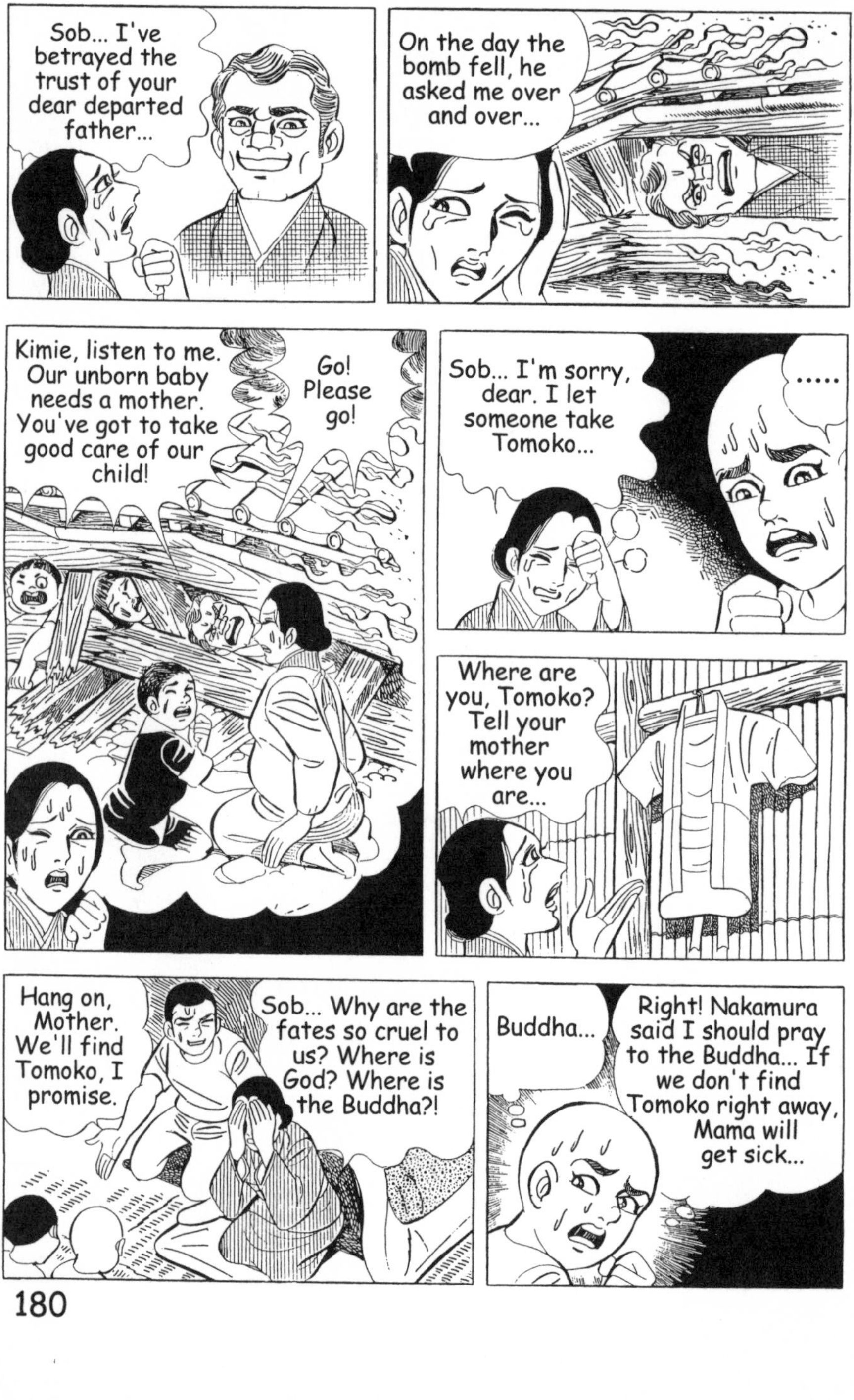

Sob... I've betrayed the trust of your dear departed father...
On the day the bomb fell, he asked me over and over...
Kimie, listen to me. Our unborn baby needs a mother. You've got to take good care of our child!
Go! Please go!
Sob... I'm sorry, dear. I let someone take Tomoko...
.....
Where are you, Tomoko? Tell your mother where you are...
Hang on, Mother. We'll find Tomoko, I promise.
Sob... Why are the fates so cruel to us? Where is God? Where is the Buddha?!
Buddha...
Right! Nakamura said I should pray to the Buddha... If we don't find Tomoko right away, Mama will get sick...

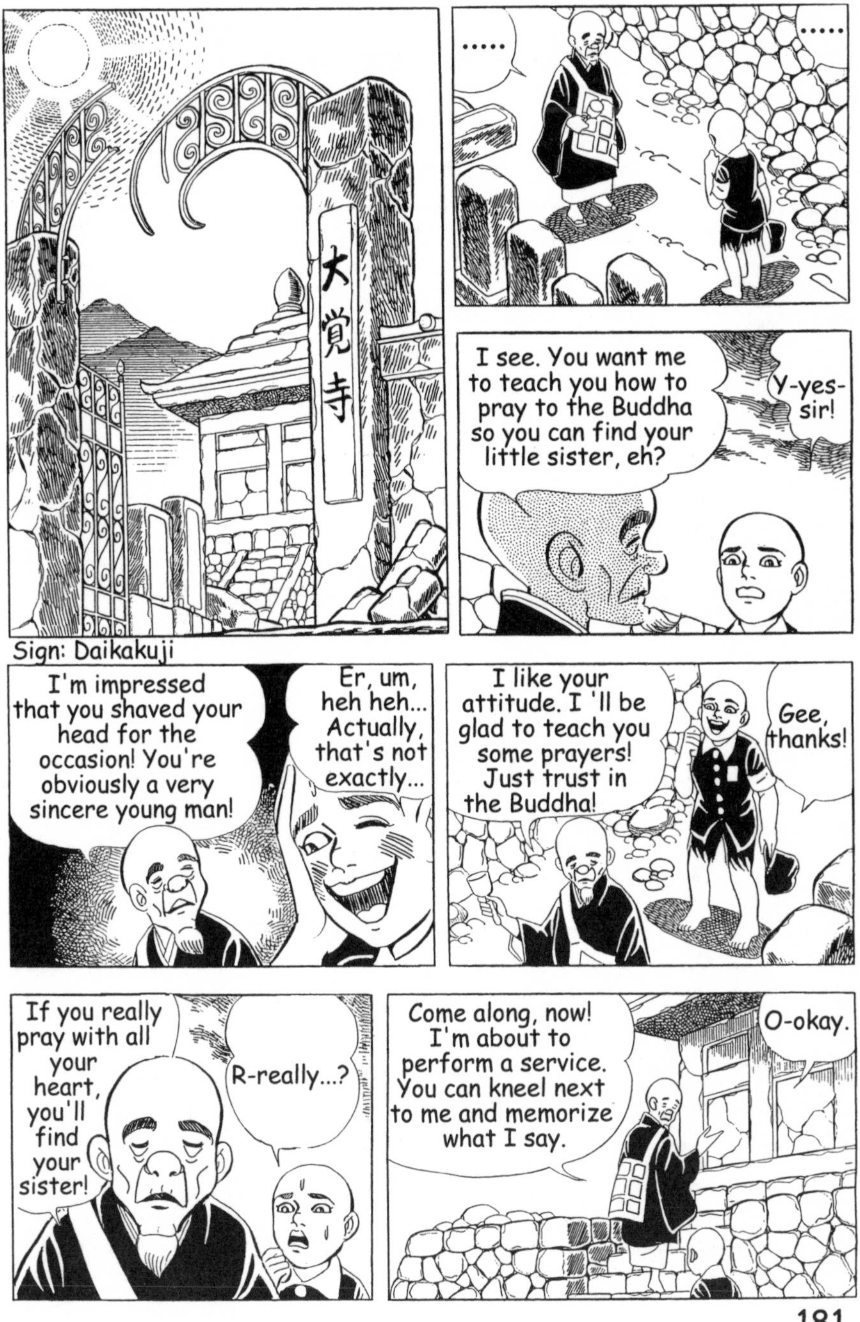
大覚寺
......
......
I see. You want me to teach you how to pray to the Buddha so you can find your little sister, eh?
Y-yes-sir!
Sign: Daikakuji
I'm impressed that you shaved your head for the occasion! You're obviously a very sincere young man!
Er, um, heh heh... Actually, that's not exactly...
I like your attitude. I 'll be glad to teach you some prayers! Just trust in the Buddha!
Gee, thanks!
If you really pray with all your heart, you'll find your sister!
R-really...?
Come along, now! I'm about to perform a service. You can kneel next to me and memorize what I say.
O-okay.

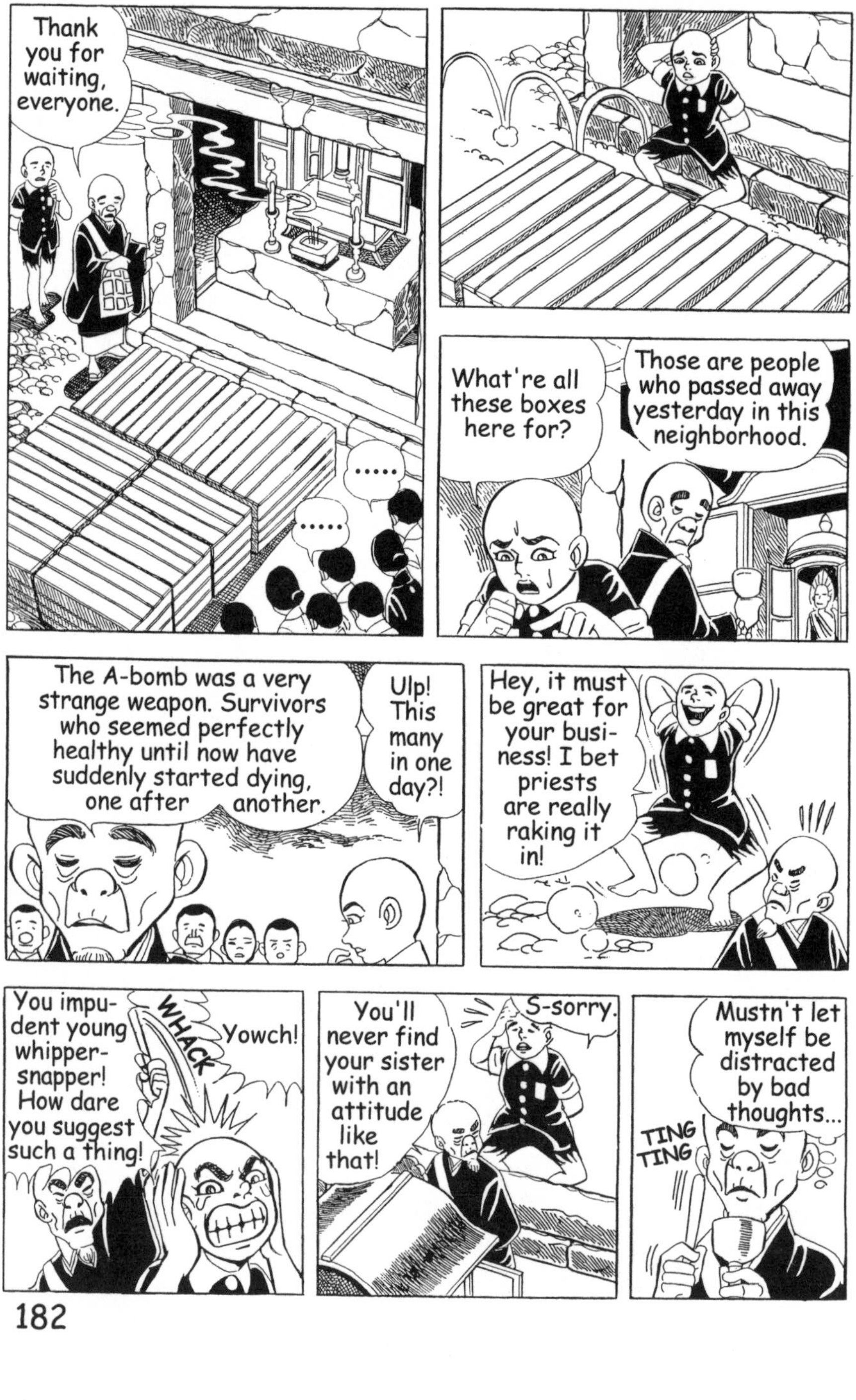
Thank you for waiting, everyone.
......
......
What're all these boxes here for?
Those are people who passed away yesterday in this neighborhood.
The A-bomb was a very strange weapon. Survivors who seemed perfectly healthy until now have suddenly started dying, one after another.
Ulp! This many in one day?!
Hey, it must be great for your business! I bet priests are really raking it in!
You impudent young whippersnapper! How dare you suggest such a thing!
WHACK
Yowch!
You'll never find your sister with an attitude like that!
S-sorry.
Mustn't let myself be distracted by bad thoughts...
TING TING

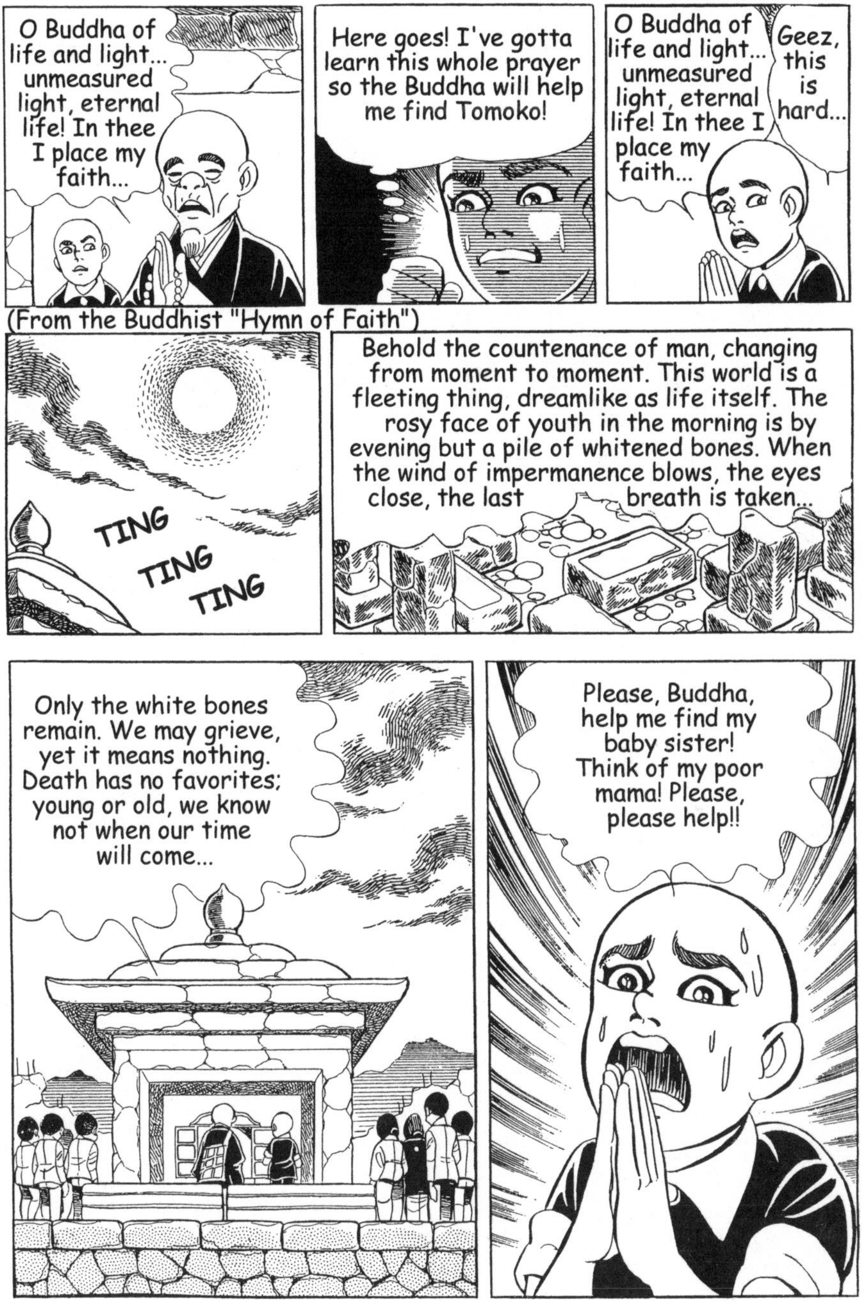
O Buddha of life and light... unmeasured light, eternal life! In thee I place my faith...
Here goes! I've gotta learn this whole prayer so the Buddha will help me find Tomoko!
O Buddha of life and light... unmeasured light, eternal life! In thee I place my faith...
Geez, this is hard...
(From the Buddhist "Hymn of Faith")
TING
TING
TING
Behold the countenance of man, changing from moment to moment. This world is a fleeting thing, dreamlike as life itself. The rosy face of youth in the morning is by evening but a pile of whitened bones. When the wind of impermanence blows, the eyes close, the last breath is taken...
Only the white bones remain. We may grieve, yet it means nothing. Death has no favorites; young or old, we know not when our time will come...
Please, Buddha, help me find my baby sister! Think of my poor mama! Please, please help!!

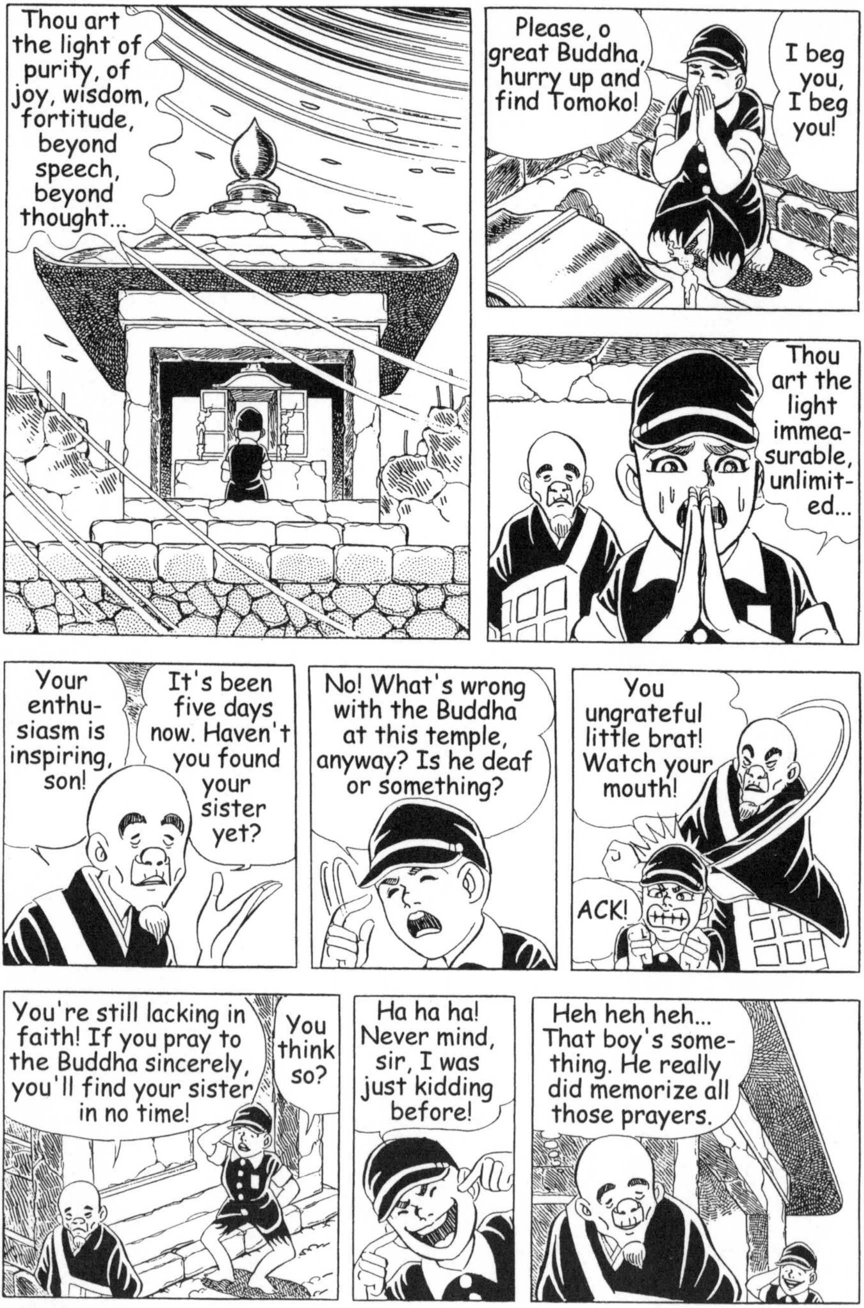
Thou art the light of purity, of joy, wisdom, fortitude, beyond speech, beyond thought...
Please, o great Buddha, hurry up and find Tomoko!
I beg you, I beg you!
Thou art the light immeasurable, unlimited...
Your enthusiasm is inspiring, son!
It's been five days now. Haven't you found your sister yet?
No! What's wrong with the Buddha at this temple, anyway? Is he deaf or something?
You ungrateful little brat! Watch your mouth!
ACK!
You're still lacking in faith! If you pray to the Buddha sincerely, you'll find your sister in no time!
You think so?
Ha ha ha! Never mind, sir, I was just kidding before!
Heh heh heh... That boy's something. He really did memorize all those prayers.

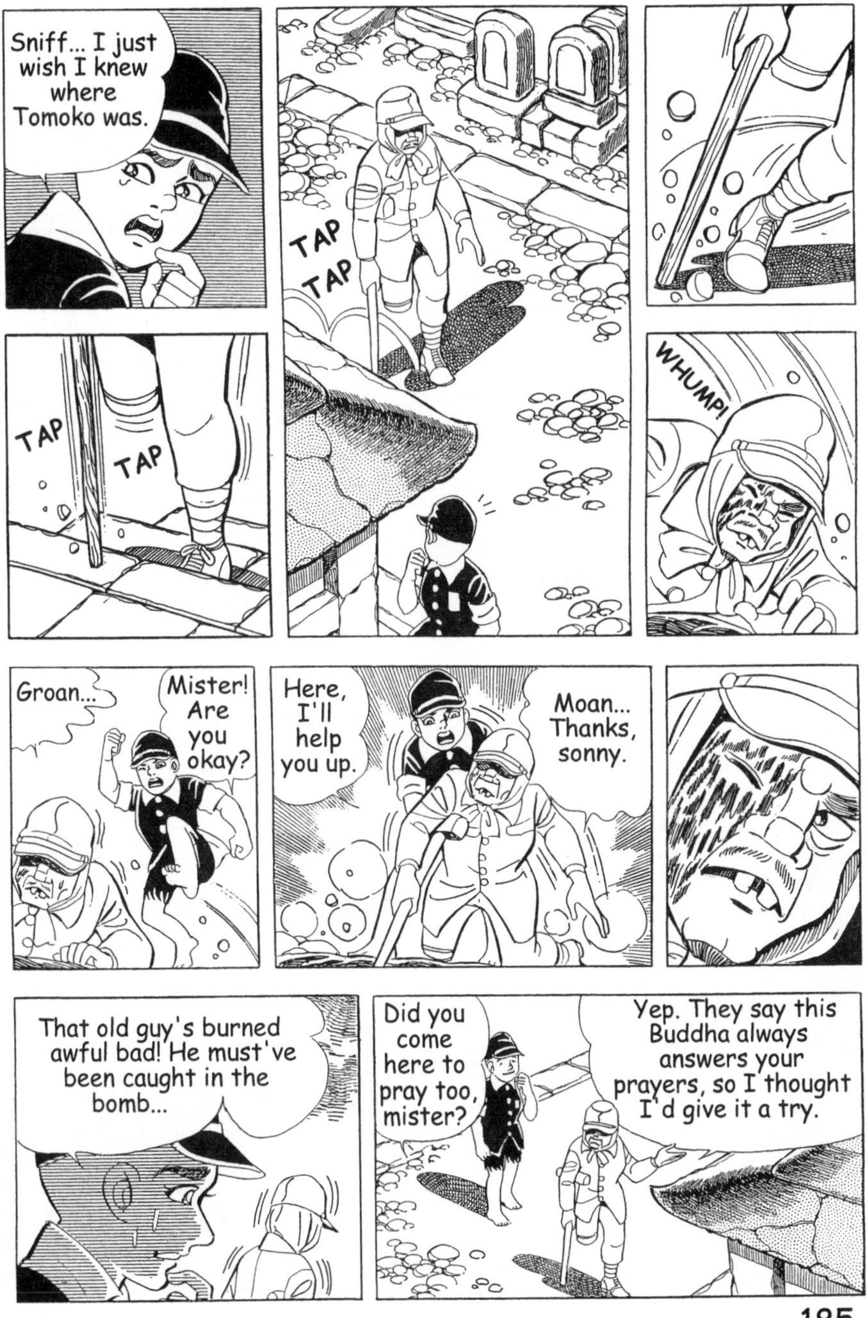
Sniff... I just wish I knew where Tomoko was.
TAP TAP
TAP
TAP
WHUMP!
Groan...
Mister! Are you okay?
Here, I'll help you up.
Moan... Thanks, sonny.
That old guy's burned awful bad! He must've been caught in the bomb...
Did you come here to pray too, mister?
Yep. They say this Buddha always answers your prayers, so I thought I'd give it a try.

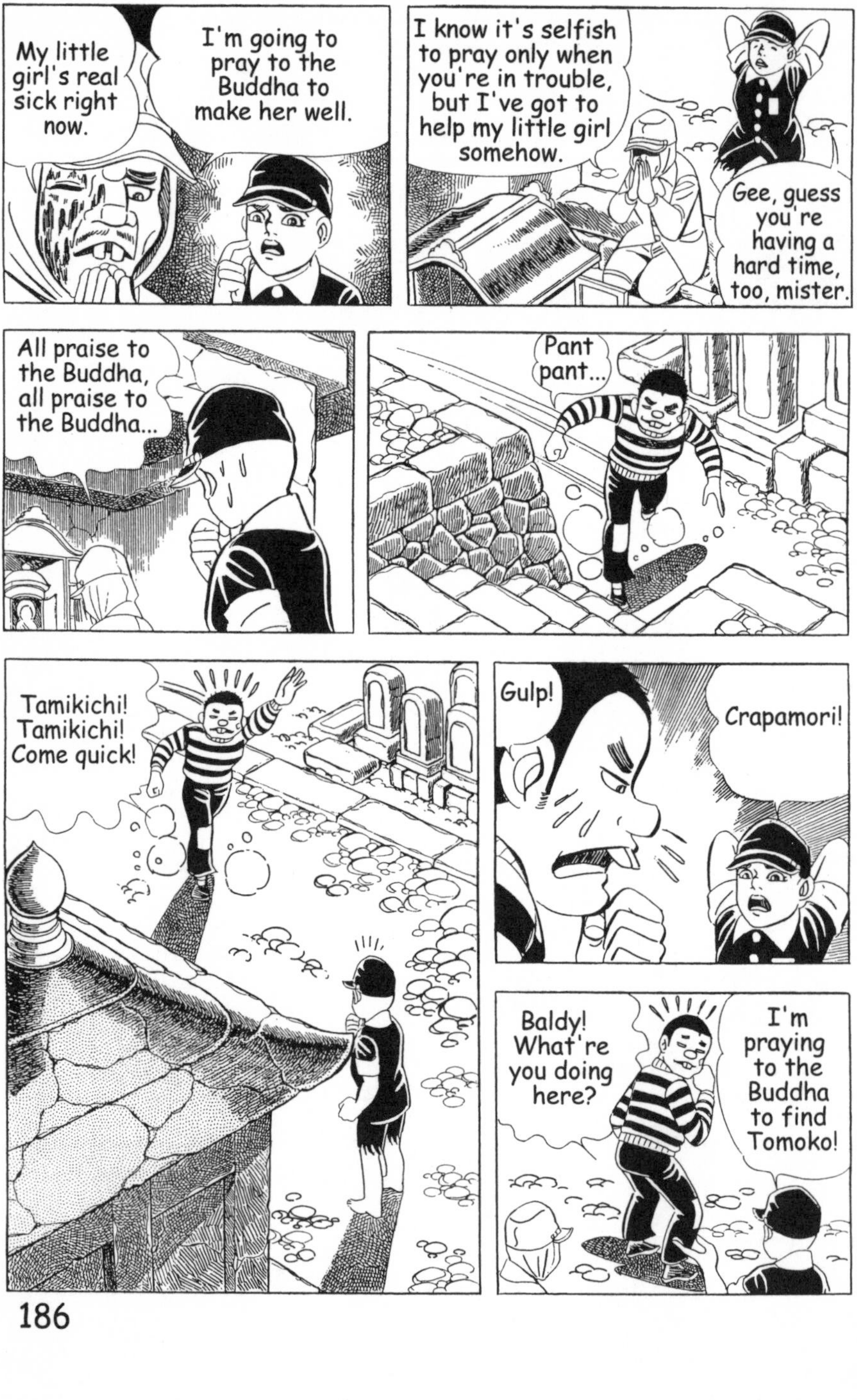
My little girl's real sick right now.
I'm going to pray to the Buddha to make her well.
I know it's selfish to pray only when you're in trouble, but I've got to help my little girl somehow.
Gee, guess you're having a hard time, too, mister.
All praise to the Buddha, all praise to the Buddha...
Pant pant...
Tamikichi! Tamikichi! Come quick!
Gulp!
Crapamori!
Baldy! What're you doing here?
I'm praying to the Buddha to find Tomoko!

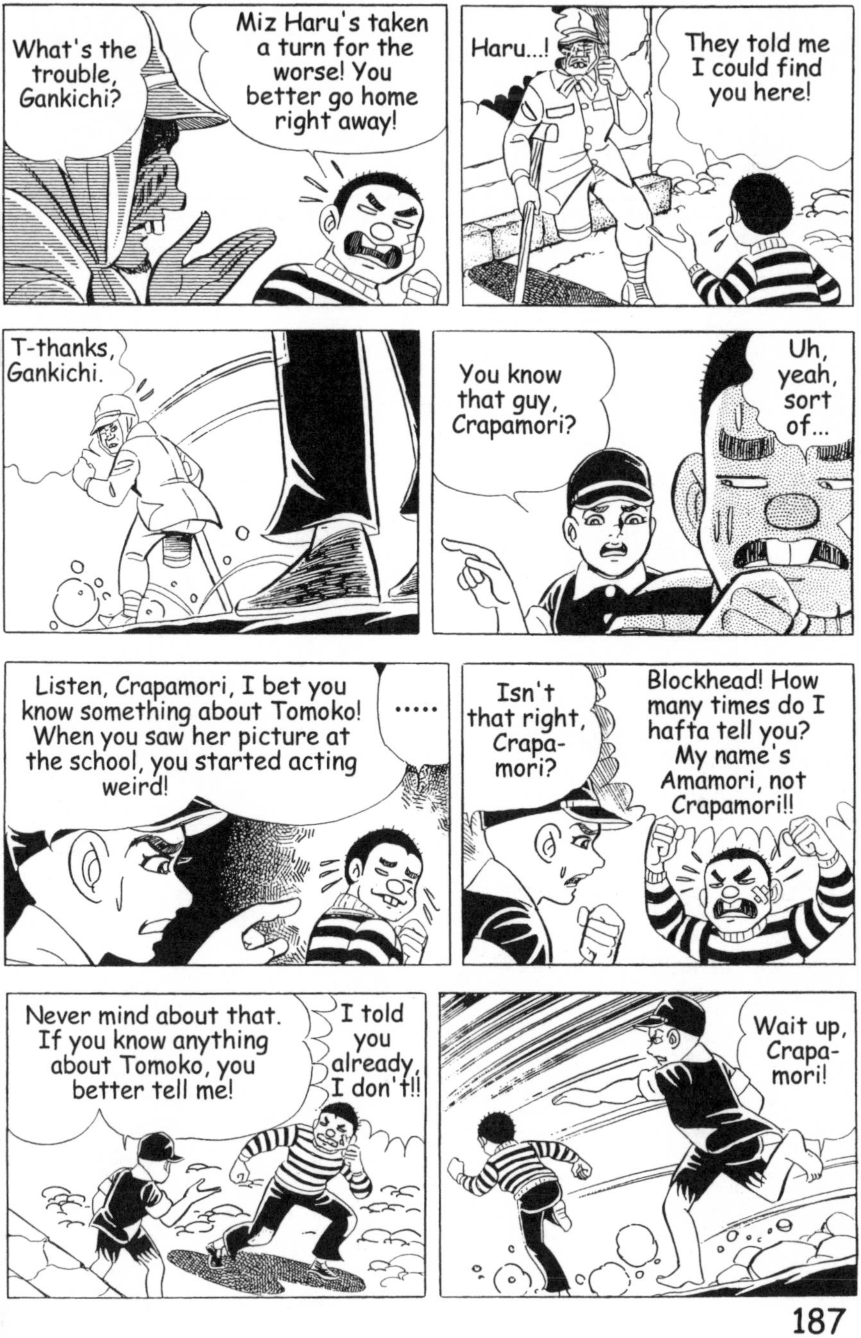
What's the trouble, Gankichi?
Miz Haru's taken a turn for the worse! You better go home right away!
Haru...!
They told me I could find you here!
T-thanks, Gankichi.
You know that guy, Crapamori?
Uh, yeah, sort of...
Listen, Crapamori, I bet you know something about Tomoko! When you saw her picture at the school, you started acting weird!
.....
Isn't that right, Crapa-mori?
Blockhead! How many times do I hafta tell you? My name's Amamori, not Crapamori!!
Never mind about that. If you know anything about Tomoko, you better tell me!
I told you already, I don't!!
Wait up, Crapa-mori!

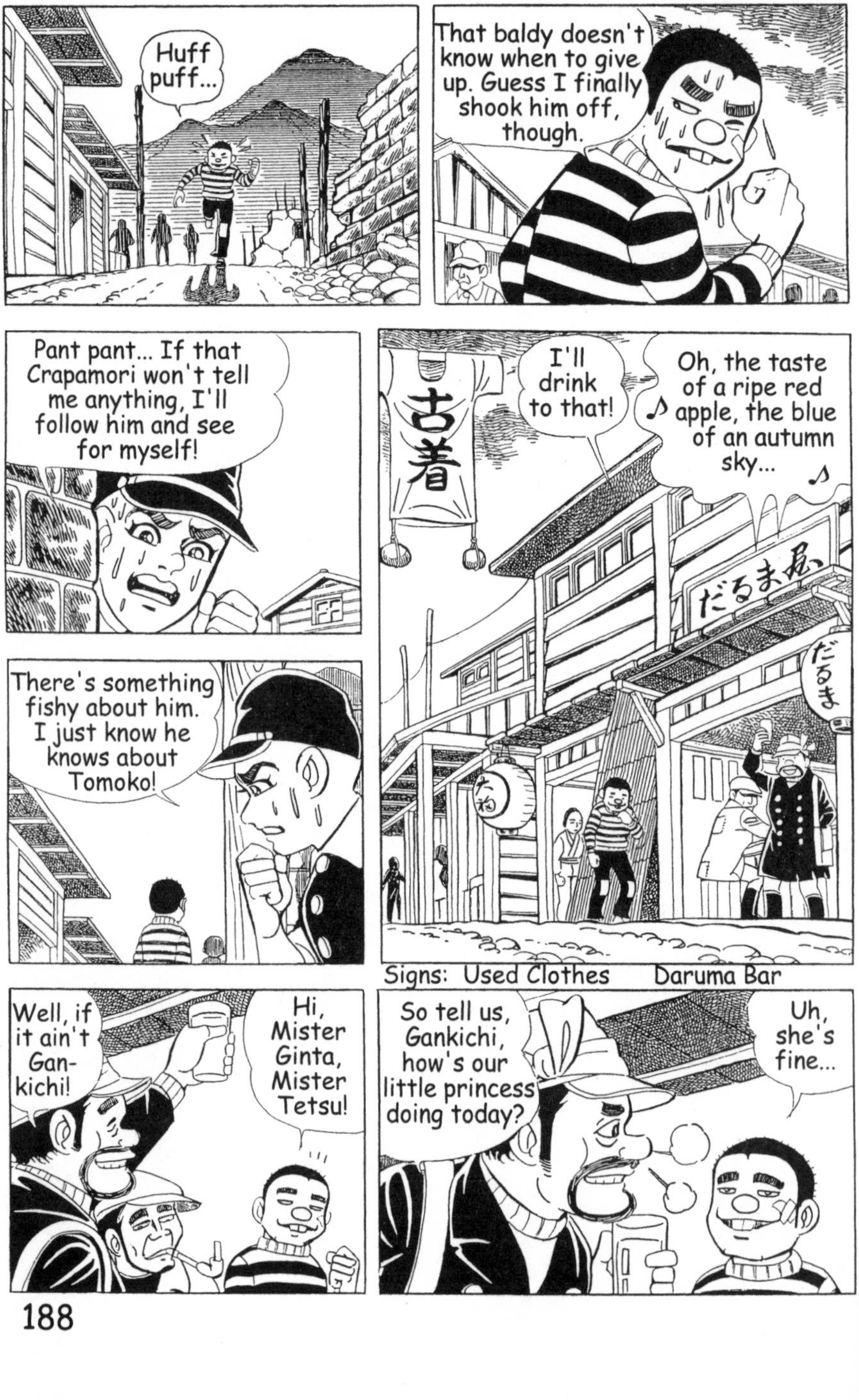
Huff puff...
That baldy doesn't know when to give up. Guess I finally shook him off, though.
Pant pant... If that Crapamori won't tell me anything, I'll follow him and see for myself!
There's something fishy about him. I just know he knows about Tomoko!
古着
I'll drink to that!
♪ Oh, the taste of a ripe red apple, the blue of an autumn sky... ♪
だるま屋
だるま
Signs: Used Clothes Daruma Bar
Well, if it ain't Gan-kichi!
Hi, Mister Ginta, Mister Tetsu!
So tell us, Gankichi, how's our little princess doing today?
Uh, she's fine...

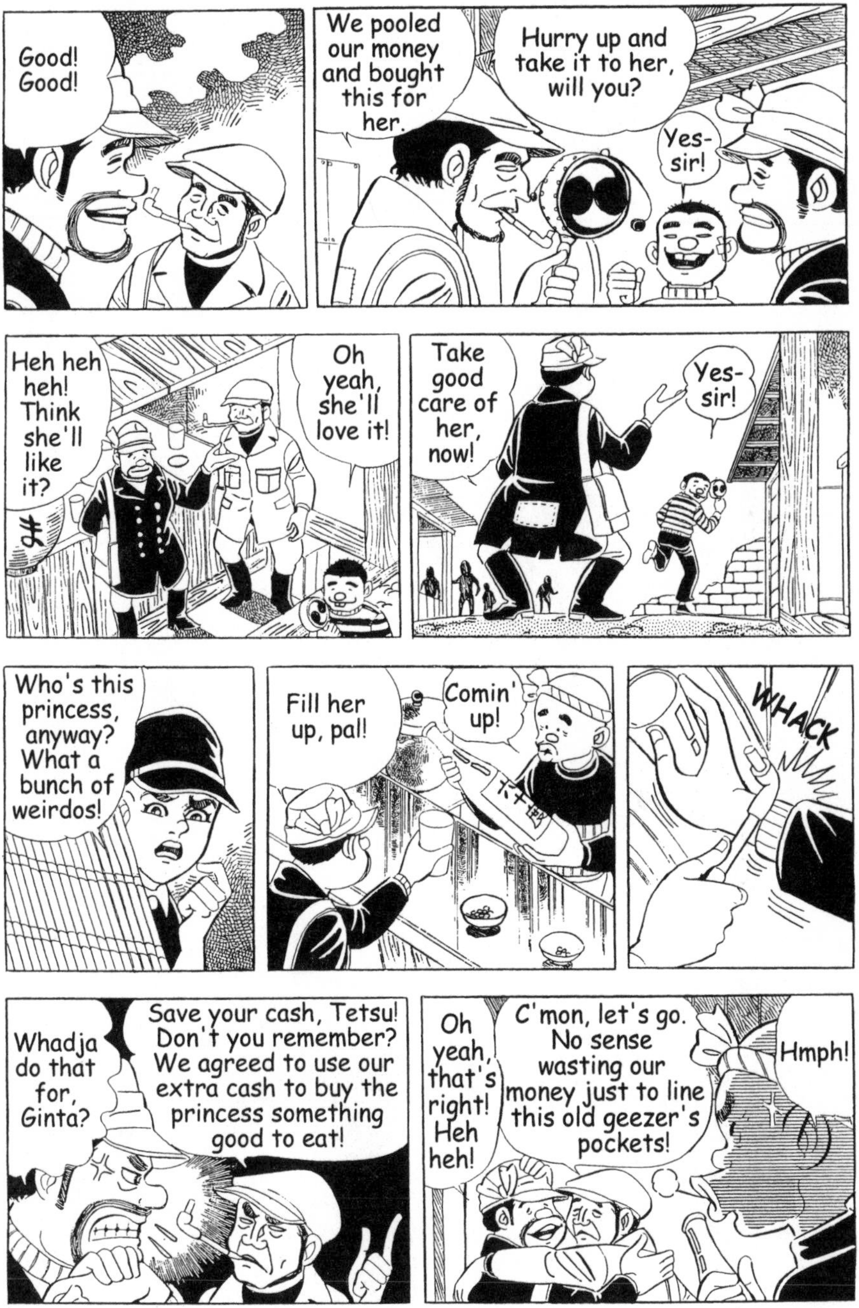
Good! Good!
We pooled our money and bought this for her.
Hurry up and take it to her, will you?
Yes-sir!
Heh heh heh! Think she'll like it?
Oh yeah, she'll love it!
Take good care of her, now!
Yes-sir!
Who's this princess, anyway? What a bunch of weirdos!
Fill her up, pal!
Comin' up!
WHACK
Whadja do that for, Ginta?
Save your cash, Tetsu! Don't you remember? We agreed to use our extra cash to buy the princess something good to eat!
Oh yeah, that's right! Heh heh!
C'mon, let's go. No sense wasting our money just to line this old geezer's pockets!
Hmph!

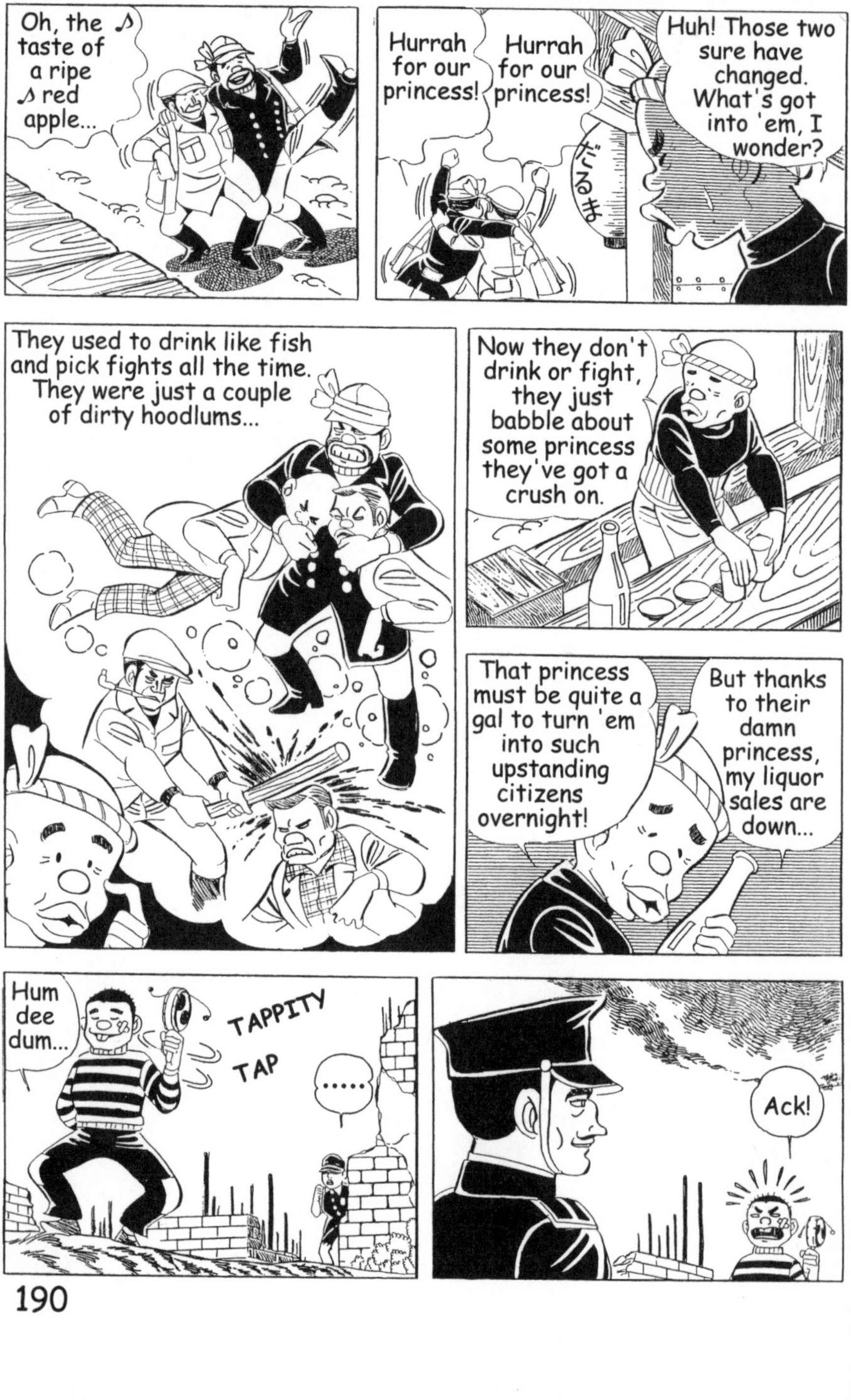
Oh, the ♪ taste of a ripe ♪ red apple...
Hurrah for our princess!
Hurrah for our princess!
だるま
Huh! Those two sure have changed. What's got into 'em, I wonder?
They used to drink like fish and pick fights all the time. They were just a couple of dirty hoodlums...
Now they don't drink or fight, they just babble about some princess they've got a crush on.
That princess must be quite a gal to turn 'em into such upstanding citizens overnight!
But thanks to their damn princess, my liquor sales are down...
Hum dee dum...
TAPPITY TAP
......
Ack!

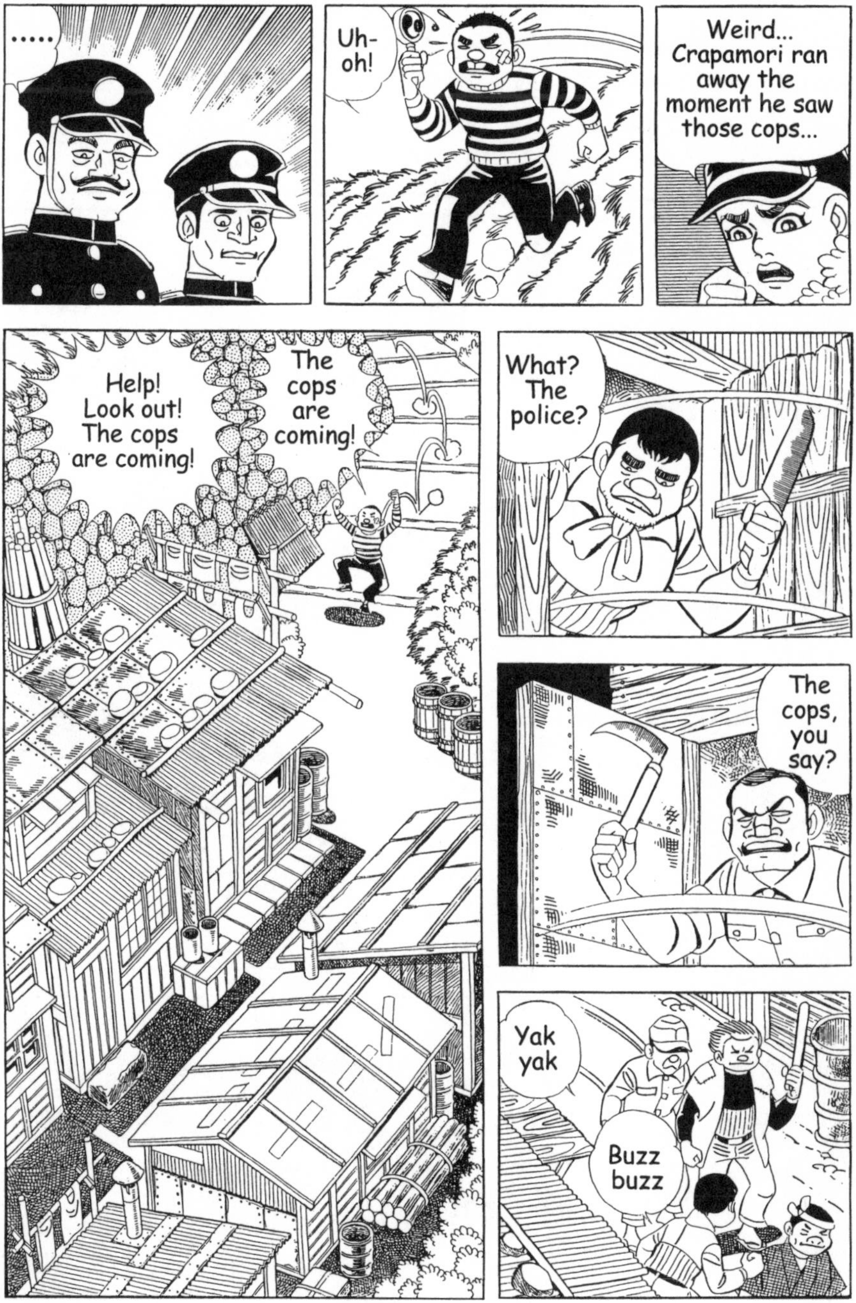
.....
Uh-oh!
Weird... Crapamori ran away the moment he saw those cops...
Help! Look out! The cops are coming!
The cops are coming!
What? The police?
The cops, you say?
Yak yak
Buzz buzz

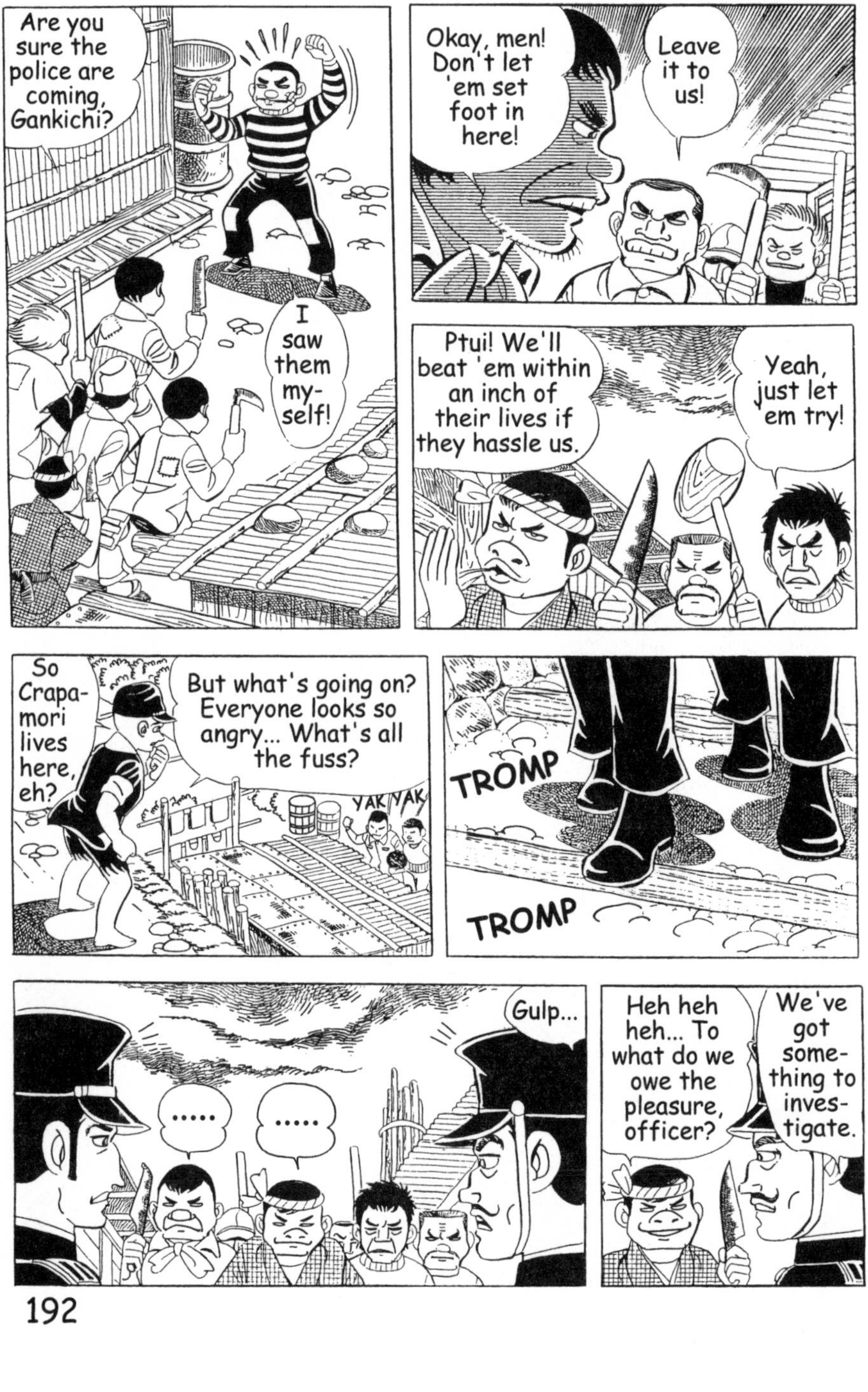
Are you sure the police are coming, Gankichi?
I saw them my-self!
Okay, men! Don't let 'em set foot in here!
Leave it to us!
Ptui! We'll beat 'em within an inch of their lives if they hassle us.
Yeah, just let 'em try!
So Crapa-mori lives here, eh?
But what's going on? Everyone looks so angry... What's all the fuss?
YAK YAK
TROMP
TROMP
......
......
Gulp...
Heh heh heh... To what do we owe the pleasure, officer?
We've got some-thing to inves-tigate.

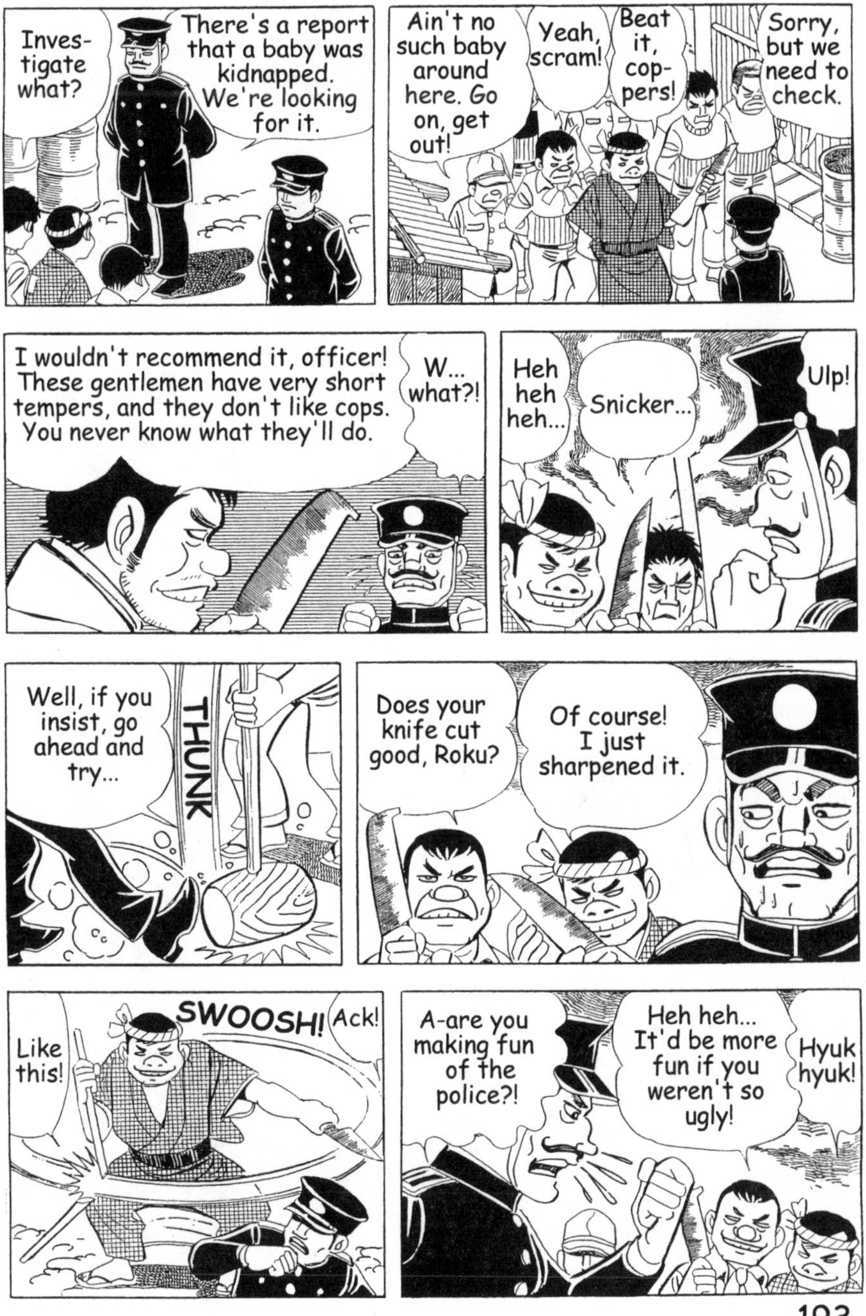
Inves-tigate what?
There's a report that a baby was kidnapped. We're looking for it.
Ain't no such baby around here. Go on, get out!
Yeah, scram!
Beat it, cop-pers!
Sorry, but we need to check.
I wouldn't recommend it, officer! These gentlemen have very short tempers, and they don't like cops. You never know what they'll do.
W... what?!
Heh heh heh...
Snicker...
Ulp!
Well, if you insist, go ahead and try...
THUNK
Does your knife cut good, Roku?
Of course! I just sharpened it.
Like this!
SWOOSH!
Ack!
A-are you making fun of the police?!
Heh heh... It'd be more fun if you weren't so ugly!
Hyuk hyuk!

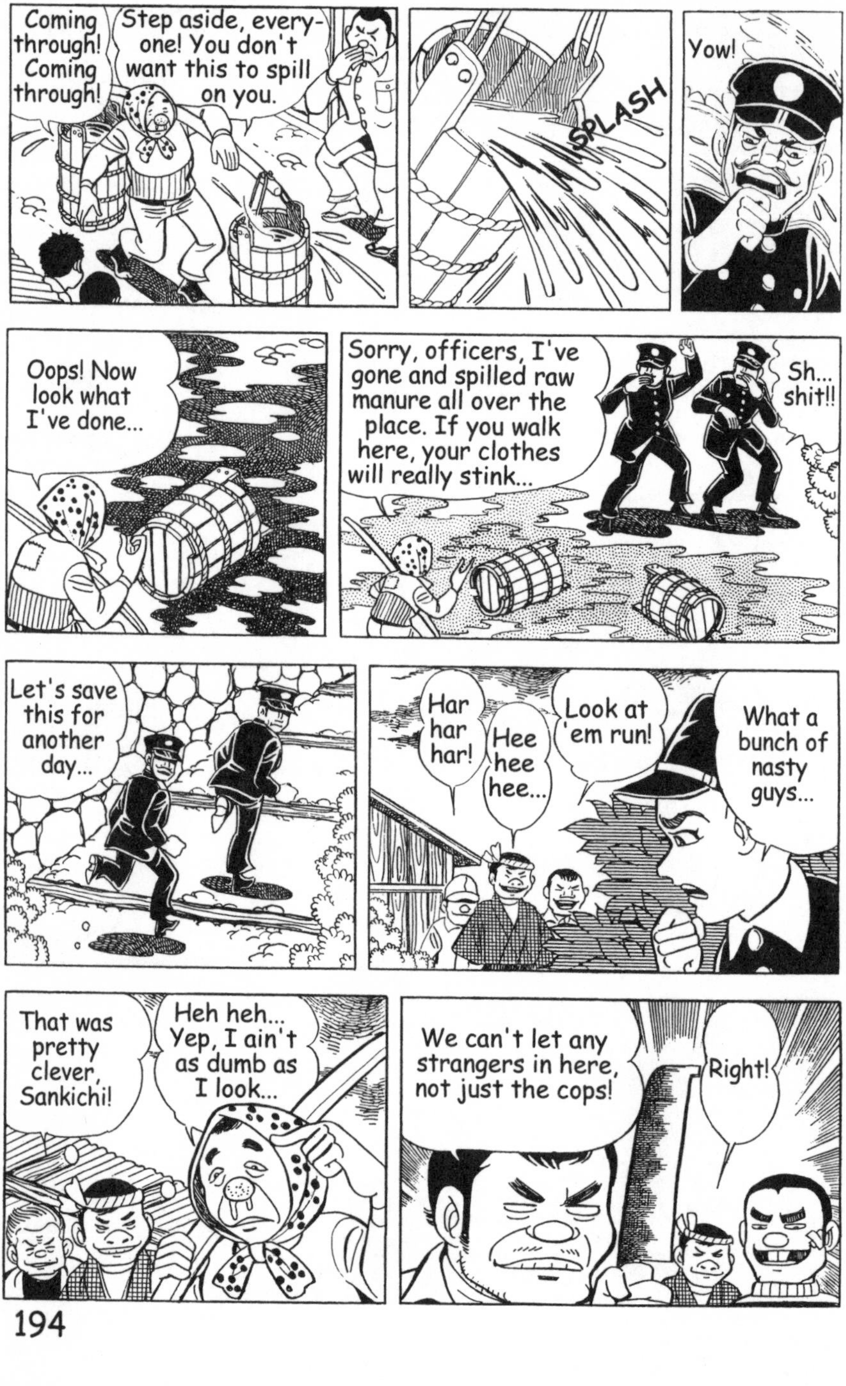
Coming through! Coming through!
Step aside, every-one! You don't want this to spill on you.
SPLASH
Yow!
Oops! Now look what I've done...
Sorry, officers, I've gone and spilled raw manure all over the place. If you walk here, your clothes will really stink...
Sh... shit!!
Let's save this for another day...
Har har har!
Hee hee hee...
Look at 'em run!
What a bunch of nasty guys...
That was pretty clever, Sankichi!
Heh heh... Yep, I ain't as dumb as I look...
We can't let any strangers in here, not just the cops!
Right!

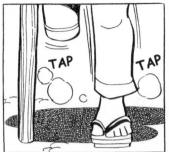

TAP TAP

I hear the police have come around asking questions.

Don't worry, Tamikichi, we won't let 'em lay a hand on you or the princess!

Sorry to cause so much trouble for you all.

Whaddaya mean? You don't have to apologize to us!

Yeah, the least we can do is protect you!

WAAHH WAAHH WAAHH

There, there.

Look, Tamikichi! Ginta and Tetsu told me to give this to the princess!

Oh my! Thank you!

Hey, princess, stop crying! This is for you!

RAT-A-TAT-TAT

Waahh! Waahh!

195

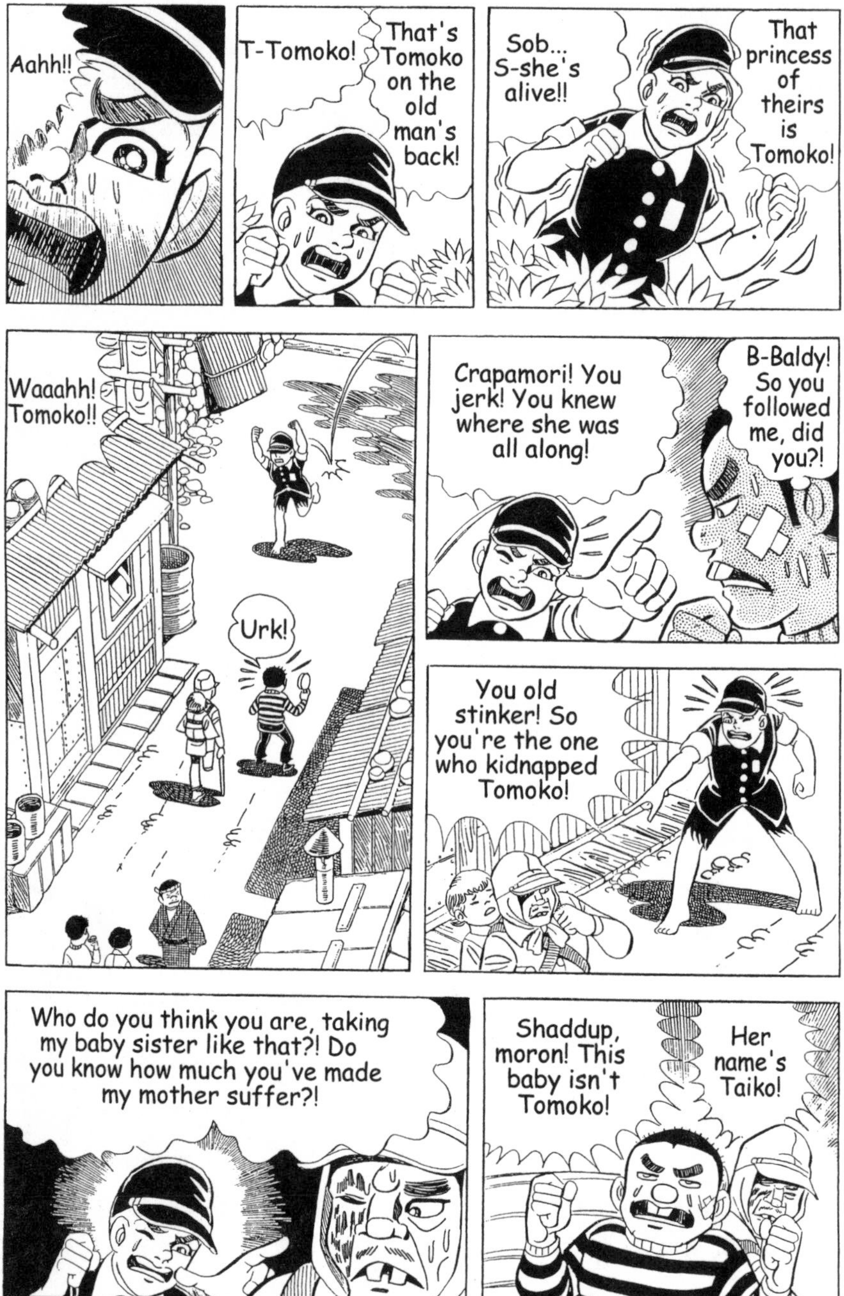
Aahh!!
T-Tomoko!
That's Tomoko on the old man's back!
Sob... S-she's alive!!
That princess of theirs is Tomoko!
Waaahh! Tomoko!!
Urk!
Crapamori! You jerk! You knew where she was all along!
B-Baldy! So you followed me, did you?!
You old stinker! So you're the one who kidnapped Tomoko!
Who do you think you are, taking my baby sister like that?! Do you know how much you've made my mother suffer?!
Shaddup, moron! This baby isn't Tomoko!
Her name's Taiko!

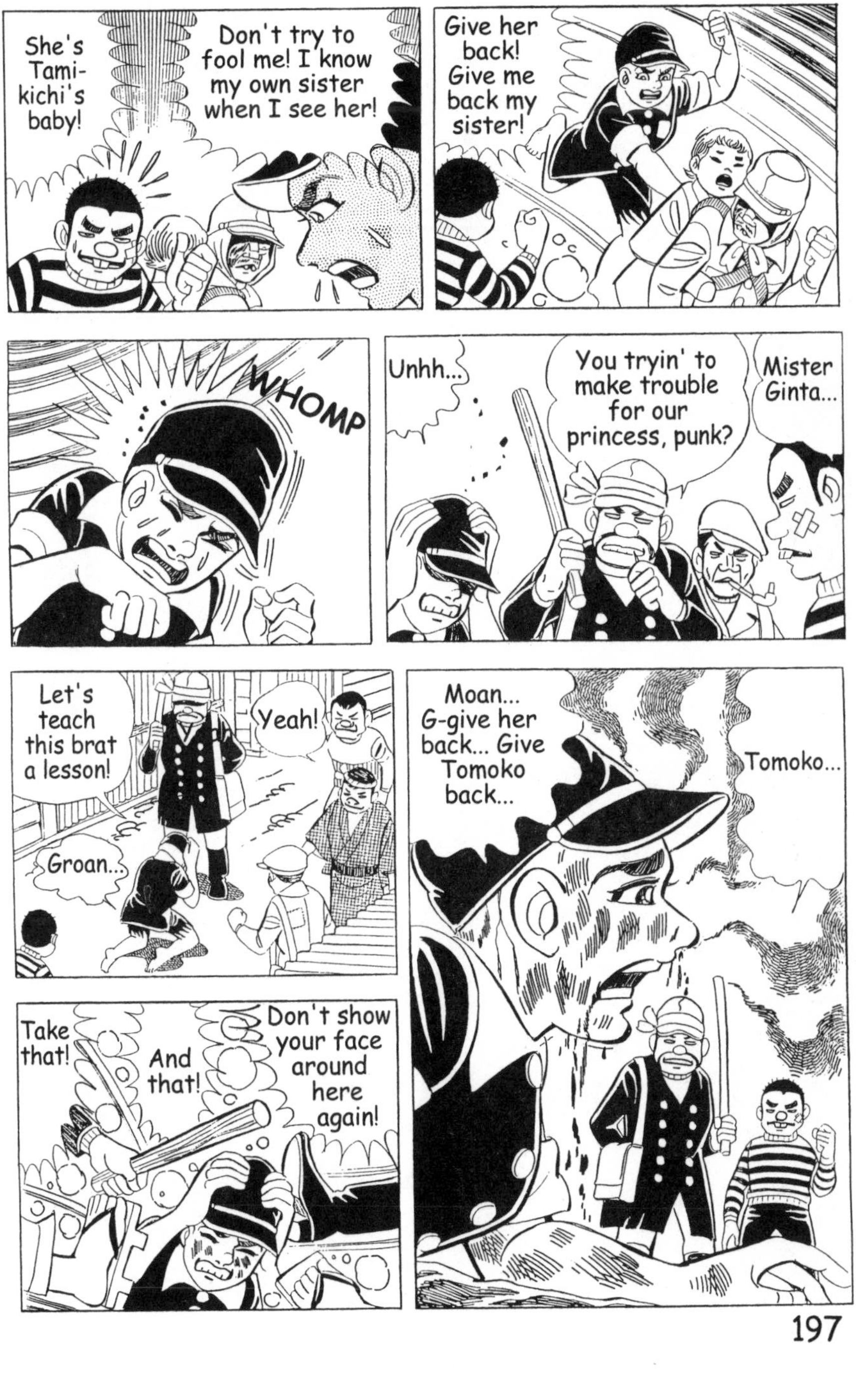
She's Tami-kichi's baby!
Don't try to fool me! I know my own sister when I see her!
Give her back! Give me back my sister!
WHOMP
Unhh...
You tryin' to make trouble for our princess, punk?
Mister Ginta...
Let's teach this brat a lesson!
Yeah!
Groan...
Take that!
And that!
Don't show your face around here again!
Moan... G-give her back... Give Tomoko back...
Tomoko...

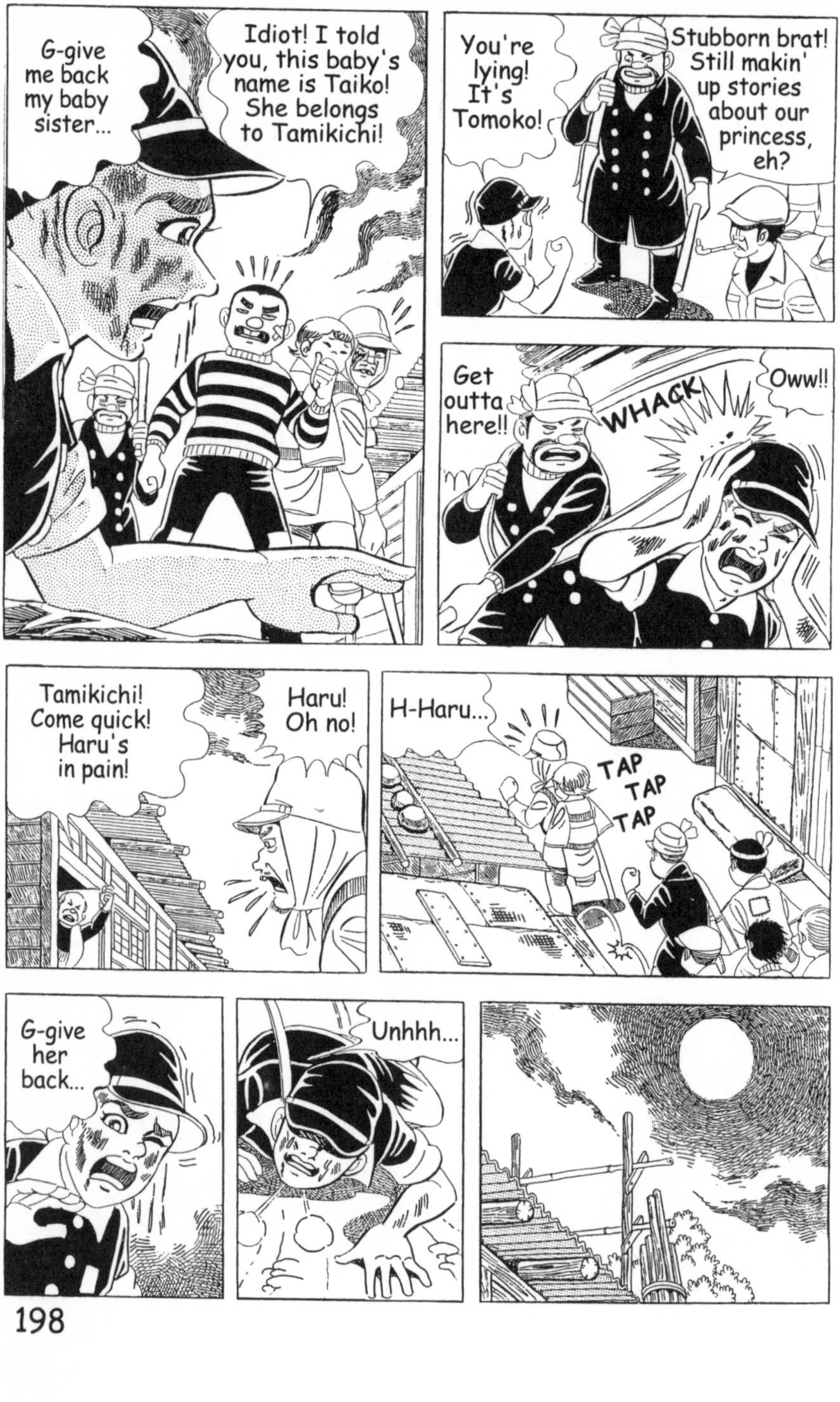
G-give me back my baby sister...
Idiot! I told you, this baby's name is Taiko! She belongs to Tamikichi!
You're lying! It's Tomoko!
Stubborn brat! Still makin' up stories about our princess, eh?
Get outta here!!
WHACK
Oww!!
Tamikichi! Come quick! Haru's in pain!
Haru! Oh no!
H-Haru...
TAP TAP TAP
G-give her back...
Unhhh...

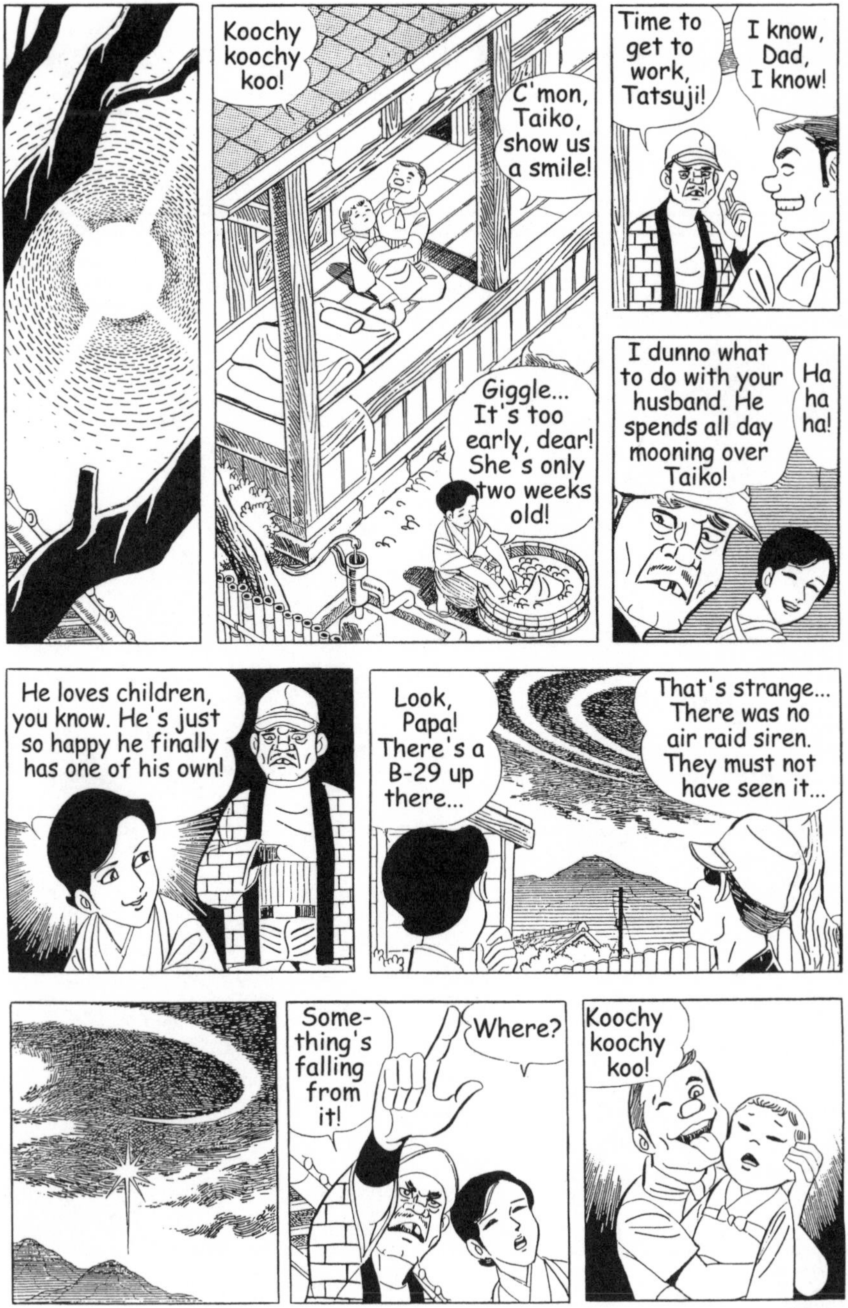
Koochy koochy koo!
C'mon, Taiko, show us a smile!
Giggle... It's too early, dear! She's only two weeks old!
Time to get to work, Tatsuji!
I know, Dad, I know!
I dunno what to do with your husband. He spends all day mooning over Taiko!
Ha ha ha!
He loves children, you know. He's just so happy he finally has one of his own!
Look, Papa! There's a B-29 up there...
That's strange... There was no air raid siren. They must not have seen it...
Some-thing's falling from it!
Where?
Koochy koochy koo!

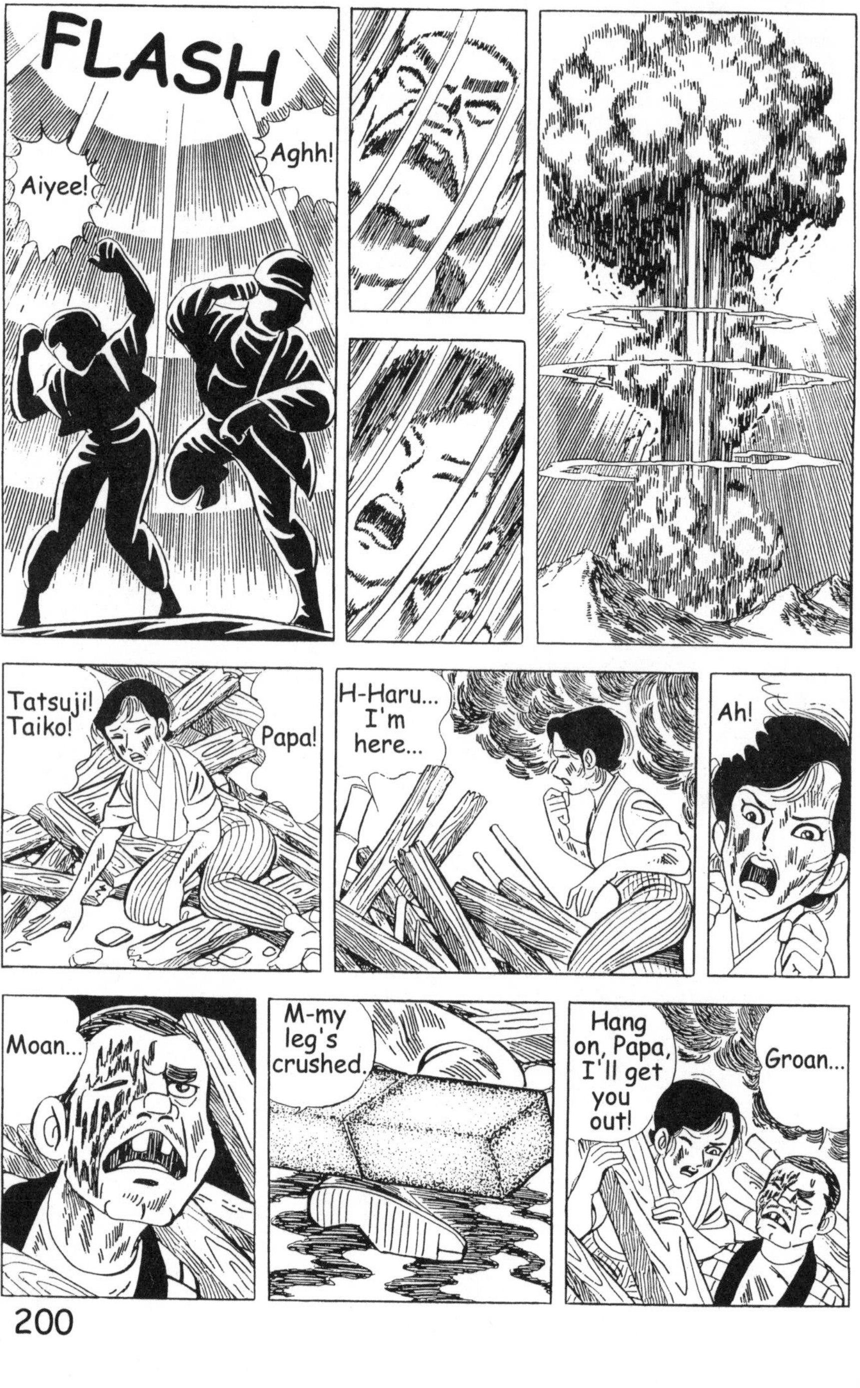
FLASH
Aiyee!
Aghh!
Tatsuji! Taiko!
Papa!
H-Haru... I'm here...
Ah!
Moan...
M-my leg's crushed.
Hang on, Papa, I'll get you out!
Groan...

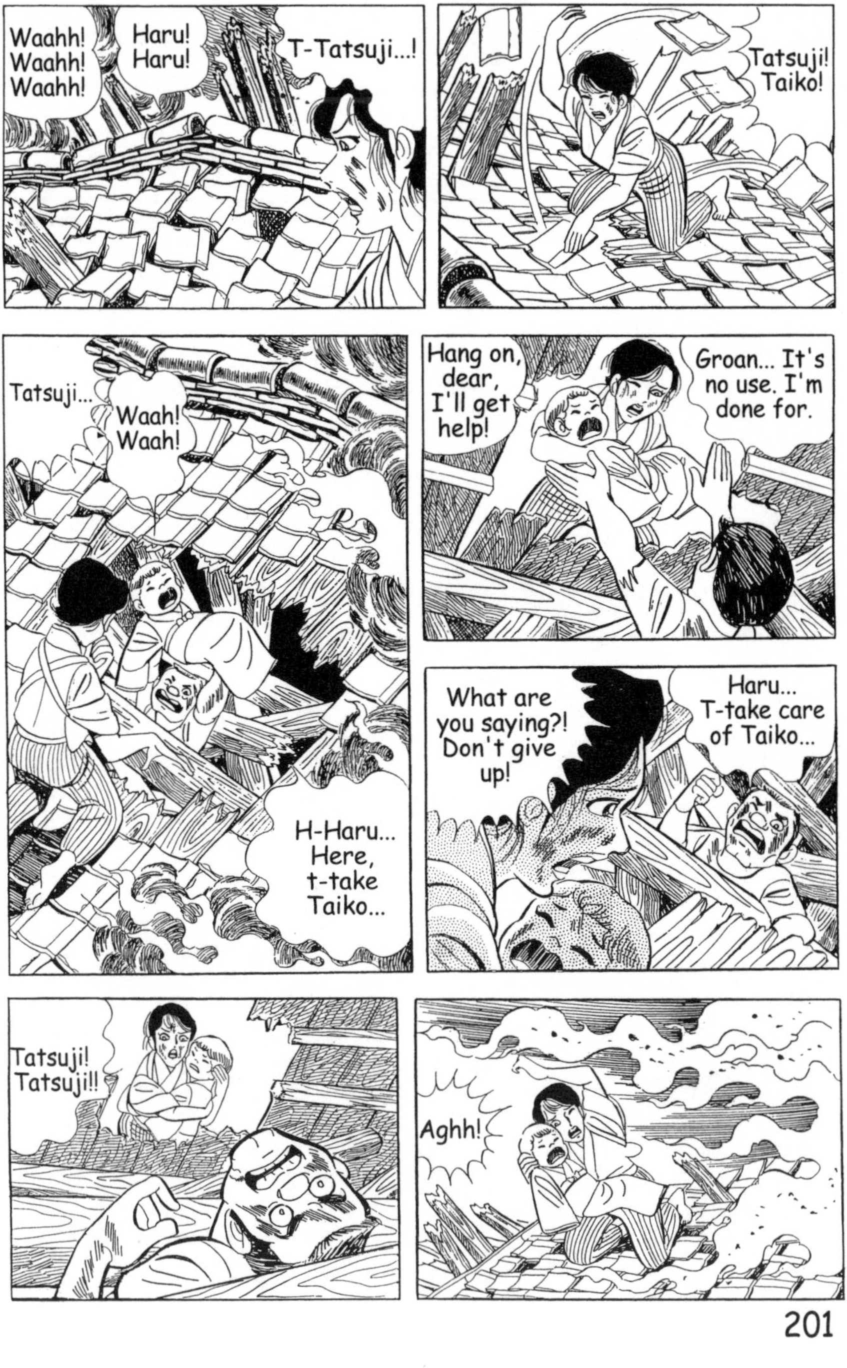
Waahh! Waahh! Waahh!
Haru! Haru!
T-Tatsuji...!
Tatsuji! Taiko!
Tatsuji...
Waah! Waah!
H-Haru... Here, t-take Taiko...
Hang on, dear, I'll get help!
Groan... It's no use. I'm done for.
What are you saying?! Don't give up!
Haru... T-take care of Taiko...
Tatsuji! Tatsuji!!
Aghh!

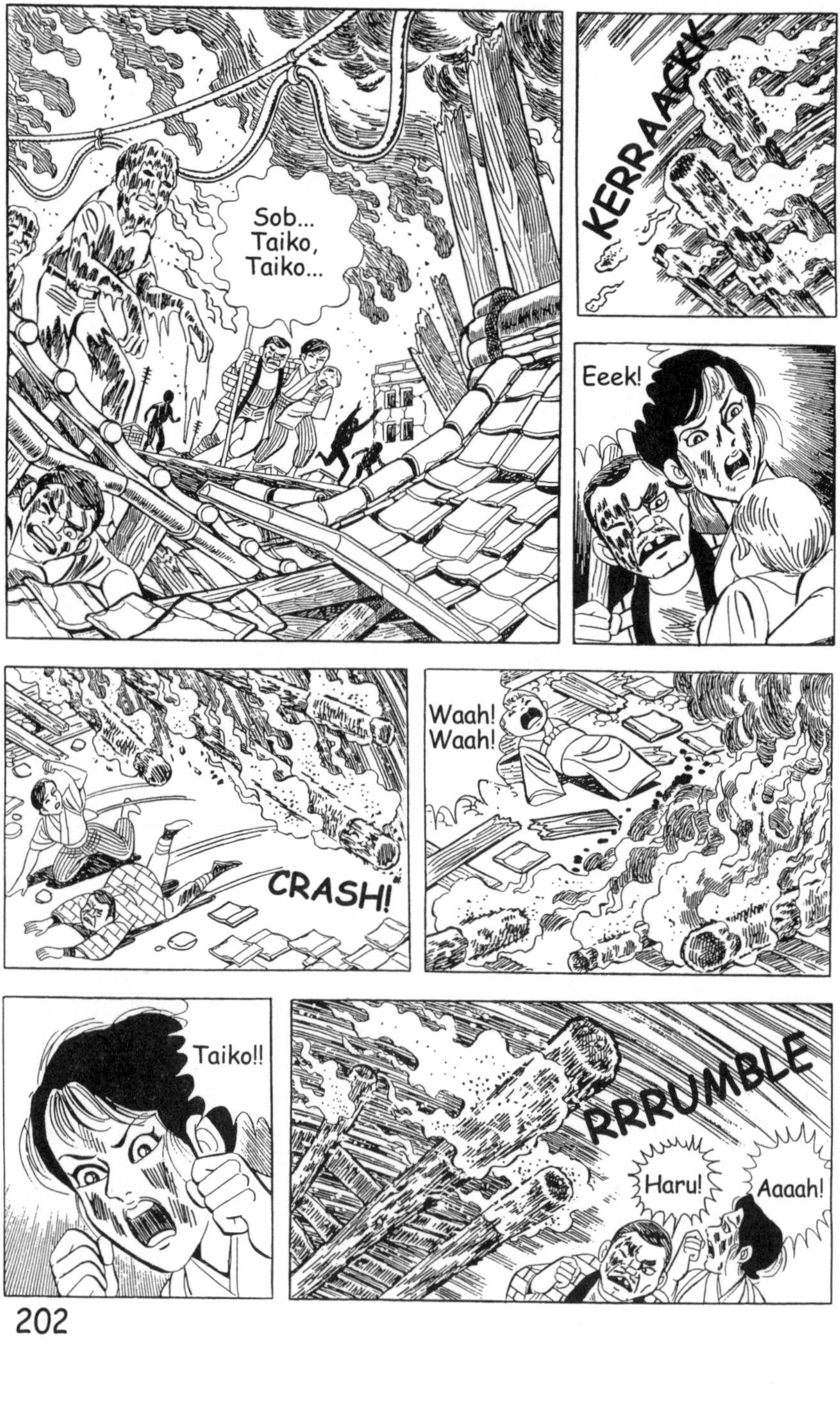
Sob...
Taiko,
Taiko...
KERRAACKK
Eeek!
CRASH!
Waah!
Waah!
Taiko!!
RRRUMBLE
Haru!
Aaaah!

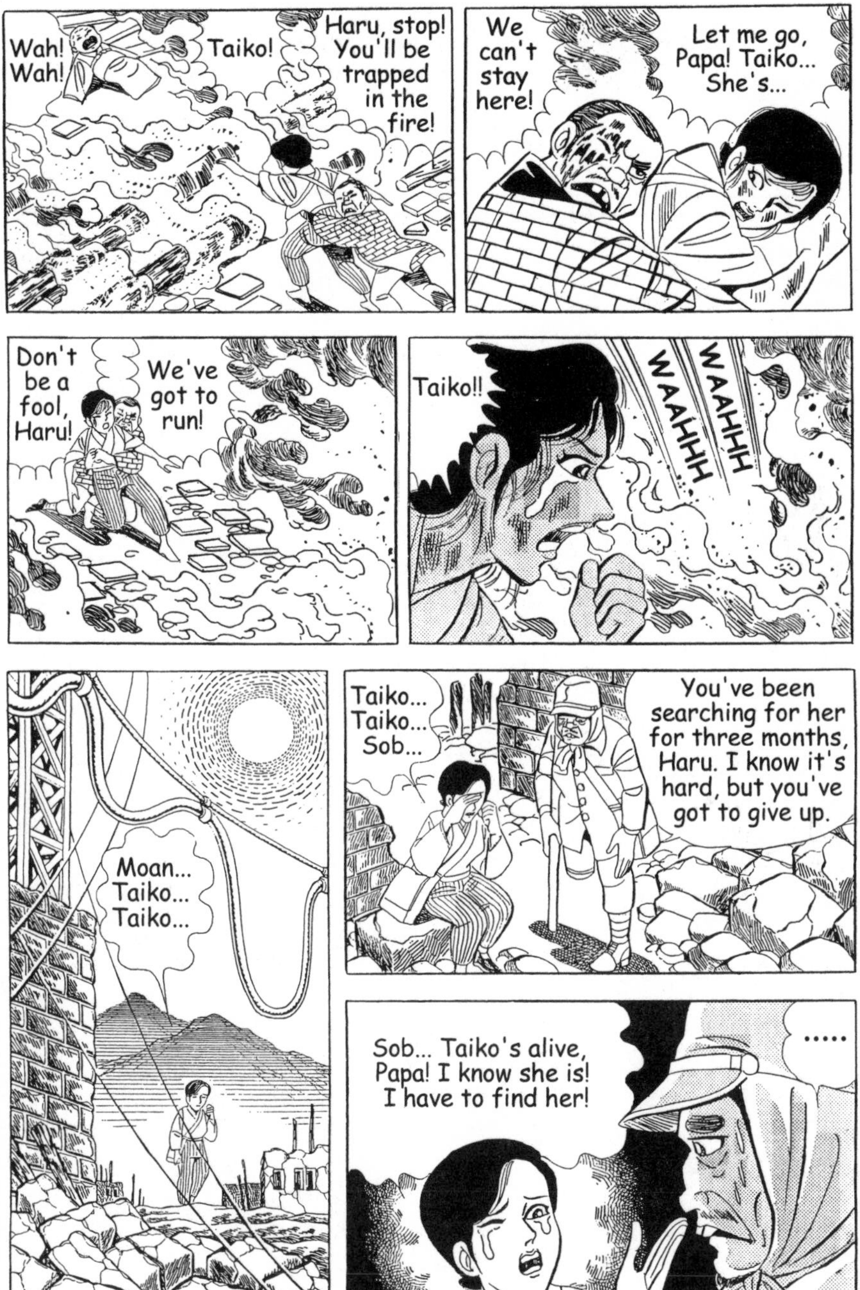

Wah! Wah!
Taiko!
Haru, stop! You'll be trapped in the fire!
We can't stay here!
Let me go, Papa! Taiko... She's...
Don't be a fool, Haru!
We've got to run!
Taiko!!
WAAHHHH WAAHHHH
Moan... Taiko... Taiko...
Taiko... Taiko... Sob...
You've been searching for her for three months, Haru. I know it's hard, but you've got to give up.
Sob... Taiko's alive, Papa! I know she is! I have to find her!
.....

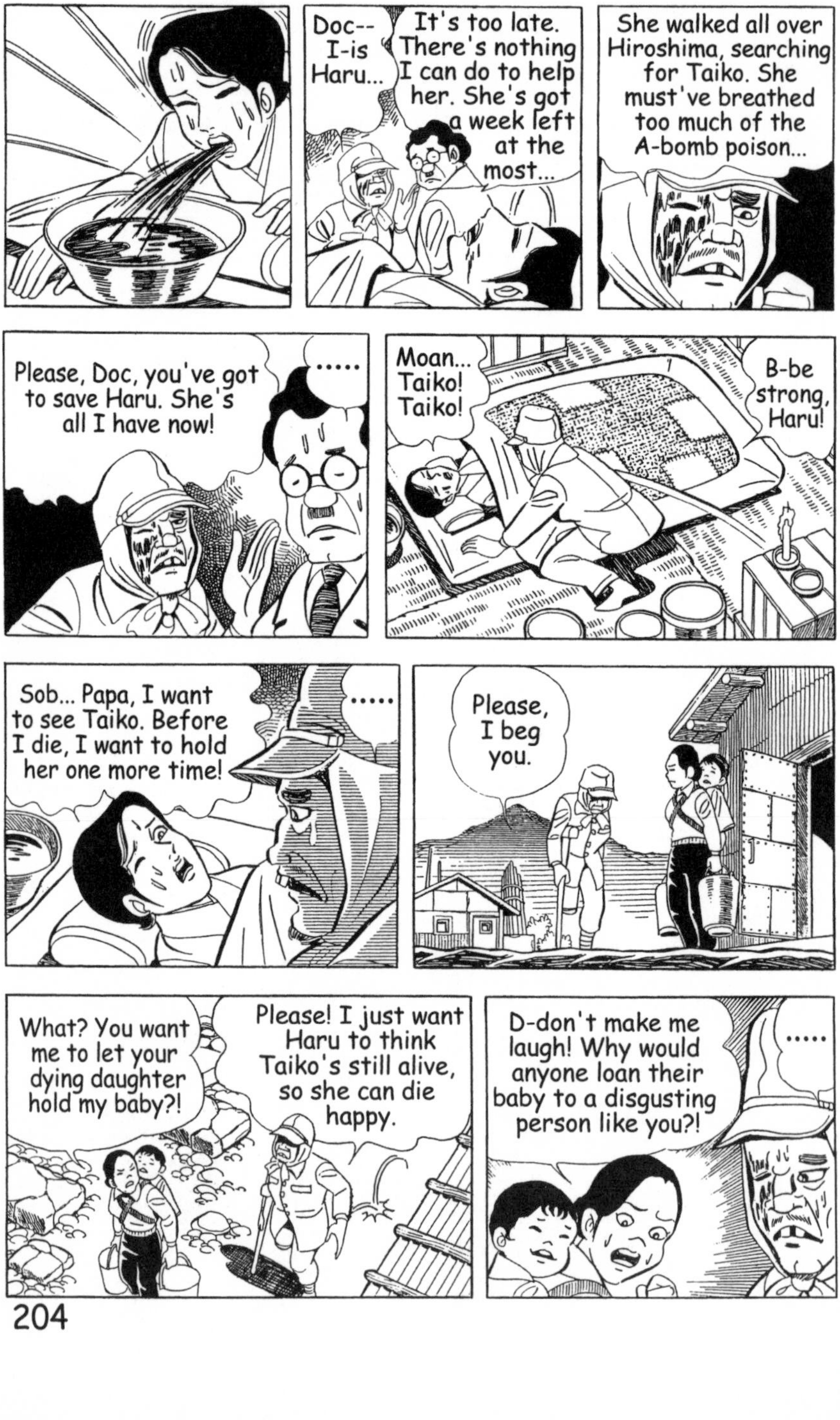
Doc-- I-is Haru...
It's too late. There's nothing I can do to help her. She's got a week left at the most...
She walked all over Hiroshima, searching for Taiko. She must've breathed too much of the A-bomb poison...
Please, Doc, you've got to save Haru. She's all I have now!
.....
Moan... Taiko! Taiko!
B-be strong, Haru!
Sob... Papa, I want to see Taiko. Before I die, I want to hold her one more time!
.....
Please, I beg you.
What? You want me to let your dying daughter hold my baby?!
Please! I just want Haru to think Taiko's still alive, so she can die happy.
D-don't make me laugh! Why would anyone loan their baby to a disgusting person like you?!
.....

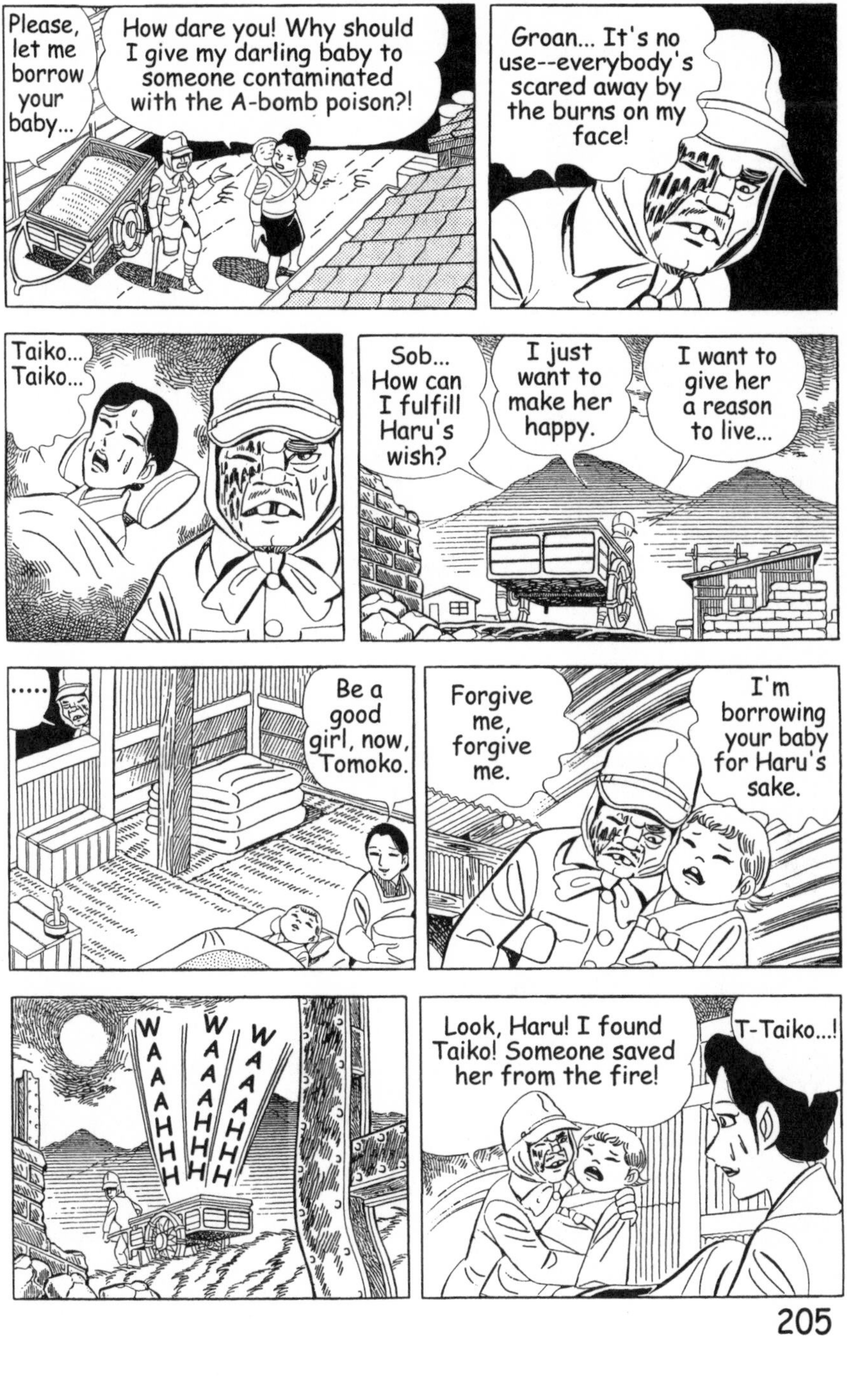
Please, let me borrow your baby...
How dare you! Why should I give my darling baby to someone contaminated with the A-bomb poison?!
Groan... It's no use--everybody's scared away by the burns on my face!
Taiko... Taiko...
Sob... How can I fulfill Haru's wish?
I just want to make her happy.
I want to give her a reason to live...
.....
Be a good girl, now, Tomoko.
Forgive me, forgive me.
I'm borrowing your baby for Haru's sake.
WAAAAHHH
WAAAAHHH
WAAAAHHH
Look, Haru! I found Taiko! Someone saved her from the fire!
T-Taiko...!

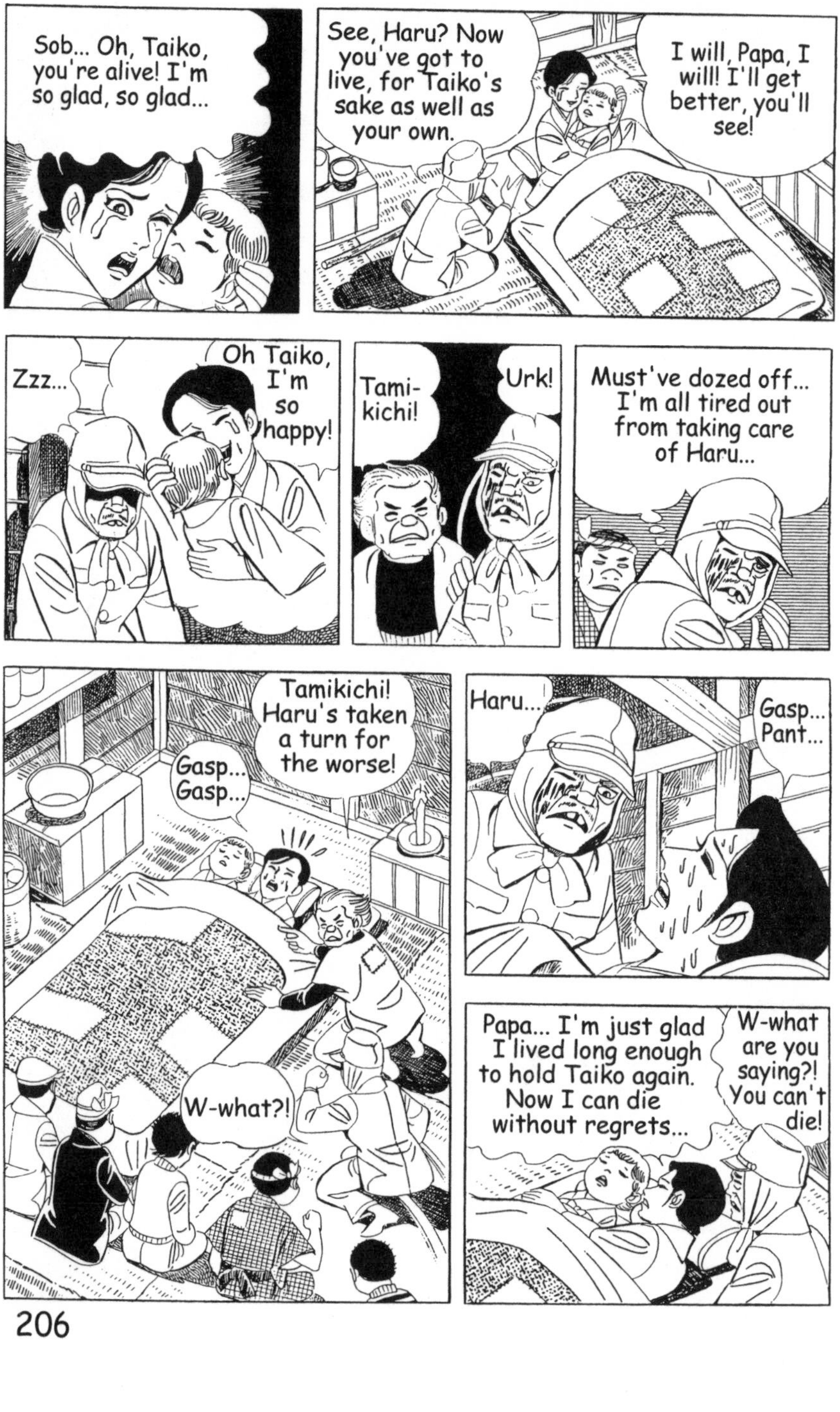
Sob... Oh, Taiko, you're alive! I'm so glad, so glad...
See, Haru? Now you've got to live, for Taiko's sake as well as your own.
I will, Papa, I will! I'll get better, you'll see!
Zzz...
Oh Taiko, I'm so happy!
Tami-kichi!
Urk!
Must've dozed off... I'm all tired out from taking care of Haru...
Gasp... Gasp...
Tamikichi! Haru's taken a turn for the worse!
W-what?!
Haru...
Gasp... Pant...
Papa... I'm just glad I lived long enough to hold Taiko again. Now I can die without regrets...
W-what are you saying?! You can't die!

Please, Papa, take good care of Taiko for me... That's all I ask...

You can't die, Haru! You've got to live!!

Gasp...

Haru! Be strong!

Don't give up now!

Gasp... T-Taiko, your mother wanted to be with you always... But she can't...

I want so badly to live, but it's no use... Gasp... Forgive me, forgive me...

WAAHHH WAAHHH WAAHHH WAAHHH

Sob... Don't cry, Taiko, don't cry!

Waah! Waah!

There, there... Let mama sing to you...

♪ Pant pant... Hush-a-bye, baby, don't you cry... ♪

Sob...

Sniff...

M-mama's going to sing you a ♪ lullaby... ♪ Sleep, my little one, sleep...

Haru!

Haru...

Miz Haru!

207

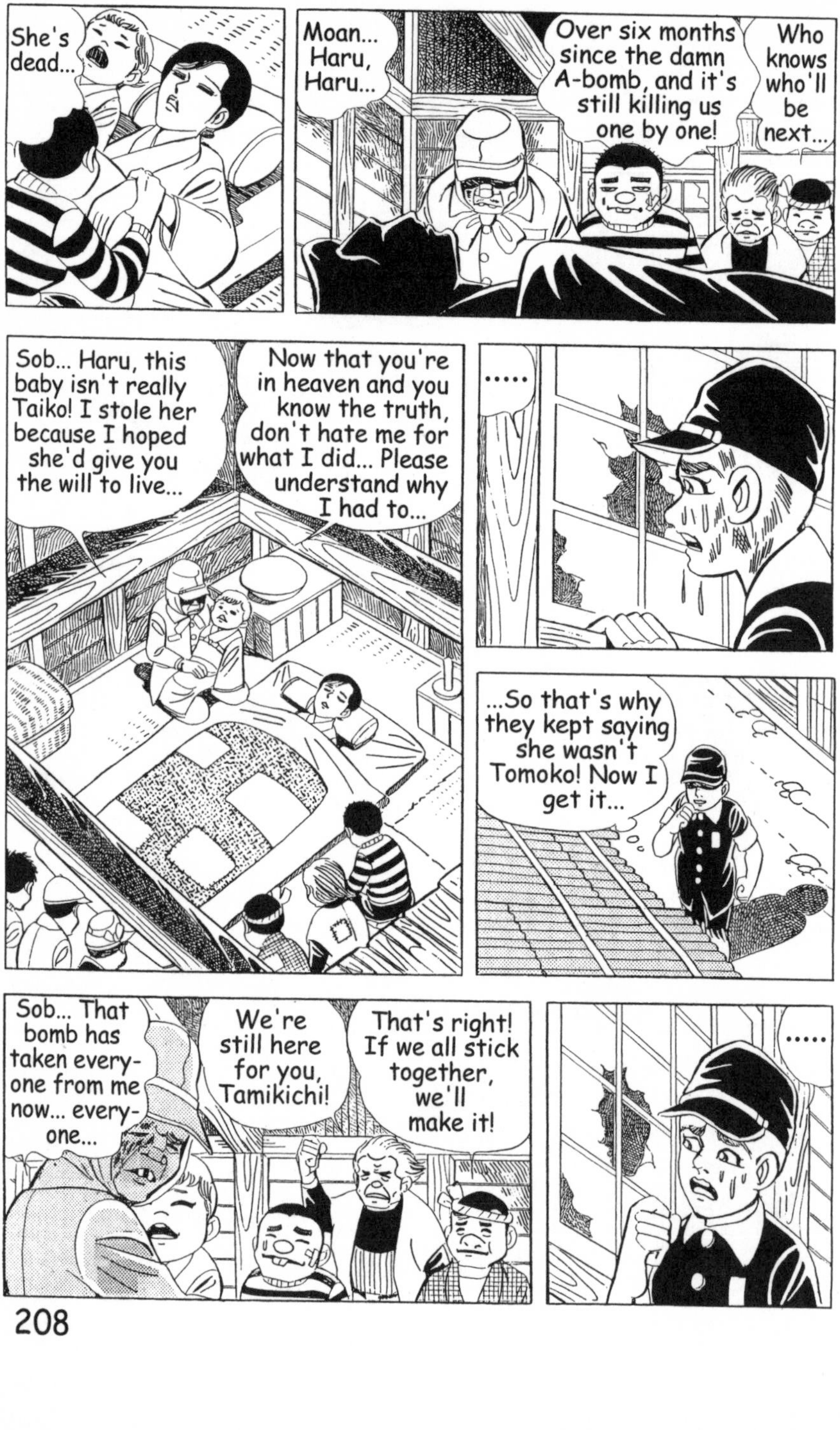
She's dead...
Moan... Haru, Haru...
Over six months since the damn A-bomb, and it's still killing us one by one!
Who knows who'll be next...
Sob... Haru, this baby isn't really Taiko! I stole her because I hoped she'd give you the will to live...
Now that you're in heaven and you know the truth, don't hate me for what I did... Please understand why I had to...
.....
...So that's why they kept saying she wasn't Tomoko! Now I get it...
Sob... That bomb has taken every-one from me now... every-one...
We're still here for you, Tamikichi!
That's right! If we all stick together, we'll make it!
.....

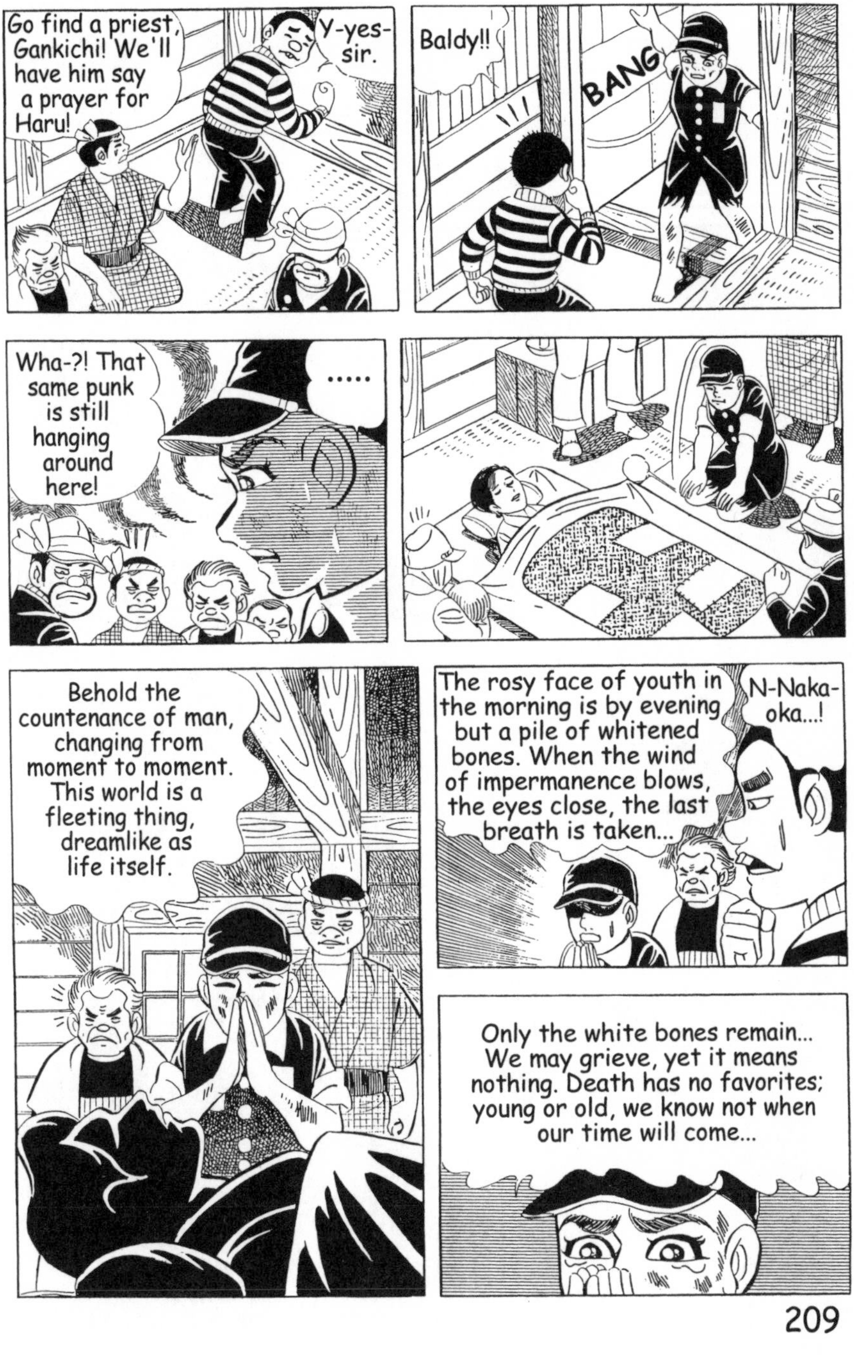

Go find a priest, Gankichi! We'll have him say a prayer for Haru!
Y-yes-sir.
Baldy!!
BANG
Wha-?! That same punk is still hanging around here!
.....
Behold the countenance of man, changing from moment to moment. This world is a fleeting thing, dreamlike as life itself.
The rosy face of youth in the morning is by evening but a pile of whitened bones. When the wind of impermanence blows, the eyes close, the last breath is taken...
N-Naka-oka...!
Only the white bones remain... We may grieve, yet it means nothing. Death has no favorites; young or old, we know not when our time will come...

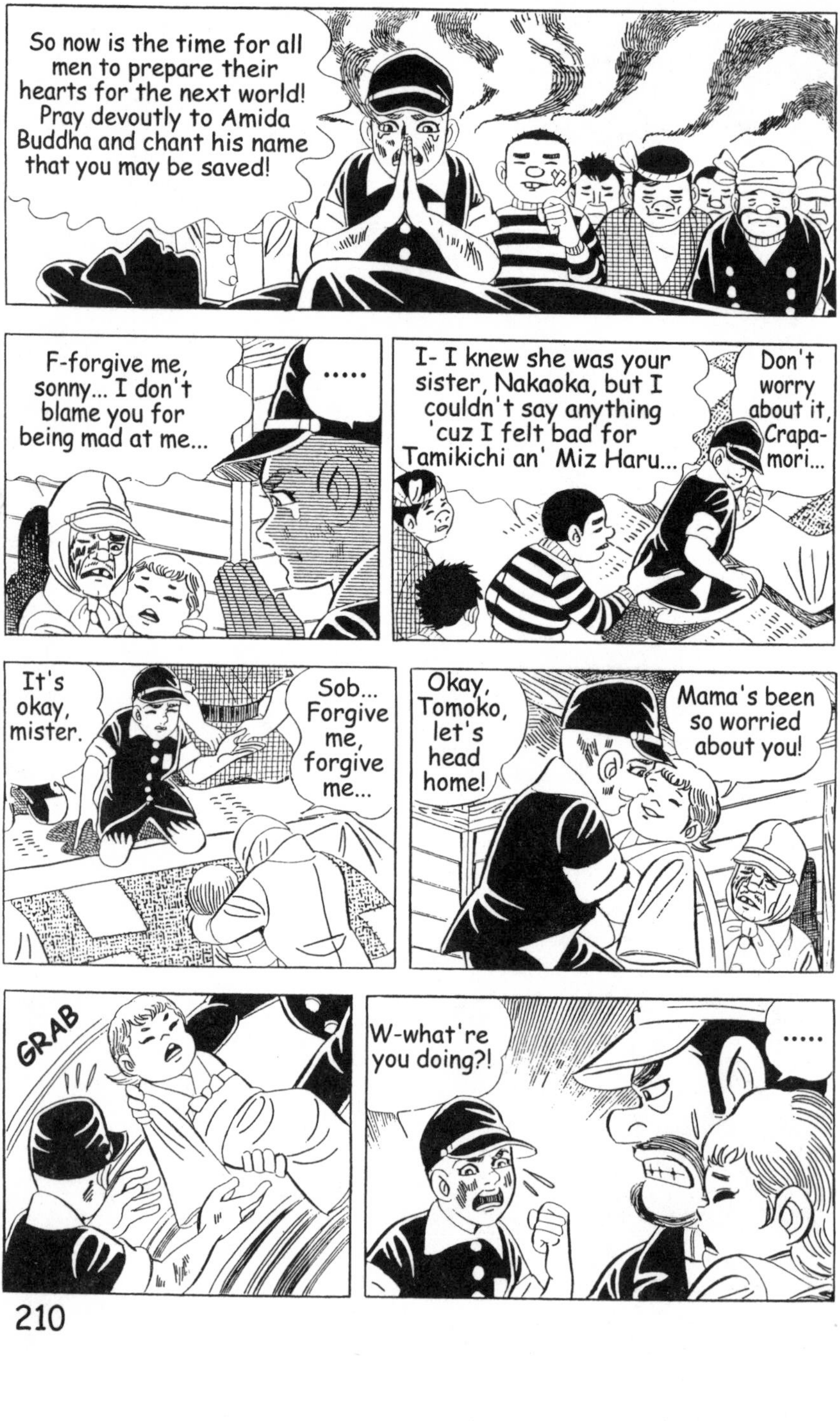
So now is the time for all men to prepare their hearts for the next world! Pray devoutly to Amida Buddha and chant his name that you may be saved!
F-forgive me, sonny... I don't blame you for being mad at me...
.....
I- I knew she was your sister, Nakaoka, but I couldn't say anything 'cuz I felt bad for Tamikichi an' Miz Haru...
Don't worry about it, Crapa-mori...
It's okay, mister.
Sob... Forgive me, forgive me...
Okay, Tomoko, let's head home!
Mama's been so worried about you!
GRAB
W-what're you doing?!
.....

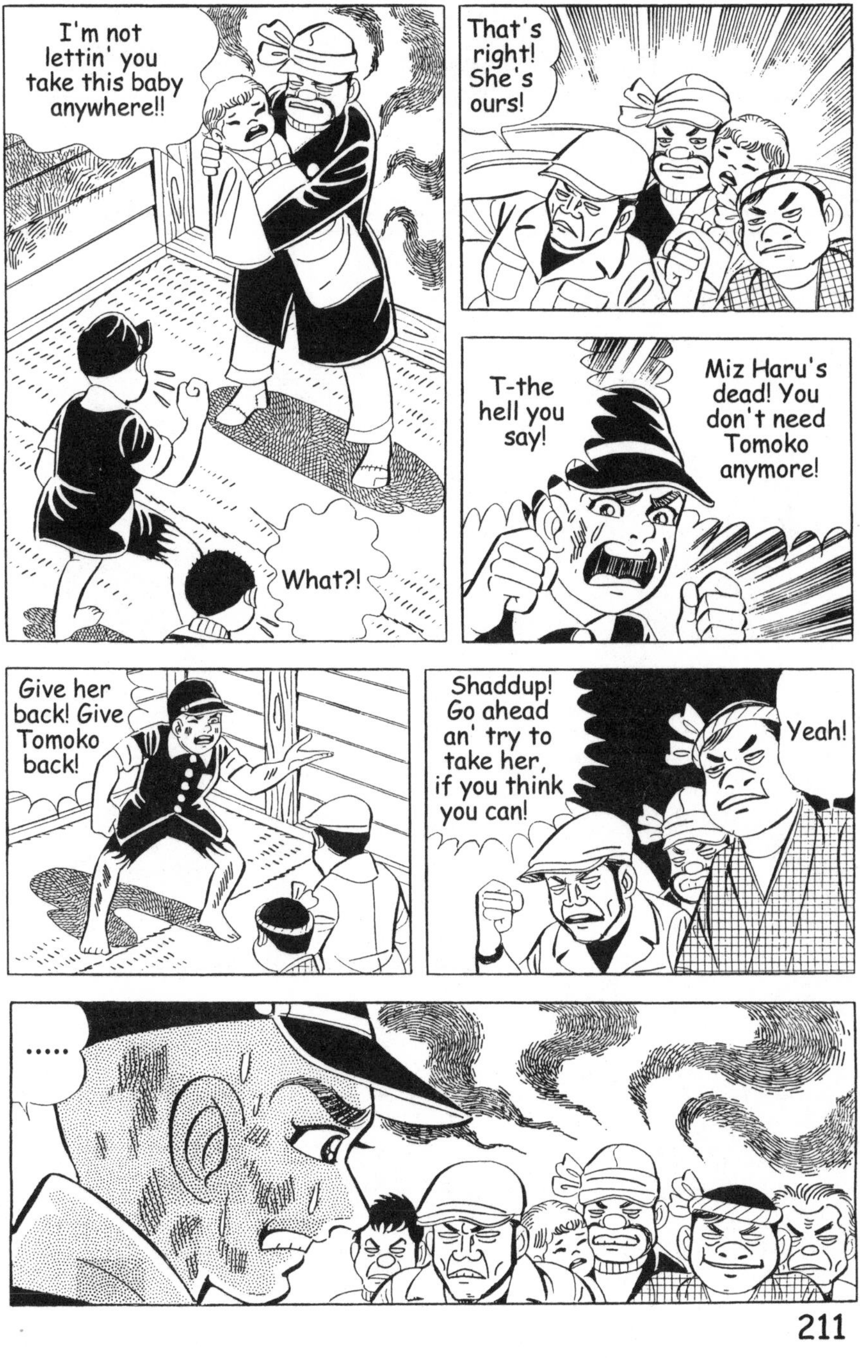

I'm not lettin' you take this baby anywhere!!
What?!
That's right! She's ours!
T-the hell you say!
Miz Haru's dead! You don't need Tomoko anymore!
Give her back! Give Tomoko back!
Shaddup! Go ahead an' try to take her, if you think you can!
Yeah!
.....

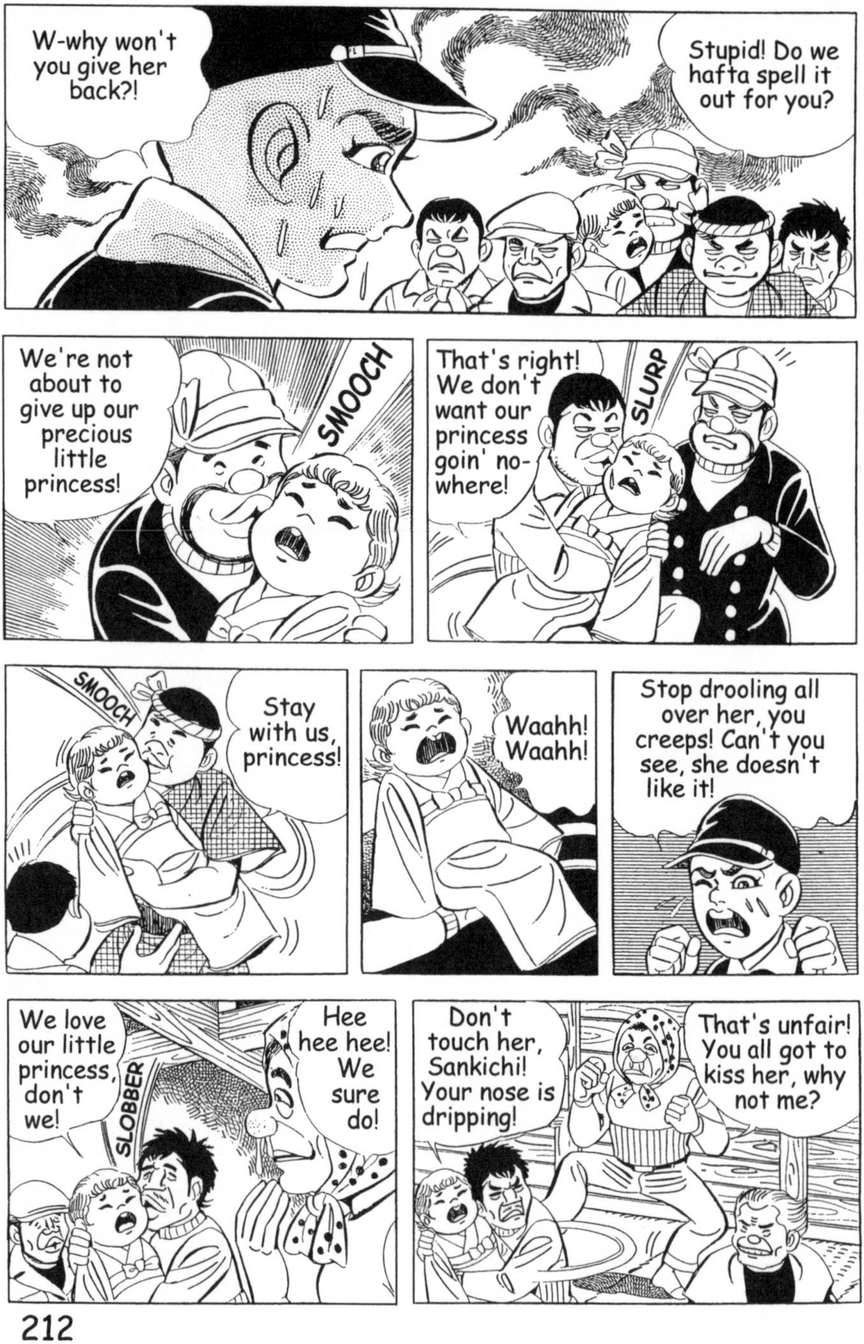
W-why won't you give her back?!
Stupid! Do we hafta spell it out for you?
We're not about to give up our precious little princess!
SMOOCH
That's right! We don't want our princess goin' no-where!
SLURP
SMOOCH
Stay with us, princess!
Waahh! Waahh!
Stop drooling all over her, you creeps! Can't you see, she doesn't like it!
We love our little princess, don't we!
SLOBBER
Hee hee hee! We sure do!
Don't touch her, Sankichi! Your nose is dripping!
That's unfair! You all got to kiss her, why not me?

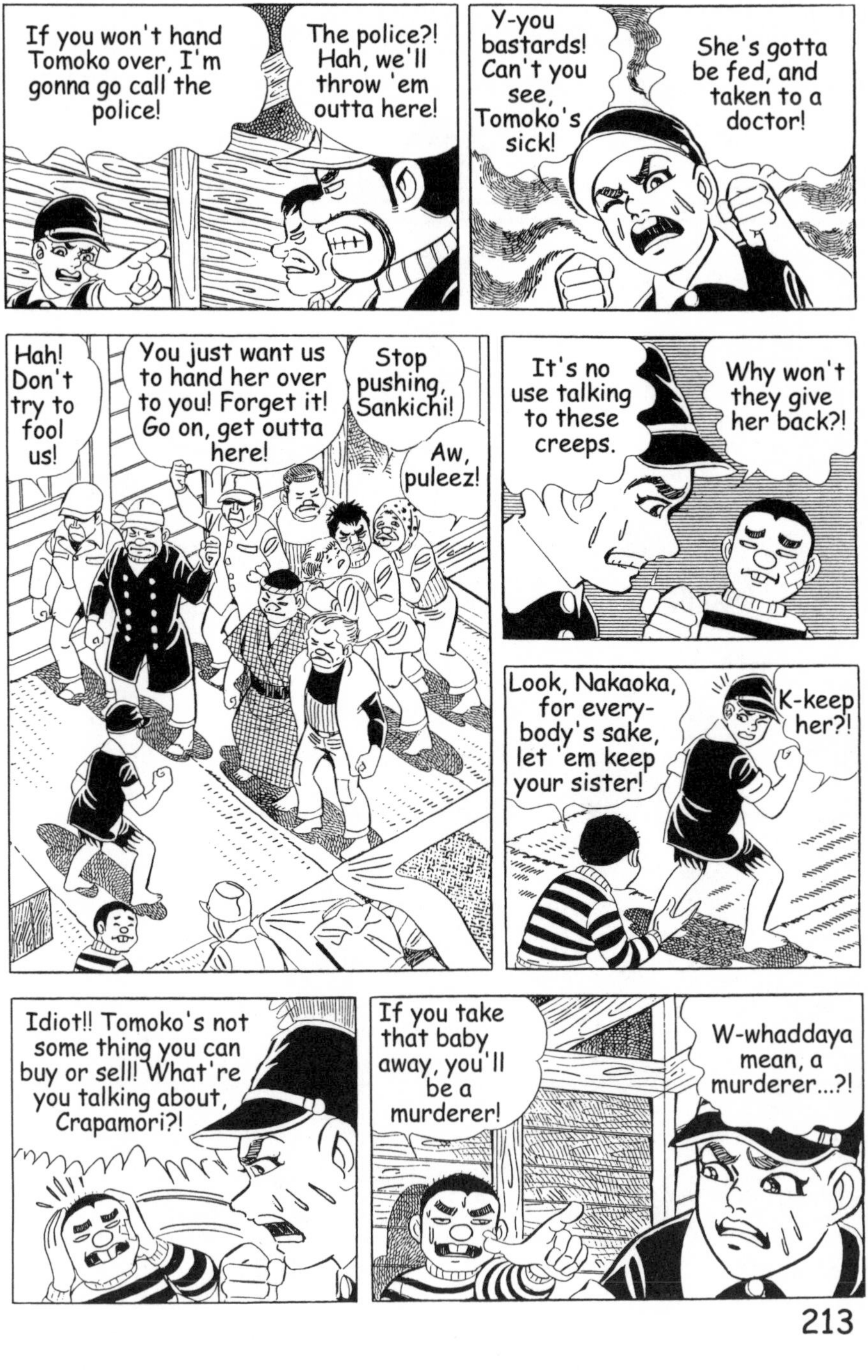
If you won't hand Tomoko over, I'm gonna go call the police!
The police?! Hah, we'll throw 'em outta here!
Y-you bastards! Can't you see, Tomoko's sick!
She's gotta be fed, and taken to a doctor!
Hah! Don't try to fool us!
You just want us to hand her over to you! Forget it! Go on, get outta here!
Stop pushing, Sankichi!
Aw, puleez!
It's no use talking to these creeps.
Why won't they give her back?!
Look, Nakaoka, for every-body's sake, let 'em keep your sister!
K-keep her?!
Idiot!! Tomoko's not some thing you can buy or sell! What're you talking about, Crapamori?!
If you take that baby away, you'll be a murderer!
W-whaddaya mean, a murderer...?!

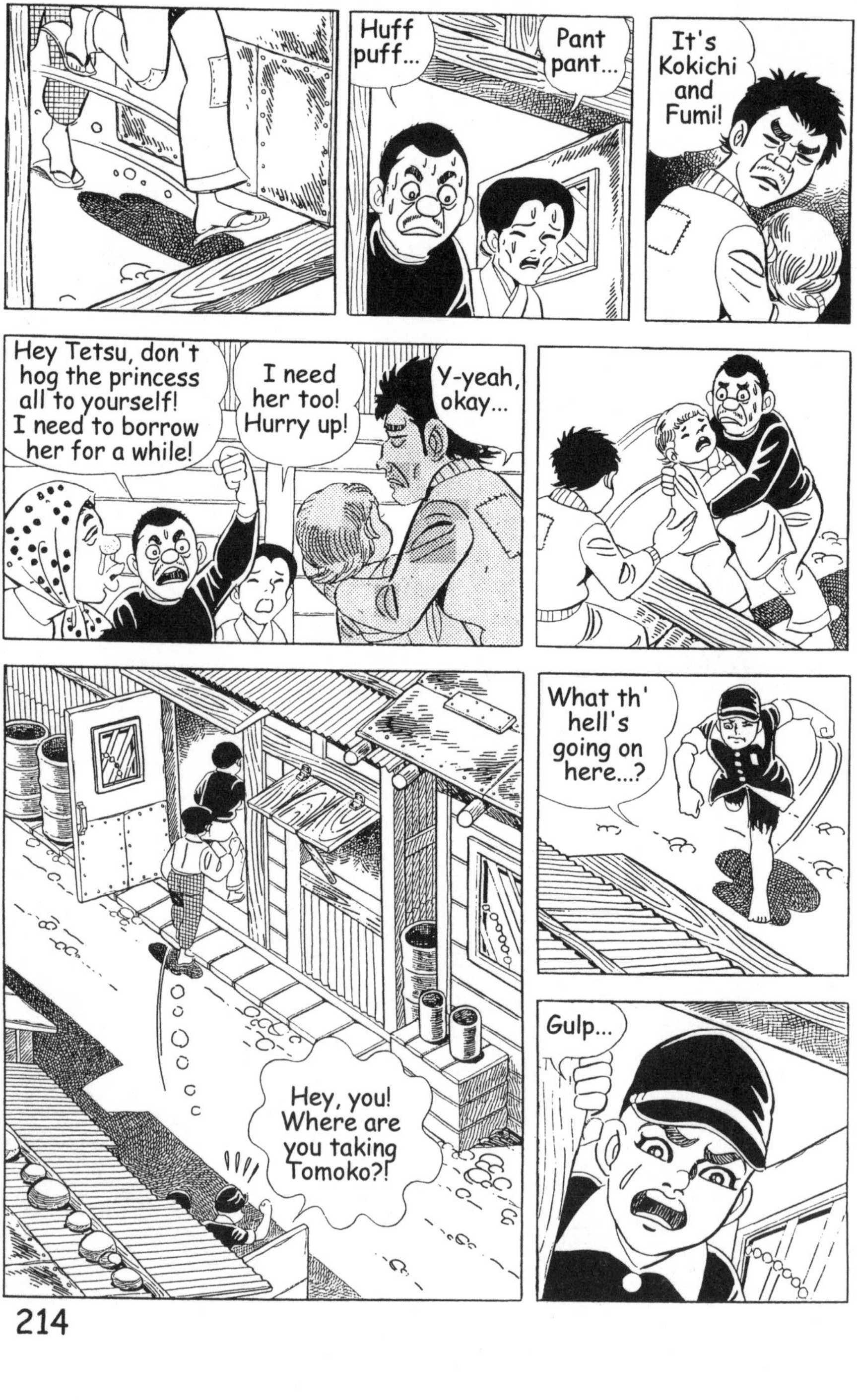
Huff puff...
Pant pant...
It's Kokichi and Fumi!
Hey Tetsu, don't hog the princess all to yourself! I need to borrow her for a while!
I need her too! Hurry up!
Y-yeah, okay...
Hey, you! Where are you taking Tomoko?!
What th' hell's going on here...?
Gulp...

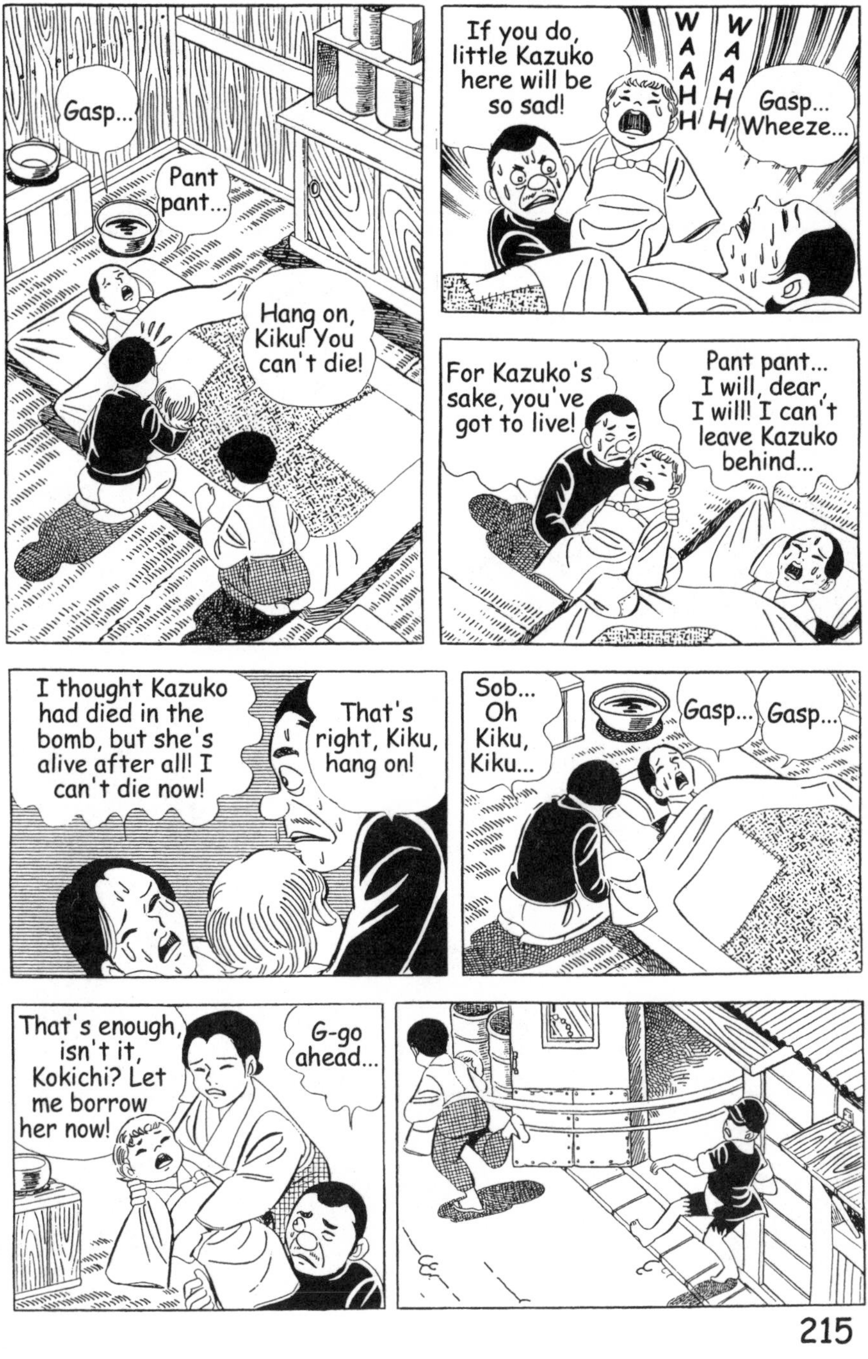
Gasp...
Pant pant...
Hang on, Kiku! You can't die!
If you do, little Kazuko here will be so sad!
WAAHH WAAHH
Gasp... Wheeze...
For Kazuko's sake, you've got to live!
Pant pant... I will, dear, I will! I can't leave Kazuko behind...
I thought Kazuko had died in the bomb, but she's alive after all! I can't die now!
That's right, Kiku, hang on!
Sob... Oh Kiku, Kiku...
Gasp... Gasp...
That's enough, isn't it, Kokichi? Let me borrow her now!
G-go ahead...

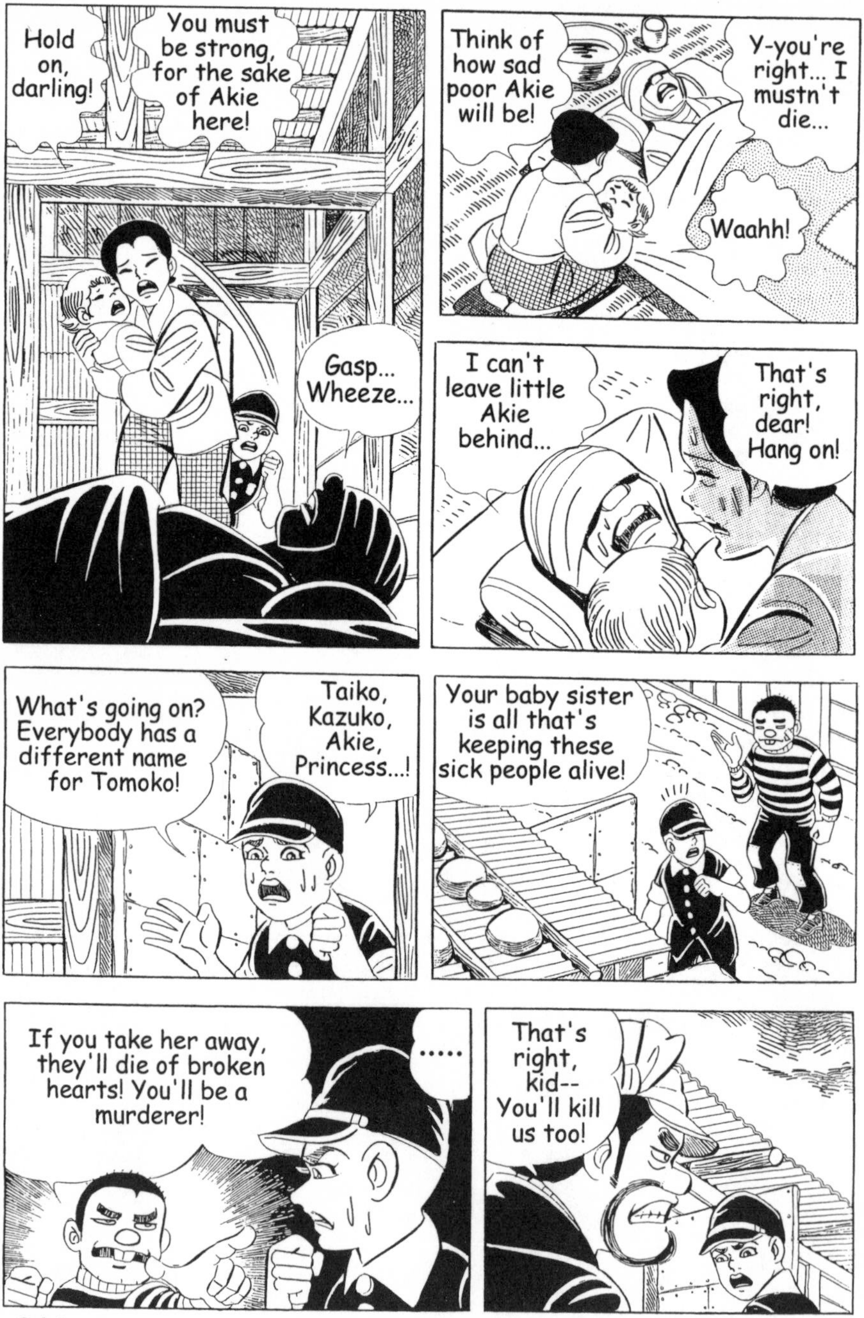
Hold on, darling!
You must be strong, for the sake of Akie here!
Gasp... Wheeze...
Think of how sad poor Akie will be!
Y-you're right... I mustn't die...
Waahh!
I can't leave little Akie behind...
That's right, dear! Hang on!
What's going on? Everybody has a different name for Tomoko!
Taiko, Kazuko, Akie, Princess...!
Your baby sister is all that's keeping these sick people alive!
If you take her away, they'll die of broken hearts! You'll be a murderer!
.....
That's right, kid-- You'll kill us too!

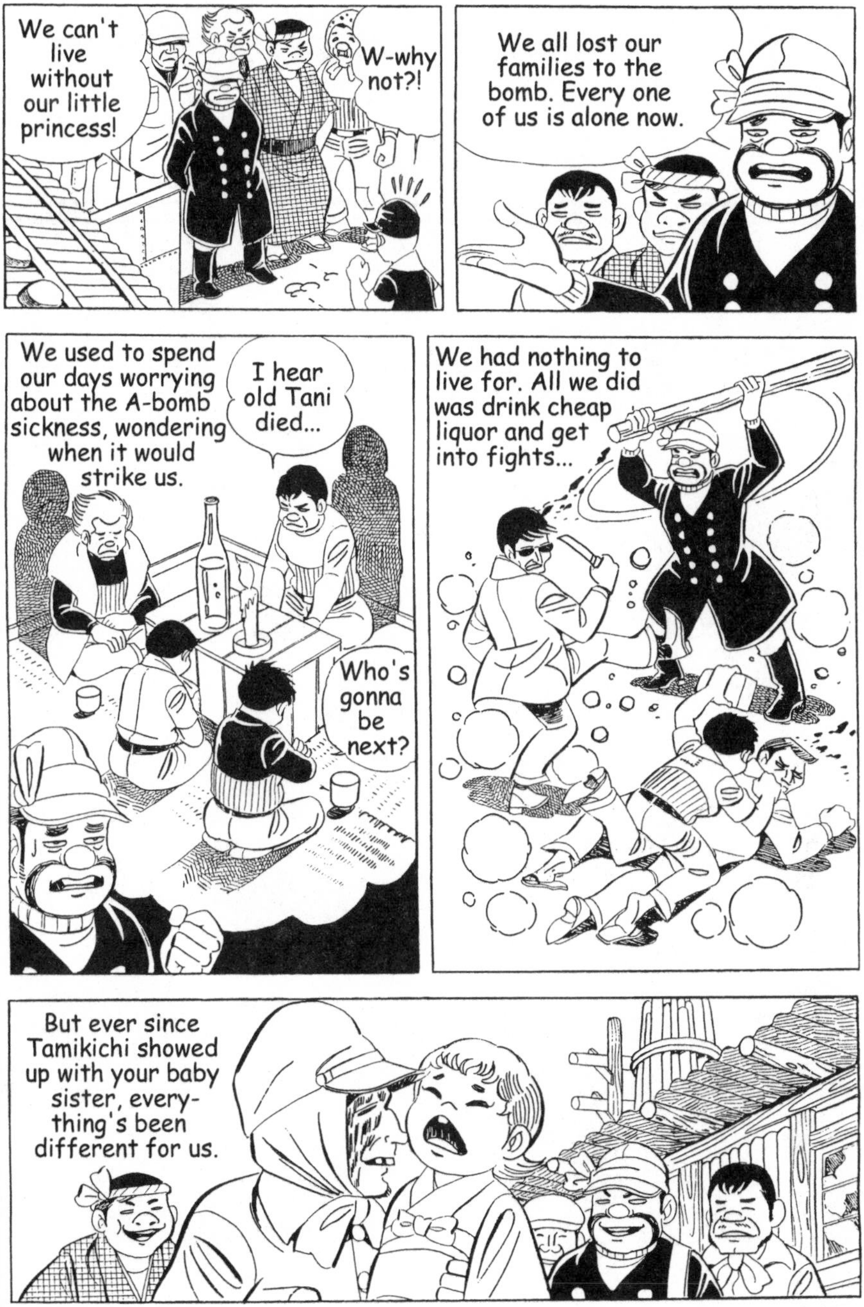
We can't live without our little princess!
W-why not?!
We all lost our families to the bomb. Every one of us is alone now.
We used to spend our days worrying about the A-bomb sickness, wondering when it would strike us.
I hear old Tani died...
Who's gonna be next?
We had nothing to live for. All we did was drink cheap liquor and get into fights...
But ever since Tamikichi showed up with your baby sister, every-thing's been different for us.

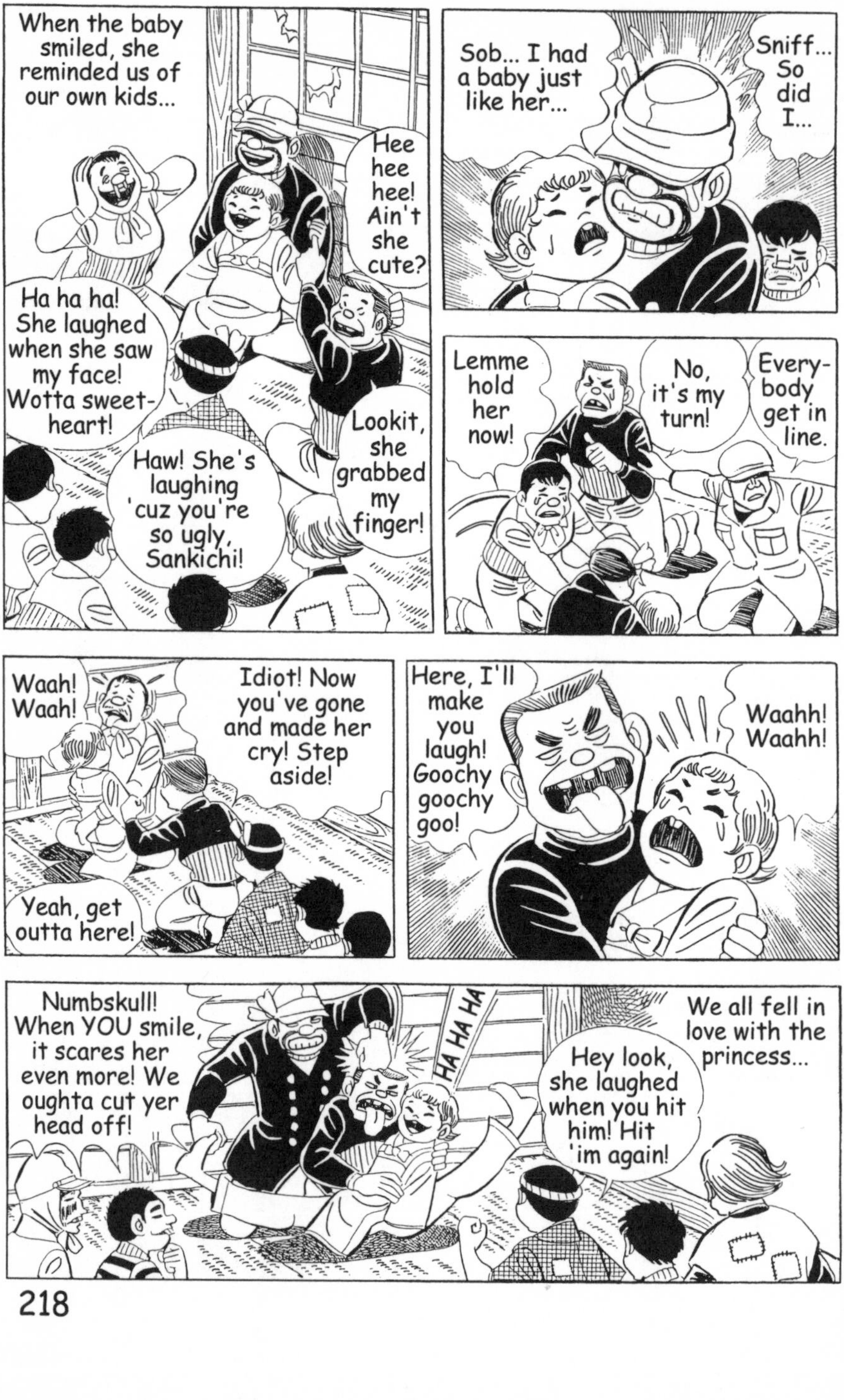
When the baby smiled, she reminded us of our own kids...
Hee hee hee! Ain't she cute?
Ha ha ha! She laughed when she saw my face! Wotta sweet-heart!
Lookit, she grabbed my finger!
Haw! She's laughing 'cuz you're so ugly, Sankichi!
Sob... I had a baby just like her...
Sniff... So did I...
Lemme hold her now!
No, it's my turn!
Every-body get in line.
Waah! Waah!
Idiot! Now you've gone and made her cry! Step aside!
Yeah, get outta here!
Here, I'll make you laugh! Goochy goochy goo!
Waahh! Waahh!
Numbskull! When YOU smile, it scares her even more! We oughta cut yer head off!
HA HA HA
Hey look, she laughed when you hit him! Hit 'im again!
We all fell in love with the princess...

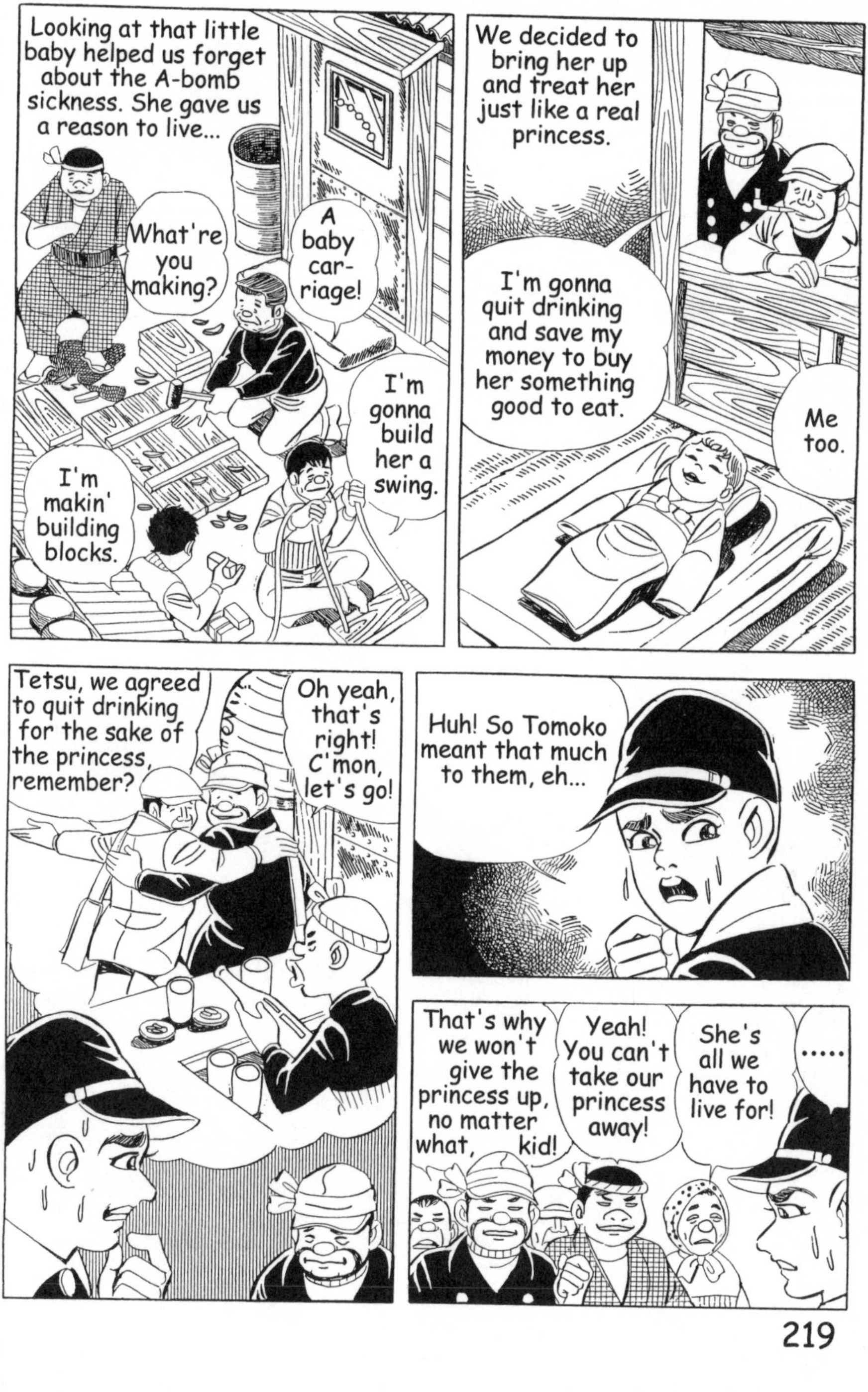

Looking at that little baby helped us forget about the A-bomb sickness. She gave us a reason to live...
What're you making?
A baby car-riage!
I'm makin' building blocks.
I'm gonna build her a swing.
We decided to bring her up and treat her just like a real princess.
I'm gonna quit drinking and save my money to buy her something good to eat.
Me too.
Tetsu, we agreed to quit drinking for the sake of the princess, remember?
Oh yeah, that's right! C'mon, let's go!
Huh! So Tomoko meant that much to them, eh...
That's why we won't give the princess up, no matter what, kid!
Yeah! You can't take our princess away!
She's all we have to live for!
.....

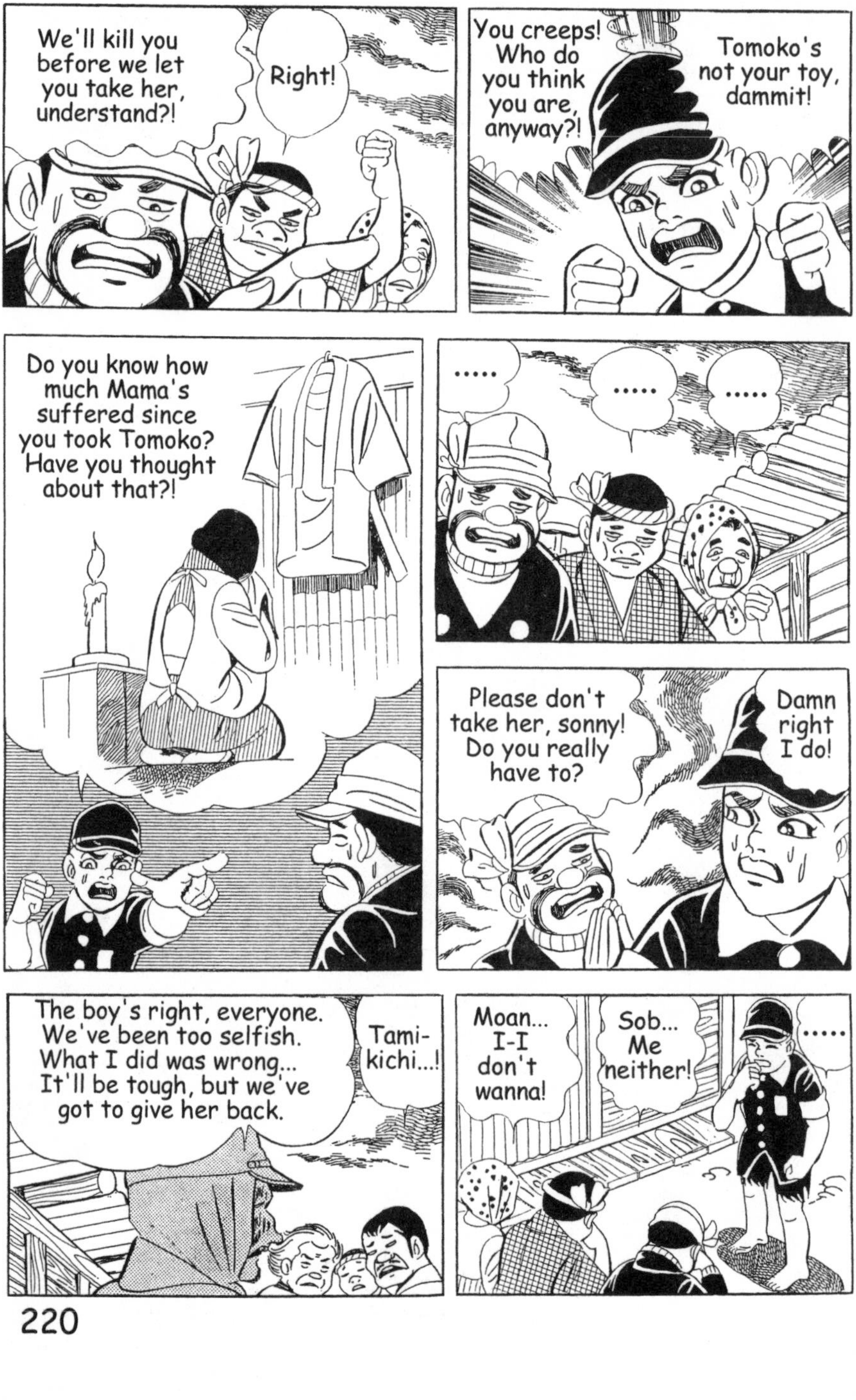
We'll kill you before we let you take her, understand?!
Right!
You creeps! Who do you think you are, anyway?!
Tomoko's not your toy, dammit!
Do you know how much Mama's suffered since you took Tomoko? Have you thought about that?!
.....
.....
.....
Please don't take her, sonny! Do you really have to?
Damn right I do!
The boy's right, everyone. We've been too selfish. What I did was wrong... It'll be tough, but we've got to give her back.
Tami-kichi...!
Moan... I-I don't wanna!
Sob... Me neither!
.....

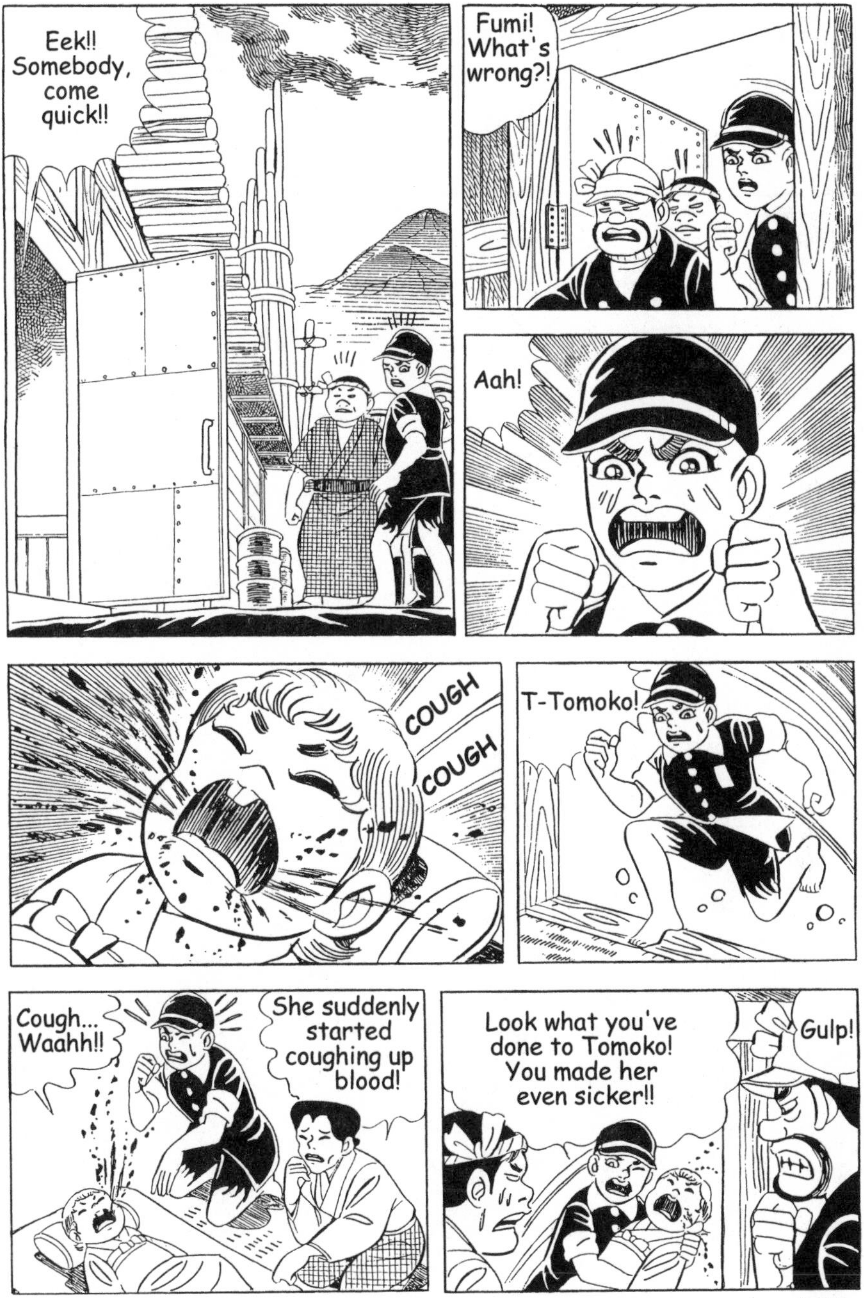
Eek!! Somebody, come quick!!
Fumi! What's wrong?!
Aah!
COUGH
COUGH
T-Tomoko!
Cough... Waahh!!
She suddenly started coughing up blood!
Look what you've done to Tomoko! You made her even sicker!!
Gulp!

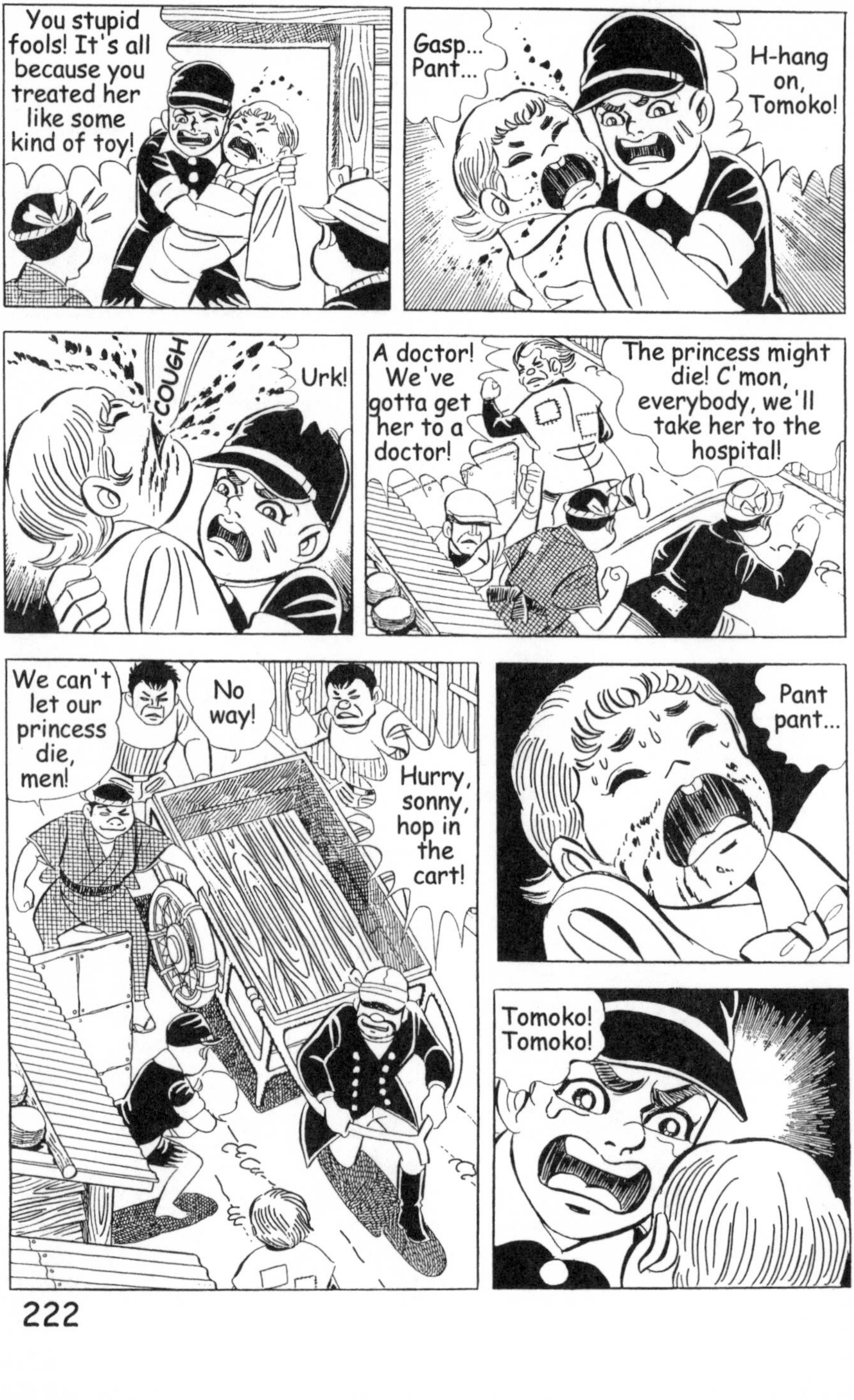
You stupid fools! It's all because you treated her like some kind of toy!
Gasp... Pant...
H-hang on, Tomoko!
COUGH
Urk!
A doctor! We've gotta get her to a doctor!
The princess might die! C'mon, everybody, we'll take her to the hospital!
We can't let our princess die, men!
No way!
Hurry, sonny, hop in the cart!
Pant pant...
Tomoko! Tomoko!

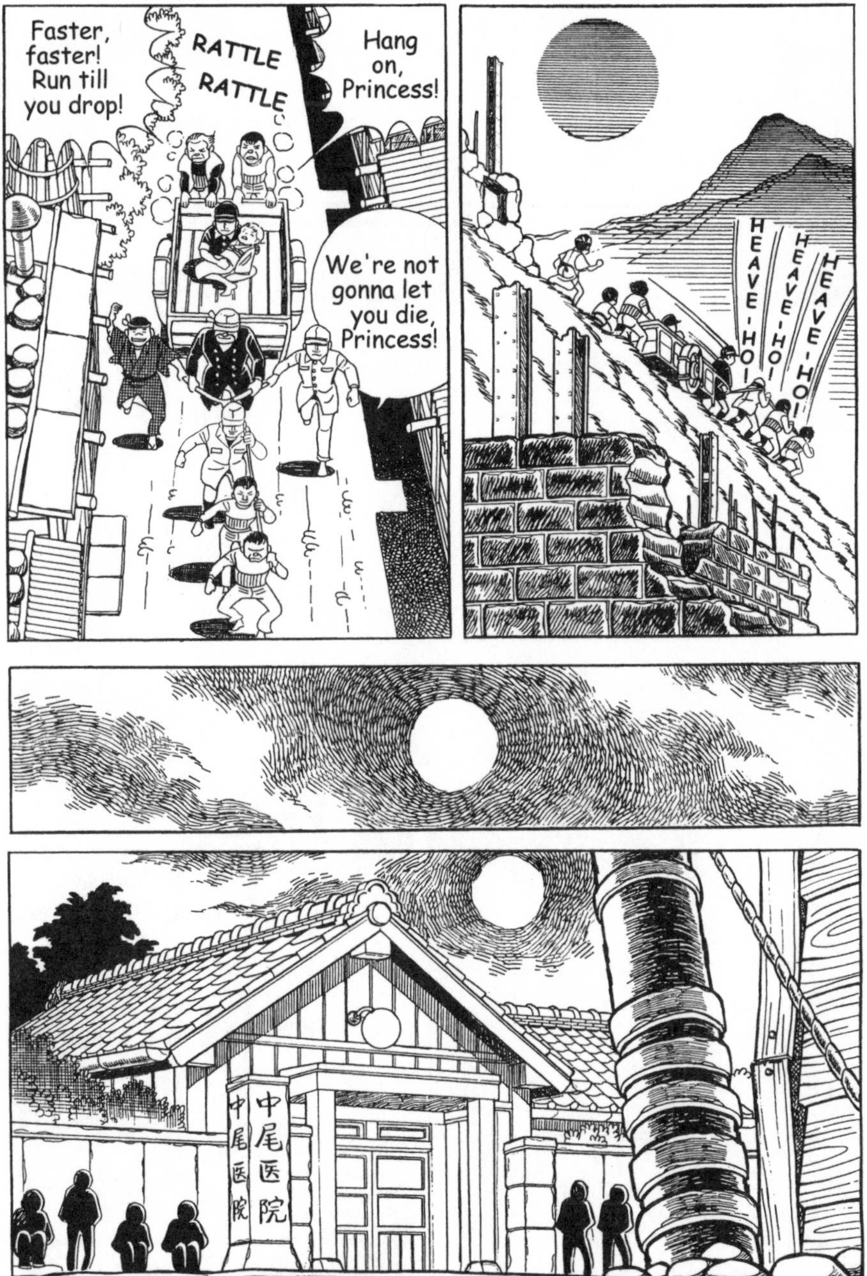
Faster, faster! Run till you drop!
RATTLE RATTLE
Hang on, Princess!
We're not gonna let you die, Princess!
HEAVE-HO!
HEAVE-HO!
HEAVE-HO!
中尾医院
中尾医院

Sign: Nakao Clinic

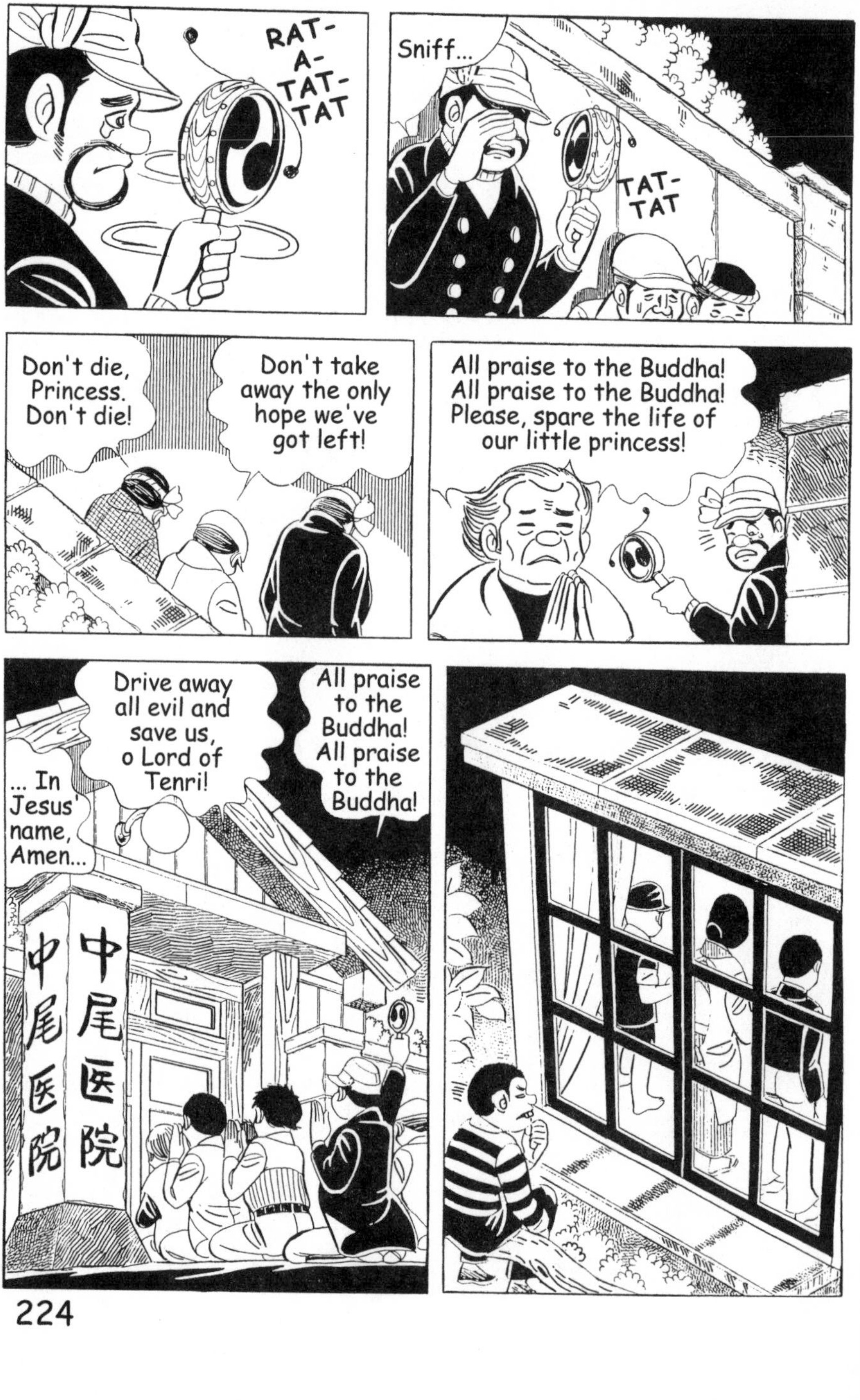
RAT-A-TAT-TAT
Sniff...
TAT-TAT
Don't die, Princess. Don't die!
Don't take away the only hope we've got left!
All praise to the Buddha! All praise to the Buddha! Please, spare the life of our little princess!
... In Jesus' name, Amen...
Drive away all evil and save us, o Lord of Tenri!
All praise to the Buddha! All praise to the Buddha!
中尾医院
中尾医院

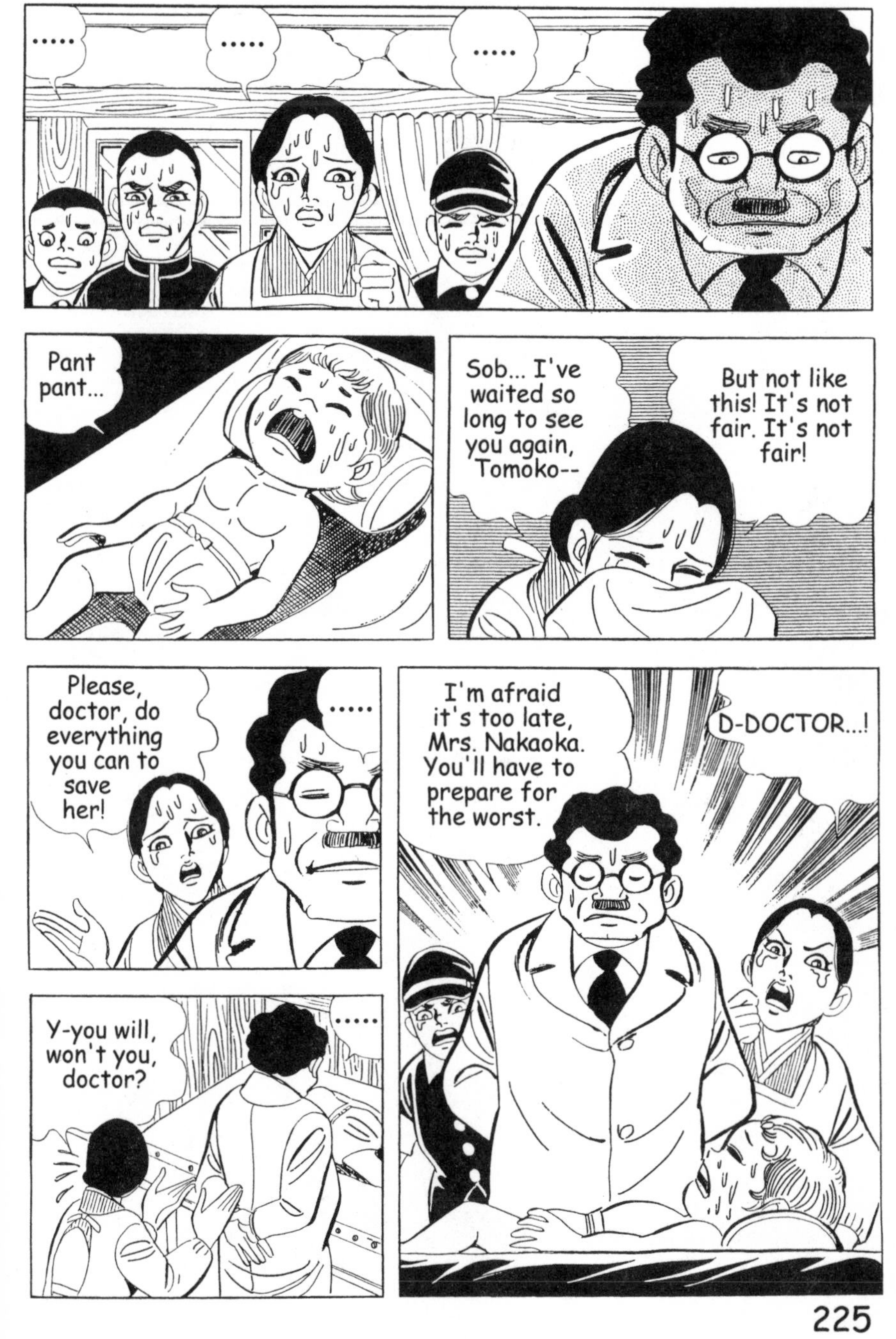
.....
.....
.....
Pant pant...
Sob... I've waited so long to see you again, Tomoko--
But not like this! It's not fair. It's not fair!
Please, doctor, do everything you can to save her!
.....
Y-you will, won't you, doctor?
.....
I'm afraid it's too late, Mrs. Nakaoka. You'll have to prepare for the worst.
D-DOCTOR...!

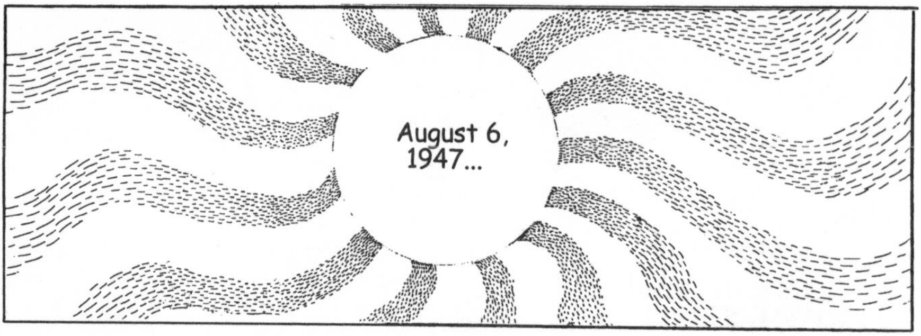
August 6,
1947...

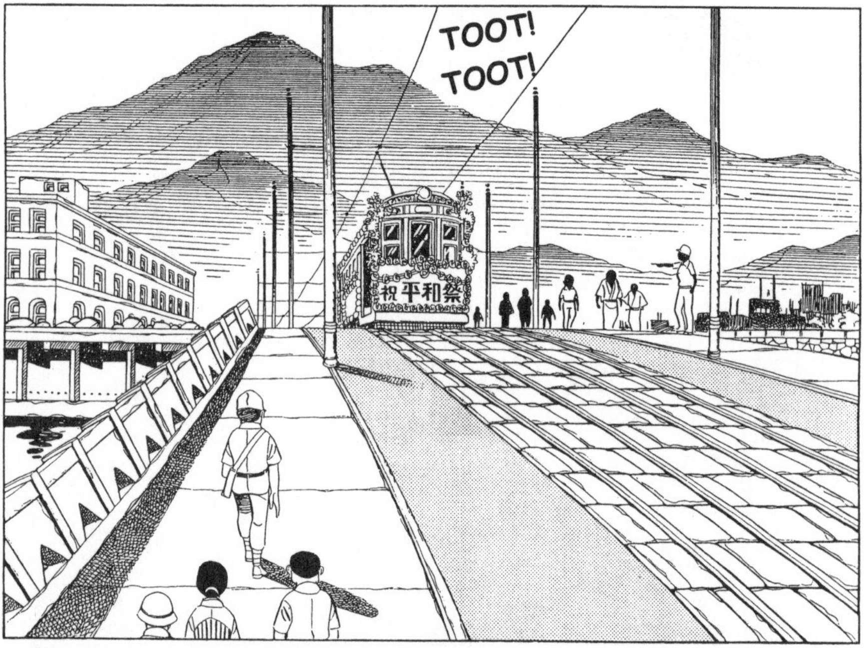
TOOT!
TOOT!
祝平和祭

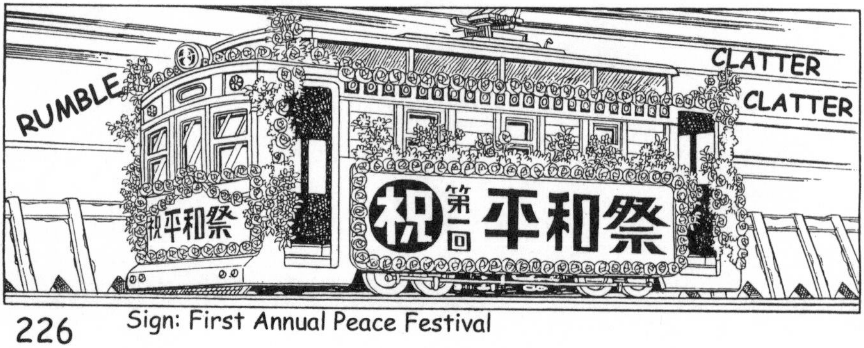
RUMBLE
CLATTER
CLATTER
祝平和祭
祝 第一回 平和祭


Sign: First Annual Peace Festival

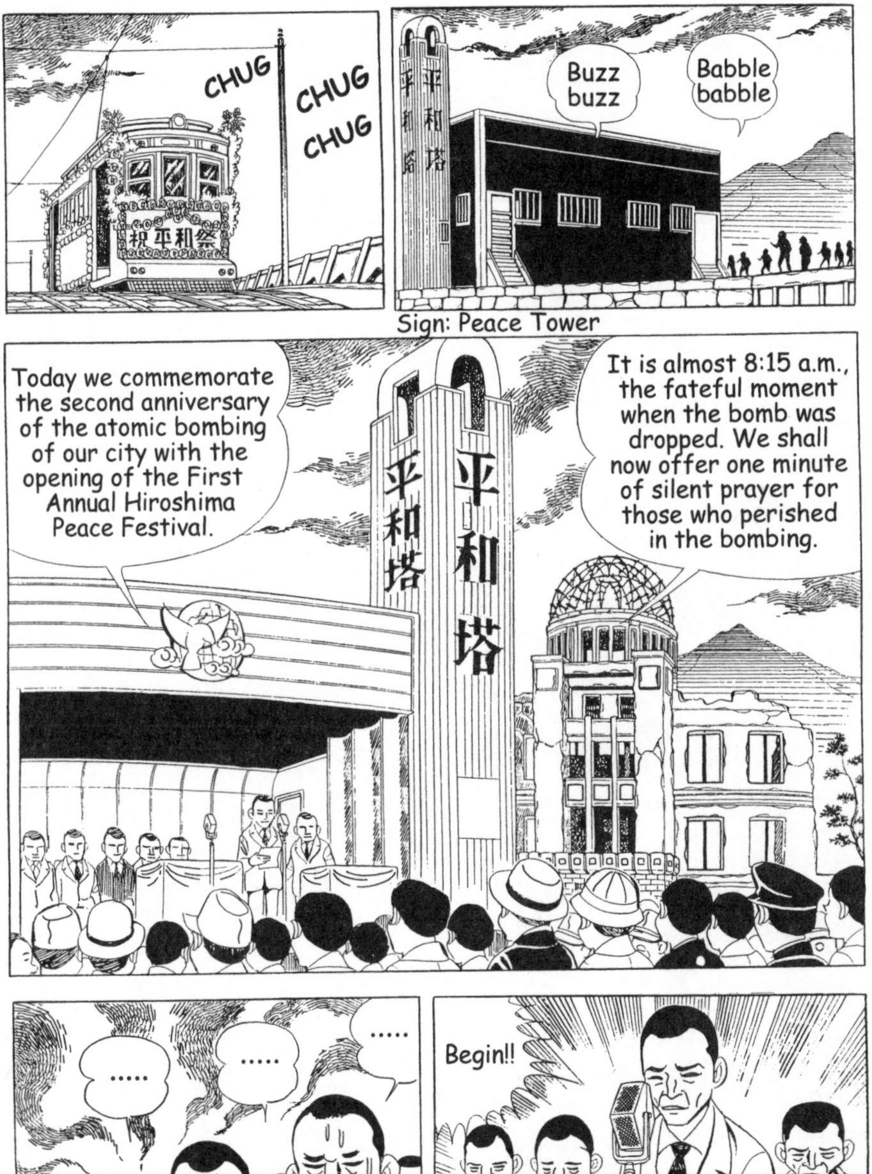
CHUG
CHUG
CHUG
祝平和祭
平和塔
Buzz buzz
Babble babble
Sign: Peace Tower
Today we commemorate the second anniversary of the atomic bombing of our city with the opening of the First Annual Hiroshima Peace Festival.
平和塔
It is almost 8:15 a.m., the fateful moment when the bomb was dropped. We shall now offer one minute of silent prayer for those who perished in the bombing.
.....
.....
.....
Begin!!

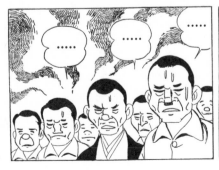

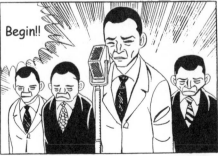

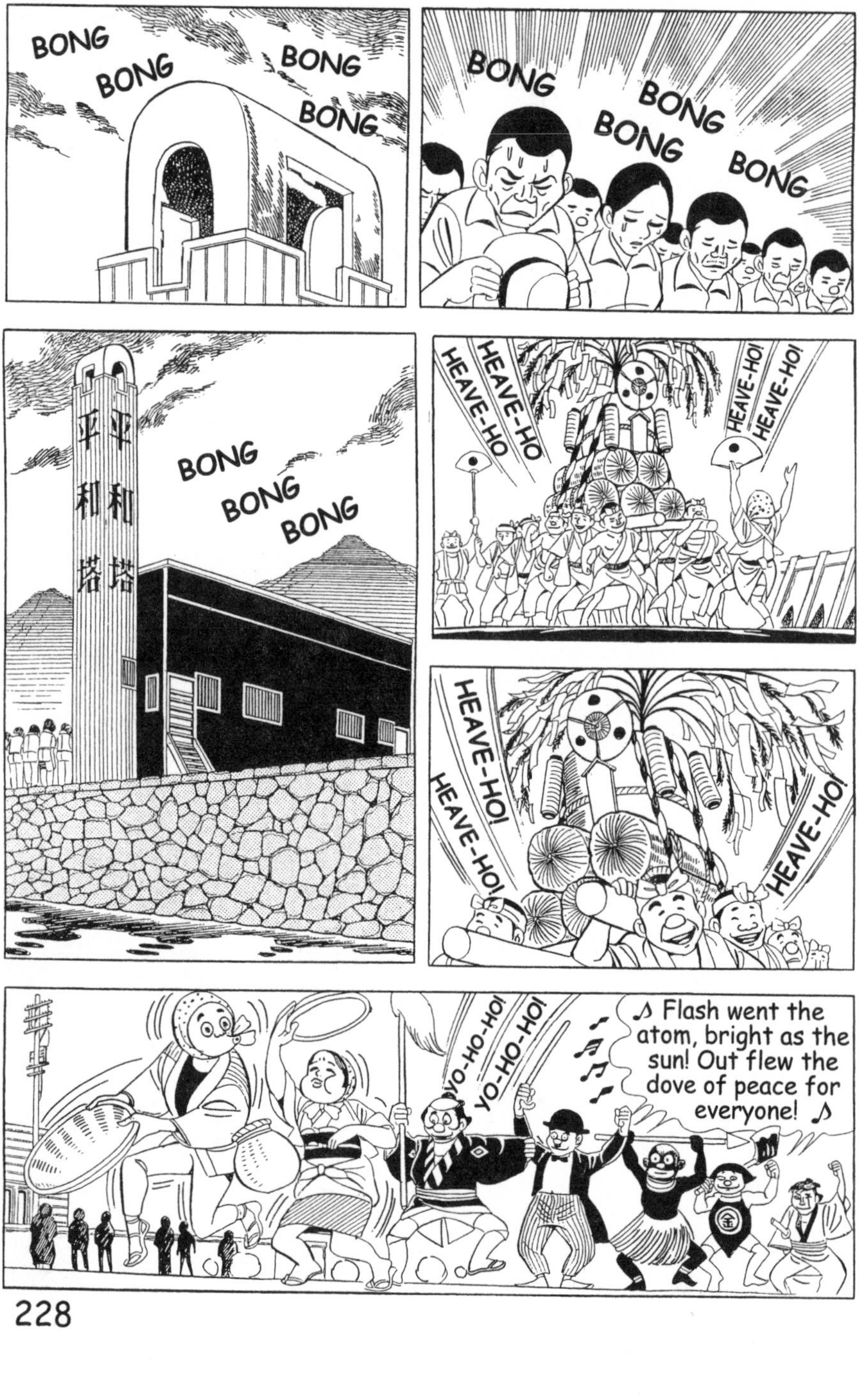
BONG
BONG
BONG
BONG
BONG
BONG
BONG
BONG
平和塔
平和塔
BONG
BONG
BONG
HEAVE-HO
HEAVE-HO
HEAVE-HO!
HEAVE-HO!
HEAVE-HO!
HEAVE-HO!
HEAVE-HO!
YO-HO-HO!
YO-HO-HO!
♪ Flash went the atom, bright as the sun! Out flew the dove of peace for everyone! ♪

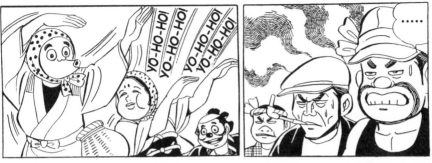

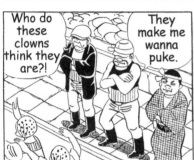

YO-HO-HO!
YO-HO-HO!
YO-HO-HO!
YO-HO-HO!
.....
Who do these clowns think they are?!
They make me wanna puke.
Prancing around in those dumb masks--and on this day, of all days!
Singing and carrying on as if they're glad the bomb fell!
The people who died in the bomb must be turning over in their graves!
Hell, these jokers don't give a damn about the bomb victims.
祝 平和祭
福引大売り出し
Folks are still dying left and right from the A-bomb disease! This is too much!
These people are morons. They've already forgotten how horrible the war and the bomb were!
No wonder we keep having wars over and over again...
祝 平和祭
福引売り出し

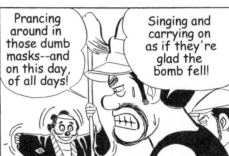

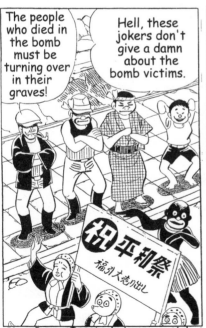

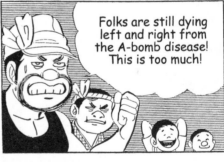

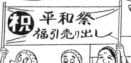

Sign: Peace Festival--Lottery tickets on sale

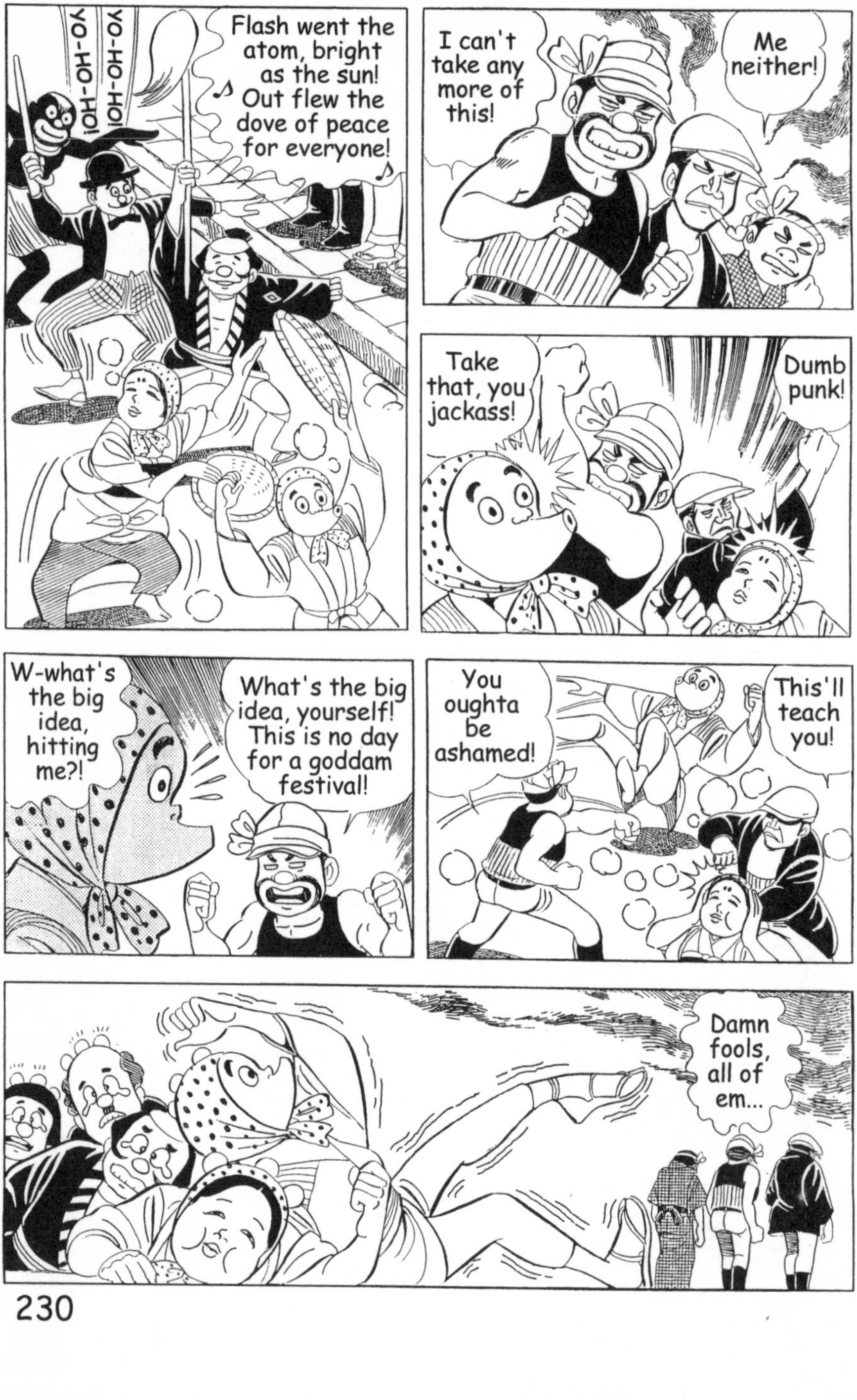
YO-HO-HO!
YO-HO-HO!
Flash went the atom, bright as the sun! ♪ Out flew the dove of peace for everyone! ♪
I can't take any more of this!
Me neither!
Take that, you jackass!
Dumb punk!
W-what's the big idea, hitting me?!
What's the big idea, yourself! This is no day for a goddam festival!
You oughta be ashamed!
This'll teach you!
Damn fools, all of em...

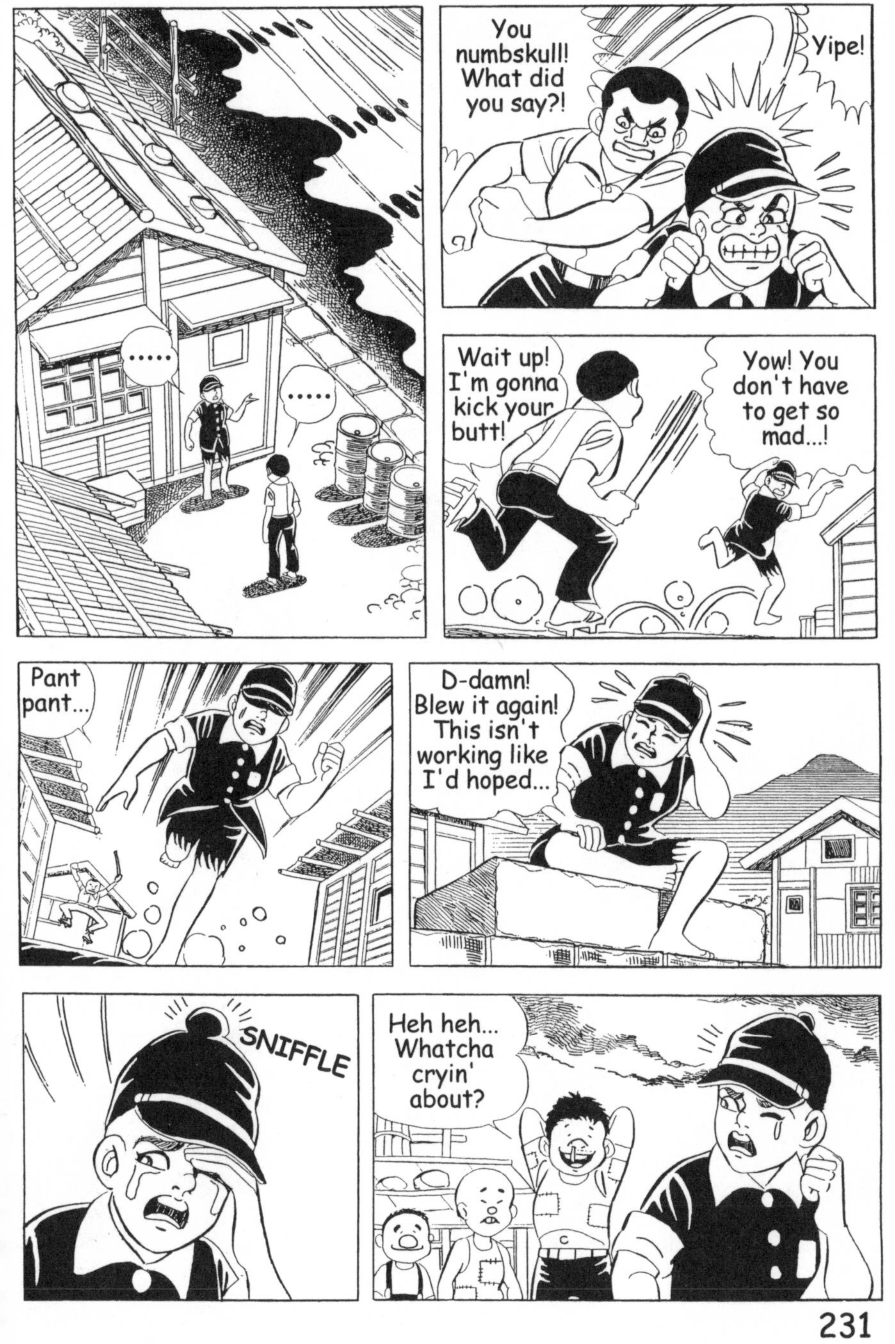
.....
.....
You numbskull! What did you say?!
Yipe!
Wait up! I'm gonna kick your butt!
Yow! You don't have to get so mad...!
Pant pant...
D-damn! Blew it again! This isn't working like I'd hoped...
SNIFFLE
Heh heh... Whatcha cryin' about?

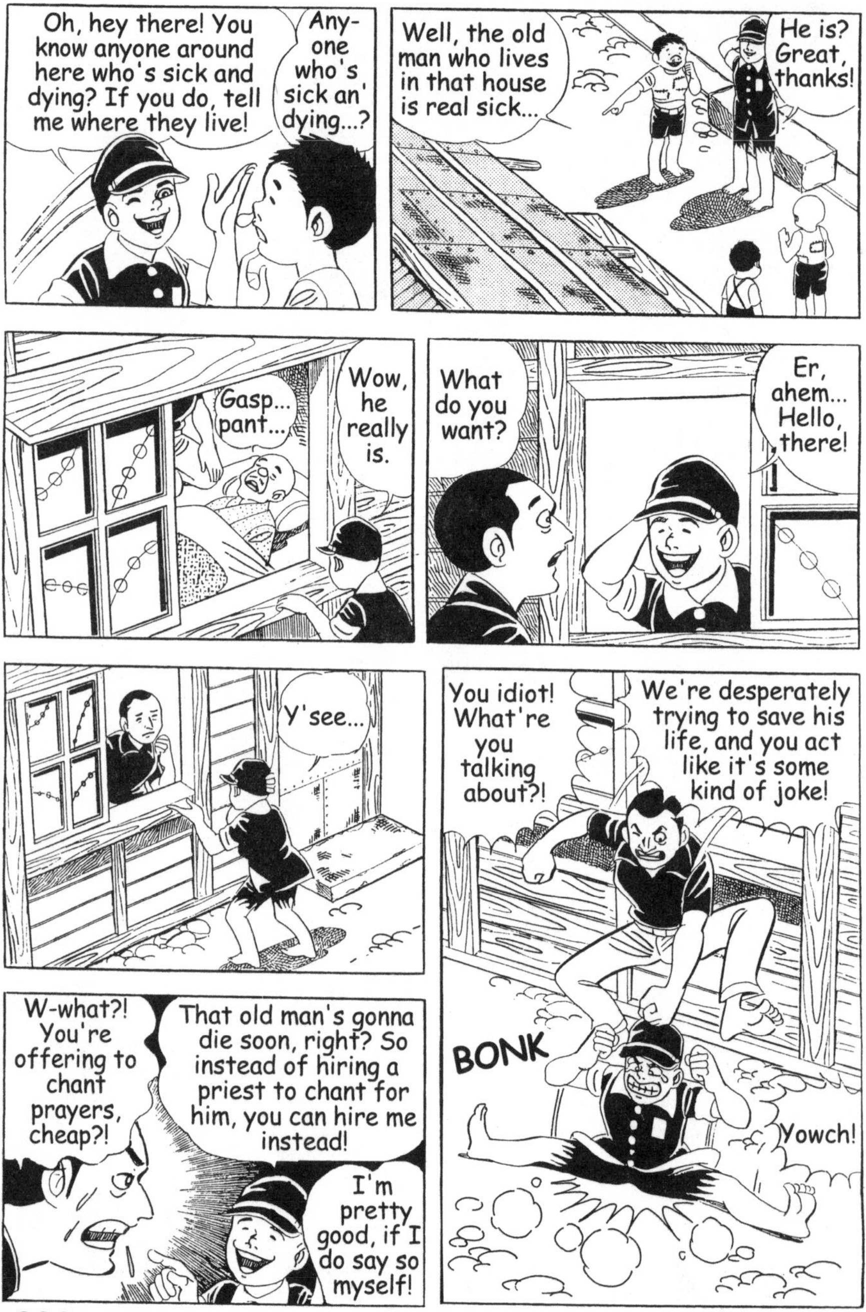
Oh, hey there! You know anyone around here who's sick and dying? If you do, tell me where they live!
Any-one who's sick an' dying...?
Well, the old man who lives in that house is real sick...
He is? Great, thanks!
Gasp... pant...
Wow, he really is.
What do you want?
Er, ahem... Hello, there!
Y'see...
You idiot! What're you talking about?!
We're desperately trying to save his life, and you act like it's some kind of joke!
W-what?! You're offering to chant prayers, cheap?!
That old man's gonna die soon, right? So instead of hiring a priest to chant for him, you can hire me instead!
I'm pretty good, if I do say so myself!
BONK
Yowch!

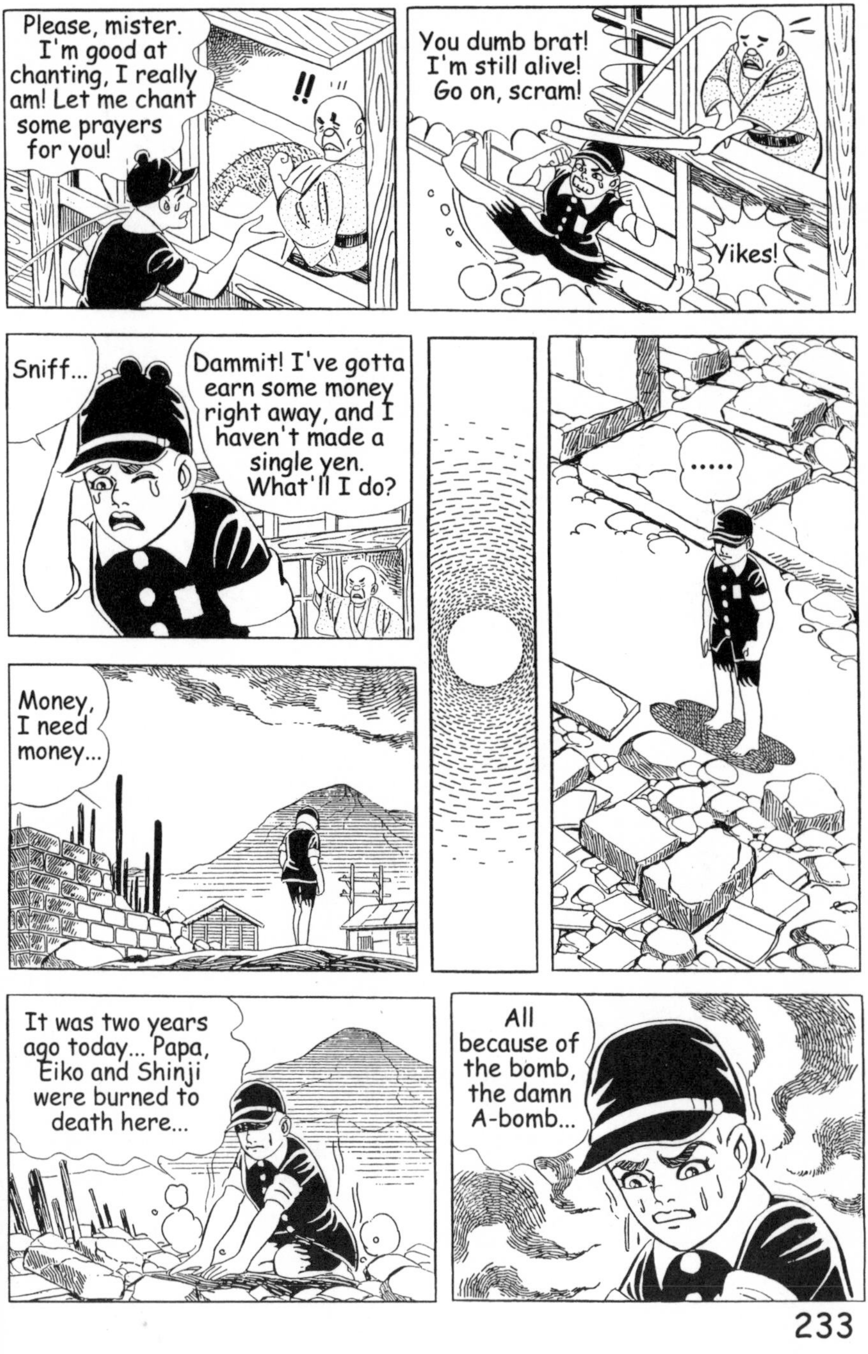
Please, mister. I'm good at chanting, I really am! Let me chant some prayers for you!
!!
You dumb brat! I'm still alive! Go on, scram!
Yikes!
Sniff...
Dammit! I've gotta earn some money right away, and I haven't made a single yen. What'll I do?
......
Money, I need money...
It was two years ago today... Papa, Eiko and Shinji were burned to death here...
All because of the bomb, the damn A-bomb...

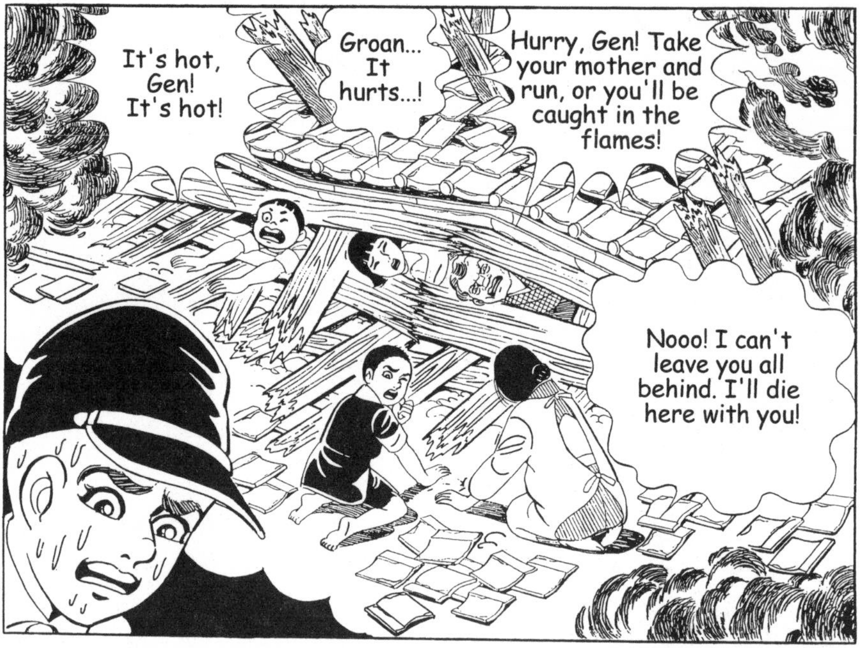
It's hot, Gen! It's hot!
Groan... It hurts...!
Hurry, Gen! Take your mother and run, or you'll be caught in the flames!
Nooo! I can't leave you all behind. I'll die here with you!
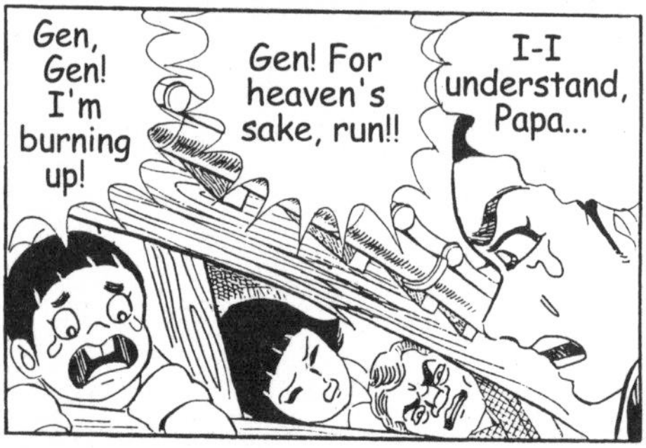
Gen, Gen! I'm burning up!
Gen! For heaven's sake, run!!
I-I understand, Papa...
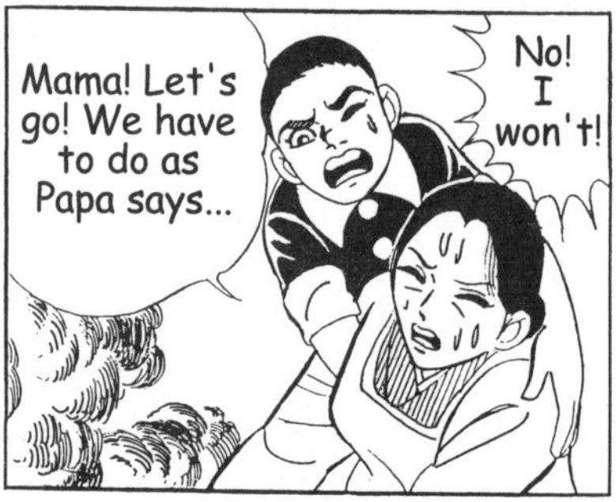
Mama! Let's go! We have to do as Papa says...
No! I won't!
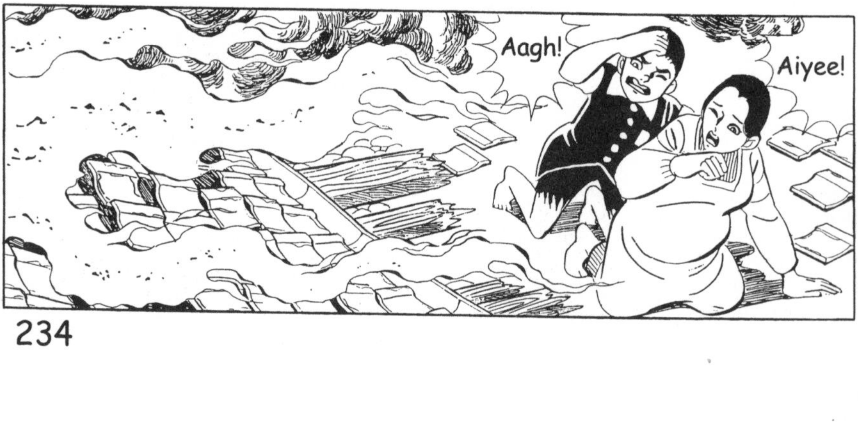
Aagh!
Aiyee!

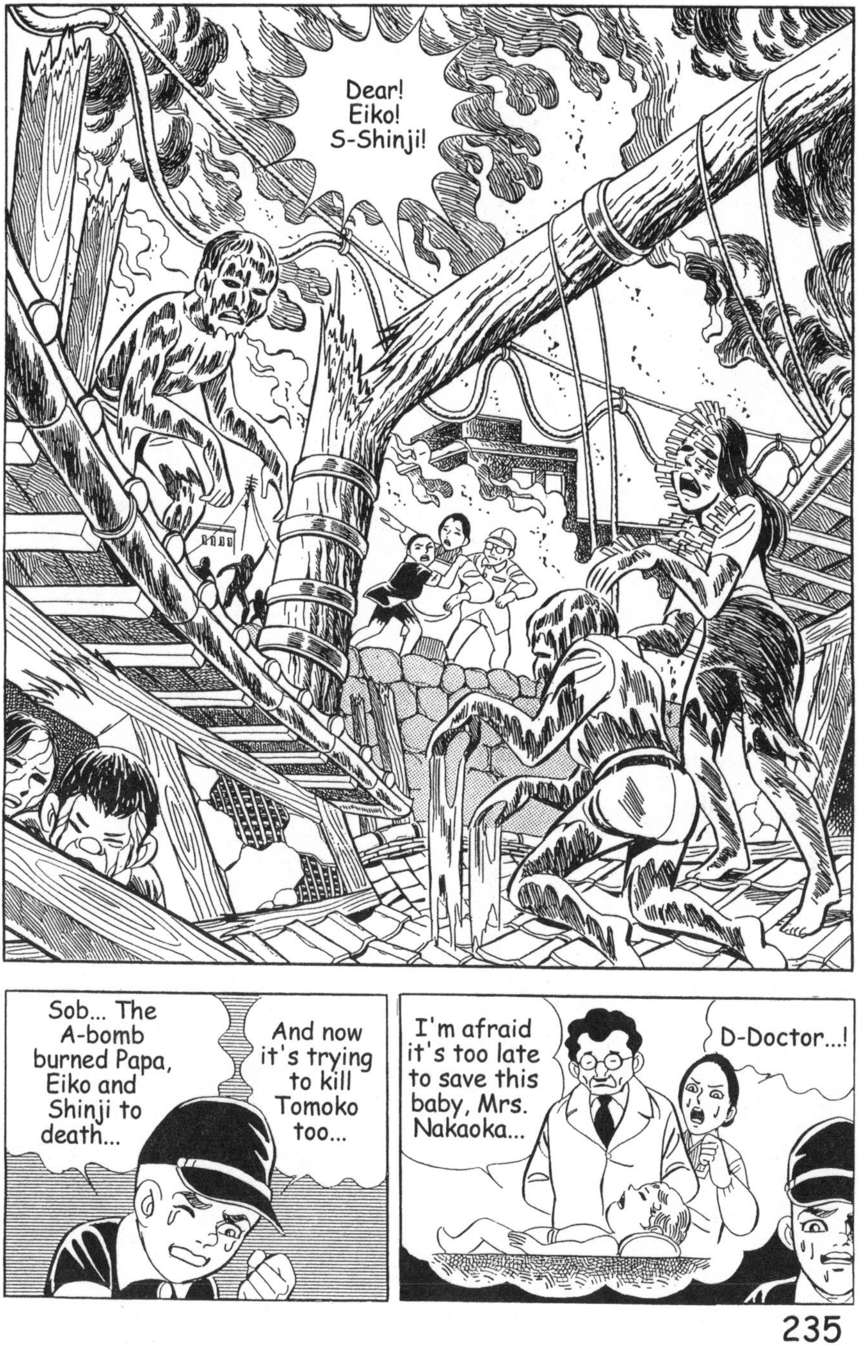
Dear! Eiko! S-Shinji!
Sob... The A-bomb burned Papa, Eiko and Shinji to death...
And now it's trying to kill Tomoko too...
I'm afraid it's too late to save this baby, Mrs. Nakaoka...
D-Doctor...!

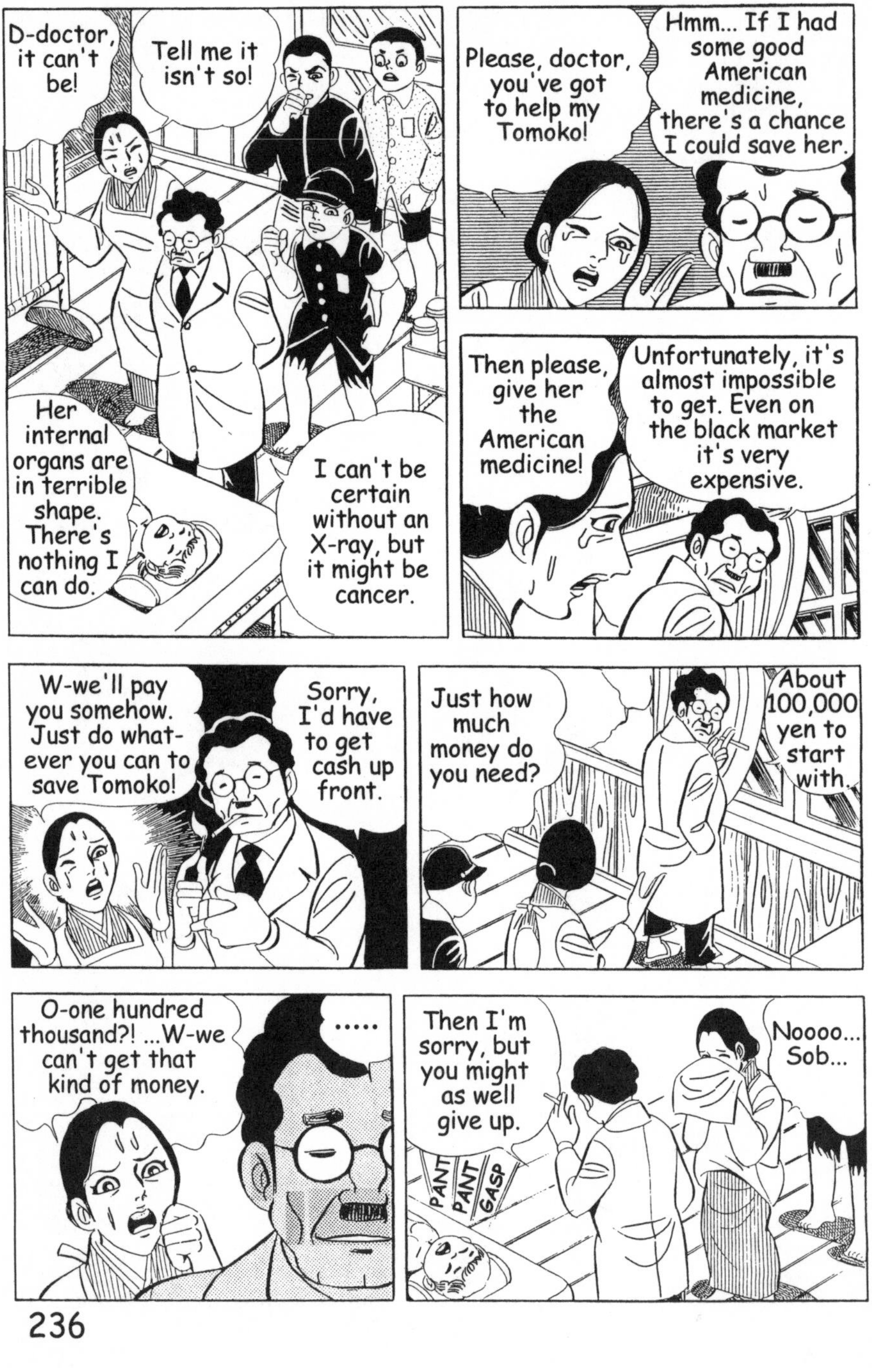
D-doctor, it can't be!
Tell me it isn't so!
Her internal organs are in terrible shape. There's nothing I can do.
I can't be certain without an X-ray, but it might be cancer.
Please, doctor, you've got to help my Tomoko!
Hmm... If I had some good American medicine, there's a chance I could save her.
Then please, give her the American medicine!
Unfortunately, it's almost impossible to get. Even on the black market it's very expensive.
W-we'll pay you somehow. Just do whatever you can to save Tomoko!
Sorry, I'd have to get cash up front.
Just how much money do you need?
About 100,000 yen to start with.
O-one hundred thousand?! ...W-we can't get that kind of money.
.....
Then I'm sorry, but you might as well give up.
PANT
PANT
GASP
Noooo... Sob...

You quack! You better help Tomoko! If you let her die, I'll kill you!

Stop it, Gen!

Sob...

.....

P-please, doctor. You've got to save her! Please!!

.....

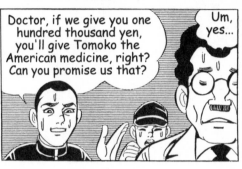

Doctor, if we give you one hundred thousand yen, you'll give Tomoko the American medicine, right? Can you promise us that?

Um, yes...

Pant pant...

Sob... Tomoko, Tomoko...

Ohhhh... Money, if only we had money...

Don't worry, Mother, we'll scrape the money together.

That's right, Mama! We'll all pitch in!

We'll make sure Tomoko gets that American medicine!

So we need a hundred thousand yen to save the princess, eh?

.....

Okay, men, if that's what it's gonna take, let's go make some money!

Awright! Let's get going!

I'll quit drinking, by golly!

237

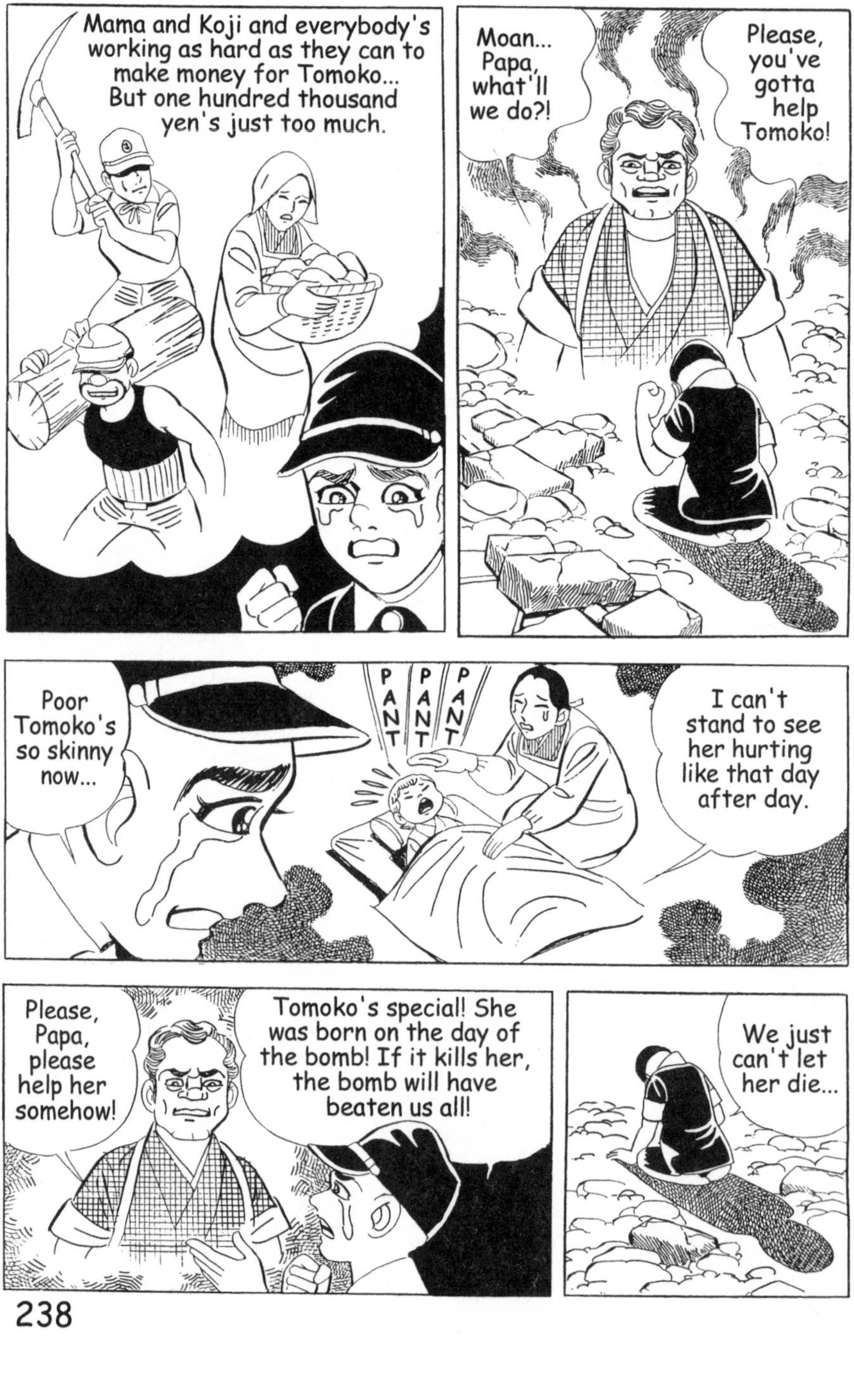
Mama and Koji and everybody's working as hard as they can to make money for Tomoko... But one hundred thousand yen's just too much.
Moan... Papa, what'll we do?!
Please, you've gotta help Tomoko!
Poor Tomoko's so skinny now...
PANT PANT PANT
I can't stand to see her hurting like that day after day.
Please, Papa, please help her somehow!
Tomoko's special! She was born on the day of the bomb! If it kills her, the bomb will have beaten us all!
We just can't let her die...

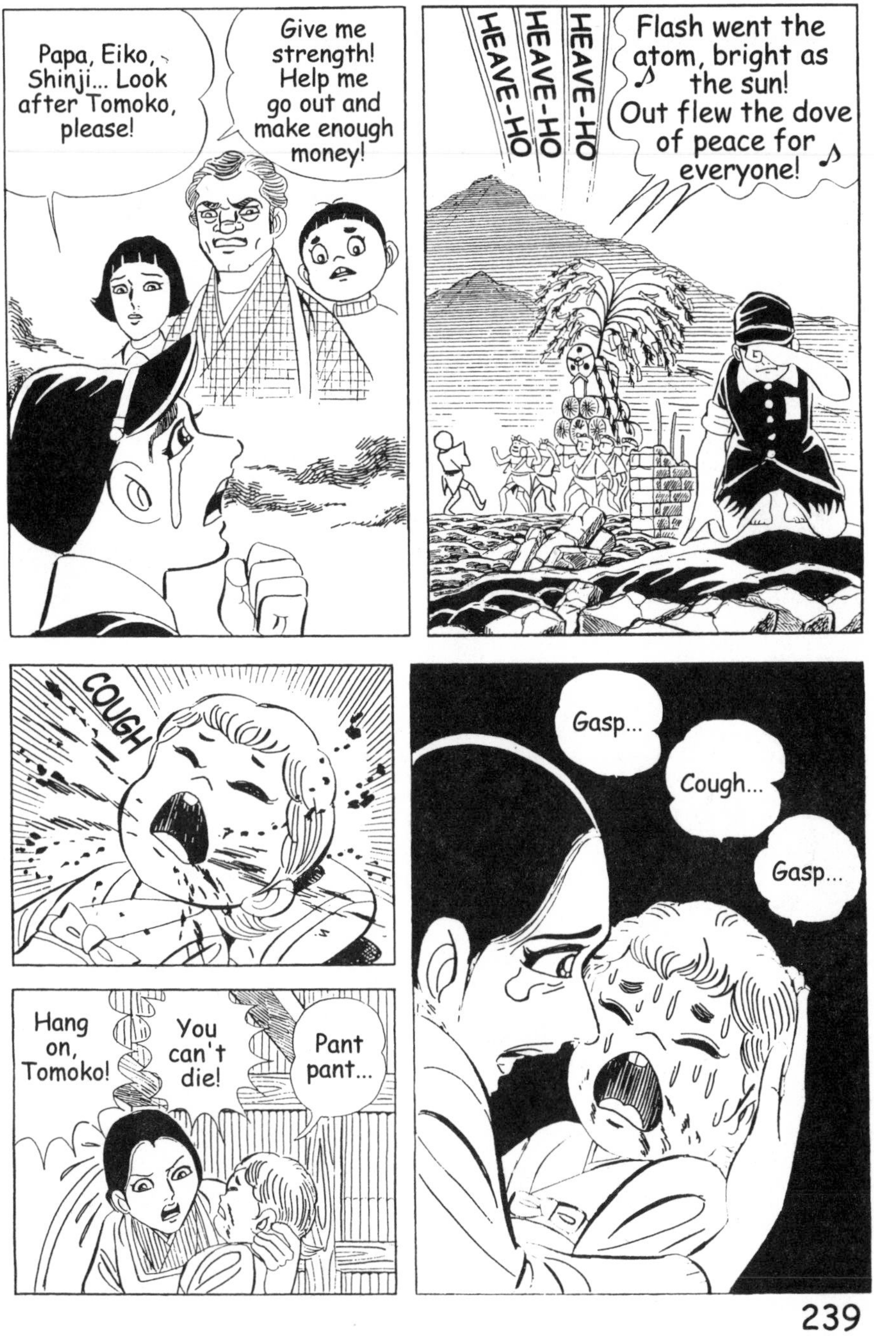
Papa, Eiko, Shinji... Look after Tomoko, please!
Give me strength! Help me go out and make enough money!
HEAVE-HO
HEAVE-HO
HEAVE-HO
Flash went the atom, bright as the sun! Out flew the dove of peace for everyone!
COUGH
Hang on, Tomoko!
You can't die!
Pant pant...
Gasp...
Cough...
Gasp...

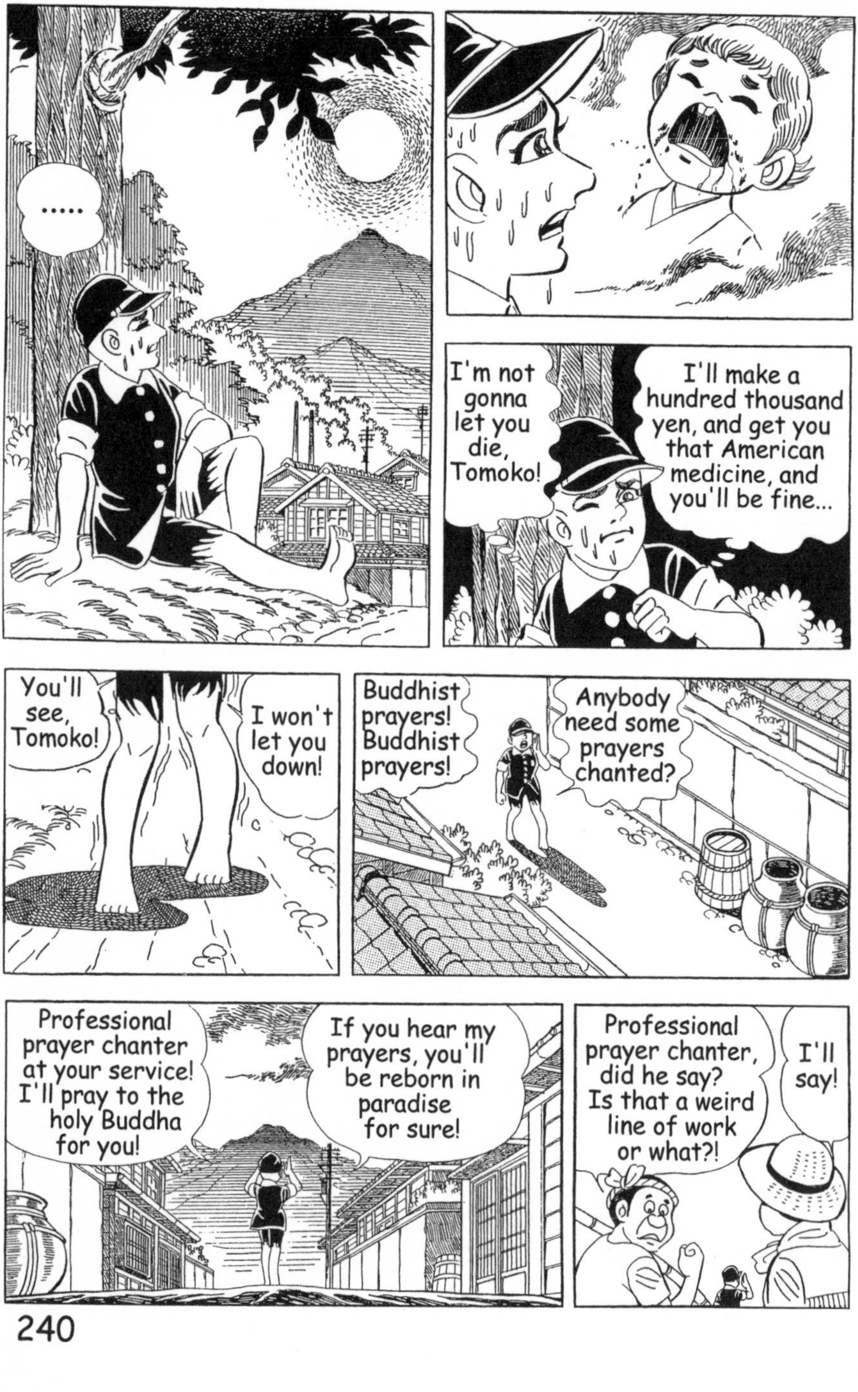
.....
I'm not gonna let you die, Tomoko!
I'll make a hundred thousand yen, and get you that American medicine, and you'll be fine...
You'll see, Tomoko!
I won't let you down!
Buddhist prayers! Buddhist prayers!
Anybody need some prayers chanted?
Professional prayer chanter at your service! I'll pray to the holy Buddha for you!
If you hear my prayers, you'll be reborn in paradise for sure!
Professional prayer chanter, did he say? Is that a weird line of work or what?!
I'll say!

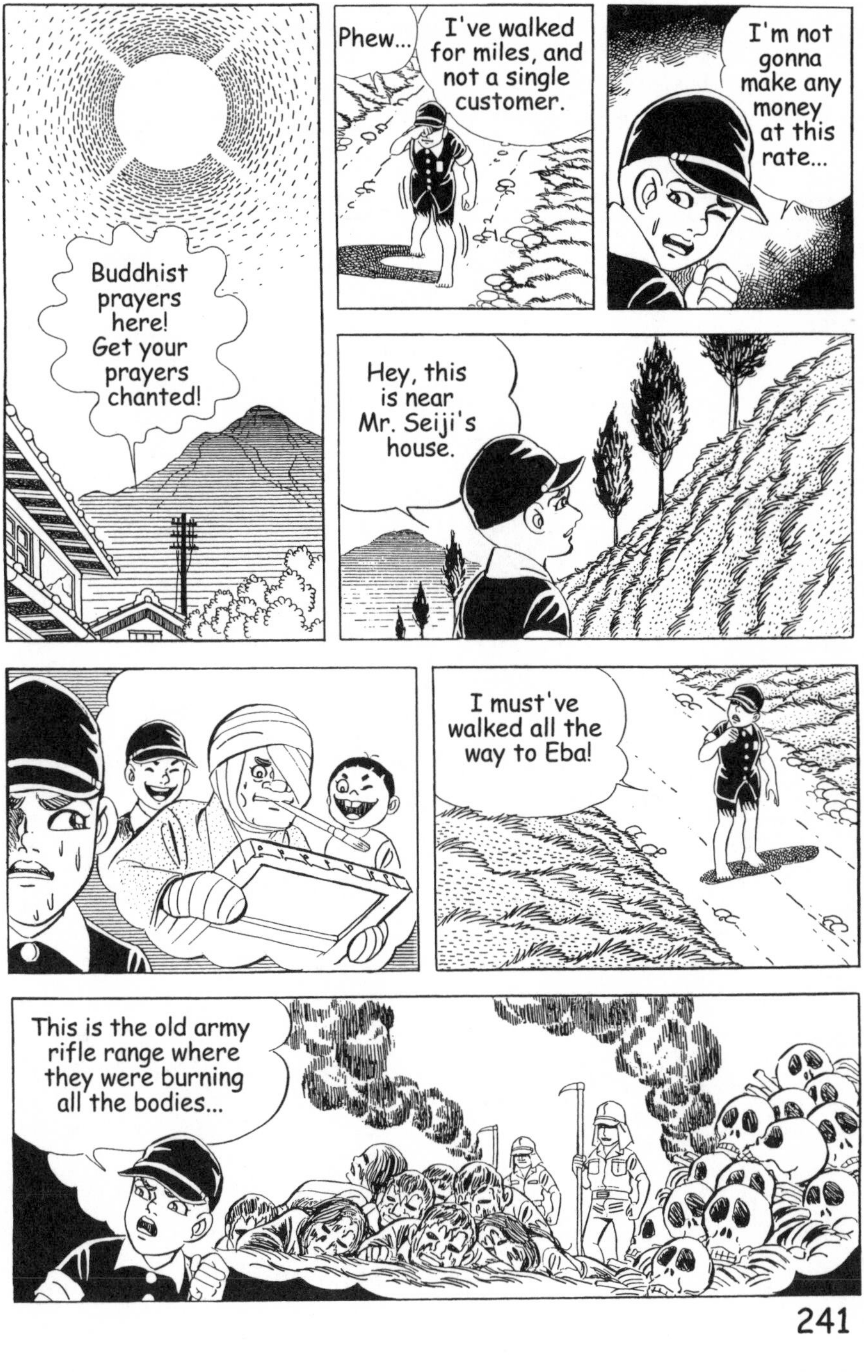
Buddhist prayers here! Get your prayers chanted!
Phew...
I've walked for miles, and not a single customer.
I'm not gonna make any money at this rate...
Hey, this is near Mr. Seiji's house.
I must've walked all the way to Eba!
This is the old army rifle range where they were burning all the bodies...

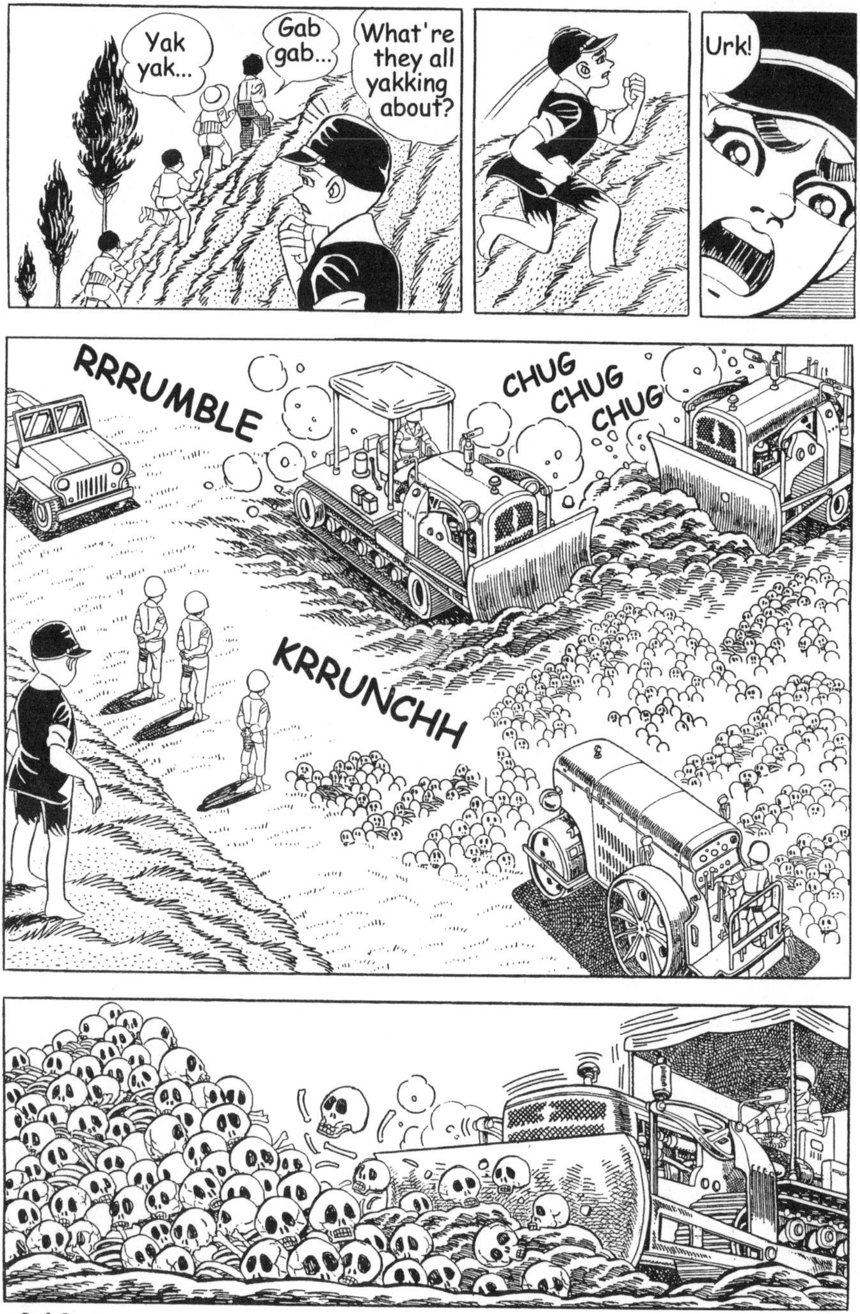

Yak yak...
Gab gab...
What're they all yakking about?
Urk!
RRRUMBLE
CHUG CHUG CHUG
KRRUNCHH

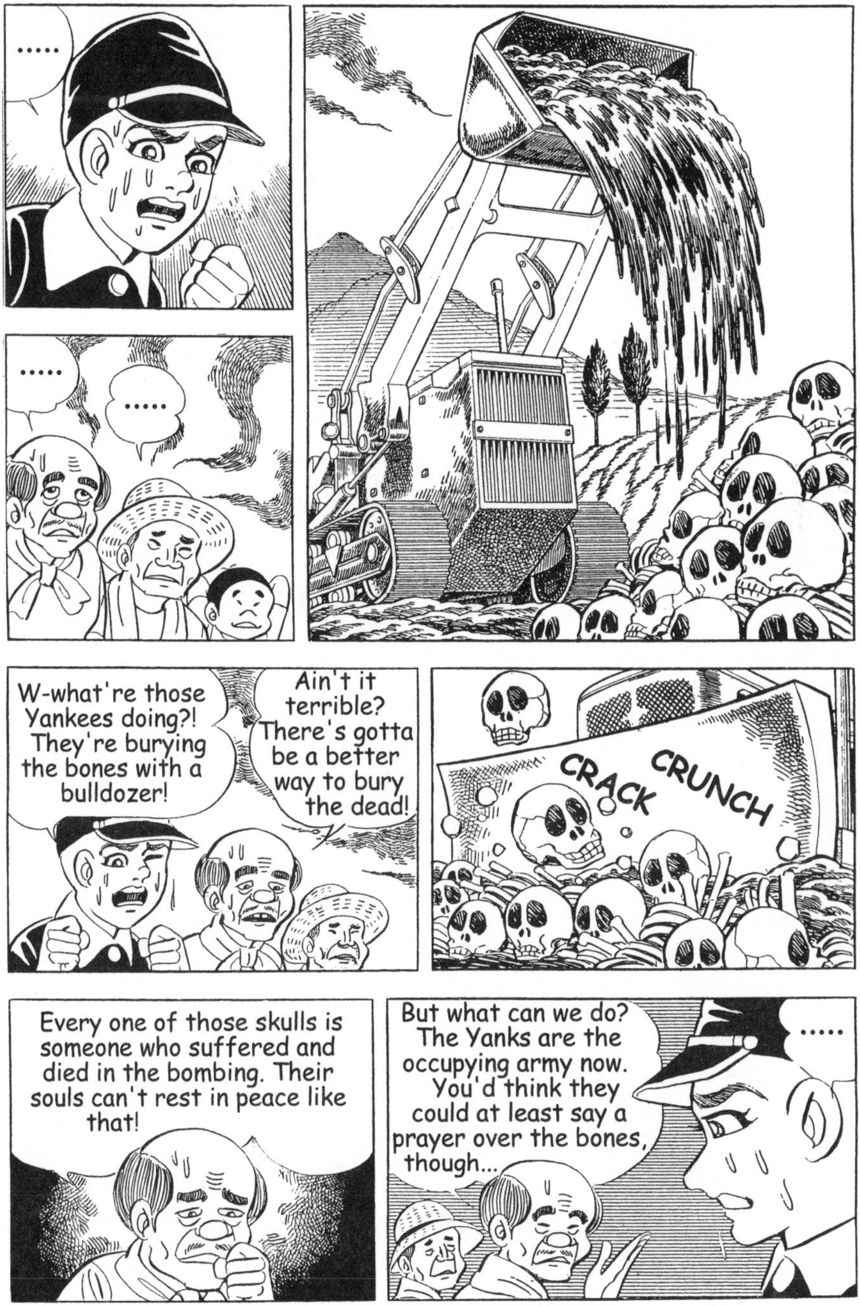
.....
.....
.....
W-what're those Yankees doing?! They're burying the bones with a bulldozer!
Ain't it terrible? There's gotta be a better way to bury the dead!
CRACK
CRUNCH
Every one of those skulls is someone who suffered and died in the bombing. Their souls can't rest in peace like that!
But what can we do? The Yanks are the occupying army now. You'd think they could at least say a prayer over the bones, though...
.....

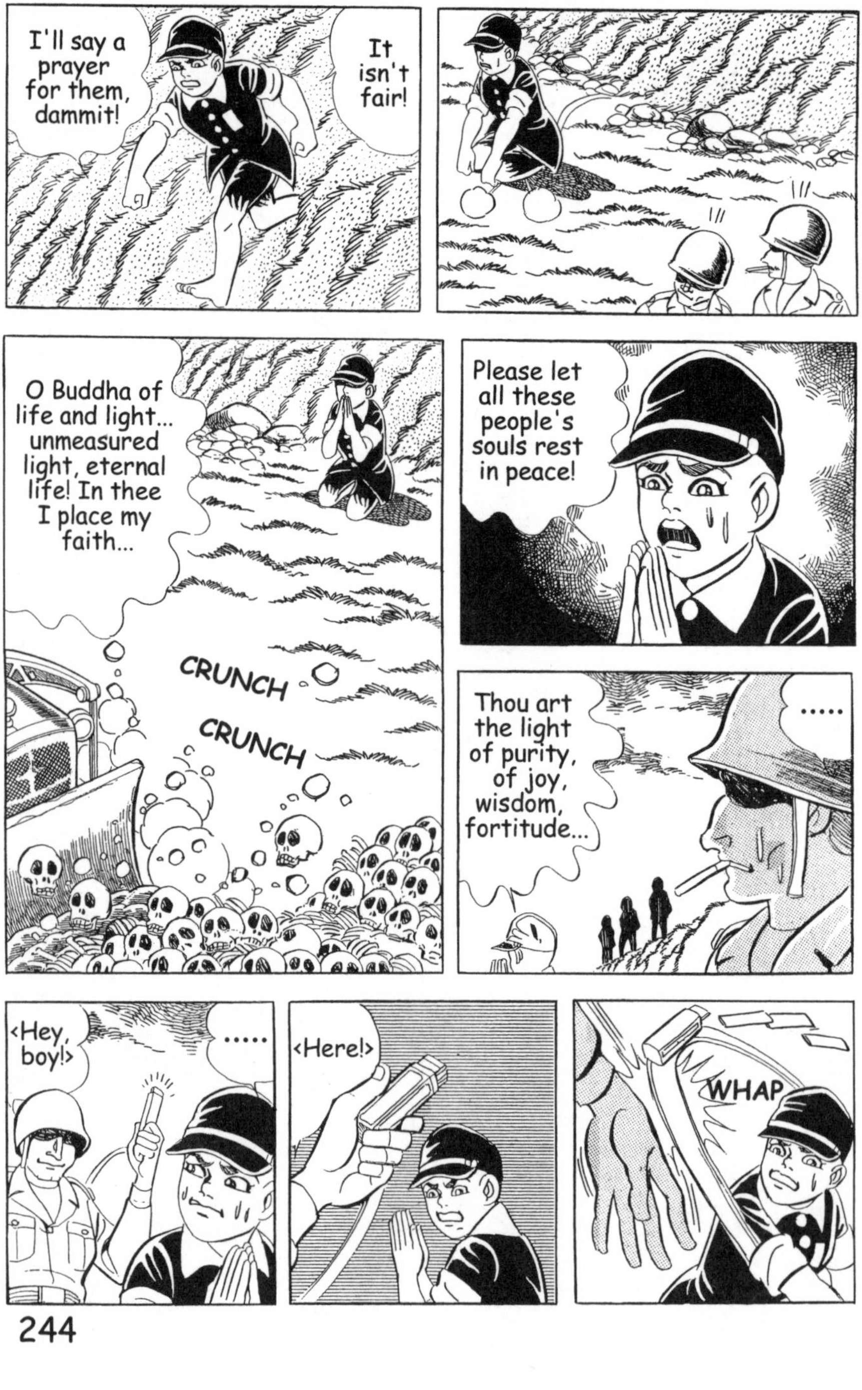
I'll say a prayer for them, dammit!
It isn't fair!
O Buddha of life and light... unmeasured light, eternal life! In thee I place my faith...
CRUNCH
CRUNCH
Please let all these people's souls rest in peace!
Thou art the light of purity, of joy, wisdom, fortitude...
.....
‹Hey, boy!›
.....
‹Here!›
WHAP

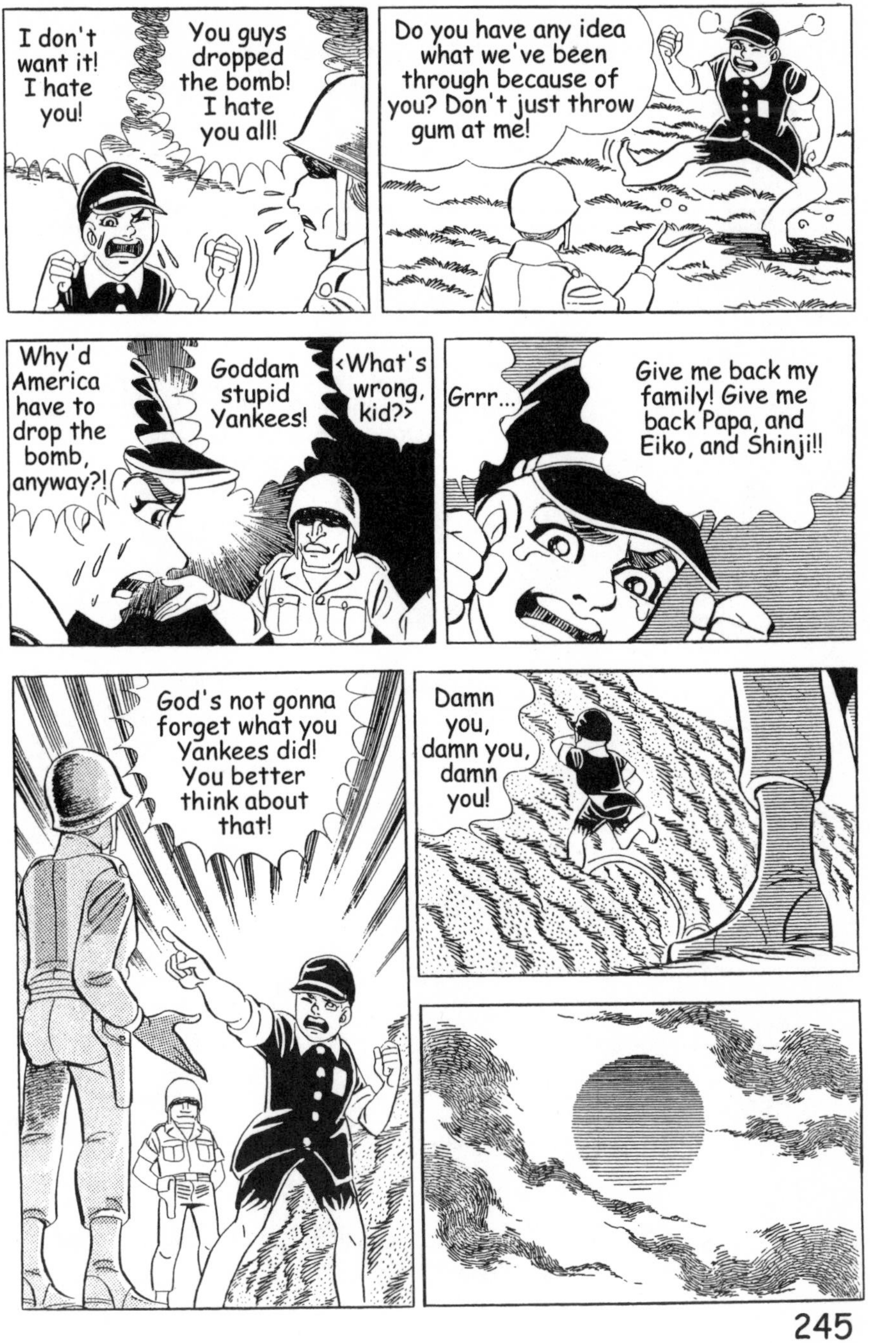
I don't want it! I hate you!
You guys dropped the bomb! I hate you all!
Do you have any idea what we've been through because of you? Don't just throw gum at me!
Why'd America have to drop the bomb, anyway?!
Goddam stupid Yankees!
<What's wrong, kid?>
Grrr...
Give me back my family! Give me back Papa, and Eiko, and Shinji!!
God's not gonna forget what you Yankees did! You better think about that!
Damn you, damn you, damn you!

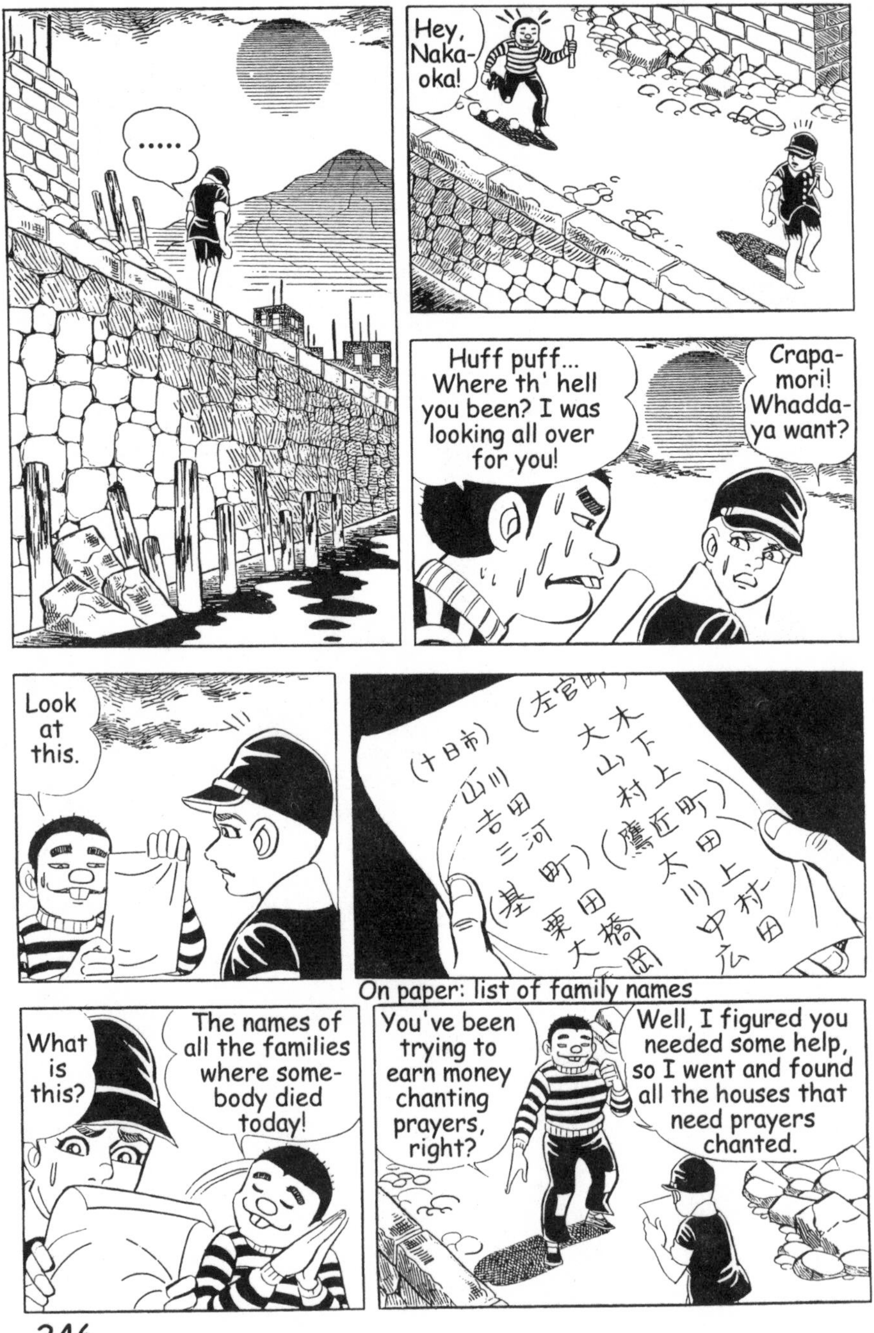
......
Hey, Naka-oka!
Huff puff... Where th' hell you been? I was looking all over for you!
Crapa-mori! Whadda-ya want?
Look at this.
(十日市) 山川 吉田 三河
(左官町) 大木 山下 村上
(基町) 栗田 大橋
(鷹匠町) 太田 川上 中村
On paper: list of family names
What is this?
The names of all the families where some-body died today!
You've been trying to earn money chanting prayers, right?
Well, I figured you needed some help, so I went and found all the houses that need prayers chanted.

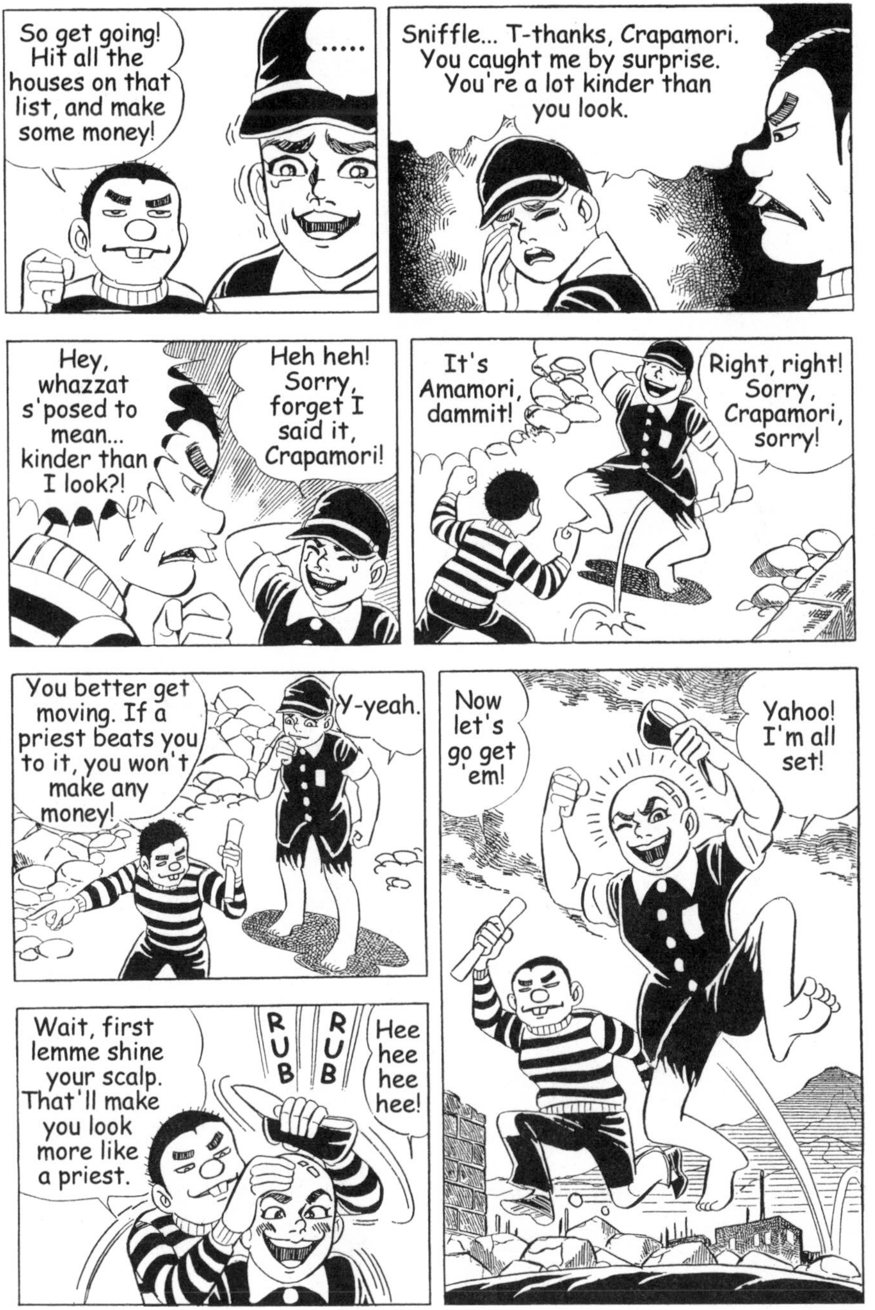
So get going! Hit all the houses on that list, and make some money!
.....
Sniffle... T-thanks, Crapamori. You caught me by surprise. You're a lot kinder than you look.
Hey, whazzat s'posed to mean... kinder than I look?!
Heh heh! Sorry, forget I said it, Crapamori!
It's Amamori, dammit!
Right, right! Sorry, Crapamori, sorry!
You better get moving. If a priest beats you to it, you won't make any money!
Y-yeah.
Wait, first lemme shine your scalp. That'll make you look more like a priest.
RUB RUB
Hee hee hee hee!
Now let's go get 'em!
Yahoo! I'm all set!

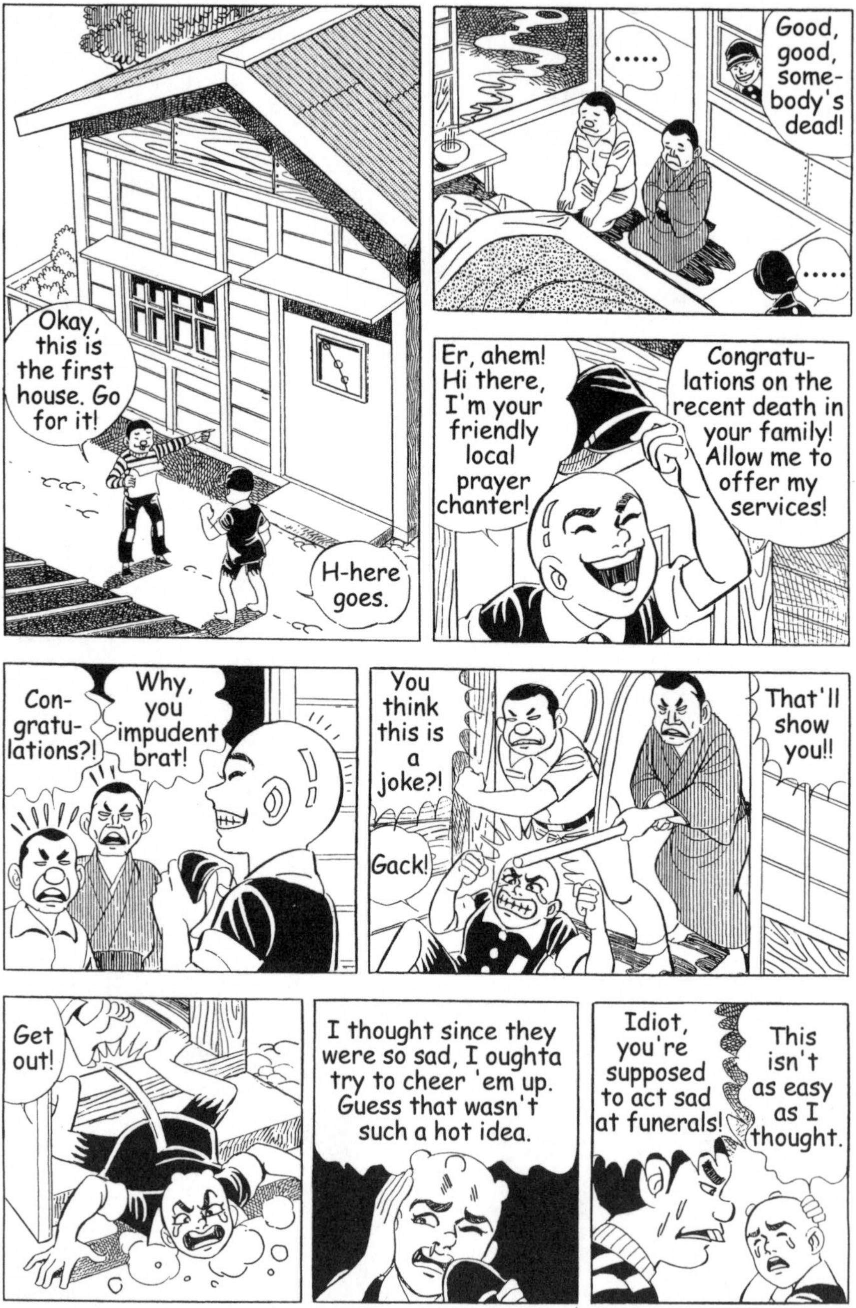
Okay, this is the first house. Go for it!
H-here goes.
.....
Good, good, some-body's dead!
.....
Er, ahem! Hi there, I'm your friendly local prayer chanter!
Congratu-lations on the recent death in your family! Allow me to offer my services!
Con-gratu-lations?!
Why, you impudent brat!
You think this is a joke?!
That'll show you!!
Gack!
Get out!
I thought since they were so sad, I oughta try to cheer 'em up. Guess that wasn't such a hot idea.
Idiot, you're supposed to act sad at funerals!
This isn't as easy as I thought.

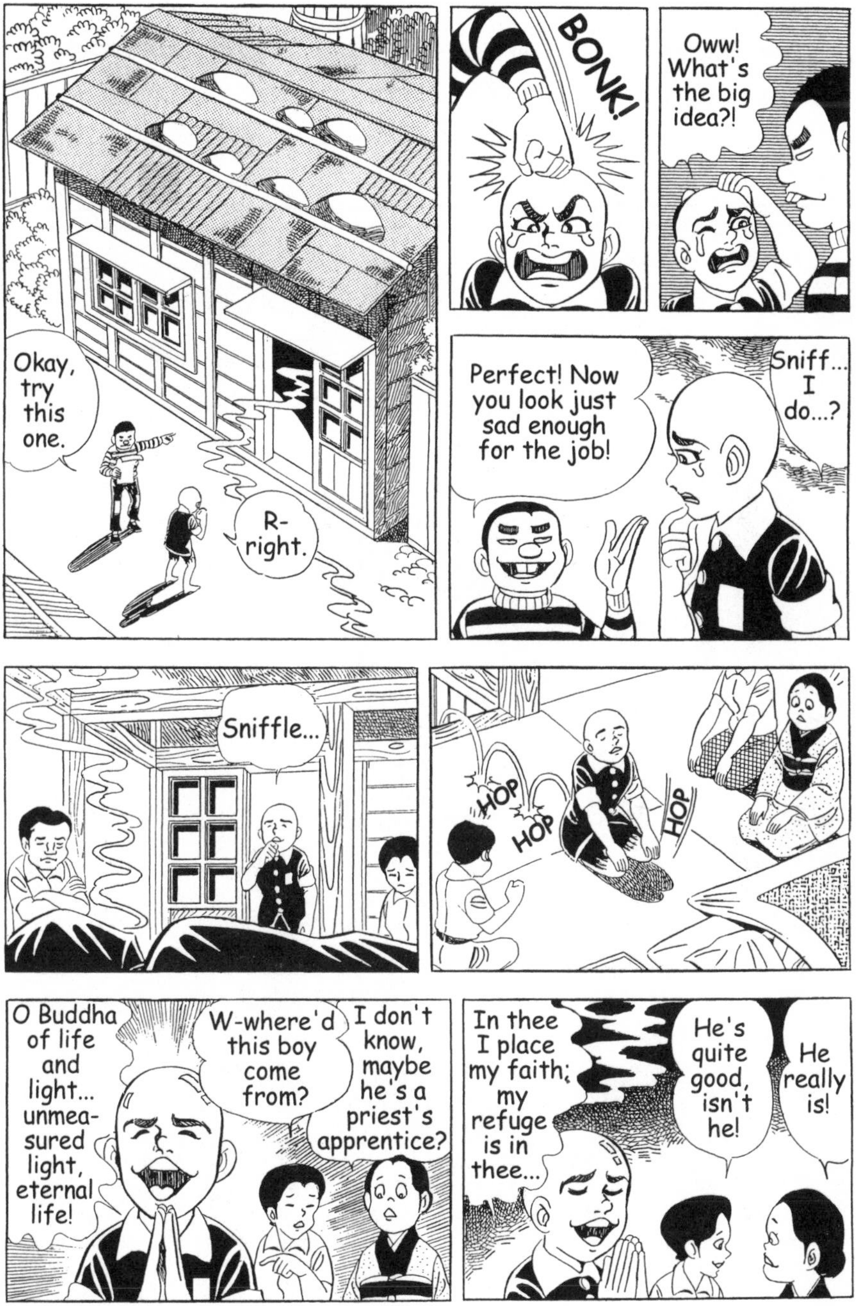
Okay, try this one.
R-right.
BONK!
Oww! What's the big idea?!
Perfect! Now you look just sad enough for the job!
Sniff... I do...?
Sniffle...
HOP
HOP
HOP
O Buddha of life and light... unmeasured light, eternal life!
W-where'd this boy come from?
I don't know, maybe he's a priest's apprentice?
In thee I place my faith; my refuge is in thee...
He's quite good, isn't he!
He really is!

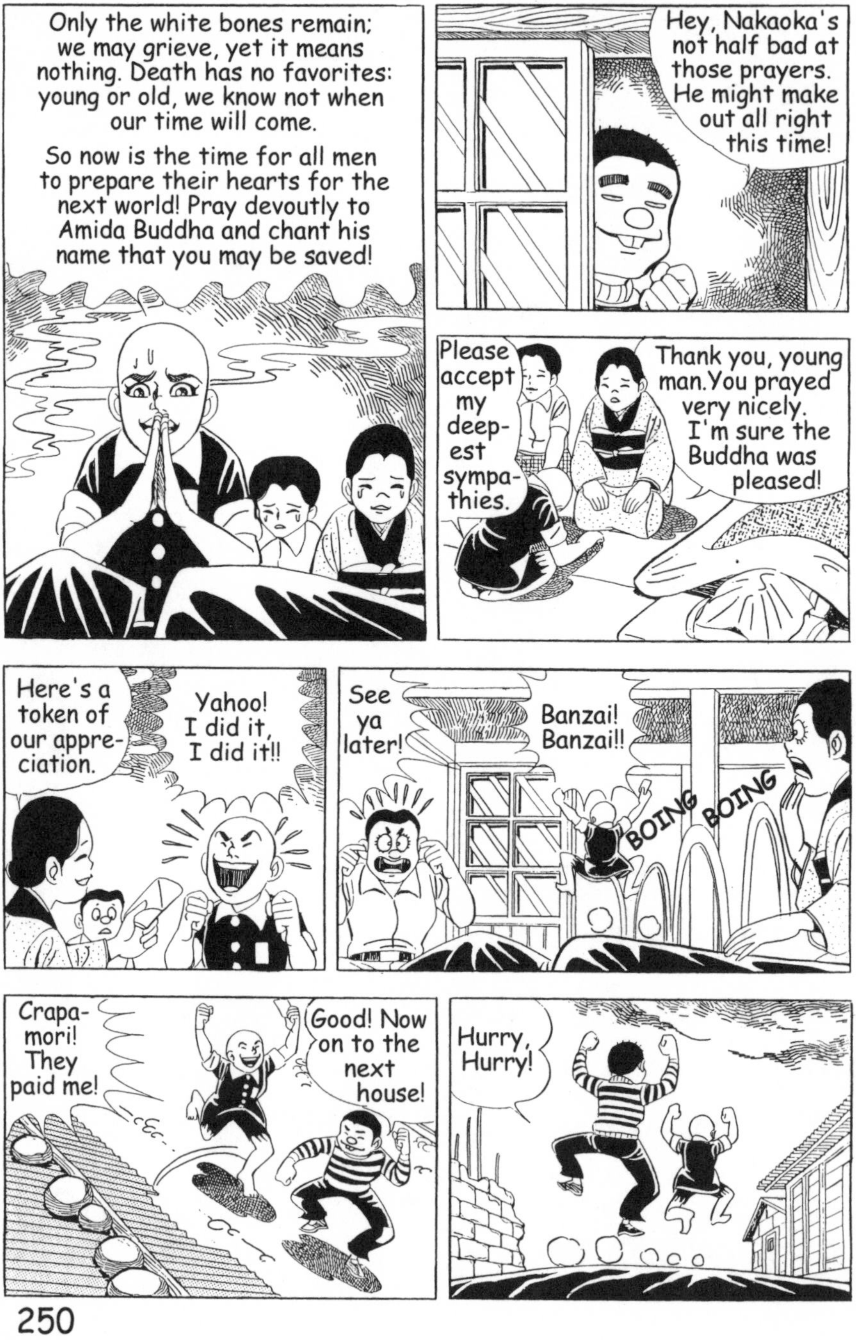
Only the white bones remain; we may grieve, yet it means nothing. Death has no favorites: young or old, we know not when our time will come.
So now is the time for all men to prepare their hearts for the next world! Pray devoutly to Amida Buddha and chant his name that you may be saved!
Hey, Nakaoka's not half bad at those prayers. He might make out all right this time!
Please accept my deepest sympathies.
Thank you, young man. You prayed very nicely. I'm sure the Buddha was pleased!
Here's a token of our appreciation.
Yahoo! I did it, I did it!!
See ya later!
Banzai! Banzai!!
BOING BOING
Crapamori! They paid me!
Good! Now on to the next house!
Hurry, Hurry!

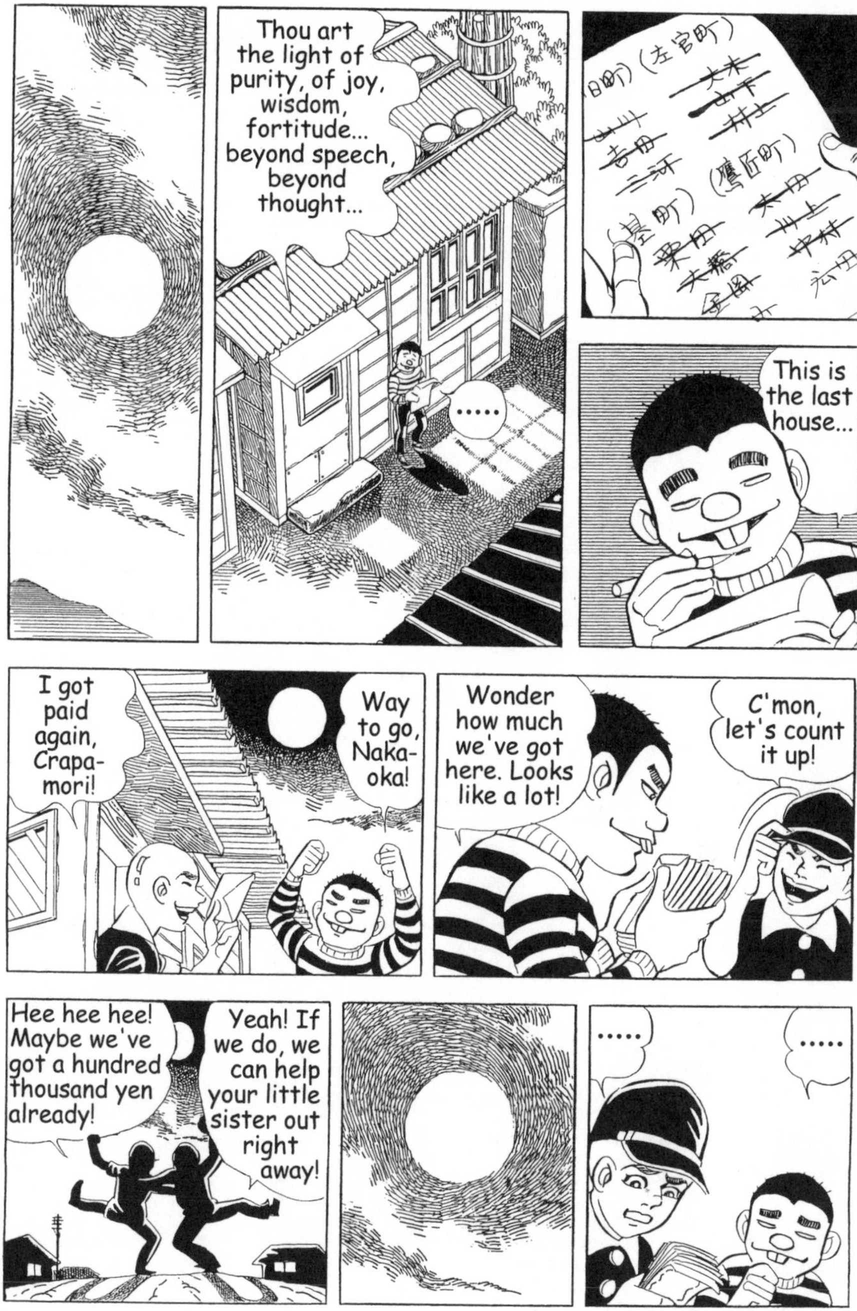
Thou art the light of purity, of joy, wisdom, fortitude... beyond speech, beyond thought...
.....
This is the last house...
I got paid again, Crapa-mori!
Way to go, Naka-oka!
Wonder how much we've got here. Looks like a lot!
C'mon, let's count it up!
Hee hee hee! Maybe we've got a hundred thousand yen already!
Yeah! If we do, we can help your little sister out right away!
.....
.....

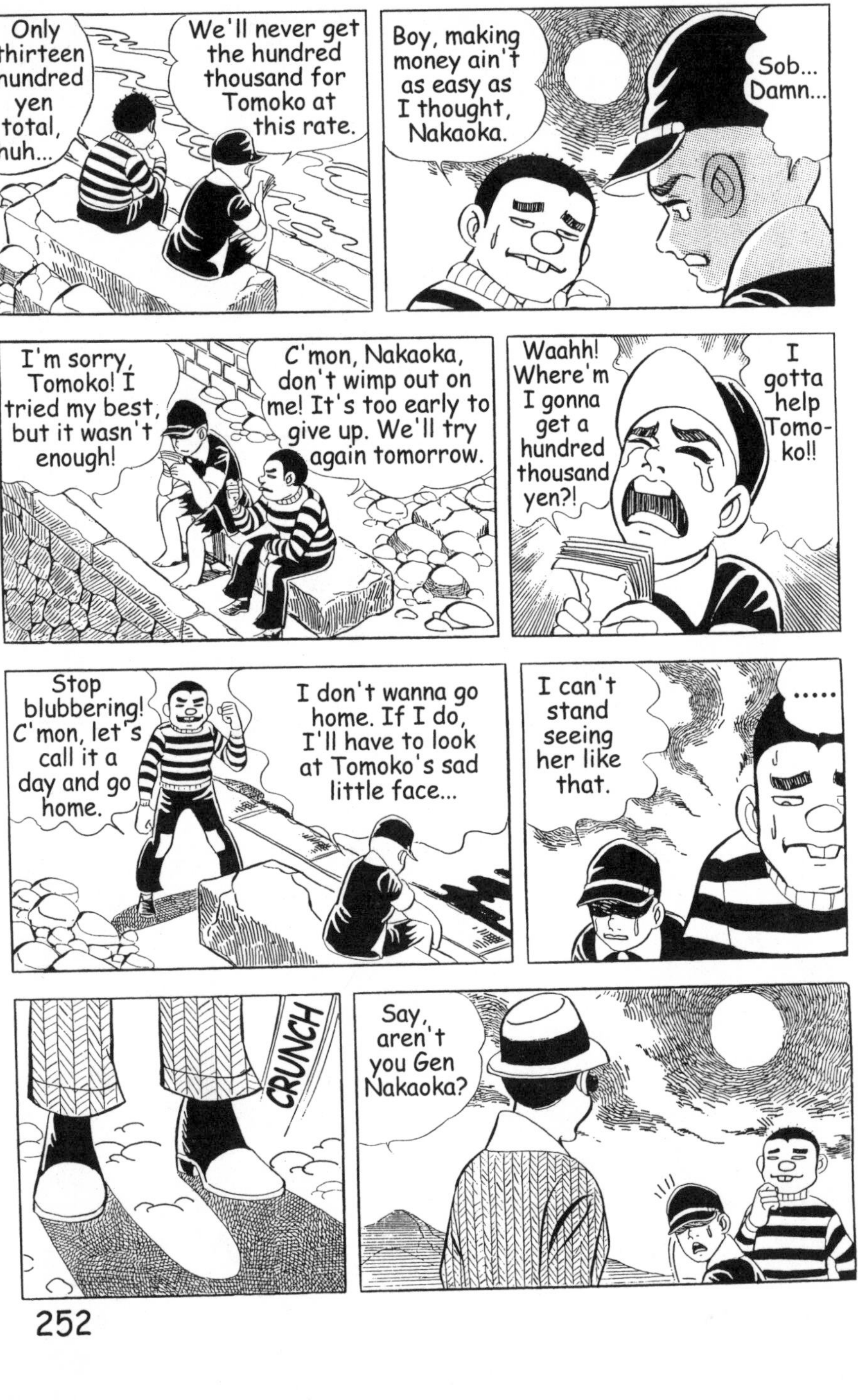
Only thirteen hundred yen total, huh...
We'll never get the hundred thousand for Tomoko at this rate.
Boy, making money ain't as easy as I thought, Nakaoka.
Sob... Damn...
I'm sorry, Tomoko! I tried my best, but it wasn't enough!
C'mon, Nakaoka, don't wimp out on me! It's too early to give up. We'll try again tomorrow.
Waahh! Where'm I gonna get a hundred thousand yen?!
I gotta help Tomo-ko!!
Stop blubbering! C'mon, let's call it a day and go home.
I don't wanna go home. If I do, I'll have to look at Tomoko's sad little face...
I can't stand seeing her like that.
.....
CRUNCH
Say, aren't you Gen Nakaoka?

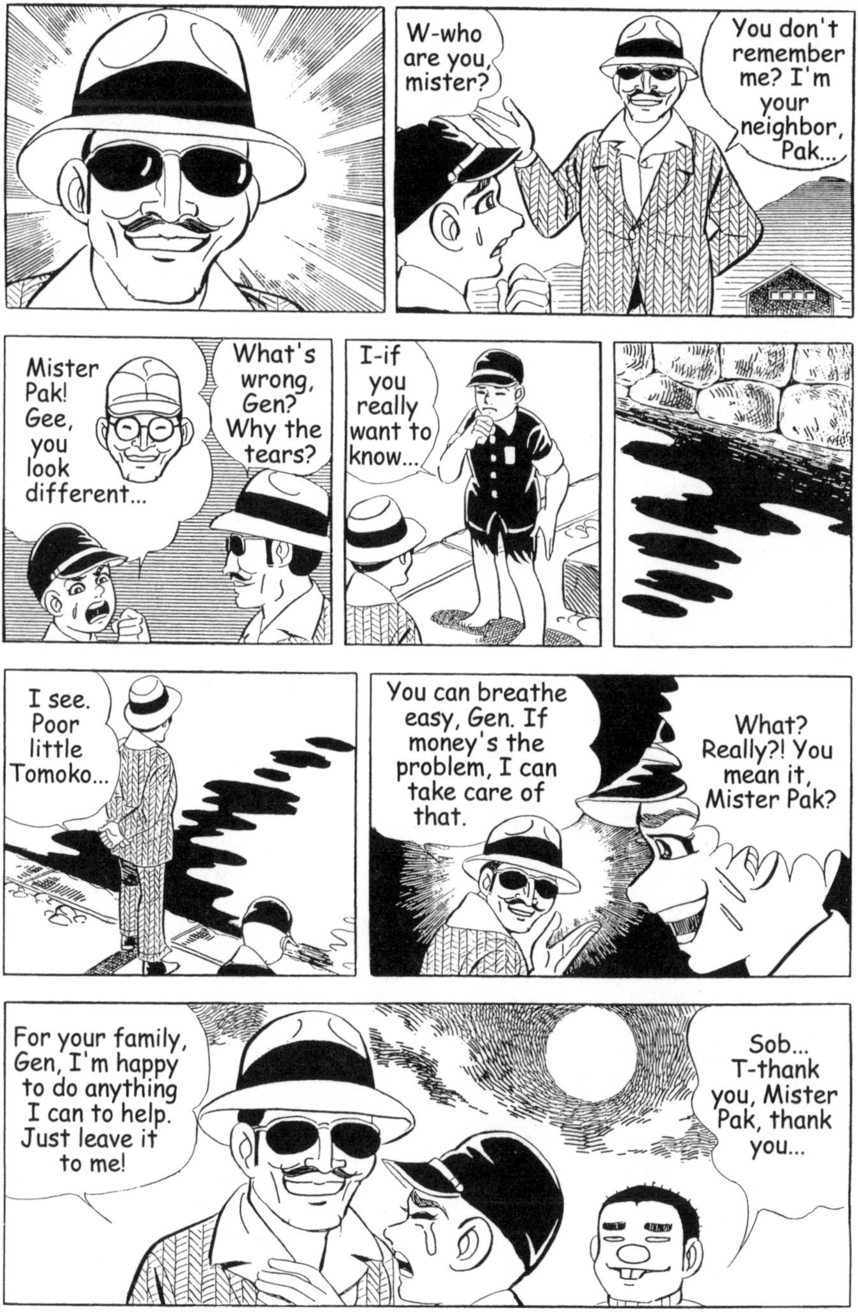

W-who are you, mister?
You don't remember me? I'm your neighbor, Pak...
Mister Pak! Gee, you look different...
What's wrong, Gen? Why the tears?
I-if you really want to know...
I see. Poor little Tomoko...
You can breathe easy, Gen. If money's the problem, I can take care of that.
What? Really?! You mean it, Mister Pak?
For your family, Gen, I'm happy to do anything I can to help. Just leave it to me!
Sob... T-thank you, Mister Pak, thank you...

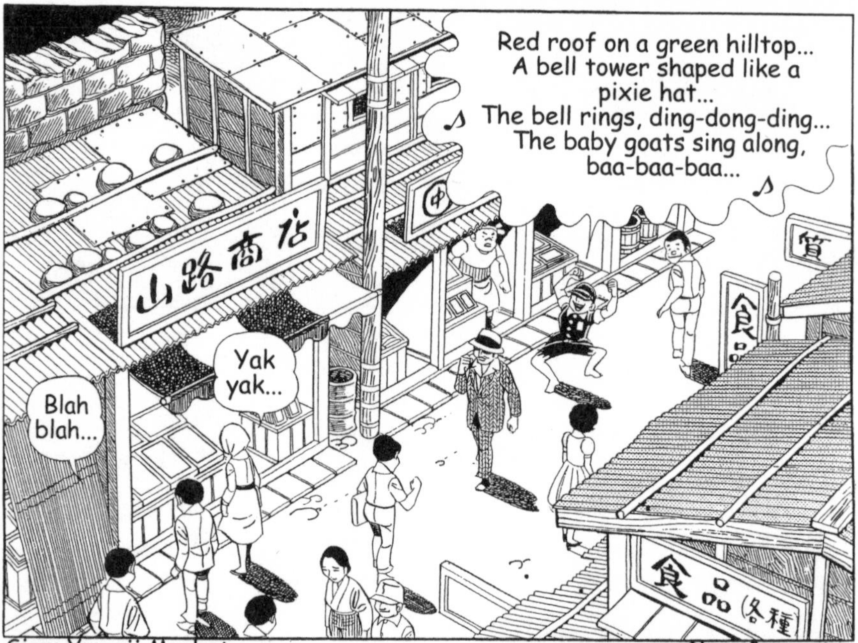
Red roof on a green hilltop... A bell tower shaped like a pixie hat... The bell rings, ding-dong-ding... The baby goats sing along, baa-baa-baa...
山路商店
Yak yak...
Blah blah...
食品(各種)

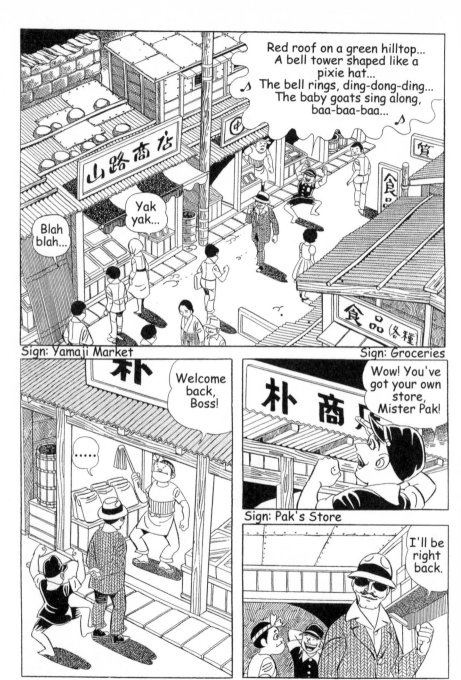

Sign: Yamaji Market

Sign: Groceries

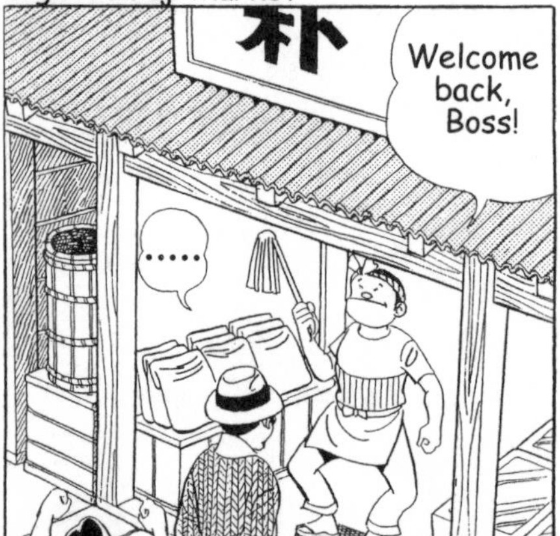
朴
Welcome back, Boss!
......

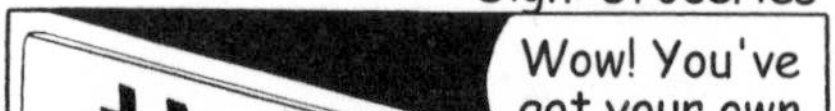
朴商
Wow! You've got your own store, Mister Pak!

Sign: Pak's Store

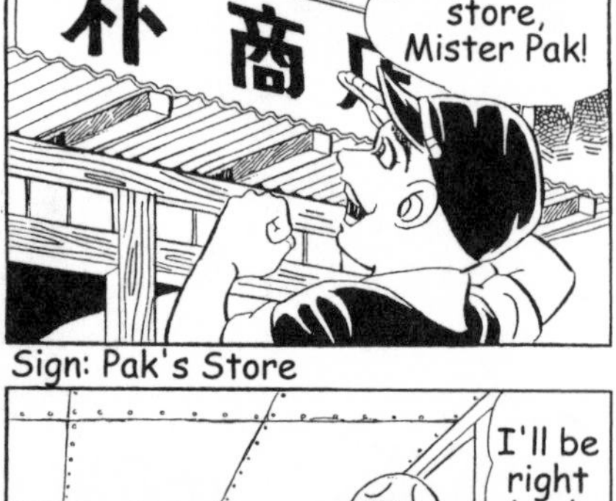
I'll be right back.

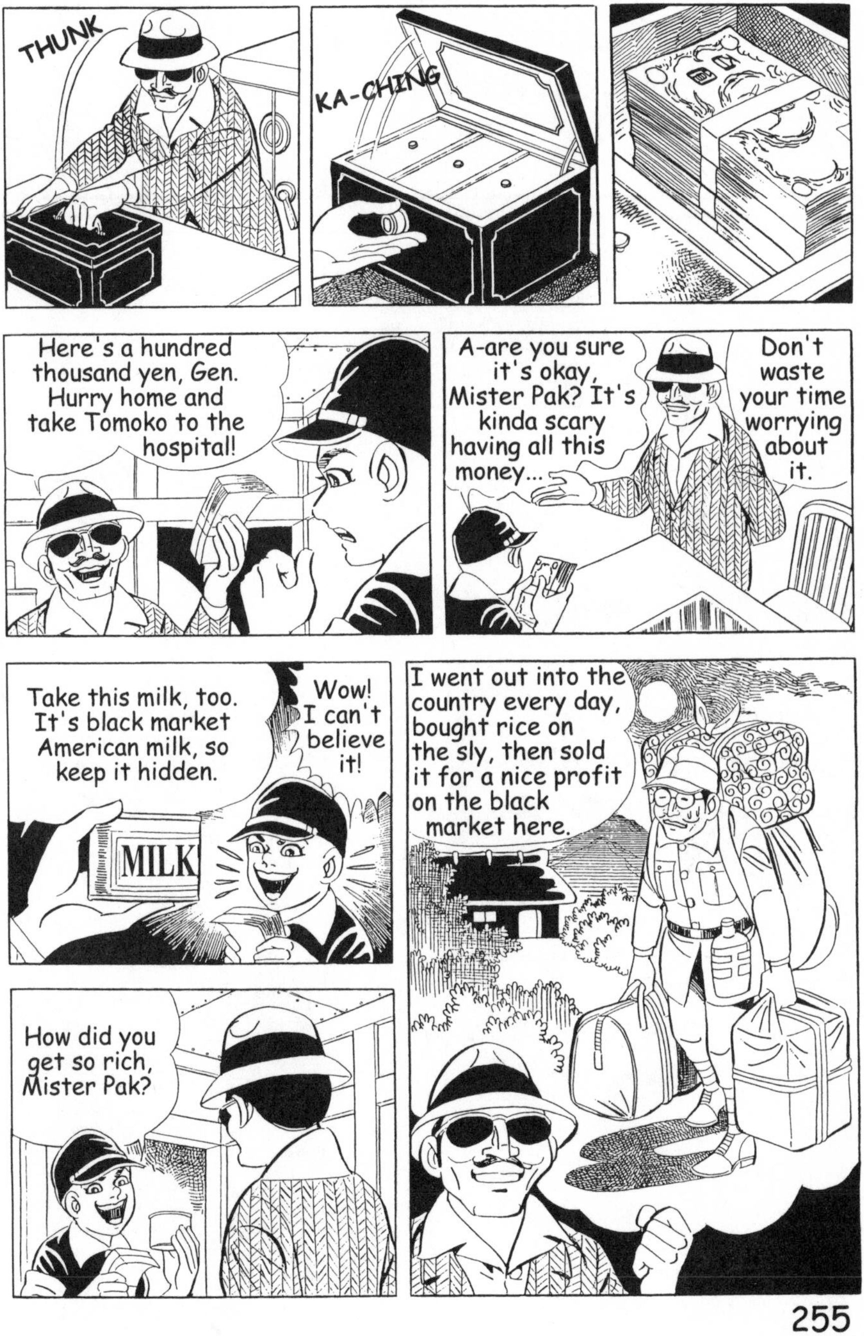
THUNK
KA-CHING
Here's a hundred thousand yen, Gen. Hurry home and take Tomoko to the hospital!
A-are you sure it's okay, Mister Pak? It's kinda scary having all this money...
Don't waste your time worrying about it.
Take this milk, too. It's black market American milk, so keep it hidden.
Wow! I can't believe it!
MILK
How did you get so rich, Mister Pak?
I went out into the country every day, bought rice on the sly, then sold it for a nice profit on the black market here.

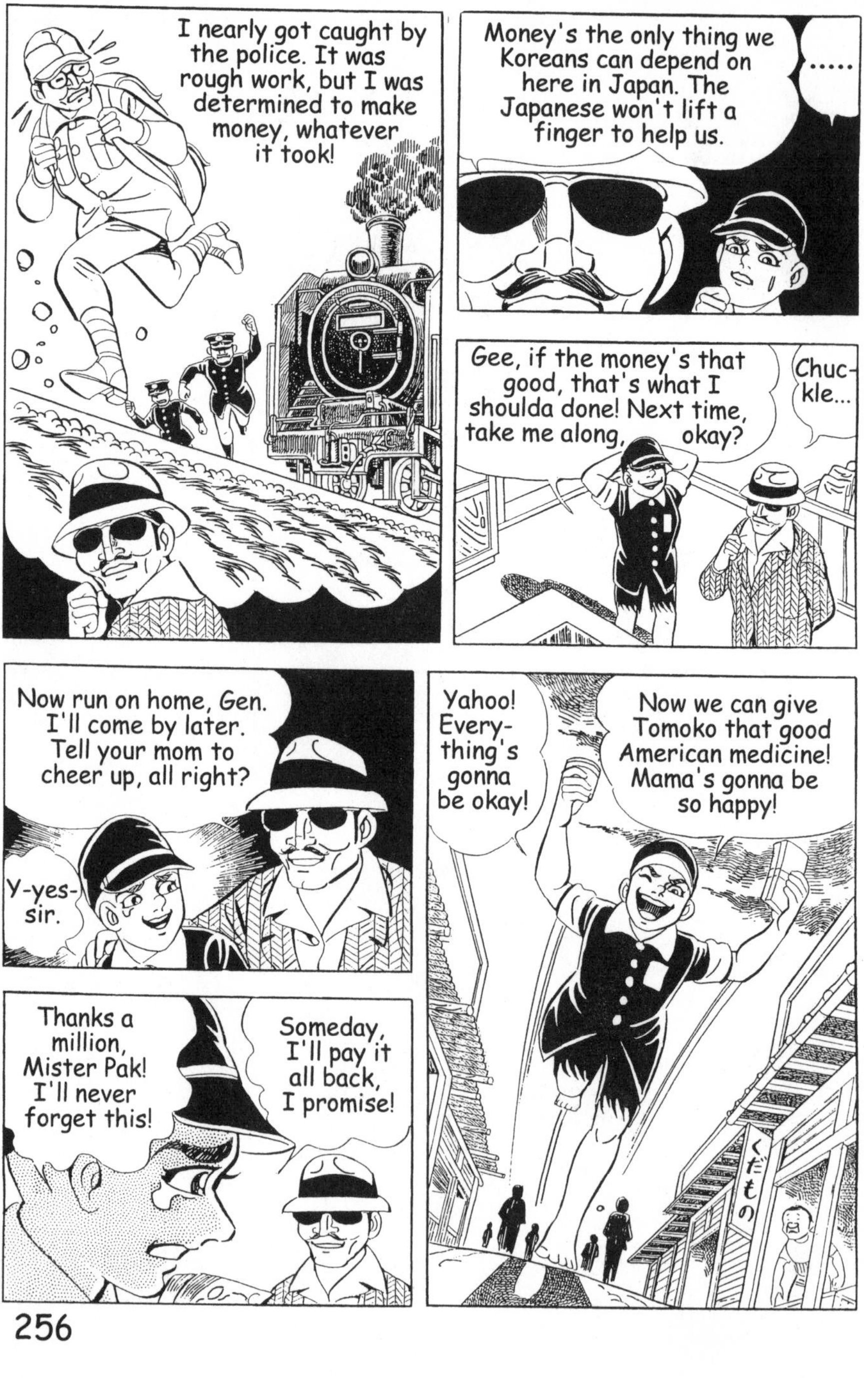
I nearly got caught by the police. It was rough work, but I was determined to make money, whatever it took!
Money's the only thing we Koreans can depend on here in Japan. The Japanese won't lift a finger to help us.
.....
Gee, if the money's that good, that's what I shoulda done! Next time, take me along, okay?
Chuc-kle...
Now run on home, Gen. I'll come by later. Tell your mom to cheer up, all right?
Y-yes-sir.
Thanks a million, Mister Pak! I'll never forget this!
Someday, I'll pay it all back, I promise!
Yahoo! Every-thing's gonna be okay!
Now we can give Tomoko that good American medicine! Mama's gonna be so happy!
くだもの

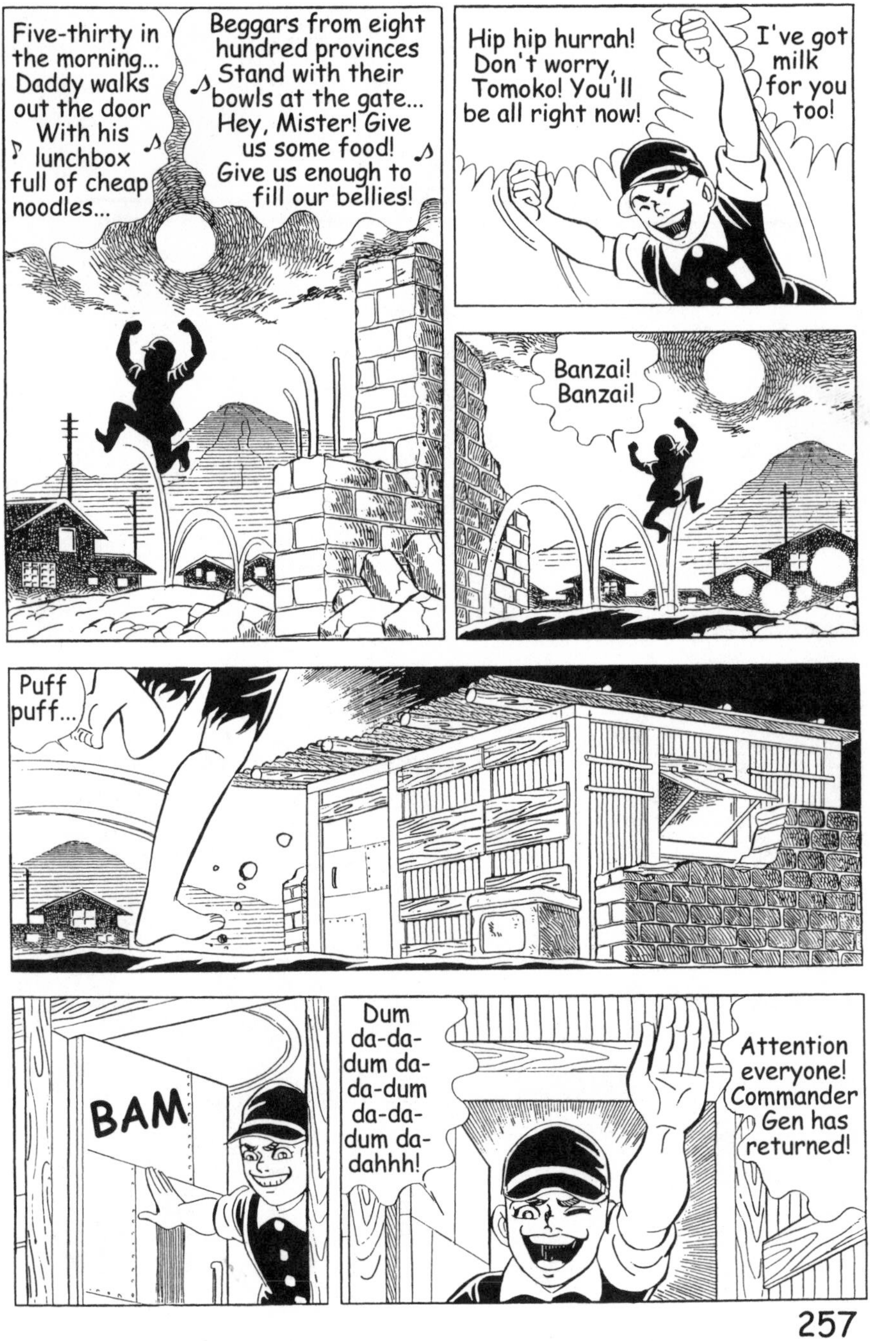
Five-thirty in the morning... Daddy walks out the door With his lunchbox full of cheap noodles...
Beggars from eight hundred provinces Stand with their bowls at the gate... Hey, Mister! Give us some food! Give us enough to fill our bellies!
Hip hip hurrah! Don't worry, Tomoko! You'll be all right now!
I've got milk for you too!
Banzai! Banzai!
Puff puff...
BAM
Dum da-da-dum da-da-dum da-da-dum da-dahhh!
Attention everyone! Commander Gen has returned!

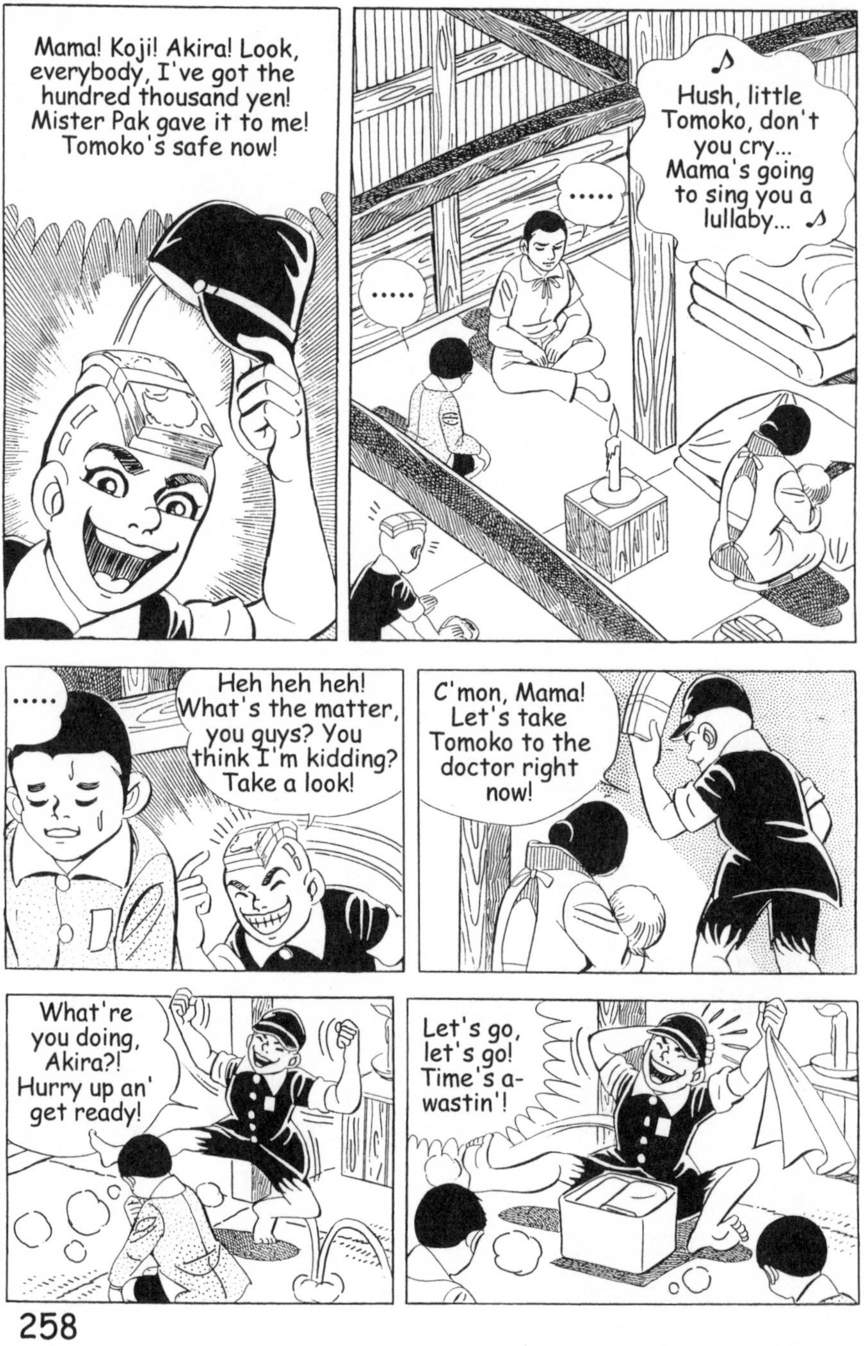

Mama! Koji! Akira! Look, everybody, I've got the hundred thousand yen! Mister Pak gave it to me! Tomoko's safe now!
Hush, little Tomoko, don't you cry... Mama's going to sing you a lullaby...
.....
.....
.....
Heh heh heh! What's the matter, you guys? You think I'm kidding? Take a look!
C'mon, Mama! Let's take Tomoko to the doctor right now!
What're you doing, Akira?! Hurry up an' get ready!
Let's go, let's go! Time's a-wastin'!

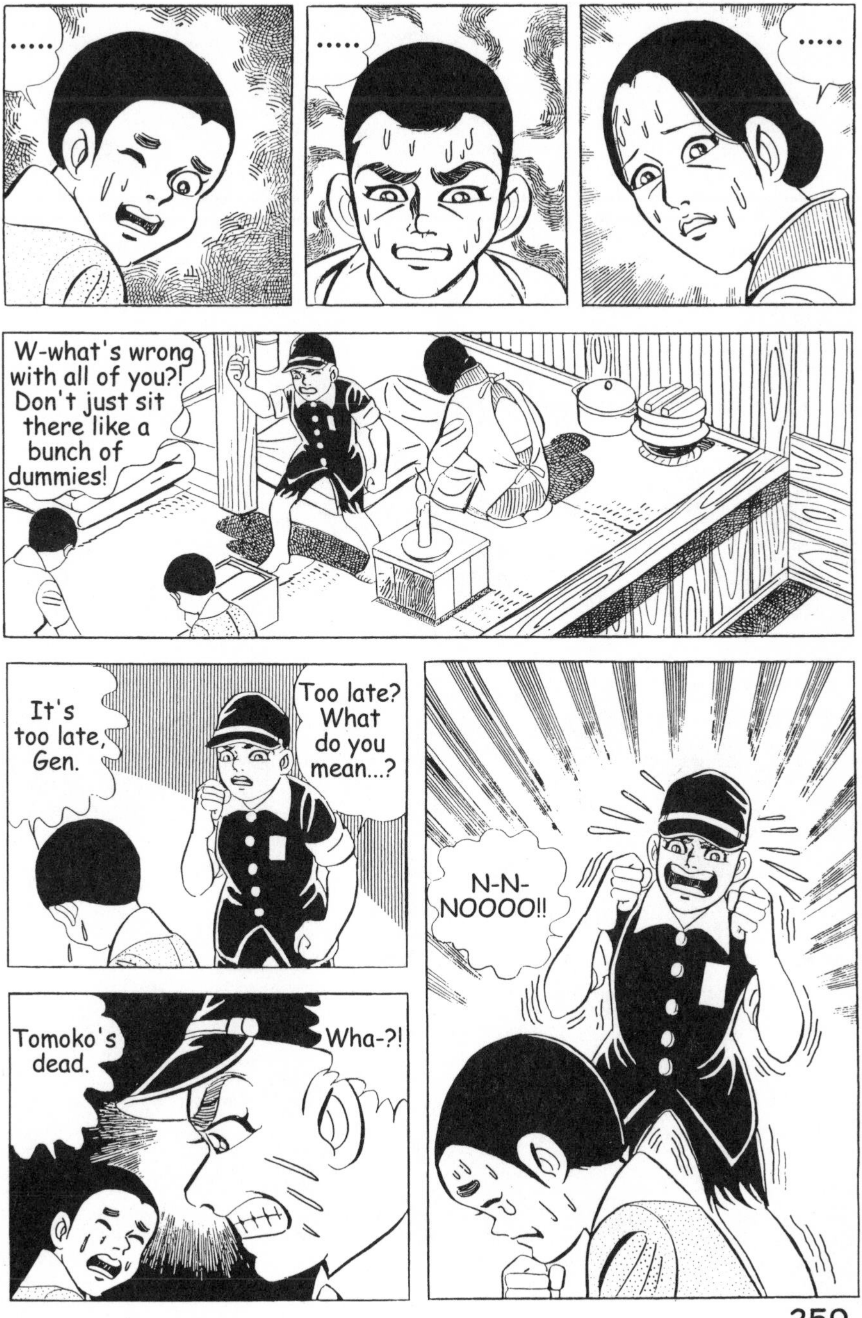
.....
.....
.....
W-what's wrong with all of you?! Don't just sit there like a bunch of dummies!
It's too late, Gen.
Too late? What do you mean...?
N-N-NOOOO!!
Tomoko's dead.
Wha-?!

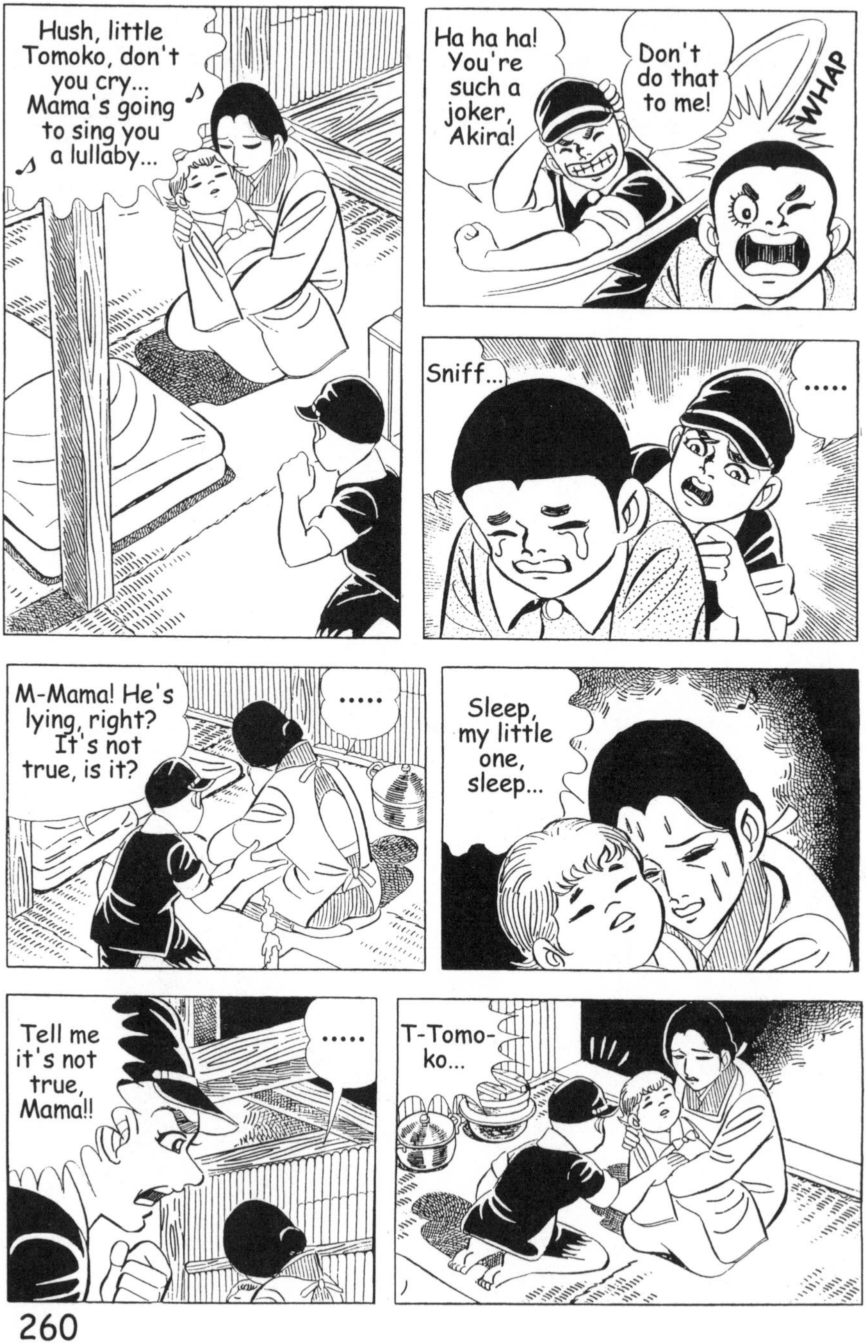
Hush, little Tomoko, don't you cry... Mama's going to sing you a lullaby...
Ha ha ha! You're such a joker, Akira!
Don't do that to me!
WHAP
Sniff...
.....
M-Mama! He's lying, right? It's not true, is it?
.....
Sleep, my little one, sleep...
Tell me it's not true, Mama!!
.....
T-Tomo-ko...

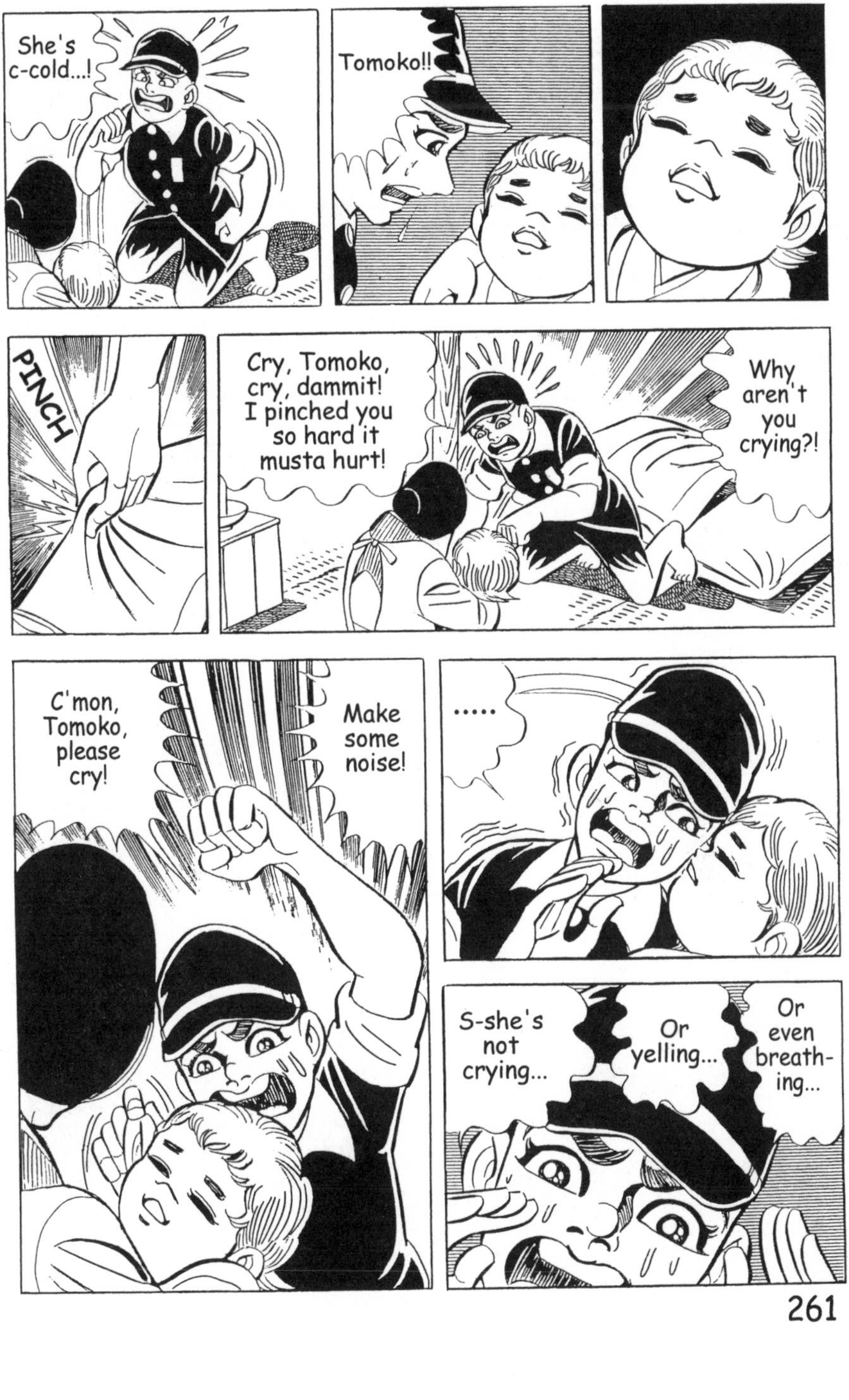
She's c-cold...!
Tomoko!!
PINCH
Cry, Tomoko, cry, dammit! I pinched you so hard it musta hurt!
Why aren't you crying?!
C'mon, Tomoko, please cry!
Make some noise!
.....
S-she's not crying...
Or yelling...
Or even breath-ing...

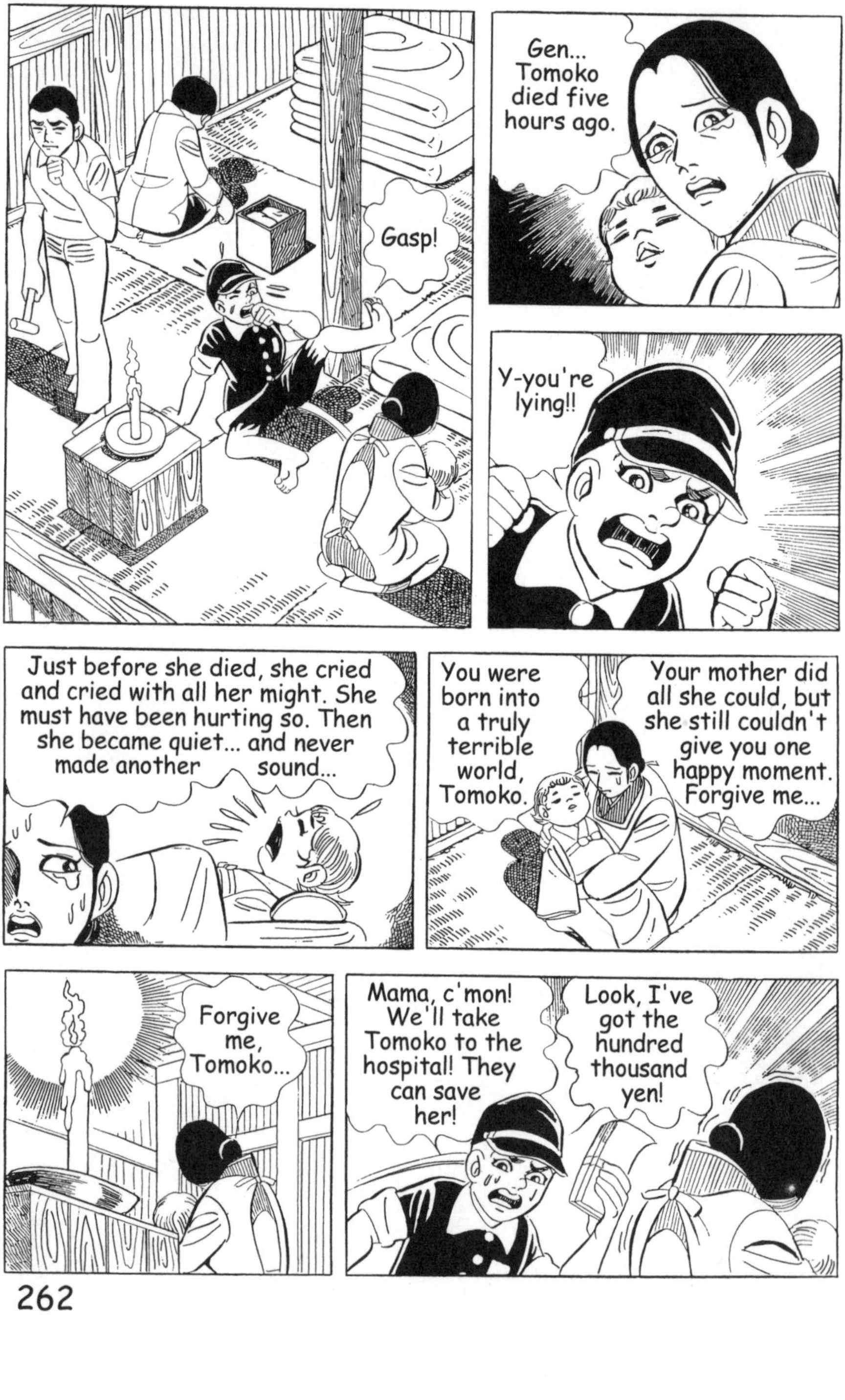
Gasp!
Gen... Tomoko died five hours ago.
Y-you're lying!!
Just before she died, she cried and cried with all her might. She must have been hurting so. Then she became quiet... and never made another sound...
You were born into a truly terrible world, Tomoko.
Your mother did all she could, but she still couldn't give you one happy moment. Forgive me...
Forgive me, Tomoko...
Mama, c'mon! We'll take Tomoko to the hospital! They can save her!
Look, I've got the hundred thousand yen!

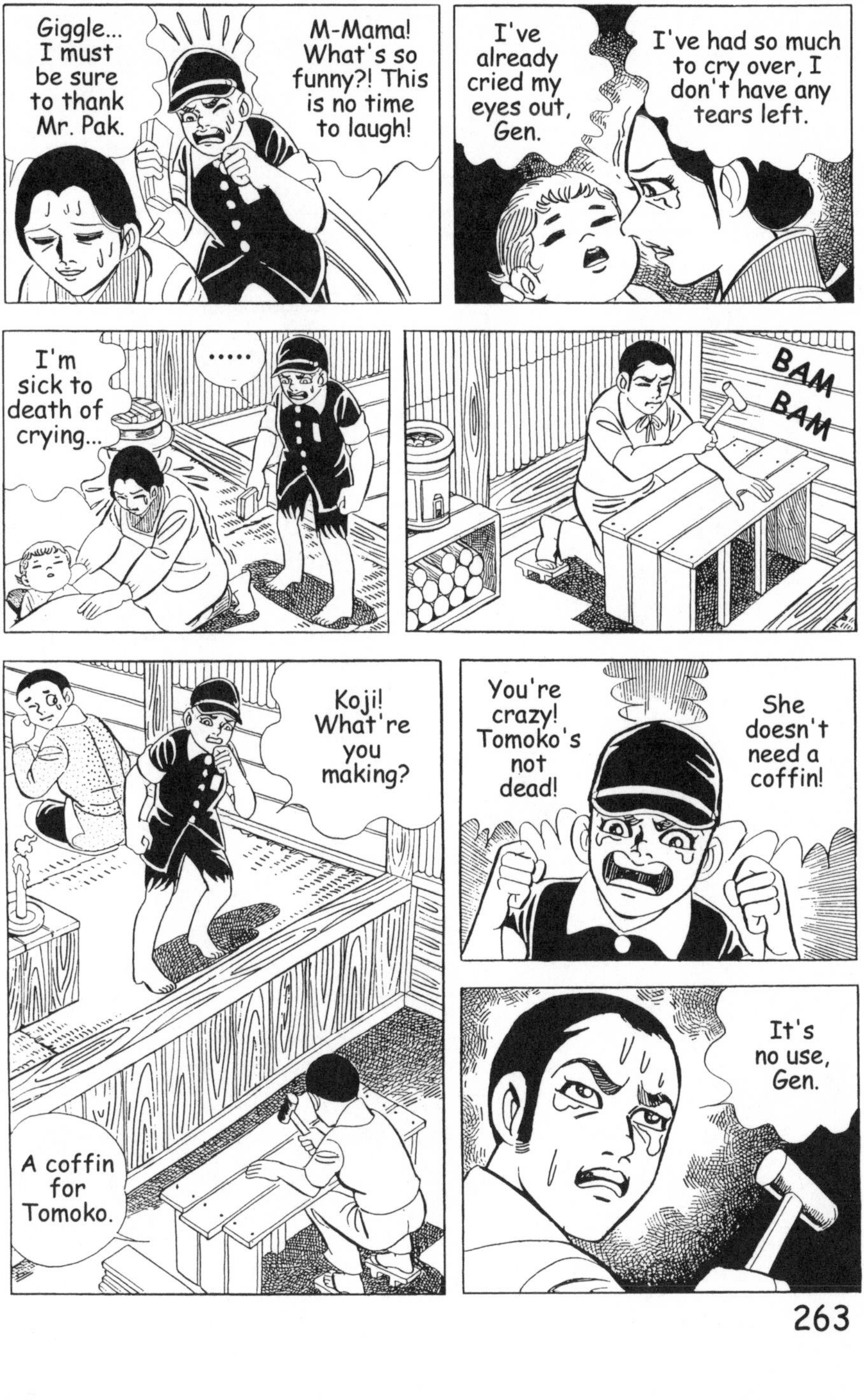

Giggle... I must be sure to thank Mr. Pak.
M-Mama! What's so funny?! This is no time to laugh!
I've already cried my eyes out, Gen.
I've had so much to cry over, I don't have any tears left.
I'm sick to death of crying...
......
BAM
BAM
Koji! What're you making?
A coffin for Tomoko.
You're crazy! Tomoko's not dead!
She doesn't need a coffin!
It's no use, Gen.

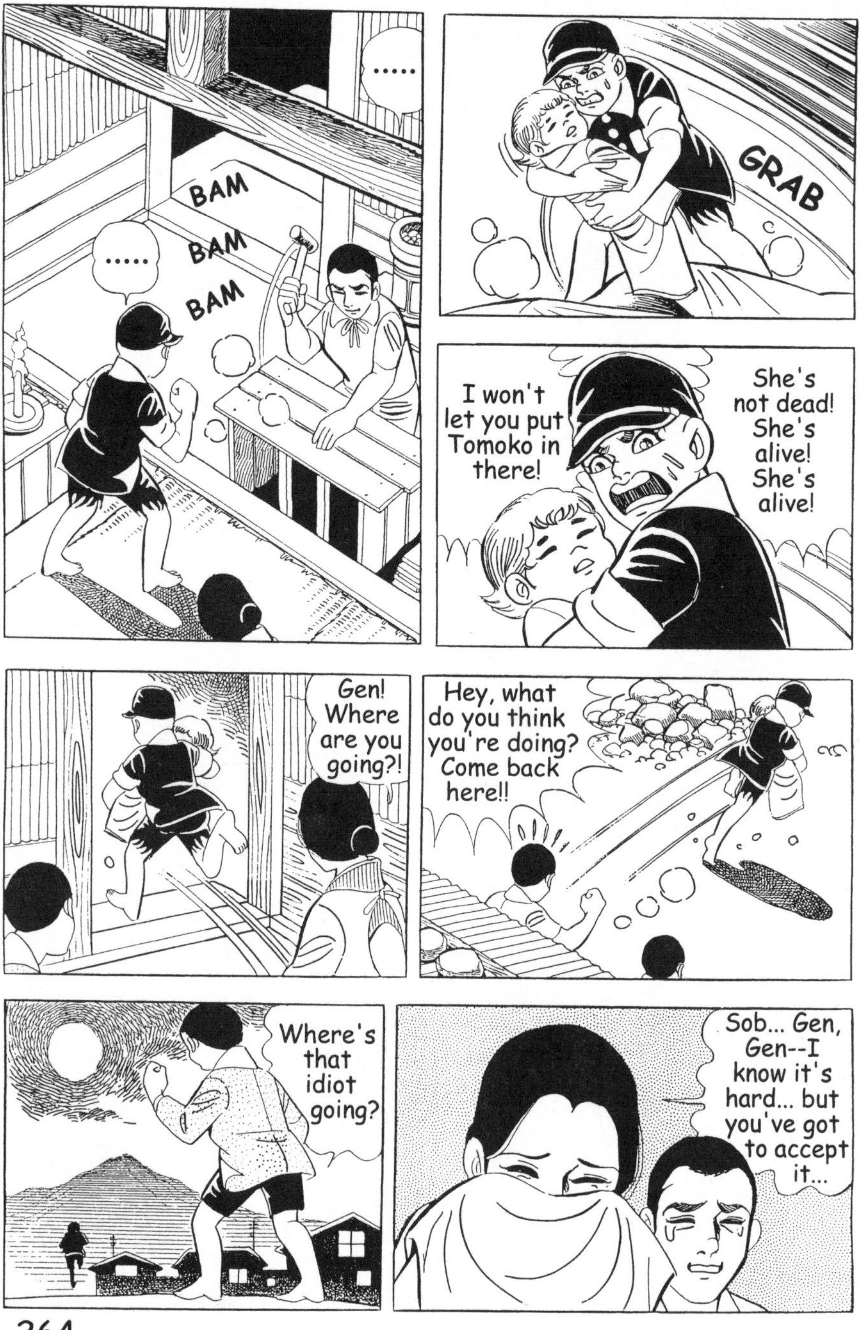
......
BAM
BAM
BAM
......
GRAB
I won't let you put Tomoko in there!
She's not dead! She's alive! She's alive!
Gen! Where are you going?!
Hey, what do you think you're doing? Come back here!!
Where's that idiot going?
Sob... Gen, Gen--I know it's hard... but you've got to accept it...

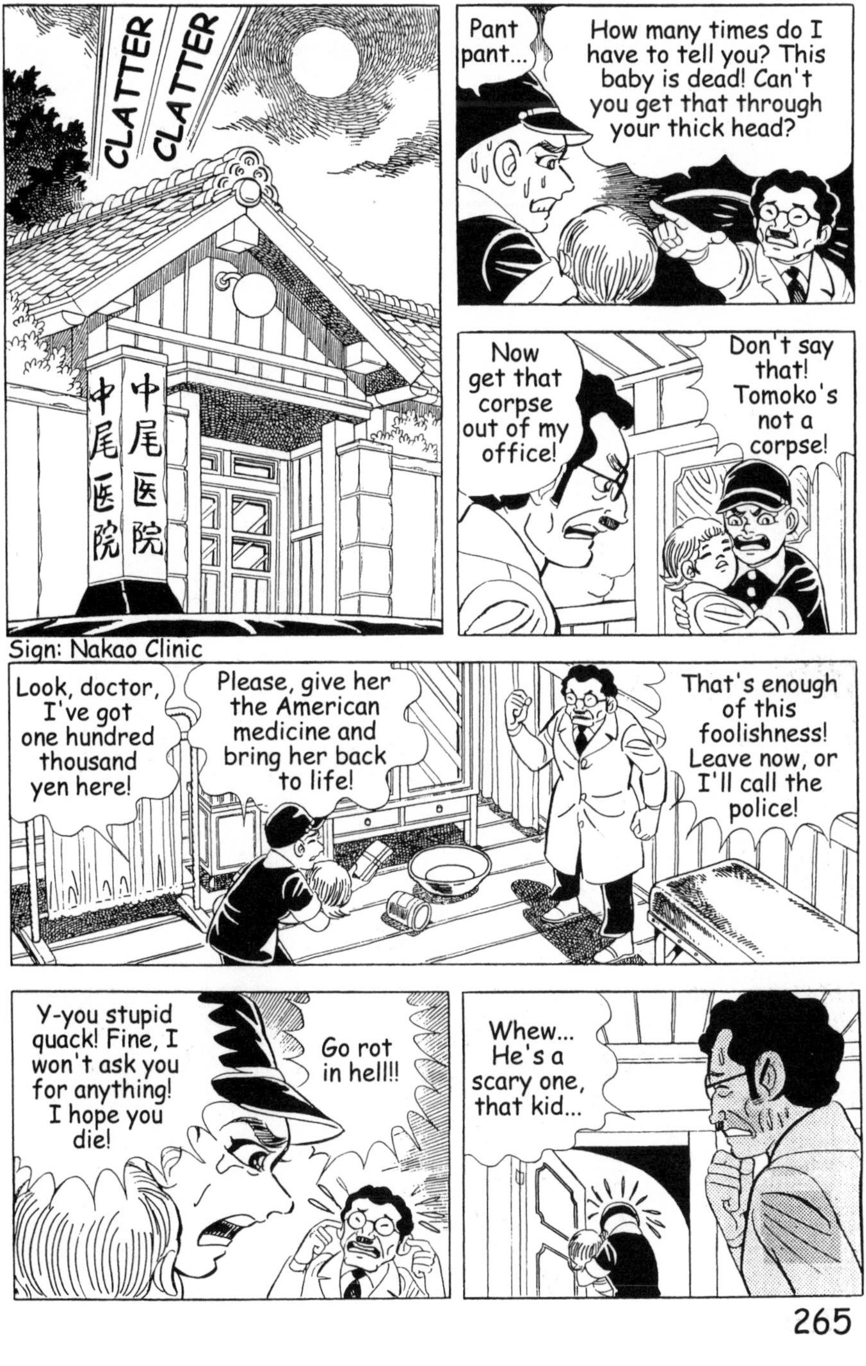
CLATTER
CLATTER
中尾医院
中尾医院
Sign: Nakao Clinic
Pant pant...
How many times do I have to tell you? This baby is dead! Can't you get that through your thick head?
Now get that corpse out of my office!
Don't say that! Tomoko's not a corpse!
Look, doctor, I've got one hundred thousand yen here!
Please, give her the American medicine and bring her back to life!
That's enough of this foolishness! Leave now, or I'll call the police!
Y-you stupid quack! Fine, I won't ask you for anything! I hope you die!
Go rot in hell!!
Whew... He's a scary one, that kid...

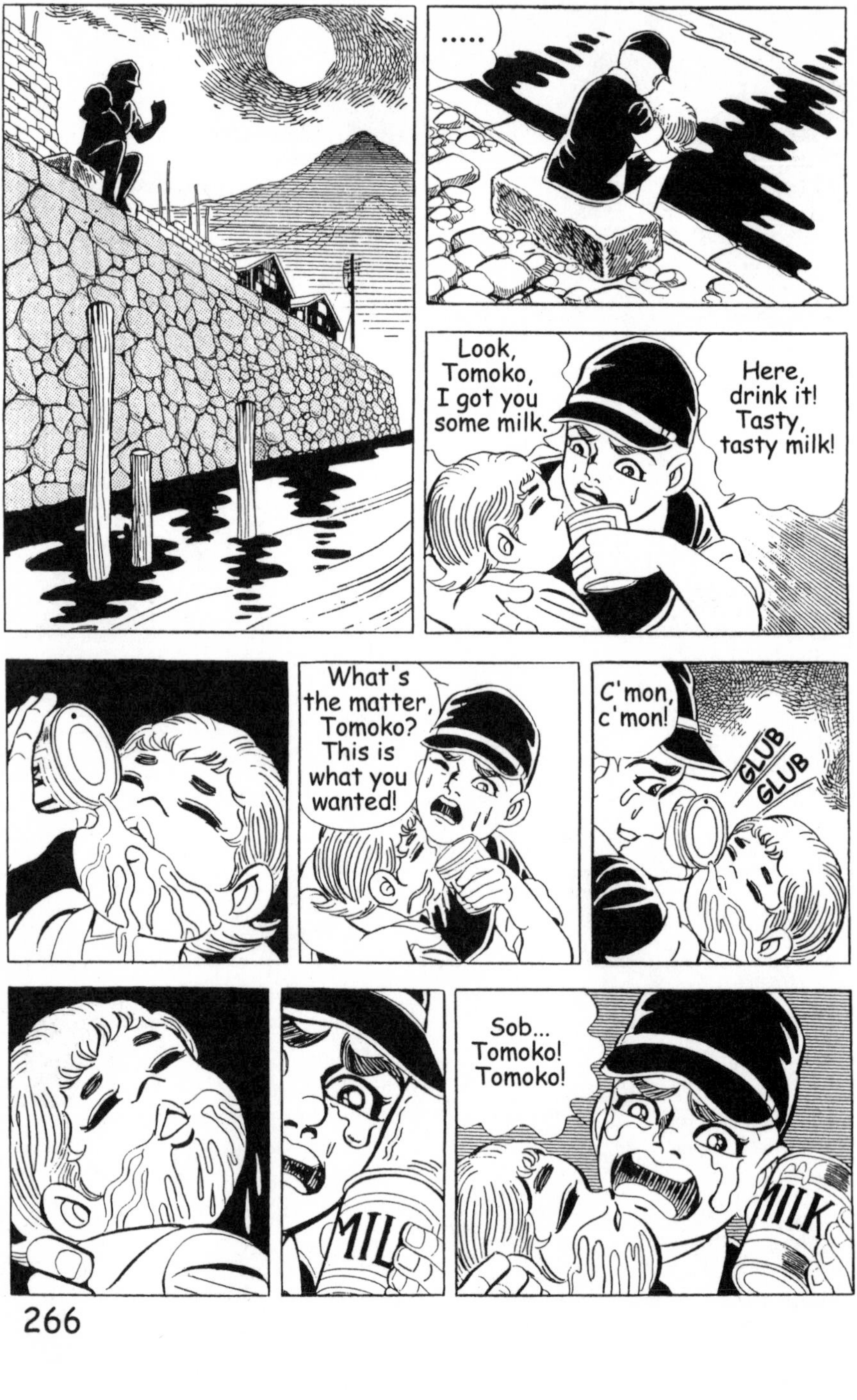
......
Look, Tomoko, I got you some milk.
Here, drink it! Tasty, tasty milk!
What's the matter, Tomoko? This is what you wanted!
C'mon, c'mon!
GLUB
GLUB
MIL
Sob... Tomoko! Tomoko!
MILK

WAAHH! WHY WON'T YOU DRINK THE MILK, TOMOKO?!

DRINK IT, PLEASE DRINK IT!

Noooo! It's not fair, Tomoko! You can't die on me now!

Not after everything I did to save you!

WAAAHHH
WAAAHH
WAAAHH

267

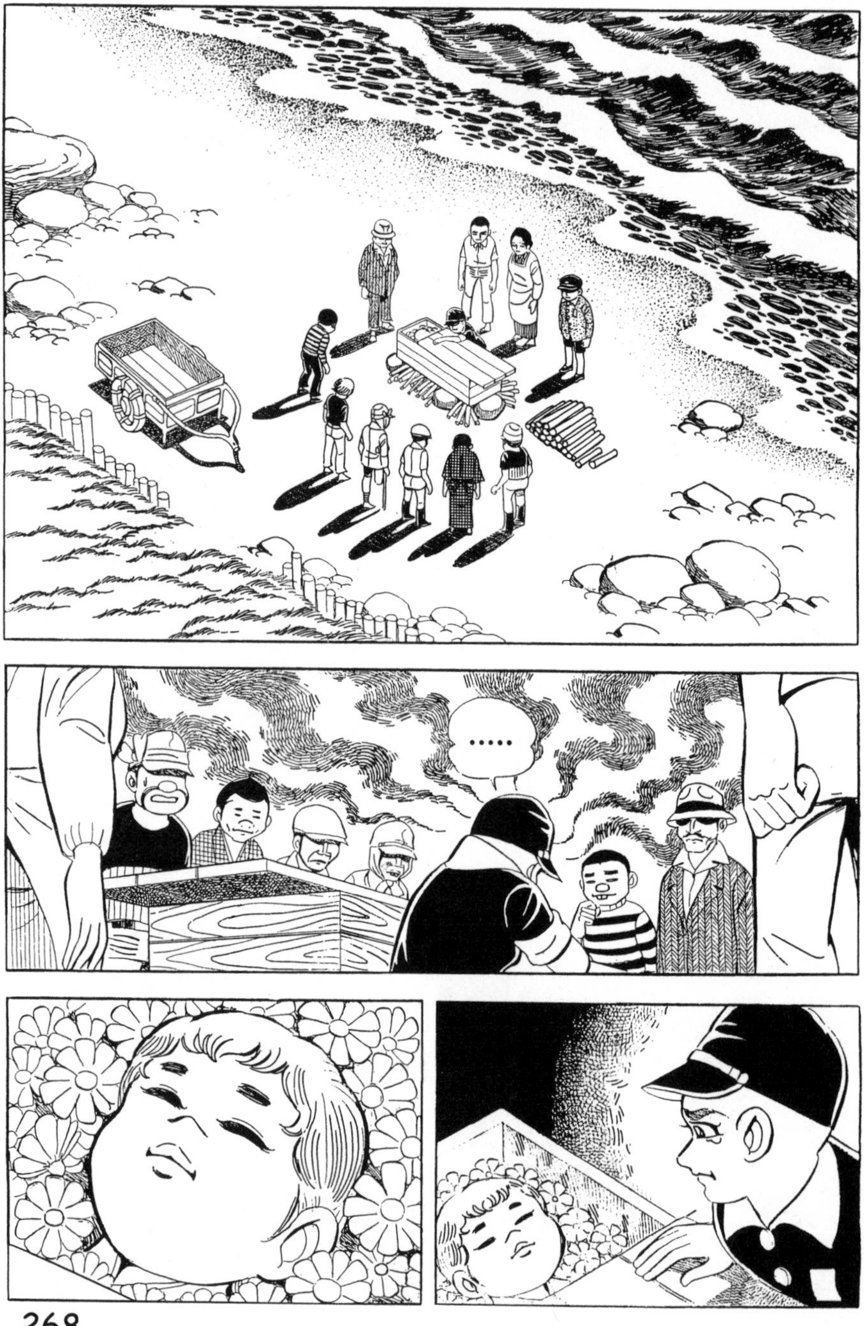
......

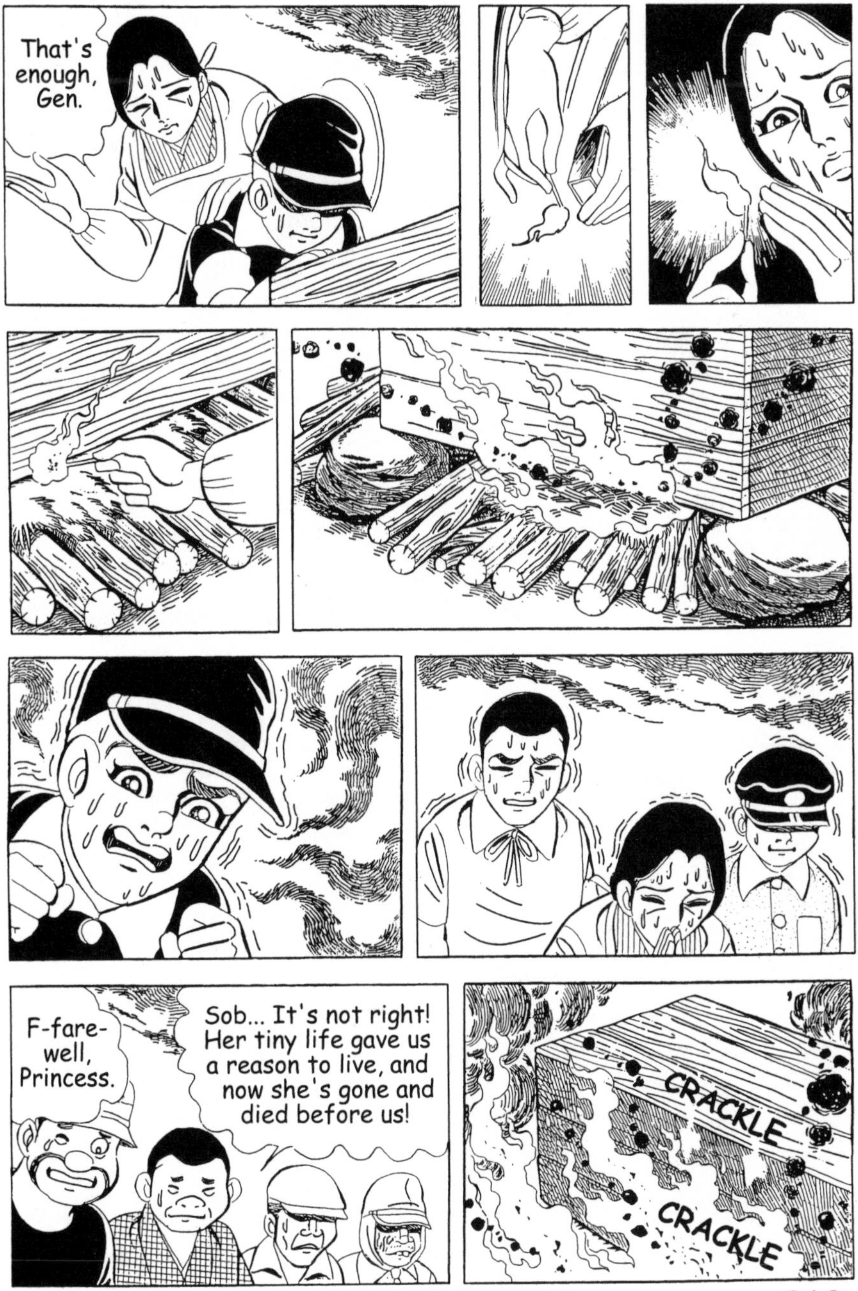
That's enough, Gen.
F-fare-well, Princess.
Sob... It's not right! Her tiny life gave us a reason to live, and now she's gone and died before us!
CRACKLE
CRACKLE

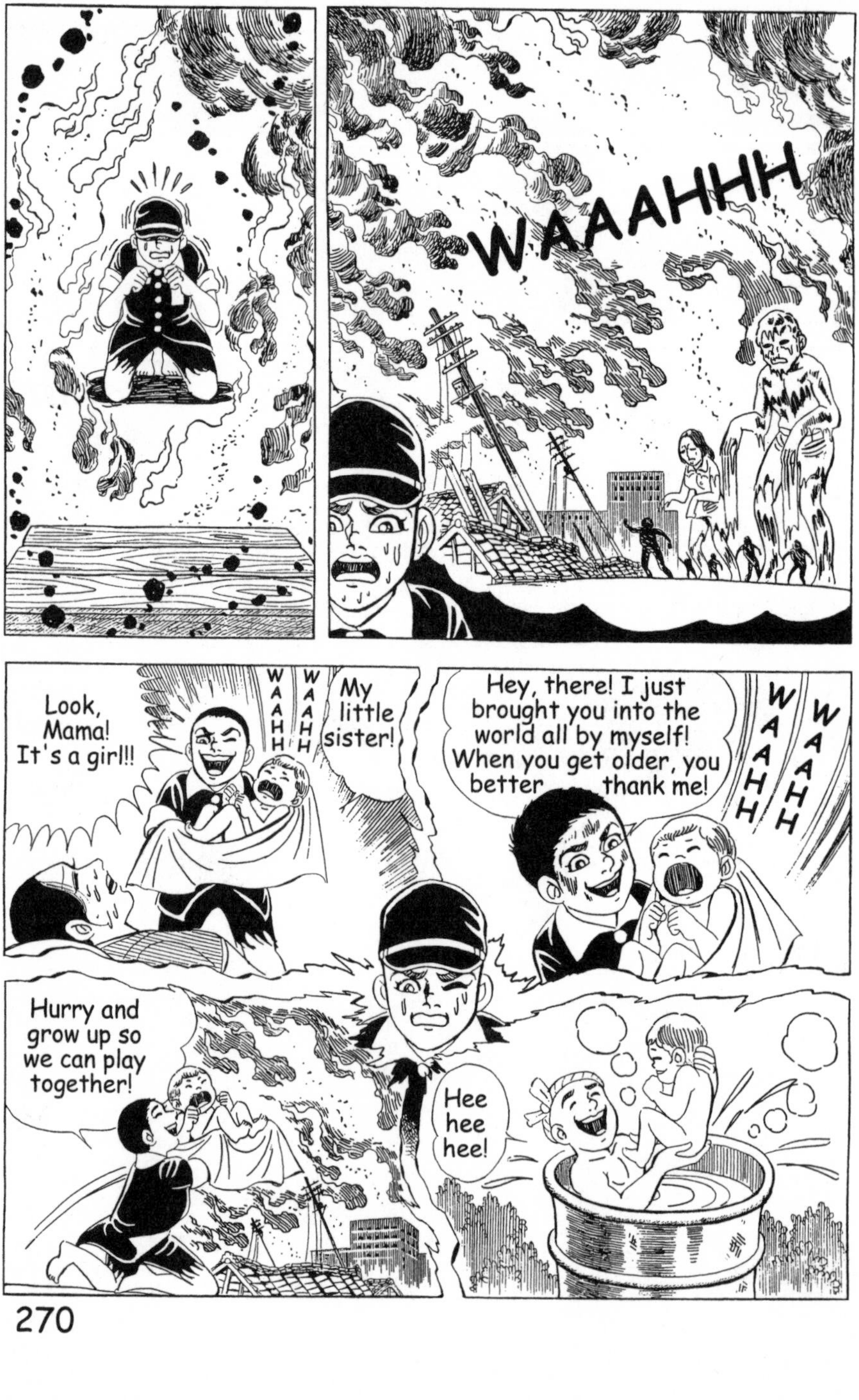
WAAAHHH
Look, Mama! It's a girl!!
WAAAHH
WAAAHH
My little sister!
Hey, there! I just brought you into the world all by myself! When you get older, you better thank me!
WAAAHH
WAAAHH
Hurry and grow up so we can play together!
Hee hee hee!

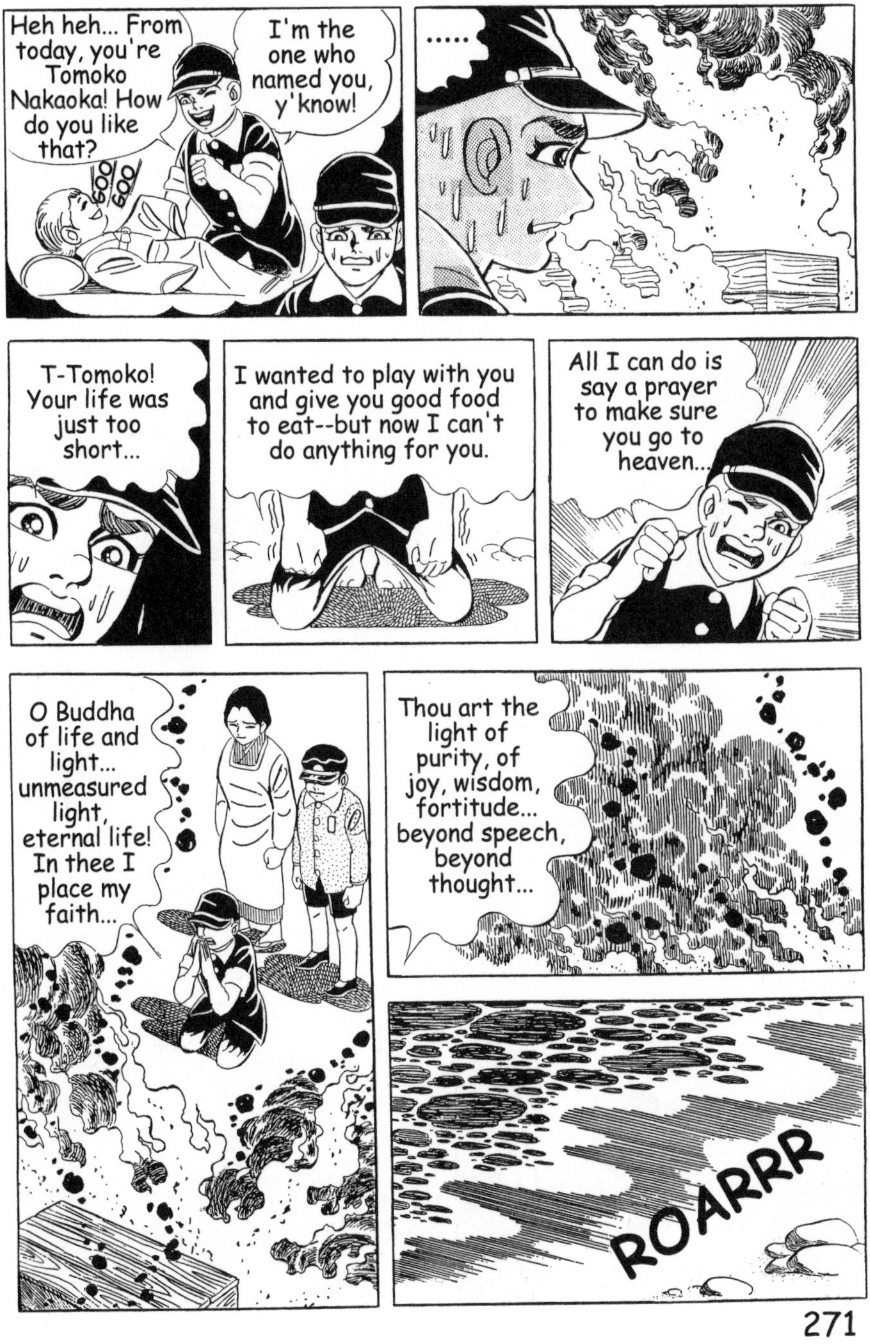
Heh heh... From today, you're Tomoko Nakaoka! How do you like that?
I'm the one who named you, y'know!
GOO GOO
.....
T-Tomoko! Your life was just too short...
I wanted to play with you and give you good food to eat--but now I can't do anything for you.
All I can do is say a prayer to make sure you go to heaven...
O Buddha of life and light... unmeasured light, eternal life! In thee I place my faith...
Thou art the light of purity, of joy, wisdom, fortitude... beyond speech, beyond thought...
ROARRR

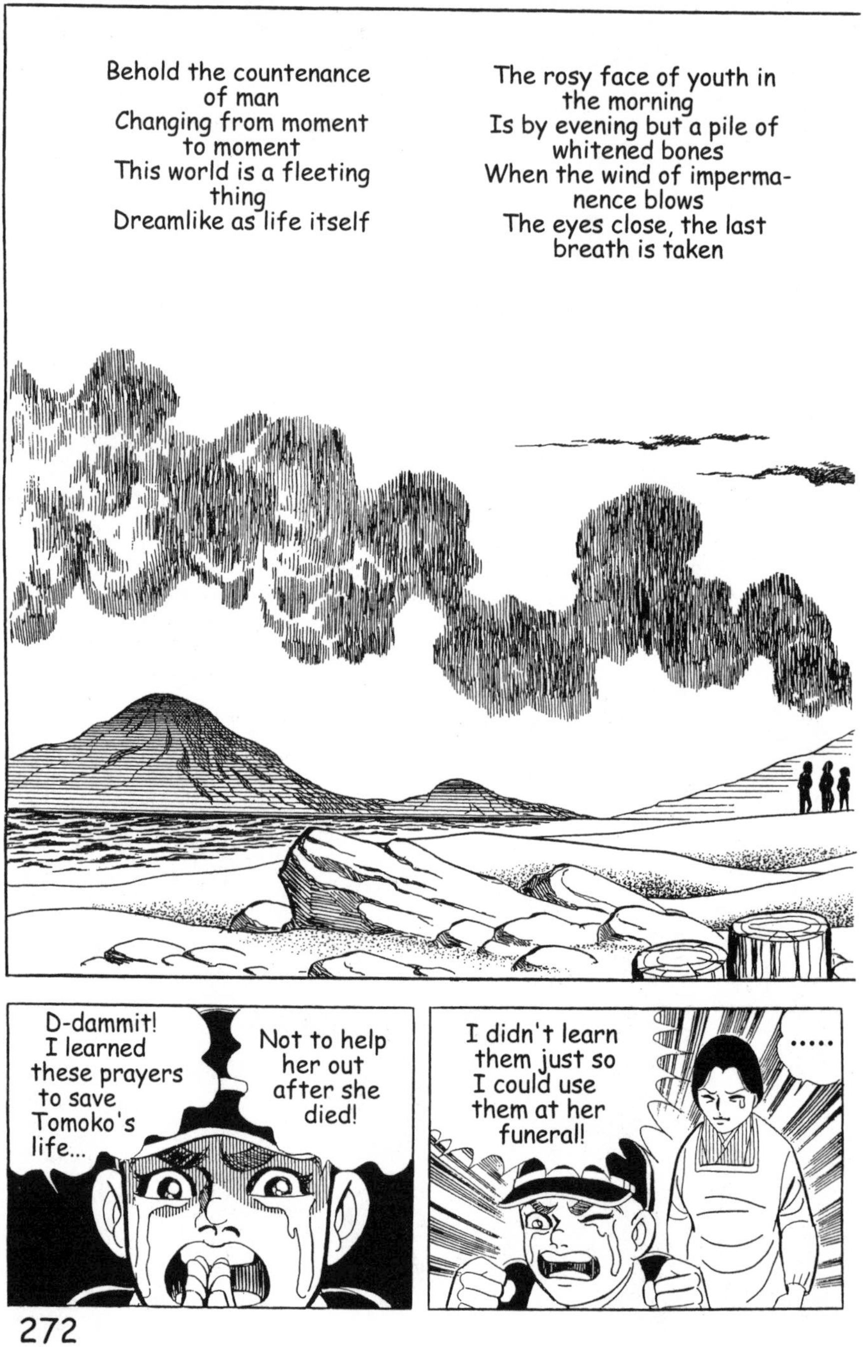
Behold the countenance of man
Changing from moment to moment
This world is a fleeting thing
Dreamlike as life itself
The rosy face of youth in the morning
Is by evening but a pile of whitened bones
When the wind of impermanence blows
The eyes close, the last breath is taken
D-dammit! I learned these prayers to save Tomoko's life...
Not to help her out after she died!
I didn't learn them just so I could use them at her funeral!
.....

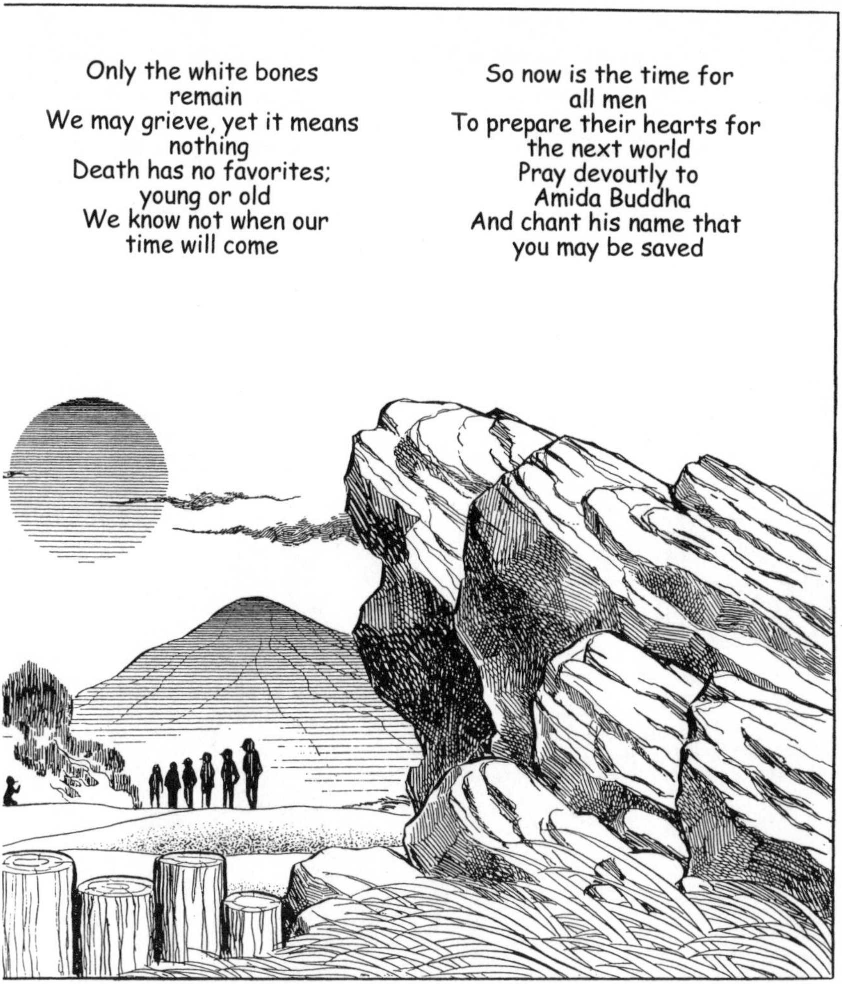
Only the white bones remain
We may grieve, yet it means nothing
Death has no favorites; young or old
We know not when our time will come
So now is the time for all men
To prepare their hearts for the next world
Pray devoutly to Amida Buddha
And chant his name that you may be saved

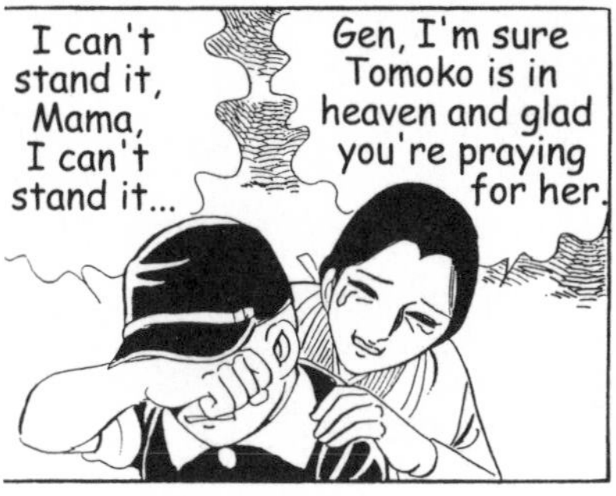
I can't stand it, Mama, I can't stand it...
Gen, I'm sure Tomoko is in heaven and glad you're praying for her.

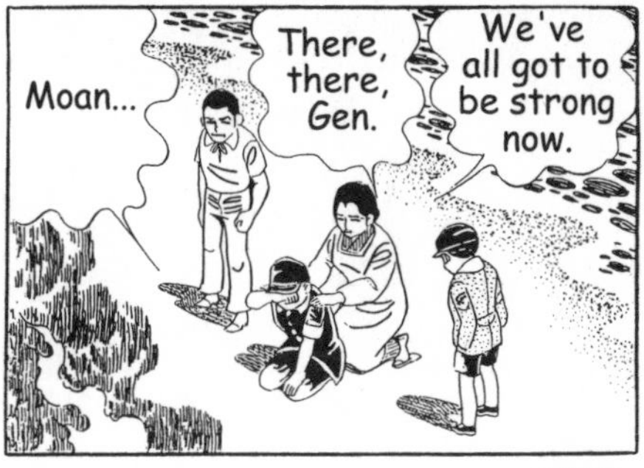
Moan...
There, there, Gen.
We've all got to be strong now.

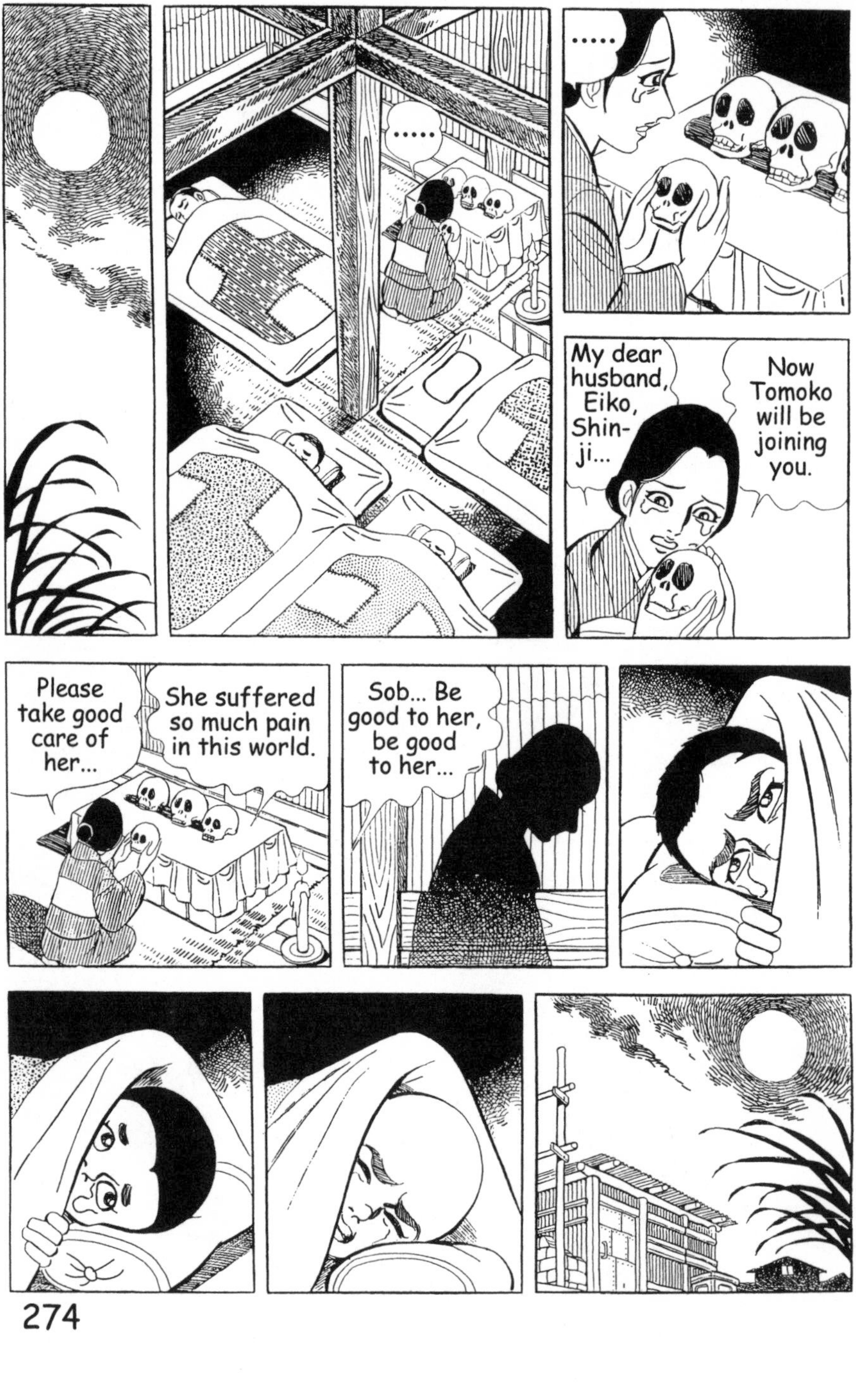
......
......
My dear husband, Eiko, Shin-ji...
Now Tomoko will be joining you.
Please take good care of her...
She suffered so much pain in this world.
Sob... Be good to her, be good to her...

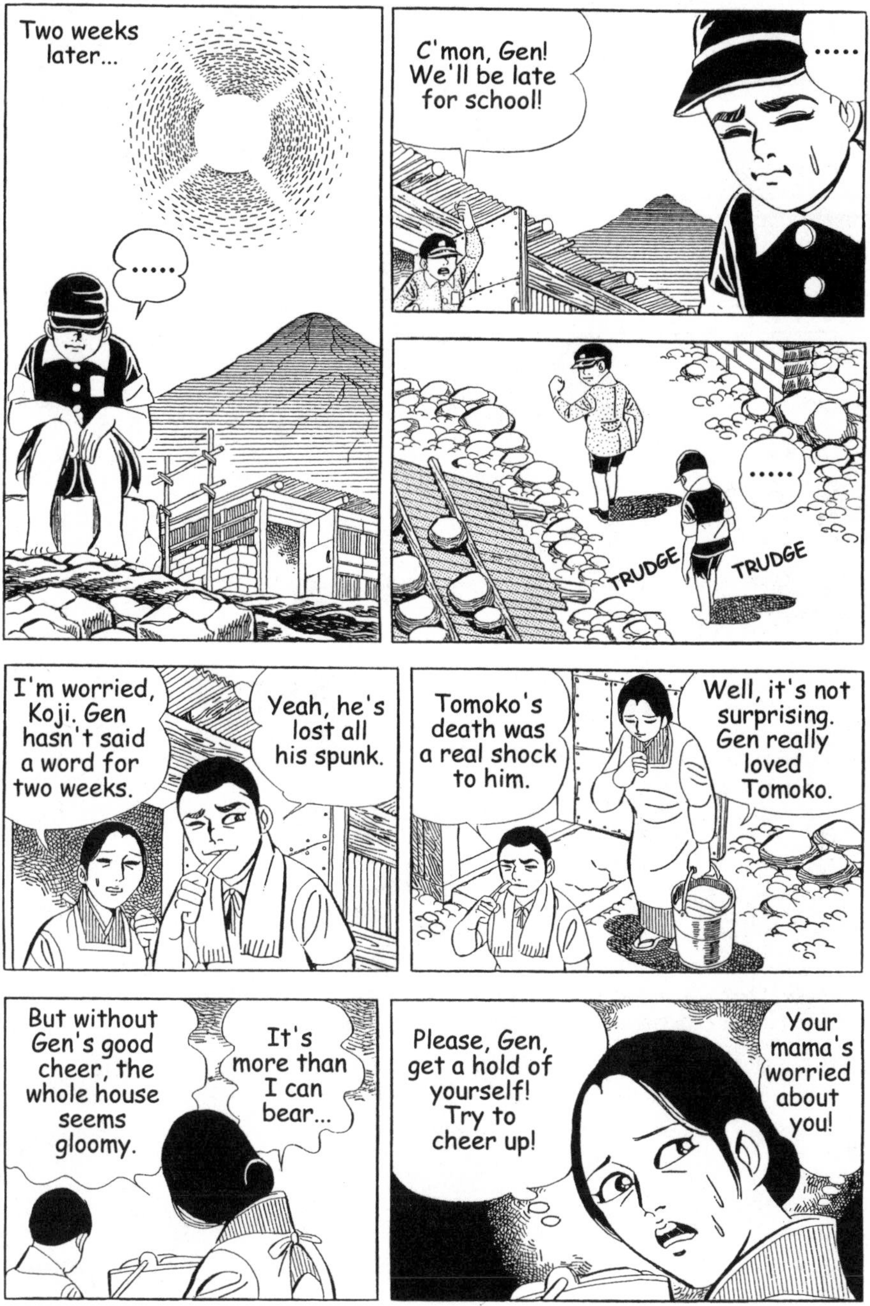
Two weeks later...
......
C'mon, Gen! We'll be late for school!
.....
......
TRUDGE TRUDGE
I'm worried, Koji. Gen hasn't said a word for two weeks.
Yeah, he's lost all his spunk.
Tomoko's death was a real shock to him.
Well, it's not surprising. Gen really loved Tomoko.
But without Gen's good cheer, the whole house seems gloomy.
It's more than I can bear...
Please, Gen, get a hold of yourself! Try to cheer up!
Your mama's worried about you!

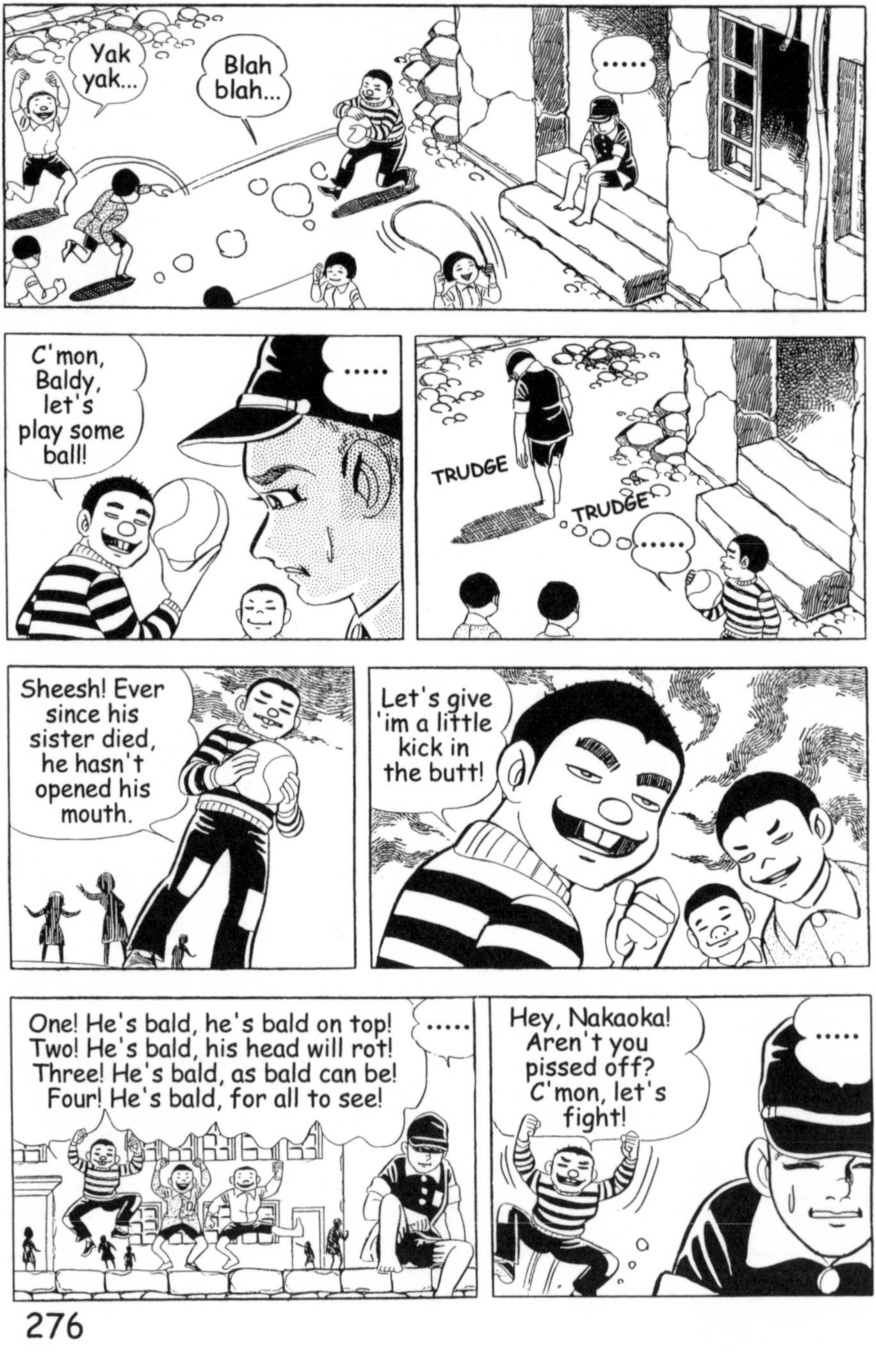
Yak yak...
Blah blah...
.....
C'mon, Baldy, let's play some ball!
.....
TRUDGE
TRUDGE
.....
Sheesh! Ever since his sister died, he hasn't opened his mouth.
Let's give 'im a little kick in the butt!
One! He's bald, he's bald on top! Two! He's bald, his head will rot! Three! He's bald, as bald can be! Four! He's bald, for all to see!
.....
Hey, Nakaoka! Aren't you pissed off? C'mon, let's fight!
.....

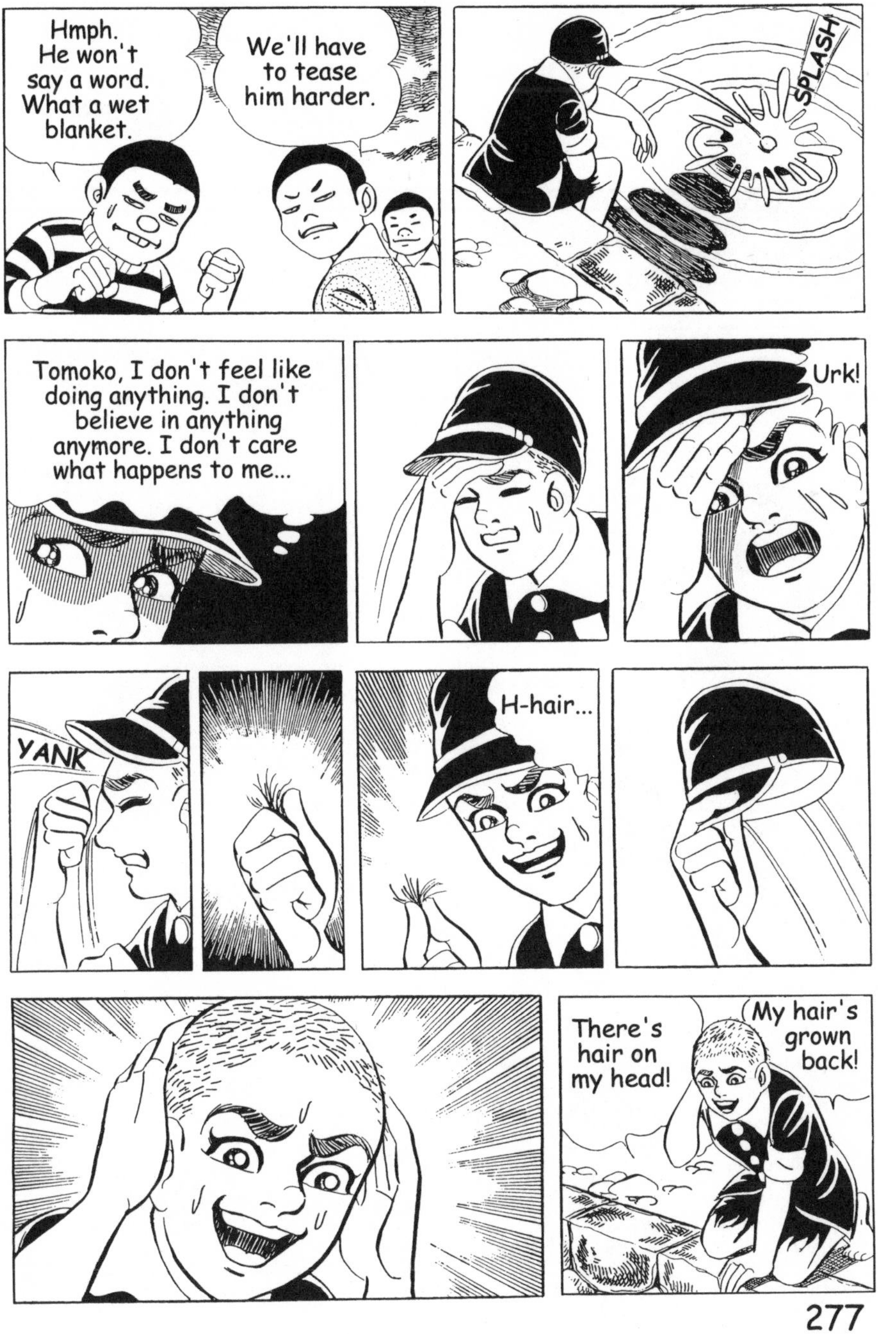
Hmph. He won't say a word. What a wet blanket.
We'll have to tease him harder.
SPLASH
Tomoko, I don't feel like doing anything. I don't believe in anything anymore. I don't care what happens to me...
Urk!
YANK
H-hair...
There's hair on my head!
My hair's grown back!

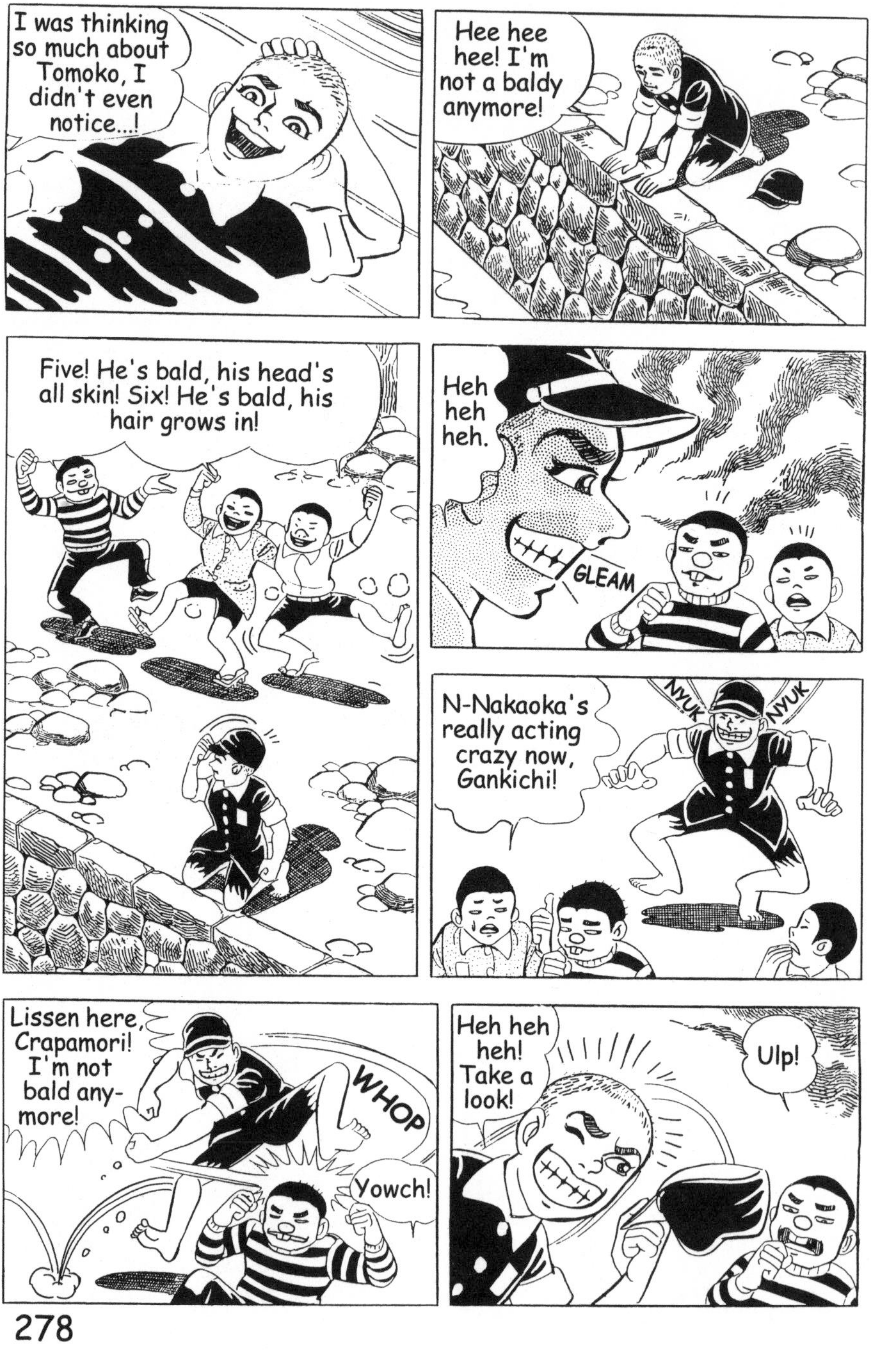
I was thinking so much about Tomoko, I didn't even notice...!
Hee hee hee! I'm not a baldy anymore!
Five! He's bald, his head's all skin! Six! He's bald, his hair grows in!
Heh heh heh.
GLEAM
N-Nakaoka's really acting crazy now, Gankichi!
NYUK
NYUK
Lissen here, Crapamori! I'm not bald any-more!
WHOP
Yowch!
Heh heh heh! Take a look!
Ulp!

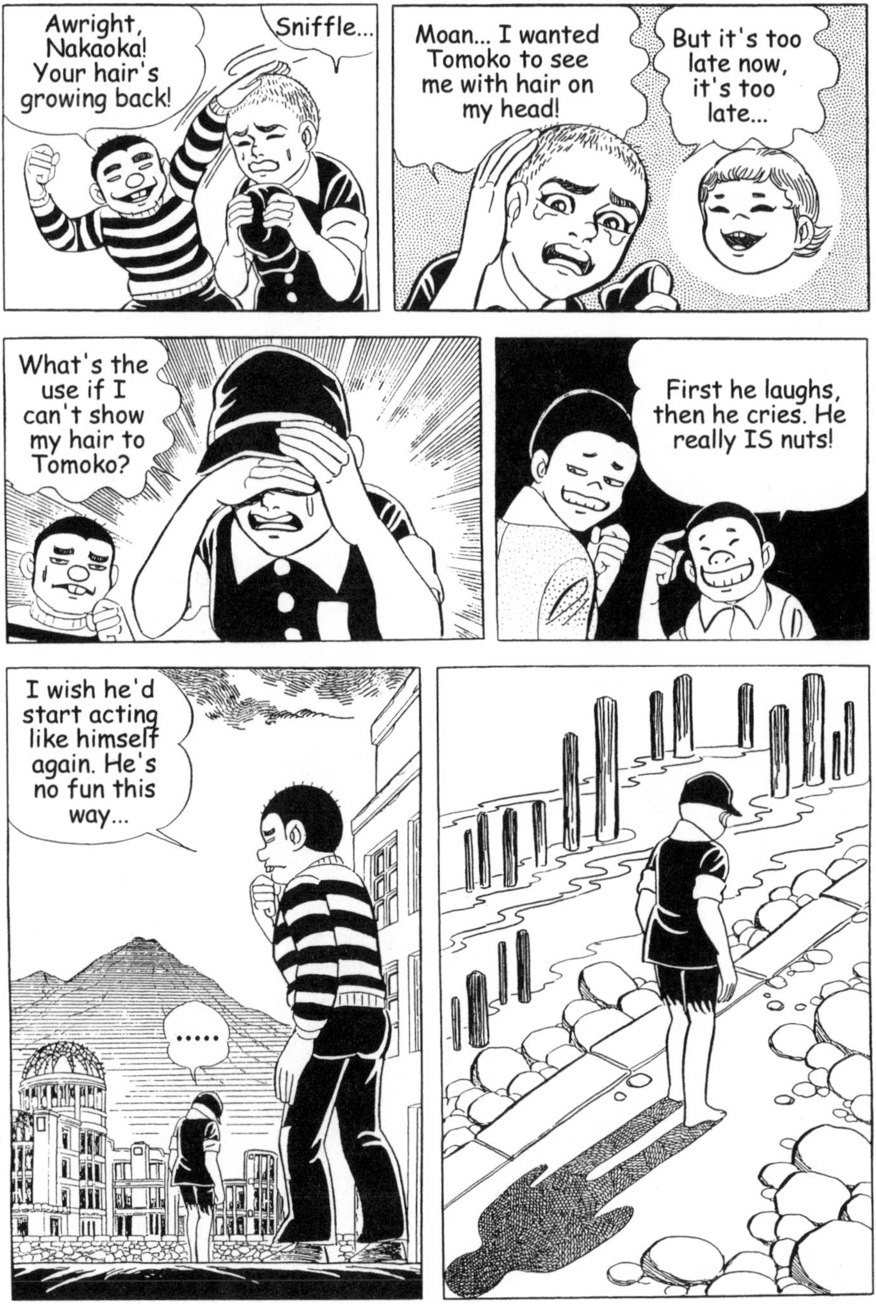
Awright, Nakaoka! Your hair's growing back!
Sniffle...
Moan... I wanted Tomoko to see me with hair on my head!
But it's too late now, it's too late...
What's the use if I can't show my hair to Tomoko?
First he laughs, then he cries. He really IS nuts!
I wish he'd start acting like himself again. He's no fun this way...
......

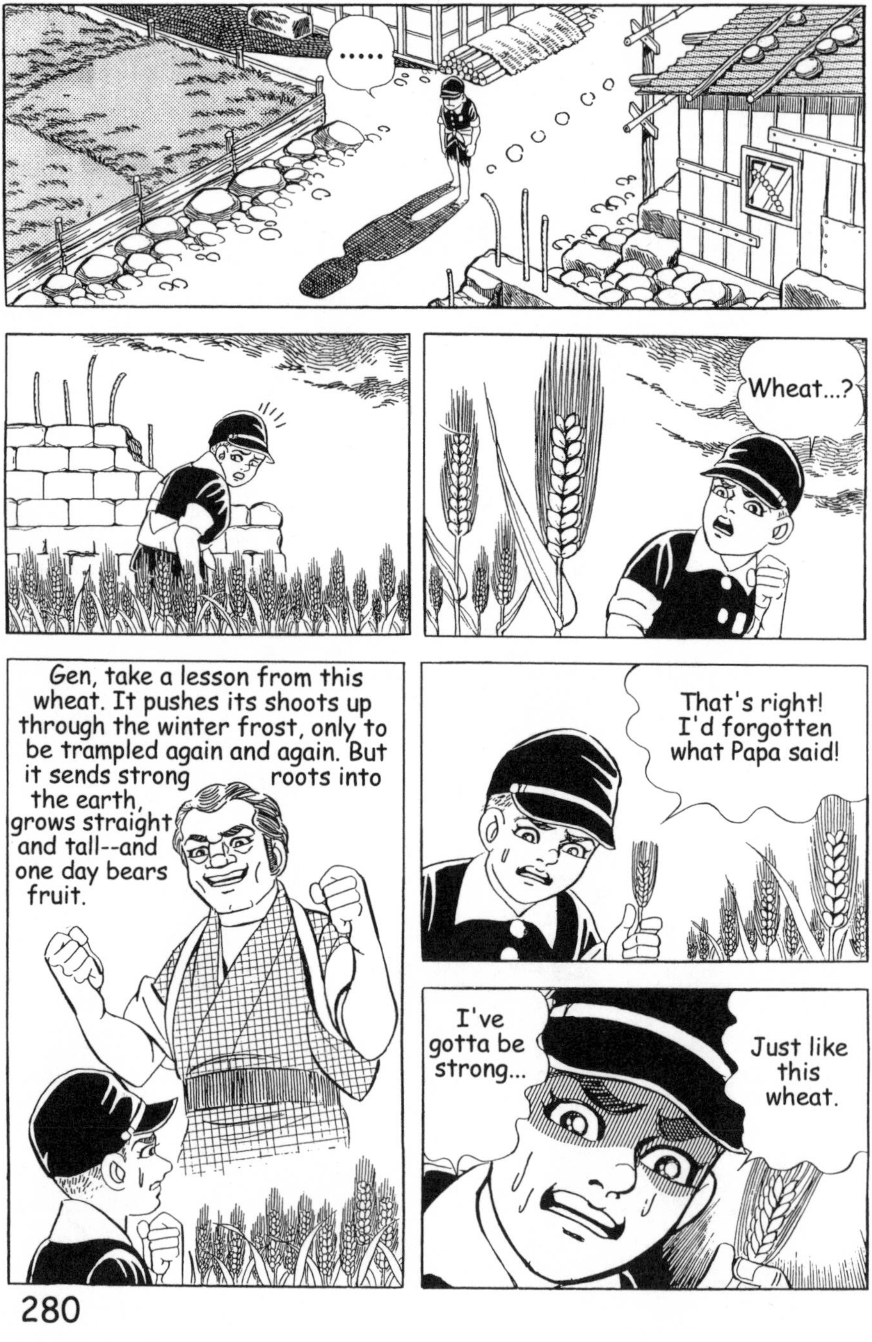
......
Wheat...?
Gen, take a lesson from this wheat. It pushes its shoots up through the winter frost, only to be trampled again and again. But it sends strong roots into the earth, grows straight and tall--and one day bears fruit.
That's right! I'd forgotten what Papa said!
I've gotta be strong...
Just like this wheat.

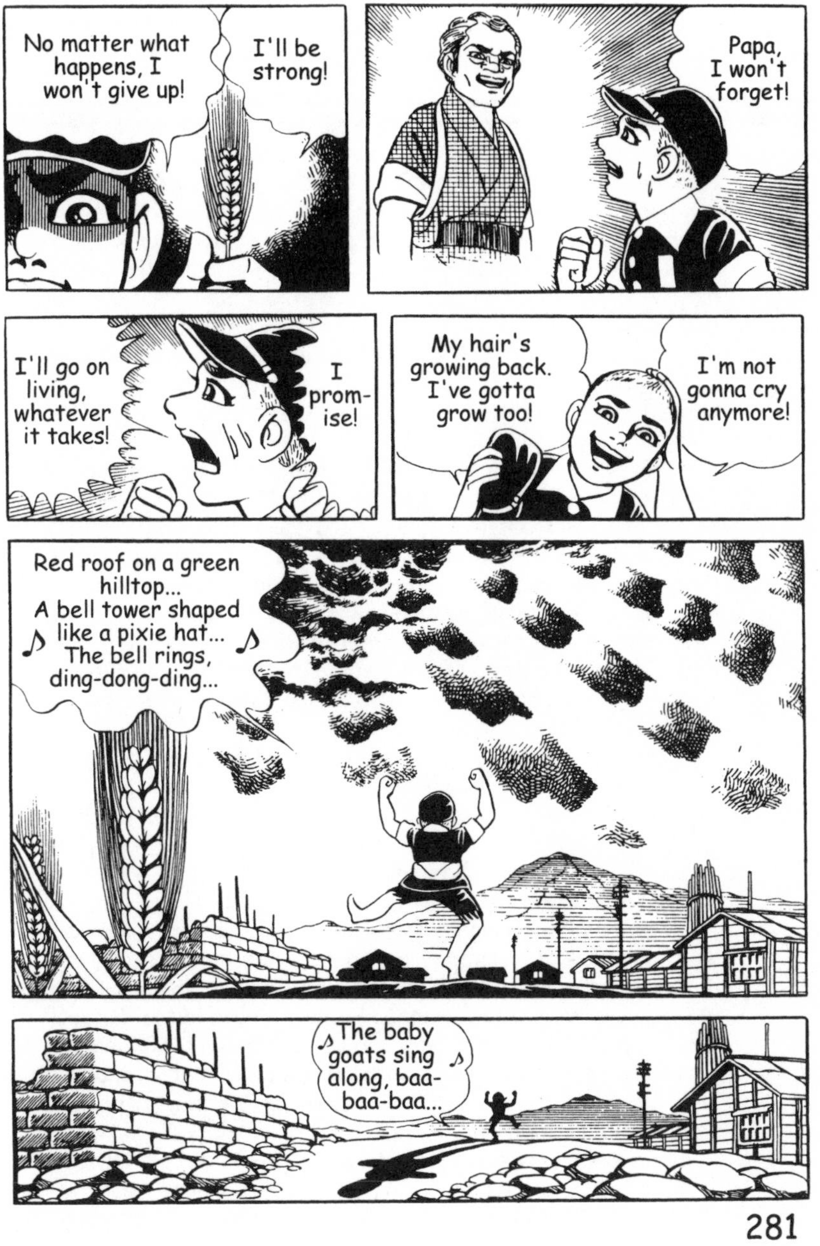
No matter what happens, I won't give up!
I'll be strong!
Papa, I won't forget!
I'll go on living, whatever it takes!
I promise!
My hair's growing back. I've gotta grow too!
I'm not gonna cry anymore!
♪ Red roof on a green hilltop... A bell tower shaped like a pixie hat... The bell rings, ding-dong-ding... ♪
♪ The baby goats sing along, baa-baa-baa... ♪

# About Project Gen

Namie Asazuma
Coordinator, Project Gen

In the pages of *Barefoot Gen*, Keiji Nakazawa brings to life a tragedy unlike any that had ever befallen the human race before. He does not simply depict the destructive horror of nuclear weapons, but tells of the cruel fate they visited upon victims and survivors in the years to come. Yet Gen, the young hero of this story, somehow manages to overcome one hardship after another, always with courage and humor. *Barefoot Gen's* tale of hope and human triumph in the face of nuclear holocaust has inspired volunteer translators around the world, as well as people working in a variety of other media. Over the years *Gen* has been made into a three-part live-action film, a feature-length animation film, an opera, and a musical.

The first effort to translate *Barefoot Gen* from the original Japanese into other languages began in 1976, when Japanese peace activists Masahiro Oshima and Yukio Aki walked across the United States as part of that year's Transcontinental Walk for Peace and Social Justice. Their fellow walkers frequently asked them about the atomic bombing of Hiroshima, and one of them happened to have a copy of *Hadashi no Gen* in his backpack. The Americans on the walk, astonished that an atomic bomb survivor had written about it in cartoon form, urged their Japanese friends to translate it into English. Upon returning to Japan, Oshima and Aki founded Project Gen, a non-profit, all-volunteer group of young Japanese and Americans living in Tokyo, to do just that. Project Gen went on to translate the first four volumes of *Barefoot Gen* into English. One or more of these volumes have also been published in French, German, Italian, Portuguese, Swedish, Norwegian, Indonesian, Tagalog, and Esperanto.

By the 1990s Project Gen was no longer active. In the meantime, author Keiji Nakazawa had gone on to complete ten volumes of *Gen*, and expressed his wish to see the entire story made available to non-Japanese readers. Parts of the first four volumes had also been abridged in translation. A new generation of volunteers responded by reviving Project Gen and producing a new, complete and unabridged translation of the entire Gen series.

The second incarnation of Project Gen got its start in Moscow in 1994, when a Japanese student, Minako Tanabe, launched "Project Gen in Russia" to translate *Gen* into Russian. After publishing the first three volumes in Moscow, the project relocated to Kanazawa, Japan, where volunteers Yulia Tachino and Namie Asazuma had become acquainted with *Gen* while translating a story about Hiroshima into Russian. The Kanazawa volunteers, together with Takako Kanekura in Russia, completed Russian volumes 4 through 10 between 1999 and 2001.

In the spring of 2000, the Kanazawa group formally established a new Project Gen in Japan. Nine volunteers spent the next three years translating all ten volumes of *Gen* into English. The translators are Kazuko Futakuchi, Michael Gordon, Kyoko Honda, Yukari Kimura, Nobutoshi Kohara, Kiyoko Nishita, George Stenson, Michiko Tanaka, and Kazuko Yamada.

In 2002, author Keiji Nakazawa put the Kanazawa team in contact with Alan Gleason, a member of the first Project Gen, who introduced them to Last Gasp of San Francisco, publisher of the original English translation of *Gen*. Last Gasp agreed to publish the new, unabridged translation of all ten volumes, of which this book is one.

In the hope that humanity will never repeat the terrible tragedy of the atomic bombing, the volunteers of Project Gen want children and adults all over the world to hear Gen's story. Through translations like this one, we want to help Gen speak to people in different countries in their own languages. Our prayer is that *Barefoot Gen* will contribute in some small way to the abolition of nuclear weapons before this new century is over.

Write to Project Gen c/o Asazuma, Nagasaka 3-10-20, Kanazawa 921-8112, Japan

## Special Acknowledgement

The following people (as well as many who wish to remain anonymous) contributed generously to our Kickstarter campaign and made these hardcover editions of *Barefoot Gen* possible.

A. Macbride

A. T. Warren

A. Waller Hastings

Aabra Jaggard

Aaron B Reiser

Aaron Diamond

Aaron J. Schibik

Abhilash Sarhadi

Ada Palmer

Adam Christopher Bryant

Adam Doochin

Adam Meyers

Adrienne Marie Núñez

Agustin Chancusi

Akio Duffy

Alan Zabaro

Alenka Figa

Alex Fitch

Alex Ponomareff

Alex Stevenson

Alexander Hoffman

Alexis A Candelaria

Ali T. Kokmen

Alison Davila

Alok Karande

AM

Amanda Burdic

Amanda, Keagan, and Andromeda O'Mara

Amberly Maxwell

Amy Heaney

Amy Rachels

Amy Watson

Andrea Peitsch

Andrew Lohmann

Andrey Novoseltsev

Andy Holman

Angela Bacchi

Anne-Scott Whitmire

Annie Koyama

Arianne Hartsell-Gundy

Arthur Murakami

Asahiko Matsuda

Ash Brown

Ashley Hernandez

Avelino Morais

Avi Finkel

B. Wilks

Badou Jobe

Barbara Lindsey

Bears Den Mountain Lodge

Ben Laverock

Benjamin Sussman

Benjamin Woo

Bernd the Anon

Beth Campbell

Beth Lonsinger

billy pete

Blue Delliquanti

Bob Culley

bowerbird!

Brad Ander

Brent Van Keulen

Bryan Gaffin

Cabel Sasser

Caitlin Huddleston

Candise Branum

Cara Averna

Carl K.H.

Carlos Bergfeld

Cedric Tisserand

Chikada, Hibiki (fireworks.vc)

Chris Lepkowski

Chris Patti

Chris Shepard

Christian Kaw

Christopher Charles Reed

Clay Nash

Cody Billings

Corey Proft

Cynthia Oshiro

dajomu

Dan and Ellen Wasil

Daniel Cahill

Daniel Oliveira Carn

Daniel Schneider

Daniella Orihuela-Gruber

Danielle Keenan

Dave Johnston

David & Sinda Eggerman

David Lee

David Toccafondi

Denise Larson

Dennis Smith

Derick Peterson

Deter Clawmute

Don Van Horn

Donald Scott

Donna Almendrala

Dorian Bell

Doug Redway

Doug Wilder

Douglas Candano

D-Rock

Dus T'

Dylan Cheung

Dylan Fields

Eileen Kaur Alden

Elaine Loftus Loeb

Eleanor Walker

Elisha Rush

Ellen Jane Keenan

Ellen Power

Ellen Yu

Elliott Walker

Emily Hui

Emily Lakin

Emmanuel D'Hoop

Eric Agena

Eric Kim

Eric Phipps

Erick Reilly

Erika Ray

Evan Ritchie

Eve Turner-Lee

Eyeball Kicks

Fred Burke

G.M. Harvey

Gabe Lowendick

Gabriel Bravo Gallardo

Gary D. Simmons

Gary Tanigawa

Genta Mochizawa

George Peter Dimos

Gina Curtice

Graham Kolbeins

Gregory Prout

Guy Thomas

H.Dannoue

Hans Eric Svensson

Harris Fish

Hart Larrabee

Heather Skweres

Heidi von Markham

Helen Koyama

Hikky Yoshida

Hillary Harris Moldovan

Holly Tomren

Hollyann Wood

Ian Harker

Isabel Samaras

Ismael F. Salazar Jr.

Ivory Madison & Abraham Mertens

J. Christina Smith

J. Driscoll

J. Torres

J.R. Pas

Jackie Fox

Jackie Z.

Jacob Ryan Larson

Jake Pushinsky

James A. Hardi

James Prevott

James R. Bradshaw

James Turnbull

James Wight

Jane Mahoney

Jared Brock

Jared Konopitski

Jason beirens

Jason Tuason

Jay Perry

JB Segal

Jeff Newelt

Jeffrey Kahn

Jeffrey Meyer

Jen Crothers

Jen Propst

<3 Jeska Kittenbrink

Jill DeLong

Jim DelRosso

Jim Kosmicki

Jingran Wang

Jocelyne Allen

John "Boother" Booth

John Kyritsis

John Madigan IV

Johnny Mayall

Jon Kelly

Jon Parrish

Jonathan Shaver

José Loureiro

Joseph Kurachi Luk

Joseph P. Young

Joshua Drescher

Joshua Dunh

Julian Khaw

Julie Reiser

Julitta R. McIntire-Federico

Junko Mizuno

Justin Harman

Karin Wilson

Karl Brian Arcadio

Kat Kan

Katy Costello

Kayoko.A

Kazue Evans

Kelly Winquist

Kelsey C

Kendell Briggs

Kent K. Barnes

Kevin J. Maroney

Kevin Robinson

Kimberly A. Gordon

Kimiaki Suzuki

Kohji 'osa' Osamura

Kory Cerjak

Kristina Elyse Butke

Kristine Anstine

Kumar Sivasubramanian

Kurtis Ray Foster

Kwame N. Akosah

Leanna Lucas

Leen Isabel

legalmoon

Linda Stevens

Linda Yau

Lisa Martincik

Liz Davis

Loren Rhoads

Luan Resende

Lucas Aubrey Paynter

Luke White

Lynne Wooddell and Family

M

M. Griffiths

M.R. Innes

Maggie Young

Mahlon Landis

Maiji/Mary Huang

Marc Escanuelas

Marc Lee

Marc St-Jacques

Marcel Wienen

margaret miller

Mariell Leniuk

Marisa McFarlane

Mark Hartsuyker

Marla Greenwald and Erin Sparling

Mary C. Carroll

Masahiro Kitagawa

Masako I.

Matt Adrian

Matt Parrillo

Matteo Gilebbi

Matthew and Crystalyn Hodgkins

Matthew Mizenko

McCausland

Meagan Lowell Phillips

Mel Smith

Melanie Gillman

Michael Arroyo

Michael C. Stewart

Michael Czobit

Michael John Constantine

Michael MacBride

Michael Pang

Michael Rock

Michael Tannenbaum

Michael Thaler and Inna Guzenfeld

Michelle C.

Michelle Stoliker

Michiko Byers

Mike Borch

Mike Davis

Mike Dawson

Mission: Comics & Art

Monique G.

Naadir Jeewa

Nancy Chan

Nancy Ruan

Nathan Schreiber

Nathan Young

Nathaniel Merchant

Niall John James MacDougall

Nicole Compliment

Nicole Fabricand-Person

Nina Matsumoto

Odette Christensen

Odyssey Publications

Olivia Eirene Luna

Olivia Rohan

Olivia Tai

Omar Pineda

Óscar Morales Vivó

OYAJIHAHA

Pascal Hamon

Patricia Wakida

Patrick King

Patrick Leahy

Patrick Montero

Pattie Piotrowski

Paul Freelend

Paul J Hodgeson

Pete Goldie

Peter Munford

Petey Rave

Phaedra Risher

Philip Kinchington

Priya Ananthasankar

Pual N

R Evans

R. Sikoryak

R. Todd Crockett

R~

Rachel "Nausicaa" Tougas

Raina Telgemeier

Rebecca Boldes

Renzo Adler

Richard J. Neil III

Richard Wesley Hooper

Rob Reger

Robert Altomare

Robert Duncan

Robert Paul Weston

Robert Rosendahl

Rochelle Claire Brown

Rodrigo Ortiz Vinholo

Ronald Stewart

Rosanne Nagy

Royce Engemann

Russell Martens

Ruth Ilano

Ryan Lynch

Ryan Sands

Sadie McFarlane

Samuel Henley

Sarah Rich

Sawa Hotta

Scott Rubin

Sean C Kershaw

Sean Kleefeld

Seiko Yoshina

Sergio Goncalves Proenca

Sergio Segovia Cervantes

Sharon Leong

Shaun Huseman

Shelby McGowan

Shervyn

Shiro H.

Siddharth Gupta

Soko Yamamoto

Sonia Harris

Sophie Muller

Stacey Ransom & Jason Mitchell

Stephen Schloss

Steve & Ana Hart

Steve Laflef

Steve Leialoha and Trina Robbins

Steven Darrall

Steven M. Jankowski

Susanna Hough

Sutter Kane Haggblom

T.M. Finney

Tabi Joy

Takahiro and Molly Kitamura

Tatsuo  Senshu Ph.D

Terry W. McCammon II

Tetsuya Ishibashi

The Beguiling Books & Art

The Chou Malpicas

The Hoffman Family

The Kostelecky Family

The Land of Obscusion

theRat

Thomas Lloyd

Thomas Pand

Thorsten Gruber

Timothy Rottenberg

Tomislav Jelenkovic

Tony Bennett

Torsten Adair

TOUYAMA Jun-ichi

Treve Hodsman

Tshihide Satoh

Tsuyoshi Ogawa

Tyler Bibbey

Varun Gupta

Vivian Kokot

W.Schiller

Wesley Holtkamp

Wilma Jandoc Win

Yellow T

Zac Clarke

Zach Powers

Zach Van Stanley

Zach Von Joo

Zachary Clemente

Zack Davisson

琴線計画

近田火日輝